Rebellion to Integration

West Sumatra and the Indonesian Polity
1926 - 1998

Audrey Kahin

Amsterdam University Press

Cover design: Wat-ontwerpers, Utrecht
Lay-out: Adriaan de Jonge, Amsterdam

ISBN 90 5356 395 4

© Amsterdam University Press, Amsterdam, 1999

Table of Contents

Acknowledgements 9
Maps 12
Introduction 15
Prologue 21

Section I: Late Colonial Rule

Chapter 1: Background and Eruption of the 1927 Rebellion 31
The Brink of Rebellion 31
Background to the Unrest 33
Centres of Opposition 36
   Padang Panjang 37
   Silungkang/Sawahlunto 42
   Padang 43
The Uprising 46

Chapter 2: The Crisis of the Early 1930s 50
Repercussions of 1927 51
Religious Nationalism 51
The Socialist Stream 57
   Youth Groups 57
   Hatta's Followers 59
   Tan Malaka's Pari 62
The Dutch Crackdown 65
Aftermath 67
   Cat and mouse 68

Chapter 3: Nationalism in Prewar West Sumatra 71
Parties and Leadership 71
The Role of the Entrepreneurs 75
Schools in West Sumatra 78
Societal Divisions 84
The Closing Years of Dutch Rule 89

Section II: Achieving Independence

    Chapter 4: West Sumatra under the Japanese 95
The Early Occupation 95
  Sukarno's Role 96
  Japanese Governor Yano Kenzo 98
Giyu Gun 99
  The Character of the Giyu Gun 100
The Closing Phase 103
Japanese Legacy 105

    Chapter 5: Independence Proclaimed 107
Facing the British 108
Establishing a Republican Administration 110
Crises in Early 1946 114
  The Return of Tan Malaka 114
  The People's Front in West Sumatra 116
  The Baso Movement 118
  Compromise with the Front 120
Islamic Dissension 122
  The March 3 Affair 123
The Military Side 126
Clashes with the Centre 127
  Sumatra's Civilian Government 128
  Rationalization of the Armed Forces 131
Political Alignments in Java and Sumatra 133
  Tan Malaka and His Influence 135

    Chapter 6: Independence Achieved 138
West Sumatra under the Dutch Occupation 138
  The Attack 138
  The Republic's Emergency Government (PDRI) 138
Situjuh Batur and the Death of Chatib Suleiman 142
The Local Struggle 144
  Military Collapse and Internal Conflict 144
  Internal Defence and Security 146
  Revolutionary Trade 148
Failure of Dutch Plans for a Minangkabau State 152
End of the Armed Struggle 153
Legacy of the Revolution 156

6

Section III: Region versus Capital

    Chapter 7: Disillusionment 165
Rejection of Federalism 165
   Establishment of a Unitary State 165
   Failure of Moves for Greater Regional Autonomy 167
Reaction in Sumatra 169
   Disillusionment in Aceh 170
   Freezing of West Sumatra's Civilian Institutions 171
Failure of the Electoral Road 175
   Religious Disaffection 175
   The 1955 Elections 176
Toward the Banteng Council 178
   Dissolution of the Banteng Division 179
The Banteng Council 182

    Chapter 8: Defiance 184
Unrest in the Military 184
Success of the Banteng Council: December 1956 - July 1957 188
   Military Achievements 189
   Economic Decentralization 189
   Political Support 190
      The Indonesian Communist Party 191
      Riau and Jambi 191
Repercussions at the Centre 193
   Hopes for Compromise 195
Impingement of Outside Forces & Moves toward a Break 197
   The Palembang Charter 198
   MUNAS 200
   The Issue of Communism 202
   Crises in Jakarta 204
   Toward the Break 206

    Chapter 9: Defeat 211
Onset of the Civil War 211
Jakarta's Military Success 215
Parallels with the Revolution 218
Establishment of the Federal Government (RPI) 221
Defeat and Humiliation 225
Aftermath of the Rebellion 228

Section IV: Integration under the New Order

Chapter 10: Overthrow of the Old Order 233
The 1965 Upheaval 233
West Sumatra's Political Climate in the Early 1960s 234
The Role of General Mokoginta 238
The September 30 Movement in West Sumatra 240
Period of Transition 242
Suppression of the Communists in North Sumatra 243
Consolidating Jakarta's Power in West Sumatra 245
Advent of a New Regime 249

Chapter 11: Accommodation with the Centre 252
New Order Rule 252
Destroying the Political Parties 254
Destruction of the Nagari 257
Social and Economic Changes 261
   Governor Hasan Basri Durin 261
   The Changing Economy 262
   Role of the Perantau 263
Erosion of the New Order 265
   Fifty Years of Independence 266
Suharto's Resignation 269

Conclusion 271
'Reformasi' in West Sumatra 272
   Resignation of the Governor 273
The Era of Reform 274
   The Issues of Decentralization 275
   Elections 277

Bibliography of Secondary Sources 279
Notes 287
Index 357

Acknowledgements

My debts over the years of carrying out the research for this book are immense, too great for the names of all those who helped me to be listed here.

I am indebted to dozens of people in West Sumatra and Jakarta who have assisted me in many ways over the past twenty-five years. It is difficult to single out any individuals, but in West Sumatra, I am particularly grateful to Azmi and Buchari Nurdin who were my assistants for my initial dissertation research in 1976 and have been unstinting in their help since then; to Imran Manan and Fatimah Enar who have also been a constant source of information and assistance; and to Mestika Zed, who is proving himself to be one of the ablest young historians of his country's history. I owe a particular debt to Leon Salim who did so much to help me understand the early years of the struggle in West Sumatra; the late Sjamsul Bahar, who allowed me to read and copy much valuable material from the PDRI archives; Ny. Karelmanier and her brother, who gave me another perspective on one of the more troubling episodes in West Sumatra's history; A.A. Navis, who provided me with his valuable insights on Minangkabau culture and history and also with many written materials; Ibu Naimah Djambek, who shared her memories of her brother, Dahlan Djambek, and introduced me to many of his colleagues; and Yunidar Chatib Suleiman and Sudarman Khatib Dt. Berbangso, who provided me with records and photographs of Chatib Suleiman. In Jakarta, I am especially grateful to Taufik Abdullah, whose writings are essential to an understanding of the modern history of West Sumatra, and who did much to ease my way when I first embarked on research in Jakarta and West Sumatra and to Mr. St. Mohd. Rasjid, who gave freely of his time and also arranged for interviews with so many of his colleagues and friends, to all of whom my thanks.

Although I cannot mention by name here all the other Indonesians who granted me interviews, or helped me in other ways, their names recur frequently throughout the book as clear evidence of my obligation to them. I hope they will feel I have managed to convey some of the reality of their land and people over the past three quarters of a century.

I wish also to thank the archivists and curators of the documentary collections I have consulted in Padang Panjang, Jakarta, The Hague, Washington, London, Kuala Lumpur and Singapore, particularly to Ch'ng Kim See in the ISEAS library in Singapore, and Alan Riedy and Rohayati Barnard in the Echols Collection at Cornell University. I am grateful to the Social Science Research Council which provided me with funding for research in 1981 and 1995 and the Fulbright Hays Program, which supported my initial dissertation research in 1975-1976 and provided me with a further research fellowship in 1985-1986.

Thanks also go to Rudolf Mrázek and Barbara Harvey, who read an earlier version of the manuscript and provided me with many useful comments and criticisms.

My largest debt of gratitude is to my husband, George McT. Kahin, who first introduced me to Indonesia and whose love, advice, knowledge and patience over the years have had the greatest influence on this book.

To George

Map of Sumatera Barat

0   50 km

——— Major road
━━━ Railroad
- - - - Provincial boundary
······· District boundary
△ Mountains
     1. Mt.Singgalang
     2. Mt.Merapi
     3. Mt. Kerinci
     4. Mt. Sago

Rao

Airbangis

PASAMAN

Lubuk Sikaping

Bonjol

LIMAH
PULUH
KOTA

Suliki

Dangung-
dangung

Payakumbuh

AGAM

Maninjau

Lake
Maninjau

Matur

Baso

4

Halaban

Bukittinggi

TANAH
DATAR

1△

△2

Batu
Sangkar

Padang Panjang

Lake
Singkarak

Sawahlunto

Sijunjung

Pariaman

Kayutanam

Lubuk
Alung

Tabing

Solok

Silungkang

Sungai
Dareh

Padang

Indarung

Teluk
Bayur

Alahan Panjang

SOLOK

Painan

Muara Labuh

3

PESISIR SELATAN

Inderapura

© UMAK

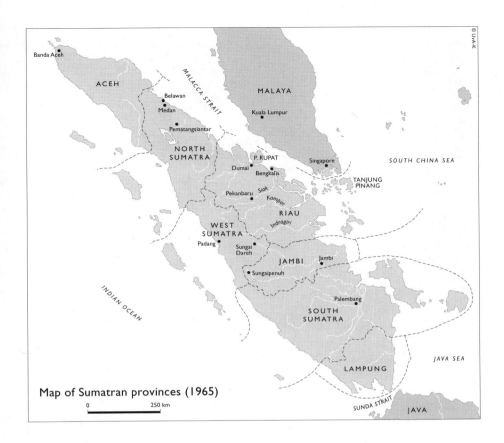

Map of Sumatran provinces (1965)

0 ——————— 250 km

Labels on map:
Banda Aceh
ACEH
MALACCA STRAIT
MALAYA
Belawan
Medan
Kuala Lumpur
Pematangsiantar
NORTH SUMATRA
P. RUPAT
Dumai
Bengkalis
Singapore
SOUTH CHINA SEA
Pekanbaru
Siak
Kampar
TANJUNG PINANG
RIAU
Indragiri
WEST SUMATRA
Padang
Sungai Dareh
JAMBI
Jambi
Sungaipenuh
INDIAN OCEAN
Palembang
SOUTH SUMATRA
JAVA SEA
LAMPUNG
SUNDA STRAIT
JAVA
© UvA-K

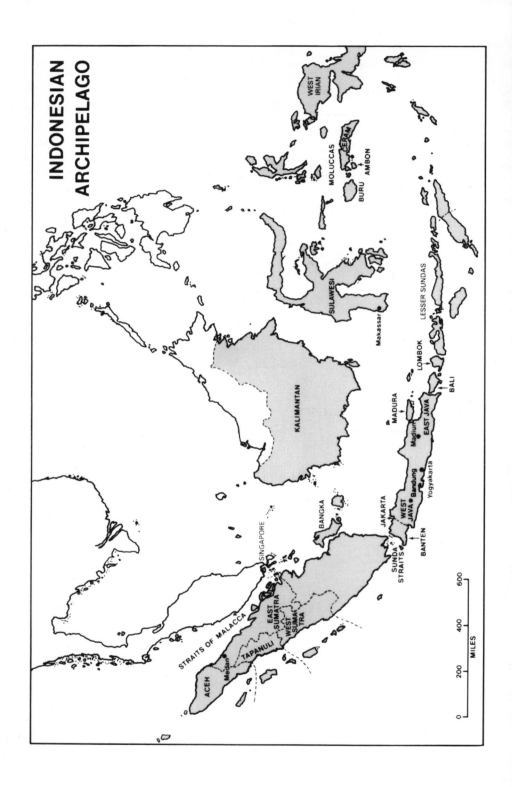

INDONESIAN ARCHIPELAGO

WEST IRIAN

CERAM
MOLUCCAS
BURU
AMBON

SULAWESI

LESSER SUNDAS

KALIMANTAN

Makassar

LOMBOK

MADURA

Madiun
EAST JAVA
BALI

BANGKA

Yogyakarta
WEST JAVA Bandung

SINGAPORE
JAKARTA

BANTEN

SUNDA
STRAITS

STRAITS OF MALACCA

EAST SUMATRA
WEST SUMATRA

TAPANULI

ACEH
Medan

600

400

200

MILES

0

Introduction

The decision, in 1950, to transform the newly independent United States of Indonesia (RIS, Republik Indonesia Serikat) into the unitary Republic of Indonesia was a fateful one. Such a form of government seemed ill-suited to an archipelago made up of more than three thousand islands and many cultural groups and languages. Yet despite this incongruity and the many centrifugal challenges Indonesia has faced, its government succeeded for fifty years in maintaining the Republic's unity. This unity was always enforced by the sheer weight of military power and repression exercised from the centre. But of almost equal importance in holding the disparate societies together was the fact that by the time the country had gained its independence, the idea of a unified Indonesia was deeply embedded within the consciousness of so many of its peoples.[1]

How the concept of Indonesia became such a potent force throughout the archipelago during the final decades of Dutch colonial rule is, then, essential to understanding the success of Indonesia's postindependence governments in maintaining control. Equally salient is the nature of the allegiance felt by the different peoples of the country toward the Indonesian state. Thus far, most studies of Indonesia have viewed these problems largely from the perspective of the centre of power in Java. Only recently has this perspective been balanced by regional histories of other parts of the archipelago, most of which have dealt primarily with the period of Dutch colonial rule, for which reliable archival materials are more accessible. There has been little consideration of how societies in the outer islands have adapted to independent Indonesia.

One such society is that of West Sumatra's Minangkabau people who live on the western periphery of the Indonesian archipelago. Their world (*Alam* Minangkabau) stretches some two hundred miles down the central coastline of western Sumatra on either side of the equator, extending up to a hundred miles inland to embrace the interior highlands of the Bukit Barisan, the mountain chain that divides much of the island of Sumatra on a north-south axis. The heartland (*darek* or *darat*) of the Minangkabau lies at the centre of this mountain range and consists of the three fertile upland plains of Agam, Tanah Datar, and Lima Puluh Kota, each with its own volcano,[2] and separated from one another by rugged hills. A fourth upland valley, that of Solok, stretches south from Tanah Datar along the banks of Lake Singkarak and encompasses the mineral-rich regions of the Ombilin river. The Singkarak/Solok region, together with other upland regions to the north and south of the three core valleys, form part of the *rantau* (fringe) areas of the Minangkabau, as does the narrow coastal plain stretching from Air Bangis in the north to Inderapura in the south.

During the anticolonial struggle and in the early years of independence, West Sumatra differed in many ways from other non-Javanese societies of the outer islands of the Indonesian archipelago, for despite its small geographical size and population (consisting of less than two million in a total Netherlands Indies population of about sixty million in 1939), it played a significant role in national Indonesian politics. The position of Minangkabau leaders in the nationalist movement and independent Indonesian government was second only to that of Javanese (who constituted about 60 percent of Indonesia's total population).

To a remarkable degree, the two ethnic groups, the Javanese and Minangkabau, exemplify two contradictory concepts of state government that have struggled for dominance in postindependence Indonesia. The hierarchical unitary ideal of the Javanese has always been triumphant.[3] But the dissident strands of the Minangkabau, expressing both a more egalitarian and a more decentralized concept of government, have provided a balance and dynamic tension that are still visible today and which, since the overthrow of the Suharto regime, hold the potential for an ultimate reordering of the polity in a form less influenced by the hierarchical 'feudal' structure that characterized precolonial Java, the colonial state, and the postcolonial Republic of Indonesia.

The traditional Javanese belief is that the well-being of the state depends on the strength of the ruler at the centre. Ben Anderson has described this well in his perceptive analysis of Javanese political conceptions and their influence on the postcolonial state:

> The welfare of the collectivity does not depend on the activities of its individual components but on the concentrated energy of the center. The center's fundamental obligation is to itself. If this obligation is fulfilled, popular welfare will necessarily be assured.[4]

In the traditional Minangkabau view, in contrast, the welfare of the polity depends on the harmony and agreement amongst its components – the extended villages (*nagari*), which were the 'highest order of human settlement acknowledged by the adat [traditional custom]'.[5] These *nagari*, which have often been described as 'village republics', exercise their own political and consensus democracy, a form of government very distant from that of the Javanese ideal.

Nearly two centuries ago, Sir Thomas Stamford Raffles encountered the frustrations inherent in the Minangkabau system of consultative government when he first visited the upland interior of West Sumatra in 1818. There he was greeted by a party of local chiefs (*penghulu*) and tried to elicit from them a swift decision regarding the amount of money he should pay to pass through their territory.

> [B]eing informed of my wish to proceed without delay, [they] very quietly stated that they had already taken the subject into consideration, that they had been discussing it since daylight, and had at last come to the resolution, that as they were only two-thirds of the Chiefs, and the other third had not arrived, they would come to no decision at all, but pro-

posed as an accommodation that I should remain where I was for three days, after which, a final decision should be immediately passed.[6]

It was only after the remaining third of the chiefs arrived and they had all debated further for an hour or two, that an amount was agreed upon and Raffles' party was allowed to proceed on its journey.[7]

***

The present study deals with West Sumatra's political history from the late colonial period up to the present, focusing on the course and degree of the Minangkabau people's integration into the contemporary Indonesian state. It provides a local perspective on the growth and development of the nationalist movement in Indonesia, the struggle for independence, and the trauma involved in adapting to an Indonesian polity based on very different concepts of government from those from animated the anticolonial struggle in the region.

West Sumatra was a principal locus of one of the most important rebellions against Dutch colonial rule in the present century (the 1926/27 Communist uprisings) and of the major rebellion against the Indonesian government in the postindependence period (the PRRI/Permesta rebellion of 1958-61). Yet during the nation's struggle against the Dutch, it was one of the most loyal of Indonesia's regions, one that nurtured a remarkably high proportion of the country's preindependence nationalist leaders as well as the first generation of independent Indonesia's political leaders – men whose views ranged across the ideological spectrum.

Of the unique characteristics of West Sumatran society, probably the most striking is the coexistence of one of the strongest remaining matrilineal systems alongside a devout adherence, by most Minangkabau people, to Islam. Some of the conflicts inherent in this coexistence are paralleled in other aspects of West Sumatra's modern history, most notably, the development of strong and seemingly contradictory ideological streams in the late colonial period, wherein, between the 1920s and 1940s, popular Islamic political parties were able to cooperate with a powerful radical/communist coalition. Equally significant during the late colonial period, when Indonesian nationalism became deeply rooted in this society, was the Minangkabau record in establishing private systems of modern elementary and secondary schools (*Diniyyah* and *Sumatra Thawalib*) considerably earlier than such efforts in most of the rest of Indonesia.

A major theme throughout the book is the contrast between Minangkabau and Javanese perceptions of the nature of the postindependence Indonesia that was to replace the colonial Netherlands East Indies. While the Javanese believed that maintenance of a unified Indonesia depended on strong central control, the Minangkabau had always assumed that Indonesia would emerge as a democratic egalitarian state, with its component provinces enjoying a considerable degree of local autonomy. The clash between these two concepts has heavily affected developments not only during Sukarno's presidency but also up to the present day and has largely determined West Sumatra's place within postindependence Indonesia.

After a prologue sketching the region's early history, the book is divided into four major sections. The first section, 'Under Colonial Rule', focuses on the late colonial period (early 1920s to 1942) and emphasises the peculiar character of the nationalist struggle in West Sumatra. Beginning with the background and course of Indonesia's 1926/27 Communist rebellion, it explains both why the rebellion broke out in West Sumatra and the factors preventing it from posing any real threat to the colonial government. It goes on to describe the political movements which subsequently developed in the region and led to a Dutch crackdown on all political activity in 1932/33. In dealing with the events of both periods, I concentrate on the peculiar constellation of political forces in West Sumatra which conditioned the struggle there and which does not conform with the general assumptions regarding the impetus and leadership of the Indonesian nationalist movement. In particular, I stress the importance of the nationalist political activities based in the private (non-Western, non-governmental) educational institutions; the cooperation and interdependence of religious, trading and educational groups in forging the concept of an independent nation, and their views of the place of the Minangkabau region within that nation. I then contrast the political movements, tensions, and nature of leadership in the 1926/27 uprising and the events of the early 1930s. The section closes with an analysis of the apparent calm of the closing years of colonial rule.

The second section, 'Achieving Independence', deals with the Japanese occupation of West Sumatra and the postwar anticolonial revolution, closing with the transfer of sovereignty at the end of 1949. In analysing the dynamics of the local political situation up to that point, I describe the nature of the military forces in West Sumatra, which developed out of the Japanese-sponsored people's army (*Giyugun*), and how they differed from analogous organizations in other parts of the archipelago. I also assess the political and economic strategies used for combatting attempts by the Dutch to reimpose their control. This is followed by an examination of how local plans for pursuing the military struggle differed significantly from those which the Republic's leaders in Java attempted to implement, and a close look at the conflicting views within Minangkabau groups regarding the shape of the independent nation that was emerging from the struggle.

In dealing with the history of the 1940s, I compare the nature of the political parties, tensions, and leadership during the revolution with parallel factors during the prewar nationalist movement. I examine how the independence struggle in West Sumatra and its leadership depart from the picture of the Indonesian revolution most prevalent in previous studies, and analyse the view of West Sumatran nationalists regarding the character of the independent Indonesian state and the importance of their region within it.

The third section, 'Region versus Capital', deals with the history of postindependence Indonesia up to the violent overthrow of the Sukarno regime, describing the events leading up to the regional rebellion of 1958-61, its course, and its aftermath. The section begins with the destruction during the early 1950s of West Sumatran hopes that an Indonesian state and nation could be created which conformed to the earlier concepts that had guided the local nationalist movement. It describes the Jakarta government's dismemberment of West Sumatra's Banteng Division and how the resulting disillusionment within the local military was matched by dissatisfaction among civilian groups with the centralized character of the new Indonesia, the lack of regional autonomy, and Java's political and economic domination of the Republic. The section concentrates on the development of dissension from the time of the transfer of sovereignty up to the outbreak of the 1958 rebellion and the destruction of much of West Sumatran society that took place in the course of, and following, the defeat of that rebellion.

The final section, 'Integration under the New Order', deals with West Sumatra under the Suharto regime. It describes the events in West Sumatra that accompanied and followed the 1965 coup in Jakarta, and their impact on the region's political alignments and its relationship to the centre. It analyses the policies of local leaders who attempted to restore a level of self-confidence to the people of the region after the trauma of the previous decade, during which they had experienced rebellion, defeat, and occupation by Javanese troops. The section focuses on the destruction of the political parties and on how the law, making the national state ideology (the *Pancasila* or Five Principles) the sole basis for all political organizations in Indonesia, removed any remaining political legitimacy from the Islamic parties. It also assesses the local implementation and consequences of the 1979 Village Law, aimed at creating a uniform system of administration (with common norms) at the village level throughout Indonesia.

The superficial harmony between the region and centre during the final decades of Suharto's rule seems to have only been achieved by the Minangkabau people lowering their expectations and accepting West Sumatra's place as merely one of many provinces within Indonesia, rather than as an influential arbiter of the character of the postrevolutionary state. However, in the later years of Suharto's rule, despite policies forged in Jakarta which largely destroyed some of the particular characteristics of local Minangkabau society – most notably the 1979 village law – the relationship of the local to the national level gradually regained a dynamic quality. Through the actions of Minangkabau people both in West Sumatra and in Jakarta (the migrants or *perantau*), the region achieved a level of prosperity and national influence strikingly out of proportion to its relatively small population and economic resources.

The overthrow of Suharto and Indonesia's tentative moves toward creating a democratic decentralized state gave some hope of reversing the trend that had characterized the country's postindependence history. The conclusion describes the events between Suharto's resignation and Indonesia's first free national elections in forty years, and explores the possibility that the 'Era of Reform' might bring about an Indonesian polity more in accord with the ideals of West Sumatra's people during the nationalist struggle and realization of the independent state.

Prologue

The Minangkabau Political Order

The origins of Minangkabau perceptions of government lie far back in its mythical history. According to legend, it was in the mountainous heartland of the Minangkabau that its people were born. At the time of Alexander the Great (Iskandar), when a flood covered the earth, three of Alexander's sons sailed toward the land of the Rising Sun (*benua cina*). After a dispute over their father's crown, the brothers separated, with two of them departing to the east and west to found kingdoms in China and Anatolia, while the ship of the third, the Maharaja di Raja, ran aground on the summit of West Sumatra's highest mountain, Gunung Merapi.[1] As the waters receded, the Maharaja di Raja and his followers descended to found their first settlement, the *nagari* (extended village) of Pariangan Padang Panjang. The core area of their settlement was concentrated around three wells (*luhak*), which became the three upland districts (*luhak nan tigo*) of the heartland – Agam, Tanah Datar, and Lima Puluh Kota.[2]

Two of Maharaja di Raja's descendents, Datuk Ketemanggungan and his half-brother Datuk Perpatih nan Sebatang,[3] formulated the customary (*adat*) forms of government in the Minangkabau world. According to some versions of the story, dissension between the brothers arose when in the mid-fourteenth century, Adityavarman, a prince from Sumatra who had been educated in Java, attempted to bring the Minangkabau region under Javanese control. Arriving with an armada of ships and a large army to impose Majapahit's rule, Adityavarman was greeted not by armed force but by dances and songs. He was wooed by the people and persuaded to send his Javanese troops away. Adityavarman married a sister of Datuk Ketemanggungan and Datuk Perpatih nan Sebatang. But the brothers disagreed over his rightful place in the established system of government, with followers of Dt. Ketemanggungan acknowledging his royal status, while those of Perpatih nan Sebatang refused to recognize him as king.[4] The conflict between the brothers

> resulted in a permanent institutional conflict between their heirs, the
> Koto Piliang (Datuk Ketemanggungan) and the Bodi Tjaniago (Datuk
> Perpatih nan Sebatang). The political system of the Bodi Tjaniago is
> based on 'egalitarian' principles in the sense that the nagari of this tradi-
> tion is ruled by a group of penghulu as the representatives of their re-
> spective *suku* [Minangkabau kinship group]. The Koto Piliang recog-
> nizes the position of a *puntjak* – a chief – as the *primus inter pares*, and it is
> thus assumed to be more autocratic.[5]

This difference is reflected in the council halls (*balai*) of the two traditions:

> a Bodi-Tjaniago *balai* has a level floor, so that, as the proverb says of the *panghulu*, 'when they sit they are equally low, when they stand they are equally tall'; a Koto-Piliang *balai* has a raised dais at each end for the heads of the hierarchy.[6]

Despite differences in the philosophies of the Bodi Caniago and Koto Piliang, in practice, both had to be accommodated within Minangkabau society. According to Darwis Thaib Dt. Sidi Bandaro, the more hierarchical ideas of the Koto Piliang, in particular, had to be adapted to the egalitarian order of the Minangkabau, resulting in a situation where 'the laws are made from below although the orders come from above'.[7] The tension between the two traditions of governing is one of the dichotomies that maintain a balanced tension within the society. P.E. de Josselin de Jong has characterized the relationship between the two traditions as, frequently, a 'sharp rivalry, with nevertheless an underlying sense of unity, as one cannot exist without the other, and the co-operation of both is needed to make up the total community'.[8] In general, each *nagari* (extended village) is considered to belong to one or other of the traditions, although representatives of both exist within it.

The *nagari* varied widely in their internal organization, in part dependent on whether they primarily adhered to the Bodi Caniago or the Koto Piliang tradition. All, however, followed a matrilineal system of inheritance, all were governed by a village council, and all had to meet certain criteria to be recognized as *nagari*. Each *nagari* had its own territory with clear geographical limits and its own council hall (*balai*), mosque, road, public bathing place, and open field. The Adat Consultative Council (Dewan Kerapatan Adat) heading the village drew its members from the traditional heads (*penghulu andiko*), representing the family (clan [*kaum*] or group [*suku*]).[9] In addition, however, the religious scholars (*ulama*) and intellectuals (*cerdik pandai*) also exerted recognized legitimate authority and formed part of the *nagari* leadership. The strands in the society represented by the three categories of leaders were woven together to form a unity, expressed in the saying '*Adat* is led by the *penghulu*, religion by the *ulama*, the government by the *cerdik pandai*, and all three entwine together to form one'.[10] The strands are not mutually exclusive and all three elements are not infrequently combined within a single individual, who is at the same time a traditional leader, an Islamic scholar, and an intellectual.

The *nagari* of the region existed in a loose federation headed by the Minangkabau raja who, from the beginning of the fifteenth century, had his seat in the interior kingdom of Pagarruyung, in the *luhak* (district) of Batipuh Tanah Datar. Despite the existence of this royal family, however, 'kingship never functioned as a governing institution',[11] and the position of the Pagarruyung raja could not be likened to that of rajas in other parts of the archipelago, such as the raja of Mataram in Java, for in practice he had no authority or executive, legislative, or juridical power whatsoever with respect to the *luhak* and *nagari*.

When the Minangkabau people began moving from the core upland regions to the coastal areas of West Sumatra, the settlements they established there were fre-

Statue of Adityavarman in the National Museum, Jakarta

quently less democratic than those in the heartland.[12] These coastal areas were also more open to outside influence, and from the mid-sixteenth to mid-seventeenth century many of those north of Padang came under virtual domination of the kingdom of Aceh at the northern tip of Sumatra. Even today, these coastal regions display the most extensive vestiges of a hierarchical order of society with inherited titles.

As the Minangkabau intellectual and writer A.A. Navis has noted, ambivalent feelings toward Adityavarman and his place in West Sumatra's history extend to the present day. Despite the important role he played in bringing glory to the Minangkabau kingdom, and even though from the point of view of the matrilineal order he himself was a Minangkabau,[13] his affiliation with the Javanese rulers render him controversial. In the early 1950s, Minister of Education Muhammad Yamin wanted to establish an Adityavarman University, but the people rejected the name, changing it to Andalas [Sumatra] University in 1956. Similarly, in 1975, Governor Harun Zain refused to allow the museum then being constructed in Padang to be called the Adityavarman museum, a decision reversed by his successor.[14]

The most famous legend of West Sumatra deals with the relationship between the Minangkabau and the Javanese. It probably originates in an incident during the Javanese expedition sent by King Krtanagara of Singasari against Sumatra in the late-thirteenth century, several decades prior to the coming of Adityavarman. Confronting the invading Javanese forces, the two Minangkabau rulers (Datuk Ketemanggungan and Datuk Perpatih nan Sabatang) were aware that they could not be successful on the battlefield, and so decided to win by a trick. They proposed that the ultimate result of the war should rest on the outcome of a contest between two buffalo, one selected by each side. The Javanese commander accepted the proposal, and chose a huge, fierce animal to represent his forces. The Sumatrans, on the other hand, chose a small calf, which they did not feed for several days prior to the contest. They also fixed sharp knives to the stubs of its horns. When the hungry calf entered the arena, it thought the buffalo waiting there was its mother, so it rushed over, thrust its knife-tipped horns into the huge animal's stomach, and disembowelled it in trying to get milk.[15] From this contest the people of West Sumatra derived their name, Minangkabau (Victorious Buffalo), and their conviction of superior intelligence to the Javanese.

Religion and Colonialism

An intrinsic part of Minangkabau society for the past several centuries has been Islam, which was introduced into the west-coast ports of the region in the early-sixteenth century by Indian Muslim traders from Gujarat. Gold traders from both the west and east coasts of Sumatra carried their religion with them to the Minangkabau highlands, and the centres of the gold trade became the first to be converted to Islam.[16] Islam added another apparently contradictory element to Minangkabau society, for its patrilineal line of inheritance stood in seeming conflict with the traditional matrilineal order of the Minangkabau. Until the early-nineteenth century, Muslim communities tended to form enclaves not fully incorporated within Minangkabau society.[17]

By the eighteenth century, two major Sufi orders were active in the Minangkabau region – the Naksyabandiyah and the Syattariyah.[18] These *tarekat* (religious brotherhoods) organized schools (*surau*) whose students were characterized by their utter devotion to their teacher (*syekh* or *guru*) who taught his pupils the Islamic faith.

> In addition to teaching the reading of the Koran and of the commentaries, the *syekh* and the various *guru* who gave instruction in a large *surau* would teach the particular rules, methods and religious practices which constituted the 'path' laid down by their own order for the seeker after God. The *syekh* would also teach his own secret *ilmu* (esoteric knowledge) concerning methods of self-defence, means of making oneself invulnerable in the face of weapons, and ways of consulting numerological treatises to decide upon auspicious days, such learning, with its pre-Islamic overtones and magical colouring having been readily assimilated by Minangkabau Islam.[19]

The relationship between religion and Minangkabau society underwent a critical change with the coming of the Paderi movement in the early-nineteenth century.

Three Minangkabau studying in Mecca in the late-eighteenth century witnessed the city's occupation by forces of the Islamic fundamentalist movement founded by Ibn 'Abd al/Wahhab, known as the Wahhabis. Impressed by their teachings, these three haji – Haji Miskin, Haji Abdur Rahman, and Haji Muhamad Arif – on their return to West Sumatra in 1803, used the Wahhabis as their model when they founded the Paderi movement which flourished in the Minangkabau for the next thirty-five years.[20] The movement aimed at purifying Islam in West Sumatra from its superstitious accretions.

Some of the most important Paderi leaders, including one of the pioneers of the reformist movement in the late-eighteenth century, the renowned Syattariyah *syekh* Tuanku Nan Tuo, recognized the need to compromise with traditional local leaders when acting to remove the alleged corruption from the society and win adherents. His moderate attitude was also adopted by the most famous second generation Paderi leader, who was to head the struggle against the Dutch, Tuanku Imam Bonjol.[21] However, many of the Paderi followed the Arabian model in espousing religious war (*jihad*) as the principal means for extending their influence, and this provided the pretext for the entry of Dutch colonial rule to the Minangkabau highlands.

The Paderi movement tended to exert greatest strength in the districts of Agam and Lima Puluh Kota. Many of its opponents among the traditional village leaders and religious conservatives fled these Paderi-controlled upland regions and sought refuge with the *adat* princes, whose coastal kingdoms formed centres of opposition to the Paderi. There they sought assistance from the Dutch.

Since the late-seventeenth century, the Dutch had exerted some influence in West Sumatra, but this had been mainly restricted to a few coastal trading ports, particularly Padang, through which the Dutch East India Company (voc) could obtain gold, and to a lesser extent pepper, in exchange for Indian cotton. Largely replaced by the British in these areas, from the 1780s until the end of the Napoleonic wars, the Dutch only regained the port of Padang in May 1819. Soon afterwards, they began receiving requests from both coastal princes and refugees from the highlands for aid against the Paderi.[22]

With the ostensible aim of restoring peace to Sumatra, the Dutch began military actions in 1821, and by 1825 were concentrating their efforts on closing off the Paderis' sea communications on the West Coast. However, it was only after they defeated a rebellion in Central Java headed by Prince Diponegoro that they were able to amass sufficient strength on Sumatra to drive back the Paderi forces. Even then, it took them more than six years to defeat Imam Bonjol and his supporters. The two sides reached an uneasy settlement in late 1832, but less than four months later, rebellion again broke out in the mountain stronghold of Bonjol and in the other Paderi regions of northern Agam.[23] After a two-year siege, Bonjol finally fell to the Dutch in August 1837. Three months later, they captured Imam Bonjol, exiling him and other Paderi leaders from the Minangkabau.[24]

For the rest of the nineteenth century, the Dutch ruled West Sumatra in accordance with the Long Declaration (*Plakaat Panjang*) of 1833, under which they had promised the anti-Paderi leaders not to impose any direct taxation in the Minangkabau. This enabled the leaders who cooperated with the Dutch to maintain the fiction that they were their partners, not their subjects.[25]

Outsiders had initially been attracted to West Sumatra because of its gold, and to a lesser extent, its pepper. By the late-eighteenth century, however, gold supplies were largely exhausted, and from then on, by far the most valuable of West Sumatra's export crops was coffee. To improve collection and delivery of this crop, in 1847 the Dutch introduced forced cultivation into the region.[26] Under this system, either traditionally selected or Dutch-appointed *adat* leaders acted as colonial agents charged with collecting the coffee harvest. In many *nagari*, the Dutch created a new position, that of *penghulu suku rodi* (lineage chief for forced labour), to carry out the government's corvée policies.[27] The salaries of Dutch-appointed officials were determined as a percentage of the coffee production of their area.

To assist them in governing West Sumatra, the Dutch attempted to make use of the traditional order of Minangkabau society, distorting the character and shape of the institutions to conform with their own needs. The traditional *kerapatan nagari* (village council) became the lowest level of the colonial administration; the *penghulu* in each *nagari* who had previously jointly governed its affairs, now had to select one of their number to serve as village head (*nagarihoofd*). By appointing individuals to head the village, the Dutch introduced a far more authoritarian cast to the Minangkabau village polity, for previously, even within the more hierarchical Koto Piliang villages, the village head had been merely first among equals. The colonial authorities shaped traditional village federations (*laras*), which had been loose alliances among a group of *nagari* for mutual benefit, into the subdistrict level of the Dutch administration, with a *laras* head (*larashoofd*) selected from the heads of the component *nagari*.[28] A hierarchical system of government was thus created, consistent with the fact that real power now lay with the top level of the West Sumatra government, the Dutch Resident, and no longer in the *nagari*.

The colonial administration's use of the traditional order of Minangkabau society to enable it to exercise its authority and exploit the area's resources more easily, continued into the present century, with the Nagari Ordinance of 1914. Although ostensibly aimed at reestablishing an 'autonomous village community', this ordinance restricted membership of the *nagari* council to 'core *penghulu*' – men whom the government recognized as 'original *penghulu*'[29] – who would be the only traditional leaders allowed to hold authority in the *nagari*. By assuming the right to select these *penghulu* the Dutch encroached upon *adat* prerogatives and also created divisions among the *adat* leaders between those who did and did not receive government recognition.

The Beginnings of Anticolonial Nationalism

Historians of Indonesia generally trace the 'awakening of the nation of Indonesia' to the founding in 1908 of the 'first national organization in Indonesia', the Budi Utomo (Noble Endeavour).[30] Made up almost entirely of Javanese administrators and intellectuals, the Budi Utomo served 'as a bridge between enlightened colonial administrators and Javanese intellectuals'.[31]

> the Budi Utomo was predominantly Javanese-cultural. It sought the stimulation and advancement of the Javanese people (whom it regarded as the Javanese, Sundanese, and Madurese language-groups, all of whom

had adopted a form of Javanese culture) toward a more harmonious development. It sought to strengthen them to face modern life by rejuvenating Javanese culture.[32]

Despite the exclusively Javanese focus of the organization and its elite character, the date of its foundation, May 20, is still celebrated in Indonesia as 'National Awakening Day'.

In that same year, 1908, an anti-Dutch rebellion broke out in the Minangkabau, primarily in reaction to the introduction of direct taxation into the region. In the early years of the century, a decline in the value of coffee production had led the Dutch to disregard the promises they had made in the Plakaat Panjang and to abolish the cultivation system in favour of a direct tax. Their action sparked violent uprisings in many parts of West Sumatra during 1908, led by religious scholars particularly of the Syattariyah mystical brotherhood, as well as by *adat* leaders who felt betrayed by the unilateral Dutch abrogation of the agreement and saw their own positions undermined by the new taxation system.[33] In subsequent decades, many of those who led the independence struggle against the Dutch in West Sumatra recalled the 1908 uprising together with the Paderi wars as the two most significant episodes in the course of their people's nationalist awakening. There would indeed seem to be equally valid grounds for considering the tax rebellion in the Minangkabau as an early manifestation of anticolonial nationalism, and viewing the foundation of the Budi Utomo in this light.

The first Indonesia-wide vehicle for the anti-Dutch nationalist movement, however, was the Sarikat Islam (SI, Islamic League), established in Surakarta in 1912 as a protective association for indigenous batik merchants. Attracting support from a broad spectrum of society, it grew rapidly, claiming more than two million members throughout the archipelago by 1918, and calling for complete independence for the Netherlands Indies. The first West Sumatran branch of the SI was founded in Padang and soon spread throughout much of West Sumatra.[34] Although the SI embraced a wide range of political ideologies, in both Java and Sumatra it was the Islamic leaders who dominated the association in its early years. Increasingly, however, this dominance was challenged by Marxist and non-Marxist radicals among its members. Their association, the ISDV (Indies Social Democratic Association), founded in 1914, was transformed in 1920 into the Indonesian Communist Party (PKI, Partai Komunis Indonesia). From then on, a bitter struggle developed between Muslim and Communist leaders for control of the Islamic League's regional branches and the growing trade union movement allied with the League.[35]

This struggle took place in an atmosphere in which the Dutch colonial government was taking the first steps toward granting very limited autonomy to the Netherlands East Indies with the establishment of the Volksraad (People's Council) at the end of 1916, which had its first meeting in May of 1918. Leaders of the Budi Utomo enthusiastically participated in the Council, as did, to a lesser extent, the more moderate members of the Islamic League.[36] The evolutionary parliamentary path toward greater autonomy inherent in the Volksraad, however, was strongly opposed by the younger, more radical members of the League, particularly by

Semaun and members of the Communist faction. This inevitably led to the split within the League in the early 1920s, and the Communist Party's more active pursuit of a revolutionary path that would eventually lead to the 1926/27 Rebellion, which had one of its two principal centres in West Sumatra.

Late Colonial Rule

CHAPTER I

Background and Eruption of the 1927 Rebellion

The Brink of Rebellion

The early 1920s were a period of unrest throughout the Netherlands East Indies. Hopes raised in World War I that the Dutch would begin to allow Indonesians some role in governing themselves had been disappointed. The influence of Communist and socialist ideas had sparked strikes and political conflict to which the Dutch had responded with further repression. The unrest was felt throughout the Indies, no more so than in the province of Sumatra's West Coast.

By 1926, West Sumatra was in a state of turmoil. The political, religious, and educational ferment that had developed over the preceding years was initially centred in Padang Panjang – a small windy town lying in the foothills of Mounts Merapi and Singgalang, at the upper gateway to the Anai Pass which leads precipitously down from the fertile Minangkabau highlands to the Padang coastal plain. In the early decades of the twentieth century, Padang Panjang was a major crossroads for traders transporting their goods between the highlands and the coast, and also for political, religious, and educational ideas arising from within or penetrating from outside the region.

Innovative non-governmental religious schools had made their first appearance in this small town more than a decade earlier, attracting students from throughout the Malay world, and establishing branches in other parts of Sumatra and beyond.[1] A so-called People's School was also founded there in 1924, modeled after the radical school network first established in Semarang by the outstanding Communist leader Tan Malaka, who had been born in West Sumatra and was now in exile in the Philippines.[2]

In the religious field, Padang Panjang was the place where the reformist or modernist generation of Muslims, the so-called Young Group (*Kaum Muda*), fought many of their intellectual battles, not only with the region's older, more conservative religious scholars (*Kaum Tua*), but also with their own contemporaries and with their increasingly radical students. Dissension in the schools merged with disagreements among political activists as – in the early months of 1926 – rumours began to circulate of an impending Communist rebellion against Dutch rule throughout the Indies.

The Indonesian Communist Party's short history had been a turbulent one. Initially part of the mass Islamic League (Sarikat Islam), the Communists were expelled in 1923, after which they struggled to replace the League as 'the only major representative of the Indonesian popular movement'.[3] During its meeting at Prambanan in December 1925, the Communist Party Central Committee called for a nation-wide uprising against the Dutch, to begin in Sumatra during July 1926.[4] But government counter-measures, together with dissension among the Party's members and branches, delayed the rebellion's outbreak.

Most outspoken in criticism of the Party's decision to revolt was Tan Malaka, its former chairman, who sent a message from his exile in Manila arguing that a successful rebellion could only be mounted after a period of preparation and organized mass action. Contending that the Party was heading for a putsch, not a rebellion, he warned that its actions would only provide the colonial authorities with an excuse to crack down on all political activity. The letter Tan Malaka sent outlining his arguments against the proposed rebellion did not reach the Communist Party's Central Committee before plans had gone so far that many of the leaders and some of the Party branches were too committed to be willing to draw back.[5] Consequently, preparations went ahead, though when the rebellion did not break out on the scheduled date, Tan Malaka's campaign against it began to exert a growing influence on the Party branches, particularly in Bandung and West Sumatra.[6]

In West Sumatra, the Communists were torn between their loyalty to the Party organization in Java, which was calling for rebellion, and the conflicting orders they were receiving from Tan Malaka. This issue split the section of the Communist Party in Padang, which had close ties with the Java-based party, from that in Padang Panjang, which was more strongly influenced by Tan Malaka and his followers. As tension grew in the region, sporadic terrorist actions broke out in which several lower administrative officials were assassinated. In response to the unrest, the Dutch began to crack down on all their perceived opponents, arresting or exiling not only the well-known Communist or 'extremist' religious leaders but also many ordinary members of the burgeoning radical movements.

On June 28, 1926, the political and religious ferment was echoed in the natural world when a violent earthquake, followed by an eruption of Mt. Merapi, devastated much of Padang Panjang and the surrounding area, destroying most of the buildings, including the barely completed Islamic School (*Diniyyah*) for girls which had opened just two days earlier.

Padang Panjang was not the only focus of unrest in West Sumatra, and in the aftermath of the earthquake, it lost its place as the major centre of rebellious activity against the Dutch. This position was assumed by Silungkang, a small weaving town of about three hundred households, lying in a narrow, desolate valley about forty miles southeast of Padang Panjang. Located on the railroad line between Solok and the mining town of Sawahlunto, Silungkang was famous for its textiles throughout the archipelago. A local trader, Sulaiman Labai, had established a branch of the Islamic League (*Sarikat Islam*) there about ten years earlier, and this had been transformed into the People's League (*Sarikat Rakyat*) in 1924, after the Communists' expulsion from the Islamic League. Sulaiman Labai and his followers had close ties with union leaders at the Ombilin coalmine in nearby Sawahlunto. Silungkang was to become the major centre of the 1927 rebellion in West Sumatra.

When the Indonesian Communist Party first began to plan for an uprising, its West Sumatra branches were among the most vocal in pressing for speedy action. It therefore seemed likely that preparations would proceed apace once the Padang leader Sutan Said Ali, who represented West Sumatra at the December 1925 Pram-banan meeting of the Communist Party, brought back the orders for the revolt.[7] This did not happen, in part because Said Ali was dilatory in returning and did not actually reach Padang until the end of January 1926. By this time, rumours circulat-ing about his relations with a girl to whom he was not married had undermined his authority, making several local Communist sections, including those at Sawahlunto and Silungkang, reluctant to follow his orders. His position in Padang too was weak-ened, and the cohesion of the PKI section there further eroded when in May of 1926 he moved to Medan and was arrested by the Dutch on the 22nd of that month.[8]

In August 1926, the head of the subdistrict of Sicincin in the Anai valley was assassinated,[9] and in September, an *adat* head was murdered in Kamang, near Bukit-tinggi, and a village head was shot in the Solok area.[10] In response, Dutch authorities accelerated their round-up of suspected Communists, and on October 13 they arrested the two major Silungkang leaders, Sulaiman Labai and Dt. Bagindo Ratu.[11]

Background to the Unrest

West Sumatra was one of only three areas where the projected nation-wide Commu-nist uprising actually broke out in the form of an armed conflict, however disorga-nized, chaotic, and unsuccessful.[12] The rebellion occurred even though many local radical leaders had already fled to other parts of Sumatra and across the Malacca Strait – in response to Tan Malaka's orders – and although most of the remaining key leaders had been arrested during the closing months of 1926. Despite all these set-backs, the idea of armed opposition to Dutch rule still exerted a strong appeal; the reasons for this, and the general nature of the unrest throughout the region, can per-haps best be understood if we examine the character of West Sumatra's political life at the time, and the different economic, social, political, and religious streams that converged there.

First, the Minangkabau, whom Ch. O. van der Plas described as 'a restless people with a long tradition of revolt and resistance',[13] had always been proud of their his-tory of opposition to outside forces, whether from Java or from Europe. In fanning the current unrest, West Sumatran revolutionaries recalled their two major previ-ous revolts against the Dutch – the Paderi Wars between 1820 and 1837, when the Minangkabau resisted the Dutch extension of their authority over much of the high-lands, and the tax rebellion of 1908, when the rural religious leaders of the Syat-tariyah mystical Islamic brotherhood spearheaded protests against Dutch efforts to impose direct taxes on the local people, in contravention of the Long Agreement which had ended the Paderi wars nearly seventy years earlier.[14] Although one author has asserted that 'The [1908] rebellion's failure sealed the demise of traditional forms of resistance,' which from then on 'would develop through other institutions such as political parties, unions, and national (Indonesian) religious organisa-tions',[15] these institutions provided a thin veneer over what was essentially a contin-uum between this rebellion and the events of 1926/27. The revolutionaries fre-quently evoked both the 1908 rebellion and the Paderi Wars as they fanned the dissatisfaction of the early 1920s.

In the years preceding the uprising, the dynamic which most strengthened cohesion among anti-Dutch groups in West Sumatra stemmed from the overlapping interests and membership of many of the differing streams making up the society – the religious leaders, the teachers and students in the private schools, the trading community, the political activists, and even some of the traditional village authorities. Members of the merchant community, through their connections with people in all strata of Minangkabau society, oiled the wheels of anticolonial activity. But it was the traders' interaction with the teachers and students at the religious schools that had the greatest impact on the local nationalist movement. The trading community was particularly close to West Sumatra's Islamic leaders, a closeness that was increased by their shared fears and grievances. As the Minangkabau intellectual A.A. Navis has noted, in the early years of the twentieth century, the merchants in the market towns, such as Padang and Padang Panjang, supported the modernist Islamic movement, which spread quickly from these centres to the traders' home bases in the villages and countryside.[16]

Both Minangkabau merchants and the Muslim community as a whole felt squeezed out by Dutch protection of European and Chinese traders in Sumatra's west coast ports and by the new 'Ethical' policy, under which secular Western education became the major vehicle for the indigenous people to gain access to positions of wealth and influence. Local Muslims saw this policy as part of an effort to undermine Islam and strengthen Christian missionary proselytizing throughout the colony.

Fears over Dutch intentions provided a major impetus for the propagation and expansion of the private Islamic schools throughout West Sumatra. These school networks, particularly those of the Sumatra Thawalib and Diniyyah Schools, provided a political fulcrum for anticolonial ideas. Their role echoed the one played earlier by the *tarekat* networks in both the Paderi wars and, more importantly, in the 1908 uprising. With respect to the latter, Ken Young has noted that the political potential of the religious schools 'lay in their extended organisational links across nagari [extended village] boundaries, and in their independence from the authority structures of nagari, laras [district] and the colonial government... [T]heir religious pupils enjoyed high mobility and fellowship with fellow tarekat members throughout the heartland.'[17] This was as true of the modernist schools in 1926/27 as it had been of the tarekat *surau* in 1908.

The networks of schools – whether of the traditional *tarekat* of the Sufi orders in the nineteenth century or of the Sumatra Thawalib and Diniyyah in the twentieth – overlapped with the Minangkabau trading networks. In fact, many private schools could only survive financially by carrying out commercial activities, so the teachers and students were themselves often also traders, and most of the schools received financial support from the trading community.[18] In addition, travelling merchants boarded at the *surau* on their journeys both within West Sumatra itself and between the region and the outside world.[19]

In contrast to the situation in other parts of the archipelago, in West Sumatra most entrepreneurs were indigenous: this was the case with all of the small traders, and by the end of the nineteenth century also with some of the large-scale entrepreneurs, though the most important cash-crop merchants were often Chinese.[20] The Minangkabau traders had many grievances. Throughout the nineteenth century, in their efforts to achieve territorial control over Sumatra during and after the Paderi wars and also to implement their coffee cultivation system, the Dutch pursued policies aimed at destroying the traditional Minangkabau trading routes which had run to the east coast of the island and across the Malacca Strait to Penang and Singapore. The colonial administration hampered these trading operations, cutting off the indigenous traders' access to the east-coast ports, and thus forcing them to shift their trade to the west coast, particularly the overseas ports of Padang and Pariaman, where Dutch authority was most secure.[21] The Padang traders themselves felt discriminated against by Dutch policies which favoured the business operations of Europeans and the Chinese.

In the Islamic world, the profession of a trader is respected, almost as much as that of a religious scholar or *ulama*; 'For Muhammad before he became a prophet had also been a trader'.[22] Indonesian Muslims contend that the Qur'an's prohibition of *riba*, which can be translated as usury or interest from loans, has meant that Muslim traders behave differently from those in the capitalist system. Islam frowns on the accumulation of wealth through ruining others, counselling that 'If any one is in difficulty let there be a delay till he is able to pay'.[23] Modernists have argued that the interpretation of the prohibition of *riba* is a moral one:

> Roughly speaking, the opprobium of *riba* (in the sense in which this term is used in the Qur'an and in many sayings of the Prophet) attaches to profits obtained through interest-bearing loans involving an *exploitation of the economically weak by the strong and resourceful*... With this definition in mind, we realise that that question as to what kinds of financial transactions fall within the category of *riba* is, in the last resort, a moral one, closely connected with the socio-economic motivation underlying the mutual relationship of borrower and lender.[24]

So, at least theoretically, trading in an Islamic society is characterized by more cooperation and less competition than in the liberal and capitalist world. In West Sumatra it has been noted that, even though merchants trade individually, when they start out they receive support and capital from established traders until they themselves are in a position to stand on their own feet, and it is rare to find a merchant living alone on a grand scale among poorer neighbours.[25] Recognizing this characteristic, Communist propaganda in the early 1920s emphasized that traders and capitalists were not necessarily synonymous. Indonesian Communists defended the role of the small-scale merchants, arguing that '... although they trade, they are not capitalists themselves but rather victims of capitalism. They do not seek riches with the sole purpose of growing fat and lazy, they merely seek a bowl of rice, and they are suppressed by capitalist enterprises which have swallowed up their entire livelihood'.[26]

After World War I, opposition to Dutch rule was widespread in West Sumatran society – in the trading community, schools, and among religious leaders, as well as members of the radical political parties. Only the native officials of the Dutch administration, and the officially recognized office-holders in the *adat* community, appear to have openly sided with the colonial authority. Opposition to colonial rule was strengthened by influences coming from outside the region, for even the most remote villages in West Sumatra often had ties with other parts of the Indies, and some also with the Malay peninsula and with Europe and the Middle East.[27]

These ties sprang in part from the Minangkabau tradition, known as *merantau*, of young men migrating to seek their fortune outside their home territory, where matrilineal inheritance laws meant that 'land essentially belonged to women'.[28] As a result of this migration, Minangkabau traders were found in many other parts of Sumatra, in Java and the eastern archipelago, as well as in Malaya and Singapore. In addition, many young men from the region went to the Middle East to continue their schooling – to Mecca where the leading religious teacher at the Masjid al Haram (Mecca mosque) was Ahmad Chatib, an Islamic scholar from West Sumatra,[29] and to the Al Azhar University in Cairo which in the early decades of the twentieth century attracted growing numbers of Minangkabau students. The fact that the Dutch established no tertiary educational institutions in West Sumatra meant that the most able and ambitious young men who wished to acquire a Western education were also forced to leave their home area and continue their schooling in Java, or in the Netherlands. Few of these Western-educated intellectuals returned to their home region, but many became leaders of political movements in Java, while maintaining ties and followers in West Sumatra. Notable among these in the years following World War I were Abdul Muis and Haji Agus Salim of the Islamic League; the nationalist Communist Tan Malaka; and Mohammad Hatta, leader of the Indonesian nationalist students' organization, Perhimpunan Indonesia, in the Netherlands.

The young Middle-Eastern-educated Muslims returned to Sumatra more often than their Western-educated counterparts. More than a century earlier, three such returnees from Mecca had brought back Wahhabist teachings and had sparked the Paderi wars.[30] In the early years of the twentieth century, three pupils of Ahmad Chatib in Mecca – Syekh Abdul Karim Amrullah (Haji Rasul), Haji Abdullah Ahmad, and Syekh Mohd. Djamil Djambek – began to spread modernist Islamic teachings when they returned home. In accordance with the views of their teacher, however, although they embraced many of the teachings of the Egyptian religious reformer Muhammad Abduh, these three Minangkabau *haji* limited their propagation of these ideas strictly to the fields of religion and education, and were extremely reluctant to embrace the political ideas of Abduh's colleague, Jamal al-Din al-Afghani, that were sweeping Egypt and Turkey at the time.[31] Such a separation of religion and politics, however, was not respected by many of their students.[32]

Centres of Opposition

In the years leading up to the rebellion of 1927, there were three main centres of radical politics and opposition to colonial rule in West Sumatra – Padang Panjang, Silungkang, and, to a lesser extent, Padang. The context of this political activity and the character of the movements in each of the towns differed markedly.

Padang Panjang:

The Islamic reformists established the most famous of their modernist schools, the Sumatra Thawalib, in Padang Panjang. It was successor to a traditional religious school, the Surau Djembatan Besi (Iron Bridge Surau) which had been founded around the turn of the century by Syekh Abdullah, who was succeeded first by Syekh Daud Rasjidi and then, in 1911, by Haji Rasul after his return from the Middle East.[33] Schools in other parts of the region adopted the Sumatra Thawalib name, and by the early 1920s there were a total of five schools within the system.[34]

The most influential teacher at Padang Panjang's Sumatra Thawalib, Zainuddin Labai el Junusiah, had not studied in either Mecca or Cairo, but had received his entire schooling in West Sumatra. Born in Padang Panjang in 1890, he left government elementary school after less than four years, over a disagreement with his teacher. He then studied with his father, and after his father's death spent a couple of years as a young vagabond (*parewa*) wandering around the villages.[35] Returning to his studies, he taught himself Dutch and English, as well as Arabic, and then spent some years as the pupil and assistant of Syekh Abbas of Padang Jepang. Zainuddin returned to Padang Panjang in 1913 to teach at the Iron Bridge *surau*.[36] He was instrumental in transforming the *surau* into the Sumatra Thawalib, a school organized along modern lines with desks, classes, and a curriculum which included non-religious subjects.[37] In 1915 Zainuddin also established an even more modern school for both boys and girls, which he named the Diniyyah school. While the Sumatra Thawalib schools still laid their greatest stress on religious education and Arabic, the Diniyyah schools emphasized general subjects, such as writing, reading, mathematics, astronomy, geography, health, botany, and education. But the two school systems cooperated closely, and students often attended the Thawalib in the morning and the Diniyyah in the evening.[38]

Zainuddin Labai was much more radical than his older colleagues. He was very attracted to the Cairo modernists, and was 'probably the greatest reader of Said Rasjid Ridha in Minangkabau'. He was also an admirer of the Turkish nationalist leader Mustafa Kamal (Kamal Attaturk), translating a biography of him and teaching classes at the Diniyyah about Kamal's nationalist movement in Turkey.[39] (The biography was widely read among young people in West Sumatra both then and later.) Labai refused the offer of a subsidy from the Dutch Assistant Resident to support his Diniyyah school,[40] and he made no attempt to persuade his students against the radical and Communist ideas to which they were increasingly attracted. In 1918 he founded *Al Munir*, an Islamic journal brought out by the students of the two schools, and continued to publish it until his death in 1924.[41] The office of this journal became one of the major centres in West Sumatra where young Muslims could debate and exchange their ideas. A former pupil, who was to become an influential Muslim leader, Mansur Daud Dt. Palimo Kajo, recalled it as follows:

> It was full of newspapers from all over Indonesia, sent in exchange for copies of the Al Munir magazine. In that office all the students of Thawalib and Dinijjah gathered to read the newspapers, and expand

their view of the situation both within the country and abroad. And that office also became a 'debating club' both as training for discussing religious problems and for religious proselitizing. In short Al Munir's office was the Dinijjah and Thawalib students' most influential meeting place, not only in spreading intellectual ideas but also in strengthening friendship, comradeship and unity.

The atmosphere became even livelier when a lunch counter, called 'Boffet Merah' [Red Canteen] was set up on Komidi Street in Pasar Usang [Padang Panjang], as a place for slaking one's thirst and also for supplying study materials, both to the Thawalib and Dinijjah students and to the general public. That was the first result from the cooperative efforts of the Thawalib and Dinijjah students. It was truly delightful. The more so when from time to time Tuan Zainuddin Labaj el Junusij came out with one of his jokes. Ah... there are too many memories of those past times. The Thawalib and Dinijjah students who are now old must be truly moved when they recall the atmosphere of that past golden age.[42]

The recollections of Djamaluddin Tamin, a teacher in the Sumatra Thawalib schools – who would later become a leader of the People's League and one of Tan Malaka's chief lieutenants – provide a contrasting view of the activities of the Islamic schools and of the 'Red Canteen'. In recalling Padang Panjang in 1920, he too remembers this meeting place:

Padang Panjang, a small town in Central Sumatra, was the gathering place and centre of Religious schools and students of mysticism from all of Sumatra, and there from the beginning of 1920 the Socialism-Communism of the Red League [Sarikat Merah] began to be discussed. So, from the beginning Padang Panjang became the centre of the red group, became the *red town* in Sumatra, simply by establishing the BOPET MERAH [*sic*.: Red Canteen] as the Red group's cooperative branch there, that is five or six months before the PKI [Indonesian Communist Party] was born in Semarang in 1920.[43]

From 1920, the religious schools, particularly in Padang Panjang, became places where religion and radical politics overlapped and reinforced each other in the face of opposition from the schools' more conservative founders. This was particularly the case in the Sumatra Thawalib schools, whose stubborn and autocratic founder and headmaster, Haji Rasul, attempted to curb what he saw as the atheistic ideas being propagated by his students. Even his son, Hamka, acknowledged that Haji Rasul's attitude alienated his pupils, and noted that Zainuddin Labai, who greatly admired Haji Rasul's scholarship, 'did not want to become close to him. Because as a young man who was also stubborn and had his own opinions, he [Labai] did not want to subject himself to my father'.[44] In contrast to Labai, who never openly opposed Communist ideas, Haji Rasul had violent arguments about Communist ideology with two of his brightest and most radical pupils and assistants, Djamaluddin Tamin and H. Datuk Batuah.[45]

Born in 1900, Djamaluddin Tamin had graduated from government elementary school in 1913 and was a founder of the Islamic League (Sarikat Islam) in West Sumatra, joining the Communist Party in 1922. He cooperated with Haji Dt. Batuah in editing the newspaper, *Pemandangan Islam* (Muslim Viewpoint).

H. Datuk Batuah was born in 1895 in Kota Lawas, near Padang Panjang. He graduated from Dutch elementary school, studied for six years in Mecca (1909-15), and then returned to West Sumatra to become a pupil of Haji Rasul. He was regarded as one of the most intelligent and dynamic of Haji Rasul's students, and assisted him in the Thawalib school after 1915.[46] In 1923, on a tour through parts of Sumatra and Java, he met with Natar Zainuddin in Aceh,[47] and with leaders of the Communist Party in Java, including Haji Mohammad Misbach, an influential member of the Islamic League (SI) in Surakarta (who, when released from jail in 1922, chose to join with the Communist side in the Islamic League split).[48] This Muslim leader clearly had the greatest influence on Dt. Batuah. According to Takashi Shiraishi, Misbach argued that by choosing the Communist side he was 'proving his true Islamness,'[49] explaining his position in a Congress of the Communist Party and the Red SIs held in early March 1923:

> ... basing himself on the Koran, [Misbach] made an argument for several points of agreement between the teachings of the Koran and those of communism. For example, the Koran declares that it is the duty of every Muslim to acknowledge the rights of human beings, and this point also appears in the principles of the communists' program.
> Furthermore, it is God's command that [we] fight against oppression and exploitation. That is also one of communism's objectives.
> Thus it is correct to say that he who cannot accept the principles of communism is no true Muslim.[50]

These ideas appealed to Dt. Batuah, and on his return to West Sumatra he spread them in the Thawalib school and in *Pemandangan Islam*, the newspaper he established and co-edited with Djamaluddin Tamin. This paper 'succeeded in reconciling the "science of the regulation of the community for the benefit of the masses living in misery and poverty", with the "intentions and the requirements of the true Islamic faith!"'.[51] Natar Zainuddin, who returned to West Sumatra in May 1923, espoused similar ideas in his newspaper *Djago-djago*, although its appeal was more openly directed toward the 'proletariat'. Both journals, however, sought the common ground between Islam and communism in their struggle against capitalism and colonialism.[52]

Like Haji Misbach, Dt. Batuah remained a faithful Muslim and apparently never saw any incompatibility between his religion and communism. As Hamka explained it,

> It appears he became a loyal follower of 'communism' on matters concerning the economic order, but did not follow its 'historic materialism'.

So he was a true Communist who still embraced Islam. People even say that, when they were near him, Communists who were anti-religious had to be respectful! Because he was not averse to behaving 'roughly' [*keras*] toward whoever criticized religion. When he met me, [after World War II] he recalled my father as his teacher. He said: 'All Java respects him because of the firmness of his convictions and his unwillingness to submit to Japan. My religious faith is still the faith he taught me. Only in political ideology did we part company.'[53]

Dt. Batuah was not able to propagate his ideas in West Sumatra for very long. In November 1923, only a few months after his return home, the Dutch sent an armed police detachment to Kota Lawas to arrest him and Natar Zainuddin. This action was part of a general crackdown on Communist activity and also in response to rumours that the two teachers were conspiring with *adat* leaders to rebel against the government and to assassinate Europeans, including the Assistant Resident of Padang Panjang.[54] After being held in Padang for about a year, the two were exiled first to the Residency of Timor and then to the new internment camp at Boven Digul when it was established at the beginning of 1927.[55] In December 1923, Djamaluddin Tamin too was arrested for articles he published in *Pemandangan Islam*, which had most likely been protesting the Dutch arrest of his colleagues the previous month. In May 1924, he was sentenced to two years in jail and spent fifteen months in Java's Cipinang jail before being released in September 1925.[56]

Rather than stifling opposition to the Dutch, these arrests intensified the burgeoning radicalism among the students and other young people in Padang Panjang and elsewhere in West Sumatra. The Government adviser R. Kern noted in July of 1924 that, although Assistant Resident Whitlau had argued that the movement would end once Batuah and Zainuddin were removed, half a year after their detention 'there are now more Communists than before'.[57] In the Sumatra Thawalib schools, students blamed Haji Rasul for the arrests of their young teachers, ultimately forcing him to resign from the school and return for a while to his home region of Maninjau before going on to Java in 1925.[58]

It was only in 1924, after the arrests of the Sumatra Thawalib radicals, that the People's School (Sekolah Rakyat) was established in Padang Panjang, patterned on Tan Malaka's school in Semarang. Like pupils at the Sumatra Thawalib, students attending the People's School during the day often also studied at the Diniyyah school in the evening. The youth organization Barisan Muda (Young Troop) of the People's League (Sarikat Rakyat) had its centre in the People's School in Padang Panjang. It flourished throughout West Sumatra, attracting school children and students from both towns and villages, and had branches in both private and government schools throughout the region.[59] Rustam, its West Sumatra head, had been a student at the Thawalib school of Syekh Ibrahim Musa of Parabek but was expelled in November 1924.[60] In Dangung-dangung, a small village not far from Payakumbuh, three young schoolboys, Damanhuri Jamil, Suhaimi Rasyad, and Leon Salim,[61] were also expelled from the government secondary school in April 1925 for trying to establish a branch of the Young Troop there. These three boys made their way to

People's School in Padang Panjang 1925 (Photograph taken in front of the PMDS Building). (J.Th.Petrus Blumberger, *De Nationalistische Beweging*, p.107, where it is erroneously identified as the Rakyat School in Semarang)
Leon Salim is seated 2nd from R in front row (with a *peci* in his lap); standing 2nd from R is Damanhuri Jamil. Standing furthest forward 2nd from L is Mahmud.

Padang Panjang, entered the People's School, and were appointed to the Central Board of the West Sumatra Young Troop.[62]

Members of the Young Troop in Padang Panjang were very active, visiting the organization's branches in other parts of West Sumatra every weekend, taking with them copies of *Pemandangan Islam*, *Djago-djago*, and other newspapers published by their leaders. Later in 1925, the Indonesian Communist Party congress in Semarang decided that the Young Troop should be replaced by the Internationale Padvinder Organisatie (IPO – International Scouts). This was a more regimented group, modeled on the Boy Scouts Association, with its members wearing uniforms and carrying out regular drills.[63] Its slogan was 'Youth of the World Unite!' [*Pemuda Sedunia Bersatulah!*], and in Padang Panjang it published the newspaper *Signaal*, edited by Djamaluddin Ibrahim, who would later become another of Tan Malaka's principal lieutenants.[64] Damanhuri Jamil, one of the schoolboys from Dangung-dangung, became the IPO's regional leader and Leon Salim, his thirteen-year old classmate, its secretary. The Dutch soon restricted the young radicals' activities and arrested Jamil, sending him back to his home village, where he was beaten by the village head and forbidden by the Dutch Controleur to return to school in Padang Panjang.[65]

In Padang Panjang, thus, the major base of the Communist Party and its People's League lay in the schools where the younger teachers and students – particularly in the modernist religious schools – believed communism to be compatible with Muslim teachings, and perceived a similarity between the nationalist political ideas of Rasjid Ridha and Mustafa Kamal, and those espoused by some Indonesian Communist leaders, notably Tan Malaka and Haji Misbach. In Silungkang, the roots of the People's League and the Communist movement were somewhat different.

Silungkang /Sawahlunto

Radical political ideas penetrated Silungkang, in part from the town's trading links with the outside world and in part from influences from the neighbouring industrial town of Sawahlunto, situated about nine miles away. Beginning in about 1912, several traders from Silungkang had settled near the Ombilin mine at Sawahlunto. Here, to provide services for government officials, they set up new businesses and opened shops selling textiles and other general goods.[66] Most of the Silungkang women, meanwhile, stayed home weaving the cotton sarongs, ceremonial clothing, and fancy textiles, which became famous throughout the Indies and beyond.[67] The female weavers formed a cooperative organization for distributing their woven textiles, one of them reportedly attending a trade fair in Brussels in 1918 to demonstrate her weaving skill.[68] At the same time, the clothing companies of Datuk Sati and Co. and Sulaiman Labai & Zoon conducted aggressive advertising campaigns from their Silungkang offices, mailing their catalogues to all parts of the Netherlands Indies and even to countries in other parts of Asia and Europe.[69]

Thus, strong ties developed between Silungkang and the outside world. The town soon became a centre not only of trade but also of political activity. The merchants who established their businesses near Sawahlunto were also influenced by the union activity and radical politics of the workers at the Ombilin mine. When the Dutch discovered coal near Sawahlunto in 1868 they had attempted to open up this remote region of central Sumatra to large-scale international trade. In 1892 they constructed a railroad, passing through Silungkang, which carried the coal from the Ombilin mine via Padang Panjang to the Padang port of Emmahaven (Teluk Bayur). They also built a new road to serve the area. By 1913 Sawahlunto had the largest European community in West Sumatra apart from Padang, and its inhabitants also included numerous Chinese and, later, Javanese contract workers and forced labourers whom the Dutch brought in to work the mine.[70]

The trader Sulaiman Labai established a branch of the Islamic League (Sarikat Islam) in Silungkang in 1915.[71] Three years later, at the end of World War I, he spearheaded protests against Dutch regulations which restricted transfers of rice. While the inhabitants of Silungkang were suffering from hunger, freight trains filled with paddy frequently passed through the town on their way to supply government officials and administrators of the Ombilin mine in Sawahlunto. One story recounts how, in 1918, together with a few dozen followers, Sulaiman Labai forced the stationmaster to surrender two freight cars of rice from a train bound for Sawahlunto which had halted in Silungkang. He distributed the food to the hungry people of the town and gave the government a receipt, promising reimbursement and stating that the seizure had been carried out because of the emergency situation. Before confiscating the rice, Labai had studied the emergency laws and had followed them carefully, so the Dutch authorities only had grounds to detain him for a few days before being forced to release him with a warning. His bold act raised spirits in the town and attracted many new members to the Islamic League, and when in 1924 the Silungkang branch transformed itself into the Sarikat Rakyat (People's League), most members followed their leaders into that Communist-sponsored organization.[72]

There was also a branch of the Communist youth organization, IPO (*Internationale Padvinder Organisatie*, International Scouts), in Silungkang, based on an earlier youth organization, SIAP.[73] SIAP had been formed in reaction to the visit of a group of Dutch boy scouts to the town on August 31, 1924, as part of their celebrations of the Dutch Queen's birthday. The supercilious attitude of these young Western visitors toward the townspeople had spurred local youths to form their own scouting troop. The SIAP and its IPO successor were too defiant for the Dutch to tolerate, and after a meeting of the Silungkang International Scouts in September 1925, they arrested its two top leaders. Charged with teaching politics to children through the Youth Troop song, the young activists were sentenced to three months in jail.[74]

The Dutch, however, were less worried about the Silungkang traders or youth organizations than about the activists at the Ombilin mine and their political and union organizers. Most threatening, in their view, was the Sawahlunto branch of the People's League, which published a local newpaper, *Suara Tambang* (Voice of the Mine) and a monthly journal *Panas* (Heat). The editors of both publications were jailed in 1924 and 1925 respectively, on charges of contravening the press laws.[75] However, their arrests only ignited further opposition, and the Workers' League (*Sarikat Buruh*) at the mine increased its membership to three thousand, while *Suara Tambang*'s readership expanded to ten thousand.

When terrorist activities began to break out in the Padang highlands in the early months of 1926, the Dutch responded with further repression. To evade such Dutch reprisals, leaders of the radical groups in the Silungkang/Sawahlunto region tried to smooth over the grievances of the local mine workers and persuade union members not to strike or demonstrate. At the same time, they followed orders from the Communist Party leadership and took their operations underground, setting up small workshops in isolated areas to manufacture rudimentary bombs and hand grenades, and other primitive weapons, in preparation for the impending rebellion.[76] The situation became more tense as rumours spread among both the Dutch and Indonesians that the planned uprising against the Dutch would take place in August, and false reports circulated that Tan Malaka had returned and was hiding in Sungai Dareh on the border between West Sumatra and Jambi.

Padang

In Padang, the third major centre of political activity in West Sumatra, it was the large-scale indigenous traders who, through their support of schools and social and religious societies, provided the base for development not only of Communist political organizations but also of anticolonial activities in general. In 1914, a group of them founded the *Sarikat Usaha* (Entrepreneurs' League).[77] The major impetus behind its formation was similar to that of the Islamic League in Java: an attempt to protect the indigenous merchants against both Dutch and Chinese trading dominance.[78] The League's executive body included as its secretary Muhamad Taher Marah Sutan, who was a shipping agent in the port of Padang, 'a hard-working idealist', who made the Entrepreneurs' League 'the meeting place of a number of leaders and intellectuals in Padang'.[79] Its other leader, Sutan Said Ali, was a teacher at the Adabiah School and member of the Islamic League. He would later leave the party and become the major Communist Party organizer.[80]

Executives of the Entrepreneurs' League were by no means all anticolonial. One of its founders, H. Abdullah Ahmad, who had also established the Adabiah school in Padang, was one of the three older-generation Kaum Muda leaders. Like his friends, Haji Rasul in Padang Panjang and Syekh Djamil Djambek in Bukittinggi, he strongly opposed communism and was viewed by the authorities as loyal to the Netherlands Indies government.[81] Hatta had a high regard for both him and Marah Sutan, writing that 'if Haji Abdullah Ahmad was outstanding in the religious movement, Taher Marah Sutan was foremost in social affairs'.[82]

The Entrepreneurs' League operated in many social fields – education, trade, funeral management, construction contracting, religious magazine and book publishing, and movie-house management.[83] The first issue of its four-page, twice-monthly tabloid, *Sjarikat Oesaha* (Entrepreneurs' League) appeared in April 1914. The League established branches in other towns in West Sumatra, and entrepreneurs, both in the League and outside, financed not only trading activities, but also political parties, religious organizations, publications of all kinds, private schools, and youth organizations. One of the most active Padang merchants was Abdullah Basa Bandaro. Taufik Abdullah has described him as a man who 'maintained good relations with Dutch officials in Padang' and worked closely with Abdullah Ahmad in establishing his Adabiah school.[84] But Basa Bandaro had also brought the Islamic League (Sarikat Islam) to West Sumatra, and in the early 1920s was the principal financial backer of *Djago-djago*, *Pemandangan Islam*, and other newspapers published by the People's League (Sarikat Rakyat) in Padang Panjang. He was one of Tan Malaka's key supporters and the prime conduit for distributing his works and pamphlets to his followers on Java.[85] By the early 1920s, the Entrepreneurs' League had become an umbrella organization for political and religious groups inclining toward the politics of Tan Malaka.[86]

In March 1923, the League's leader in Padang, Sutan Said Ali, left to become one of the founders of the local branch of the Communist Party. After his switch the Dutch soon arrested him, and he spent much of the rest of the year in jail. Padang, however, remained important to the Communist movement, for the Indonesian Communist Party (PKI) had targeted it as the centre for developing communism in West Sumatra. Magas Abdul Madjid, a young man born in West Sumatra but of a Javanese mother, was sent from Java to head the PKI section there.[87] Magas and his young followers, however, 'were not taken seriously' by the local people and they attracted little support.[88] The Dutch arrested Magas himself in early 1924, shortly after the detention of the Padang Panjang leaders, and in late 1924 he was sentenced to two and a half years in jail.[89] Sutan Said Ali, who had been released from jail in late 1923, then took over the Padang section and became the West Sumatran representative to the Central Committee of the Communist Party. Under his leadership, the Padang section, which initially had only about twenty members, became the centre of Communist operations in West Sumatra. Its membership expanded to nearly two hundred by the end of 1925,[90] by which time it was exerting about as much influence as the Padang Panjang section, which had been weakened by the wave of Dutch arrests against its leaders.[91]

Thus, in its three major centres in West Sumatra, the Communist movement diverged widely. In Padang Panjang, Muslim scholars and students constituted its backbone and their acknowledged leader and inspiration was Tan Malaka. In Silungkang, small-scale traders and entrepreneurs made up its principal leadership, but they had strong ties to the workers in Sawahlunto, and also looked to the leadership in Padang Panjang for guidance. The movement in Padang also drew on the Muslim scholars and the schools, but was most reliant on the trading community – though in Padang, it was the larger-scale merchants who wielded most influence. The Padang movement, too, maintained stronger ties to the official leadership of the Communist Party in Java than had been forged in either of the upland centres.

The expulsion of the Communist members from the national Indonesian Islamic League (Sarikat Islam) in the early 1920s, had had less impact on its branches in West Sumatra than on those in Java. Two Minangkabau leaders of the Islamic League in Java, Haji Agus Salim and Abdul Muis, had led the purge of its Communist members, and, during the months he spent in Padang in 1923, Abdul Muis frontally opposed the newly formed Communist Party there.[92] Nevertheless, most branches of the Islamic League in West Sumatra were little affected by its internal divisions. Their members sympathized with Tan Malaka's contention that 'Communism was the natural ally of Islam in the struggle against imperialism', a position iconoclastic in the Comintern but consistent with the one he had nevertheless asserted at its Fourth International Congress in 1922.[93] Most of his followers saw no contradiction in becoming members of the People's League (Sarikat Rakyat) rather than staying with the Islamic League.

More difficulties arose in December 1924, when the Central Committee of the Indonesian Communist Party (PKI), considering that the Peoples' League had deteriorated into a 'petit bourgeois' movement lacking internal strength, decided that its branches should be allowed to 'wither away' while the party concentrated on developing the trade-union movement. Although this policy was ill-suited to the situation in West Sumatra, the local branch of the PKI followed Central Committee directives and issued instructions that 'Sarikat Ra'jat [People's League] members should become provisional members of the P.K.I., who would have to undergo training in Communist teachings...'.[94] These training sessions were not a success,[95] and, although the branches of the People's League were officially disbanded, in West Sumatra at least they still retained the allegiance of their members, who continued to accept an amalgam of egalitarian and anticolonial teachings compatible with their religious beliefs.

Again, their attitude was in harmony with that of Tan Malaka, who opposed the Central Committee's decision to abolish the People's League, stating that the move was a mistake which demonstrated that the Party was dominated by a small group of anarchists.[96] Tan Malaka argued that 'Our tactics vis-à-vis the nationalist and religious revolutionaries must be to attract them to the S[arikat].R[akyat]',[97] and that the Party should appeal to 'retail traders, peasants and small entrepreneurs in the Outer Islands'.[98]

The Uprising

At a meeting in mid-September 1926, Indonesian Communists in Singapore, under leadership of Tan Malaka, formally decided to repudiate the Central Committee's plans for a rebellion, and Tan Malaka sent orders to West Sumatra that all his followers should flee the region, because he anticipated that when the uprising failed, the Dutch would attempt to stamp out the Communist movement as a whole.[99] In July 1926, after both Djamaluddin Tamin and his successor Mahmud had fled to Singapore, Arif Fadlillah became the PKI section leader in Padang Panjang, initially with Djamaluddin Ibrahim as his secretary.[100] Fadlillah attended the mid-September meeting in Singapore called by Tan Malaka,[101] and when he returned to Padang Panjang he obeyed its orders, firmly opposing the PKI sections in Silungkang and particularly Padang, which were eager to join the uprising, now scheduled to begin on November 16.

As noted earlier, the Dutch arrested Sulaiman Labai in Silungkang on October 13. His inexperienced successors were subsequently reluctant to take any decisive action without acquiescence from Arif Fadlillah in Padang Panjang. But the Padang section, also under a new leader, Mohammad Nur Ibrahim, knew Fadlillah would oppose launching the rebellion. So, on November 12, Nur Ibrahim came to Silungkang to try to persuade Labai's successor, Talaha gelar Rajo Sampono, to move forward despite Fadlillah's opposition.[102] But 'Arif Fadlillah's outright prohibition to participate in the insurrection... caused Silungkang to decide in favor of awaiting the outcome of events on Java'.[103] Preparations were thrown into further turmoil when on November 14 the Dutch arrested Nur Ibrahim and confiscated the notebooks in which he had laid out his plans for the uprising. On the basis of these notes, the government was able to round up about twenty other leading activists.[104]

The rebellion had indeed broken out in Batavia (Jakarta) and Banten on November 12, and the West Sumatra Communists learned from the newspapers that the Dutch had crushed the rebels in Batavia, but that fighting was continuing in Banten. They were also well aware that most of their own top leaders had either been arrested or had fled. Nevertheless, a member of the leadership of the West Sumatra branch of the Party reportedly arrived back from Java with a message that the revolution should be launched on January 1.[105] When the Silungkang branch heard this, they sent two of their members (Haji Jalaluddin and Limin [Alimin]) to Padang Panjang to consult again with Arif Fadlillah. More than thirty of the remaining People's League members gathered on December 20 in Silungkang to make a final decision on their own course of action. According to one of the participants, Abdul Muluk Nasution, they reached the following agreement:

> 1. the branch leaders were of the opinion that it was impossible to carry out a revolution that had any possibility of success, so they could not agree to the uprising;
> 2. Still they would not impede or forbid the launching of a rebellion under the name of the People's League, led by the Struggle Committee;
> 3. The Silungkang branch was the strongest in all West Sumatra. There was a possibility that if the members of the Silungkang branch acted, then the members of other branches would follow and join the uprising.[106]

Brandishing a revolver, one participant in the Silungkang meeting, Kamaruddin gelar Manggulung, described by the Dutch as 'the most infamous gambler in Silungkang',[107] declared that it was the duty of the members to launch the rebellion. He challenged the others present to raise their hands if any of them opposed such an action. All the participants then agreed to begin the uprising on January 1, 1927, although, as Nasution notes, they were aware that it would probably fail as it had in Batavia and Banten, and 'if there had been a democratic vote without any armed threats, certainly the decision would have been different'.[108] The more reluctant among them took comfort in the fact that two Indonesian soldiers from the Dutch garrison in Sawahlunto were participating, Sergeant Major Pontoh and Sergeant Rumuat,[109] who assured the meeting that at least twenty of their comrades had joined the People's League and would rally to their side when the revolution broke out.[110]

Still uncertain, the Silungkang branch made one more effort to contact Arif Fadlillah; in the last days of December Limin (Alimin) again went to Padang Panjang and found that the Dutch had in fact already arrested Fadlillah on December 28. When he heard this, instead of returning to Silungkang, Limin fled abroad.[111]

The plan drawn up at the Silungkang meeting designated Sawahlunto as the major focus of the rebellion that was to break out at midnight on January 1. One contingent of the rebels was to bomb both the police commissariat office and the dance hall where government leaders and Dutch officials of the Ombilin mine would be celebrating the New Year. At the same time, Sergeant Pontoh and his comrades would seize the Sawahlunto garrison and jail, free all political prisoners and arrest Dutch officials. By this time, they would have been joined by bands converging on Sawahlunto from surrounding villages, who would then be armed with weapons seized from the garrison. The next morning a giant demonstration would be held, attended by all the local people and mineworkers, demanding independence from the Dutch. It was anticipated that these actions would spark parallel activity by the People's League in other parts of Sumatra, and eventually reignite the rebellion in Java.[112]

The plan was doomed before it began. Many of the rebels were still hesitant, anticipating some word from Arif Fadlillah and unaware that he was now in jail. But far more devastating was the fact, unknown to them, that the Dutch had been alerted to part of the plan, and two days earlier had already arrested Pontoh and Rumuat and twenty of their military comrades.

The rebellion broke out in about eighteen villages (*nagari*) around Silungkang.[113] Bands from Silungkang and some of the other villages made their way to Sawahlunto. En route, the group from Silungkang marched past the barracks at Muara Klaban, apparently blind to the fact that the guards, on seeing such an armed procession, would inform their colleagues in Sawahlunto that they were about to be attacked.[114] The Dutch were then able not only to suppress the rebels in Sawahlunto but also snuff out the attack on the Muara Klaban barracks before it began. Most members of the rebel group marching toward Sawahlunto fled in panic when they realized that their plans were in disarray, and many were rounded up by the Dutch and taken to their headquarters in Sawahlunto.

The son of the district head of Muara Klaban was visiting his father when the uprising broke out. According to his recollection, hundreds of Communists surrounded their house threatening to kill his father, but the soldiers arrived soon enough to save them. The following morning, 'I saw many corpses sprawled in front of the barracks. Many bodies also were floating in the Halaban river that ran in front of the barracks and across the road to Sawah Lunto'.[115] He does not make clear how many of these were victims of the rebels and how many of Dutch retaliation.

Abdul Muluk Nasution was captured by the Dutch and brought to the jail at Sawahlunto. When he was dragged in with the body of one of his slain comrades, the Assistant Resident was there to meet him, flanked by the highest indigenous administrator, Roesad Dt. Perpatih Baringek, who was enraged and probably frightened by the assassinations of local officials that had taken place that night. Roesad threatened Abdul Muluk with a pistol and interrogated him 'with kicks and blows'.[116] Ironically, Roesad, who was known for his rough treatment of opponents of the Dutch in West Sumatra, was the elder brother of Dahlan, the major Communist leader of the uprising in Batavia, who had been arrested by the Dutch and was later exiled to Digul.[117]

After the flight of the main contingent, two rebel groups from surrounding villages rode into Silungkang in cars and buses flying red flags. Met by government fire, they were taken into custody.[118] Dutch reinforcements were brought in by rail and road convoy. These too came under attack from the rebels. Near the railway bridge at Padang Sibusuk a rebel force numbering about sixty to seventy men, headed by 'General' Abdul Munap, ambushed one convoy from Fort de Kock (Bukittinggi), which was making its way to Sijunjung via Payakumbuh. The Dutch commander, Lt. W.F.H.L. Simons, who was in the lead car, was killed in the attack by a bullet to his heart.[119]

The bloodiest actions took place in Silungkang itself. There, on January 3, after an initial withdrawal of Dutch forces, rebels killed the Dutch foreman of the Department of Public Works, Mr. Leurs, and executed several teachers, lower officials of the agricultural service, goldsmiths, and the stationmaster – a total of about twenty-four people.[120] In the coastal area around Padang and Pariaman, and in Agam and other parts of the highlands, village heads in particular became targets for assassination.[121] The Dutch responded in kind and, according to the British Consulate General in Jakarta, at least a hundred Communists were killed in the Padang highlands.[122]

Scattered skirmishes and assassinations continued for days and in some places for weeks, while the Dutch carried out widescale sweeps and rounded up thousands of suspects. By August 1927, they reported that 1,363 Communists had either been tried or were awaiting sentencing by the court at Sawahlunto alone.[123]

Of the total of about three thousand who were actually arrested, several hundred were released after initial interrogation. Three of the leaders were sentenced to death – Kaharuddin Manggulung, M. Jusuf Sampono Kajo, and Ibrahim Melawas – and they were hanged at the Durian jail in Sawahlunto.[124] Trials continued in the Sawahlunto court until the middle of 1928. Those sentenced to less than two years were imprisoned in Sawahlunto, and the others sent to jails in Java, such as Glodok, Cipinang, and Ambarawa,[125] while many were also exiled to Digul.[126] Already under Dutch arrest before the rebellion broke out, Sulaiman Labai was exiled to Ambarawa. Abdul Muluk Nasution was in the cell next to his in 1937, and at the time Nasution was released in early 1938, Labai was already over sixty years old and still had fifteen years of his sentence to serve – even if he were not sent to Digul at the end of his sentence, as was quite common practice.[127] When the Japanese took over in 1942, Labai continued his sentence, refusing to be released because he viewed the Japanese, like the Dutch, as colonizers. He finally died in jail on August 15, 1945, two days before the proclamation of Indonesia's independence.[128]

As can be seen from the above description, the uprising in West Sumatra in the early days of 1927, though bloody and traumatic, did not reflect either the strength or character of the major streams opposing Dutch rule in the region in the early decades of the twentieth century. By the time the rebellion broke out, few of the prominent anti-Dutch leaders in the area remained free and active, and their place had been taken by a motley collection of young activists and discontents who had been on the periphery of political movements and several of whom used the uprising to settle old scores.

The effect of Tan Malaka's campaign against the rebellion was seen most clearly in Padang Panjang, where virtually all the major radical political leaders opposed it. Most of those loyal to Tan Malaka had fled the region months earlier and the remainder were arrested by the Dutch before the rebellion finally broke out. The leadership vacuum had been exacerbated by the physical destruction of Padang Panjang with the eruption of Mt. Merapi on June 25, 1926. Consequently, the centre of support for the rebellion shifted to Silungkang and Padang, and as the more seasoned leaders in these two places were arrested, the initiative passed to lower-level activists with little political background.

The rebellion's major impact was the excuse it offered the Dutch to crack down not only on Communist Party members, but on all political activity in the region. It was also the precipitating factor in permanently splitting Tan Malaka from the Indonesian Communist Party, which held him responsible for the rebellion's failure.

CHAPTER 2

The Crisis of the Early 1930s

Dutch suppression of all political movements in the wake of the 1927 Communist rebellion fell as heavily on those activists and organizations that had not participated in the rebellion, as upon the insurgent members of the Communist party. Despite this repression, opposition to Dutch policies soon resumed, and by 1932 West Sumatra was once more a volatile region, with religious scholars now at the helm of antigovernment political activity. Although the most knowledgeable Dutch officials were aware that the renewed activism was unlikely to lead again to armed revolt, the government grew alarmed as Minangkabau religious political leaders became more outspoken in their criticisms of Dutch rule and openly advocated an independent Indonesia. Government reports increasingly warned that the uprising of 1927 was about to be repeated, and they drew parallels between the attitudes of religious political organizations in the early 1930s and those of the Communists in the months before the 1927 rebellion.[1] A few years later, Governor A.I. Spits recalled that

> the bloody lesson provided by the suppression of the disturbances at the beginning of 1927 seemed already to have been forgotten, or better perhaps, the facts had not been forgotten, that could not yet be, but the large mass had not drawn the correct lesson from them. The freedom ideal presented by reckless popular leaders still seemed to possess such a great attraction that they let themselves be pushed on to a road that could lead to repetition of the occurrences of 1927.[2]

Finally, in 1933, as part of a general crackdown, the government took measures against the outspoken religious political leaders, similar to those imposed six years earlier against the Communists. Several religious leaders were arrested and sent to join the earlier political exiles in the recently established detention camp at Boven Digul, in the jungles of West Irian.

The arrests in the early 1930s were part of a more general policy of political repression in the Netherlands East Indies, focused primarily on two centres – West Sumatra and Batavia. The patterns of both political activity and government repression, however, were markedly different in the two regions. Whereas in Batavia it was the secular nationalist parties – Sukarno's Partindo (Partai Indonesia), and Hatta and Sjahrir's Pendidikan Nasional Indonesia or PNI Baru (Indonesian National Education or New PNI) – that were the major targets of Dutch reprisal, in West Sumatra, two religious-based parties and their leaders were seen as the government's most dangerous opponents. The two parties targeted were the Permi or Persatuan Muslimin Indonesia (Union of Indonesian Muslims), and the Minangkabau branch of the Partai Sarikat Islam Indonesia (PSII – Indonesian Islamic League Party) – the successor of the old Islamic League (Sarikat Islam). Both of these parties had been founded or revived after 1928.

Before going on to examine the place of these two parties in the political constellation of the region at the time – the dangers they posed for the Dutch, and the ties and relationships between politics in West Sumatra and those in the capital of Dutch rule – we will begin by tracing political developments after the suppression of the 1927 Communist uprising, particularly the ways in which the two most radical religious parties grew during the succeeding years, attracting both a following within the region and the antagonism of the colonial power.

Repercussions of 1927

In the aftermath of the widespread arrests and repression of 1927, most of West Sumatra's population was intimidated and reluctant to invite further retribution from the colonial rulers. But it was the Dutch themselves who did much to precipitate the resurgence of political activity within the region, unintentionally promoting alliances among religious students, teachers, and scholars, whose political allegiances had split them apart in the early- and mid-1920s. The Dutch inadvertently encouraged such alliances both in 1928 and in 1932 through their efforts to gain control over religious schools and private education in general. A *guru ordinansi* (teachers' ordinance), which forbade Islamic scholars from teaching religion without previously obtaining permission from the government, had been in effect in Java and Madura since 1905. In 1925, the ordinance was moderated to require scholars teaching religion merely to notify, not to request permission from, the Dutch authorities. Soon afterwards, the government attempted to extend the weakened ordinance to other regions of the archipelago, including West Sumatra. However, Minangkabau Islamic scholars believed that if the ordinance were put into effect, their 'freedom to spread their religion, preach, teach, board students [*berpondok*] and conduct other religious affairs would disappear'.[3] Aware of the sensitivity of the issue, local Dutch officials approached some of the leading Muslim scholars in West Sumatra to explain the government's intention to extend the ordinance to the region, and they won agreement to the proposal from several traditionalist (*kaum tua*) and modernist (*kaum muda*) scholars, including the senior modernist teacher Haji Abdullah Ahmad, at the Adabiah school in Padang. At the same time, they apparently secured at least the neutrality of Syekh Djamil Djambek in Bukittinggi.[4]

But the third of the outstanding older-generation modernist leaders, Haji Rasul, saw the ordinance as a direct threat to the teaching and propagation of Islam. In contrast to Abdullah Ahmad and Djamil Djambek, Haji Rasul was willing to confront the Dutch as fiercely as he had earlier opposed the Communists when he felt that they threatened his religion. He pushed the Islamic social organization Muhammadiah and other religious groups into opposing the teachers' ordinance, organizing meetings in August 1928 which attracted more than two thousand Islamic scholars from throughout the Minangkabau.[5] Dutch irritation at Haji Rasul's stance was reflected in a 1929 report on the religious streams in West Sumatra by Ch. O. van der Plas, one of the government's most influential advisers, which noted that, according to the Assistant Resident of Agam, Haji Rasul was

> 'a troublesome and exceedingly querulous figure,... who is extremely ambitious,... [and is] completely unreliable', a description which from his own deeds and from the experience of his former colleagues is completely confirmed. In short he is a person with whom no-one in the long run can cooperate.[6]

Nevertheless, partly as a result of Haji Rasul's activities, traditionalists and modernists, radicals and moderates allied themselves in opposition to the Dutch policy. Put on the defensive, the Dutch postponed, for the time being, any further efforts to introduce the ordinance into West Sumatra.

Even before the eruptions over the teachers' ordinance, the Dutch had already in 1927 united much of the religious community against them when they arrested Syekh Tahir Djalaluddin, 'the most distinguished theologian among the Kaum Muda'.[7] Although born in Bukittinggi, after studying and teaching in Cairo and Mecca, Syekh Tahir had lived for many years in Malaya, holding high positions within the Sultanate of Perak as well as gaining widespread respect as a teacher and publisher. On one of his rare visits to his home area, the Dutch imprisoned him for suspected Communist activities, detaining him for several months and threatening to exile him to Digul.[8] This action outraged Muslims across the political spectrum in both Sumatra and Malaya, and the incident has been credited with encouraging renewed political activity among the students at the Sumatra Thawalib schools.[9]

Despite the government's defeat in 1928 on the teachers' ordinance, four years later, in September 1932, it promulgated the 'Wild Schools Ordinance' – yet another attempt to gain greater control over private education. This new ordinance stipulated that all teachers had to obtain government permission before they could teach in private schools. Widespread opposition to this ordinance in Java and West Sumatra resulted in alliances being forged not only between the traditional and modern Islamic scholars but also between them and non-religious organizations, radical political parties, and leaders of the Taman Siswa and other non-religious nationalist schools – notably, in West Sumatra, the innovative INS (Indonesische Nederlandsch School) of Mohammad Sjafei.[10] The vigorous campaign against the Wild Schools Ordinance enabled political and non-political organizations to present a united front against the Dutch, alarming the colonial government and preparing the way for the repression that would occur in mid-1933. As John Ingleson has noted, there would not be 'any other single issue in the remainder of the colonial period which drew such vehement opposition from as wide a cross-section of Indonesian religious, cultural and political organisations'.[11] Haji Rasul was again a leading opposition spokesman in West Sumatra. He founded a committee to combat the ordinance which by February 1933 embraced 123 regional political and educational organizations.[12] That same month, the Attorney General forbade any further public meetings concerning the Wild Schools Ordinance, but at the same time, the government felt compelled to suspend all attempts to enforce it.

In 1927, the initial beneficiary of the political alliances forged to combat Dutch efforts to extend the teachers' ordinance to the region, was the newly formed branch of the Yogyakarta-based Muhammadiah. Haji Rasul, aided by his son-in-law A.R. Sutan Mansur, had introduced this organization into West Sumatra in 1925, after he had been forced out of his Sumatra Thawalib school in Padang Panjang.[13] The local Muhammadiah branch was patterned on its Java parent organization, and, in its early years of existence, was a purely social and educational body.[14] However, after the Dutch clampdown in 1927, many of the Thawalib school students, who had earlier belonged to the radical People's League (Sarikat Rakyat) and had been attracted to the teachings of its leaders (Tan Malaka, Djamaluddin Tamin, and Haji Datuk Batuah), now turned to the Muhammadiah for protection against possible Dutch reprisals. Neither the branch's two founders nor the Muhammadiah's central leadership in Java were happy with the political activism of these new members. Dutch officials, too, warned the executive board in Java that its militant Minangkabau branch was pursuing a dangerous course.

By spearheading opposition to the teachers' ordinance, the Muhammadiah reached a high point in its popularity in West Sumatra in 1928.[15] At the same time, the success of its campaign against the ordinance emboldened the Muhammadiah's younger members and encouraged them to think of establishing their own less-circumscribed organization. When A.R. St. Mansur – the newly appointed head of the Muhammadiah's West Sumatra consulate – demoted its more militant members, most of them took the opportunity to break away and help in forming the Sumatra Thawalib Union.[16]

This union was established in November 1928 at a conference of representatives from all of the Sumatra Thawalib schools. Its aims were not only to improve the school system but also to organize activities in the political, economic, and social fields.[17] At its third conference in May of 1930, the Sumatra Thawalib Union transformed itself into the Indonesian Muslim Party (Partai Muslimin Indonesia or Permi), which soon became the strongest and most influential political party in West Sumatra, and, in many ways, most representative of the political character of the region during the late-colonial period. Unlike all other nationalist organizations of the time, it was founded on two specific principles – Islam and Nationalism.

As we have seen in the previous chapter, the nationalist Islamic ideas of Rasjid Ridha, 'the most influential Muslim thinker of his generation',[18] had had a powerful impact on Islamic scholars in West Sumatra, particularly on Zainuddin Labai el Junusiah, who had founded the Diniyyah schools in the late 1910s.[19] But these ideas did not find a really suitable political vehicle until the formation of the Permi and after two Cairo-educated Minangkabau intellectuals, Iljas Jacub and Muchtar Luthfi, returned (in 1930 and 1931 respectively) to take up its leadership.[20]

In the early 1920s, political activists at the Thawalib schools had been attracted to the Communist Party's People's League, in part because such Communist leaders as Tan Malaka and Haji Misbach were careful to stress the compatibility between the egalitarian ideas of communism and those of Islam. At that time, no other political party existed which embodied the beliefs and ideals of the teachings given at the Diniyyah and Thawalib schools. Now Permi in many ways fulfilled this role. Resident Gonggrijp described the new party as attracting those 'religious intellectuals and small traders most receptive to Communist preaching'.[21] But he was wrong in seeing Communist preaching as the motivating force either of the earlier movement or of the current one. Government adviser Ch. O. van der Plas had recognized this a couple of years earlier, when he showed due respect for the power of the movement stemming from the private Islamic schools. After carrying out an investigation into the religious streams in West Sumatra in 1929 he described them as follows:

> These 'Muslim intellectuals' (the term is Demang Roesad's) form a spiritual power, which the old group [*kaum tua*] can put up nothing against; a spiritual power, that the Netherlands government also cannot eliminate and with which it would thus serve it to come to terms.[22]

Immediately after its first conference in Payakumbuh, the Permi shifted its headquarters to Padang, which, in the opinion of Governor Gonggrijp, meant that West Sumatra's 'political - religious nationalist centre [was] shifting from Padang Panjang to Padang'.[23] Abdullah Basa Bandaro, who had played an important role in maintaining communications among Tan Malaka's followers in West Sumatra, and whom Gonggrijp described as 'behind all political activity in Padang', became its adviser, and through him, Permi established relations with the Himpunan Saudagar (Merchants' Group) in Padang,[24] as well as with trade unions, religious organizations, and other traders' associations. This is one aspect of the Permi and other political organizations that we shall examine further below.

Throughout its brief heyday, beginning in 1930, the three Permi leaders who most attracted Dutch ire were Iljas Jacub, Djalaluddin Thaib, and Muchtar Luthfi. Of the three, only Djalaluddin Thaib had not been educated in Cairo. He was born near Bukittinggi into a family of religious scholars, and after studying at the Iron Bridge *surau*, the precursor of the Sumatra Thawalib, he continued his schooling in religion and Arabic in Mecca, from 1914 to 1916. He became an assistant to Haji Rasul and was active in the Sumatra Thawalib schools as well as founding a Diniyyah school in his own village. In 1917, he went to teach for a year in Malaya.[25] He left the Thawalib schools because he opposed Communist influences there and became a founder, together with Abdullah Ahmad, of the moderate Association of Islamic Teachers (PGAI, Persatuan Guru-guru Agama Islam) in 1925,[26] as well as a writer and publisher of school textbooks. In the late 1920s, van der Plas described him as a 'conciliatory figure' among the religious groups.[27] He had, then, been prominent in the modernist Islamic educational sphere for more than a decade when he helped revive the Sumatra Thawalib Union and, in 1930, joined in founding the new Permi party.

Iljas Jacub was probably the most prominent intellectual in the Permi. Born near Painan, on the southern coast of West Sumatra, the son of a textile trader, Jacub graduated from government elementary school and worked as a clerk in the Ombilin mine in Sawahlunto from 1917-1919. He resigned in protest against the poor treatment of the workers, and turned to religious study – going first to Mecca in 1921, and then on to Cairo where he attended courses at Al Azhar and joined the political party allied with the Turkish nationalist Kamal Mustafa. He became prominent in both social and political affairs, and edited a students' political magazine, *Seruan Azhar*. In October 1927, he founded and edited *Pilihan Timoer*;[28] a journal, printed in Cairo, that was openly political and was aimed at 'the land and the people of Indonesia and Malaya'. Almost immediately, *Pilihan Timoer* was banned from Indonesia, and, in April 1928, under pressure from the British High Commissioner, the Egyptian government also forbade its publication.[29]

In Cairo, Iljas Jacub had been joined in 1926 by Muchtar Luthfi. Born near Bukittinggi in 1900, Luthfi was a cousin of Djalaluddin Thaib, and the son of H. Abdul Lathif, a teacher at the Iron Bridge *surau*. At the age of only eight he had accompanied his uncle, H. Daud Rasyidi, to Mecca.[30] Luthfi studied in several schools in West Sumatra, including the government elementary school and the Sumatra Thawalib, and in all the schools he attended was a notorious mischief-maker. But, as he grew up and was more deeply immersed in studying the Qur'an, he became famous as a political orator and religious preacher, not only in West Sumatra but also in Tapanuli. He founded a Diniyyah school and also taught at the Sumatra Thawalib. Well known for his opposition to colonialism, he did not, however, join the strong Communist stream in the Thawalib schools.[31] Nevertheless, his book *Al-Hikmatul Muchtar*, which discussed problems of politics and tradition, was so openly anticolonial that the Dutch banned it and sought to arrest Luthfi on charges of communism. His friends smuggled him out of West Sumatra, reportedly dressed as a woman, and he fled to Malaya where he taught for several months before going on to Cairo, via India and Mecca, in 1926.[32]

In Cairo, Luthfi joined Iljas Jacub in his political and publishing activities, and after *Pilihan Timoer* was banned, both men became active in the Egyptian nationalist movement. Ultimately, each of them was pronounced *persona non grata*, and they were forced to leave Egypt. They went first to Mecca, then Jacub returned to Minangkabau in 1930, followed by Luthfi the subsequent year. On their return, both immediately joined the top leadership of the Permi party.[33]

From its foundation in 1930, Permi attracted a broad spectrum of political activists in West Sumatra, and it expanded rapidly, numbering by 1932 about ten thousand members in about 160 branches spread not only over West Sumatra itself but also Bengkulu, South Sumatra, Aceh, East Sumatra, and Tapanuli.[34] It appealed to the people of West Sumatra in large part because it was not afraid to marry religion and politics in its platform. Its leaders were in tune with other Indonesian nationalist parties in emulating the Indian nationalist movement's espousal of *swadeshi* and self-reliance, but they argued against following India's lead in establishing a purely secular basis for the nationalist movement. They pointed out that, whereas in India the major line of tension ran along the Hindu - Muslim rift so that nationalists there needed a secular base on which adherents of both religions could unify, in Indonesia the situation was very different. The country was 90 percent Muslim, so that their religious homogeneity provided Indonesia's people with the potentially strongest unifying factor in their nationalist struggle. To be afraid of using Islam as a basis for the nationalist movement was like 'a tiger fearing to flee to the jungle or water fearing to flow to the sea'.[35]

Permi was in many ways unique in the nationalist movement in Indonesia. Not only did it have its foundation and major following in West Sumatra, but its espousal of the twin pillars of Islam and Nationalism differentiated it from all the other national political parties. In this, its philosophy differed from that of the foremost Minangkabau leader on the national political stage, Mohammad Hatta, who, despite his own strong devotion to Islam, believed that political parties should not be based on religion. This dispute, between Hatta's followers and those of the Permi and its successors, was one that characterized Minangkabau politics throughout the anti-Dutch struggle. The courage and outspokenness of the Permi leaders in challenging Dutch authority did, however, gain it admirers in Java, including Sukarno and his Partindo party, with whom – through the businessman Abdullah Basa Bandaro – it established ties.[36] Eventually, these ties became so close that Permi and Partindo agreed not to compete in each other's areas of strength, and Partindo refrained from establishing branches in West Sumatra.

Women stood among Permi's most influential and outspoken members. Prominent among them was Rasuna Said, a former student and teacher in the Sumatra Thawalib and Diniyyah schools, who was one of the most fervent nationalists in West Sumatra. She quarrelled with the founder of the Diniyyah school for girls, Rahmah el Junusiah, younger sister of Zainuddin Labai, over whether political issues should become part of the school's curriculum. After the school board supported Rahmah in rejecting the younger woman's proposal to introduce political subjects, Rasuna Said moved to Padang and devoted herself full-time to Permi activities.[37] She was a courageous and outspoken orator. In one of the protest meetings organized by Permi against the Wild Schools Ordinance, she called openly for independence:

> The door to independence is already open, and we hope that when you return to your homes you will whisper this to your religious and racial fellows. We all have one aim: to pioneer the road to our rights, that is to an Independent Indonesia free from foreign rule.[38]

Women were the first of the Permi leaders to be imprisoned by the Dutch. At the end of 1932, Rasuna Said was sentenced to fifteen months in jail and shortly afterwards, her colleague Rasimah Ismail was jailed for nine months for a speech made at a meeting the previous October.[39] Both were imprisoned in the Bulu jail in Semarang.[40]

Permi leaders encouraged their branches to cooperate with the one other radical Muslim party in West Sumatra, the successor of the Islamic League, now known as the PSII (Partai Sarikat Islam Indonesia). Although officially part of the Java-based Islamic League, the PSII branch in West Sumatra, like the local branch of the Muhammadiah, assumed a very different character from its parent organization. It was revived in 1928 under leadership of Dt. Singo Mangkuto and H. Uddin Rahmany, two traditional leaders from a village near Lake Maninjau.[41] This West Sumatra branch of the new Islamic League espoused goals similar to those of the Permi, and it too attracted members from among the students at the local Sumatra Thawalib schools. Its anticolonial stance was at least as strong as that of the Permi. For example, in December 1928, Dt Singo Mangkuto issued a programme with the following four points: (1) refusal of school subsidies; (2) determination not to become 'slaves of capitalism'; (3) disapproval of government education that would make Indonesians 'slaves of imperialism'; and (4) the position that 'Indonesia cannot advance so long as it is not free from the Netherlands'.[42] But, in contrast to the essentially Minangkabau character of the Permi, the PSII's local leaders were conscious of, and took pride in, the Indies-wide character and history of their party. They also differed from the Permi in that they drew greater support from traditional village leaders.[43] Dt. Singo Mangkuto's speeches were so 'fiery and anti-Dutch' that the government arrested him in 1929, jailing him for two years. On his release, the party revived and expanded beyond Maninjau, though its regional membership never exceeded three thousand. Because the Minangkabau branch of the new Islamic League was more militant than its parent organization, Dt. Singo Mangkuto attempted to secure it greater autonomy. But the League's head office in Java refused to allow this, and disavowed various decisions of the local party congresses in West Sumatra.[44] Tensions in this case, between the parent organization and its Minangkabau branch, were not only due to disagreements regarding anticolonial activity. In addition, while the Islamic League leaders in Minangkabau were close to the traditional (adat) village elders, those at the centre – notably Haji Agus Salim – took explicitly anti-adat positions, targeting in particular the matrilineal social order in Minangkabau.[45]

The Socialist Stream

Youth Groups

Although Permi was by far the strongest noncooperating political organization in West Sumatra in the early 1930s, there were many others that were active during those years. Youth organizations had been the first to revive after the debacle of the 1927 uprising. We have seen how the students at the Sumatra Thawalib schools formed the nucleus of the Permi. Similarly, the Students' League of the Diniyyah Schools – the PMDS, headquartered in Padang Panjang – soon regrouped, with eleven of its members coming together in July 1927 and swearing that, 'in the name of God, with all our strength and by whatever path, we will continue the ideals and struggle of our people'.[46]

Several of these students, including Mohamad Junus (Kotjek), Leon Salim, Damanhuri Jamil, Hasanuddin Yunus, and Mahyuddin Tonek, had been members of the earlier Communist youth organizations Barisan Muda (Young Troop) and IPO (International Scouting Organization).[47] They had earlier studied with Djamaluddin Tamin and Djamaluddin Ibrahim at the Sumatra Thawalib and People's School in Padang Panjang, and they retained their ties with their former teachers. When

Tan Malaka established his new radical nationalist party, Pari (Partai Republik Indonesia), in Bangkok in 1927, Djamaluddin Tamin was one of its founders, together with Subakat. Djalamuddin Ibrahim also became a leading member of the party, and both he and Tamin maintained contact with their former students in West Sumatra.[48] They sent the leaders of the Diniyyah youth organization (PMDS) copies of Pari's magazine, *Obor*, as well as manuals to help them organize and train members of their movement.

The two major leaders of the youth organization, Leon Salim and M. Junus Kotjek, were unable to make use of these manuals because neither of them had received a Western education and the manuals were written in English, Dutch, and French.[49] So in 1929, on the advice of the Padang entrepreneur (and Permi and Tan Malaka supporter), Abdullah Basa Bandaro, they invited a young musician from Padang, Chatib Suleiman, to join them in Padang Panjang to help develop the organization.

Chatib Suleiman was a protegé of Basa Bandaro, who had taken over the boy's education when his father, Haji Suleiman (another Padang trader), had gone bankrupt at the end of World War I. Although Chatib studied for only two years at the MULO, the advanced elementary school in Padang, he gained a good knowledge of both English and Dutch, and so was in a position to read the training manuals for the Diniyyah youth organization. At the time Basa Bandaro recommended him to Salim and Kotjek, Chatib was earning his living as a violinist accompanying the silent films at a movie-house in Padang. Despite his minimal schooling, Chatib Suleiman had a brilliant mind and from then on until his death twenty years later, he became the nationalist movement's foremost political theoretician and strategist in West Sumatra.[50]

To avoid attracting suspicion from government authorities as they rallied their members in the wake of the Dutch repression, the student leaders of the PMDS had first emphasized their sporting and musical activities, forming a flute orchestra which in 1928 marched in the government-sponsored parade celebrating Queen Wilhelmina's birthday.[51]

The organization soon spread to embrace students from schools other than the Diniyyah and Thawalib, as well as nonstudents. Because of its broader character it was renamed the El Hilaal (Crescent Moon).

Although the schools and youth associations were the driving force behind many of the nationalist organizations in the region, they were also responsible for some of the rifts in the movement. In May 1930,[52] at the founding Congress of the Permi, a quarrel arose between Djalaluddin Thaib and the leaders of the El Hilaal, particularly Leon Salim.[53] As a result of this quarrel, most of the Diniyyah school students refused to ally with the Permi. The youth organization split in two, with the Crescent Moon (El Hilaal) retaining its ties to the Permi leaders, and the Diniyyah school students forming a new organization, the Indonesian Muslim Scouts (KIM – Kepanduan Indonesia Muslim), headed by Leon Salim, Chatib Suleiman, and M. Junus Kotjek.

The youth leaders did not completely sever ties among their different organizations, and immediately after a conference where efforts to reunite them broke down, the young people nevertheless joined together to march in a parade through

Padang Panjang. All the major West Sumatran scouting groups participated – not only the Crescent Moon (El Hilaal) and Indonesian Muslim Scouts (KIM), but also the youth organizations tied to the Islamic League (SIAP) and the Muhammadiah (Hizbul Wathan) – as a sign of their continuing solidarity. The hundreds of young people marching through the streets alarmed the Assistant Resident, and he ordered the arrest of the parade's leaders – Leon Salim, Junus Kotjek, and Mahyuddin Tonek of the Indonesian Muslim Scouts, together with Hasanuddin Yunus – now a leader of the El Hilaal – and two of the Hizbul Wathan leaders.[54]

The KIM became the largest independent youth organization in the region, numbering two thousand members in thirty sections by 1932.[55] Its open allegiance to the Tan Malaka stream of nationalism was reflected in the fact that its patrols were given such names as the Zainuddin troop, the Datuk Batuah troop, the Haji Miskin troop, as well as the Imam Bonjol troop and the Arif Fadlillah troop.[56] Leon Salim, upset by the dissension that he had helped to create, soon left West Sumatra. He stowed away on a trading vessel crossing the Malacca Strait and spent the next year in Singapore and Kuala Lumpur, together with the Pari activists who had fled Padang Panjang in 1926/27.[57]

Hatta's Followers

During the early 1930s, events in West Sumatra were strongly conditioned by political developments in Batavia, the centre of Dutch rule. Following Sukarno's arrest by the Dutch in 1929, Sartono and other leaders of the Indonesian National Party (PNI) halted the party's activities. Then, after Sukarno was sentenced to four years in jail, Sartono dissolved the PNI, replacing it in May 1931 with the Indonesian Party (Partai Indonesia, Partindo). Meanwhile, National Party (PNI) members who opposed Sartono's suspension of the party's activities had formed independent groups (*golongan merdeka*) to continue their efforts in the social and educational field. During the months following Sukarno's arrest, Mohammad Hatta, still studying in Holland, refrained from criticizing Sartono's suspension of PNI activities, but once Partindo was established, he came out publicly in opposition to the course adopted by the National Party leadership which had allowed itself to be intimidated by the government's actions against Sukarno. Hatta then led the independent groups to form a competing organization, the New PNI (PNI Baru – the initials PNI standing for Pendidikan Nasional Indonesia, or Indonesian National Education, therefore not technically a party).

The split within the National Party was a fundamental and enduring one, but, as John Ingleson has convincingly argued, initially at least, the differences between the two wings were principally 'in their reading of the contemporary situation and in their assessment of the strength of the nationalist movement'. According to Ingleson's analysis, Hatta and his colleagues opposed the Sukarno PNI's reliance on a mass action base, because they did not feel the Indonesian people were yet ripe for such a movement:

The PNI *Baru* leaders believed that the [nationalist] movement was still organisationally weak and had not yet obtained solid and committed support from its nominal members. In their view, it was senseless and irresponsible to indulge in mass action before the movement was strong enough to bring it to a successful conclusion. Mass action must be the final stage of action after first obtaining a correctly educated, politically aware mass membership, which in turn was only possible if membership recruitment was carried out step by step with the development of a solid leadership core of party cadres.[58]

Then, as later, Hatta's standing in the Nationalist movement was second only to that of Sukarno, and during his years in Holland his writings and speeches exerted a major influence on developments in his home country. When the New PNI was founded, Hatta was still completing his studies in the Netherlands, and he sent his younger colleague and fellow Minangkabau, Sutan Sjahrir, back to Indonesia to oversee the establishment of the organization.

Sukarno was released from jail on December 31, 1931, after serving only a small part of his sentence. Over the next seven months he made efforts to bridge the disagreements between the leaders of the Partindo and New PNI, but when these ultimately failed, Sukarno chose to join with the Partindo and became its head.[59]

Hatta returned from Holland in August 1932, and shortly afterwards visited his family near Bukittinggi. During that visit, in November 1932, he presided over the inauguration of the West Sumatra branch of the New PNI. Prior to his visit, Chatib Suleiman, together with Leon Salim (who had recently returned from Malaya), had established a branch of the New PNI in Padang Panjang, and other sections were eventually formed in Padang, Pariaman, Maninjau, and Bukittinggi.[60] In contrast to the Islam and Nationalism bases of the Permi, the New PNI was founded on the principles of Nationalism and Democracy, and it concentrated on educating cadre rather than mobilizing a mass base. The New PNI in West Sumatra immediately came under bitter attack, particularly from Permi, in part because some Permi leaders, notably Darwis Thaib of Maninjau, defected to the new party's ranks.

Forty years later, Darwis Thaib took pride in the fact that he had shifted his allegiance among the major political parties in the 1920s and 1930s, noting that he had belonged to the People's League (Sarikat Rakyat) in 1924 and had responded to Tan Malaka's wishes by not joining the Communist Party, and later became a member of the Pari. In 1928 he joined the new Islamic League (PSII), but left it in 1930 to become secretary of the Permi. He explained that in his view, 'a party was only a bridge to the struggle to achieve the ideals of independence, and because of this I moved from party to party if it became clear that one more clearly reflected my ideals'.[61] Thus, when Hatta's party was formed at the end of 1932, Darwis Thaib had no compunction about leaving the Permi and joining the new party's leadership.

Permi's attacks against the New PNI in West Sumatra focused not only on its local leaders, but also on the small membership of its branches and even on the character of and positions taken by Hatta himself. But the most potent and potentially damaging charge was that the party was antireligious. Both Permi and the new Islamic

League (PSII) charged that 'its neutrality on religion was antireligious, its nationalism in conflict with Islam, its self-help a denial of God, and its collectivism in flagrant opposition to Islam'.[62] In his capacity as its West Sumatra chairman, Chatib Suleiman replied publicly to the accusations in late 1932. He stressed the similarity in aims and methods among the noncooperating parties, but at the same time laid out some of the principal lines of division among them, stating that, while the two radical religious parties based themselves on religion or religion and nationalism, the Education party (New PNI) looked only to nationalism and democracy. (The new party's leader, Hatta, was to remain true to the principle that, however personally devout he himself was, he could not support or belong to a party based on religion.) With respect to the New PNI's leaders defecting from other parties, Chatib Suleiman noted that a shift from a radical to a less-radical party could open a person to criticism, but a move in the opposite direction should not; regarding the small membership of the party, he asserted that the New PNI emphasized quality rather than quantity and had no desire to build a large following. Turning to the accusations regarding its opposition to religion he continued:

> It is not that we look down on the present political parties in Minangkabau, such as the PSII and PMI [Permi], not at all, but rather that we recall the human principle, that we have the right to choose our own basis for action according to our own convictions. Without minimizing or discounting the basis of the PSII, that is Islam, or the basis of the PMI [Permi], that is Islam and Nationalism, yet we are convinced and hold strongly to our own basis of Nationalism and Democracy (Sovereignty of the People).
> We have no intention of opposing or impeding other political movements, but rather we always count on competition and distance ourselves from rivalry. Do not forget that the PSII, PMI [Permi], PI [Partai Indonesia, Partindo] and also the PNI [Indonesian National Education, New PNI] all use the weapons of non-cooperation to achieve an Independent Indonesia.
> We base ourselves on that Nationalism, meaning that we do not involve religion in the political struggle, we look only at the people and homeland of Indonesia. We are not turning our backs on our religion; and our organization is not telling its members to abandon their religion.[63]

Chatib Suleiman's defence of the new PNI also illustrated one of the personal qualities that enabled him to remain perhaps the most influential politician in West Sumatra over the next two decades. Rather than exacerbating tensions by his response to criticisms, he searched for the area of agreement among the contending forces – he found that common ground in the noncooperative stance of both the New PNI and its critics.

It is worth noting here that there was no inconsistency in the fact that two founders and leaders of the West Sumatra branch of the New PNI, Leon Salim and Darwis Thaib, were followers of Tan Malaka. Many similarities existed at the time between Mohammad Hatta's New PNI and Tan Malaka's Pari, in addition to the fact that each was headed by a Minangkabau: both parties were nationalist, anticolonialist, and socialist; both emphasized cadre organization; and neither paid any allegiance to Moscow. The reader has probably already noticed parallels between the analyses and criticisms of the political situation in Indonesia, offered by Hatta and Tan Malaka. In criticizing the strategies pursued by Sukarno's National Party, Hatta argued that Indonesia had not yet reached a sufficiently advanced stage in its independence struggle for the type of mass action being proposed by Sukarno's party; he contended that, at the current stage, the focus of the nationalist movement should not be on developing mass organizations, but on creating an educated cadre to lead the struggle. These arguments echo those of Tan Malaka in 1926 when he criticized the Indonesian Communist Party for moving too swiftly to rebellion before the groundwork had been laid, and he too stressed the need to build momentum more gradually through organization and education.

In the early 1930s there was mutual respect among the Minangkabau leaders of the Pari and the New PNI, and in fact when Hatta was in Bukittinggi in November 1932, a local businessman, Anwar Sutan Saidi (who was to become one of Hatta's closest friends in the region), introduced him to Kandur St. Rangkayo Basa, an emissary from Tan Malaka, who brought him a copy of the Pari's political organ, *Obor*.[64] Personal and family ties between Tan Malaka's followers and the New PNI leaders were also close: Anwar himself was younger brother of Djamaluddin Ibrahim, former teacher in the Padang Panjang schools and now the main Pari contact between Singapore and Java; and Jazir, younger brother of Tan Malaka's principal lieutenant, Djamaluddin Tamin, became chairman of the Padang Panjang section of the New PNI in mid-1934.[65]

The amorphous, conspiratorial, and underground character of the Pari makes it very difficult to track down its actual activities. The party's principal impact was through its distribution of Tan Malaka's writings and its publication and distribution of the party journal, *Obor*, copies of which were produced and circulated at least until 1936. Throughout the prewar period Tan Malaka himself exerted an immense spiritual influence on the Indonesian independence struggle, not only through his writings but also through the myths and legends that surrounded him and his activities.[66]

The three founders of the Pari constituted its chief executive: Tan Malaka in Amoy, Subakat in Bangkok, and Djamaluddin Tamin in Singapore. Tamin was responsible for activities in the Indies, and his organization in Singapore and Malaya had strong ties and frequent interaction with the political, religious, economic, and educational streams within West Sumatra, particularly in the late 1920s and early 1930s. One basis for this cooperation was the network of schools established by the modernist Islamic scholars who had returned to West Sumatra and Malaya in the early years of the twentieth century. When Djamaluddin Tamin, who was a former teacher at the Sumatra Thawalib school in Padang Panjang, went to Bangkok in May 1927 at the time the Pari was founded, one of the first people he contacted was Syekh Ahmad Wahab. Syekh Wahab had studied in Mecca with the three older-generation modernist scholars from West Sumatra, Abdullah Ahmad, Haji Rasul, and Syekh Djamil Djambek, as well as with their Minangkabau colleague, Syekh Tahir Djalaluddin, who had chosen to go to Malaya rather than return to his home region. At the time of their meeting in 1927, Syekh Wahab already knew of Djamaluddin Tamin through his articles in *Al Munir*, published in Padang Panjang between 1918 and 1921, while

> On the other hand, I myself had already known the name of Syekh Ahmad Wahab since 1913, that is I had known from my teacher in religion and politics, Zainuddin El Junusey Labay, that Syekh Chatib alias Syekh Wahab and Syekh Taher were the anti-Dutch Islamic scholars, that is they were pro politics and anti-Dutch colonization of Indonesia while the other three [modernist scholars]... were pro-Dutch...[67]

Syekh Ahmad Wahab had established modernist schools in Siam similar to those of Zainuddin Labai in Padang Panjang, and he helped Tamin and his colleagues find funds, friends, food, and lodging while they were in Bangkok.[68] Wahab was especially close with Subakat, who was later arrested while staying with a member of Wahab's family.[69] Tamin's ties were also strong with Syekh Tahir in Perak, and when the Dutch arrested Tahir during his 1927 visit to Sumatra and threatened to exile him to Digul (see above), Tamin, under the alias Tunarman, wrote a series of articles in *Bintang Timur* arguing for his release.[70]

Tamin drew a sharp distinction between the two reformist Islamic scholars who had chosen exile (Syekh Tahir and Syekh Wahab) and the three who had returned to West Sumatra. He viewed Haji Rasul, Abdullah Ahmad, and Djamil Djambek as pro-Dutch, citing the fact that two of them had been awarded medals by the Dutch government.[71] He differentiated them from Zainuddin Labai and other younger Islamic teachers who had embraced the nationalist movement and never faltered in their opposition to the Dutch.

In the immediate aftermath of the 1927 rebellion, when dozens of Tan Malaka's followers fled West Sumatra, many of the exiles went on to the Middle East, and Tamin encouraged those who remained in Malaya to become sailors on the trading ships plying the Malacca Strait and the Indonesian archipelago. He himself also worked frequently on the ships, usually when the British authorities were hot on his heels and he was in danger of arrest. Djamaluddin Ibrahim (alias Rachman Djamal) was one of the very few exiles who Tamin felt were capable of continuing the struggle. Tamin expressed an affection and admiration for Ibrahim and his consistent willingness to go anywhere to help Pari activities,[72] sending him to Amoy at the beginning of 1928 to study for several months with Tan Malaka.

After he returned to Singapore in the middle of that year, Djamaluddin Ibrahim coordinated his work as courier with that of Kandur St. Rangkayo Basa. Kandur

Kandur St. Rangkayo Basa in the 1950s
(Leon Salim)

travelled particularly between West and East Sumatra while Ibrahim travelled between Batavia, Singapore, Pekanbaru, and Padang.[73] Tamin reported that Djamaluddin Ibrahim and Kandur were able to get valuable books and documents from Tan Malaka to the young intellectual nationalists such as Assaat, Amir Sjarifuddin, Muhammad Yamin, and Jahja Nasution.[74] At the end of 1928, Djamaluddin Ibrahim, with two other Pari members, opened a store on Geylang Road in Singapore, where they sold cigarettes smuggled in from Riau. Profits from this store helped fund Pari activities.[75] Kandur, the son of an important merchant in Karimun, Riau, had a trader's passport. In Singapore he was an art dealer,[76] and during the late 1920s he was able to travel between Pekanbaru and Singapore, pursuing his business activities while acting as Tan Malaka's courier.[77]

By 1930, however, communications between the peninsula and Indonesia had been reduced. According to Tamin, Kandur no longer visited Singapore, and spent most of his time in Bukittinggi, though he did travel from there to Batavia and Medan. He finally emerged again in Singapore in July 1932, and reported to Tamin that at the request of Abdullah,[78] he had established contact with such leaders as Yamin and Assaat in Batavia and with various Minangkabau intellectuals in Medan, while within West Sumatra he was in touch with H. Djalaluddin Thaib, Gani Sjarif, and H. Uddin Rahmany, one of the leaders of the Islamic League (PSII).[79] Tamin then supplied Kandur with books and Pari documents.

On his way home from Holland in August 1932, Hatta had hoped to see Tamin in Singapore, but the meeting did not take place because Tamin feared that Hatta would be under close surveillance by the British CID throughout his stay.[80] It was for this reason that three months later Tamin sent Kandur to pass on the copy of *Obor* to Hatta in Bukittinggi. According to Hatta, they talked for about half an hour, with Kandur telling him that there were not many Pari members in Indonesia itself and he himself did not know all of them.[81]

Thus, in mid-1933, when the Dutch instituted their ban on assembly (*vergader verbod*) the two parties they targeted in West Sumatra, the Permi and the PSII, were by no means the only centres of anticolonial political activity. However, they were the largest and attracted the widest following throughout West Sumatra and beyond. The colonial government viewed Permi in particular as its most dangerous opponent, because it contained within itself elements the Dutch felt to be most threatening – its combination of radicalism and religion attracted committed followers throughout West Sumatra, and its leaders exerted an appeal unmatched by the other parties in the region.

After Rasuna Said's arrest at the end of 1932, tension increased between the government and the Permi, and travel restrictions were instituted against leaders of the party. In April 1933, the Dutch issued a limited ban on public meetings of both the Permi and Islamic League (PSII). In July, government officials warned Djalaluddin Thaib, Iljas Jacub, and particularly the most articulate of the Permi's orators, Muchtar Luthfi, that antigovernment speeches would no longer be tolerated.[82] Luthfi defied them at a public meeting on July 9, when

> he claimed that the immediate goal of Permi was to create a new Indonesia, 'to be ruled by the *Dang Tuanku*, as the President of the Republic of Indonesia.' This reference to the legendary just and wise ruler of Minangkabau made his statement the most quoted political speech in Minangkabau.[83]

Two days later, on July 11, Luthfi was arrested and his papers seized.[84] At about the same time, the government imposed travel restrictions on other Permi leaders, and on August 5 proclaimed a full ban on all meetings of both the Permi and PSII, as well as their youth organizations. Within a month, both Iljas Jacub and Djalaluddin Thaib were in jail for attempting to avoid the ban by sending out written courses to Permi members.[85] At the same time, Islamic League (PSII) leaders Uddin Rahmany and Sabilal Rasjad were arrested for violating the ban on assembly. After being held in jail for over a year, these Permi and PSII leaders were exiled to Digul in December 1934, to the shock of their followers in West Sumatra who had believed the detention camp to be restricted to Communist opponents of the colonial government.[86]

Meanwhile in Batavia, in mid-1933, the Dutch had also imposed severe restrictions, including the one on assembly (*vergader verbod*), on both the Partindo and the New PNI. Sukarno was again arrested on August 1, 1933, and was sent to exile in Flores the following February. Hatta initially saw the government's actions as confirming the wisdom of his own political strategy in not establishing a mass-based party, and he hoped that the cadre character of the New PNI would protect its leaders from arrest. But, though recognizing that the New PNI's leaders posed no immediate threat, in February 1934 the Indies government detained not only Hatta and Sjahrir, but all of the party's major leaders in Batavia and exiled them to Boven Digul, a much harsher place of exile than Flores.[87] The fact that the government ultimately

Djamaluddin Ibrahim
(Roestam Anwar)

took sterner measures against the leaders of the New PNI than against the Partindo, was perhaps in part a result of Sukarno's alleged statements of remorse from jail.[88] But it may also have indicated that the Dutch regarded the methods of Hatta and his colleagues as, in the long run, more dangerous than those of Sukarno and his mass-based parties. As the government's adviser for Native Affairs, Gobée commented: 'leaders of the mentality of such as Mohammad Hatta are always dangerous. In comparison a revolutionary figure such as Dr. Tjipto Mangunkusumo is a child'.[89]

In West Sumatra the New PNI was subject to the same restrictions as the party in Batavia, but in contrast to the arrests of senior leaders in Batavia, no moves were initially taken against its local leaders. Aware of the danger, however, branch leaders restricted the party's political activities in accordance with instructions they received from their central headquarters.[90]

The Dutch were moving successfully against the major nationalist organizations that opposed them, not only in Batavia and West Sumatra but also in Singapore and Malaya. Subakat, one of the three founders of Tan Malaka's Pari, had been arrested as early as September 1929, and died in Glodok jail in February 1930– either by his own hand or that of the Dutch.[91] Before his death he was apparently forced to disclose information on the structure and membership of the Pari organization.[92] From then on, British intelligence services in Malaya and Singapore were hunting and harassing Tamin and the other Pari members. In cooperation with the British, between 1932 and 1934 the Dutch succeeded in capturing several important Pari members, leaving Tan Malaka himself, who was travelling between Manila and ports on the Chinese coast, almost completely isolated.[93] Djamaluddin Tamin was detained in Singapore by the CID on September 13, 1932, together with three other colleagues who had just completed a number of Pari pamphlets.[94] They and twelve other Pari members were brought to court four days later, accused of carrying out illegal political actions against the British government. After initial interrogations by British officials, four of the detainees were released on September 19. Tamin, however, was handed over to the Dutch and shipped to Batavia, where he was jailed for several months before being exiled to Digul, arriving there on October 8, 1933.[95]

After the arrest of Tamin and several of his colleagues, leadership of Pari was left in the hands of Djamaluddin Ibrahim and Kandur St. Rangkayo Basa, together with Dawood, whom Ibrahim had recruited in West Sumatra.[96] Kandur himself was arrested in Bukittinggi in June 1933 and sent to Batavia, before being exiled to Digul the following year.[97] Djamaluddin Ibrahim remained free. He had spent some time in Bandung, but after Tamin's arrest sought refuge in Singapore, taking over leadership of the Pari there. He continued to travel between Java and Singapore, and was able to continue publication of the party's magazine, *Obor*.[98] The success of Djamaluddin Ibrahim and Dawood in maintaining Pari's activities led the Dutch to arrest many additional suspected Pari followers in Java on May 11, 1936. That wave of arrests, which snared nearly all remaining members, again missed Djamaluddin Ibrahim and Dawood. But both were finally seized in Batavia in January 1937.[99] Although suffering from tuberculosis, Ibrahim was initially kept shackled and chained in prison in Cipinang. But the doctor treating him refused to let him be sent to Digul.[100] The authorities agreed to his being transferred to the Cisarawa hospital in Bogor, though they remained intent on exiling him to Digul as soon as he recovered.[101] He did not recover, however, but finally died, still in Dutch detention, shortly before the Japanese invasion.[102]

Aftermath

From the time of the Dutch crackdown in 1933, the character of political activity in West Sumatra, as in all other parts of the archipelago, had to change. The Dutch succeeded in crushing Permi as a political party although its educational institutions, particularly in Padang, perpetuated its influence and ideas. Despite the restrictions, the Islamic League (PSII) continued to exist, though it exerted relatively little influence locally, while the major wing of this national party adopted policies of cooperation with the colonial power.

During 1934 and 1935 the Dutch strengthened their surveillance of the New PNI. In response to government pressure, the party leaders decided that the now highly visible Chatib Suleiman should be replaced as chairman by Leon Salim, who together with Tamimi Usman[103] succeeded in holding the Bukittinggi and Padang Panjang sections together in the face of the internal chaos and suspicion that arose in response to the Dutch pressure. Dutch interception of their mail forced the party to send correspondence between its leaders and sections by courier.[104]

A flavour of the atmosphere in Padang Panjang during the mid-1930s can be caught from Leon Salim's account of the secret visit by a New PNI leader to West Sumatra in January 1935.

We, the leaders of the West Sumatra branch of the New PNI, received news from the general leadership that St. Nur Alamsjah was secretly planning to visit West Sumatra. St. Nur Alamsjah is Bung [St.] Sjahrir's elder brother. Under the orders of the Netherlands Indies government he was not permitted to enter West Sumatra.

Salim describes how the local party leaders arranged for St. Nur Alamsjah to stay a week in Padang, in the house of a party member, Suleiman, who lived at the edge of the market place, where the big and bustling night market was held. Meanwhile, the Dutch Intelligence Services (PID) were searching for St. Nur Alamsjah throughout West Sumatra, questioning all his former friends and acquaintances. The Head of Police in Padang Panjang, Dt. Kraink, upon receiving reports from Padang that St. Nur Alamsjah was on his way to Padang Panjang, came to question Leon Salim concerning his whereabouts:

> I shook my head as if I was really trying to solve a difficult problem. Then I said to him: 'It's not possible for anyone to slip secretly into this town. There are only two entrances. First, the railroad and second the main road through the Anai valley. Both are tightly guarded by the police. It's impossible for anyone to come in through the jungle at the foot of Tandikat mountain. Now I wonder if you have searched the houses of all St. Nur Alamsjah's family in Padang Panjang. Have you searched the house of Demang Palin (Demang Palin was the boss of this Police Chief)? He is a member of St. Nur's family.'
>
> Hearing this, the Head of Police, Demang Palin's subordinate, got up and left without saying another word.
>
> I laughed to myself.
>
> I hurriedly pulled on a few clothes because night was falling. I had to know whether Sdr. St. Nur Alamsjah had arrived safely in Padang Panjang yet. On the corner of Pasar Usang street, in the cafe (*kedai kopi*) where we usually drank tea, I should be able to get an evening report on him. I went straight there and found Sdr. Sjamsuddin Dt. Bandaro Batuah... playing dominoes surrounded by a crowd of people.
>
> He glanced cheerfully at me and as if commenting on the domino game said:
>
> 'This evening I'm really lucky. I will certainly win. I've got enough sixes. I'm going to win. All of you are going to have to buy me drinks this evening...'
>
> Everyone gathered round the domino players, encouraging the game. I joined in. Meanwhile I understood that St. Nur Alamsjah had safely arrived in Padang Panjang.
>
> I contentedly sipped my tea, knowing that across from me sat a police 'cockroach' of the Netherlands Indies Intelligence services, who was

well known to us. I offered him a drink.

In the billiard saloon across the street, absorbed in his game, was the champion billiard player of the town of Padang Panjang, Sdr. Chatib Suleiman.

I smiled with contentment.

Plan for the Visit of Sdr. St. Nur Alamsjah to Padang Panjang

1. Monday evening (market day in Padang Panjang) Sdr. St. Nur was in a sedan at Silahi (outside Padang Panjang).

2. A farmer with a young assistant gets out of the sedan carrying a small basket filled with vegetables.

3. He enters the town on foot going directly to the New Market (at the time the market was very busy as everyone was getting ready to go home for the sunset prayer).

4. St. Nur with his young escort enters the bustling market, goes out through the east gate under the two-storey guard post, in the crowds hurrying home.

5. He has to cross the street.

6. He crosses it, directly in front of the two-storey guard post. There people are busy packing up their wares. St. Nur enters. He goes straight through the shop to the back and climbs to the upper floor.

7. All the party members who are well known to the police have to be patient – keep their distance, aware of the Intelligence spies.

8. For four days and nights the members are organized to visit him one by one without raising suspicion.

9. On Friday night St. Nur is ready to be swept up in the wave of humanity going home at the end of the Friday market day in the direction of Bukittinggi, in the same manner as he entered Padang Panjang.

10. His car is waiting outside the town.

11. St. Nur safely arrives in Bukittinggi.

But...

The next day we received a report that St. Nur Alamsjah had been arrested in Bukittinggi. Who can describe our dismay on hearing the news. Our comrades in Bukittinggi were less skillful than the Dutch secret police.

Finally the cat had caught the mouse.

Salim goes on to note that Nur Alamsjah was sentenced to three months in jail for disobeying the travel ban. But the Dutch also arrested the leader of the Padang branch of New PNI, M. Nur Arif, who had made the arrangements for the visit, and he was sentenced to exile in Digul, in Salim's view in revenge for making fools of the colonial police.[105] Salim continues:

In 1935 Nur Arif left for Digul as a progressive, revolutionary young man, a smart youth of about 26 or 27, dazzlingly bright.

Digul destroyed him completely. He returned to Jakarta, a skeleton wrapped in skin. His nerves were shattered by the climate of Digul. He was my friend, my comrade, also my teacher when I was young. I well knew his contribution to the struggle. In the society he was always in the forefront, wielding power with restraint. Now the Colonial Government made him into a useless human being.

His eyes were always gazing forward, far into the distance,... vacant. He seemed empty.[106]

The difficulties of evading Dutch surveillance restricted the political education efforts of the New PNI, and its relatively small influence decreased even further. Salim himself, as leader of the local branch, was subjected to raids, house searches, and police questioning, until finally in January 1936 he was imprisoned for a year, accused of organizing the students of the two schools in singing 'the extremist song, "Marhaen March"'.[107] When he was released the atmosphere had calmed down. By that time, the Dutch had succeeded in destroying the strongest political parties, and until the Japanese occupation, nationalist activity in West Sumatra was forced to assume a different character.

CHAPTER 3

Nationalism in Prewar West Sumatra

Parties and Leadership

As can be seen from the previous chapters, anticolonial nationalism in West Sumatra during the early decades of the twentieth century had many characteristics that differ from those usually associated with that phenomenon in Indonesia during the late-colonial period. Exerting as much influence as Western ideas of modern nationalism were stories handed down the generations about Minangkabau struggles against outside aggressors. Equally influential were concepts deriving from Minangkabau ideals of equality expressed in the social principle of 'sitting equally low, standing equally high',[1] and egalitarian and community concepts based in Islam. In addition, the *merantau* tradition both enriched the local culture with outside influences and brought to West Sumatra a wider understanding of the disparate societies making up the Indonesian archipelago.[2] All of these combined to become intrinsic parts of a Minangkabau perception of nationalism that stretched beyond the island of Sumatra to embrace the entire Netherlands Indies. Certainly, the dynamic for the nationalist movement in West Sumatra rested less on the modernizing instincts of a narrow, Western-educated bureaucratic elite, than on the overlapping interests of religious, educational, and entrepreneurial elements in the region, which embraced the ideals of an Islamic trading society. Their interests were channeled through a nexus of relationships which accorded less with the colonial network of Batavia, West Sumatra, and the Netherlands, than with an alternative web of contacts tying Sumatra with Malaya/Singapore and Cairo/Mecca, often via Bangkok and India.

The potency of these extracolonial interrelationships of religion, commerce, and education was reflected in stories that formed part of the popular literature of the closing years of Dutch rule, particularly in the cluster of novels published in Medan and Bukittinggi (Fort de Kock), which narrated the exploits of the Indonesian Scarlet Pimpernel (*Pacar Merah*), Tan Malaka.[3] At least five novels appeared between 1938 and 1940,[4] telling the fantastic adventures of the Scarlet Pimpernel and his comrades (among them Yamin, Djamulin [Djamaluddin Tamin], Alminsky [Alimin], and Semaunov [Semaun]), as they struggled against the machinations of the Dutch and British intelligence services in a world that stretched from West Sumatra across the Malacca Strait to the Malay Peninsula, and from there to Cairo and Teheran and other places in the Middle East.

Often under the guise of a small trader, usually a fruit seller, Tan Malaka as the Scarlet Pimpernel is endowed in these novels with magical qualities and 'slippery as an eel' (*licin sebagai beloet*) appears and disappears at will, disarming his opponents with his calm and patient demeanour.[5]

Fact and fiction are combined in the novels, where fantastic exploits take place against the background of the 1927 rebellion and the later reality of the independence struggle. No wonder that this mixture of fact and fiction permeates the supposedly factual history of the period. Exploits narrated in the novels are picked up in contemporary newpapers, the Padang newspaper *TimoerBaroe* reporting the arrest by the Dutch PID of Tan Malaka, together with Alimin, in Teheran,[6] an incident apparently derived from the novel *Rol Patjar Merah Indonesia*.[7] Also, in his biographies of Indonesia's leaders, Tamar Djaja refers to Tan Malaka as the Pacar Merah, seeming to rely on the novels to trace his activities in the late 1930s:

> His skill at concealing himself is clear in that through all the time he was in Singapore he was never detected by the Dutch and English police. This was his final place after the many countries in East and West he travelled through in his wanderings.
> The name of Tan Malaka is connected with his experiences in the countries of his wanderings during these years, which if they are put in order become a string of words that intertwine to form something beautiful and magical such as in Siam, Egypt, Kalimantan, the Malay Peninsula, Arabia, Iran-Persia.[8]

Some of the region's foremost leaders embodied the distinctive characteristics of the anticolonial movements in West Sumatra. They consciously distanced themselves from European-influenced nationalist politics because they were disillusioned with what they perceived to be the self-seeking nature of the professional nationalist politicians they saw in Batavia. For example, Mohammad Sjafei, the founder of the INS school in Kayutanam (who would later become a leading political figure in West Sumatra), had been politically active in his youth with the Insulinde party in Batavia. But he was alienated by what he felt was the way many of the nationalist political leaders in the capital merely used the political parties to pursue their personal ambitions.[9] When he returned to West Sumatra, he conceived the school he founded there as a place where the students would be trained to become productive citizens within their own societies, rather than forming an elite separated from their fellow Indonesians.

This attitude was paralleled by a consciousness and resentment of what was perceived as Dutch manipulation of Western education. For example, Zainuddin Labai el Junusiah, the founder of the Diniyyah schools, strongly opposed what he considered were Dutch efforts to encourage divisions in Indonesian society by creating a Western-educated elite, which felt separated from and superior to their fellows. His attitude toward Dutch efforts in this direction is reflected in a story Zainuddin's daughter often heard from her mother:

> One day my father got on the train from Padang Panjang to Padang. After the train left, there were by chance two men, one a Dutchman and the other an Indonesian who was fluent in the Dutch language. They were laughing cheerfully [raucously?] while they talked, and that sound

was all that could be heard. Father was annoyed at the two men; it was very clear that they regarded the other passengers as just stupid.

Feeling irritated he went up and down the train looking for a companion so that he could counter them by speaking in Arabic. By chance there was a passenger wearing a white kopiah, which meant that he had returned from the holy land of Mecca with the title 'Haji.' Father approached the haji and began speaking fluent Arabic in a loud voice in competition with the sound of the other two men talking in Dutch. Strangely the haji only smiled and nodded his head as if he understood perfectly what Father was saying in Arabic. Even though Father well knew that the haji he was using in his competing conversation didn't understand a single sentence of Arabic, Father still felt satisfied with the way he was combatting the men speaking fluent Dutch by conversing in Arabic with an ignorant haji. After Father started speaking, the Dutchman and his *inlander* [native] fell silent.[10]

It was not until four years after Zainuddin's death that Indonesian was adopted as the universal language used by the nationalists in competition with Dutch. So to combat the Dutch language of the elite, Zainuddin then used the equally scholarly language of Arabic. (One would assume that his fellow passengers were using Minangkabau.)

Ideological currents penetrating the region from outside – whether from Java, Europe, or the Middle East – had a strong influence on West Sumatra. But these influences assumed overwhelming Minangkabau characteristics as they were absorbed into the society. The Communist movement's People's Leagues (Sarikat Rakyat) adapted to the religious climate in the region and continued to exist in open defiance of the orders coming from the PKI's Central Committee in Java.[11] Similarly, the Muhammadiah and the new Islamic League (PSII) in West Sumatra assumed completely different and more political, nationalist, and radical characteristics than their parent organizations in Java. The strongest political organizations in West Sumatra were either indigenous to the area (Permi) or gained their strength from the loyalty of their followers to a party leader who was from the region and enjoyed high prestige as a native son – for example Tan Malaka's Pari and Hatta's New PNI.

Throughout the prewar period and right up until the disastrous regional rebellion of 1958, a disproportionately high number of Indonesia's top political leaders, both in the nationalist movement and in the post-independence Republican government, came from West Sumatra. Ties with these leaders further increased Minangkabau consciousness of their connections and interrelationship with other parts of the archipelago, and their awareness of the considerations of Indies-wide politics. This consciousness had a strong impact on the nature and development of the nationalist movement in West Sumatra, as did the harmony or dissonance between the ideas and perceptions of Minangkabau leaders at the national level and those who remained in West Sumatra itself.

The roots of any dissonance between Minangkabau leaders in Batavia or Holland and those who remained in West Sumatra clearly lay in the fact that those outside the region frequently adapted to the pressures of the societies in which they now lived. They often adopted the more rigid black and white classifications of their new home areas in confronting problems, adhering to these starker dichotomies rather than the more shaded, ambiguous classifications that pervaded Minangkabau society, where seemingly contradictory concepts often coexisted within a dynamic tension.

Many Islamic scholars who left their home region and received their education either in Europe or the Middle East opposed those elements of traditional Minangkabau customs (*adat*) that did not accord with a stricter interpretation of Islam or with the more 'modern' ideas of Westernized societies. Haji Agus Salim, for instance, who was born in Kota Gedang near Bukittinggi, had far greater influence on the national scene than within his home region, in large part because his antagonism toward Minangkabau *adat* led him to pressure the central leadership of the New Islamic League (PSII) to take a strong stand against traditional practices which he felt were in opposition to Islamic law.[12] Haji Agus Salim's Minangkabau colleague in the Java-based headquarters of the Islamic League, Abdul Muis, in 1923 strongly opposed efforts by radical leaders in the Minangkabau to seek areas of compatibility between Islam and communism.[13] Another Minangkabau Muslim who was influential on the national scene, Mohd. Natsir – in the early 1930s one of the leaders of the Persatuan Islam (Islamic Union, Persis) – opposed Permi's efforts to embrace both Islam and Nationalism. He argued that Islam recognizes that inherent in man's nature is a love for his community, but that it is only through the teachings of Islam that the love for one's own people can 'be safeguarded from falling into low and intolerant fanaticism of *kebangsaan* [nationalism]'.[14]

Surprisingly, it was frequently the 'socialist' leaders who retained greatest influence in their home area, in large part because they felt the need to harmonize their socialist ideas with the strong religious and traditional currents in the Minangkabau. Of these national-level leaders, those who exerted most influence were Tan Malaka, Muhammad Yamin, and Mohammad Hatta. We have seen how Tan Malaka's vision accorded so closely with that of many of the younger Minangkabau Islamic scholars in stressing the elements of communism that were in harmony with Islam, and in emphasizing how the aims of radical nationalism were compatible with the egalitarian and entrepreneurial aspects of Minangkabau society. Both he and Hatta also stressed the necessity of organization and education as bases for developing the nationalist movement. Although some dissension later developed between Hatta and local nationalist leaders, he retained a dominant influence among the people of West Sumatra. His ties and those of Yamin with entrepreneurs in the region strengthened and mediated their ideas vis-à-vis their local followers.[15] At this stage, Sutan Sjahrir, although subordinate only to Hatta in the New PNI, exerted less influence in his home region. However, during the 1930s his stature grew, and during the Japanese occupation, when he directed policies of noncooperation, his influence became very strong in West Sumatra.

The Role of the Entrepreneurs

As had been the case in the previous decade, in the 1930s the trading community helped provide the various strands of the nationalist movement with financial backing and means of communication from West Sumatra to Java and the Malay peninsula. As we have seen in the case of the entrepreneur Abdullah Basa Bandaro, although he was treasurer of the Permi party and its major link with Sukarno's party in Java, his principal allegiance was to Tan Malaka and his Pari party.[16] The same was true with many of his fellows. Despite impediments from the Dutch, the Minangkabau entrepreneurs maintained strong trading links with the business world of the Malay peninsula and had family ties with both leaders and followers of the radical Pari party based there.

The leading Padang entrepreneur was still Mohd. Taher Marah Sutan, the shipping agent who in 1914 had helped found the Entrepreneurs' League and was a close friend of Mohammad Hatta. Marah Sutan was deeply involved not only in business but also in Padang's schools and social organizations.[17] Many indigenous traders suffered as a result of the 1927 uprising, and in its wake, Dutch economic policies tended to favour the Chinese and Eurasian communities to an even greater extent than before. The late 1920s and early 1930s, thus, were years that were particularly difficult for the indigenous entrepreneurs, more so than for the business community as a whole. It was to strengthen their position that Marah Sutan in June 1930 established a new trading organization in Padang, the Indonesian Merchants' Group (Himpunan Saudagar Indonesia – HSI).[18] A few months later a branch was formed in Bukittinggi.

Establishment of the Bukittinggi branch of the Indonesian Merchants' Group brought to the fore another Minangkabau entrepreneur who would have an enormous impact on the economic and political aspects of the nationalist movement in West Sumatra into the independence period. This was Anwar St. Saidi, at the time a young man of only twenty years, who was a founding member of the Bukittinggi branch of the Merchants' Group.[19] Anwar was born in 1910 in Sungai Puar, an ironworking village on the slopes of Mount Merapi, between Bukittinggi and Padang Panjang. He did not complete secondary school but entered the business world at the age of sixteen when he first went to work with his uncle in Payakumbuh.[20] Despite his lack of education, Anwar was a young man with broad vision and unusual energy. His political consciousness had undoubtedly been heightened by his elder brother, Djamaluddin Ibrahim, one of the former teachers at the Thawalib schools and by 1930, a leading member of Tan Malaka's Pari.

Anwar's attention was initially focused on how to develop the trading potential of the upland areas of West Sumatra for the good of the Minangkabau people. Aware of the range of goods made in the hillside villages (nagari) of Agam, where the agricultural land was poor – ironworking and woodcarving in Sungai Puar, clothing in Empat Angkat, furniture in Kamang, and silverwork in Kota Gadang and Guguk – he proposed creating an association which could coordinate the marketing of these items both within and outside West Sumatra. When he brought this idea to Taher Marah Sutan, however, the older man discouraged him, pointing out that the spe-

Anwar St. Saidi (Roestam Anwar)

cialized trading networks of the individual *nagari*, rooted in local traditional social and cultural ties, could not be easily, and perhaps should not be, superseded. He advised Anwar to concentrate on the traders in the towns and on their needs, the greatest of which was to increase their capital resources.[21]

That same year, 1930, Dr. Sutomo had established the first Indonesian National Bank in Surabaya, and Anwar was eager to found a branch of the bank in West Suma-tra. When he proposed this to the Indonesian Merchants' Group in Padang and Bukittinggi, however, problems were immediately raised about the acceptability of such banking practices as lending money (*rente*) which were considered doubtful (*subahat*) under Islamic law.[22] In combatting this reluctance, Anwar eventually had to settle temporarily for establishing an institution that concentrated on building up savings reserves. It was called Abuan Saudagar, or Merchants' Savings Bank, and was founded on December 27, 1930.[23]

None of the first ten founding members of the Bank's board had received formal education beyond elementary level, though most of them had studied religion. Three were book traders, two were printers and publishers, and the remaining five were cloth traders, mostly in batik.[24] All founders agreed that for the first five years the bank's profits would not be divided, but would be redeposited to become new banking capital.

Anwar struggled for the next years to make the bank viable. The directors of the National Bank of Indonesia in Surabaya refused to agree to a branch of their bank being established in West Sumatra, a reluctance which Anwar blamed on their suspi-cions of the Bukittinggi bankers, none of whom had received a Western education, but 'had only received their schooling under "a banana tree"'.[25] At the end of 1931, the Surabaya directors asked Anwar to postpone establishing a bank because of the difficult economic situation, and the following year excused their continuing reluc-tance to countenance a West Sumatra branch by stating that the minimal starting capital needed for a branch was F25,000, while the directors in Bukittinggi had only succeeded in collecting F15,000.[26] Finally, with the help of a legal adviser, Mr. Datuk Djamin, recommended to him by Muhammad Yamin, Anwar and his colleagues were able to evade the need for government permission by giving their new bank the official title of Bank Nasional Abuan Saudagar or National Bank of Merchants' Savings. The last two words were soon dropped and it became known merely as the National Bank. Until 1940, however, when it was transformed into a limited company, its character remained more that of a cooperative than a bank, with small traders lending capital, which the bank could use for loans which had to be repaid within a very short time, usually a week.[27] At the celebrations for its tenth anniversary in 1940, its aims were described as follows:

> The goal contained in the establishment of the National Bank was actually very large indeed. It was hoped that it would not only be a centre for the gathering and activity of capital, and a quick and easy place for lending money; but that its founding would act as a bond and a unifying factor for the merchants and would become a body that was capable of giving the necessary explanations with regard to the problems of trade and economy in general. Apart from that it was further hoped that it could support social activity for the general public, such as schools, national buildings and so on.[28]

Despite its limitations, the Bank became the major organization defending indigenous traders in their competition with the Chinese, and providing them with trading capital.[29]

Through his family relationships and his banking and trading activities, Anwar's nationalist and political contacts were extensive. His connections with Tan Malaka's Pari party brought him to the attention of the Dutch, and in September 1932, a visit from his brother Djamaluddin Ibrahim led to Anwar's arrest for hiding a political fugitive. Fortunately, he had been warned that the Dutch were planning to raid his house and had succeeded in smuggling his brother out of the town on a vegetable truck to Pekanbaru, from where Ibrahim was able to make his way directly to Singapore. Though the Dutch seized letters and books from the Bank's offices, they had insufficient evidence to charge Anwar and had to release him after a day and a half in jail.[30]

Through his economic activities, Anwar also developed close ties in Batavia with Mohammad Hatta and Muhammad Yamin. Anwar's mentor in Padang, Marah Sutan, initially sent him to Yamin, a close associate of Sukarno, for a recommendation to the National Bank's head in Surabaya, Dr. Sutomo. Anwar became strongly attracted to Yamin's romantic political ideas of a Greater Indonesia (Indonesia Raya) and would possibly have moved to work in the field of national politics in Batavia, had Yamin not advised him to remain in West Sumatra and to concentrate on economic affairs. In Yamin's view, Anwar was unique in that position, while there were already too many politicians in Batavia. Yamin did, however, urge Anwar to retain his broad vision and ideals and not let his regional base lead to parochialism.[31]

Anwar did not meet Hatta until that leader's visit to West Sumatra at the end of 1932, but subsequently, they became very close friends. A few years later, while Hatta was in exile on Banda Neira in the eastern archipelago, Anwar sent two young economics students from Bukittinggi to study with him there, while Hatta sent Anwar written courses on economics and banking.[32] From Hatta, Anwar acquired a knowledge of the theory of capitalist economy 'that originates from imperialists who never think of helping the people'. In Hatta's view, 'Capitalism finally gave birth to communism – the two are the same because they were born from the same cultural pattern'. Hatta emphasized the differences between a capitalist and a cooperative economic system, which never enriches just one or two people and does not become strong by killing other businesses. When the bank did not expand as rapidly as Anwar hoped, Hatta reminded him of its social foundations and encouraged him to return to these by collecting money for earthquake victims in South Sumatra and lending money to small businesses that were unable to give the kind of guarantees most banks demand.[33]

Schools in West Sumatra

Despite the differing degrees of influence wielded by Minangkabau actors on the national scene, the character and strength of the anticolonial movement within West Sumatra remained to a considerable degree autonomous of external direction, and was developed largely in accord with and in response to indigenous political, social, and cultural factors by men and women who remained in the region.

It is particularly noteworthy that in the years leading up to the uprisings of 1927, very few of the men who played the major roles in the anti-Dutch movements in West Sumatra had received any of their education outside the region – whether in Java or in Europe. This was true of Zainuddin Labai, the largely self-educated founder of the Diniyyah schools in Padang Panjang, whose early death cut off what might have been the decisive moderating influence he could have wielded on the conflagrations of 1925-27. It was similarly true of Sulaiman Labai, the trader and paramount leader of the People's League in Silungkang before his arrest in October of 1926, and of Djamaluddin Tamin and Djamaluddin Ibrahim, who fled the region to join with Tan Malaka. The most notable exception to this rule was Datuk Batuah, who had six years of schooling in Mecca. None of the traders who guided the political activities in both Padang and Bukittinggi during the 1920s and 1930s – Basa Bandaro, Taher Marah Sutan, Sutan Said Ali, or Anwar St. Saidi – had had any education outside of West Sumatra.

In 1933, a number of the principal leaders opposing Dutch rule did study abroad, but this was in the Middle East, rather than Europe or Java. In fact, none of these leaders – Muchtar Luthfi, Iljas Jacub, Djalaluddin Thaib, Djamaluddin Ibrahim, Rasuna Said, Chatib Suleiman, Darwis Thaib, or Leon Salim – attended Western schools beyond the advanced elementary (MULO) level.

In analysing the strength and character of the nationalist movement in West Sumatra in the decades preceding World War II, and how it can be differentiated from the movement in Java and in other parts of the archipelago, we this need to look more closely at the range of schools and other educational institutions in the Minangkabau, and the extent to which they were responsible for fostering ideals of Indonesian independence in their pupils. These schools played an influential role in the years leading up to 1933, and after the repression that year they became the major locus of nationalist activities. The government's failure in its efforts to gain control over private educational institutions through the Teachers' Ordinance and the Wild Schools Ordinance, meant that even after the suppression of political party activity 'it was the thousands of national schools that kept alive and promoted the national ideals for which these parties had stood'.[34]

The educational system which played such an important role in shaping the nationalist movement, and in helping it penetrate deeply into the urban and rural society of West Sumatra was not an elite Western-style education, aping the language, attitudes, and values of the colonial power. Certainly, that style of education existed, particularly in the teachers' training institute (*kweekschool*, known as the *Sekolah Raja*) and the training school for officials (Mosvia) in Bukittinggi,[35] but most of the West Sumatrans who graduated from such schools and from the more advanced Western schools in Java – with a few notable exceptions – remained aloof from the nationalist movement. These Western-educated graduates generally took up positions in the colonial administration either within West Sumatra or in other parts of the archipelago. Indeed, in the early 1930s, when the government decided to move its two elite schools from Bukittinggi to Java, the Permi party welcomed their departure. The Permi journal, *Medan Ra'jat*, commented that the move would provide an impetus for the local people to build similar schools for themselves, thus deepening the Minangkabau young people's love for their fatherland, 'because a single school established by its own people is worth more than ten schools built by foreigners'.[36]

The two earlier chapters have dealt in some detail with the role played by the network of Sumatra Thawalib and Diniyyah schools which spread so widely across the towns and countryside of West Sumatra and beyond, attracting pupils not only from all regions of Sumatra but also from other parts of the archipelago and from Singapore and the Malay peninsula.[37] These schools did indeed adopt such Western teaching methods as a curriculum embracing non-religious subjects, desks, and graded classes. While continuing to teach religion, they introduced such secular subjects as history, geography, languages, and mathematics. But these borrowings were generally adapted to the needs of West Sumatran society, and the teachers always strove to differentiate their schools from government schools. The language of instruction for all subjects was Indonesian (Malay), with the exception of religious subjects which were taught in Arabic, while Dutch and English were taught as foreign languages.[38] Many of the schools were thoroughly politicized. Kamaluddin Muhamed (Krismas), a well-known Malaysian novelist, attended the Thawalib school in Payakumbuh from 1931-35, and after two years in Malaya he returned to study at the two branches of the Islamic College in Padang and Payakumbuh in 1937. His education in those schools had a profound impact on him, and several decades later, in Kuala Lumpur, he described the spirit pervading them during the period of Dutch repression:

When the teachers taught history they would use Dutch books, but teach them in Indonesian and give them a different slant; for example, the First Governor General was described as the first Dutch pirate who came to Indonesia. The teachers were sent to jail, perhaps for a week or two then they came back. Someone else would take their place teaching school. Then they too would be arrested. If the schools were shut down another school would open. I have never seen spirited people like that here [i.e. in Malaya]...

The organizers were all political people. Two or three or four of the top leaders really knew about Permi and also about modern education. They would pick cadres in the kampung. Would explain to them what their stand was, and the cadre would have this in common. Thousands were organized by the people in the kampung; no overall organization bound them but they understood each other and established organizations just like the others. Cadres of the party would become teachers... At the time everybody went to these schools – only a few of them, perhaps 5 to 10 percent to government school.[39]

But the Thawalib schools were not alone. As we have seen, the Diniyyah schools founded by Zainuddin Labai el Junusiah became very political in the early 1920s. Although Zainuddin did not participate personally in political activity, his students were free to do so, and the students' organization attached to the Diniyyah school became the most radical of the youth groups in the region. Zainuddin had founded the Diniyyah as a coeducational institution, but his younger sister Rahmah el Junusiah persuaded him to let her establish a branch of the school exclusively for girls in November 1923. After her brother's death the following year, the girls' school under Rahmah's leadership gradually became far more important than that for boys, until the two were again joined in 1932.[40]

In contrast to her brother, Rahmah was determined to maintain her schools as non-political institutions, free from both party and government ties. We saw earlier that she forbade Rasuna Said from introducing political subjects into the curriculum. She argued that the religious instruction the pupils received in the schools would form a basis for their later judgments, and that, as far as politics were concerned,

> the children would automatically become involved after their graduation because of the Islamic basis which they had been given in the school and which would also serve as guidance in their activities. One's love for one's fatherland and one's political attitude in general, Rahmah believed, would not be shaken if based on *iman* [religious belief]. On the other hand, any skills in the political movement would be used in contradiction to the interest of Islam, if not accompanied by faith.[41]

Rahmah therefore refused to let her school be tied to any political organization, rebuffing proposals from Muchtar Luthfi to align it with Permi, and also refusing

Students from the Diniyyah and Thawalib schools, Padang Panjang,
February 1955

attempts to absorb it within any larger grouping of Muslim schools.[42] But this attitude was largely to protect her school from government reprisals, for she also was an early leader and staunch backer of the Diniyyah schools' students organization. Its former head, Leon Salim, had replaced Chatib Suleiman as head of the West Sumatra New PNI in 1934.[43] After he was released from a year in Padang's jail in 1937, Rahmah employed this radical political activist as her private secretary and as an administrator in her school.[44] Like her brother, she too refused offers of a subsidy from the Dutch administration, determined to keep the school independent, although it meant that she had to make endless trips through Sumatra and Malaya in her efforts to raise funds for its support, and was brought before the court when she was unable to repay some loans made to the school.[45]

A Malaysian woman, who was later to achieve a position of importance in her own country, recounted the nature of the Diniyyah school as she remembered it in the late 1930s:

> The schools were so different from those in Malaya; although they were religious schools they taught economics, science, maths, and other subjects. There was also vocational training in the Diniyyah. They really prepared the girls to become women, teaching weaving, domestic science, and making them know something about everything and gave them a sense of responsibility. There were about five to six hundred... in the hostel. Rahmah was very strict and life in the Diniyyah Putri was so very confined and under very strict supervision.[46]

In the religious field, the Thawalib and Diniyyah were the largest independent non-

Western schools, whether openly political or not. Their influence pervaded urban and rural areas of West Sumatra, and beyond. Less than a year after its own foundation, the Permi political party – together with prominent Padang businessmen, including Basa Bandaro – sponsored the establishment of an Islamic College in Padang with the aim of expanding the opportunities for a tertiary education to young graduates of these independent religious schools.[47] The college, initially headed by Sjamsoeddin Rassad, was opened on May 1, 1931.[48] It offered a four-year course in four main subject areas: languages (including Indonesian, Dutch, English, and beginning German and French, as well as Arabic and religious understanding); mathematics (including arithmetic, algebra, and geometry); general studies (including geography, cosmography, history, political science, domestic science, gymnastics, sport, and hygiene); and vocational subjects (painting, music, agriculture, teaching, trade, and journalism).[49]

The Islamic College continued to exist long after the crackdown on the Permi political party, and even long after the party finally succumbed to Dutch pressure and dissolved itself on October 18, 1937.[50] Indeed, the college expanded its influence, establishing an Islamic Teaching College in Payakumbuh. During the 1930s, the numbers of Islamic tertiary-level schools in West Sumatra, including those also founded by the Muhammadiah, reached at least fifteen.[51] Many of the young people receiving this more advanced education became teachers in the village schools of the Thawalib and Diniyyah throughout West Sumatra.

The most notable school outside what can broadly be described as the Thawalib network was the famous INS (at this time, the acronym denoted Indonesische Nederlandsch School), which Mohammad Sjafei founded in Kayutanam on October 31, 1926.[52] Born in West Kalimantan in 1893, Sjafei was the adopted son of Ibrahim Mara Sutan.[53] Sjafei graduated from the Sekolah Raja in Bukittinggi, then studied painting in Batavia and taught at the Kartini School, joining his father in his political activities and in a training school he founded for political cadre. In 1922, Sjafei used his own funds to go to study in Holland, where he soon joined the Indonesian students' nationalist association, Perhimpunan Indonesia, heading its education section. In Holland, he became close to Mohammad Hatta, with whom he shared many characteristics and ideas, particularly with respect to the importance of education for the development of Indonesian nationalism. He argued that 'for the nationalist movement to be successful in confronting Dutch colonialism, *the people's education has to be broadened and deepened*'.[54]

He was respected by the Dutch, who offered him teaching and administrative positions within the government education system. Refusing these offers, Sjafei returned to West Sumatra in 1925, determined to establish a school which would develop the individual talents of its pupils and would be adapted to the needs of the Indonesian people, in both town and countryside. The school he founded the following year could be described as a 'vocational school' and its philosophy was encapsulated in the saying: 'What I hear I forget, what I see I remember, what I do I know'.[55]

As was the case with the Thawalib and Diniyyah schools, Sjafei too refused to accept subsidies from the Dutch government, and financed the school through publishing educational books,[56] donations from his parents and other sympathizers, and a variety of fund-raising methods such as theatrical performances, football games, and lotteries and sales of the artifacts made by the school's pupils. Classes, which were conducted in Indonesian, with English taught as the principal foreign language, emphasized subjects that would be of use to the pupils when they returned to their homes in the small towns and countryside of West Sumatra. So education in the schools embraced the following fields:

> Manufacturing [*perusahaan*] (wood, iron, clay, yarn, rattan, rubber, and so on); arts (painting, carving, dance, staging plays, music, and so on); graphics (printing, writing, journalism, and so on); all kinds of sports; management; agriculture; husbandry; fishing; forestry; technology; military and police basics; trade; cooperatives, and so on.[57]

Fearful that his school would be harassed by the Dutch, Sjafei, like Rahmah el Junusiah, refused to let it be used for political activities; at least one of his advanced students left for this reason, going instead to teach at the Taman Siswa schools, recently established in West Sumatra.[58] Through his work in education, Sjafei became one of the most respected men in West Sumatra, respected by both the nationalists and the Dutch administration. Trained to rely on their own talents and abilities, many of his pupils became known not only in the nationalist movement and as traders and industrialists, but also in the fields of art, literature, and journalism.[59]

One of the major financial backers for the non-government schools in West Sumatra during the 1930s was Anwar St. Saidi's National Bank, which gave 2.5 percent of its profits as *zakat* (tithe) to support schools in the region. Initially, most of these donations went to the private religious schools via the *ulama* (Islamic scholars) who headed them,[60] but from 1936 Anwar became increasingly convinced that many of the religious schools were being used to enhance the prestige of the *ulama* who headed them rather than for the good of the Islamic community as a whole. So he began to direct much of the bank's support toward some of the other private schools, particularly the nationalist Taman Siswa schools which had entered West Sumatra in 1932, after the campaign against the Wild Schools Ordinance. By the mid-1930s there were branches of the Taman Siswa in Bukittinggi, Padang, Payakumbuh, Sungaipuar, and Matur. Some of the bank's support was also directed to the Merapi Institute in Padang Panjang, which Chatib Suleiman had established after ceasing to teach at the Muhammadiah's Dutch Native School, because he was dissatisfied with its leadership.[61] Two years later, together with the young political activist Junus Kotjek and a maverick Islamic scholar Adam B.B., Chatib Suleiman set up a 'Modern Islamic Seminary' in Padang Panjang (probably again with support from Anwar St. Saidi), which trained graduates of the Diniyyah and Thawalib schools to become religious teachers.[62]

Some of the other religious schools – for instance most of the Muhammadiah schools – accepted financial subsidies from the Dutch administration. This may well have been why Chatib Suleiman found it impossible to work within them. The religious education was separate from the secular subjects, and for religious subjects the language of instruction was Arabic. In contrast to the Thawalib and Diniyyah schools, the secular education taught in the Muhammadiah schools was based on the curriculum of the Dutch schools and was taught in Dutch. As the Malaysian novelist Krismas noted, 'The Muhammadiah schools were always liked by the Dutch while the Thawalib were suspected'.[63]

Finally, in the 1920s and 1930s the leaders of many of the traditionalist Islamic schools were also adapting to the modern age, and their numbers too were expanding. As early as 1918, conscious of the challenges posed by modernist Islamic teachings, Syekh Siradjuddin Abbas of Padang Lawas had begun to introduce modern teaching methods into his schools, while retaining their traditional religious teachings. In 1928, he persuaded other leading traditionalists (Syekh Suleiman Arrasuli of Candung and Syekh Muhammad Djamil Djaho of Padang Panjang) to reorganize and coordinate their schools. Two years later, traditionalist scholars founded the Persatuan Tarbiah Islamiyah (Union of Islamic Education, PTI or Perti),[64] a social organization to which the schools were allied. By the end of the 1930s there were about 127 of these traditionalist schools with about twenty thousand pupils.[65]

With the exception of the government schools and those of the Muhammadiah and Perti, private schools in West Sumatra, whether they allowed political activities within the schools themselves or not, were largely independent of Dutch control, allowing their pupils the opportunity to perceive themselves as part of an Indonesian-speaking society whose ties with the Islamic and Malay world were stronger than those with the Dutch-dominated colonial Indies.

Societal Divisions

In analysing both the 1927 rebellion and the repression of the religious parties in 1933, there is a danger of misrepresenting the situation by portraying a Minangkabau society divided into discrete compartments – such as *adat* and Islamic groups, or capitalists and Communists – and seeing such a division as the key to differentiating the supporters and opponents of Dutch rule in the different periods. These are false dichotomies, particularly in the decades preceding Indonesia's attainment of independence, when resentment of many characteristics of colonial rule drew together apparently antagonistic political forces in opposition to the Dutch.

In attempting to understand the phenomenon of anticolonial nationalism in West Sumatra in the aftermath of the 1927 rebellion, one British official, like the Dutch, saw it as based in part on the internal splits within the society between the forces of traditional custom (*adat*) and the religious Islamic forces. Noting that the disturbances in West Sumatra had been more serious than those occurring elsewhere, Consul General Crosby wrote:

> It is becoming clear that communist agitation, though it was certainly the immediate, was not the only or the ultimate, cause of the rising in this district, where antagonism towards the Government has always been latent. This antagonism arises in large measure out of the opposition, dating since many years past of the more progressive section of the

local population (the Minangkabau Malays) to the curious system of ma-
triarchal succession and of the common possession of family property
which still continues to be observed in their midst. Years ago, the Dutch
Government, in order to strengthen its hold upon the country, chose to
take the side of the upholders of tradition in this matter.[66]

There was an element of truth in this statement. A dynamic tension had always
existed within the society resulting from the apparent contradiction between certain characteristics of traditional Minangkabau society and Islamic teachings, particularly the 'purer' forms of Islam introduced by the modernists. Clearly, the Dutch
had exacerbated these tensions by attempting to strengthen traditional village elders
against the Muslim scholars, and building the colonial administration as far as possible on cooperative members of the *adat* hierarchy, while at the same time freezing
and codifying the essentially fluid set of laws and traditions that had shaped traditional Minangkabau society. The extent to which the Dutch had succeeded in sharp-
ening internal tensions within the society through this policy was evidenced in the
bloody actions taken by the rebels against the native officials in the Dutch administration during the 1927 uprising.

But neither 'the more progressive section of the local population' nor the 'upholders of tradition' were single blocs. The Dutch themselves clearly had great difficulty in characterizing the leaders of the 1927 rebellion, and were reduced to
describing them merely as 'discontents'. They thus wrote in their investigative
report on the rebellion's causes:

> The communist leaders derived from the following groups of socially
> disillusioned persons: elementary school teachers, impoverished mem-
> bers of the nobility [e.g. Mhd. Joesoef Gelar Sampono Kajo in Silo-
> engkang], men who had wanted to become *penghulus* but had failed
> [Soetan Said Ali, Arif Fadlillah], discontented *penghulus* without written
> appointment [Padang Pandjang], ambitious members of the nobility
> anxious to satisfy their ambition in the popular movement [Dt. Gangin-
> do Ratoe in Siloengkang], socially stranded people [Soelaiman Labai in
> Siloengkang], people dismissed from government service, [de op-
> komende 'middelklasse' (Siloengkang)], minor teachers of religion wish-
> ing to increase their importance, numerous relatives of former regional
> chiefs, dismissed head *penghulus* [Padang Pandjang, Fort van der
> Capellen], and so forth.[67]

In this Dutch assessment, the rebel leaders derived from virtually every social
group, and were united only in their discontent or disillusionment.

The colonial government had attempted to build its administration on amenable
members of the village hierarchies which, it should not be forgotten, included religious as well as *adat* functionaries,[68] and Dutch policies were directed not only
against the Muslim scholars but also against noncooperative members of this traditional leadership. In their 1914 Nagari Ordinance, the Dutch had attempted to

reorganize the system of village government,[69] making a distinction between 'core *penghulu*', supposedly descendents of the original founders of the *nagari* from whom the *nagari* head was to be elected, and 'non-core *penghulu*' who were excluded from village government. As Akira Oki has commented:

> To the government's surprise, the selection of core penghulus turned out to be very difficult in many places. To settle disputes, Dutch officials gradually intervened in the selection of the council members and some-times enforced their opinions on the basis of Dutch investigations. However, penghulus who did not receive authorization as members of the new council claimed the investigations to be unfair... Dissatisfaction arose among non-authorized penghulus, particularly in Bodi-Caniago nagaris because such nagaris possessed a more democratic political structure than did Koto-Piliang nagaris.[70]

Dutch policy had led to a growing body of dissatisfied *penghulu* who, willingly or unwillingly, remained outside the Dutch administrative system.

In the early 1930s, the government commissioned Demang Roesad (Dt. Perpatih Baringek) to analyse the reasons why some *adat* leaders were attracted to political movements, and he attributed their actions to four essentially self-serving motiva-tions: first, general discontent; second, the leaders' wish to exercise more influence in their extended village (*nagari*); third, their weakness because of their fear of the influence of political leaders; and fourth, because they could see no alternative as all their followers had already joined a political movement.[71] He also thought that *adat* leaders might see membership in a political party as useful in obtaining *penghulu* titles. He noted that many of the more militant *penghulu* had come together in a Minangkabau Penghulu Council (Dewan Penghoeloe2 Minangkabau [DPM]) set up in mid-1931, in opposition to proposals for leasing land to Indo Europeans, and several of the council's members were also leaders of Permi and the new Islamic League.[72]

The dividing lines between the cooperating and noncooperating groups did not always run along religious/*adat* lines. Divisions among social groups had become even more blurred when the introduction of Communist ideas further split the reli-gious community – with most of the leading Muslim scholars of the older generation of Islamic reformists (*kaum muda*) perceiving the evils of communism as greater than those of colonialism, while their more radical students were in the forefront of opposition to the colonial government.[73]

The turbulence and tension of the late 1920s and early 1930s sowed the seeds for many of the alliances and antagonisms that would characterize the region's political life – at least until the Dutch transferred authority to the independent Indonesian government at the end of 1949.

Some of the major rifts in the political society of the Minangkabau were, in fact, amongst those who shared modernist religious beliefs. We have looked at the split between Mohammad Hatta's followers in the New PNI and the nationalist parties that adopted religion as their base, notably the Permi and PSII. There was a further enduring split that emerged between the followers of the Permi (known as the 'M' stream) and those of the Muhammadiah (or 'MM' stream).[74] This could perhaps be characterized at this period as a rift between the political and apolitical modernist Muslims, exacerbated by the fact of the personal antagonisms that had developed between Haji Rasul, now a leader of the Muhammadiah, and many of his former students now prominent in the Permi, who had been influenced by radical and communist leaders in the early 1920s. As Deliar Noer points out:

> It was not uncommon to hear Permi leaders accuse the Muhammadijah of not having the courage to participate in politics and that the Muhammadijah was close to the Dutch as the subsidies it received from the government showed. On the other hand, the Muhammadijah in the area abhorred Permi and judged them as not fully abiding by Islam.[75]

Given that the disagreements were as much personal as ideological, the antagonisms that developed between these two groups endured to a later period, when labels based on nationalist ideology did not necessarily apply.

Rifts within the modernist streams of Islam were also evident among the students from Cairo. Both Muchtar Luthfi and Iljas Jacub were strongly influenced by the nationalist political movement that was raging in Cairo while they were there, while another student, Mahmud Junus, 'only came to Cairo to study and while there permitted himself no activity other than demanding knowledge'.[76] During his years in Cairo (1925-1930), Mahmud Junus became a recognized scholar, and when he returned to the Minangkabau, he refused to join with Iljas Jacub and Muchtar Luthfi in their political activities, but focused all his attention on improving the quality of the modernist religious schools in West Sumatra.[77]

There were similar disagreeements within the Muhammadiah, where, even in the early 1930s, there was a powerful element – headed by Saalah J. Sutan Mangkuto – which was as firm in its opposition to colonial rule as were any within the Permi or the New Islamic League (PSII).[78] But the majority of the Muhammadiah's local leadership under A.R. St. Mansur adhered to the principles of its Central Javanese headquarters, and eschewed political acts that could attract Dutch retribution, concentrating instead on religious, social, and educational matters.

The fact that Islamic scholars rather than *adat* leaders more often headed the nationalist movement in West Sumatra – at least after the 1908 uprising – reflects, in part, the differing perceptions of leadership between the two groups.[79] As A.A. Navis has pointed out, the *adat* leader or *penghulu* saw his major duty as guarding and protecting his group (*kaum*) and extended village (*nagari*) from outside attack. As each village had a population of no more than about two or three thousand people, it could not easily defend itself against such a threat through physical force; so when facing danger, the village leaders generally chose the route of discussions to seek a compromise. Under colonial rule, in order to save their followers from disaster, the *adat* leaders were willing to grant large concessions to the Dutch in return for their not interfering with the village or its traditions and customs. Village leaders would usually instruct their followers to obey the government if possible, and if not, to migrate (*merantau*).[80] As their most important aim was to protect their village from destruction, the *adat* leaders were usually willing to accept whoever wielded authority in the area.

In contrast, the prime function of the religious scholars was to show their followers how to lead their lives in accordance with God's will. In fulfilling this function they could adopt a radical attitude in facing a Dutch (*kafir*) government, in part, because Islam accepts the concept of fighting a holy war (*jihad*) and dying a martyr's death, embraces the concepts of egalitarianism and social justice, and also because as Muslims their sense of community transcended territorial boundaries. In the interests of religion and the Islamic community, 'property and village can become dust'.[81] It is in part for these reasons that in West Sumatra, most efforts to oppose authority, particularly that of a non-Islamic government, have been impelled by the religious leaders.[82]

Nevertheless, most of the traditionalist stream of Islam stood outside the main political arena in West Sumatra. Its major representative was the Perti, which in opposing modernist Islamic teaching frequently cooperated with Minangkabau *adat* leaders,[83] and also with the colonial government. But the Perti's conservative teachings did not attract a wide following among the younger generation.[84] The Perti was to develop into one of the most enduring political parties in West Sumatra, and continued to play a small but frequently influential role on the national stage until after the fall of Sukarno, thirty-five years later. A continuing characteristic of the party was its ability to accommodate whichever government exerted power at the centre.

Among the traditional sects, however, there were also divergent viewpoints. While most of the Naksyabandiyah allied with the Perti, the more mystical Syattariyah adherents were attracted to Tan Malaka and his teachings, and would later form the backbone of the Islamic Communist Party, the PKI Lokal Islamy.[85]

The fissures among the different groups within Minangkabau society, though they became more acute under Dutch manipulation, were never unbridgeable. They were always counteracted in part by personal and family ties, as well as regional and economic connections. This can be seen throughout the first half of the twentieth century, when at the national level, Minangkabau leaders headed political parties across the ideological spectrum, and within a family, siblings or parents and children often embraced conflicting ideologies.

It was, indeed, possible for a single person to embrace many of the apparently contradictory streams within himself, being at the same time the traditional head of a lineage (*penghulu adat*), a good Muslim, a merchant, and a radical nationalist or Communist. It was a variation on this conjunction which so alarmed the Dutch and their local administrative officials with respect to the young Communist leader in the early 1920s, Haji Datuk Batuah, who was not only a religious teacher who had undertaken the pilgrimage to Mecca, but was also a traditional leader (*penghulu*) who, it was feared, was in a position to influence his *penghulu* colleagues.[86]

The capacity for the different streams to work together became evident even in the late 1930s when the Dutch introduction of measures threatening both religious and traditional aspects of Minangkabau society spurred the traditional and religious forces to cooperate in opposing these measures. Most important was the Dutch attempt to introduce a Marriage Registration Bill into West Sumatra in mid-1937. Religious groups of all persuasions protested that this bill conflicted with Islamic law,[87] while *adat* leaders too saw the ordinance as not in accord with Minangkabau traditions.[88] A meeting opposing the ordinance, attended by 360 *penghulu*, established the MTKAAM (Majelis Tinggi Kerapatan Adat Alam Minangkabau, High Consultative Council of the Adat of the Minangkabau World), a new *adat* organization which was neither conservative nor cooperative with the colonial authorities. All five of its committee leaders had been members of the Muhammadiah, with one of them having also belonged to the Permi.[89] As the organization developed, the Dutch viewed it as 'made up of discontented, troublesome elements among the penghulus', later commenting that 'more and more people of dubious reputation' were joining it.[90]

Another such unifying issue was the Dutch plan to repeal the ordinance (Law 177IS) limiting Christian missionary activity in mainly Islamic areas. Fear that the law might be repealed drew together nationalist, *adat*, and religious groups from across the political spectrum. An organization established to oppose these Dutch plans included among its leaders members of Permi, the new Islamic League (PSII), Muhammadiah, the *adat* MTKAAM and New PNI, together with educators and businessmen.[91]

Here, one can note a contrast which existed between some of the highest native officials of the Dutch administration in the region. As noted above, Demang Roesad Dt. Perpatih Baringek, one of the Dutch government's most loyal and trusted henchmen in West Sumatra, had a brother who headed the Communist uprising in Batavia, while he himself always had ties of loyalty to his former schoolmate, Tan Malaka.[92] On the other hand, Landjoemin Dt. Toemenggoeng, whom the Dutch had brought to West Sumatra after the 1927 uprising as a minister (*patih*) to assist the Dutch Resident in Padang,[93] did not appear to encompass any such ambiguities. Apparently Dt. Toemenggoeng was resented by the people of West Sumatra and was unable to get on with his Indonesian colleagues in the administration, and so was sent back to Batavia. When he returned for the congress of the MTKAAM in March 1939, he irritated his fellow *penghulu* by standing by his earlier acts of suppression against the *pergerakan* (nationalist movement) in the 1920s, and blaming it for all the sufferings of the people of the region.[94]

The Closing Years of Dutch Rule

As we saw at the end of the previous chapter, the colonial government's repression of political activity in West Sumatra did not end with the arrests of the leaders of the Permi and Islamic League in 1933, but continued throughout the remainder of the decade. As one Sumatran newspaper wrote at the end of 1939:

> The earlier blazing era of activity was extinguished through banishments, prohibitions and arrests. The police, working together with state officials and also with traditional leaders [*penghoeloe2 Adat*] to pacify

Minangkabau, used all their powers and abilities to scoop up everything that had the slighest odor of opposition to the government. Whenever the police were unable to implement these duties, government officials came forward to carry them out, and if they had insufficient ways of completing the task then the *penghulu* emerged to exert their rights in accordance with tradition as leaders [*mamak*, lit. uncles] toward their followers [*kemanakan*. lit. nephews].[95]

The calm political atmosphere in the region in the final years leading up to World War II was thus largely a result of political repression – the nationalists had tried armed opposition in 1926/27 and democratic political party methods in the early 1930s. The Dutch had permitted them no leeway, and had repressed political activity as harshly as they had armed opposition. Local nationalists had of necessity to limit any further action to underground activities or the narrow parameters sanctioned by the colonial power. Reluctance to challenge the Dutch was further exacerbated by the harsh economic conditions that had battered the region sporadically since the onset of the Depression at the end of 1929. Even in 1939, headlines appeared in Sumatra newspapers bemoaning 'The Sufferings of the People of Minangkabau',[96] and calling on representatives in the Volksraad and Minangkabau Raad to take steps to ease their hardships.[97]

It was not until 1938 that the Dutch set up the Minangkabau Council (Minangkabau Raad) for West Sumatra, which was then headed by the Dutch Resident and had Roesad Dt. Perpatih Baringek as its secretary.[98] It had a total membership of forty-nine of whom thirty-eight were Indonesians, though their selection was strictly controlled and the government severely restricted the issues the council could discuss. Establishment of the council was not opposed by the previously noncooperative parties, and members of the Permi, New PNI, and PSII all put forward candidates for the body. [99]

Soon after it was formed, members of the Minangkabau Raad requested that Muhammad Yamin represent their region in the Volksraad in Batavia. He agreed to this, though it meant his ejection from the Gerindo (Gerakan Rakyat Indonesia) which was pledged to noncooperation with the Dutch government.[100] Yamin became the clearest voice articulating the demands of West Sumatrans at the national level, and raising their complaints in the Volksraad.[101] He was a man trusted by the Minangkabau and with good ties particularly with educators and the business community.[102]

During the closing years of Dutch colonial rule, Chatib Suleiman's influence spread beyond the political sphere to the business, religious, and educational communities in West Sumatra. After ceding chairmanship of the New PNI to Leon Salim in 1934, he devoted much of his time to teaching, while continuing his writing and speaking activities. In early 1939, Anwar St. Saidi persuaded him to move from Padang Panjang to Bukittinggi, to become his secretary and help him to run the batik import company (Inkorba) which he had established the previous year.[103] Chatib Suleiman also later participated in Anwar's trading company, Bumiputera,[104] and was instrumental in setting up agricultural and fishing cooperatives with

A group of *ulama* and nationalist businessmen, 1940, at the establishment by the National Bank of the Comite Mukimin Minangkabau (Roestam Anwar)
Seated from left: Syekh Abbas, Padang Jepang; Syekh Ibrahim Musa, Parabek; Syekh Suleiman Arrasuli; Syekh Mohd. Djamil Djambek; Syekh Daud Rasjidi.
Standing from left: Nasaruddin Thaha; Siradjuddin Abbas; unknown; Anwar St. Saidi; Chatib Suleiman; unknown; Mr. Mohd, Nasrun; Moh. Rasyid Khalidi; H. Nurman Dt. Nan Sati; Leon Salim

branches as far away as Penang and Singapore.[105] He remained, however, principally a teacher and political leader, using his business offices as places where he could meet with local people and discuss and propagate his ideas.[106] In all of his activities Chatib stressed the importance of cooperation and unity in strengthening a powerless people. He remained a follower of Hatta, but gradually became more strongly influenced by Sjahrir's ideas, even naming his first son after him.[107]

During these years, Chatib Suleiman developed a wide circle of friends and colleagues, but his closest friend was probably still Leon Salim. With financial support from Anwar St. Saidi, in 1939 the two men founded a magazine, *Sinar*, which focused on economic affairs and had a readership among merchants and students. Chatib himself was its most frequent contributor.[108] He also remained close to Junus Kotjek, a fellow leader of the youth organizations and the New PNI, who, like Chatib Suleiman, was a musician and played the violin.[109] In addition to Anwar St. Saidi, his other close colleagues were Mr. Nasrun, who had preceded Chatib as Anwar's secretary, and among teachers and religious leaders Marzuki Yatim, Adam B.B., and Mohammad Sjafei of the INS vocational school in Kayutanam.

During the closing years of colonial rule, Chatib Suleiman moved more aggressively on to the political scene, making public speeches against Dutch plans to cancel

Law 1771S forbidding Christian proselytizing.[110] He also cooperated with *adat* leaders, particularly Dt. Simarajo, the young head of the newly established, more radical *adat* organization MTKAAM, in opposing Dutch introduction of a marriage law which contravened traditional practices.[111]

Events in West Sumatra during the two decades leading up to World War II do much to belie – at least in this part of Indonesia – the frequent contention that the Indonesian nationalist movement was restricted to a narrow, educated urban elite in Java, sparking little interest or genuine support among the rural masses on that island and elsewhere. The history of this period in West Sumatra flies in the face, for example, of John Ingleson's assertion that

> the nationalist movement was essentially a Java movement, the product
> of a western-educated élite who, whatever their ethnic origins, made
> their careers in Batavia or in one of the other major Javanese cities.[112]

There is some truth to the fact that the cooperative wing of the nationalist movement in the mid- to late 1930s was drawn in large part from the Dutch-educated elite. But the mainstream of the nationalist movements which were forced out of the political arena in the early 1930s was deeply embedded in Indonesian society. The emphasis on the narrowness and the Western-educated nature of the nationalist movement in Indonesia which permeates much of the scholarly writing concerning its development, at least after the decline of the Islamic League (Sarikat Islam) in the late 1910s, stems in large part from the fact that most writers rely so heavily on Dutch reports. These stress the limited and elite nature of the movement, and naturally downplay both its indigenous features and broad appeal. Had Dutch officials not portrayed those who opposed them in this way, it would, of course, have been more difficult for them to justify their rule and the repressive policies they enforced against the nationalists who were asserting Indonesia's right to independence. It is less understandable why in the postcolonial period scholarly writers have continued to propagate this view, and assumed similar patronizing attitudes toward the Indonesian movements for independence that developed not only in the major Javanese cities but also in small towns and the countryside in other parts of the archipelago. Their strength and character would become clearer after the Japanese invasion.

SECTION II

Achieving Independence

CHAPTER 4

West Sumatra under the Japanese

In February 1942, the Japanese began their invasion of Sumatra, sending advance parachute units into Palembang apparently to preempt Dutch plans to sabotage the nearby oil installations. These Japanese units spread over south and central Sumatra. In mid-March, more substantial military forces landed on the island's north and east coasts and advanced rapidly southwards.[1] The first Japanese troops entered Padang on March 17, 1942, and ten days later the commander of the Dutch forces in Sumatra surrendered unconditionally. The island was immediately put under the Department of Military Administration (*Gunseibu*) of the 25th Army in Singapore, which for the first year of the occupation governed Sumatra in conjunction with Malaya.[2]

During this first year, the Japanese were concerned with creating a functioning administrative apparatus in Sumatra so that they would be able to make efficient use of the island's vital resources, particularly the oil fields near Palembang and the rubber estates in east Sumatra. To this end, they reinstituted the colonial system of government, reappointing most of the Indonesian officials who had earlier served the Dutch. The Japanese 25th Army soon found it impossible to administer Sumatra from Singapore, particularly in view of the need to provide protection to areas around vital installations, including the oil refineries in Palembang.[3] So on May 1, 1943, it moved its headquarters from Singapore to Bukittinggi, and Sumatra became the sole area under its administration. The 29th Army was now in charge of administering Malaya and the 16th Army Java. They, together with the 25th Army in Sumatra, were all under the 7th Area Army stationed in Singapore, which formed part of the Southern Expeditionary Forces, headquartered in Saigon.

With East Indonesia as a separate zone governed by the Japanese Navy, the Indonesian archipelago became subject to three military administrations. These administrations pursued very different policies, for it was envisaged that Sumatra and East Indonesia would be incorporated into the Japanese empire, while Java, with less economic and strategic importance, might well ultimately be granted autonomy.

The Early Occupation

The Governor General of the Netherlands Indies, A.W.L. Tjarda van Starkenborgh Stachouwer, and the Commander of Netherlands forces in the Indies, Lt. Gen. Hein Ter Poorten, surrendered unconditionally to the Japanese on March 9, 1942, at Kali Jati airfield in West Java, but the Dutch Governor of Sumatra, A.I. Spits, declared that the Dutch forces on that island would continue their struggle 'to the last drop of blood'. He ordered a scorched earth policy in Sumatra to impede the Japanese advance. Protesting that this would destroy their country and cause wide-spread suffering among the people, Chatib Suleiman, Leon Salim, and some of their supporters planned to hold mass demonstrations against the policy. These protests were to be centred in Padang Panjang, and were scheduled to take place on March 12, 1942. They would demand that, before the Japanese crossed into West Sumatra, the Dutch hand over power to the Indonesians, who could then negotiate in their own right with the Japanese invaders.

Learning in advance of the plans for the demonstrations, on the night of March 11 the Dutch arrested Chatib Suleiman, Leon Salim, and four of their comrades. They forced the six men to accompany Dutch troops as they retreated northwards to what was to become their final holdout at Gunung Setan (Devil's Mountain) in Aceh. (The Dutch had earlier intended to make their last stand in the mountainous areas of the West Sumatran interior, but under Japanese military pressure were forced to revise their plans.) After a long trek north, the Dutch and their prisoners reached Kota Cane in southern Aceh on March 18. There, the Dutch authorities jailed and interrogated the six Indonesians, but before they could pronounce their sentence, Japanese bombs began falling on the town. Abandoning their prisoners, the Dutch troops fled toward Gunung Setan. Advancing Japanese forces encountered no Dutch resistance when they occupied Kota Cane, and freed all the prisoners in the jail.[4]

Chatib Suleiman and his five companions were allowed to make their way back to West Sumatra. When they reached Kaban Jahe in the Karo Batak area they met messengers from Padang who had been sent to find out what had happened to them. The Padang envoys accompanied the liberated prisoners on the final stages of their return home. The whole group arrived back in Padang Panjang on April 2.

Sukarno's Role

During these early days of the Japanese occupation, events in Padang were strongly influenced by the presence there of Sukarno, whom the Dutch had brought from Bengkulu, where he had been interned since 1938. At the time of the Japanese landing in Palembang, the Dutch arranged Sukarno's evacuation to Padang, initially hoping to fly him to Australia. But events moved too quickly and he was still in Padang when Japanese forces entered the town on March 17.

From the beginning, Sukarno decided that the Indonesians should endeavour to make use of the Japanese to achieve their own goal of Indonesian independence. And through his cooperation with these new rulers he was able to diminish the harshness of their behaviour toward the local people of West Sumatra.

Later Indonesian accounts of the Japanese takeover of Padang describe that harshness and show the rapid rise in tensions between the invading forces and the town's inhabitants:

Colonel Fujiyama led the Japanese army's entry into Padang after the Dutch had apparently been willing to surrender unconditionally.[5] From dawn on March 17, 1942, fully armed Japanese troops could be seen entering the streets of Padang, and occupying strategic positions. Some were on foot, some on bicycles. Not a single explosion was heard. The long and 'glorious' era of the Dutch was seemingly now over. When that morning as usual the people left their houses, they saw Japanese soldiers on every corner of the town of Padang. At first the people were not afraid of them, and many even gave them friendly smiles. So in a very short time, Padang was flooded with people from the surrounding areas, who wanted to see close up the newly arrived Japanese army. But soon the situation began to change and tensions rose as those admired soldiers seized and confiscated every bicycle they came across. Watches were also their targets. And whoever tried to stop them was certain to receive a kick or a punch. As quick as lightning the people began to hide any possessions that the newly arrived forces might covet.[6]

Sukarno met with Colonel Fujiyama, the commander in charge of setting up an administration there, and it was he who persuaded the Japanese authorities to send out a party to search for Chatib Suleiman and his comrades. A few days later Sukarno had to intervene again, this time on behalf of Anwar St. Saidi, whom the Japanese arrested on April 3, the day after the Kota Cane prisoners arrived back in Padang Panjang. Indonesians in Bukittinggi had raised the Red and White Indonesian flag alongside the Rising Sun of the Japanese. When the occupying forces ordered it lowered, Anwar protested and was put in jail.[7] According to Anwar's own account, the Japanese already suspected him of working for the Dutch. This was because, shortly before flying to Australia, Ch. O. van der Plas – the Dutch Adviser for Native Affairs and member of the Council for the Indies – had summoned Anwar to meet with him and West Sumatra Resident Bosselaar in Padang. At this meeting, Anwar tried to persuade van der Plas that the Dutch should release Hatta from his exile on Banda Neira and return him to Java before they themselves withdrew. Some of Anwar's enemies (he suspected a Chinese business competitor and some Indonesian officials in the colonial administration) used the account of this meeting which Anwar had published in the Padang newspaper *Persamaan* to convince the Japanese that he was pro-Dutch.[8]

Hearing that Anwar had been arrested and was being tortured, Sukarno approached the Japanese to plead for his release. In his autobiography, Sukarno recalled the incident:

> One unfortunate I knew intimately. His name was Anwar. Anwar had been tortured. The *Kempeitai*, the Japanese Secret Police, were eager to make an example of him since he was the first subversive caught. They pulled his fingernails out....
> Two days running I returned to plead for Anwar. I said, 'I know him well. While you honor your vow of cooperation with Indonesia's nationalist

aspirations, he and the other nationalists will not plot against you... If you let him out I'm sure I can make of him a good worker. I personally vouch for his patriotism.'

Two hours after this second visit they released him.[9]

Although Sukarno was in Padang only until May 1942, when he was allowed to return to Java, his presence in these early weeks of the occupation was clearly important in persuading most of the Indonesian leaders in West Sumatra to cooperate with the Japanese. When Japanese forces forbade any flag being flown other than the Japanese Rising Sun, it was Sukarno who had to instruct the people 'to lower their flags until "such time as we may fly our colors free of all foreign domination"'.[10]

Leaders of the local branch of the New PNI (the party of Hatta and Sjahrir), which used the Bumiputera office in Bukittinggi as its meeting place, split over whether or not to work with the Japanese.[11] Anwar St. Saidi, as head of the National Bank and the trading organizations, eschewed any political role but worked in the the economic field to gather funds and, later, arms for the independence struggle.[12] Tamimi Usman led those who followed Sjahrir's path of noncooperation and underground activities.[13] But the group headed by Chatib Suleiman and Leon Salim followed the line of Sukarno and Hatta, and saw cooperation with the Japanese as the best method of moving toward their ultimate goal of Indonesian independence, 'travelling on the same ship as the Japanese while carrying their own trading merchandise'.[14]

Several groups came together in support of the Japanese. Sukarno helped form a People's Committee (*Komite Rakyat*) to ensure calm in the region as the Japanese consolidated their control, and Chatib Suleiman and Leon Salim brought together all existing youth organizations to form the Pemuda Nippon Raja (Youth of Greater Japan).[15] The Japanese, however, were suspicious of this support, and soon after Sukarno's departure, they abolished the People's Committee and not long afterwards disbanded the youth organization. Its leaders were arrested on November 14, 1942, charged with pretending to work with the Japanese while actually being opposed to them. They were, however, released after a week in jail.[16]

Japanese Governor Yano Kenzo

In the early months of the occupation, Colonel Fujiyama and his assistant I. Wakamatsu, who were responsible for establishing a functioning administration in West Sumatra, relied on advice from a local official, Dt. Madjo Orang, in appointing new officials.[17] They also helped Sukarno return to Jakarta while arranging for a Padang journalist, Madjid Usman, to be brought back to West Sumatra in exchange.[18]

The arrival of Yano Kenzo in August 1942 to take up his appointment as governor of West Sumatra provided local nationalists with further scope. A former Prefecture Governor of Toyama, Yano was an independent man who disagreed with many aspects of the policies of the 25th Army in Sumatra. Fascinated by Minangkabau society, particularly its tradition of matrilineal inheritance, he enjoyed being pho-

tographed in Minangkabau traditional costume and founded both a cultural association and a religious organization to instruct him on the area's traditions and history.[19]

Most important, however, was an organization named Kerukunan Minangkabau
(Minangkabau Harmony), which he established and used as his personal liaison with
the West Sumatran people. This consultative body met regularly at the governor's
house, and its members included Chatib Suleiman, the educator Mohammad Sjafei,
Dt. Madjo Orang, and the Islamic scholar Syekh Djamil Djambek, as well as Colonel
Fujiyama and his assistant Wakamatsu. Yano encouraged members of the group to
criticize openly all aspects of Japanese rule, and perhaps for this reason he apparently did not inform the military headquarters in Bukittinggi of its existence.[20]
Members of this informal advisory council to the governor later formed a majority
in the representative assembly for the province, the Shu Sangi Kai, and ultimately in
the provincial branch of the Hokokai (Patriotic Service Association) which was
established in Sumatra in early 1944. Mohammad Sjafei chaired these associations,
and he selected Mr. St. Mohd. Rasjid as his chief of staff in the Hokokai, with Chatib
Suleiman, Dt. Madjo Orang, and Roesad Dt. Perpatih Baringek as other members.[21] They worked closely with the religious groups through Mahmud Junus[22] and
Syekh Djamil Djambek and with the *adat* groups through Dt. Simarajo, Dt. Perpatih Baringek, and Dt. Madjo Orang. These associations enabled Chatib Suleiman
and his colleagues to become regular advisers to the governor, and they soon began
to exert growing influence on his policies in the region.

Giyu Gun

On June 29, 1943, the Japanese government issued a general policy directive that
indigenous volunteer armies should be formed in Java, Sumatra, North Borneo, and
Malaya, to assist Japanese forces in defending the region against an anticipated
Allied counterattack.[23] The directive reflected Tokyo's rising fears that the Allies
intended to launch a large-scale offensive within a year, directed either at the oil
fields of Sumatra or along the Burma coast toward Siam.[24] The specific Japanese
order of early October, 1943 for establishment of the 'People's Armies' (Giyu gun or
Lasykar Rakyat) signalled a shift in emphasis from consolidating Japanese control
over the areas they had occupied to preparing to defend these territories against a
future Allied invasion.

It was as part of this general policy that the Giyu gun was established in West
Sumatra, an event that was one of the most important watersheds in the region's
modern history. This 'people's volunteer army' would become the nucleus of the
Banteng Division that would head West Sumatra's military struggle against the
Dutch and later, in the 1950s, the regional rebellions against the Sukarno government. Most important at the time was the role it played in providing a means
whereby local nationalist leaders were able to bypass the formal administrative
structure still dominated by conservative Dutch-trained Indonesian officials, and
create an atmosphere more hospitable to their aim of ultimate independence from

both the Dutch and the Japanese. As conceived and developed in the Minangkabau region, the Giyu gun and its support groups provided a network of connections and organizations to ensure solidarity among the Minangkabau people as they faced threats from outside the region.

The specific character of this local Giyu gun was in many ways shaped by the West Sumatran leader Chatib Suleiman and the Japanese Governor of West Sumatra, Chokan Yano Kenzo.

It had been in meetings of the Minangkabau Harmony group in late 1942 that Chatib Suleiman first proposed to Yano that the Japanese create a volunteer army in West Sumatra, an idea to which Yano was sympathetic and which he passed on to the 25th Army commander Tanabe in Bukittinggi.[25] Yano's sympathy with local aspirations for independence and his disappointment that his government did not share his attitude appear clearly in an article he wrote twenty years later:

> The Minangkabau tribe of Sumatra, which was under my jurisdiction at the time of the war, seemed the most intelligent and economically developed tribe of its kind; and at the same time their interest in politics was remarkable. It is, therefore, no wonder that they had such a strong desire to put an end to the 350 years of Dutch oppression, and to become fully independent. Believing that the Japanese occupation army would help fulfill their long-cherished dream, they cooperated willingly. However, after nearly two years of occupation, nothing was changed. The Japanese army well realized Indonesia's unlimited resources, and was determined to continue their possession of this land of rich resources; even if it meant releasing their strong hold on the Philippine and Burmese territories. Keeping Indonesia under its control was, thus, the army's major concern.[26]

It was not until Allied military successes forced Tokyo to authorize the formation of indigenous military forces in several parts of Southeast Asia that the idea of a local volunteer army could be implemented. Propaganda meetings on behalf of the Giyu gun started in Sumatra in October 1943. Yano later wrote:

> Previously the army had tried a mercenary system to supplement the army, which had failed. This was because only the dream of independence, not money, was enough to motivate the native people to fight. Therefore, in *this* voluntary army recruitment campaign, I freely encouraged their dream of independence, with my superior's (Commander Tanabe's) approval.[27]

The Character of the Giyu gun

As soon as orders came down from the Japanese for the formation of auxiliary volunteer militias, in October 1943, Chatib Suleiman sponsored the establishment of the

Indonesian militias in training (Sudarman Khatib)

Headquarters for the Formation of Giyu gun. Its members cooperated with the Japanese in selecting the first candidate officers for the new volunteer army. Chatib Suleiman headed the organization, and his major colleagues were the educator Mohammad Sjafei, Islamic Council leader Mahmud Junus, and the young leader of the *adat* association, Dt. Simarajo.[28] They chose their candidate officers from men who were already mature and whose earlier experience in the nationalist movement made it unlikely that they would succumb to Japanese propaganda. The background of these young officers would help them keep in mind that their goal was Indonesian independence, not Japanese victory in the war against the Allies. Chatib Suleiman travelled around West Sumatra during the next few months, recruiting candidates to lead the new volunteer army.[29]

There was always a geographical split within the West Sumatra Giyu gun. The main Japanese aim in establishing the force was to help defend the region against a possible seaborne Allied invasion. To this end, the first units were recruited in Padang and along the coast. The 37th Infantry Regiment of the Japanese 4th (Osaka) Division stationed in Padang was in charge of training the Giyu gun's coastal units, and junior officers were brought in from Japan as instructors, most of them not professional soldiers.[30] Seven companies under their Japanese trainers were strung out along the coast from Air Bangis in the north to Muko Muko in the south, with separate units guarding Padang and the cement factory inland at Indarung, a total force of about three-thousand men.[31] Only in the closing months of 1944 did the Japanese 25th Army in Bukittinggi organize Giyu gun units directly under its own command in the highland interior regions of West Sumatra. Their purpose was to strengthen defence of the 25th Army after some of its units had been transferred to Burma to help repel Allied attacks on the mainland. The Giyu gun soldiers in these upland units, then, had less experience and cohesion than their colleagues in the coastal areas.

The first group of Japanese-trained officers in West Sumatra included four men who would become the major founders of the region's independence army in 1945, three of whom had already achieved prominence in the local Muslim community during the closing years of Dutch rule. These were Dahlan Djambek, then twenty-six years old, who was the son of the influential modernist Islamic scholar Syekh Djamil Djambek; Sjarief Usman, also twenty-six and the son of an Islamic scholar, who had been active in nationalist youth organizations in the 1930s and whose political writings had led to his arrest by the Dutch; and Dahlan Ibrahim, who was a year older and had been a religious teacher and student at the Islamic College in Padang. The oldest candidate officer was twenty-nine-year-old Ismael Lengah, a teacher in the technical school in Padang, who had been educated in both Jakarta and Holland. He was a former pupil of Abdullah at the Adabiah school in Padang, who recommended he be included among the senior officers.[32]

From the beginning, in recruiting the candidate officers, Indonesian leaders stressed the nationalist character and aims of their volunteer army. Chatib Suleiman and Junus Kotjek wrote a marching song for them in 1943, which, while treading a careful line, emphasized the Giyu gun's nationalist aims. Its first verse and refrain ran:

> In the past our warriors' blood
> Was shed to destroy the Enemy
> Thousands of young souls were sacrificed
> So that our fatherland should not fall
>
> Refrain:
> Giyu gun, Army of the People
> Army of the Fatherland
> Always ready with blood and life
> To pound the enemy to destruction
> Final Victory will surely be ours[33]

In recruiting and supporting the People's Army, Chatib Suleiman and his colleagues in the support organization enlisted the help of traditional village elders and religious leaders. The Association for Supporting the Giyu gun (Giyugun koenkai) acted as liaison between civilian and military leaders and collected food and supplies for the soldiers from the *nagari* (extended villages).[34] A parallel and equally important women's organization was established to raise food supplies and organize social and welfare support for the Indonesian soldiers. Named the Hahanokai, it was headed by Rasuna Said and Ratna Sari, who, it will be recalled, had earlier taught in the Islamic schools and, as leaders of Permi, had spent months in Dutch jails.[35]

As noted earlier, Giyu gun military units were organized separately in the upland and coastal areas, but differences between them were not duplicated in their support organizations. Chatib Suleiman travelled throughout West Sumatra, dividing most his time between Padang and Bukittinggi, where he left Leon Salim in charge of the support organization for the town and surrounding district of Agam.[36] Leon Salim had wished to join the Giyu gun but Chatib Suleiman thought he would be more useful playing an organizational role outside the army.[37]

There were several notable differences between the West Sumatra Giyu gun and the volunteer armies the Japanese established in Java (Peta) and in other parts of Sumatra. First, it does not appear that nationalist leaders in other regions had such an important voice in selecting their officers. Certainly, in Java these officers were usually drawn from the local nobility or from the families of administrative officials. In addition, while none of the West Sumatran officers had received prior military training from the Dutch, in Java, the most senior officers – including future Indonesian army commanders Nasution, Kawilarang, and Simatupang – had all attended Dutch military academies in the last years of colonial rule. Most important was the fact that the Giyu gun was the only military force that the Japanese created in West Sumatra. They did not establish a separate Islamic army (the Hizbullah) as they did in Java, nor did they promote any units independent of the Volunteer Army, such as those formed in East Sumatra in the early months of 1945 to act as shock troops against the feared imminent landing of the Allies.[38]

Thus, whatever rivalries and bitterness separated regular army officers in West Sumatra from the political parties' militias in the years after the Independence Proclamation, all military leaders had personal ties and relationships based on their period of common training under the Japanese. This shared experience made it easier for them to bridge the ideological barriers which emerged between political groups in the early years of independence. Moreover, the cooperation between traditional, religious, and secular leaders in recruiting and supporting the People's Army under the Japanese, provided both territorial links and bases of understanding that were invaluable in the years after 1945.

The Closing Phase

The impact of Japan's military reverses began to be felt drastically from the first half of 1944. One exacerbating factor was that the Japanese command increased the money supply without the necessary backing of real assets, a policy that led to ever-greater inflation.[39] The catastrophic potential of these monetary policies struck Governor Yano, who loudly protested their effect on the local people, arguing:

> As anyone can find on the first page of any textbook on public finances, the prices of goods increase in relation to the increase in war currency. Doubling the amount of war currency has resulted in a threefold rise in the price of goods.[40]

Throughout the occupation there had been tension between the Japanese military administration headquartered in Bukittinggi and Governor Yano Kenzo, who headed the West Sumatra provincial government in Padang. Governor Yano opposed many 25th Army policies while maintaining a friendly personal relationship with the Bukittinggi commander Tanabe.[41] As a result of his outspoken opposition to the Army's economic policies, Yano resigned as governor in March 1944,[42] and was replaced the following month by Hattori Naoaki, 'a more prudent, cautious person', who had been head of education in Sumatra.[43]

Japanese military reverses multiplied over the following year, and the Japanese administration resorted to imposing even greater demands on the Sumatran people. Local Indonesian officials were charged with raising fixed quotas of food and materials from their districts, and they were also responsible for drafting villagers to work as coolies on Japanese defence construction projects.[44]

In late 1944, however, the deteriorating military situation also led the Japanese to make concrete moves to try to attract Indonesian political support. Through the Koiso Declaration of September 7, 1944, Tokyo promised future independence to an Indonesian state embracing the whole of the former Netherlands East Indies. The 25th Army in Bukittinggi objected to Sumatra being incorporated within such a state, and until almost the end of the occupation it tried to keep the island from being included in these plans.[45] Within the context of creating a separate Sumatra, military authorities in Bukittinggi took tentative steps toward establishing a Central Advisory Council (Chuo sangi in) for the whole island, which held its first meeting in May 1945, with Mohammad Sjafei as its chairman, and Chatib Suleiman as its secretary. Any possibility that the council could play a real role in determining Sumatra's future was, however, undermined not only by the limitations placed on it by the 25th Army but also by the history of the previous years. Since the Japanese invasion, there had been only minimal contacts between the provinces (*shu*) of the island, and it was only at this lower *shu* level that indigenous organizations had developed any real substance.

It was only in the final weeks of the occupation that the 25th Army in Sumatra finally began cooperating with its counterpart in Java to take steps toward granting independence to the whole of Indonesia. It appointed three Sumatrans to participate in the meetings of the Committee for the Preparation of Indonesian Independence (PPKI, Panitia Persiapan Kemerdekaan Indonesia), formed in Jakarta in late July, 1945.[46] But none of the Sumatran delegates to the committee had any real standing outside his own province, and two of them had not even been members of the Sumatran Central Advisory Council.[47]

On August 9, Marshal Terauchi summoned Sukarno and Hatta to meet with him in the Vietnamese town of Dalat, where he told them that the Japanese government had decided to grant independence to Indonesia, with Sukarno as chief of state and Hatta as his deputy.[48] On their journey back from Vietnam, Sukarno and Hatta stopped over in Singapore, where they met the three Sumatran delegates. On August 14, the day of the Japanese surrender to the Allies, a Japanese military plane carried all five to Jakarta. Three days later, on August 17, the Sumatran delegates were present when Sukarno and Hatta proclaimed the independence of the Republic of Indonesia.

Mural of the Japanese occupation on wall of a tunnel in Bukittinggi

Japanese Legacy

The Japanese legacy to West Sumatra was a mixed one. By isolating the region from other parts of Sumatra, as well as from Java, they had encouraged the development of organizations whose strength was rooted in their local regions. The lack of a leadership or indigenous administration embracing the whole of Sumatra left responsibility for waging the independence struggle on the island during most of the first year after the Japanese surrender almost exclusively in the hands of local-level organizations. At the same time, however, this isolation from other parts of Indonesia, particularly from the heartland of Java, does not appear to have loosened the psychological ties and loyalty felt by West Sumatrans both to the Indonesian nationalist leaders in Java, particularly to those of Minangkabau origin, and to the goal of an independent Indonesia.

The Japanese had provided basic military training to a large group of Minangkabau young men. This, together with the humiliating Dutch defeat at the hands of the Japanese, meant that West Sumatrans no longer viewed colonial rule as a fact of life that had to be accepted. From their Japanese instructors they had gained self-confidence and pride in being Asian, while their Indonesian officers and political leaders had made sure that these feelings were directed toward attaining the goal of Indonesian independence.

Under the Japanese, nationalists – from both the secular and religious streams – were given the opportunity to emerge as political leaders. Particularly under the supportive protection of Governor Yano, men who had been nationalist activists since the late 1920s were allowed to attain public stature in the region. Although not permitted any concrete responsibility for administering the area, Mohammad

Sjafei, Chatib Suleiman, and their colleagues were able to organize area-wide support associations and use their speeches to instill nationalist ideas among those of their people who had previously been little aware of an Indonesian nationalist movement.

On the other hand, by maintaining the Dutch administrative apparatus, the Japanese helped ensure that the men who were already suspected by the local people because they had been officials under the Dutch were now further tarnished by their role as agents of the Japanese. These officials became the targets of a bitter and angry population who, after the hardships of the final years of Japanese rule, were determined to reverse the whole range of injustices they saw in their society.

CHAPTER 5

Independence Proclaimed

News of the Japanese capitulation to the Allies on August 14, 1945, filtered only gradually into West Sumatra. But despite the ensuing confusion, people responded remarkably quickly when immediately afterwards, rumours and radio broadcasts from Java brought reports that Sukarno and Hatta had proclaimed the Republic of Indonesia in Jakarta on August 17, 1945. Local activists seized the opportunity presented by the vacuum of power between mid-August and the Allied landings in mid-October to set up a Republican administration in the region. By the end of August, Indonesian members of the Japanese-sponsored Patriotic Service League (Hokokai) in Padang had followed Jakarta's lead and renamed themselves the Indonesian National Committee (KNI-Komité Nasional Indonesia). On August 29, Mohammad Sjafei issued a public declaration on behalf of the people of Sumatra welcoming Indonesia's Independence Proclamation. After reading the text of the Proclamation, Sjafei stated:

> We, the Indonesian people on Sumatra, herewith acknowledge Indonesian independence as laid down in the above proclamation and accept the supremacy of those two Indonesian leaders [i.e. Sukarno and Hatta].[1]

Two days later, on September 1, the National Committee held its first meeting in Padang, at which it elected Mohammad Sjafei as the first Republican Resident of West Sumatra.

These events stood in sharp contrast to what was occurring in other parts of the island. Only at the end of September did the newly appointed Governor of Sumatra, Mohd. Hassan, finally announce publicly in Medan that a Republic had been proclaimed in Java, and it was the Communist leader Karim M.S. who pledged support to the Republic.[2] The lack of leadership at the Sumatra-wide level, and the poor communications with the other parts of Indonesia, intensified the situation that had existed under the Japanese – whereby all strong organizations and links were established at the local (*shu*, now residency) level.[3] In the early months of independence local leaders made all of the decisions regarding West Sumatra's response to the rapidly changing situation. Prominent among them were members of the West Sumatra branch (KNI) of the National Committee (KNIP) and of the military and civilian organizations established by the Japanese – particularly the People's Army (Giyu gun) and its support organizations – as well as a few local followers of Sjahrir who had refused to cooperate with the Japanese.[4]

The impact of the Japanese occupation both helped and hindered the ability of those West Sumatran leaders who had been prominent under the Japanese to consolidate their position in the residency government. Men who had served in the representative bodies established by the Japanese (Shu sangi kai and hokokai), and in the earlier Minangkabau Council (Minangkabau Raad) which the Dutch had set up in 1938, initially assumed positions of authority in the new Republican regime. They formed a majority of the members in the local branch of the Indonesian National Committee (KNI), which was established in Padang in the first days of independence. (This body had both a legislative and executive function.) Thus, most of the initial officeholders in the Republican regime were officials and traditional (*adat*) leaders who had cooperated with the colonial government, making them out of tune with the desire for change that was sweeping the region.

Because of this, leaders of the National Committee tended to pursue policies that were too moderate for the society around them that wished to see independence marked by a clean break with the past. Clashes between the new Republican government and the local people resulted in widespread unrest that tore the region apart. But out of the turmoil there emerged a central core of leadership characterized by pragmatism, moderation, absolute loyalty to the Republican national leadership, and opposition to the Dutch.

Facing the British

When news of the independence proclamation reached West Sumatra in late August, 1945, groups of demobilized soldiers from the People's Army (Giyu gun) began to reassemble in various parts of the region. In Padang, First Lieutenant Ismael Lengah led other former soldiers and members of the support organization (Giyugun koenkai) in establishing an Indonesian Youth Information Office (BPPI), nearly all of whose members had previously served in the Giyu gun. Within its framework Lengah began to recruit a militia officered by the former soldiers. This later became the nucleus of the People's Security Body (BKR), the forerunner of the Republic's armed forces. Dahlan Djambek, who had also been a first lieutenant in the Padang Giyu gun, established a branch of the People's Security Body (BKR) in Bukittinggi. In the following weeks, leaders of the Youth Information Office (BPPI) went out to the villages around Padang, gathering together former comrades and subordinates and supervising the establishment of local security forces. As Padang had been the major centre for recruiting and training the People's Army under the Japanese, the best organized military units of the new Republic were stationed in and around the town.

The hiatus between the Japanese surrender on August 14 and the Allied landings in Indonesia several weeks later strengthened the ability of the Republicans in both Java and Sumatra to gain a foothold on independence, from which they were never completely dislodged. British forces in Southeast Asia under Lord Louis Mountbatten were not only inadequate but also ill-prepared to carry out the postsurrender tasks in the additional territories of the Netherlands East Indies and southern Indochina assigned to them under the Potsdam Agreements.[5] Viewing their most important and immediate task as the release of Allied prisoners of war, British commanders accepted the necessity of cooperating with the Indonesians who actually administered the territory where their prisoners were held.[6]

The British contingent that landed in Padang on October 10, 1945, was commanded by Major General H.M. Chambers, and was accompanied by Major General A.I. Spits (former Governor of Sumatra) as Netherlands Representative.[7] On October 21, these Allied officers accepted the surrender of all Japanese forces in Sumatra signed by Lt. General Moritake Tanabe, Commander of the 25th Army, and Vice Admiral Sueto Hirose.[8]

Throughout the thirteen months that the British forces were in West Sumatra (from October 1945 to November 1946), relations between them and the Indonesians remained tense. When they first landed at the Padang port of Teluk Bayur, the disembarking Allied troops were accompanied by Dutch officials. This fact made the Indonesians suspicious as to whether the British would restrict themselves to their assigned tasks of freeing Allied prisoners of war and repatriating the Japanese, or would allow themselves to be used to facilitate the return of Dutch rule. Despite their misgivings, however, Republican officials maintained the public stance of believing the Allied troops were there only to carry out their assigned tasks.

The British forces successfully established enclaves within Padang, but were never able to extend their control outside the town.[9] Until August 1946, they concentrated on ensuring security within these enclaves. Here too they sheltered evacuees from other parts of the town, who had reason to fear the Republican authorities. The British had another major security priority – keeping open their lines of communciation with Tabing airfield to the north of Padang and the seaport of Teluk Bayur about five kilometres to the south. Padang was the only town occupied by the Allied forces during their fifteen months in West Sumatra, and for nearly the first two years of independence was virtually the only place where the Indonesian armed forces clashed with the British, and later the Dutch. Indonesians came to regard Padang's periphery as the front line of the independence struggle against the Dutch in West Sumatra.

Although there was no really large-scale fighting between the two sides, there were frequent minor skirmishes. The most serious incident was a particularly brutal murder that occurred in early December, 1945. At Sungai Beramas, on the southern borders of Padang, a group of Indonesians attacked and killed a British Major Anderson who had been swimming with a Red Cross nurse, who was raped and beaten to death.[10] In reprisal, the British burned down three nearby villages and attacked the Indonesian military barracks and the Youth Information Office in Padang.[11] Though the level of violence subsequently declined, these incidents carried a legacy of bitterness into the later period. Nevertheless, Indonesians were still aware that the British occupation was of some advantage to them, for the Allied forces provided a temporary buffer, allowing them to build up their strength for their eventual struggle against the Dutch.

On October 5, 1945, Indonesia's new President Sukarno ordered the establishment of the Republic's military arm, the People's Security Forces (TKR, Tentara Keamanan Rakyat). The People's Security Body (BKR) in West Sumatra then adopted that name. Later that month, the Republican Resident of Palembang, A.K.

Gani, was appointed coordinator of all Republican forces in Sumatra, and he in turn named the former police chief in Lampung, Suhardjo Hardjowardojo, commander of the People's Security Forces for the whole of the island. These Republican armed forces in Sumatra were officially divided into six divisions. Central Sumatra, consisting of West Sumatra and Riau, became the territory of Division 3, the Banteng (Buffalo) Division. Dahlan Djambek was appointed as the division's first commander.

During the early months of independence, however, these official steps had little impact on the local units operating around Padang. Many of the armed bands which sprang up were essentially autonomous, and it was up to their commanders whether or not they allied with the regular army or with the militias of the newly formed political parties. Many independent units joined with the Islamic parties' militias, particularly the Hizbullah, and these irregular forces were especially active in the peripheral areas of Padang. The Republican army command frequently tried to bring the militias and other armed bands within its jurisdiction, but for the first few months its efforts were largely unsuccessful. The militias continued to act independently, often in defiance of the more cautious instructions coming from the army's higher echelons.

Soon, however, leaders of both the regular army and the party militias became aware of the danger inherent in so many units operating outside the official military chain of command. In early 1946, they attempted to coordinate their forces, establishing a 'struggle council' on the outskirts of Padang to synchronize the actions and areas of operation of all front-line units, and to organize their supplies. In mid-1946, still dissatisfied with their degree of coordination, Banteng Division commanders tried to amalgamate the irregular forces into a single unit directly under regular army officers. They succeeded in doing this with most of the nonreligious militias, including the Communists and the 'extremists'. But the strongest militias, those of the Islamic parties – the Hizbullah, the Sabilillah, and the Lasjmi[12] – remained autonomous and continued to hold independent responsibility for several portions of the front line around Padang.

Despite this lack of overall control, most irregular units were willing to acknowledge the general authority of the regular army commanders and to cooperate with them. They agreed to form other 'struggle councils' to help coordinate military operations. These were headed by Sjarief Usman, a regular army officer who had been a strong Muslim activist before the war and maintained close ties with the Islamic parties.[13] Branches of these struggle councils were set up throughout West Sumatra. They incorporated all the militias in a given region and were commanded by regular army officers.[14]

Establishing a Republican Administration in West Sumatra

In the early weeks of independence, the officials who had earlier served the colonial administration would have preferred to adopt a neutral posture until it became clear whether their former Dutch masters, with the aid of the British, would succeed in reestablishing their rule. But young radicals, particularly from the Japanese-sponsored People's Army, persuaded these more cautious leaders to come out openly in support of the Republic. During the tumultuous months that followed the declaration of Indonesian independence, the West Sumatran National Committee (KNI) attempted to create a Republican government in the region. Even after it succeeded, grassroots dissatisfaction was frequently expressed against the character of the residency's leadership, first against its conservative character and later against the dominant position of members of the Socialist Party (PS), the successor to Hatta and Sjahrir's prewar party, the New PNI.[15] The upheavals of the first months of 1946 eventually pushed many of the traditional leaders and former officials out of leadership positions, if not out of the Republic altogether.

From the beginning, the socialist, religious, and traditional streams of Minangkabau society were represented in the National Committee's leadership. It incorporated the former colonial officials Dt. Madjo Orang and Roesad Dt. Perpatih Baringek, and cooperated with the old Muslim reformist (*kaum muda*) leader, Syekh Mohd. Djamil Djambek, the Islamic educator Mahmud Junus, and traditionalist religious (Perti) leader H. Siradjuddin Abbas. But dominant in its policy-making were Mohammad Sjafei and Chatib Suleiman, together with Anwar St. Saidi, Mr. St. Mohammad Rasjid – a lawyer who had returned to Padang in 1944 – and Mohammad Djamil, a medical doctor who had become secretary of the committee, and whose fiery speeches attracted a following in the region.

Thus, the followers of Hatta, Sjahrir, and Tan Malaka dominated the residency government. As had been the case in the 1920s and 1930s, few of those in top positions during the revolution had received a Dutch education beyond the junior high-school level. Major exceptions, however, were the four men who were successively selected to head the residency of West Sumatra, all of whom had received advanced Western education. Three of these Residents remained in office for only a few months, but the fourth, St. Mohd. Rasjid, who was appointed in July 1946, held the position until the end of the independence struggle in 1949.

As we have seen, the first Resident of West Sumatra in independent Indonesia was Mohammad Sjafei, the highly respected founder and headmaster of the INS school in Kayutanam[16] who, during the Japanese occupation, had been appointed to head most of the indigenous organizations they had permitted to exist. In the early days after the proclamation of independence, his colleagues in these bodies pressured him to accept the post of Resident.[17] A teacher and educator, but not a politician, Sjafei was unable to cope with the tensions and antagonisms that tore the region apart, as British forces arrived to take over from the Japanese, and on November 15, 1945, he resigned as Resident and returned to his school.

Over the objections of the more committed nationalists, Mohammad Sjafei, together with the local branch of the Indonesian National Committee (KNI), insisted that Roesad Dt. Perpatih Baringek be appointed as his successor. A senior official in the colonial administration since the 1920s – when he had played a key role in suppressing the 1927 rebellion[18] and had been appointed Wedana (district head) of the Dutch government's Political Information Service [PID] – Dt. Perpatih Baringek had made too many enemies in West Sumatra and was identified too closely with the Dutch administration for his period of governance to be an easy one. The pragmatic members of the National Committee, many of whom had been his colleagues under the Japanese and Dutch, supported his appointment. They were preoccupied with avoiding anarchy by setting up a functioning government in West Sumatra as soon as possible, and they saw Dt. Perpatih Baringek as the most experienced administrator in the region and, therefore, capable of consolidating Republican governance. In the eyes of even some of his more radical colleagues he was acceptable, in part because of his boyhood friendship with Tan Malaka. His position had always been an ambiguous one because of this, and because his brother had been a leader in Batavia of the 1926 uprising and had died in exile in Digul.[19] But though these connections made him acceptable to some of his colleagues in the upper reaches of the administration, they did nothing to alleviate the suspicions and hostility felt by villagers and townspeople throughout West Sumatra, who saw Roesad Dt. Perpatih Baringek as the very epitome of the Indonesians who had loyally served the Dutch and had no place in the newly independent Indonesia.

Even before Roesad took over as Resident in mid-November, 1945, many of the officials who had been appointed to head the districts and subdistricts of West Sumatra had been repudiated by people in the towns and countryside, who identified the hardships they had suffered under the occupation with these officials, who had been the Japanese government's agents in carrying out its policies. In the months after the Japanese capitulation, many of the officials had been forced to flee their positions and several had been killed by villagers.

In January 1946, Roesad's administration attempted to broaden the Republican government's base in the society. As district heads (*bupati*), they appointed so-called popular leaders, who were usually representatives of the strongest group or party in the district. At the same time, however, to ensure administrative efficiency, they still named as deputy district heads former colonial officials, usually from another part of West Sumatra. These efforts at compromise were insufficient to reconcile the population with the new Republican administration, particularly as it was proving unable to alleviate the deteriorating economic conditions throughout the region. In the face of the popular unrest, Roesad could not long prevail in his post.[20] He resigned as Resident in March 1946, and the National Committee had to appoint yet a third residency head.

On March 17, 1946, the National Committee held its fifth meeting in Bukittinggi to elect a new Resident. Mr. St. Mohd. Rasjid emerged as by far the strongest vote-getter, receiving thirty-eight votes, as against four for Chatib Suleiman and two for Djamil, the doctor-orator who was secretary of the National Committee. Rasjid was a skillful politician, and when the Committee elected him Resident, he refused the appointment for health reasons. (He was hospitalized for a month and returned to the government in June.) His decision not to accept the residentship was a wise one given the anarchic situation at the time.

It is rather difficult to account for Rasjid's popularity among the Committee members throughout the early months of the revolution, though he would later prove their assessment correct. Born in Pariaman in 1911, he was the son of a district officer and had received most of his education in Java, graduating from the Law Faculty in Batavia with the title of Master of Law. He continued his professional life in

Wedding of Chatib Suleiman and Yunidar, 1946 (Sudarman Khatib)

Java and in 1938 worked for six months as a law partner of Amir Sjarifuddin in Sukabumi before returning to West Sumatra to practise law in 1939. He was on his way back to Java in December 1941 at the time of the Japanese attack on Pearl Harbour, and for the final three months of Dutch colonial rule he became the only Indonesian serving on the high court in Batavia. When the Japanese invaded the Indies, he retained the position and, according to his own account, became the highest Indonesian official in the whole of West Java. He was one of about twenty Sumatran lawyers whom the Japanese brought back to the island in 1944, to fill the many gaps in the legal system left by the internment of the Dutch officials. In Padang, he was appointed Public Prosecutor, and Sjafei selected him as Chief of Staff of the Patriotic Service Association (*Hokokai*) when it was established later that year.[21]

After Rasjid refused to become Resident, Chatib Suleiman too withdrew his candidacy for the post, writing in his diary, 'In the pleno session of the regional National Committee, I resigned my executive position and refused to let my candidacy for Resident go forward, as it would further have increased the lack of harmony in the National Committee'.[22] After the very prominent role he had played during the Japanese occupation, Chatib Suleiman had withdrawn somewhat to the background after their defeat. His open collaboration with the Japanese had led to resentment against him, particularly among those of his former colleagues in the New PNI, who had followed Sjahrir's lead during the occupation and had, actively or passively, opposed the occupation authorities. At the end of the war, some of these men even planned to assassinate Chatib Suleiman because of his close collaboration with the Japanese. However, he was highly respected by the former soldiers of the People's Army and the members of its support organization (Giyugun koenkai), whom he had recruited and who knew his devotion to the struggle for Indonesian independence. These forces now formed the backbone of the Republican army in West Sumatra. Nor did his pro-Japanese activities alienate Chatib Suleiman from his governmental colleagues, nearly all of whom had also cooperated to some extent during the occupation. He remained a member of the National Committee's executive board until the March 1946 meeting, but nevertheless seemed to feel that were he to be appointed Resident, this would shatter whatever fragile unity had by then been forged among the contending groups in the National Committee.[23]

And so, the remaining candidate, Dr. Mohd. Djamil, became West Sumatra's third Resident in March 1946, but only after Rasjid had assured him of his support and assistance in carrying out his duties. Djamil's disastrous tenure will be dealt with below. It lasted only three months, at the end of which Rasjid ultimately became fourth Resident, and put together an administration that was able to survive the remaining years of the revolution and maintain a relatively unified and strong society capable of withstanding both internal pressures and those exerted by the Dutch, as they tried to re-impose their rule.

Crises in Early 1946

The Return of Tan Malaka

In the early months of independence, in West Sumatra as in the Republic's capital in Java, there were two basic disagreements among the Indonesian leadership with regard to the nature of the struggle against the Dutch. At the national level, these disagreements pitted Tan Malaka against his Minangkabau compatriots, Mohammad Hatta, now the Republic's vice president, and Sutan Sjahrir, the Republic's first prime minister. In this confrontation, President Sukarno was not too closely identified with either side, retaining his freedom of movement, while quietly encouraging Hatta and Sjahrir in their moves against Tan Malaka. The major strategic splits were, first, Sjahrir's emphasis on the importance of diplomacy in winning independence, as opposed to Tan Malaka's advocacy of total struggle; and second, Hatta's desire to create a democratic multi-party state in contrast to Tan Malaka's view that political parties were divisive and that a national front should be established, capable of uniting the Republic in a demand for 100 percent independence from the Dutch.

In mid-May, 1942, five months after the Japanese takeover, Tan Malaka had left Singapore, where he had been living since 1937. He travelled through Sumatra, stopping briefly in Bukittinggi and Padang,[24] then crossed the Sunda Straits to Java, where he lived anonymously for the rest of the occupation, first on the southern fringes of Jakarta and then as a clerk at a coalmine in south Banten. In the early days of independence, he gradually moved to centre stage. The myths and legends surrounding him and his exploits during the twilight years of colonial rule had kept him in the public eye, and he attracted a following as soon as he appeared again on the national scene. There were rumours that it was he who was leading the struggle against Allied forces in Surabaya in November 1945, rumours supported by Muhammad Yamin in a pamphlet he published the following year. Yamin here pro-

Tan Malaka (Leon Salim)

claimed Tan Malaka 'Father of the Indonesian Republic', and likened his exploits over the previous twenty years, 'on the fringes of the Western Pacific, from Shanghai, Manila, Bangkok, to Singapore, Medan, Bukittinggi and Jakarta', to new tales from *A Thousand and One Nights*.[25]

In September Tan Malaka met with Sukarno on two occasions. At one of these, Sukarno signed a political testament bequeathing leadership of the revolution to Tan Malaka, Sjahrir, and two other leaders, should Sukarno and Hatta lose their ability to exercise power.[26] A month later, Tan Malaka strongly opposed Hatta's November 3, 1945 directive calling for the establishment of political parties. He was even more adamant in opposing the negotiating path with the Dutch being pursued by the Sukarno government and its prime minister Sutan Sjahrir. In a speech to a conference of parties and struggle groups at Purwokerto on January 4, 1946, Tan Malaka argued that the Republic should not fracture its united front against the Dutch by disagreements over various 'isms'. Only after 100 percent independence was in their hands should Indonesians allow ideological differences to divide them. In his view, such political divisions would only weaken the struggle and lower the spirits of the people, as had happened in the quarrels between the Islamic League and the Communist Party in the early 1920s. Islamic, Nationalist, and Socialist groups could all unify behind a short programme to which all of the people could agree:

> We cannot accept an independence that is less than 100 percent. We do not wish to negotiate with anyone at all before 100 percent independence has been achieved and before the enemy has in an orderly fashion left our shores and our seas. We do not want to negotiate with the burglar in the house. Let it not be thought that the people do not under-

stand diplomacy. We do not want to negotiate as long as the enemy is
still in our country.[27]

A second conference of struggle groups was held in mid-January, 1946, which neither Sukarno, Hatta, nor any government ministers attended, though they had been
invited. In his speech to the conference, Tan Malaka issued an open challenge 'criticizing the mushrooming parties as being divisive and very difficult to control'[28] and
urging instead a Struggle Union (Persatuan Perjuangan) which he envisaged as uniting all political and economic forces in Indonesia. The demands of Tan Malaka and
his Struggle Union attracted wide support across the political spectrum, with parties of all colorations flocking to join, ultimately forcing the resignation of Sjahrir's
cabinet in late February.

Sukarno and Hatta made some gestures of conciliation toward Tan Malaka, but
they were unwilling to countenance either his militant stance vis-à-vis the Allied
forces, or his contention that in the economic field the Republic's declaration of 100
percent independence necessitated the takeover of the Western-owned plantations
and industrial complexes. When it became clear that compromise was impossible,
Sukarno again appointed Sjahrir to head the government, and attempted to persuade political party leaders who had joined the Struggle Union to enter Sjahrir's
cabinet.

After announcing his cabinet's formation on March 12, Sjahrir immediately
moved to a new stage of negotiations with the Dutch. Tan Malaka and his Struggle
Union continued to call for the Allied troops to be ejected by force from Indonesia,
and this agitation clearly hampered the Republic's attempts to appear as a moderate
and accommodating partner in its negotiations with the Dutch. On March 17, on
orders of defence minister Amir Sjarifuddin and interior minister Dr. Soedarsono –
and with Sukarno's approval and assistance – Tan Malaka was arrested, together
with some of his most prominent supporters, including Muhammad Yamin and
Chaerul Saleh.[29]

The People's Front in West Sumatra

In West Sumatra, too, this struggle was played out. In response to Hatta's call in
November 1945, political parties were formed across the political spectrum, and
most of these established their own militias. Of major importance were the Islamic
parties – the Masjumi,[30] with its Hizbullah and Sabilillah militias, and the traditional Islamic party Perti, with its military arm Lasjmi.[31] Of the nonreligious parties, a branch of the Socialist Party (PS) – led at the national level by Sutan Sjahrir
and Amir Sjarifuddin – was founded in West Sumatra at the beginning of 1946 and it
incorporated most of the former members of Hatta and Sjahrir's prewar New PNI.[32]
Although the Socialist Party did not have its own militia, its leaders commanded the
loyalty of many officers in the West Sumatra division of the Indonesian National
Army. The strongest Communist Party leader was Bachtaruddin, who also initially
headed the forces of the party militia Temi (*Tentera Merah*, Red Army).[33] These

were only the largest of the plethora of parties that were founded in late 1945 and early 1946.

Chatib Suleiman saw these parties competing with each other and splintering the people's unity in confronting the outside enemy. Although a follower of Hatta and Sjahrir, he was much more drawn to Tan Malaka's vision of a national front which could unite all groups irrespective of their political, social, or religious orientation. So two days before Tan Malaka's arrest, and unaware of developments on Java, he took the initiative in urging the National Committee of West Sumatra to establish a People's Front (Volksfront),[34] very similar to Tan Malaka's Struggle Union (Persatuan Perjuangan).

> Chatib Suleiman stressed that this Struggle Union now would direct the energies and desire of the people to defend the sovereignty of their country and the right of their people [to be free] from all corrupt efforts from without and within to besmirch the independence of the state.[35]

Proposals for establishing the People's Front (Volksfront) were made at the same mid-March, 1946 National Committee meeting that appointed Djamil as West Sumatra's third Resident.

Members of the Front's leadership committee came mostly from the more radical side of the political spectrum, including – in addition to Chatib Suleiman and the journalist Bariun A.S.[36]– Bachtaruddin, head of the Communist Party, Suleiman of the Youth Party, and Iskandar Tedjasukmana of the Socialist Party, with the army being represented by the Muslim officer Lt. Col. Dahlan Ibrahim.[37]

Established by the National Committee, and with broad political and economic powers, the Volksfront in West Sumatra was a stronger and more unified coalition than the Struggle Union in Java, and in Resident Djamil it was balanced by a very weak executive authority. Thus, with its formation, a dual system of government developed. Soon it was difficult to differentiate between the residency government and the Volksfront. The National Committee (KNI) had handed over economic powers to the Front, which assumed the right to collect taxes and supplies, imposing duties on goods being brought in and out of some of the major towns.

The Front's most drastic measure was to invalidate the 100-rupiah note, because they suspected that the Dutch were trying to undermine the Republic's economy by flooding the region with forged notes. Freezing the currency led to rapid inflation and a growth in the black market.[38] In response, Resident Djamil countermanded the Volksfront's orders and withdrew the economic powers earlier granted it by the National Committee. But uncertainty continued, and Djamil's actions did little to resolve the unrest that was sweeping the area, and reached its peak in April 1946.

By this time, it seemed possible that the social revolution that had been racking East Sumatra since January might spread to the Minangkabau region.[39] Local resentment against Republican officials was still erupting in several parts of the region, and it was becoming difficult for the government to maintain control. This was particularly the case in the region of Baso, a district a few miles east of Bukittinggi on the road to Payakumbuh.

In Baso lived a religious scholar, Abdul Rahman Tuanku Nan Putih, who had been active in the movement for Indonesian independence since the 1920s. Born in 1898, he had attended religious school at Sianok, studying under Syekh Daud Rasyidi of Balingka. He was a member of the Islamic League (SI), and joined with the Communist branch (*Sarikat Rakyat*, People's League) when the League split in the early 1920s. He was arrested by the Dutch at the time of the 1927 rebellion and exiled to Pamekasan in Madura, where he was imprisoned for about three years. Although a follower of Tan Malaka, after his release from jail, Tuanku Nan Putih joined various other political parties, including Permi and the New PNI, moving from one to another as each was suppressed.

In early 1942, Tuanku Nan Putih encouraged his followers to hasten the Dutch departure and welcome the Japanese invaders. He formed a branch of the scouting organization Pemuda Nippon Raya in Baso.[40] Although he was arrested for a time by the Japanese because of charges by former Dutch officials that he was a Communist, he continued to urge his people to support the authorities, collecting supplies and encouraging his young followers to join the People's Army (Giyu gun) when it was established.

Hearing of the sufferings of the people sent to the notorious forced labour camp at Logas, near Pekanbaru, he persuaded Japanese authorities in 1943 to let him put his followers to work on building a new airfield at Padang Gadut near Bukittinggi, rather than being sent to Logas.[41] His wife had inherited extensive landholdings around Baso, and during the occupation Tuanku Nan Putih encouraged her to start a collective farm on nearby Subarang Hill to grow such crops as corn, cassava, and sugar cane.[42] After the Japanese defeat, Tuanku Nan Putih brought back a few dozen Javanese *romusha* (forced labourers) from the Logas labour camp and settled them on the farm.[43] In late 1945 or early 1946, a government delegation, headed by Sumatran Governor Hassan, visited Baso to inspect the condition of the *romusha* and apparently approved of the way the farm was organized.[44]

At the time of the Japanese surrender, Tuanku Nan Putih was joined at Baso by his younger half-brother, Boerhan Malin Kunieng, whose nickname was Tuanku Nan Hitam.[45] During the occupation, Boerhan had been in Bangkinang, where he married, and when he and his family returned to Baso three Japanese officers accompanied them, with two cars and two trucks. The Japanese officers had had technical training and agreed to work with the villagers, starting a machine shop where they taught the local people how to repair machines and make weapons, as well as instructing them in battle techniques.[46] Boerhan and his followers used their trucks to go to outlying areas, as far as Lubuk Sikaping, where they were able to barter firewood for rice, which they brought back and distributed among the local people.

In the early months of independence, the Baso leaders sided with Tan Malaka's demands for 100 percent independence. But Boerhan Tuanku Nan Hitam interpreted this call far more radically than his half-brother, urging revolutionary action and accusing Tuanku Nan Putih of being too moderate.[47] Tuanku Nan Putih gradually lost influence to his more radical brother, as many of his followers were attracted to Boerhan's revolutionary calls. They began waylaying and robbing travellers on the road between Bukittinggi and Payakumbuh and stealing cattle from neighbouring areas.[48] Local officials became fearful of travelling along the main road, as several of them were kidnapped and a few killed.[49] Those put to death included the police chief and another official from Suliki, as well as Landjoemin Dt. Toemenggoeng, father-in-law of Chaerul Saleh, and probably the highest Minangkabau official in the prewar Dutch administration.[50]

Initially, the local Republican authorities tolerated the revolutionary actions in Baso, for Tuanku Nan Putih's followers were good fighters and several of the young men trained by the Japanese went to help the struggle against the Allied forces in the area around Padang. But as their excesses increased, the atmosphere changed, and wild rumours circulated regarding the situation in and around Baso. Accusations spread that on the communal farm, the people shared not only their food and supplies, but also their wives.[51] West Sumatra Resident Djamil and those close to him were clearly fearful that the movement at Baso was getting out of hand. Their control over the residency was already being undermined by the radical proposals and activities of the Volksfront, and they saw the Baso movement as an even more immediate threat to their authority.

On April 16, Divisional commander Dahlan Djambek ordered Abdul Halim's battalion to eradicate the Baso movement.[52] Tuanku Nan Putih and Tuanku Nan Hitam were first seized and taken away, and although the army troops encountered no resistance they then arrested most of the brothers' followers. They took them all to Bukittinggi, where they were jailed and most were beaten and tortured and many killed. Among those put to death were three of the Japanese, nearly all of the Javanese *romusha*, and many of the brothers' local followers – Halim claimed a total of 113 deaths.[53] Although both half-brothers were executed, their families were never officially told of their fate and the bodies were never returned to them.

Resident Djamil clearly ordered the crackdown. Dahlan Djambek and Sjarief Usman were the officers making the military plans, and Halim the principal commander implementing them. Almost certainly, the original order had come from the central government, in line with its earlier moves against Tan Malaka and his colleagues in Java – and those soon to be taken against the West Sumatran leaders of the People's Front.[54]

The crisis period of March and April 1946 in West Sumatra also marked the peak of the social revolution in the neighbouring residency of East Sumatra. There the local Republican authorities completely lost control and young militias ran riot – killing prominent aristocrats, arresting officials, and seizing property. The principal targets were the traditional aristocracy and the local officials who had served the Dutch regime.[55] From the Republic's capital of Yogyakarta came a delegation, under the leadership of defence minister Amir Sjarifuddin, charged with calming the violence in East Sumatra. En route, this group spent a few days in Bukittinggi, arriving on April 17 – the day after the Baso movement had been crushed. Halim has stated that when he was presented to Amir, the defence minister asked him if all had gone well at Baso, which he interpreted as indicating government support of the movement's suppression.[56]

During its visit to West Sumatra, Amir's delegation met with the residency leaders of the People's Front, who assured them 'that we had no idea of rebellion; we were only revolutionary'.[57] Nevertheless, the centre's representatives apparently urged Resident Djamil and his administration to suppress the Front. On April 25, a couple of days after Amir and his party left the region, Djamil ordered that Chatib Suleiman and his five colleagues be arrested, and they were imprisoned initially in Bukittinggi but then sent to the outskirts of Padang – to what was in effect a combat zone.

In his confrontation with the Volksfront leaders, however, Djamil had little local support. During the month-long struggle which followed its leaders' arrest, the Volksfront declared its willingness to make concessions to the government; and when Djamil still refused to release Front leaders, its sympathizers – both from the political parties and army – responded by arresting Resident Djamil himself on May 17. Banteng Division commander Dahlan Djambek then ordered his troops to return the Volksfront prisoners to Bukittinggi, where they and Resident Djamil confronted each other in face-to-face meetings. At its May 20 conference, the Front restated its loyalty both to the Republican government and to the leadership of the Sjahrir cabinet, and ordered Resident Djamil's release.[58] Two days later, Djamil finally agreed to free the six Volksfront leaders.

But the crisis between the residency government and the Volksfront was not yet resolved. Two further meetings of the National Committee were held in Padang Panjang on June 2 and June 20. At these, the government and the Volksfront aired their differences and finally reached a compromise. Officially, the Volksfront's powers, particularly over the economy, were curbed, but their leaders retained top positions in the National Committee, while it was agreed that Djamil would soon be replaced as Resident. At the end of June, he was prevailed upon to accept the largely honorary position of subgovernor of the newly established province of Central Sumatra and was succeeded as Resident of West Sumatra on July 20 by Mr. St. Mohammad Rasjid, who received support from 90 percent of the National Committee.

Rasjid was a follower of the Socialist party of Sjahrir and Amir Sjarifuddin and was close to the People's Front leaders. He was politically astute and possessed the innate ability to mediate and compromise among the contending forces in the residency. Thus, with his appointment as Resident and the reincorporation of the Front's leadership into the government, the situation in West Sumatra stood in sharp contrast with that at the centre, where Tan Malaka, Muhammad Yamin, and their followers were to remain under arrest until August or September 1948, while Sukarno, Hatta, and Sjahrir determined the Republic's strategy for gaining independence.

The history of the Front in West Sumatra cannot be separated from the attitude of the central government toward Tan Malaka, nor from the more revolutionary actions being carried out by some of his followers in the region. The Front's fate and that of the Baso movement can be seen as resulting from basic splits both within

West Sumatran society and between the region and a central government that was trying to bring the West Sumatra administration to conform with the priorities of the Republic in Java. The events of March, April, and May 1946 highlighted some of the dynamics governing the situation in West Sumatra, and the contrasts between the alliances and antagonisms there and at the centre.

The most striking difference was the collaboration in West Sumatra between the followers of Tan Malaka and those of Hatta/Sjahrir. Overlapping allegiances between the two groups had been evident in the early 1930s when many people were adherents both of Tan Malaka's Pari and of Hatta/Sjahrir's New PNI. These dual allegiances continued into the revolutionary period. In contrast, in Java, where the Republican government faced basic strategic dilemmas over the course to follow in its interaction with the Western powers, earlier compatability between the Socialist and Marxist ideas of Tan Malaka, Hatta, and Sjahrir had broken down, resulting in open confrontation between them and eventually in Tan Malaka's arrest.

In West Sumatra, the struggles between Resident Djamil and the Volksfront did not really represent a confrontation between the residency government and the Front. Djamil's only real backing came from the centre, in the form of the delegation which visited the area under leadership of Amir Sjarifuddin immediately before the arrest of the Front's leaders. It was, in fact, the West Sumatran government in the form of the National Committee (KNI) that had established the Volksfront and granted it broad powers. Other than Djamil, the most important leaders of the government were generally friends, colleagues, and allies of the Front's leaders. The men heading the Volksfront were also supported by the military leaders, most of whom had been chosen and guided by Chatib Suleiman in their early training under the Japanese.

So the splits among the Nationalist/Socialist/Communist leaders that loomed so large on the national scene were little evident in West Sumatra, where the differences between these leaders were disagreements over tactics rather than strategy. Astute leaders such as Rasjid and Chatib Suleiman could forge compromises that enabled these tactical differences to be subsumed within an overall strategy that unified the region in the face of an outside enemy.

But if such a strategy were to be implemented it had to be through compromise and a considerable degree of tolerance. 'Extreme' movements, such as that at Baso, had no place. The people at Baso adhered more closely to Tan Malaka's radical vision of 100 percent independence, and saw a social revolution as the only way of achieving the goals they had set themselves. Tuanku Nan Putih was himself unable to control the actions of his erstwhile followers, and a government struggling to establish order in the region it officially controlled believed the movement had to be eradicated – in the same way as the central government had felt obliged to move against Tan Malaka's Struggle Union, in part as a sign that extremist activities could not be tolerated.

In crushing the Baso movement, the military and civilian leaders were doubtless urged on by those who had earlier compromised with the Dutch and had been shamed by Tuanku Nan Putih's consistent adherence to the principles he derived both from his religion and his socialism. The survivors at Baso attributed the fact that two officers identified with the Muslim parties (Dahlan Djambek and Sjarief Usman) should have acted against such a respected religious scholar as Tuanku Nan Putih, in part, on the basis of divisions among Muslim leaders during the colonial period. Tuanku Nan Putih's son contrasted his father's life with that of his Muslim opponents, such as Syekh Mohd. Djamil Djambek (father of Colonel Dahlan Djambek) and Perti leader Syekh Arrasuli of Candung, saying his father was in favour of the ordinary people while Syekh Djambek collaborated with and made concessions to both the Dutch and Japanese, while Arrasuli also collected funds from his followers to build himself a house.[59] Tuanku Nan Putih had always combined his Islamic teaching with a strong anticolonialism and championship of the poor. A police officer from Baso who participated in suppressing the movement retained his respect for the Islamic leader, stating: 'Tuanku Nan Putih based himself on religion because according to the Qur'anic verses you must help the poor people, you must help orphans, so he tried to put that into practice'.[60]

Djamaluddin Tamin, the Pari leader from West Sumatra, later blamed the suppression of the Baso movement on the fact that both Tuanku Nan Putih and Tuanku Nan Hitam were followers of Tan Malaka, stating that religious, Socialist, and Communist forces had combined to crush them.[61] And, less plausibly, some analysts have portrayed the earlier removal of Roesad Dt. Perpatih Baringek as Resident as partially stemming from a similar alignment of forces brought about by Roesad's continuing sympathies with Tan Malaka.

But once the Baso movement, at one extreme, had been exterminated and, at the other, Resident Djamil had been effectively removed from a pivotal power position, the Volksfront was once more incorporated into the residency government which pursued policies having much in common with those advocated by Tan Malaka. When the West Sumatra branch of the Regional Defence Council (DPD) was established in June 1946 as the effective executive body in the region, it was headed by the Resident, with the commander of the Banteng Division as his deputy. But the party representatives, chosen by the National Committee to serve on the Council, were Duski Samad from the Masjumi, Abdullah from Tan Malaka's party, and Communist Party leader Bachtaruddin.[62] So out of the upheavals that racked the region during the early months of 1946 emerged a residency leadership now dominated by an alliance between Socialist and Communist leaders, supported by some of the more moderate Islamic scholars.

Islamic Dissension

The early months of independence had demonstrated that the people of West Sumatra as a whole felt alienated from the local Republican leadership and were demanding more radical action than the government had thus far been willing to take. The residency leadership, therefore, felt it needed to make a strong effort to shore up its support in the rural areas, and it did this in June and July of 1946 by holding direct elections throughout the residency at the lowest level of the administration – the nagari or extended village – for new nagari councils (Dewan Perwakilan Nagari) and *nagari* heads (Wali Nagari). The elections were based on universal suffrage for all citizens aged eighteen and over.[63] In these elections, where the political parties and other social groupings campaigned on behalf of their candidates, the Masjumi party was overwhelmingly successful. Many of the traditional village elders, who in the eyes of the people were still tied to the Dutch and Japanese, were defeated and replaced by men who were respected and trusted largely because of their earlier unwillingness to cooperate with the colonial powers.[64]

These elections marked a major shift in power at the lowest level of government. As a result, members of the Muslim Masjumi party to a large extent replaced the traditional lineage heads (*penghulu*) in leadership positions.[65] Of the newly elected village heads, around 90 percent now belonged to the Masjumi party,[66] which also held a solid majority on most of the *nagari* councils. While these elections succeeded in consolidating Republican support in the rural areas they also, however, highlighted the discrepancy between Muslim strength at the village level and their continuing lack of influence at the top of the residency leadership. This discrepancy was one of the several causes of another major eruption that shook the government of West Sumatra in early 1947, an upheaval that came to be known as the 'March 3 Affair'.

The March 3 Affair

On March 3, 1947, units drawn mainly from the Muslim militias rose up against the local Republican government in Bukittinggi and several other major towns. They planned to kidnap Resident Rasjid, Army Commander Ismael Lengah, and other top residency officials, and seize power from this civilian and military leadership. The attempted coup took place just at the time when the Indonesian National Committee was meeting in Java to endorse the Linggajati agreements with the Dutch.

Under the Linggajati agreements the Dutch government recognized the Republic as the *de facto* authority in Java and Sumatra, and both sides pledged to work toward the establishment of 'a sovereign, democratic, federal state', the United States of Indonesia, that would form part of the Netherlands-Indonesian Union.[67] In West Sumatra, the Linggajati agreements called on the Indonesian army to withdraw from Padang and the surrounding areas, leaving only a small contingent of police and a skeletal administrative apparatus within the town.[68] Feeling ran high in West Sumatra against these provisions.

Resentment against the Linggajati concessions formed part of the background to the March 3 Affair. It also had its roots in a number of grievances that extended far beyond the Islamic militias who were the major actors in the coup attempt. First, dissatisfaction at the discrepancy revealed after the local elections of mid-1946 between Muslim political strength in the village administrations and their weak representation in the residency government. Second, the accusation that many residency leaders had too-close ties with the previous Dutch colonial administration and, as a result, were trying to slow the pace of the revolution. Third, the resentment felt by front-line troops, whether regular army or militias, against higher-ranking officers who were accused of leading a luxurious and immoral life in Bukittinggi, while their soldiers were dying at the front around Padang. And fourth, the militias' anger at the fact that virtually all supplies for the armed forces were allocated to the regular army soldiers, while the militias at the front received virtually nothing.[69]

The group that led the challenge to the residency leadership was drawn mostly from the Islamic political parties and the religious and secular militias. It was headed by the old Muhammadiah radical, Saalah J. St. Mangkuto[70] and the maverick scholar and teacher Adam B.B. from Padang Panjang,[71] together with a number of leaders from the Islamic militias, the Hizbullah, Sabilillah, and Lasjmi. The principal leader of the Islamic forces on Sumatra, Bachtiar Junus, reportedly arrived from Medan to persuade local Hizbullah leaders to participate.[72] Also involved was Nazaruddin Dt. Rajo Mangkuto, head of the militia of the traditional *adat* party (MTKAAM), who had been secretary to its founder and leader, Dt. Simarajo.[73]

Also among the instigators of the March 3 movement were members of an intelligence mission, headed by Captain Rachmat Tobri, sent from the Republic's Sumatra military command in Medan. This mission was charged with investigating the 'Singkarak Charter' and other loyalty oaths that several prewar Minangkabau officials had allegedly made to the colonial government before the Dutch surrender in 1942.

> [News of] the Singkarak meeting between [the former colonial officials] and the Dutch side had leaked and was widely known among the groups of struggle leaders and political leaders in West Sumatra, and greatly stimulated the already existing atmosphere of extremism and fanaticism. The Singkarak Charter was likened to a betrayal of the revolutionary struggle. The passive attitude among a number of the ex-district heads and officials, even an attitude of siding and working with the Dutch or sympathizing with them and having hidden ties with them, helped create such an impression.[74]

One of the members of Captain Tobri's mission, Zubir Adam, established close ties with the local Islamic leaders and soon became involved in the so-called Movement against the Enemies of Indonesian Independence (Paki). In several towns in West Sumatra, members of the movement held meetings at which they castigated residency civilian and military leaders, accusing them of still maintaining close ties to the former Dutch regime. They also charged the military command with corruption and loose living.[75] In addition, it was alleged that too many of both the civilian and military leaders were leftist in orientation.[76] For all these reasons they had to be replaced.

Resident Rasjid had been warned earlier that a coup would be launched against him. On the eve of the uprising, both he and Colonel Ismael Lengah addressed a meeting of Islamic scholars in Padang Panjang and tried to persuade them that their charges were unjustified. Alerted in advance to the conspirators' plans, Rasjid's guards from the Police Mobile Brigade were able to thwart the rebels when they tried to seize both him and Commander Lengah, but other government officials were kidnapped in several towns of West Sumatra. Most of those captured were civilian administrators, many from among the group known coloquially as 'officials of three eras' (*pegawai tiga zaman*) – the Dutch, the Japanese, and the Republican – against whom so much popular hostility had been directed since independence.[77] A majority of the top military officers and civilian officials, however, were well enough guarded to evade capture.[78]

Despite the broad military support and the depth of the dissatisfaction behind the uprising, its execution was surprisingly weak and disorganized. In Bukittinggi, after an exchange of fire lasting only a few hours, the Hizbullah units surrendered before they even reached the centre of the town. One regular army soldier was killed and one of the attackers was wounded. In the other towns, too, the uprisings were evidently feeble and uncoordinated. Nevertheless, the Republican army had to withdraw about two-hundred men from their units around Padang to help quell the various outbreaks.[79]

By the morning of March 4, it was clear that the coup attempt had failed. The principal leaders had been arrested, including members of the Masjumi and Hizbullah, as well as Zubir Adam and Anwar Doos from the Sumatra command delegation.[80] During the morning hours, intermediaries – including Mohammad Sjafei and such Muslim military and civilian officials as Dahlan Ibrahim, Darwis Taram, and Sjarief Usman – tried to get the two sides to compromise. Although the army's commander Ismael Lengah rebuffed these efforts, other top residency officials who were lawyers by profession, including Resident Rasjid, were determined that the rebels should not be treated arbitrarily. Eventually, only two of the political leaders, Saalah St. Mangkuto and Nazaruddin, were brought to answer for their actions in a court of law. In their trial, which began on August 28, the court sentenced Nazaruddin to a year in jail and Saalah to a period of probation. The government arrested many of the rebel soldiers and confiscated most of their weapons, but after being disarmed and detained for a few days, the men were sent home with a gift of money and clothing.[81]

Reports of the uprising reached Java while the Central National Committee was meeting there to ratify the Linggajati agreements.[82] Alarmed at the news, leaders of the Masjumi party sent a team to investigate the causes of the affair. On March 23, a delegation led by Masjumi head Mohd. Natsir, who was himself a Minangkabau and was minister of information in the Republican government, arrived in Bukittinggi.[83] His investigation team decided that the Masjumi party as a whole was not involved though some of its members were. But Colonel Ismael Lengah refused to return the weapons he had confiscated from the Islamic units even when Mohammad Natsir, and later Vice President Hatta, personally demanded that he do so.[84] Lengah's inflexibility on this issue confirmed Muslim hostility toward him, which had been a major factor in the rebels' dissatisfaction with the residency leadership. Despite the lenient treatment they received, the rebels remained deeply suspicious of Lengah and other leaders.

The significance of the incident lay less in the actual threat it posed to the residency government than in the way it indicated the balance of forces in West Sumatra, and the ongoing tensions both within the society and between its leaders and those at the centre. The importance of the March 3 Affair also lay in the way it was interpreted at the local and national level. It made a lasting impact on the relationships among the competing forces within the residency and also on the attitude of leaders at the national level toward West Sumatra.

The Military Side

The March 3 Affair not only highlighted the tensions between the Islamic parties and the Socialist and Communist parties, but also those between the political parties' militias and the command headquarters of the Republican army division in West Sumatra. So before examining more closely the basic disagreements between the views of the residency leadership and those of the national Republican leadership in Java regarding West Sumatra's place within the Indonesian struggle for independence, we should first turn to the character of the military forces that had developed in the region during the early years of independence. The nature of the armed forces in West Sumatra had a critical impact on the relations between the region and the centre, not only during the revolution but for more than a decade following the Dutch transfer of sovereignty to the Republic.

For the first year of the struggle, as we have seen, there was a degree of accommodation between regular and irregular forces in West Sumatra. This was based chiefly on the earlier relationships among their commanders, most of whom had received their first military training together in the Japanese-sponsored People's Army (Giyu gun). Many Muslim officers in the Giyu gun had chosen to join the Republic's regular army (TRI, Tentara Republik Indonesia, Indonesian Republican Army) rather than the Hizbullah or other militias affiliated with Islamic parties. These included Banteng Division commander Dahlan Djambek and regimental commanders Sjarief Usman and Dahlan Ibrahim, who were all very close to the Muslim party leaders. Dahlan Djambek was revered as son of Syekh Djambek, while both of the others had been active Muslim nationalists in the 1930s. Many of the next echelon of Army commanders (including Ahmad Husein, who headed the Banteng forces on Padang's eastern front), were also closely allied to the Muslim groups[85] and were able to provide a constant bridge between the divisional command and the independent militias, so that most of these militias willingly accepted the overall authority of the regular army officers.

From the summer of 1946 this situation began to change. In July 1946, the Sumatra Command was reorganized into three subcommands: North, Central, and South Sumatra. In this reorganization, Dahlan Djambek was appointed to head the Sub Command of Central Sumatra,[86] Dahlan Ibrahim became headquarters chief of staff, and Sjarief Usman became head of the section responsible for liaison between the militias and the regular army.[87] Two months later, Ismael Lengah succeeded Dahlan Djambek as commander of the Banteng Division.[88] From then on, although the Islamic officers continued to hold influential command positions, the most senior of them no longer had continuous direct contact with either regular or irregular troops in the front lines.

The uneasiness of the Muslim militias vis-à-vis the army command was exacerbated by Ismael Lengah's appointment to head the Banteng Division. He was from Padang and exerted most influence there, but his education had been secular and technical, and he had few ties with the Islamic groups in West Sumatra, who viewed him as a socialist and follower of Tan Malaka. Brusque and impatient in manner, he made few efforts to conciliate his opponents (whether these were the Muslim leaders or the Dutch), and resentment against him clearly played a role in the tensions among the regular and irregular forces, which reached their peak in the March 3 Affair. After the rebellion was put down, both the residency government and the Banteng Division command felt it imperative that the Muslim militias be brought under direct operational control of army headquarters, and they welcomed the order issued by President Sukarno on June 3, 1947, for all militias in the Republic to be merged with the regular army, now named the Indonesian National Army (TNI).

Sjarief Usman was charged with incorporating the West Sumatra militias into the Banteng Division. He first consolidated all of them into a Special Regiment, a process that was completed by the end of 1947. Then he began the more difficult task of absorbing this Special Regiment into the command structure. The Islamic militias, in particular, did not wish to lose their identity completely, and the party political leaders were equally reluctant to relinquish control over their military forces to the regular army leadership.[89] When it became clear that many of the militias' basic supply problems would be solved by being amalgamated within the division, however, most of their individual commanders reluctantly agreed to this course.

Fusion of the militias and the regular forces was never completely successful. A few of the militia commanders never did agree to forfeit their independence, and even among those units that were integrated into the division, many still offered their primary loyalty to their militia commander and political party. Nevertheless, incorporation of the irregular forces into the Banteng Division was more successful and faced fewer problems than in analogous situations in most other parts of Indonesia. Its end result was that, with the assent of the political party leaders, by early 1948 the armed militias were – officially at least – integrated into the regular army command.

By this time, however, it had become clear that however successful West Sumatra's leaders felt they had been in overcoming the internal challenges they faced and in maintaining a unified front against Dutch attempts to extend their power beyond their base in the coastal area around Padang, the leaders of the Republic in Java were unhappy with the way the military and political situation was developing in West Sumatra.

Clashes with the Centre

Sumatra's Civilian Government

From early 1946, when social revolutions erupted in both East Sumatra and Aceh and lesser upheavals occurred in West Sumatra, the Republic's central government made several attempts to strengthen its control over that island's government. In the aftermath of the First Dutch 'Police Action' in July 1947,[90] areas under Republican control in Java shrank, and the Yogyakarta government began to look to Sumatra as the potential fall-back area should the Dutch overrun its remaining centres in Java. But the island's viability as a secure bulwark for the Republic was weakened by Sumatra Governor Hassan's evident inability to exert any real authority over its component residency governments.

Even at the August 1945 meetings of the Committee for the Preparation of Indonesian Independence, Vice President Hatta had been one of the strongest opponents of Sumatra being made into a single province, arguing instead for the establishment of three provinces on the island. He believed Sumatra was too vast and diverse for a single government to exercise effective control. And during the early years of independence Governor Hassan's ineffectiveness had proven him right. The Republic's central leadership in Yogyakarta became increasingly dissatisfied as the residencies in Sumatra monopolized virtually all governmental power and displayed ever more independence vis-à-vis the Sumatran provincial government. Yogyakarta determined to make the residency governments in both Java and Sumatra more responsive to the Republic's national priorities.

Initial moves were made in this direction in Sumatra in April 1946 by the Amir Sjarifuddin delegation, which proposed creating three subprovinces – North, Central, and South Sumatra. But these too proved ineffective, as Hatta later noted:

> ...in practice, the Governor of Sumatra is only the Governor of Pematang Siantar, because of the lack of communication with the Residents. The Residents continue to function like their predecessors in the Japanese period. The position of the Sub-Governor is not clear. The regencies [i.e. subprovinces] have been established but nobody knows what their duties are.[91]

The central government then proposed transforming the three subprovinces into fully fledged provinces. As such a move meant both abolishing the province of Sumatra and also weakening the residencies, the proposal was not received enthusiastically by any of the current office holders in Sumatra and was effectively ignored.

Until mid-1947, West Sumatra lay in a backwater of Indonesian national politics. As a result, during this first two years the course of the revolution within the region developed largely independently of outside control. The local military and civilian leaders, although loyal and generally obedient to the central government, were able to observe their own priorities, carrying out their own interpretations of Yogyakarta's orders at their own pace. At the same time, in part due to their isolation from the Indonesian central government in Java, leaders in West Sumatra remained steadfastly loyal to the Indonesian Republic as they themselves perceived it. And although enjoying almost complete freedom of action, they elected to carry out their interpretation of most of the orders which did arrive from the Republican capital of Yogyakarta.

From the middle of 1947, the relative isolation of the governments in Sumatra began to change. The change in part resulted from the impact of the first Dutch 'Police Action' of July 21, 1947. In West Sumatra, prior to their advance out of their

Padang enclave, the Dutch moved against the Republic's civilian and police apparatus within the town. They arrested many of the local officials, and the mayor of the town, Aziz Chan, who had adopted a confrontational stance toward the Dutch throughout the months of his tenure, was killed. His death occurred on July 19, when Dutch officers intercepted him as he was leaving for his regular weekend visit to Bukittinggi and persuaded him instead to accompany them to the demarcation line at Kandis to investigate an alleged Republican violation. A few hours later his family was informed that he had been involved in an 'incident', and his body was being taken directly to the military hospital in Padang. The Dutch maintained that 'extremist' Republican militias had shot him accidentally, but the Republicans disputed this version and accused the Dutch of murdering him by a blow to the back of his head.[92]

Two days later, Dutch forces advanced in three directions from Padang, to occupy virtually all of West Sumatra's coastal lowlands. In other parts of Java and Sumatra, their troops penetrated even deeper into Republican territory, particularly in West and Central Java, but also in South and East Sumatra, where they succeeded in achieving their major economic objectives – the oil fields near Palembang and the vast rubber plantations outside Medan.

At the time of the Dutch advance in July 1947, Sumatran Governor Hassan and his provincial government were forced to flee to Bukittinggi from their capital at Pematang Siantar. Vice President Hatta, who was also in Pematang Siantar at the time of the Dutch attack, accompanied Governor Hassan and his entourage in their flight. Thereafter, Hatta remained in Bukittinggi until January 1948, heading the Republican government in Sumatra while President Sukarno headed it in Java. From this upland town, Hatta exerted a powerful influence over all of Sumatra and particularly over his home region of the Minangkabau. As a result of his presence, West Sumatra's politics were no longer isolated from those at the national level, and the two coexisted uneasily side by side, with national priorities increasingly impinging and being imposed on local ones.

Hatta's low opinion of Sumatra's government was strengthened during his six-month stay in Bukittinggi, and his view that the island needed to be reorganized administratively received strong reinforcement. His growing disapproval of the Sumatran authorities was probably in large part based on the natural frictions that must have arisen among the government leaders when so many different levels of administration overlapped within a single small town. For during the last half of 1947, Bukittinggi was the residence not only of Vice President Hatta and Governor Hassan, but also of Central Sumatra Subgovernor Nasrun[93] and West Sumatra Resident Rasjid. The Sumatra military command was also transferred there from its headquarters in Prapat, so in the military field too the various command levels overlapped, with Bukittinggi the headquarters of the Sumatra command as well as of West Sumatra's Banteng Division.

Given this situation, it was inevitable that antagonisms would develop among the many military and civilian leaders attempting to exert their authority in their own field. The confusion must have been compounded by the fact that, in the face of the Dutch advance, large numbers of refugees had fled from the coastal areas into terri-

Mohd. Hatta

tory still controlled by the Republic, swelling the population of Bukittinggi from about thirty thousand to about a hundred thousand.[94]

The Dutch use of force in their military advances of July 1947 was in defiance of the earlier Linggajati agreements. Their actions received general condemnation from the world community, and Australia and India brought the issue before the United Nations. The Security Council set up a Good Offices Committee with the task of settling the Dutch/Indonesian conflict by peaceful means.[95] Under the auspices of this Committee, delegates from the Republic and from the Netherlands met for talks in December 1947 on neutral territory – the US ship *Renville* anchored off the Java coast. There, Amir Sjarifuddin, who had been the Republic's prime minister since the previous July, ultimately felt compelled to sign the 'Renville Agreement'. This agreement proclaimed a ceasefire between the two sides but acknowledged Dutch control over the territory their forces had penetrated up to the so-called Van Mook ceasefire line – on condition that a plebiscite were held in the Dutch-occupied territories to determine the wishes of the people in these territories, and, accordingly, which party would ultimately rule there.[96]

Hatta was summoned to Java from Sumatra in January 1948, at the time of the Renville agreements. Later that month, widespread opposition to the agreements led to the fall of Amir Sjarifuddin's cabinet and Sukarno then appointed Hatta to head a presidential cabinet and concurrently serve as the Republic's minister of defence. In these positions he was called upon to implement the provisions of the unpopular agreements. In April 1948, Hatta introduced a law which abolished the provincial government of Sumatra, and also eliminated the residency level of the government in both Java and Sumatra, together with several lower administrative levels. In Sumatra, the new provinces of North, Central, and South Sumatra were given powers that, in theory at least, made them virtually autonomous regions.[97]

This law, however, remained mostly on paper. A province of Central Sumatra was officially established in mid-1948, and the Subgovernor, Mr. Nasrun, was appointed to head it, a snub to Mr. Rasjid, West Sumatra's Resident, who was the expected appointee but who had clashed frequently with Hatta – both over the March 3 Affair and during the vice president's months in Bukittinggi in 1947.[98] Nevertheless, the new order was not implemented, for the residencies were not officially abolished until December 18, 1948, the very eve of the Second Dutch 'Police Action' against the Republic. Following that attack the residencies were reinstated, and throughout the subsequent year they once more became the strongest units of government.

During 1948, because of its preoccupations with the many crises it faced in Java, the central government of the Republic failed in its attempts to impose its ideas on the civilian government that emerged in West Sumatra. But the situation was very different in the military field.

Rationalization of the Armed Forces

As we have noted, when Hatta became prime minister in January 1948 he also assumed the position of minister of defence. Faced with the shrinking area under Republican control, particularly in Java, he drew up plans together with Col. A.H. Nasution, the commander of the Siliwangi Division of West Java, for streamlining the Republic's armed forces.[99] Through massive demobilizations, they aimed to provide the army structure with maximum efficiency while at the same time making it less of a drain on the Republic's treasury. Overall, they planned to create 'mobile offensive systems' of 'shifting pockets' of highly trained, more fully armed regular forces, supported by territorial militias.[100]

This plan was to encompass the armed forces not only in Java but also in Sumatra, where Nasution envisaged creating four military subterritories, 'each of which was to be a self-supporting infrastructure, so that each could maintain its own defence with its own power. On top of these four would be the Sumatra command'.[101] Each of the army divisions on Sumatra would be reduced to a mobile brigade, which in West Sumatra meant that only a third of the men in the Banteng Division would be retained as fully armed regular soldiers, while the remainder would become local security forces.

Nasution accompanied Hatta on a visit to Bukittinggi in April 1948 when they presented these rationalization steps to the officers of the Sumatra command, all of whom vigorously opposed the plan. The Sumatran officers argued that while the reorganization might make sense in Java, it was completely unsuitable for Sumatra. In Sumatra, the Dutch occupied only about a fifth of the island compared with about a half of Java. The armed forces in Sumatra were no drain on the Republic's treasury, as their food supplies were raised from the local people and their weapons were either manufactured locally or acquired by their commanders through trade with Singapore and Malaya. Mobile units would be ill-adapted to the kind of people's struggle being waged in Sumatra, and the massive demobilizations would have a devastating psychological impact on the soldiers who had volunteered to fight for the Republic against the Dutch.[102]

Ismael Lengah, 1976 (in front of his portrait from the revolutionary period)

The Sumatra command's intransigent opposition to the rationalization proposals angered both Hatta and Nasution and convinced them that if the plans were to be implemented, the Sumatran officers would have to be replaced by more compliant officers from Java. Such a transfer would accord well with the fact that the Republic had agreed at Renville to withdraw from large areas of West Java, and, as a consequence, many officers from West Java's Siliwangi Division were now stranded in Yogyakarta with no territorial commands. From May 1948, army headquarters began to send Siliwangi officers to Bukittinggi to take over key positions on Sumatra. The first such officer was Daan Jahya, who was appointed chief of staff for operations in the Sumatra Command. Commander Suhardjo attempted to stymy that move by appointing Banteng Division commander Ismael Lengah to the same position. This defiance strengthened Hatta's determination to replace both Suhardjo and Ismael Lengah. On November 18, 1948, when the vice president made a further trip to Sumatra he brought Siliwangi officer Col. Hidayat with him to take over the Sumatra territorial command, and when he returned to Java at the beginning of December he ordered Ismael Lengah to accompany him. Despite protests from Lengah's fellow officers, who argued that he 'was the only officer who could coordinate the strength of the different units', Lengah had to leave on December 10, with the ostensible assignment of becoming an instructor in the military academy in Yogyakarta.[103]

The disputes between the local army officers in Sumatra and their superiors in Java were caused by their different perceptions as to the nature of the Indonesia – Dutch conflict, and the priorities they felt had to be observed to bring it to a successful conclusion.

The major aim of the national Republican leadership was to maintain the Republic of Indonesia in existence, even if the Dutch should succeed in occupying Java and overrunning the Republican capital of Yogyakarta. Since before the first Dutch advance in July 1947, the Republic had had a contingency plan whereby the vast territories of Sumatra could provide the major fall-back area for its government should Yogyakarta be occupied by Dutch forces. With Sumatra the keystone of their plans for preserving the Republic, they thought it essential that its governments and armies should be integrated into a centrally administered territorial structure responsive to the national leadership's authority.

In contrast, the local leaders in West Sumatra saw their most important goal as protecting their home area against Dutch efforts to reassert their control. Thus, they saw their major strategic priority as blocking any further Dutch advance and preventing the former colonial power from gaining a foothold in the rural areas of West Sumatra.

Colonel Hidayat, as the new Sumatran commander, faced an impossible task in attempting to implement the government's rationalization plans.[104] He was blocked at every turn by the remaining local officers, and his efforts were brought to an abrupt halt on December 19, when Dutch forces launched their second 'Police Action' against the demoralized and resentful army in West Sumatra.

Political Alignments in Java and Sumatra

These struggles in both the military and civilian fields between the central Republican government in Yogyakarta and the political and military leaders in West Sumatra reflected the different political realities existing in the two regions as well as the differing goals of the national as opposed to the local government.

After the Republic accepted the Renville Agreement in January 1948, it faced an increasingly fractured situation. Socialist Prime Minister Amir Sjarifuddin had signed the agreement, and opposition to it from both the Islamic Masjumi party and the Indonesian National Party (PNI) led to his cabinet's fall on January 23. Subsequently, however, alignments shifted. Hatta, appointed by Sukarno to head a presidential cabinet, was now faced with enforcing the agreements. The men he appointed to his cabinet on January 31 consisted almost completely of members of the Masjumi and the PNI, who now had to implement the unpopular agreements.

Within the Socialist Party there had long been friction between Amir Sjarifuddin and Sutan Sjahrir, which had intensified in mid-1947 when Amir's withdrawal of support had led to the fall of Sjahrir's third cabinet, which was replaced by a coalition cabinet headed by Amir. Thereafter, until his resignation in January 1948, Amir had led the government while Sjahrir had been the Republic's principal spokesman abroad.[105] In February 1948, Sjahrir and his followers withdrew from the Socialist Party (PS), which he and Amir had previously headed, to form a new party: the Indonesian Socialist Party (PSI). Amir's more radical Socialists who remained in the Socialist Party (PS) then formed an alliance with other left-wing and Communist parties in the People's Democratic Front (FDR). Until mid-1948, this front saw itself as a loyal opposition.

Subsequently, disagreements between Sjahrir and Amir became starker. Disillusioned with his earlier reliance on assurances by the United States that they would pressure the Dutch to implement the Renville Agreement, Amir moved closer to the international Communist bloc, while Sjahrir maintained a stance that was avowedly neutral, but in reality was increasingly allied with the Western powers.

As it became clear that the Dutch had no intention of implementing their undertaking under Renville to hold plebiscites in the areas of Republican territory they had overrun, Amir's position became more radical and he moved into open opposition to the agreements he had signed. He finally broke with Hatta's government in July 1948, when it recalled Suripno, its envoy who had negotiated a consular agreement between the Republic and the Soviet Union.[106]

The growing fissure between the Socialist parties and the Hatta government became unbridgeable when Suripno returned to Indonesia, bringing back with him Musso, who had been an important leader of the Indonesian Communist Party in the 1920s and one of the organizers of the 1926/27 uprisings.[107] Musso aligned with Amir, and soon after his return took over leadership of a fusion of Amir's Socialist party and the Soviet-oriented Communist forces (not including the more nationalist Communists that supported Tan Malaka). Armed conflict broke out in Madiun in September 1948, when disgruntled army units and militias pushed an ill-prepared Musso to challenge the Sukarno Hatta government earlier than he or Amir had planned. The challenge was shortlived, and military forces loyal to the government soon crushed the uprising, killing both Musso and Amir.[108]

These splits and upheavals in Java had no parallels in West Sumatra. In the early part of 1948, all members of the Socialist Party in West Sumatra had sided with Sjahrir in his split with Amir. Throughout 1948, the Socialists worked in conjunction not only with the local branch of the Communist Party (PKI) under Bachtaruddin, but also with Tan Malaka's followers under Abdullah. There was still tension with the Islamic parties, but many of the more moderate religious leaders cooperated with the Socialist-Democratic local government.

Similarly, the bitterness of many military units and militias in Java stemming from their demobilization under the rationalization policies (which was a large factor in the Madiun revolt), was not paralleled at this time in Sumatra. In West Sumatra, it was not until after that revolt in Java that both army and militias were really confronted with the humiliations they would have to accept under the rationalization plans of Nasution and Hatta.

These differences do much to explain why the Madiun uprisings of Communist leaders and radical army units against the Republican government in Java had few repercussions in West Sumatra. It appears that Hatta expected a rebellion to break out not only in Java but also in Sumatra. At the beginning of August, recognizing Mr. Rasjid's strong standing in West Sumatra, he overlooked his earlier irritation at the Minangkabau Resident and appointed him Commissioner of State for Internal Security in Sumatra.[109] Mr. Rasjid returned from Java to Bukittinggi to take up this post on August 7.[110]

Suripno and Musso had stopped over in Bukittinggi a few days earlier on their way back to Yogyakarta. While in West Sumatra they had met with local Communist leaders and toured the eastern front, accompanied by its commander, Ahmad Husein, spending the night at the house of Nazir St. Pamuncak.[111]

When six weeks later, news of the Madiun rebellion reached West Sumatra, Governor Hassan, Resident Rasjid, and top army commanders met with the Sumatran Communist leaders (including Abdul Karim and Bachtaruddin) and asked them to choose between Sukarno/Hatta and Musso. All chose the Republican leadership of Sukarno/Hatta.[112] A further meeting of all Socialist and Communist party leaders was held on September 22, where, together with Islamic and National party leaders, they swore their loyalty to the government and agreed to preserve the Republic's unity. As a result, the West Sumatran government did not ban the Communist party, and only a few Communists were briefly arrested.[113]

Tan Malaka and His Influence

In dealing with the differing perceptions and realities in Central Java and West Sumatra in the months leading up to the Second Dutch attack, it is necessary to look once more at the influence of Tan Malaka and the way in which the strategy developed to defend West Sumatra against the Dutch accorded with his prescriptions, rather than with those that Hatta and Nasution were attempting to impose.

When Hatta took over the prime ministership of the Republic after the Renville agreements were signed in January 1948, he announced that the jailed leaders of Tan Malaka's Struggle Union (Persatuan Perjuangan) would be brought to trial.[114] Shortly thereafter, Tan Malaka's followers, imprisoned and silenced since mid-1946, began to regroup, coming together to form the People's Revolutionary Movement (GRR, Gerakan Revolusi Rakjat). In its official newspaper, *Murba*, the GRR vociferously opposed the Renville Agreement, but supported Hatta's government.[115] The majority of Tan Malaka's followers also opposed the People's Democratic Front (FDR), the coalition of left-wing groups headed by Amir Sjarifuddin, and the Indonesian Communist Party headed by Musso after his return in August 1948. Shortly after this, Sukarno announced that all the leaders of Tan Malaka's Struggle Union, who had been in jail since 1946, would finally be released.[116] Throughout the events leading up to the Madiun rebellion, Tan Malaka's followers opposed the actions of Musso and the PKI. On September 16, the very eve of the rebellion,[117] the government finally informed Tan Malaka that they had insufficient evidence to try him, and released him from jail after more than two years' imprisonment.[118] He and his party denied that the government was using them in its attempts to suppress the Communist Party.

After the government crushed the Madiun rebellion – and with it the Indonesian Communist Party – the several pro-Tan Malaka groups allied within the People's Revolutionary Movement (GRR) decided to join together in a political party, the Murba (or Proletarian) Party which was established in early November, 1948. Seven points in the new party's constitution closely resembled those of the Struggle Union (Persatuan Perjuangan) of 1946, though the language was framed to attract the widest possible following both from former followers of Amir Sjarifuddin and a broader nationalist spectrum.[119]

On being released from jail, Tan Malaka still steadfastly opposed the Hatta gov-

Abdullah glr. Sutan Bandaro Panjang (centre) with two colleagues in the 1930s
(Lindayanti)

ernment's policy of negotiation with the Dutch, and continued to stress the importance of achieving 100 percent independence. He left Yogyakarta in early November, 1948 for East Java to set up his headquarters in Kediri, where he formed a militia
prepared to oppose the anticipated Dutch attack.

In West Sumatra, Tan Malaka's influence had been kept alive throughout the
years of his imprisonment. The type of guerrilla warfare that the regional government was preparing was patterned on the concept of total struggle involving the
whole society, outlined in Tan Malaka's writings. The creator of the policy, Chatib
Suleiman, was strongly influenced by Tan Malaka's ideas, and his fellow member of
West Sumatra's Regional Defence Council (DPD), Abdullah, who was also a close
adviser to the Resident, remained one of Tan Malaka's most loyal followers. Abdullah had been the first person allowed to visit Tan Malaka in jail in 1948. According to
Tan Malaka's own account,

> ... the People of Sumatra finally demanded our freedom. A representa-
> tive of the Sumatran People, sent by the People there, was able to break
> through the 'iron curtain' of the Government and the Prosecutor's Of-
> fice in Yogyakarta and was finally able to meet with me in the Magelang
> jail at the end of June 1948. This Sumatra representative was the only
> one that the authorities had allowed to speak privately with me up till
> that time. From his thoughts and emotions, I was able to read the
> thoughts and emotions of the People of Sumatra. The thoughts and
> emotions of the Sumatra representative (who had also been my school-
> friend when I was young) further strengthened me mentally and physi-
> cally. This voice from Sumatra also reinforced the demands for my
> freedom that had already begun to resound around the prison in Java.[120]

On returning to West Sumatra, Abdullah was probably influential in encouraging the implementation of Tan Malaka's ideas, and he established the West Sumatra branch of the Murba party and became its head. In the months preceding the Dutch attack of December 19, 1948, West Sumatran military officers cooperated in preparing for the type of warfare advocated by Tan Malaka. The Intelligence section of the Banteng Division (Pema, Penghubungan Masyarakat), headed by Leon Salim, spread pamphlets to prepare the people to carry out a 'total People's Defence'. Banteng officers Ismael Lengah and Abdul Halim arranged for Tan Malaka's book, *Gerpolek*, to be reprinted and distributed to their soldiers because they believed the strategy outlined there could be used to good effect in the coming struggle against the Dutch.[121]

On December 21, two days after the Dutch attack, Tan Malaka made a speech condemning the negotiation policies that had led to the 'second colonial war'.[122] It is ironic that his stance should have provided the Republican mission to the United Nations with strong arguments for their policy of negotiation:

> Soedjatmoko, deputy leader of the republican mission to the United Nations, was reported as saying on 14 January 1949 that 'failure of a speedy settlement of the Indonesian problem would open possibilities for Trotzky to [*sic*] the Indonesian Tan Malaka "to exploit once again the fundamental longings of the Indonesian peoples for freedom"'.[123]

Certainly, Tan Malaka's broadcasts from East Java, calling for the continuation of the struggle for 100 percent independence, put heart into those Indonesians who were shocked and disappointed at the rapid collapse of the Republican government and its military and civilian leadership before the armed might of the Dutch. These broadcasts reached as far as West Sumatra, where Hamka, the son of Haji Rasul, recalled that as the Dutch forces were advancing on Padang Panjang, he and his friends gathered at a bookshop to listen to 'the voice that for so long we had not heard: Tan Malaka':

> He began by giving his political opinions. He first regretted the discussions that had been carried on from Sjahrir and Sjarifuddin to Hatta! He then explained that from now on, he was the one who would lead the people's struggle, that would know no discussions or negotiations before the Dutch had withdrawn completely from the land of Indonesia.[124]

It was this struggle that the people and government in West Sumatra were determined to pursue.

CHAPTER 6

Independence Achieved

West Sumatra under the Dutch Occupation

The Attack

In the early hours of Sunday, December 19, 1948, coincident with their assault on the Republican capital of Yogyakarta, the Dutch launched their second 'Police Action' in West Sumatra. They outflanked the principal Indonesian lines of defence in the Anai valley, between Kayutanam and Padang Panjang, by landing four Catalinas on Lake Singkarak at 6.30 on the morning of December 19. The east shore of the lake then became the staging area from which their advance columns proceeded north to Padang Panjang and Bukittinggi, and south to Solok over relatively flat terrain.[1]

Concurrently, Dutch troops crossed the ceasefire lines near Indarung in the east and Lubuk Alung in the north. The larger of their contingents advanced east via the Subang Pass, and, encountering little organized opposition, occupied the town of Solok by the afternoon of Monday, December 20. Also that afternoon, their northern column reached Kayutanam. Between there and Padang Panjang, however, it encountered strong resistance, as the major forces of the Republic were concentrated in the hills above the narrow, precipitous Anai valley.[2] Downed bridges and tree-trunk barricades impeded the Dutch advance up the valley, and their soldiers were further harassed by sniper fire from the retreating Republican troops.[3] Using American P51s, the Dutch strafed and bombed the Republican concentrations and retreating forces, and launched air attacks against Bukittinggi and other major towns in preparation for the later ground assaults against them.[4]

By the morning of Tuesday, December 21, the Dutch had flown in sufficient troops to the eastern shore of Lake Singkarak for motorized units to be dispatched north to occupy Padang Panjang, and a smaller contingent sent south to meet up with the force controlling Solok. Early on the morning of the 22nd, they left Padang Panjang for Bukittinggi, occupying the Republican capital within a couple of hours. It was a deserted town they took over, nearly all its population having evacuated into the surrounding countryside,[5] and most of its strategically important buildings in ruins.[6]

The Republic's Emergency Government (PDRI)

The Republican leaders in Java had anticipated the possibility of the Second Dutch attack and had made contingency plans. In November 1948, Vice President Hatta

Dutch soldiers cross a downed bridge on the approach to the Anai Valley

had brought Mr. Sjafruddin Prawiranegara – the Republic's minister of prosperity (*kemakmuran*) – with him to Bukittinggi, and when Hatta returned to Yogyakarta, Sjafruddin remained to prepare for the possible establishment of an emergency government in Sumatra – should the Republic's capital on Java fall to the Dutch. In mid-December, 1948, Indian President Jawaharlal Nehru sent a plane to carry Sukarno and Hatta out of Java. En route out of the country, the plane was to stop in Bukittinggi, where Hatta would remain to head the emergency government while President Sukarno went to New Delhi, and from there to New York to plead the Republic's case before the United Nations. Before Nehru's plane even reached Yogyakarta, however, it was grounded in Singapore because Dutch authorities refused it both transit permission over their territory and landing rights in Jakarta.[7] Sukarno and Hatta were, thus, both still in Yogyakarta on December 19 when the Dutch attacked and occupied the town.[8]

In Bukittinggi, on receiving news of the Dutch attack on Yogyakarta, Sjafruddin was initially unable to believe that the Republican government could have collapsed so rapidly or that most of the cabinet, including Sukarno and Hatta, had allowed themselves to be arrested. Thinking that the reports might merely be Dutch propaganda,[9] and uncertain of his legal authority, he delayed setting up an emergency government in Sumatra until after he, together with leaders of the Sumatran provincial government and the new Sumatra military commander Hidayat, had fled Bukittinggi and retreated to the small town of Halaban, about sixteen kilometres southeast of Payakumbuh. They arrived there on December 21, and were soon joined by West Sumatra Resident Rasjid.

In Halaban, they immediately began to work out their strategy for responding to the Dutch assault. Convinced by then that the Republican leaders in Java were indeed under Dutch arrest,[10] on December 22 Sjafruddin proclaimed establishment

The Arrest of the Republic's leaders, Yogyakarta, December 19, 1948
(from left: Sjahrir, a Dutch officer, Sukarno, Hatta)

of the Emergency Government of the Republic of Indonesia (PDRI – Pemerintah Darurat Republik Indonesia), with himself at its head, Sumatra governor Mr. Tengku Mohd. Hassan as deputy head, and Mr. Rasjid as minister of security.[11] The cabinet appointed military commanders for the army, navy, and air force and named their representative in India, Mr. Maramis, as minister of foreign affairs, instructing him to plead their cause in the United Nations.[12] They later appointed a commissariat in Java, headed by Dr. Sukiman, Kasimo, and Mr. Susanto – all ministers of Hatta's cabinet who had escaped capture by the Dutch when they attacked Yogyakarta.

From then on, the Emergency Government (PDRI) played a critical role in ensuring that the struggle against the Dutch was still headed by a legal government that was recognized by Republicans throughout the archipelago. It provided a national symbol and unifying factor for guerrilla forces scattered throughout Java and Sumatra, particularly because Sjafruddin's government was recognized by the Republic's military arm (headed by Commander-in-Chief Sudirman) as the legal successor to the Sukarno/Hatta government. The West Sumatran historian Mestika Zed has posed the question as to what might have happened to the Republic's struggle for independence had the PDRI not commanded the loyalty of Sudirman and his subordinate officers on Java and Sumatra. His response was that

> The guerrilla war on Java and Sumatra would have become a war 'with no summit above and no roots down' to the people. This never happened. The integrity of the Republican leadership remained sufficiently strong and the PDRI succeeded in supporting it. Panglima Sudirman for example, in his own words expressed his loyalty when he stated that the armed forces of the Republic were as one with the PDRI in their under-

standing, will, attitude and action. [As a result] the civilian and military leaders scattered in small units throughout the outlying areas could continue the Republic's guerrilla struggle in opposing Dutch hegemony.[13]

Before leaving Halaban, the Republican leadership split up. Sjafruddin and most of his ministers went south to set up a mobile government near Bidar Alam, on the border between West Sumatra and Jambi. Colonel Hidayat and the Sumatra military command went north, stopping initially for several weeks in Rao, in the northernmost part of West Sumatra, and then continuing on a 'long march' to Aceh, where Hidayat set up the headquarters for the Sumatra military command in territory never penetrated by the Dutch. Mr. Rasjid and other members of the West Sumatra government moved to Kototinggi, a village in the hills outside Suliki, north of Payakumbuh. Accompanied by Chatib Suleiman and Anwar St. Saidi, Mr. Rasjid arrived there on December 24 and set up the military government of West Sumatra in the office of the *nagari* council.[14]

Once the leaders dispersed, Sjafruddin and Rasjid used radio transmitters to maintain contact with each other and later to broadcast messages to the outside world. Very shortly after the Dutch attack, Indonesian monitors in Singapore were receiving daily broadcasts from Sjafruddin and his emergency government, which they were able to pass on to representatives in New Delhi and Geneva.[15] Subsequently, Sjafruddin also succeeded in establishing contact with Hidayat in Aceh, and with military leaders in Java.[16]

However, from the time the Dutch occupied Bukittinggi, internal communications within West Sumatra largely broke down, and for the first few weeks most villagers only knew what was happening in their immediate vicinity. During that period, they probably never even heard the instructions continually being broadcast by the West Sumatran government. Subjected to air attacks, harassed by fleeing soldiers, and watching the Dutch forces advance against little opposition, most villagers probably did not immediately commit themselves to the Republican side.[17]

After their first assault, the Dutch established outposts throughout upland West Sumatra so that they could lay claim to controlling the whole region, but the centre of their attention and the bulk of their forces were concentrated in the Minangkabau heartland – Tanah Datar, Agam, and Lima Puluh Kota, particularly along the main road connecting Padang Panjang and Bukittinggi and running to Payakumbuh. The Republican military government of West Sumatra, established north of there, was potentially vulnerable to these Dutch concentrations.

By January 10, 1949, Dutch forces had occupied all the major towns in the highlands, and that day they succeeded in advancing from Payakumbuh to raid the village of Kototinggi. They were, however, clearly unaware that the headquarters of West Sumatra's government was located there, and they did not find the large radio transmitter which was Mr. Rasjid's principal means of communicating with the outside world. Nor did they find any of the government leaders and their families, who fled the village to hide in the surrounding hills.[18] The following day these leaders sent out an instruction, probably written by Chatib Suleiman and Mr. Rasjid, which portrayed the disarray in the immediate aftermath of the Dutch attack:

Most of our government officials did not know where to go; the lower levels of the administration, unable yet to stand on their own feet, were like chickens that had lost their mother; some of the people's leaders were frantic; and the army itself, if we are willing to face up to it frankly, was in a state of chaos. The psychological effect of the Dutch attack was temporarily tremendous. Most of all, those villages that had not previously been subject to air attack were in a state of panic.

Optimistically, the instruction concluded: 'Time is the most effective medicine, and now gradually we are beginning to rebuild our government and army'.[19]

Situjuh Batur and the Death of Chatib Suleiman

As a first step toward re-establishing Republican control in the region, the West Sumatran leaders planned to hold a meeting of local civilian and military leaders to coordinate the region's security forces and discuss how to reorganize the administration and security of West Sumatra to accord with the drastically altered situation after the Dutch attack. In addition, participants in the meeting were to make plans for restoring people's confidence in their Republican leaders, a confidence which over the previous three weeks had been severely undermined by the humiliating defeats and losses suffered by the Republican side. They hoped to draw up plans for mounting actions against Dutch lines of communication and taking some dramatic step such as recapturing a Dutch-occupied town, possibly Payakumbuh. Even if Indonesian forces were only able to hold the town briefly, they believed that such an attack would demonstrate to the Indonesian people and the outside world that Dutch claims to victory were premature, and that the Republican government and military forces were still intact and effective.

The meeting was held at Situjuh Batur on the night of January 14. Lying in the foothills of Mount Sago, Situjuh Batur was only twelve kilometres from Payakumbuh. Up until then, however, the Dutch had been unable to penetrate the Situjuh area. To make it more inaccessible, Indonesian forces dug up the approach roads, destroyed all bridges, and blockaded the entry routes with stones and tree trunks, rendering them impassable to motor transport.[20]

A total of about eighty local leaders from all over the region came on foot to Situjuh Batur on January 14. The highest ranking civilian members of the West Sumatra government who attended were Chatib Suleiman and Abdullah, the former teacher at the Adabiah school in Padang and now head of the Murba party and a member of the military governor's staff. Other members of the governor's staff and of the civilian bureaucracy were also present, as was Colonel Dahlan Ibrahim, who now headed the West Sumatra military command, and Thalib, the military commander of the Payakumbuh region.

Instead of holding their talks in the main part of Situjuh Batur where there was no building large enough to hold all the participants, they congregated at the district military commander's house, located on the edge of the village at the bottom of a

Chatib Suleiman, 1947
(Sudarman Khatib)

deep and narrow valley. The meeting continued into the early morning hours of January 15, and after it ended, many local participants began their journeys home. Those who had travelled a considerable distance, however, stayed to sleep the night at the commander's house or one of the other buildings scattered around the bottom of the valley.

Before dawn, a Dutch contingent (made up mostly of Ambonese soldiers) advanced on Situjuh, subduing the local security forces and encircling the valley where the meeting's remaining participants were sleeping. Most of the sleeping Indonesians were unaware of the enemy presence, but one or two were roused and became suspicious when they saw figures standing along the ridge above the valley. They alerted their companions, several of whom began to make their way up the hillside or along the river valley. When the Dutch soldiers saw them escaping they began to fire. The shots woke the other sleepers, some of whom were able to flee up the hill-slopes or hide themselves along the banks of the stream which ran through the bottom of the valley. Others, however, including Chatib Suleiman, were trapped by the advancing forces and returned the Dutch fire. Armed only with light weapons they were soon shot down as the colonial troops swept down into the valley. Dutch forces killed sixty-nine Indonesians that night – most of them members of the local security militia or ordinary villagers, but among the dead were Chatib Suleiman, Bupati Arisun, and a number of regional military and civilian leaders.[21]

Thus, the meeting organized to consolidate resistance to the Dutch and plan methods for raising the people's morale was transformed, through the death of Chatib Suleiman, into one of the harshest single blows against the West Sumatra leadership. It also inaugurated a period of further schism and retribution within the region.

Suspicion arose that the Dutch had targeted Situjuh Batur for attack because a traitor within Republican ranks had betrayed plans for the meeting. This suspicion focused on a first lieutenant in the Singa Harau Battalion, Kamaluddin (alias Tambiluak). It seems unlikely that these accusations were true,[22] for after escaping from local villagers who had attacked him and cut off his ear, Kamaluddin refused to seek medical treatment from the Dutch in Payakumbuh because he said they would arrest him.[23] He chose instead to try to report to the head of the division, Dahlan Djambek, in Kamang. But as he made his way along the railroad track from Payakumbuh, Republican militias intercepted and killed him.[24] Soon afterwards all other members of his family were also murdered, and from then on, security measures against any Indonesian suspected of collaborating with the Dutch were often equally swift and bloody.

The Local Struggle

I have outlined in the previous chapter the disagreements between the local and national leaders with regard to the nature of the struggle that would be waged in West Sumatra. As a result of the preparations Hatta had made before the Second Dutch attack, the plans of the central government were in one sense realized: an emergency government was established in West Sumatra, under Sjafruddin Prawiranegara, which provided effective leadership for the Indonesian Republic even though the Dutch successfully occupied its capital of Yogyakarta and captured Sukarno, Hatta, and most of their colleagues. In the military field, too, Hatta had been successful in replacing the intransigent Sumatran commanders with Colonel Hidayat and other officers from West Java's Siliwangi Division, whose view of the character of the struggle accorded with the one espoused by him and Colonel Nasution.

However, after the Second Dutch attack, Mr. Sjafruddin and his Emergency Government retreated swiftly from Bukittinggi to establish their mobile headquarters on West Sumatra's very southern border with Jambi, so that they exercised little more day-to-day authority over the Minangkabau region than over the rest of Indonesia. Similarly, almost immediately after the Dutch had occupied Bukittinggi and other towns in West Sumatra, Colonel Hidayat and his military command left the area on their 'long march' to Aceh, where Hidayat established the military headquarters for the whole of Sumatra. So, the way in which West Sumatra's struggle was waged remained in the hands of the local authorities.

Military Collapse and Internal Conflict

Under the rationalization plans for the army in Central Sumatra, the Banteng Division was to have been consolidated into a 'mobile brigade' (commanded by Abdul Halim), and 'territorial forces' (under the command of Dahlan Ibrahim, who was concurrently the titular commander of the Banteng Division). Although these plans were officially in force as of mid-December, the subsequent Dutch attack prevented most of them from ever being implemented. Ismael Lengah's removal in early December and Hidayat's departure for Aceh immediately after the Dutch attack, left the army in West Sumatra without an acknowledged leader.

Dahlan Djambek (Ibu Naimah Jambek)

In the face of the Dutch onslaught, the fragile military structure in West Sumatra shattered along the lines of its members' strongest earlier allegiances, with many of the former militias reforming under their erstwhile commanders. On the northern front, most army units scattered, retreating to the coastal regions around Pariaman or to the mountainous areas west of Bukittinggi, particularly around Lake Maninjau. The confusion was then increased by some of these bands becoming undisciplined and running wild, plundering the countryside for their needs.

The disorder was further compounded by the uncertain delineation of authority in the upper reaches of the Banteng command, where several top officers vied for influence. Dahlan Ibrahim was the official territorial commander in West Sumatra, but he was restrained in asserting his authority over his subordinate officers. He directed his major attention to the supply problems of his soldiers and to their relationship with the political parties and the society as a whole. In asserting his authority, he was hampered by the fact that most of his immediate subordinates were of at least equal rank and experience. The armed forces in West Sumatra were divided into three subcommands[25] headed by Abdul Halim in the north, Ahmad Husein in the east, and Alwi Sutan Marajo in the south.[26] Abdul Halim, who was also head of the mobile forces, was of roughly equal status to Ibrahim and attempted to exert major authority over the division's troops.

But the Banteng Division's first commander, Dahlan Djambek, also remained in the Minangkabau region, after requesting permission not to accompany Hidayat to Aceh. Djambek's presence in Kamang, a few kilometers north of Dutch-occupied Bukittinggi, further confused the lines of authority. It also, however, boosted the morale of the local people, particularly in the area north of Bukittinggi, and to them he became a hero. He helped the fleeing dispirited soldiers to regroup and successfully prevented the Dutch from extending their control north of the Republic's former Sumatra capital.[27] His courageous exploits made him famous in and around

Bukittinggi among Dutch and Indonesians alike. But there was direct confrontation between him and Abdul Halim, who was overall commander of the northern section. The main area of tension between them was on the road through Palupuh to Bonjol where their lines of command overlapped. In a January 19 order, Colonel Halim specifically subordinated Djambek's Agam Battle Command to his own northern command, but it was difficult for him to enforce such an order against his former superior officer. This was even more true as Military Governor Rasjid had appointed Dahlan Djambek military regent (*bupati militer*) of Agam (the district embracing Bukittinggi), making him the only army officer in West Sumatra to hold an important administrative position.[28]

Internal Defence and Security

The confusion over the leadership of the armed forces re-enforced the power of the civilian authorities in West Sumatra. It is noteworthy that, in contrast to the situation in Java, where military officers held most key governmental positions, in Sumatra – with very few exceptions – each level of the administration was headed by a civilian, with an army officer usually serving as his subordinate. On January 2, Colonel Hidayat had issued an order dividing the island of Sumatra into five military territories and appointing a military governor to head each of these territories. But all five governors he appointed were actually civilians, most of them having headed their residencies prior to the Dutch attack.[29] In line with this, Mr. Rasjid became military governor of West Sumatra. Hidayat's reorganization orders, therefore, removed the power recently vested in the provincial governors, and placed it firmly back in the hands of the former Residents.

As previously noted, in the aftermath of the Second Dutch 'Police Action' many of the political parties' militias re-emerged. At the time, neither the military government nor the regular army commanders exerted any control over most of these bands, and Governor Rasjid enlisted the help of the political leaders to bolster his authority. The party leaders appealed to their militias, warning them that in their efforts to undermine Republican unity the Dutch would exploit any ideological rifts in Republican ranks. Thereafter, the military government attempted to incorporate most militia members within the network of the local security forces,[30] and after May 10, 1949, forbade the existence of any military force other than regular army soldiers and the village and district security militias.[31]

These local security forces were part of a system, enforced throughout the region after the Second Dutch attack, that had been conceived and created by Chatib Suleiman. At the beginning of 1947, immediately prior to his departure for Java to attend the National Committee meetings on the Linggajati agreements, Chatib Suleiman had overseen the establishment of its most important component, the Body for Guarding the Villages and Towns (BPNK – Badan Pengawal Nagari dan Kota). All young men between the ages of seventeen and thirty-five who were not soldiers or members of the political party militias were obliged to join this body, where they received military training from regular army officers. In the wake of the armed militias' incorporation into the regular army, and the rationalization moves within the army itself during 1948, the Body for Guarding the Villages and Towns provided a place where the young people discharged from the army could still play an active role in preparing the defence of their local areas.

These defence forces formed part of interlocking systems of local security and regional defence, based on the elected village (*nagari*) authorities. Replacement of the colonially supported *nagari* heads and village councils by popularly elected leaders and organizations through the *nagari* elections of mid-1946, undoubtedly played an important role in their success. The village defence militias created in 1947 provided a means of mobilizing and exerting pressure on the rural population to participate actively in the struggle.

The principal duties of the village security body, the BPNK, were to guard village security, prepare for a Dutch attack on the village, coordinate the young people to collect and transport supplies for the army at the front lines, and investigate internal and external enemies.[32] It did not merely act as a security force, for its components also formed the major arteries of the communications network throughout the region, with its members providing 'a small army of couriers' for the government and army.[33] At the boundaries of the *nagari* its guard posts passed officials from one district to the next throughout the region. They also acted as lookout posts, customs points, and places from which the Republic could impose economic blockades on the Dutch-occupied towns.

The local security bodies that played such an important role after the second Dutch 'Police Action' had ties at all levels to the civilian administrative structure and to the regular army. But though they worked in conjunction with the armed forces, nearly all of them were headed by civilians, and, like the 'military governor', these civilians were given military titles and also military ranks.[34] Most army officers were subordinate to the militarized civilian officials, who were thus in a position to act as a buffer between army units and villagers, particularly in raising food and supplies for the soldiers.

The BPNK was the lowest rung of a security organization also existing at the district and residency level. Mr. Rasjid headed the Regional Defence Council (DPD), which was the strongest arm of the West Sumatran government,[35] and the district defence units (Pasukan Mobil Teras) were drawn from the most able members of the village security bodies (BPNK).[36] Both the district and village security forces aimed to block Dutch efforts to penetrate the rural areas and dissuade villagers who felt inclined to shift their allegiance to the Dutch. The security organizations were also an important component in the residency's attempts to raise taxes from virtually all of the people in the region in order to support the war effort.[37]

From 1947, the principal method by which the residency government raised funds internally both for the army and the civil administration was through a 10 percent war tax – the *iuran perang* 10%, which in 1946 was initially imposed on rice. Effective imposition of such a tax system demanded a supply network down to the village level. Many of the residency organizations involved in raising the taxes were built on the foundations of the support organizations for the Giyu gun established during the Japanese occupation. Prominent among them were the women's associations, which supplied and cared for the soldiers and their families, acted as intermediaries in collecting and distributing food to the armed forces, provided nursing care in army and civilian hospitals, and organized community kitchens.[38]

Immediately after the retreat from Bukittinggi in December 1948, the military government focused its attention on economic planning for the months ahead, particularly improving the collection of the 10 percent war tax that had been technically in force over the past two years. The tax was universally applied to all forms of wealth and income, and was preferably to be collected in kind, though if this were not possible it could be in cash. The Village Security Organizations (MPRN – Markas Pertahanan Rakyat Nagari), in conjunction with leading members of the village, were charged with raising the taxes, which were used to run the government and supply the needs of the government militias and armed forces.[39]

These networks ensured that the whole society participated in the struggle. They contributed to a situation where, having occupied most of the towns in West Sumatra, the Dutch came up against a brick wall. Their communications routes between the towns they had occupied remained tenuous, and within as well as outside the urban areas they continued to encounter small-scale guerrilla opposition. Despite the ease of their advance and their few casualties, they were now almost totally unable to consolidate their control of the occupied areas, being refused cooperation not only in the villages but also in the towns. As the Dutch Resident L.B. van Straten lamented:

> The struggle, stretching from the front to the kampung is a true reflection of the ideas of Tan Malaka, developed in his brochure 'Sang Guerilla dan Gerpolek' where he sought to emphasize the Murba – the common people.... [Various examples he cites] show the truth of a statement that was made in a warung [coffee stall] in Padang: 'The Netherlands army is only strong enough to hold the occupied towns; outside of these the TNI, BPNK and guerrillas rule.'[40]

Revolutionary Trade

With the Dutch controlling all major towns and ports of entry in Sumatra, Rasjid and his government faced a formidable economic challenge. To meet it they built on policies that had been formulated to cope with the economic difficulties they had already encountered during the years following the Japanese occupation. At no time since 1945 had the residency governments in Sumatra been able to rely on a stable currency to support their economies. Japanese banknotes were still in circulation during the first two years of independence, but the Allied forces introduced a new Dutch currency which they used to pay for their supplies and in all their other monetary transactions.[41] Fearing that this colonial currency would be used to undermine Republican authority, West Sumatra's government had declared this NICA (Netherlands Indies Civil Administration) money invalid, and recognized Japanese banknotes as the only legal tender in Republican areas until April 10, 1947,[42] when the

Sumatran provincial government in Pematang Siantar began printing Sumatran currency, ORIPS (Oeang Republik Indonesia Propinsi Sumatera).[43] The government of West Sumatra, too, soon began printing its own banknotes, as did several other residencies.[44] The lack of centralized control over the currency, with each Resident in Sumatra printing his own money, led to increasing inflation, and a drastic depreciation in the value of the Sumatran currency by November 1948.

As they were unable to rely on the currency, the local population turned to a system of barter within and between neighbouring villages, and to trade (or smuggling) with the Dutch-occupied areas, as well as with other pro-Republican parts of the island. For the residency government, the most important trading activities were those carried on with Singapore and Malaya.[45] Even during the Japanese occupation, this trade had never been totally cut off. As during the prewar period, Anwar St. Saidi was a major actor in this commerce. Through Chinese and Minangkabau contacts in Singapore, he had been able to arrange to have three shipments of weapons imported into West Sumatra during 1944/45.[46] Anwar stored the weapons in his own house and those of friends in Bukittinggi and Sungai Puar,[47] and handed them over to Ismael Lengah and other Banteng officers in the weeks after the declaration of independence.[48]

This trade in arms continued in the early years of the revolution. In Singapore, agents of the Republic sold Sumatra's exports for Straits dollars, and with these bought weapons from the British, as well as other items such as oil, tyres, sugar, clothing, and mosquito nets. Officially, the British were unaware that arms from Singapore were being supplied to Republican forces in Sumatra. Similarly, they never acknowledged that their supplies of confiscated Japanese weapons stored on Kudap island in the Riau archipelago were also finding their way to the Republic's soldiers.[49]

The Republican authorities in Sumatra were able to maintain a substantial volume of trade across the Malacca Strait, despite the Dutch imposition of a trading blockade on the Republic, which virtually cut Java off from Malaya and Singapore. Until December 1948, there were two major trading routes from West Sumatra to the Malay peninsula, the first of which ran from Pekanbaru via Tanjung Pinang and the Riau archipelago to Singapore, and the other north from Pariaman around the coast of Aceh to Singapore.

The first of these routes had been used by political activists and traders during the 1920s and 1930s, and since the closing months of the Japanese occupation some of the large Minangkabau traders had used it to smuggle weapons into Republican West Sumatra.[50] Most imports were brought to Sumatra by small boats following this route. Despite the traditional competition between Minangkabau and Chinese traders, this east-coast trading network throughout the independence struggle was heavily dependent on family and business connections between the Chinese merchants in West Sumatra and their counterparts in Pekanbaru and the East Sumatran port towns, as well as in Singapore and the Malay peninsula. Although in terms of volume, West Sumatran products formed an insignificant portion of the total Sumatran trade with the peninsula, Resident Rasjid estimated that in 1948 the region exported about one million Straits dollars' worth of goods and products to Singapore, and profits from these exports provided the residency with a critical source of foreign currency. During at least the early years of independence, the largest portion of West Sumatra's trade across the Malacca Strait was in the hands of the supply section of the army's Division 9 (Banteng Division), which operated from Bukittinggi and channelled importation of arms and other military supplies from Riau and Singapore via a branch office in Pekanbaru.[51]

When Vice President Mohammad Hatta came to Sumatra in June 1947, he suspected that the army's trade with Singapore was being conducted as much for the personal profit of its operators as for the benefit of the Republic. In addition, he believed that the Chinese agents were much more adept in their business dealings and were often cheating the army officers. So, in an effort to centralize Sumatra's export and import trade he helped establish the Central Trading Corporation (CTC), which eventually became the largest and most effective enterprise carrying out trade between the Republican-controlled territories in Sumatra and the Malay peninsula.[52] There were, in addition, at least two local trading organizations – the relatively small Minangkabau Trading Company and the Sumatra Banking and Trading Corporation, established in early 1947 – which depended heavily on the export of copra.[53]

Other parts of Sumatra also provided Bukittinggi with critically needed supplies. A large portion of the weapons and ammunition needed for its armed forces came from Aceh, and, until the Dutch overran the oil fields in mid-1947, the residency was able to obtain gasoline and petroleum from Jambi in exchange for rice. Trade with the Dutch-occupied cities became of greater importance after the second Dutch attack, which administered a great shock to the Republic's trading network with the Malay peninsula. With Dutch forces occupying nearly all the significant ports of entry for goods into Republican Sumatra, much of the interior was cut off from overseas trade. Because Pariaman, Painan, and virtually all of its other western ports were now under Dutch control, West Sumatra's government had to rely completely on the island's eastern outlets, routing all the region's trade via the coast of Riau. But there, too, most of the ports were now controlled by the Dutch.

After the poor harvests during the Japanese occupation, rice yields had improved rapidly after 1946, eventually providing a sufficient surplus for rice to be used as one of West Sumatra's most important trading commodities with the surrounding areas of Sumatra. Its other major exports to these neighbouring regions included quinine, copra, cloves, resin, rattan, coffee, rubber, and gold. Several of these items were also used in trading across the Malacca Strait.

In the closing years of the struggle, however, by far the most important trading commodity was opium. In early 1948, the Republican government in Yogyakarta transferred a few tons of opium to the Sumatra government, which stored it in the Chinese section of Bukittinggi under the custody of the director of the State Bank, Mr. A. Karim.[54] Part of this supply was smuggled to Singapore where profits from its sale were used to buy weapons and clothing, as well as to support Indonesian pilots studying in India and to pay for spare parts for the Indonesian air force.[55] At the time of the Second Dutch attack, about thirty-two cases of opium remained, which the Republican government carried with them as they retreated from Bukittinggi. The

Sumatra military command took control of about half of this (fifteen cases) and the Military Governor of West Sumatra the rest (seventeen cases).[56] Small in bulk and high in value,[57] the 'black gold' could be relatively easily smuggled out of Indonesia, as well as into and out of the Dutch-occupied towns where it became an item of exchange primarily with the Chinese communities, who cooperated with the Republicans by providing them with cloth and weapons in exchange for the opium.

Immediately after the Dutch advance at the end of 1948, the Republic's Emergency Government, headed by Sjafruddin Prawiranegara, formed a supply section which was given control over trade from West Sumatra and Riau to the Malay peninsula.[58] In early 1949, the Chinese network of trade with the peninsula suffered from the same impediments as did that of the Indonesians, for not only did the Dutch now control virtually all of the eastern ports, but their patrols used them as bases for policing the major river mouths which debouched into the Malacca Strait. However, in the Dutch-occupied towns there was already a large stockpile of cloth, weapons, and ammunition in the hands of local Chinese that had been brought into Sumatra over the preceding months, and the Republicans were able to use their supply of opium to ensure that these necessities found their way to them rather than to the Dutch.[59]

From the days immediately following the Second Dutch attack, both Sumatra Commander Hidayat and the Emergency Government stressed that the Republican authorities should use their opium supply principally to obtain food and clothing rather than weapons and ammunition, in the ratio of about three or four to one.[60] For some members of the army (TNI) this regulation became an added irritant to the many restrictions ensuring their subordination to civilian authority. Military commanders felt they were more capable than the civilians of guarding the opium stores, and that they, rather than Governor Rasjid, should have control over its exchange for both weapons and food. They resented the degree to which they were dependent on the civilian authorities even for their soldiers' food supplies.

During 1949, the bulk of the Republican trade was concentrated in northern Riau where Dutch control was more sporadic than in the areas further south. Supplies arriving at the Emergency Government's (PDRI) central trading headquarters at Rantau Kampar and further inland at Pasir Pengaraian were divided equally between West Sumatra, Riau, and southern Tapanuli. From about March of that year, the supply section of the PDRI felt that it was fulfilling most of the requirements of northern Riau, but the hazardous conditions along the land route to West Sumatra prevented it from meeting all the needs of that region. The fact that it took at least five weeks to transport any quantity of goods from the supply centre at Rantau Kampar to the governor's headquarters at Kototinggi meant that, after the second Dutch 'Police Action', the West Sumatran government and army could not rely on external sources for urgently needed supplies, even though they controlled major trading capital. As a result, an even larger portion of the burden of financing the struggle came to rest on the shoulders of the local people than had been the case in the earlier years of the revolution.

Failure of Dutch Plans for a Minangkabau State

In the aftermath of their invasion of upland West Sumatra, the Dutch mounted a major effort, particularly in the towns they occupied, to win support for a Minangkabau state which would become a component of the Dutch-sponsored Federal Consultative Assembly (BFO – Bijeenkomst voor Federaal Overleg).[61] The Dutch and the Republicans competed openly for the allegiance of West Sumatra's urban population, and within the Dutch-occupied towns a number of associations grew up, ranging across the spectrum from the small, openly pro-Dutch movements for a Special Region of West Sumatra (DISBA, Daerah Istimewa Sumatera Barat)[62] to outspoken groups of Republican adherents who openly opposed the Dutch authorities.

This competition in the towns differed from the struggle in the countryside in that it took place in areas actually administered by the Dutch, and was conducted by both sides more through persuasion than through physical violence. It tested earlier colonial perceptions of the character of West Sumatran society and the type of authority to which its people were most likely to pay allegiance. The basic argument of the Dutch was that the people would only accept leaders whose authority rested on traditional *adat* qualifications, and therefore that the elected *nagari* heads, if they were not also *penghulu* (clan leaders), would not command the people's loyalty.[63] They ignored the fact that colonial manipulation of the *adat* system had fatally undermined the authority of so many of the *penghulu* who had headed the *nagari* in the colonial administration and had come to be regarded as instruments of the colonial power and not as representatives of the villagers.[64]

The Dutch also contended that Java dominated the Republic and that the Minangkabau people as a whole resented that dominance. They believed that even moderate Republicans saw that geographic and economic ties with other parts of Sumatra were stronger than 'the ideological and political ties with distant Java'.[65] Thus, in the Dutch view, the most welcome as well as the most viable solution for West Sumatra was the establishment of a Sumatran federation in which a Minangkabau autonomous territory could play a large role, and where the tie with Java would be more symbolic than real.[66]

In combatting the Dutch-supported movements for a Minangkabau Special Region, there was an active underground Republican 'shadow government' within the towns, and a network of spies, suppliers, and messengers connecting it with the Republican administration and army in the surrounding countryside. Prior to the second 'Police Action', this underground network had existed even in the Dutch-controlled areas of Padang and its hinterland.[67] It became much more extensive after December 1948, with a shadow administration of officials who had sworn allegiance to the Republican side existing in nearly all of the Dutch-controlled areas. This Republican underground apparatus was paralleled by an openly pro-Republican political movement within the towns, whose leaders acted as mouthpieces for Republican positions and presented counter-arguments to those of the Dutch. Their success in these efforts was attested to by the Dutch Resident, who wrote in June 1949:

We can't close our eyes to the fact that in Bukittinggi there still exists a strongly Republican-inclined nucleus, a nucleus that has the courage of its convictions and dares to express them, a quality which the wavering advocates of a loosening of political ties with [the former Republican government in] Jogja lack.[68]

These urban Republican networks impeded Dutch consolidation of their control even within the larger towns where most of their forces were concentrated. The bulk of the urban population, although often in Dutch employment, essentially tried to lead their own lives and meet their families' needs without irreparably committing themselves to the colonial power. Indeed, most seem to have continued to give at least token material assistance to the Republican forces and pay taxes to its government.[69]

Effective functioning of the Republic's administrative, security, and economic apparatus under the Dutch occupation in both town and countryside sprang as much from the character of West Sumatran society and geography as from the foresight of the government's earlier preparations in anticipation of the attack. Traditional trading routes had been reestablished, with small boats plying the waters between small east-coast ports and Singapore, successfully evading Dutch efforts at a blockade.[70] And the fact that Minangkabau government traditionally rested on the basis of autonomous villages (*nagari*), rather than being dependent upon an administrative hierarchy, meant that the shock and disarray of the early weeks of the attack did not cripple the functioning of the Republican administration for long. So long as the military government in Kototinggi was able to issue general guidelines, the method of their implementation could effectively be left to the local authorities. Even after adequate internal communications systems were re-established, the effective working bodies remained at the *nagari* level, with higher officials serving only as supervisory agents and courts of appeal for local disputes.[71]

End of the Armed Struggle

Dutch frustration at Republican resilience in West Sumatra was replicated in many other parts of Indonesia, and the inability of the Netherlands forces to consolidate their control over the regions they had overrun in their military advance forced them to consider other options. Pressed by the United Nations, they reluctantly took the first steps toward a compromise with Republican leaders. But they made no effort to contact the Republic's Emergency Government headed by Sjafruddin Prawiranegara in Sumatra, or its military commander-in-chief General Sudirman in Java. Instead, contacts were made with the imprisoned Sukarno/Hatta leadership. In April 1949, discussions began between a delegation headed by Dr. J.H. van Royen and one headed by Mr. Mohamad Roem, a former interior minister of the Republic who had been among those arrested by the Dutch when they occupied Yogyakarta, and who since then had been detained with Sukarno, Hatta, and other Republican leaders on the island of Bangka off Sumatra's southeast coast.

As a result of the Roem-van Royen discussions, the Dutch agreed on June 22 that

Sjafruddin Prawiranegara (centre), 1948, at Kaliurang
(George Kahin at right)

the Republican leadership should be allowed to return to Yogyakarta. It was also agreed that a Round Table conference would be held in which Republican representatives, together with representatives of the Dutch-supported Federal Consultative Assembly (BFO), would negotiate with the Dutch for a transfer of sovereignty from the Dutch to the Indonesians.

The Emergency Government, headed by Sjafruddin Prawiranegara, and the armed forces leadership, headed by Sudirman, reacted angrily to the Roem-van Royen discussions and agreements. They believed that the Emergency Government (PDRI), as the lawful government of the Republic, was the body that should conduct negotiations with the Netherlands, and that the imprisoned Republican leaders were not qualified to represent the Indonesian side, as they were no longer the legal government and had no basis on which to assess the relative strength of Republican and Dutch forces on the battlefield.[72] Both civilian and military leaders were deeply suspicious of Dutch intentions, believing that the Dutch were only willing to negotiate when they were hard-pressed on the battlefield, and that as soon as they had improved their military position they would again take up arms. These leaders cited the making and breaking of the Linggajati and Renville agreements as proving their stand.[73]

Ultimately, Sjafruddin and his government only agreed to go along with the outcome of the Roem-Van Royen discussions after Hatta himself met with Sumatra commander Colonel Hidayat in Aceh, and after a Republican delegation headed by Masjumi leader Mohammad Natsir[74] came to Central Sumatra to meet with Sjafruddin and his colleagues. (An indication of the imprisoned leaders' ignorance of the situation on the ground was that Hatta had gone to Aceh to meet with Sjafruddin, believing the Emergency Government must have its headquarters there because, according to the Dutch, that was the only region of Sumatra outside their control.)

Hearing broadcast reports of the impending visit, Sjafruddin and his associates trekked north on foot from their hideout on the Jambi border. When Natsir and his delegation arrived in Bukittinggi, they received radio instructions from the PDRI to proceed to Payakumbuh, and under cover of a very uneasy local ceasefire made their way north out of the Dutch-controlled town. The group's United Nations guards left them as they entered Republican territory 'because they were in danger of being killed because they had white skin like the Dutch'. Messengers from the PDRI met the group and brought them to the small village of Dangung-dangung where Sjafruddin, Rasjid, and their colleagues were waiting. As they entered Dangung-dangung, radios were broadcasting reports of Sukarno and Hatta's arrival in Yogyakarta. A journalist who accompanied Natsir's group depicted the scene before them:

> The first building we saw in this Republican region of Dangung-
> dangung was the SMP school house and beside it the elementary school.
> Many of the people were already awaiting our arrival; school children (it
> is the Fasting holiday at the moment) were everywhere. The healthy cas-
> sava fields, the rice already harvested [in the rice barns], chickens and
> goats in the yards and information officials installing radio antennae so
> that the people can listen to the broadcast from Jogja of President
> Sukarno's arrival in the Republican capital. In contrast with the atmos-
> phere in Payakumbuh, only 15 kms to the south, where the town was de-
> serted, here in the village of Dangung-dangung crowds of people were
> listening to Republican broadcasts from Jogja. Perhaps the people of
> Payakumbuh had evacuated the town, but we can honestly say that the
> Dangung-dangung market was far more crowded than the town.[75]

Despite their misgivings, Sjafruddin and his colleagues, like their military counter-parts in Java, realized they had no choice but to accept the outcome of the Roem-van Royen talks. They recognized the importance of Sukarno and Hatta both to the image of the Republic abroad and to the maintenance of unity within Republican ranks. So Sjafruddin agreed to return to Java with Natsir and his delegation. Addressing a crowd of hundreds that gathered to hear him, Sjafruddin told them that rather than create division over the issue 'it was much better to accept an agreement which was not as favourable as we would like and remain united'. Sjafruddin left West Sumatra with the Natsir delegation, and returned his mandate to President Sukarno in Yogyakarta on July 13.[76]

Sukarno proclaimed a ceasefire to go into effect on August 17, 1949, and in West Sumatra talks began almost immediately between Republican and Dutch officers to arrange for the departure of Dutch troops and their replacement by Republican military and security forces. As the Republican underground administration in the towns came to the surface, the officials who had served in Dutch-occupied areas either made their peace with the Republicans or else left the region. Initially uncertain over their fate, these officials were relieved when Sjafruddin returned to Sumatra in early November and gave an undertaking that the Republic would allow no reprisals against administrators who had cooperated with the Dutch.[77]

After protracted negotiations, the Dutch handed over the civilian administration of most of the upland towns of West Sumatra to Republican officials in early December 1949,[78] and shortly afterward the Resident of Padang – the only remaining 'special region' in West Sumatra – surrendered his authority to the Governor of Central Sumatra.

Legacy of the Revolution

The departure of the Dutch brought to an end the anticolonial movement that had done much to define the political landscape in West Sumatra since the end of World War I. Throughout the 1920s and 1930s the colonial authorities had faced a turbulent and uneasy situation in the region. In bolstering their position, they had relied on a traditional system of local administration that they had manipulated and distorted to serve their own ends, and by so doing had undermined in the eyes of their compatriots the traditional leaders who had cooperated with the colonial authority. The revolutionary years had proved the Dutch wrong in believing that these traditional leaders were their natural allies and that the traditional system of governance was as rigid as they had tried to make it. Religious forces, political parties, and an electoral system had been embraced by the Minangkabau people as the most potent means of opposing a continuance of colonial rule. Similarly, the Dutch had been proven wrong in believing that local Minangkabau nationalism could be used to combat Indonesian nationalism, and that anti-Javanese sentiments could be used to undermine loyalty to the Republic of Indonesia. Their failure was in large part due to the fact that during the prewar period a nationalism embracing the whole of the archipelago had sunk deep roots in Minangkabau society.

Many of the group that dominated events in West Sumatra from the middle of 1946 onward were leaders of the 1930s who had survived the Dutch repression. Among them, too, were a few of the older activists from the 1920s who had been interned in Digul or jailed elsewhere in Indonesia, and a new group of young men who had been trained in the Japanese volunteer army. But the years of Dutch repression and reprisal against their Indonesian opponents had also exacted a heavy toll on many of those who had stood up against them in the prewar period.

It is probably useful here to say a word or two about the activities during the revolutionary years of some of the local leaders who had actively opposed Dutch rule in the 1920s and 1930s.

Of the Permi leaders who had been exiled to Digul in 1934, only Iljas Jacub played an important political role in Republican West Sumatra after independence. The Dutch did all they could to prevent his return, but when he finally succeeded in reaching West Sumatra in late 1946[79] he was appointed to head the Masjumi party and provided it with wise and moderate leadership, cooperating with Resident Rasjid and the other Socialist leaders who headed the regional government. He continued to play an important part in local politics in the early 1950s.

The roles played by Muchtar Luthfi and Djalaluddin Thaib were much more equivocal. After being evacuated to Australia in 1942, both these Permi leaders had cooperated with the Dutch, and returned to Indonesia with the Dutch forces. Muchtar Luthfi went to Makassar (Ujung Pandang) rather than returning to West Sumatra. There he was selected as a member of the representative body in the Dutch-sponsored State of East Indonesia (NIT). Despite this collaboration, he openly advocated Indonesian independence from the Dutch, and in the East Indonesia Parliament he was outspoken in arguing on behalf of the people of South Sulawesi. After the transfer of sovereignty, he headed the Masjumi party in Makassar. In August 1950, at the time of the exodus to the Netherlands of the Dutch-sponsored forces of the KNIL (Koninklijke Nederlandsche Indische Leger – Royal Netherlands Indies Army), one of these soldiers shot and killed Muchtar Luthfi, apparently because he had criticized the KNIL for their cruelty against the people of the region.[80]

After the Digul inmates were transferred to Australia in 1942, Djalaluddin Thaib worked for the Dutch as a public-relations officer and was given the rank of major. He returned to West Sumatra with the Dutch forces, but Republican troops kidnapped him from the Padang hotel where the Dutch had lodged him. Ismael Lengah and his military colleagues detained him in Batu Sangkar until he agreed to transfer his allegiance and work with the Republic. After his release, however, he lived in obscurity and played no further active political role.[81]

The only leader of the first generation of reformist Muslim leaders (the *Kaum Muda*) who was still alive in 1945 was Syekh Djamil Djambek.[82] During the Japanese occupation, Djambek had worked with Mohammad Sjafei and Chatib Suleiman in the Japanese-sponsored regional representative bodies. After the independence declaration he continued to act as an important Muslim leader until his death in December 1947, at the age of eighty-seven.

During the revolution, the sons of both Haji Rasul and Syekh Djambek played important leadership roles in West Sumatra. Haji Rasul's son, the famous Islamic scholar and author Hamka, had spent the years of the occupation in Medan, where he openly collaborated with the Japanese. At the end of their occupation, fearing retribution, he fled to West Sumatra, where he was given asylum.[83] He cooperated closely with the Republican leaders there, providing them with a figure of sufficient religious standing in his home region to mediate between the Socialist and religious groups.[84] For example, he was defence counsel in the trial of Saalah J. Sutan Mangkuto and Dt. Radjo Mangkuto, the leaders of the March 3, 1947 revolt.[85] Three of Syekh Djambek's sons joined the Republican army,[86] but Dahlan Djambek emerged as the most important when he became the first commander of the Banteng Division and one of the most outstanding military leaders in West Sumatra.

The Communist leaders of the early 1920s, H. Dt. Batuah and Natar Zainuddin, both returned to Sumatra. Natar Zainuddin had been released from Digul in 1937

Captain Leon Salim with his
children (1950)
(Leon Salim)

and went first to Aceh. During the Japanese occupation, he established contacts with the Japanese intelligence, but also formed an underground network, the 'Anti-Fascist Movement'. After the independence proclamation, Zainuddin was prominent in the 'extreme' wing of Communist party in East Sumatra.[87] During 1949 he worked with the radical militias operating on the the the Tapanuli – West Sumatra border. Dt. Batuah, on the other hand, came home to West Sumatra, where he was appointed titular head of the Communist Party (PKI), a position he retained until his death in 1948.[88]

Few of Tan Malaka's lieutenants and leaders of his Pari party returned to West Sumatra: Djamaluddin Ibrahim had died in Dutch detention before the Japanese invasion; Djamaluddin Tamin returned to Java from his Digul exile, was imprisoned with Tan Malaka's followers and later led the new Murba party when it was established in 1948; and Kandur was taken from Digul to Australia with the Dutch, but refused to work with them. (He was repatriated in early 1947, but then went to Bangkok[89] before returning to Indonesia to become a staff-member in Hatta's office.) However, as we have seen, Abdullah St. Bandaro Panjang, one of Tan Malaka's strongest supporters (his former schoolmate and teacher at Padang's Adabiah school), played a pivotal role in the top reaches of West Sumatra's political and economic leadership. He was part of the small group around Resident Rasjid, who together with Chatib Suleiman directed the course of the struggle against the Dutch. Anwar St. Saidi, the entrepreneur and brother of Djamaluddin Ibrahim, was a follower of Sjahrir and Hatta as well as Tan Malaka, and he helped guide economic policy in West Sumatra and obtain and store weapons for the struggle against the Dutch.

Throughout the revolution, Leon Salim played an important role in heading military intelligence activities in the region and on the staff of Governor Rasjid.[90] He remained a friend and loyal ally of Chatib Suleiman, although their differing responsibilities in the military and civilian spheres meant that their relationship was not so close as in the colonial period. A rift also developed between them over the strategy to be employed against the Dutch. During November and December 1948, Salim tried to goad the people and their leadership to prepare for war, and he openly opposed the policies of Hatta and Hidayat, who still thought it was possible to achieve a negotiated settlement with the Dutch. When the Dutch launched their second 'Police Action' on December 19, Salim felt he had been vindicated. Frustrated by the Republic's lack of preparedness, he also lost patience with Chatib Suleiman's continuing emphasis on attempting to unite all factions within the region in support of the Republic, rather than preparing the people for military struggle. After he fled Bukittinggi on the night of December 21, just before the invading forces took over the town, Leon Salim discovered that his friend was still holding discussions with groups likely to side with the colonial power, while the Republic's military units were still unready to block the Dutch advance. He described what happened when he reached Payakumbuh:

> I went directly to the house of the battalion commander. I went there and saw the group there. It was a large meeting, with Chinese, Indians, ordinary people, Islamic leaders, soldiers, and Chatib Suleiman. Perhaps he saw me coming, my closest friend. He came forward and welcomed me, put his arm around my shoulder. I asked where [Governor] Rasjid was.
> 'He's gone to Alang Lawas [near Halaban].'
> 'Why?'
> 'He's meeting with Sjafruddin. There's a meeting of the PDRI [Emergency Government] there.'
> 'Will he be returning soon? Because tomorrow the Dutch will be here!' The Dutch were already at Bukittinggi and the next morning they must reach Payakumbuh. This was what I thought. I asked if Rasjid would soon return, and he replied that he would.
> 'What are these people doing?' I asked. I was unhappy to see that meeting; seeing it, I thought that my leaders were indeed Minang people; even in a situation like this they still had to spend their time in discussions.

Seeing his friend's agitation, Chatib Suleiman drew him into an adjoining room, illuminated only by the moonlight coming through the window. There Salim upbraided him:

> 'You as leaders are mad, mad talking with these colonial dogs.... Perhaps tomorrow by *subuh* [morning prayer], the Dutch will enter here; these people will welcome them, these men you are talking with. We must just choose whether it is they who live or we.'

Leon Salim then stormed out of the room and made his way on foot back toward Bukittinggi. The two men never met again and Salim received news less than a month later that his friend had been killed at Situjuh.[91]

Chatib Suleiman's death and the departure of Mr. Mohd. Rasjid from West Sumatra in mid-September 1949,[92] left the region without the pragmatic influences that had been able to bridge the rifts within the society during the later years of colonial rule, and throughout the revolution. In praising Chatib Suleiman's role, Hamka recalled his ability to reach out to the Masjumi, and also the effectiveness of his cooperation with Mr. Rasjid:

> Chatib Suleiman was an honest man. It is a great pity that in West Sumatra my group had no one as honest as Chatib Suleiman. It is a great pity that he was not Masjumi!
> If one considers his spirit, there was gathered love for his homeland, socialist knowledge, Islamic belief, and a 'Minang' spirit. Obedient to those above, loyal to his friends and stubborn!
> He was rich with theories. He was adept at conceiving programmes and schemes. Only there had to be someone else who implemented them. It is said that many of Mr. St. Mohd. Rasjid's programmes emerged from the brain of Chatib Suleiman. And he was willing to forego the credit so long as they were carried out.[93]

No recognized leaders remained who could mediate both among the contending internal forces and between them and the centre. During the months marking the transition to Republican rule, it was not only Mr. Rasjid who responded to the shift of power by departing for the Javanese capital, but also Army Commander Dahlan Djambek and the head of the Communist Party, Bachtaruddin, who both soon left for Jakarta, along with many of the other respected leaders who had guided the revolutionary struggle.[94]

Many Minangkabau remained prominent in the central political leadership of independent Indonesia, out-numbering all other ethnic groups, with the exception of the Javanese. These national leaders, however, no longer included Tan Malaka, who after fleeing Kediri when the Dutch occupied the town on December 25, 1948, was killed in early 1949, probably on the orders of the Republican commander of East Java, Sungkono.[95] Rumours of his exploits continued to permeate West Sumatra for months and years, and for a long time, many refused to believe he had been killed. But his influence on attitudes and events in the region gradually waned. From then on the national leader who had by far the greatest impact on the course of West Sumatra's history was Vice President Hatta. His influence had already been shaping events in both the civilian and military field since his sojourn in Bukittinggi during 1947. After he returned to Java in early 1948, his orders had conditioned the character of the armed forces in West Sumatra which faced the second Dutch 'Police Action' of December 19, 1948, when Dutch forces penetrated the highland regions of West Sumatra and occupied all its major towns. And although the defence against the Dutch occupation mounted by West Sumatra's civilian and military leaders in 1949 accorded more with local perceptions of how to wage the struggle and with those of Tan Malaka, rather than with those of Hatta and Nasution, the centre's priorities reasserted themselves after the Dutch government transferred sovereignty to the Republic at the end of 1949.

Despite disturbing auguries in the military and civilian fields that the independent Indonesia emerging from the struggle was likely to have little in common with the one they had previously envisaged,[96] most West Sumatrans entered the new age self-confident and relieved after eight years of occupation and revolution. During the closing months of 1949, as they watched the Dutch armed forces and civil administration withdrawing from the territories they had occupied, and being replaced by civilian and military officials of the Republic, the Minangkabau people believed that their major goals had been achieved. Throughout the revolution they had demonstrated their loyalty to the Indonesian Republic and they trusted the national leadership with its large Minangkabau component to act in their region's best interests. Their attitude was portrayed well by the Dutch Resident of West Sumatra after the ceasefire between the Dutch and Indonesians:

> ... the ideals for which the Republic has stood are alive in the hearts of the bulk of the Minangkabau – especially in the uplands. People don't forget that the really big figures in Djokja [Yogyakarta], such as Hatta, Soetan Sjahrir and Hadji Agoes Salim are Minangs, and that the Djokja government can with almost as much justice be called a Minangkabau government.[97]

Region versus Capital

CHAPTER 7

Disillusionment

The hope and satisfaction felt in West Sumatra in August 1949, at the time of the ceasefire with the Dutch, dissipated over the following eighteen months. By January 1951, these feelings had been replaced by the seeds of disillusionment and resentment against the Republican government in Java that would grow rapidly over the ensuing years. Between 1949 and 1951 the central government took draconian measures against West Sumatra's civilian and military institutions, making the people feel they were being deprived of the fruits of the loyalty they had demonstrated throughout the independence struggle.

Rejection of Federalism

Establishment of a Unitary State

Jakarta's unpopular measures against West Sumatra, however, have to be viewed against the background of the serious challenges which threatened the form and existence of the new Indonesian government in the aftermath of the Round Table conference with the Dutch in the fall of 1949.

After long and difficult discussions, The Hague Agreement was signed, providing that no later than December 30, 1949, the Dutch government would transfer sovereignty to the Republik Indonesia Serikat (Republic of the United States of Indonesia, RIS or RUSI), which consisted not only of the revolutionary Republic but of all the states and autonomous areas set up by the Dutch in their effort to create a federal state in the archipelago.[1] Mohammad Hatta became the prime minister of this new Indonesian entity. Almost immediately, however, the representative bodies in the component states began voting to dissolve themselves and become part of the Indonesian Republic. The actions by the individual states were to some extent a natural rejection of the way the Dutch government had manipulated them in its efforts to retain control over its Netherlands Indies colony, but they were also a result of pressure from Republican adherents both at the centre and in the Dutch-sponsored states.

The situation was exacerbated by uprisings and attempted coups against the independent Indonesian government which broke out in the early months of 1950, launched by former Indonesian members of the Royal Netherlands Indies Army (KNIL), sometimes led by disaffected Dutch officers. The most serious threat occurred in Bandung and Jakarta, where the notorious Captain R.P.P. 'Turk' Westerling led an effort to topple Hatta's government and assassinate leading members of his cabinet.[2] When it was discovered that Sultan Hamid II of West Kalimantan, one of the leading proponents of federalism and a member of the RIS cabinet, had supported and perhaps instigated Westerling's attempted coup, this further discredited federalism and accelerated the movement toward a unitary state.

In reaction, many of the strongest proponents of federalism, particularly in the oldest of the federated states, the State of East Indonesia (Negara Indonesia Timur, NIT), became fearful that they would be absorbed within the Indonesian Republic, and these fears sparked separatist movements among pro-Dutch elements and soldiers of the former Netherlands East Indies Army (KNIL) in the eastern archipelago. In April 1950, KNIL units awaiting demobilization in Makassar rebelled against the Republic and in support of the East Indonesian State. Later that month, pro-Dutch elements and former KNIL soldiers in Ambon proclaimed an independent Republic of the South Moluccas (RMS, Republik Maluku Selatan).

Faced with the conflicting pressures for and against the dissolution of the federal states, all sides feared the newly born Indonesia might soon disintegrate. Hatta as prime minister of the RIS held a meeting in early May with the heads of the two strongest remaining states, the State of East Indonesia (NIT) and the State of East Sumatra (PST), and all three leaders agreed to the formation of a unitary state. On August 17, 1950, the Unitary State of the Republic of Indonesia replaced the federal Republic of the United States of Indonesia.[3]

The rapid developments of these months changed not only the character of the new Indonesian state but also the perceptions of some of its leaders. Hatta, who was one of the strongest Indonesian proponents of a devolution of powers to the local areas, now oversaw the creation of a state where power was concentrated in the hands of the central Republican government in its new capital of Jakarta. He expressed regret at the necessity of moving in this direction, writing later that 'a federal system is, in fact, suitable for such a far-flung archipelago as Indonesia, and might be expected to strengthen the feeling of unity', but that 'the manner and timing of the move by the Netherlands Indies Government had aroused such antipathy toward ideas of federation that it was found necessary to make the change from a federal to a unitary state'.[4] For several years following the dissolution of the RIS, advocacy of a federal system for Indonesia became almost the equivalent of treason.

The transformation of the federal into the unitary structure entailed measures which were also to have an important impact on future relations between the centre and the regions. Most important was the postponement of the provision in the RIS constitution for nation-wide elections to be held within a year of the transfer of sovereignty. As the years passed, the political parties exercising power in Jakarta became increasingly reluctant to organize these elections, which did not finally take place until more than four years later. Another measure influencing the future shape of Indonesia was the reinstitution of the Vice Presidency (which had not existed in the RIS). Under this provision, Hatta was in effect kicked upstairs from his powerful role as prime minister to that of vice president, a position of higher prestige, but with much less power. Furthermore, the establishment of a single House of Representatives, which absorbed members of the RIS senate as well as all other national-level representative bodies in both the Republic and the RIS,[5] meant that in any future elections representation would essentially be solely on the basis of population.

All these measures tended to run counter to the hopes of the people in the provinces that they would be able to participate in running their own affairs, and led rather to a monopolization of power at the centre and a growing distance between the inhabitants of the outer islands and their supposed governmental representatives in Jakarta. In other words, the form of government adopted by the new Republic of Indonesia strengthened the power of the central government in Jakarta and of densely populated Java, as opposed to the sparsely populated but extensive geographical regions of the 'Outer Islands'.

Failure of Moves for Greater Regional Autonomy

Although in the wake of the dissolution of the RIS there was overwhelming support for a unitary Republic, most political opinion in Indonesia still strongly favoured considerable devolution of governmental authority. Regional autonomy was a key characteristic of the envisaged Republic in the early 1950s, one to which all parties and shades of opinion adhered, and which they saw as an essential part of the democratization process. Decentralization was 'accepted as an important part of the new Indonesian democracy'.[6]

But the dissolution of the federal structure meant that the context in which regional autonomy could exist was now basically altered. Federalism has been described as 'a form of government in which sovereignty or political power is divided between the central and the local government, so that each of them within its own sphere is independent of the other'.[7] It envisages autonomous regional bodies, exercising decision-making rights over all the concerns of the regions for which they are responsible, while the federal government retains total power only in the limited fields for which it is responsible – usually defence, foreign affairs, postal services, and other communications. In a unitary state, on the other hand, decentralization can merely mean regional heads or bodies being granted the freedom to implement in ways that fit the conditions and situations in their own regions decisions reached at the centre in accordance with perceived national interests. The local bodies do not have decision-making powers outside some very limited areas.

During the early 1950s, all political parties embraced the principles of decentralization and regional autonomy, but, as Schiller has pointed out, there is 'a fundamental distinction between decentralization of authority in a unitary state and the distribution of powers in a federal state'. In a unitary state, there are no longer diverse loci of power, for both the civil-service personnel and funds derive from the centre, and the members of the bureaucracy do not necessarily have ties with the local regions where they serve. In a federal system a component state's 'civil service is made up of residents of the state. The revenue received tends to determine to a considerable extent the amount which can be expended'.[8]

During this period in the allocation of powers between the centre and the regions, the issues of personnel and finance were two of the most contentious. People were keenly aware that the just-concluded revolution had been waged successfully in part because it had been administered, financially as well as militarily, largely on the bases of separate, locally rooted institutions. As the months progressed, people in the regions began to fear that this situation was changing drastically and that political leaders at the centre were merely paying lip service to the principle of regional autonomy. There was growing resentment against what was increasingly viewed as Javanese domination of the state administrative apparatus in the regions as well as in the centre.

The government's decentralization policy was essentially based on Law 22 of 1948, which established three autonomous levels of government below the national level: the province, the district (*kabupaten*), and the village (*desa*). Under this original law and the subsequent laws passed in 1950 which set up the provinces in Java and Sumatra, the province, the district (*kabupaten*), and the village (*desa*) were to enjoy a significant range of powers to govern their own regions.[9] And it was specifically provided that these 'autonomous regions':

> ... must, as an absolute condition have a democractic organization in which power must be in the hands of the people of the region.... The highest instruments of authority must be held by a Regional Representative Council the organization of which must be determined by election.[10]

But no elections were, in fact, held for the regional councils, which either came into existence on an ad hoc and provisional basis or were appointed by the central government. The lack of elected regional bodies constituted one of the major grievances of the regions during the early 1950s. (This dissatisfaction was compounded in 1956 when the life of even the provisional bodies came to an end pending the promised elections for their replacements.)

In the years immediately following the transfer of sovereignty it was at the provincial level that there was greatest conflict between the centre's exercise of authority and local demands for greater representation in decision making. These conflicts focused on the powers of the head of the province (*kepala daerah*) and the local representative council.

Of the loci of authority, the position of the provincial head or governor was pivotal, for he stood at the margin of central and regional authority and could perceive his role either primarily as the representative of the people of the region or alternatively as an administrator responsible for carrying out the policies determined at the centre.[11] Under the 1948 decentralization law, the local representative councils should have selected candidates for the position of provincial head (*kepala daerah*). Jakarta's role was envisaged as merely choosing one of the candidates they selected.[12] However, taking advantage of a loophole in the law, Jakarta assumed the right to appoint the governor, deliberately ignoring the names proposed by the regional representative councils, and stripping those councils of some of their most significant powers.[13] Thus, despite the provisions of the 1948 law, a provincial head appointed by the central government actually held a monopoly on power in the regions, rather than this being in the hands of the envisaged elected democratic bodies. Further-

more, that head was usually a member of the civil service (*pamong praja*), and frequently not from the region to which he was appointed. The vast majority of these
officials were Javanese, so, as Mohammad Sjafei (the noted educator from West
Sumatra) declared in Parliament in 1952: 'The outer regions are getting the impression that in the placement of personnel the key positions are always reserved for our
Javanese brothers'.[14]

During the early 1950s there were a number of debates in Parliament in which
proponents of greater local autonomy fought for an arrangement more favourable to
the regions outside Java. One of their proposals was for a bicameral legislature,
where, similar to the United States, membership of one of the bodies would be
elected on the basis of population, but in the other there would be one or two representatives from each region irrespective of its population numbers. This proposal,
together with other measures aimed at increasing regional autonomy, was defeated
in Parliament,[15] and the government postponed tackling the most thorny problems
of decentralization until after the formation of an elected Constituent Assembly,
which was to follow the holding of general elections.[16]

Reaction in Sumatra

Under the laws passed in 1950 to supplement the original decentralization law of
1948, Indonesia as a whole was divided into ten provinces, three of which were in
Sumatra – North, Central, and South Sumatra.[17] As we have seen, this tripartite
division had been impossible to implement during the revolution, and residencies
had been able to retain their role as the effective governmental entities. After 1950,
too, Jakarta encountered further major problems in attempting to implement the
policy. First, the boundaries of the three Sumatran provinces were essentially arbi-
trary and the areas they incorporated made little sense ethnically, religiously,
socially, or economically. North Sumatra encompassed Aceh, East Sumatra, and
Tapanuli, the first two with large Muslim majorities and the last predominantly
Christian – all these areas having widely differing economic and cultural patterns.
The province was ethnically diverse, with a mixture of Acehnese, Malay, Batak
(Toba, Karo, and Simalungun), and a large Javanese immigrant population on the
East Sumatra plantations. Similarly, Central Sumatra incorporated not only the
Minangkabau region of West Sumatra but also the land region of Riau and its exten-
sive archipelago stretching almost to Singapore, as well as Jambi, which until 1950
had been incorporated in South Sumatra. Many of the inhabitants of Jambi and Riau
resented domination by the politically and educationally more advanced Minangkabau.[18] The new province of South Sumatra (which included the residencies of
Palembang, Benkulen, Lampung, and Bangka-Billiton), was described by Maryanov
as 'incorporating both the oil-rich Palembang areas as well as the Kubus, one of the
most primitive tribes of Indonesia. It contains huge tracts of impenetrable jungle as
well as large resettlement areas for surplus Javanese'.[19]

Mohd. Natsir

Disillusionment in Aceh

From the beginning, Aceh, at the northern tip of Sumatra, was a major centre of resentment at the course being pursued by the independent Indonesian state. Aceh's incorporation within the province of North Sumatra reversed a decree promulgated by Deputy Prime Minister Sjafruddin Prawiranegara in December 1949, which had recognized Aceh's unique history and its importance and loyalty to the Republic during the revolution by establishing it as a separate province, under a government headed by the leader of the Islamic Scholars' organization (PUSA, the All Aceh Ulama Union) Teungku Daud Beureu'eh, who had been military governor of Aceh during the closing years of the revolution.[20]

Over the following months, Daud Beureu'eh and his Islamic colleagues formed a provisional representative assembly for the region, with members drawn largely from the community of Islamic scholars. They were outraged when in August 1950 government plans were revealed for Aceh to be included in the province of North Sumatra. PUSA leaders responded by reiterating their demands for provincial status. First Sjafruddin and Interior Minister Assaat, then Vice President Hatta, and finally Prime Minister Natsir were compelled to visit the region to persuade it to accept its incorporation. These government ministers were fearful that, if Aceh succeeded in retaining its provincial status, similar demands would come from throughout the archipelago. Only Natsir's personal authority as an Islamic leader finally convinced the PUSA to reluctantly withdraw their demand for Aceh to remain a province.

During his visit to the region in January 1951, Natsir made a radio broadcast where he recalled Aceh's loyalty during the revolution and reminded its people of the threats posed to the Republic since the transfer of sovereignty by the pro-Dutch revolts:

We still remember the violence of the disturbances in several regions of our homeland caused by the problems of federalism and unitarianism, disturbances which came close to threatening the welfare of the state.

He called on them to view their inclusion in the Province of North Sumatra

not as a door that closes off forever all other future possibilities, but as a step...that we hope can later become a good contribution toward organizing our country into autonomous regions that possess duties and responsibilities in harmony with their individual strength and readiness, and furthermore in harmony with the division of duties and responsibilities between the Government and the region.[21]

In deference to Natsir's religious standing, PUSA abandoned open opposition to the centre's plans, but its leader Daud Beureu'eh refused to take up the government post offered him and retired instead to his home village in Pidie.[22]

Freezing of West Sumatra's Civilian Institutions

The developments in the civilian field in West Sumatra were not so dramatic as in Aceh, but they, too, intensified local disillusionment with the Jakarta government's policies. In accordance with Hatta's earlier ideas, the province of Central Sumatra was reconstituted to include, in addition to West Sumatra, not only the regions of Jambi and Riau on the mainland of Sumatra, but also the Riau archipelago, which had been under Dutch control for much of the revolution.[23] Political dynamics in the region changed as soon as the ceasefire was proclaimed. Mr. St. Mohd. Rasjid, who had headed West Sumatra through most of the revolution, departed to become a member of the Central Joint Commission overseeing the ceasefire, and his replacement, Mr. Nasrun (who had held the largely powerless position of Central Sumatra governor since 1948) became his ineffective and unpopular successor.

At its first session after the transfer of sovereignty, the People's Representative Council of Central Sumatra (DPRST) passed a motion demanding that Governor Nasrun be removed, and proposing as his successor H. Iljas Jacub, the respected prewar Permi leader and former Digul internee, now a leader of the Masjumi party and head of the DPRST. Jacub refused the candidacy. Immersed in its efforts to transform the RIS into the new Indonesian Republic, the Hatta government in Jakarta delayed reaching a decision on what to do about Governor Nasrun. Tensions between Nasrun and the provincial council rose as delegations from Central Sumatra were sent to meet with the Interior Ministry in Jakarta and emissaries came from the capital to Bukittinggi in an effort to settle the dispute.

The provincial council expanded its list of proposed candidates for governor by adding the names of former military governor Mr. St. Mohd. Rasjid, who was by then an official in the Indonesian foreign office; Mr. Djamil, the medical doctor who had been a disastrous Resident during the early months of 1946, but who had since been an influential educator; and Dr. A. Rahim Usman, a respected doctor, brother of the journalist Madjid Usman and a close adviser to Mr. Rasjid until the Second Dutch attack, after which he had led the group of Republican politicians within Dutch-occupied Bukittinggi. The Interior Ministry eventually agreed to Nasrun's removal, recalling him to Jakarta on August 1, 1950, but postponing any decision on appointing his successor.[24] During the interregnum the provincial legislature, headed by the old Muhammadiah leader S.J. St. Mangkuto, exercised authority in the region.

With the creation of the unitary state on August 17, 1950, Masjumi leader Mohammad Natsir was appointed Indonesia's prime minister, with Mr. Assaat as his minister of the interior. Both men came from West Sumatra. A month later, Mr. Assaat held discussions with West Sumatra's provincial authorities regarding the appointment of a new governor and other issues of decentralization. By then it was clear that neither Rasjid nor Iljas Jacub was willing to accept the governorship, 'presumably because [neither wanted] to be torn between loyalty to the central government and his own party on the one hand and popular acceptability on the other'.[25]

In the middle of the following month news reached West Sumatra that the Natsir cabinet had rejected the provincial council's nominees for governor, on the grounds that none of them, with the exception of Mr. Rasjid, had the necessary administrative experience. Instead, it was going to appoint a Javanese, Roeslan Moeljohardjo, as acting governor of Central Sumatra. Roeslan had served in Bukittinggi as Assistant Resident to the Central Government Secretariat prior to the second Dutch 'Police Action' of December 1948.[26] Natsir, Minangkabau head of the Masjumi party, later explained the decision to appoint Roeslan by saying he was a good Muslim and member of the Masjumi party, and should therefore have been acceptable to the people of West Sumatra.[27] The provincial council, however, rejected him, and Roeslan returned to Jakarta on December 29.

The Natsir cabinet then decided to pass a Law (No. 1 of 1951) applying exclusively to the province of Central Sumatra, which suspended representative government in the region ('freezing' [*pembekuan*] the local representative bodies) and transferred authority to Roeslan Moeljohardjo, who was reinstated as acting governor, and to a six-man committee appointed by the Interior Ministry. The local authorities reluctantly acceded, and on January 13, 1951, S.J. St. Mangkuto representing the government of Central Sumatra handed over authority to Acting Governor Roeslan.[28]

Over the next five years, politicians and legislators in Central Sumatra were frustrated in all their efforts to have the provincial People's Representative Council reinstituted or to have a provisional legislature replace it.[29] The Natsir cabinet had promised that the Council would be re-established in six months' time, but before those months expired Natsir's cabinet had itself fallen and been replaced by the Sukiman cabinet, which showed no interest in fulfilling the promise. (Dr. Sukiman was Javanese and had no ties to or sympathy for the Minangkabau of West Sumatra.)

From then on, the central government failed to approve any representative council in Central Sumatra. In part, this was a result of the rapid turnover of cabinets in Jakarta, and it could also to a significant degree be attributed to dissension at both the local and central level regarding which groups should be allowed to select members of representative provincial and district councils prior to the holding of a general election. But there was also a general indecisiveness and ineffectiveness in national decision-making processes, and a reluctance on the part of whichever government held office in Jakarta to grant powers to the local authorities.

These deficiencies were clearly visible in a conference on regional autonomy that took place in late 1953 between regional heads from Central Sumatra and representatives of the central government, including Professor Hazairin, interior minister in the First Ali Sastroamidjojo (PNI) cabinet. At the conference, the Sumatran delegates contended that 'tension and differences of opinion frequently arose between the district councils and the district head or the regional head because the status and powers of the district representative councils are unclear'. They demanded that within the next six months the central government should give substance to the regional representative bodies at the district and village level in Central Sumatra, as it had done over the previous year in Sulawesi. They further asked for a local election to be held as soon as possible for a People's Representative Council at the provincial level. They recalled their fruitless efforts over the previous months and years to persuade the government to take concrete measures toward some degree of decentralization. In response, Minister Hazairin stonewalled them completely. His direct response was:

> We cannot agree to issue an *instellingswet* [lit. institutional law] that applies not only to the district or town but also to the province if such a law is based on Law No. 22 of 1948, because in that law we see many things that, from the viewpoint of the current situation and development of the society, are no longer suitable and for that reason need to be changed.

After expounding on the situation and necessary changes he concluded:

> Because of this, would it not be better for the problem of the formation of a People's Representative Council [DPRD] for Central Sumatra to be postponed until the government's new administrative plans are in force?...because these problems have arisen not only in Sumatra but also in Kalimantan and other regions.

Understandably, representatives not only of West Sumatra but also of Riau and Jambi greeted these views with frustration and hopelessness, one of them complaining:

> Now what is the situation? The region of Central Sumatra is a democratic vacuum. So now the conference demands, in other words the people of Central Sumatra demand, an administration that is democratic from the centre to the regions; for 8 years the people have waited and [a decision] can no longer be avoided. If the Central Government is going to await the issuing of a new law to replace the law No. 22 of 1948, it would

be better to await a new constitution that is not provisional or just wait for the arrival of a democratization of the regional government and a new state.

A representative from Riau noted that the current situation compared badly even with the situation under the Dutch when, in addition to the Minangkabau Raad,

> there were also small councils, and in the villages a Village Council that had firm ties with those above and below. Outside Minangkabau, in Riau, it was the same. The region of Riau was made up of Sultanates that had power and could arrange their own administration, with their own finances and autonomy....
> Even if it is through an emergency law we ask the Central Government to implement this, because the people are restless. Their restlessness is clearly evidenced by the rise of rumours caused by feelings of dissatisfaction, and also in the region of Riau recently there are movements [*aliran*, lit. currents] recreating their autonomous areas, because in this way, they can order and organize their region themselves in their accustomed manner.

The local representatives clearly mistrusted government calls that they should be patient until a new law was formulated, for they suspected that such a new law, rather than granting greater autonomy, might well instead call for a greater degree of centralization. They pleaded for the government to respond to their demands for decentralization and democratization.[30]

After the formation of the unitary state in August 1950, the central government soon demonstrated that it was no longer willing to allow any real measure of local autonomy for the new provinces on Sumatra. In its fear that recently Dutch-controlled areas in other parts of the archipelago might break off from the new Republic, it singled out two of the regions that had been most loyal during the revolution, Aceh and West Sumatra, and by denying them any attributes of autonomy, attempted to demonstrate the central government's impartiality to the less reliable provinces. But these moves were counterproductive, and within three years had pushed Aceh's Muslim community into rebellion, while the issue of the lack of any representative government in Central Sumatra became a running sore between it and the central government. Furthermore, the conflicting views between Jakarta and West Sumatra regarding the place of the Minangkabau region within the Republic of Indonesia became part of a struggle that would only be resolved in the centre's favour after that region too went into armed rebellion in 1958.

At the same time, the government failed to take effective action to further the economic development of the regions outside Java, or even to address their most immediate economic problems; nor was it willing to grant sufficient administrative and fiscal decentralization for the local governments to meet their needs themselves. There was growing regional resentment at the preponderance of the country's foreign exchange being channelled to Java – rather than to the other islands where nearly three-fourths of this income was being earned.[31]

Failure of the Electoral Road

Religious Disaffection

In both Aceh and West Sumatra ethnic demands and sentiments were always closely interwoven with religious loyalties. In Aceh, during the revolution, the autonomous PUSA government had been able to institute many attributes of an Islamic state, and it was only Prime Minister Natsir's position as an Islamic leader and head of Indonesia's largest Muslim party that had enabled him to persuade the region to accede reluctantly to its incorporation within the province of North Sumatra. During the succeeding years, dissatisfaction grew as the old aristocracy (the *hulubalang*) were restored to positions of power in the government bureaucracy, replacing the Islamic scholars who had held these posts during the revolution, while at the same time the region's direct trade with the Malay peninsula, which had flourished during the revolution, was largely cut off. Regional grievances were exacerbated by the decreasing influence of the religious parties on the national scene, and dissatisfaction with the growing emphasis on the Five Principles or *Panca Sila* as the foundation of the state.[32] It was becoming increasingly obvious that there was little likelihood of the new Indonesia becoming a state based on Islam. These developments led the disgruntled PUSA leaders to make common cause with other disaffected Muslim elements who opposed the secular route they feared the Republic was pursuing.

Indonesia's earliest centre of Islamic disaffection had been in West Java, where, in 1948, units of the Republic's Islamic militias, together with several minor Masjumi politicians, had defied official Masjumi party policy and broken with the Republican government. These Muslim dissidents believed the government was betraying the revolution when, in accordance with the Renville agreement of January 1948, it withdrew its troops from areas of West Java penetrated by Dutch forces. The insurgent Muslim group, the Darul Islam (House of Islam), headed by S.M. Kartosuwirjo,[33] set up a rudimentary government structure in the region and on August 7, 1949, proclaimed the Islamic State of Indonesia (Negara Islam Indonesia). Its guerrilla units were transformed into 'the Islamic Army of Indonesia' (Tentera Islam Indonesia), which in 1950 controlled about a third of the countryside of West Java, mostly in the mountainous interior.[34]

Rebellion in South Sulawesi came later. Islamic forces there, under guerrilla leader Kahar Muzakkar (who had fought for the Republic during the revolution), after a series of negotiations with the central government eventually refused to have their units incorporated into the Republic's army. In 1951, Kahar fled with his followers to the interior mountainous areas of South Sulawesi, and in January 1952 he made common cause with Kartosuwirjo and his Darul Islam in West Java, accepting an appointment as Sulawesi commander of the Darul Islam's Islamic Army of Indonesia.[35] In August 1953, Kahar issued a proclamation that Sulawesi had become a part of Kartosuwirjo's Islamic State of Indonesia.[36]

It was in the following month, September 1953, that Daud Beureu'eh too proclaimed that Aceh had become part of the Islamic State of Indonesia.[37]

In West Sumatra, regional and ethnic loyalties were also tied closely to those of

religion, and regional dissatisfaction with the central government became inter-
twined with ideological allegiances. But the issues were not seen in such stark black
and white colours as in the Darul Islam areas. However, although they were not as
unified as their brethren in Aceh in wishing to see Indonesia's political future based
on Islamic law and teachings, the vast majority of Minangkabau people did belong to
an Islamic political party, either the modernist Masjumi or the more traditionalist
Perti. While the governments of Natsir and Sukiman held power at the centre, religious and party loyalty to the Masjumi-dominated governments in Jakarta muted
the expression of regional grievances. This remained true to some extent during the
tenure of the subsequent coalition government of Mr. Wilopo, when Masjumi
leader Mr. Mohamad Roem held the post of interior minister. In July 1953, however,
a cabinet headed by Nationalist Party (PNI) leader Ali Sastroamidjojo, came to
power, from which the Masjumi party was excluded.[38] It was at this point that, in
Aceh, religious and regional allegiances coalescing in opposition to the central government provided the spark to ignite Islamic rebellion.[39]

In Central Sumatra, the impact of the government changes in Jakarta was not so
drastic. During his first two years as governor, Roeslan Moeljohardjo's membership
of the Masjumi party had ensured that he acted as a loyal spokesman for the central
government, while at the same time, this, and his attempts to understand local grievances, had moderated Islamic criticism of him locally. With the Masjumi out of
power, Governor Roeslan was in a less ambiguous position, and he became an
unequivocal champion of the regional interests of Central Sumatra vis-à-vis the centre, protesting in particular the funds allocated to the regional government which
were insufficient for it to run the administration and embark on rehabilitation and
economic development.[40] Regional feelings against the centre began to be interwoven with ideological and religious conflicts, for the Ali cabinet was supported not
only by the Nationalist parties, but also to some extent by the Communist Party.
The West Sumatran Communist leader Bachtaruddin, now a member of the PKI
faction in Parliament in Jakarta, described the Ali cabinet as 'the best cabinet so
far'.[41]

The 1955 Elections

As the date approached for nation-wide general elections, finally slated for September 29, 1955, religious allegiances merging with regional dissatisfactions strengthened opposition to the centre. At the same time that ideological animosities sharpened, internal confrontations emerged within West Sumatra, particularly between
the two major religious parties on the one hand – the Masjumi and Perti – and the
largest of the local secular parties, the Indonesian Communist Party (PKI), on the
other. The PKI's Central Sumatra branch, supported by other nonreligious parties,
spearheaded an effort to remove Roeslan as governor 'because he was no longer
acceptable to the people of West Sumatra'. Their objections to Roeslan were clearly
as much because of his membership in the Masjumi party as because he was a
Javanese, and it was Masjumi adherents, as well as the Perti, Nahdlatul Ulama (NU),
and other religious parties who now came to his defence.[42]

In August 1955 in Jakarta, the Masjumi party again replaced the Nationalist Party's Ali Sastroamidjojo cabinet at the head of the coalition government. Burhanuddin Harahap's Masjumi-led cabinet held power from then until March 1956, throughout the months immediately preceding and following the holding of national elections. However, in the elections, to the dismay of most Muslims outside Java, the Masjumi party did not, as hoped and generally expected, emerge as Indonesia's largest political party. Instead, it came in second to the Nationalist Party (PNI) and could therefore not hope even to head a coalition government, at least in the immediate future.

One major reason behind the Masjumi failure was the fact that the Nahdlatul Ulama party, which had split off from the Masjumi coalition in 1952, decisively defeated the Masjumi for the Muslim vote in East and Central Java.[43] In Central Sumatra, however, the Masjumi was overwhelmingly successful, capturing 52 percent of the vote (797,692 votes). Its nearest rival was the local traditionalist Islamic party Perti (351,768 votes), distantly followed by the Communist PKI with 90,513 votes. (The PKI had more than twice as many votes as its nearest rival the Nationalist PNI, which received 42,558 votes.[44])] From this time on, the Masjumi, which received nearly 50 percent of its vote outside Java, was increasingly seen not only as the party of the modernist Indonesian Muslims, but as the representative of the regions outside the Javanese heartland.[45]

But politically conscious Muslims still hoped that the Constituent Assembly issuing from the Constituent elections scheduled for December 1955 would bring about a constitution more in accord with religious tenets than the Provisional Constitution of 1950. It was hoped that the new constitution would at least assign greater weight to Islamic law, even if it did not take steps toward establishing an Islamic state, an ultimate goal that few Muslims were willing to acknowledge.

Following the nationwide elections, sentiments in West Sumatra bore many similarities with those experienced in the aftermath of the village elections held in the residency in 1946. Then, after the Muslim parties had been overwhelmingly victorious in these local elections, they saw themselves as still excluded from the residency-level positions of power, a situation that was one of the most important causes of the attempted coup on March 3, 1947. Now, in Central Sumatra Muslim parties had captured at least 70 percent of the vote, but this success was not reflected at the national level, where in March 1956 the second cabinet of the PNI's Ali Sastroamidjojo replaced Burhanuddin Harahap's Masjumi cabinet.

West Sumatrans were disillusioned not only at the return to power of a cabinet in Jakarta dominated by the Nationalist party and enjoying the support of the Communist and other non-Muslim parties, but also at the realization that the election had not solved the problem of the continuing 'democratic vacuum' in West Sumatra itself. The government in Jakarta envisaged that the Constituent Assembly elections of December 1955 would result in a body that could decide the kinds of democratic changes that should be instituted in Indonesia. But the head of the West Sumatra branch of the Masjumi party, Mansur Daud Dt. Palimo Kayo, was voicing the views of most other parties when he argued that, rather than waiting for the outcome of Constituent Assembly decisions – a process that could take years – the provincial council in Central Sumatra should be re-established, with its membership based largely on the parties' strength in the general elections, while attention was also paid to representation for the small parties. There was general agreement with this stance among the political parties of Central Sumatra, and the organization representing the parties (PPST) stated that the formation of a new Provincial Representative Council should 'be accomplished through compromise without waiting for a new regional autonomy law', and that Representative Councils should also be established on a similar basis at the district and village levels.[46]

In Jakarta, Hatta was becoming increasingly frustrated at his limited powers as vice president. His threats to resign, which he began to voice in July 1956, further exacerbated worries that the regions were losing representation at the centre, reinforcing the feeling that, not only was hope for any improvement disappearing, but it was now more than likely that, at least for regions outside Java, the situation would in fact worsen. West Sumatra's newspapers voiced the growing dissatisfaction, charging 'that the central government was either inefficient or corrupt or both; that the province was being treated badly in comparison with Java, considering its production of revenue; that this was part of a deliberate effort to develop Java and the Javanese at the expense of the province and people of Central Sumatra; and that the region was beginning to feel that it was being governed as a colony by a colonial power'.[47] As long as the Masjumi party had played a major role in the government in Jakarta, and as long as Vice President Hatta at least symbolically represented Sumatra in the central government, people in West Sumatra retained their hope that eventually the new civilian order developing in Indonesia would conform more to the perceptions they had clung to during the revolution. But both these situations changed during 1956.

Toward the Banteng Council

The feelings of betrayal that permeated Minangkabau society in the early 1950s reverberated also in the military field. In many ways, West Sumatra's military command, the Banteng Division, personified the disappointment and feelings of injustice which were widespread in West Sumatra in the immediate aftermath of the revolution. As late as 1995, in a meeting of Banteng Division veterans, a former officer expressed the Banteng soldiers' bitterness, seemingly still as sharply felt as in the early 1950s.

> The region of Central Sumatra had led the struggle for independence on Sumatra, with the governor and military commander moving to Bukittinggi, with all the Sumatran political parties in Bukittinggi – so Bukittinggi or West Sumatra was the centre for the struggle command. And the moment this command was no longer useful in heading the struggle against the Dutch it was this command, the Banteng command, that was abolished. The Bukit Barisan command [Territorial Division 1] in the North and the Srivijaya command in the South [Territorial Division 2],

both of which had had West Sumatra as their centre – these were not abolished. This was the fuel that ignited the confrontation with the centre in the PRRI [the 1958 rebellion].[48]

Although reduced and dismembered after the revolution, it was the Banteng Division that provided the impetus and consolidating factor that gave West Sumatra the leverage to confront Jakarta over the issue of regional autonomy, appearing to provide a possible way out of the political impasse between the regions and the centre.

Dissolution of the Banteng Division

The Banteng Division's postrevolutionary history was a sad one. Almost immediately after Sjafruddin Prawiranegara's departure with other members of the Emergency Government (PDRI) in early July 1949, it became clear that central army headquarters had not forgotten its plans for rationalization of the armed forces in Sumatra, particularly in Central Sumatra. Its actions were accelerated by the need to incorporate units of the Dutch Colonial Army (KNIL) within Indonesia's Armed Forces,[49] and also by fears that elements within the Indonesian National Army (especially former militia members) might react negatively to the central government's compromises with the Dutch.[50] It was anticipated that former militia soldiers now serving in the regular army would oppose the emerging agreements, both from political conviction and also because they realized the fragility of their own positions – that in any overall postwar rationalization of the armed forces they would be the most expendable units.

The changing situation was becoming clear as early as July 1949. Lieutenant Colonel Dahlan Djambek presided over a meeting of officers on the ninth to eleventh of that month, at which it was agreed that, in conformity with the rationalization program, the strength of the former Banteng Division would be reduced to that of a brigade.[51] A few days earlier, Djambek, who had distinguished himself as a brave and able commander in the final stages of the anti-Dutch struggle, had reassumed his former position at the head of the Banteng Division after persuading Dahlan Ibrahim, the titular divisional commander, to step down.[52] According to later accounts, in the meeting with the Banteng officers Djambek was carrying out the instructions of Sumatra commander Hidayat, reportedly sent to him in Dutch, threatening that 'I will shoot you dead with my own hands if you don't put everything there in order'.[53]

At this time, some of the regular army officers apparently hoped that consolidation of the Banteng Brigade's units into 'fully armed' battalions would be a way of strengthening West Sumatra's military forces.[54] It soon became clear, however, that the primary goal of the policy was to force most of the Banteng units to disband. During November, while Indonesian forces entered the major towns to take over authority from the Dutch, thousands of soldiers returned home to their villages. By the end of the year, many other officers and men had voluntarily left the army to return to civilian life.[55]

At the end of December 1949, the Banteng Division was officially reconstituted as the Brigade EE Banteng, consisting initially of four and later of six battalions.[56] Throughout 1950 changes continued, until a division previously numbering between twenty- and thirty-thousand men had been reduced to a brigade consisting of five- to seven-thousand soldiers.[57] Units from West Java's Siliwangi Division were also brought into West Sumatra and amalgamated with the brigade. At the same time, there were various changes in the numbers and composition of the local battalions and companies, with several of these units sent out of West Sumatra to serve tours of duty in areas of unrest in other parts of the archipelago.[58]

On November 1, 1950, the slimmed-down brigade was incorporated as a subterritory within the newly formed First Military Territory (TTI), covering the northern half of Sumatra, which had its headquarters in Medan. The following month, Dahlan Djambek informed his subordinates that he was being reassigned to Armed Forces Headquarters in Jakarta. Outraged that their commander would depart immediately following his acquiescence to the centre's policies, a situation which Captain Sjoeib likened to 'when a ship is about to sink, its captain first saves himself in a rowing boat', the officers sent Sjoeib and Sofyan Ibrahim to Jakarta to protest the orders directly to Army Chief of Staff, General Nasution. Nasution, however, merely reprimanded them for questioning their brigade commander's orders and told them that any complaints should be directed to their superiors in Medan.[59]

During 1950, three Banteng battalions were sent out of West Sumatra to help quell uprisings in other regions of the archipelago: one to West Java, one to Pontianak (West Kalimantan), and one to Ambon. This practice continued through the early 1950s, with units dispatched in particular to Aceh and West Java to combat the Islamic rebellions in those regions.

The situations the Banteng units faced in suppressing these local uprisings made them even more resentful toward central army headquarters. Most unhappy was the experience of the Pagar Ruyung battalion. At the beginning of 1950, five of the battalion's eight companies were sent to West Kalimantan, and having completed this assignment, the whole battalion was transferred to West Java to fight against the Darul Islam.[60] It was incorporated within the West Java Siliwangi Division and its ties cut with the Banteng Division. By 1953, the battalion had suffered about twenty-five men killed, and it learned that the central command had plans to divide it further and to disperse its remaining forces. This proposed dismemberment sparked protests from West Sumatran groups and political parties, and Governor Roeslan attempted to persuade the central government to reverse its plans.[61] Soldiers in the battalion demanded to be returned to West Sumatra, and there were reports of mutiny. Whatever steps were actually taken by the unhappy members of the Pagar Ruyung battalion, their forces were surrounded and disarmed by the Siliwangi command, which also arrested one of their most outspoken officers, Lt. Abubakar, alleging that he was mentally disturbed.[62] Within a couple of months, most of the units had been allowed to go back to Sumatra, some of the soldiers had returned to civilian life, and the remainder had been incorporated into other Siliwangi detachments in Bandung.[63]

In West Sumatra, Lt. Col. Thalib had succeeded Djambek as commander of the

Vice President Hatta being greeted by Police Chief Kaharuddin
Dt. Rangkayo Basa on a visit to West Sumatra, 1956. In the centre are Lt. Col.
Ahmad Husein and Central Sumatra Governor Roeslan Moeljohardjo
Source: From the collection of Djohari Kahar (courtesy Hasril Chaniago)

Banteng Brigade at the end of 1950, and when Thalib himself was appointed chief of
staff of the North Sumatra Command in Medan a year later, Ahmad Husein was his
successor. The Banteng Brigade was dissolved in April 1952 and, still headed by
Husein, became Regiment Four of the North Sumatra Command (TTI).

Ahmad Husein now assumed a leading role in West Sumatra's history. Prior to
this time he had been a supporting player, one of the younger generation of Japanese-trained officers who led the Banteng Division during the struggle with the
Dutch. His career as a soldier had, however, been noteworthy. A flamboyant and
courageous fighter, he had risen to prominence among his contemporaries while
still in his early twenties. He had headed the units based in Solok which had been
responsible for the eastern front bordering on the occupied town of Padang, and for
his battalion's exploits Husein earned the name 'Tiger of Kuranji ' (*Harimau Kuranji*). By 1949, he had attained the rank of lieutenant colonel, but with the transfer
of sovereignty and the disbanding of the Banteng Division, he was reduced to the
rank of major. In 1950 his Kuranji battalion was assigned to West Java to fight the
dissident Darul Islam.[64] In late 1951, Husein was appointed to replace Ahmad
Thalib as commander of the Banteng Brigade and he returned to West Sumatra,
with his battalion following soon afterward.[65] In 1954 he was promoted again to the
rank of lieutenant colonel.

Ahmad Husein was clearly one of the young Minangkabau officers whose hopes for power, prestige, and wealth were frustrated by the military retrenchment and the downgrading of the Banteng Division after the transfer of sovereignty. As the son of a leading member of the Muhammadiah, Husein was a devout Muslim,[66] and he must have been further disillusioned during his stint in West Java by being called upon to fight rebels who were equally fervent Muslims. Throughout his career, Husein's ties with his men had been close, and this and his earlier experiences during the occupation and revolution clearly influenced his response to the situation facing the soldiers under his command during the early 1950s.

The living conditions and welfare of the soldiers in West Sumatra, as in other parts of Indonesia, declined during these years. After serving frequent tours of duty in Aceh and West Java, Banteng soldiers returned home to barracks where their living quarters were in poor repair, the sanitary conditions primitive, and their children were suffering from a shocking amount of disease and death.[67] Husein lodged frequent complaints with Jakarta concerning these poor conditions, and in mid-August 1956, he and Governor Roeslan led a delegation to Jakarta to protest the situation and seek redress. When they returned on September 9, Governor Roeslan reported their mission had been successful, but no evidence of improvement was forthcoming over subsequent weeks.

While Husein was in the capital, he was approached by some of his former colleagues and superior officers from West Sumatra then studying at the Military Law Academy (AHM – Akademi Hukum Militer), who urged him to organize a reunion of the former Banteng Division. (Active in this, according to Husein, were a number of former officers of the division, including Nusjirwan, Jusuf Noer, Dahlan Djambek, and Sjoeib.[68]) On September 21, former and active Banteng officers held a series of meetings in Jakarta and Padang, and they decided to organize a reunion of members of the old West Sumatran division.[69] Husein appointed Major Sofyan Ibrahim to head the organizing committee, and two months later, from November 20-24, a Banteng Reunion was held in Padang.[70]

Officers and men flocked to attend, including three of the Banteng Division's commanders – Dahlan Djambek, Ismael Lengah, and Dahlan Ibrahim. Also present were North Sumatra Commander Simbolon and his counterpart for South Sumatra, TT II Commander Lt. Colonel Barlian, as well as Colonel Sadikin, representing Army Chief of Staff Nasution.

The Banteng Council

The final session of the Reunion on November 24, 1956, produced a Charter signed by the 612 Banteng Division veterans who were present. The so-called Banteng Charter focused its demands in four major fields: problems of the country in general; problems specific to the province of Central Sumatra; problems of regional defence; and social and economic problems of the region's people. On the national level, it demanded 'immediate implementation of progressive and radical improvements in all fields, especially in the leadership of the Army and henceforth in the leadership of the State'.[71] For Central Sumatra, it demanded broad autonomy in form and content. It called for a regional defence command and reinstatement of the former Banteng Division, as well as the abolition of Indonesia's centralized system of government, which, it held, had resulted in an unhealthy bureaucratic system, stagnation in regional development, and a loss of local initiative.[72]

The Reunion established a 'Banteng Council' (Dewan Banteng), charged with implementing the Banteng Charter; a council, it was emphasized, that could, in extraordinary circumstances, take matters 'into its own hands'. Only eight members of this seventeen-man Banteng Council were active or retired military officers.[73] Two others were from the police,[74] while the remaining seven were civilian, religious, or political leaders or officials.

The broad spectrum of Central Sumatran society represented in the Council demonstrated that the Banteng leaders were determined that their action should be seen not as part of a military initiative, but as a widely based regional movement, representing the dissatisfaction and aspirations of West Sumatrans who had participated in the Nationalist movement and independence struggle, while attempting not to alienate the peoples of Riau and Jambi. It also showed the extent to which disillusion had spread among so much of Minangkabau society.

In the weeks following the Reunion, members of the Banteng Council attempted to present its demands to the central government, attempts which they felt were rebuffed.[75] When Mohammad Hatta finally resigned his position as vice president on December 1, 1956, this provided the final impetus for decisive action in West Sumatra. Less than three weeks later, on the evening of December 20, members of the Banteng Council and other civilian and military officials gathered in Bukittinggi for a ceremony at which Central Sumatra Governor Roeslan Moeljohardjo formally handed over his powers to Banteng Brigade Commander Lt. Col. Ahmad Husein.

In yielding his office, Governor Roeslan stated he was certain that 'the revolutionary forces in Central Sumatra who are still struggling for the ideals of the [Independence] Proclamation are not driven by hunger for power....' He was completely convinced, he said, that

> the Banteng Council in particular and the people of Central Sumatra in general have no wish to build a State within a State, because relations between the Regional and the Central Government of the Republic of Indonesia will certainly return to normal when there is a Cabinet that can eliminate all the feelings of confusion, tension and dissatisfaction that threaten the security of the Indonesian State and People.[76]

CHAPTER 8

Defiance

The Banteng Council which was to lead the government of West Sumatra over the subsequent year was formed with the explicit task of implementing the Banteng Charter, and it measured its success by the degree to which it achieved this goal. On the local level, the Charter's principal aims were to gain greater economic, social, and political autonomy for the region, and to reinstate the former Banteng Division. On the national level, its main goals were the restoration of the joint leadership or duumvirate (*dwitunggal*) of Sukarno/Hatta, improvement of the civilian government, and reorganization of the armed forces leadership.

Unrest in the Military

The previous chapter examined West Sumatra's internal sources of unrest and dissatisfaction with the central government. But these specific complaints cannot be separated from the national Indonesian context, particularly the struggles within the armed forces, where similar disaffection soon led to parallel seizures of power by local commanders in North Sumatra, South Sumatra, and Sulawesi.

Unrest in the military was not a recent phenomenon. It had characterized the armed forces since the transfer of sovereignty and the death immediately thereafter of General Sudirman, the one charismatic Indonesian military leader who enjoyed the allegiance of all its troops. Although dissatisfaction in the military during the early 1950s focused on the figure of A.H. Nasution, Chief of Staff of the Army, it was also directed against all those who had received their initial military training from the Dutch during the late colonial period, which meant practically all officers at the apex of the military hierarchy.[1] The tensions first erupted into direct confrontation in 1952, when officers who had received their training as members of the former Japanese-sponsored Java-based militia, Peta (Pembela Tanah Air, Defenders of the Fatherland), tried to enlist President Sukarno's help in challenging Nasution and his policies.[2] Under Nasution's policy of rationalization, the armed forces which then numbered two-hundred thousand were to be reduced by eighty-thousand men by the end of 1952,[3] and it was mostly these less-educated, ex-Peta officers and soldiers who were scheduled for dismissal. In addition to being close to President Sukarno, the ex-Peta soldiers also had vocal defenders within the Parliament. But when Parliament interfered on their behalf, directly supporting them in what the armed forces leadership believed to be a matter of internal military discipline, a group of senior officers, including Nasution, went to the Palace on October 17, 1952, to confront Sukarno. They called for Parliament to be dissolved and nationwide elections to be held. Sukarno was able to rally his own forces against the challenge, and reject the group's demands. But Nasution's involvement in the affair, which was widely interpreted as an attempted military coup, led to his dismissal on December 18, 1952.[4]

For most of the next three years, Nasution was not involved in army affairs, and devoted his time to writing and to developing a new political party, the League of Upholders of Indonesian Independence (IPKI) made up mostly of military veterans.[5] During the years that Nasution was out of power, the army territorial commanders, particularly in Sumatra and Sulawesi, strengthened their authority over their local regions. Parliament, however, continued to control the purse strings, and it restricted defence allocations to less than 20 percent of the national budget. In his writings, Nasution charged that, for lack of funds, the army was being deprived of new equipment and weaponry, and 'soldiers were badly fed, provided with inadequate medical care, and living in ever more dilapidated barracks'.[6]

The territorial commanders responded to the deteriorating economic situation by turning to barter trade and smuggling to meet the needs of their soldiers. These operations were carried out on a large scale in Sulawesi, where military commanders had long been struggling to gain control over the copra trade, and in North Sumatra where Colonel Maludin Simbolon's command organized extensive rubber smuggling across the Malacca Strait.[7] Their barter operations gave the territorial commanders 'a financial base independent of the centre, one which sometimes was so strong that even if the military budget had been restored the commanders would have lost income by giving up their local arrangements'.[8] It was only when, following the 1955 elections, the Burhanuddin cabinet approved Nasution's reinstatement as army chief of staff on November 7, 1955, that the growing autonomy of these territorial commanders was threatened.

Determined to stamp out the warlordism that he saw now rampant in much of the archipelago, Nasution on his reinstatement immediately renewed his efforts to rationalize and streamline the army, and shore up his own control and that of central army headquarters. He immediately began rotating long-established territorial commanders, replacing them with officers on whose loyalty he could rely. Among those scheduled for transfer were Col. Maludin Simbolon in North Sumatra and Colonel J.F. Warouw in East Indonesia (both notable for their success in the barter trade), as well as Colonel Alex E. Kawilarang, commander of West Java's Siliwangi Division, and Colonel Zulkifli Lubis, who had served as army deputy chief of staff since December 1953.[9]

Lubis was in a special position. He had himself been one of the principal contenders for Nasution's current post, and as deputy chief of staff of the army had been responsible for running Army Headquarters during the long interregnum between the resignation of the previous chief of staff, Bambang Sugeng, on May 2, 1955, and Nasution's appointment in December of that year. Trained in intelligence by the Japanese during their occupation, Lubis had been responsible in 1945 for setting up the Republic's intelligence services, which he headed throughout the revolution. A Mandailing Batak born in Aceh, he was a devout Muslim and a cousin but strong opponent of Nasution, who returned his enmity in good measure. Nasution always viewed Lubis as the prime instigator of the opposition that developed against him in the army, stating:

> We were enemies already from the Yogya period [i.e. during the revolution]...He still had people from this period and also ties with the regional commanders. I tried to move them round, but I could not get these measures through. For the military this was the most urgent problem. Some people in sskad [the Army Staff and Command School in Bandung] were very close to Lubis, some had been his people earlier. Sumual [later to lead the rebellion in Sulawesi] trained there.[10]

The Army Staff and Command School (sskad) in Bandung was at the centre of opposition to Nasution. Set up during the revolution to provide middle-ranking officers with staff training, it was regarded as 'an intellectual and ideological center for the army', and its officer corps offered frequent criticisms of the policies of army headquarters.[11] Lubis himself stated that the regional councils in Sumatra and Sulawesi developed 'after discussions at sskad', though he believed that the idea came from outside, 'from Simbolon, from Rasjid'.[12] Whatever the case, in response to Nasution's moves to transfer long-established regional commanders, Lubis launched an unsuccessful coup against both the army chief of staff and Prime Minister Ali Sastroamidjojo on November 15, 1956. Nasution, as well as Ali, successfully weathered the attempt, and Lubis went into hiding. But Nasution did arrest several Lubis supporters at an anniversary celebration of the sskad held in Bandung from November 21-24, an action which further alienated much of his officer corps, and consolidated opposition to him in the regions.[13]

Several North Sumatran officers who had attended the Staff and Command School's anniversary celebration in Bandung at which the arrests took place, gathered with their fellow graduates and other officers in the north Sumatra town of Medan in early December. There they discussed proposals raised by sskad officers for restoring unity to the army by changing its leadership, dissolving the cabinet, and reorganizing and reducing the number of members of Parliament. The North Sumatran officers resolved to take radical action to implement these measures, an undertaking known as the 'December 4 Idea'.[14] Forty-eight officers of the North Sumatra military region, including its commander, Simbolon, and Banteng commander Husein, signed an oath that they would become 'pioneers in the struggle to realize the Independence Proclamation of 1945' and implement the December 4 Idea.[15] Measures espoused in the December 4 Idea became an integral part of all later demands by the local military councils that defied the central government.

When Colonel Ahmad Husein seized control in West Sumatra on December 20, 1956, his action was only the first in a series of regional upheavals led by dissatisfied army officers. Its most immediate successor was in Medan, where Simbolon launched a coup on December 22 with the announcement that he had taken over authority from the acting governor. He established an Elephant Council (Dewan Gajah), proclaimed a state of war and siege for the province of North Sumatra, and severed the ties between his military command and the central government in

Colonel Maludin Simbolon
(courtesy of *Kompas*)

Jakarta.[16] The government immediately responded by dismissing Simbolon and ordering his deputy, Lt. Colonel Djamin Gintings, to replace him as North Sumatra commander. After some initial hesitation, Gintings' troops surrounded Simbolon's home in Medan. Lacking sufficient local support to prevail, Simbolon fled to Tapanuli and eventually sought sanctuary with Husein in Padang.[17]

It was not until mid-January that Colonel Barlian, the South Sumatra commander, followed the example of his colleagues further north by proclaiming formation of a Garuda Council in Palembang. Because of his proximity to Java and the presence of a large number of Javanese troops in his territory, Barlian needed to exercise caution, and the Garuda council did not sever its ties with the central government or take any further actions for another couple of months. Finally, on March 9, Barlian announced that he had ousted the governor and taken over control of the civil administration of South Sumatra. Jakarta made one attempt to overthrow Barlian, encouraging a Javanese regimental commander stationed in Palembang to move against him, but the attempt failed miserably. In response, Barlian called on the Banteng Council for support and Husein promised to send him 1,200 troops in the event of an attack by the central government. Jakarta then backed down, and Barlian was able to consolidate his position in Palembang.[18]

The other major regional power seizure occurred in Sulawesi, the headquarters of Territorial Command VII, which embraced the whole of East Indonesia. It was led by Lt. Colonel H.N. Ventje Sumual, a Christian Minahasan whom Nasution had appointed to succeed Colonel Warouw as division commander in August 1956.[19] Sumual had participated in the SSKAD reunion in Bandung in November 1956 and had criticized Nasution's arrests of Lubis's supporters there. Since then, Sumual had been carefully watching the events in Sumatra. On March 2, 1957, he proclaimed a state of emergency in East Indonesia, declared himself 'military administrator', and instituted martial law. One of his officers, Saleh Lahade, read a 'Charter of Inclusive Struggle' (Piagam Perjuangan Semesta Alam) or Permesta (which was adopted as the name for the movement). The Charter incorporated East Indonesia's demands for greater local autonomy, economic development, and control of revenue, and, on the national level, for decentralization and the restoration of the Sukarno – Hatta duumvirate (*dwitunggal*.) Nasution bided his time in responding to the Permesta declaration, and it was not until June that he moved to oust Sumual. He accomplished this by dissolving the East Indonesia command which Sumual headed, splitting it into four military regions, and appointing Sumual merely as temporary chief of staff of the coordinating command. Unwilling to accept this demotion, Sumual, on June 19, with several of his loyal officers, transferred Permesta headquarters to northeastern Sulawesi, his home region where a sympathetic officer was still in command. From this Minahasa base, Sumual renewed his defiance.[20]

Success of the Banteng Council: December 1956 - July 1957

The nature of the Banteng Council and its actions differed in several ways from the seizures of power by local military commanders in other parts of the archipelago, and also from the Islamic rebellions that were already racking Aceh, West Java, and South Sulawesi. The Banteng Council was much more cohesive than the other military-led councils and was supported by a broader spectrum of the society. Its history was less tied to personal antagonisms against Nasution, and more based in the long-standing grievances of local civilian groups, as well as former members of the Banteng Division, with respect to West Sumatra's position in the postindependence Indonesian state. Its widespread support in the society also derived from the homogeneity of the Minangkabau people in West Sumatra, a homogeneity which did not extend to the other components of Central Sumatra – Riau and Jambi – where resentment of Minangkabau dominance led to definite fissures in the Council's support. At the same time, the autonomy movement in West Sumatra differed from the Darul Islam rebellions in Aceh, West Java, and South Sulawesi in that the Banteng Council did not head a primarily Islamic movement, although the modernist Islamic Masjumi party provided the broadest of its bases of local support. It was even less able to use Islam as a rallying cry when it joined with the other regional military councils, led by such Christian officers as Simbolon and Sumual.

In contrast to the situation in other parts of the archipelago, the Banteng Council's breadth of support in West Sumatra made the central government and the army command unwilling to confront it directly. In fact, rather than make efforts to oust Husein, as it had the dissident colonels in North and South Sumatra and in Sulawesi, Jakarta appeared willing to accept his authority at least in West Sumatra. Over the six months following its formation on December 20, 1956, the Banteng Council succeeded in realizing many of its aims, and it looked as if the central government might be willing to cede to it a considerable degree of the local autonomy it demanded in both the military and civilian fields.

Military Achievements

In contrast to his swift and harsh actions against both Simbolon and Lubis, Nasution always seemed to treat Husein with kid gloves. In fact, Husein has expressed the opinion that Nasution if anything encouraged him in his initial actions, when in early 1957 the army chief of staff condoned Husein's seizure of a shipment of weapons that were scheduled to go to Gintings' forces in Medan.[21] The first major success for the Banteng Council was when, at a meeting of Sumatra commanders held in Palembang at the end of January 1957, Nasution announced that Sumatra would be divided into four commands, including two new commands for Central Sumatra and Aceh. At the same time, he appointed former Banteng commander Dahlan Djambek to head a commission to look into the military problems on the island.[22] Two months later, this success was consolidated when Nasution inaugurated Husein as commander of the newly created military region of Central Sumatra and Sjahmaun Gaharu as commander in Aceh.[23] By conceding to the autonomy demands in the two dissident areas that were ethnically and culturally the most homogeneous, Nasution was clearly attempting to undercut efforts, particularly by Simbolon, to unify all the military forces in Sumatra in opposition to the central army command.

At the same time, in response to the territorial commanders' proclamation of martial law in their own regions, Nasution prevailed upon Sukarno to declare a national state of siege, hoping thereby to control further regional dissension and contain the growing splits within the armed forces.

Economic Decentralization

As has been noted, one of the major complaints of the regions was that most of their export earnings were channelled to the central government in Java, with none of the economic fruits of their independence struggle being enjoyed by the regions themselves. Local leaders demanded that earlier promises be fulfilled and the provinces be granted wider autonomy in financial affairs, with a more just balance maintained between the centre and the regions. As John Legge has noted, West Sumatra had less justification for its complaints in this regard than other Sumatran areas, for its export earnings were much lower than those for North or South Sumatra.[24] However, leaders of the Banteng Council based their own figures on the taxes raised and foreign exchange earned within the whole province of Central Sumatra (of which West Sumatra was the major political component), which considerably changed the picture.[25]

One of the promises made by Republican leaders during the revolutionary period that remained most vivid in the minds of the local people focused on electricity being brought to remote areas of West Sumatra. As late as 1995, the widow of revolutionary leader Chatib Suleiman could still recall how her husband in the months before his death told her how wonderful things were going to be after the Dutch departure, saying that now we are struggling but afterwards good things will come, including light to all the villages.[26] It was to this same promise that Husein returned when he reproached Sukarno and the central government in the speeches he gave around West Sumatra in 1957. In a speech in Solok he stated:

> When Bung Karno visited here in 1947 [sic] he said that independence for our country was for the prosperity of the people, so that within 10 years those who live in the mountains, in distant villages and even in isolated islands all will be illuminated with electric light.[27]

Husein and other members of his Banteng Council moved swiftly to make the people of the region feel the beneficial effects of local autonomy. Their most dramatic move in the months after their takeover was to give a million Rupiah to each district (*kabupaten*) for local development.[28] Ceremonies were held in district towns, where Council representatives handed over the money to local officials. Results were immediate. The funds sparked community efforts and resulted in new roads, irrigation projects, bridges, schools, and hospitals being built throughout the region. These accomplishments were still visible in West Sumatra in the 1990s, and local people still recalled them then as among the Banteng Council's major achievements.[29]

Political Support

From the date of its formation the Dewan Banteng attempted to enlist support from all political groupings in West Sumatra. Included in the seventeen-member Council, in addition to military and police officers, were an *adat* leader, representatives of both the traditional and modernist religious communities, as well as a local government official and a representative from Jambi and one from Riau.[30] Members of the Council always pointed to their Javanese General Secretary, Soeleiman, as evidence that they were not Minangkabau chauvinists and not anti-Javanese.[31] Advisers to the council included lawyers and teachers,[32] and among their outspoken supporters were Mohammad Sjafei of the INS and Abdullah, teacher at the Adabiah school and follower of Tan Malaka.[33]

Husein and his Council made major efforts to ensure that influential figures within various West Sumatran organizations understood the limited nature of the Council's aims and publicly supported it. When the chairman of the students' organization of the Faculty of Agriculture made no statement in support of the Council, Husein, together with Simbolon and police chief Kaharuddin Dt. Rangkayo Basa, came to his home in Padang Luar 'to explain to me that there were disparities in the distribution to the regions and that this move was just a reminder to the central government and also for the development of the region'. The student leader then agreed to make a statement of support in the Faculty of Agriculture.[34]

During the early months of the council, there appear to have been only two major sources of opposition to it: (a) the Indonesian Communist Party (PKI), and (b) sections of the population in Riau and Jambi, whose disaffection spread to Pesisir Selatan Kerinci on the southern border of West Sumatra.

a) The Indonesian Communist Party

From the beginning, antagonisms flared between the Council and the Communists. Immediately after the proclamation of the Banteng Council, the head of the Communist party's Politbureau in Jakarta, D. N. Aidit, charged that the affair in Central Sumatra had been instigated by the Masjumi and Socialist (psi) parties, and did not have support of the people. Colonel Ismael Lengah (former commander of the Banteng Division), as the Council's liaison to the authorities in Jakarta, met with Aidit to try to persuade him to moderate his views. Though Lengah subsequently stated that he had got a promise from Aidit to withdraw his earlier statement, the Politbureau in fact reiterated its charges on December 27, 1956, accusing the Council of being anti-democratic and reactionary.[35]

Communist leaders later expressed pride that their party was the only political group within West Sumatra that opposed the Banteng Council:

> When in the months of December, January and February, the 'Dewan Banteng' was at the peak of its power, when our society acted as if it were overcome by an overwhelming wave, when the Dewan Banteng moved to the forefront with all kinds of initiatives, at that time it was only the Communist Party that never stopped explaining the reality of the situation and never stopped issuing commands to the People that they not believe the false slogans of the fascist group and that they mount opposition to it.[36]

In the early weeks of 1957, the Banteng Council arrested several members of labour unions affiliated with the Communist party in Pekanbaru. They were brought to West Sumatra and imprisoned in Bukittinggi and Padang on charges of carrying out verbal and written attacks on the Council, and infiltrating government agencies to undermine the administration.[37] Protests against the arrests came from the Jakarta headquarters of the Indonesian Communist Party (pki) and of the Communist Labour Federation, SOBSI, and were backed up by a spokesman for the provincial committee of the pki in Central Sumatra, Djamhur Hamzah, before he too was detained by local authorities.[38] From then on, antagonism between the Banteng Council and the Communist Party in Jakarta became ever more bitter.[39]

However, within West Sumatra itself, for the time being, the issue was not so clear-cut. Despite exhortations from Party headquarters, several local Communist Party branches supported the Council, and many Communists deserted the party.[40] Many West Sumatran families had both Masjumi and Communist Party members who freely discussed their differences of opinion regarding the Banteng Council, with individual Communists torn between their ideological and local allegiances.[41]

b) Riau and Jambi

The province of Central Sumatra consisted not only of West Sumatra but also of the mainland and island regions of Riau to the east, and to the southeast the previous residency of Jambi. During the revolution, while the land area of Riau had been within the military command of the Banteng Division, the Dutch had retained control over the myriad islands making up the Riau archipelago. Both during the revolution and subsequently, military forces in Jambi were incorporated in the South Sumatra (Garuda) division, which had its headquarters in Palembang. Riau and Jambi had both been traditional settlement (*rantau*) areas for the Minangkabau people, who often held a disproportionate degree of power in both the economic and administrative affairs of these less-developed regions. There then existed sufficient tensions within the two regions to provide fertile ground for central government attempts to undermine the authority of the Dewan Banteng there.

But the Council, too, was conscious of these dangers, and it made consistent efforts to retain allegiance from the peoples of both areas. Only a few weeks after formation of the Banteng Council, Husein declared that it would grant autonomy to Riau and Jambi, and instructed that committees be set up in each region to prepare the way for establishing the two new provinces. A few days later, the Committee for Formation of Riau Province declared it would 'sink or swim' with the Banteng Council.[42] Although several civilian political leaders within West Sumatra opposed the division of the province of Central Sumatra, the Council went ahead with its plans.[43]

The central government moved equally swiftly, instructing the Resident in Riau to deal directly with Jakarta on all government matters, rather than via the provincial capital in Padang. At the same time, it transferred the Resident of Jambi, who supported the Banteng Council, to Jakarta.[44] From then on, the central government made a major effort to detach both Riau and Jambi from allegiance to the Banteng Council, passing an emergency law to create separate provinces of West Sumatra, Riau, and Jambi.[45] Husein for his part inaugurated the first governor of Riau on October 15.[46]

It is difficult to assess the relative success of Jakarta and Padang in attracting loyalty from the people of the two new provinces, but J.D. Legge concludes:

> It was, perhaps, natural that the mainland part of Riau should go along with the Husein regime. Conversely Djambi, since it had been militarily tied to South Sumatra even when it had been included within Central Sumatra politically, continued to look to Palembang rather than to Padang and remained loyal to the central government after it had become a separate province.[47]

This may have been the case at an official level, but even after South Sumatra commander Barlian later refused to join Husein in rebellion, many people, particularly in the areas of Jambi close to the West Sumatra border, actively supported the rebel forces.

Repercussions at the Centre

The various local military councils shared a number of national aims, including removal of the Ali Sastroamidjojo government, restoration of Hatta in the nation's leadership, increased regional autonomy (preferably including the establishment of a second legislative body in Jakarta to represent the regions), and in the military sphere, reorganization of the armed forces leadership. The Banteng Council put far less emphasis on the last of these than did the military leaders in the other regions. As has been noted, Husein had reasonably good relations with Nasution, and once the Banteng Division had been reinstated and a new military command established in Central Sumatra with Husein at its head, he had little inclination to pursue further reorganization of the armed forces leadership or any replacement of Nasution as army chief of staff. His attitude was very different from that of the other colonels, particularly Simbolon and Lubis, both of whom had lost their earlier powerful positions and had little hope of regaining leadership posts unless there was a drastic reorganization in the armed forces and Nasution was removed from the scene. Nevertheless, from March of 1957, Husein provided sanctuary within West Sumatra to Simbolon, and frequently also to Lubis, even though his aims and theirs diverged quite markedly.

The aim of replacing the Ali Sastroamidjojo government was soon accomplished, though the regional unrest was only one of several causes for his cabinet's collapse. In part as a consequence of the formation of the regional councils, support for the cabinet was undermined as parties sympathetic to the councils, notably the Masjumi and Perti, withdrew their representatives from the government.[48] Sukarno soon moved to respond to the crisis. On February 21, he formally advocated his conception (*konsepsi*) of a new political system, under which there would be a four-party cabinet, made up of the Nationalist (PNI), Islamic (Masjumi and Nahdlatul Ulama), and Communist (PKI) parties. This new cabinet would be advised by a National Council consisting of functional groups drawn from all segments of Indonesian society.[49] There was a strong reaction both in the regions and in Jakarta against the proposal to include the Communist Party within the cabinet. As noted above, less than a month later, on March 14, Nasution prevailed on Sukarno to proclaim a state of emergency, and the Ali cabinet tendered its resignation.[50]

The fall of Ali Sastroamidjojo seemed to open the way for fulfilment of what was the most heartfelt of the demands of the Banteng Council – the return of Hatta to a position of real power in the government, either through his resumption of the post of vice president or as head of a new cabinet. The regionalists, particularly in West Sumatra, had laid their principal emphasis on Hatta rejoining Sukarno at the head of the state in a restoration of the *dwitunggal*. Mohammad Sjafei voiced this widespread sentiment in West Sumatra when he noted that while Javanese had always seen Sukarno as the just king (*ratu adil*), the regions outside Java saw the *ratu adil* as a combination of both Sukarno and Hatta.[51]

Hatta, however, would not be content with a return to nominal co-leadership with Sukarno, for he had experienced the frustrations of occupying the largely symbolic position of vice president during the years preceding his resignation. He outlined his thinking on the subject in an extensive article which was carried in *Haluan* on March 20, only a few days after the Ali cabinet resigned. Here he wrote:

> In searching for a suitable way out, it is good for us to accept the existing

reality and not hope to achieve a solution by holding to a certain myth, such as the resuscitation of the dwitunggal Myth....

I can understand it when several regions demand the return of the Sukarno Hatta dwitunggal at the head of the government of the state as it was at the beginning of our National Revolution. This expresses the regions' loss of faith in the capacity of the Central Government....

But implementation of these hopes and desires is in conflict with the present reality that differs from the earlier one. According to the letter and spirit of the First Republic of Indonesia Constitution, the administration of the state was based on a Presidential Cabinet under the leadership of the President and Vice President, who in all matters had the same status. This gave birth to the dwitunggal.

He goes on to note that under the present (1950) constitution it is the cabinet that has the authority to govern and the Head of State is only a symbol.[52] Thus, demands for restoration of the earlier *dwitunggal* were in conflict both with the present constitution and with 'the reluctance of President Sukarno himself to directly head the government'. Stressing that this did not mean 'that it is impossible for Bung Karno and me to work together in the interests of the state, in a different way than we did earlier', he urged his supporters to search for a solution based on the current reality:

> *First*, establish a capable and authoritative Government made up of men who are respected and are able to restore the political morality that has disappeared....
> *Second*, establish an efficient administration in both the centre and the regions....
> *Third*, [provide for] a suitable division of labour between the centre and regions, based on a system of autonomy that is democratic, and free from hierarchical levels, and [for] a just division of finances....
> This is the realistic road that should now be followed to bring us together again as a people, firmly united and not shattered by dissension [*berpeceh-belah*], in a climate of unity in diversity [*bhineka tunggal ika*].[53]

Despite Hatta's elucidation of the unreality of hopes for its restoration, the *dwitunggal* remained the popular formulation put forward in demands made by West Sumatra and other regions for Hatta's return to a position of leadership in the Indonesian state.

After several weeks of manoeuvring, regional hopes for Hatta's return were dashed when in early-April, 1957, Sukarno appointed Djuanda Kartawidjaja, a respected nonparty independent, to head a new cabinet which the president described as a Kabinet Karya (working cabinet).[54] Husein and others in West Sumatra expressed their disappointment at Sukarno's selection process, where Hatta had been ignored and during which slanders had circulated regarding his earlier business dealings.[55] However, Djuanda, the new prime minister, was a moderate and a Sundanese from West Java who had made the pilgrimage to Mecca and was thus potentially more sympathetic to non-Javanese and Islamic attitudes than the previous PNI-headed government had been. One of Djuanda's first official acts as prime minister was to visit West Sumatra and meet with the regional dissidents to discuss their grievances.[56]

Hopes for Compromise

Formation of the Djuanda government led to a period of negotiation and discussion, when it appeared as if some compromise might be reached between the two sides. During his April visit to West Sumatra, Djuanda assured the Banteng Council that he had come to remove suspicions between centre and region. Acknowledging that previous cabinets had thought in a centralist way, he stressed that he and his colleagues were now determined to abandon this way of thinking. Djuanda's words were given added weight by the fact that for the past few months the Parliament in Jakarta had been passing legislation outlining steps for decentralizing the country's administration. Though as yet few results were visible, Jakarta promised to speed up implementation of these decentralization laws, which granted greater regional administrative and fiscal autonomy. Shortly after his appointment, Prime Minister Djuanda also promised an expanded public works programme for areas outside Java.[57]

During Djuanda's visit to West Sumatra, Husein put forward three major sets of demands from the Banteng Council: (1) broad autonomy; (2) financial balance between centre and regions, removal of centralism, formation of a pre-senate made up of regional representatives; and (3) improvement in the leadership of the armed forces.[58] He expanded on these demands when, immediately afterwards, he visited Jakarta to participate in an All Indonesia Military Conference attended by Nasution and regional commanders from throughout Indonesia. There, Husein reiterated the Banteng Council's loyalty to the ideals of the Independence Proclamation, and, after declaring that actions in the regions were a response to decay in the state, called again for a return of the *dwitunggal*.[59] He warned that it would be a national tragedy if the central government responded with force to the regions' demands.

In his speeches before Djuanda and before the military conference, Husein opened up one of the possible avenues for compromise between the regions and the centre. He and others saw Sukarno's call for formation of a National Council representing all functional groups in Indonesia as a potential vehicle through which to realize their own wish for a pre-senate which would include representatives from the regions and thus balance the majority representation of the Parliament (DPR). In Padang, Djuanda had supported the idea, stating that he favoured a National Council that would have the form of a pre-senate representing the regions.[60]

Although these ideas did not accord with Sukarno's perception of the National Council, for a while it looked as if this formulation could provide a ground for compromise between the two sides. When appointed by Sukarno to sit in the Council as a representative of Central Sumatra, Abdullah, the respected educator and former Tan Malaka follower, at first refused, stating that he could not participate before a normalization of relations was reached between the regions and the centre. Sukarno went so far as to invite Abdullah to the Palace where after a two-hour meeting Abdullah was eventually persuaded to sit in the National Council, not as a representative of the region, but as an individual citizen of West Sumatra and on condition that force was not to be used against the region – a promise Sukarno guaranteed in writing.[61] When Rasuna Said agreed to sit in the Council as a representative of West Sumatra, she was chided by her old comrade Ratna Sari, who said that Rasuna Said had lived too long in Jakarta and no longer understood the feelings of the people of her home region.[62]

In late June and early July, there seemed still to be a real possibility of compromise, at least between Husein and the central government. Despite his adamant stand against readmitting Hatta to any form of shared power, Sukarno seemed to be willing to take some steps toward assuaging the grievances of the regions. Djuanda, the new prime minister, was openly seeking some basis for compromise, stating to Parliament at the end of May his government's 'willingness to fufill the demands of the regions as far as possible', contending that it had 'already realized several of those wishes while bearing in mind the financial position of the country'.[63] Husein, too, seemed to see some possibility of compromise. In a speech in mid-July, he discussed Sukarno's *konsepsi*, stating that this did not yet fulfil the wishes of the people of the regions because 'in addition to the DPR [People's Representative Council (or Parliament)] that currently exists, the regions should have representatives either in the form of a senate or pre-senate that can better guarantee the interests of the regions. For what is the meaning of the National Council if all its members are only appointed from the people around Bung Karno himself?'[64] Some reshuffling of Sukarno's ideas of a National Council then seemed the major area on which some compromise could be based.

The people of West Sumatra saw the Banteng Council restoring some measure of dignity to their region in the national arena after the series of slights they had been subjected to over the previous years. They noted the respect accorded Husein during his trips to Jakarta, where military and civilian leaders, including Hatta and the Sultan of Yogyakarta, invited him to meet with them and paid attention to his views, and where he was able to argue in public for greater regional autonomy. So far, Husein had emerged triumphant in his challenge to the central government, and rather than being weakened by his severance of ties with Jakarta, was apparently strengthened both in his relations with the centre and in his control over the local government.

But the seeds of the future tragedy were already visible both in Jakarta and in Padang. Although the civilian government and the top army command appeared to be searching for compromise with the dissidents, other political forces at the centre clearly opposed any concessions. Shortly after Husein attended the military conference at the end of April, the Banteng Council's commissioner in Jakarta was arrested and held in custody for several weeks. Rumours were spread throughout the capital that the Banteng Council was providing assistance to dissident regional forces in West Java, with Lubis clearly suspected of being their leader.[65] Violence erupted in Jakarta, as grenades were thrown against both Communist headquarters and the houses of regional sympathizers.[66]

Dr. Sumitro Djojohadikusumo

In Padang, Husein himself was being pressured by his less-successful colleagues to assume a more confrontational stance toward the central government. Since Simbolon's flight from Medan at the end of 1956, Husein had granted him asylum in West Sumatra. Although Lubis spent much of his time in hiding in Jakarta, he, too, frequently came to both West and South Sumatra. And in May, Dr. Sumitro Djojohadikusumo, fleeing charges of financial fraud in Jakarta, also sought sanctuary with the Banteng Council in West Sumatra, while making frequent trips abroad.[67] None of these men would be willing to accept a peaceful outcome based merely on Hatta's return to the government, and greater autonomy for the regions, with more regional influence and representation at the centre. And several of the fugitives now hiding in the dissident regions were openly courting outside powers, particularly the United States, in the hope of obtaining sufficient support to challenge Sukarno's government. Their pleas were falling on fertile ground in Washington, where the Dulles brothers and other American policy makers were happy to find local allies in their struggle against the forces of communism or neutralism in Southeast Asia.[68]

Impingement of Outside Forces & Moves toward a Break

A watershed was reached in August and September 1957. During these months, the possibilities for compromise were explored, but the pressures from both extremes – the Communist Party in Jakarta on one side, and the dispossessed colonels and their foreign supporters, together with Lubis' fanatically anti-Communist organizations, on the other – polarized the situation so that by the end of September, the opportunity for a peaceful agreement between the centre and the regions had been lost. The events of the succeeding months would only further exacerbate the situation until the dissension turned into armed rebellion after the declaration of a competing government in February 1958.

In August, Prime Minister Djuanda was initiating real efforts to bridge the differences between the centre and the regions. He proposed a National Conference (Musyawarah Nasional or Munas) to normalize the situation in the Republic of Indonesia and strengthen its unity.[69] Spokesmen from the regions voiced tentative hopes for the outcome of such a conference, but also expressed their misgivings as to the sincerity of the government's search for a peaceful solution. Husein asked why such military leaders as Lubis, Simbolon, and Djambek had not been invited to participate in the conference. He also regretted the government's recent proclamation of emergency laws dividing Central Sumatra into three autonomous territories, and the fact that it had sent invitations to attend the conference not only to five representatives from West Sumatra, but also the same number from both Riau and Jambi. He likened these actions to the 'divide and rule' tactics the Dutch employed against the Republic during the revolution.[70]

Djuanda's cabinet made some moves to alleviate at least Husein's concerns, when it decided to 'invite only provincial officials by name and allow them to select advisers', thus opening the door for the regional commanders to bring along their dissident military colleagues who no longer held commands, such as Colonels Simbolon and Lubis.[71]

The Palembang Charter

But even before the conference opened on September 10, the military were ranging themselves firmly in opposing camps. Nasution had called a conference of territorial commanders, which was held on August 29 in Bandung.[72] From Padang, Dahlan Djambek commented that Nasution's convening this conference in Bandung, and an earlier one in Semarang, raised suspicions that the army chief of staff was trying to divide the armed forces into two blocs.[73] At the same time, Sumual proposed that the military heads of all the dissident councils meet in Palembang on September 4.[74] Nasution forbade the regional commanders from participating in such a meeting. Nevertheless, under cover of an ongoing conference of Islamic scholars,[75] the dissident colonels and Dr. Sumitro met in Palembang on September 7-8. At the end of their meeting they drew up a declaration, the so-called Palembang Charter, which was signed by the three dissident colonels still holding commands – Colonels Barlian, Husein, and Sumual (but with Colonels Djambek, Lubis, and Simbolon, as well as Dr. Sumitro, also participating). The Charter included six major demands:

> 1. restoration of the Sukarno – Hatta duumvirate;
> 2. replacement of the existing central military leadership (meaning Nasution's resignation);
> 3. implementation of a policy of decentralization by granting extensive autonomy to the regions;
> 4. formation of a senate;
> 5. general rejuvenation and simplification of the government;
> 6. banning of 'internationally oriented Communism'.[76]

So for the first time the colonels were apparently calling in this charter for banning the Indonesian Communist Party (PKI). It seems evident that they took this stand not merely, as Simbolon has recently asserted, 'because the PKI could not possibly be accepted within the Pancasila ideology',[77] but at least in part as an appeal to the colonels' American audience. The phraseology of the demand, however, directed as it was to 'internationally oriented communism', would also seem to target the PKI specifically, implicitly excluding Tan Malaka's national Communist party Murba.[78]

After their Palembang discussions, Sumitro told a visiting American that once the Munas conference in Jakarta was over, he expected to get 'full powers' from Barlian and Husein. He then planned to go first to Singapore to see 'U.S. Consul General Foster Collins, an old friend' (and widely regarded by Indonesian leaders as being the area's top CIA agent) and subsequently to the United States 'to inform U.S. officials at [the] highest possible level of developments in dissident areas'.[79] It was the anticommunism paragraph in the Palembang charter that Sumitro's lieutenant, Roland Liem, stressed in these subsequent efforts to attract foreign support for the dissident movement. In approaching both the British and the Americans, he described the Palembang Charter as providing for a 'National Front against communism' which would 'join with any other bloc which wishes to crush communism'.[80] Although Sumitro appears to have been the dissidents' major channel to foreign supporters, Simbolon also met with American intelligence agents, as did Sumual and Lubis and later probably Husein.[81]

The meeting of the dissident commanders in early September coincided with an all-Indonesia conference of Islamic scholars also held at Palembang. This meeting was equally vocal in condemning communism and proposing concrete measures to combat it, while calling upon President Sukarno to ban the Indonesian Communist Party.[82] The Islamic leaders made these statements in the face of a much more reasoned critique of communism set out by Hatta in his message to the conference. There, the former vice president emphasized that, while Marx should be rejected because he was a materialist who was antireligious, the truth of much of his social analysis should also be recognized, as should the fact that

> the main reasons for the development of communism lie in the poverty of the people which increases day by day. Communist successes are not caused by their actions to promote their ideology, an ideology that is not understood by most people, but rather is the result of their activities in working with the people and their promises that they will divide landholding and improve the lot of the poor.[83]

Hatta's informed and balanced attitude toward communism possibly contributed to the colonels' expressed disillusionment with him during their meetings at Palembang. The guidelines they drew up for the future struggle rejected the 'myth of the *dwitunggal*', and abandoned 'the idea that everything can be solved if only the *dwitunggal* were re-established'. They resolved, however, that, as Colonel Lubis' secret papers noted, their disillusionment should 'be kept secret because the change in attitude toward Bung Hatta will have a great effect that could be used by our opponents'.[84]

The agreements they made at Palembang with their dissident comrades made it less likely that Husein, Barlian, and Sumual would be flexible in their discussions with national leaders at the Munas conference held in Jakarta from September 10-12, and diminished whatever area of compromise had previously existed between the regions and the centre.[85] Nevertheless, all three colonels initially felt that they received a fair hearing at the National Conference in Jakarta and that it made some progress toward settling the centre - regional dissension.

Twenty-one regions were represented at the National Conference, but major interest among the press and public focused on the Banteng delegation, and particularly on Colonel Husein.[86] Participants were impressed by the speech Husein made to the conference. Stressing that the unrest in the regions was merely aimed at correcting the centre's mistakes, he downplayed the dissatisfaction within the armed forces, and defined the major problems faced by the country as, first, the splitting of the *dwitunggal*, and, second, 'the problem of a National Council versus the idea of a pre-senate'. With respect to the first, he 'prayed that our Duumvirate [of Sukarno and Hatta] can be restored so that together they can give leadership to the people and armed forces as they did in earlier times'. Then, emphasizing that the essence of the dissension was the regions' lack of faith in the centre, he stated that 'With the formation of a pre-senate where a majority of the members are chosen by the regions, then perhaps harmonious relations can be re-established between the regions and the centre'. The body, he said, could still retain the name 'National Council' (Dewan Nasional) envisaged by Sukarno in his *konsepsi* 'so long as its content accords with the reality within our society'.[87]

Throughout the conference all regional representatives were in accord in their major demand that the Sukarno/Hatta duumvirate be restored. But this hope was again disappointed, for although at the end of the conference President Sukarno and former Vice President Hatta joined together in a ceremony at the site of their earlier Proclamation of Indonesian Independence in 1945, where they now pledged to 'cooperate with the entire Indonesian people' for the good of the country, they signed no actual agreement. Moreover, any possibility that the broad sentiment expressed at the conference for restoration of the *dwitunggal* might ultimately have pressured Sukarno into yielding some concrete role to Hatta was undermined by Hatta's departure immediately afterwards on a 40-day trip to the Republic of China.[88]

The Munas deferred discussion of economic problems to a meeting to be held a few weeks later. It did, however, establish a seven-man committee to study military questions and 'recommend actions to end differences between Army Headquarters and Regional Commanders'.[89] Despite the paucity of concrete results from the conference, there was a sense of relief that it had 'ended on at least [a] surface note [of] national unity', and that the first tentative steps had been taken toward a rapprochement between Hatta and Sukarno and between the regional dissidents and the central government.

The three commanders who had attended the conference were all guardedly optimistic at its results. Husein, in particular, had enjoyed his position in the limelight and later admitted 'we were satisfied at the decisions' reached there.[90] Immediately after the conference, he declared that he was hopeful that the principles for solution outlined at the conference would be implemented and was encouraged by the religious feelings that influenced the discussions, but he regretted that Hatta's absence in China would prevent his participating in the decisions of the Committee of Seven that the conference had appointed to investigate the situation.[91]

His military colleagues who had remained in Sumatra were, however, far more critical of the conference's results, and they, together with Dr. Sumitro, voiced these criticisms in a meeting they held with Husein and Barlian in Padang shortly after the two returned from Jakarta. According to Sumitro, at that meeting:

> It was the unanimous conclusion of the regional leaders that the National Conference had turned out to be nothing more than a diversionary move on the part of the Centralists. Worse still, it had developed into a signal victory for Sukarno's skill at political maneuvering.[92]

The participants at the Padang meeting drew up a statement which characterized the Munas conference as a victory for Sukarno that had further restricted Hatta's position. The statement also criticized Nasution's appointment to the Committee of Seven, stating that his position as chief of staff of the army 'should have ruled him out for membership'.[93] It emphasized that 'the composition of this Committee...was heavily weighted in favour of Sukarno and Nasution'.[94] Nasution's presence on the committee may indeed have impeded its work, for, according to another of its members, Hamengku Buwono IX, Sultan of Yogyakarta, it did reach a face-saving compromise, which was supported by the Sultan and Sukarno but was opposed by Nasution's staff and some of the younger territorial commanders, who insisted that army unity could not be restored unless Simbolon was dismissed from the army.[95]

Yielding to the opinions of his colleagues in Padang, several of whom were more senior in the army hierarchy and had previously been his superior officers, Husein now began to express a far more skeptical attitude toward the National Conference. 'We should not be too impressed by the resolutions and decisions and the emergence of Sukarno/Hatta together as the two national leaders from the Munas', he now said, 'for all of this was merely a puppet show. What gives it content is the realization and implementation of these decisions'.[96] Simbolon used the same simile, describing the conference as a theatrical play (*sandiwara*) and accusing the central government of talking about discussions while trying to impose its wishes unilaterally on the regions.[97]

It is worth noting that Hatta was equally disillusioned with the Munas conference, but his disillusionment focused on the role the regional dissidents played there. In discussions with President Sukarno prior to the conference, the former vice president had been pressing him to form a presidential cabinet, presumably with Hatta at its head. Sukarno had refused, only agreeing that Hatta should head a National Planning Council. Hatta had hoped that the conference would strengthen his hand, and was disappointed when the regional representatives – despite all the calls at the conference for a restoration of the *dwitunggal* – did not press for the former vice president to be assigned an important government position. He wrote later to Dahlan Djambek:

> I am actually the one who should be dissatisfied with the results of the National Conference that bound me to an ambiguous position. If some of the regions now feel dissatisfied, this is a result of their having partici- pated in the unanimous acceptance of the imprecise formula presented to them.

He described the joint oath made by Sukarno and himself as meaningless, like enter- taining children with a dead sparrow, and accused the regional representatives of being unwilling to recognize their own responsibility: 'if a decision was not accept- able and would not be followed, it should not have been agreed to'.[98]

The Fact-Finding Commission of the Committee of Seven, set up at the National Conference, did, however, appear to be genuinely trying to carry out its investiga- tions impartially and seriously, interviewing military opponents of the central gov- ernment, both those in jail and those in the regions. It went so far as to call on the authorities to revoke their order for Zulkifli Lubis' arrest.[99] Despite these signs of good faith, the dissident colonels were not willing to give the Commission the bene- fit of the doubt. Even while it was carrying out its investigations in West Sumatra, Djambek was bewailing that 'the more time passes the more gloomy the results of the Munas appear, and we are beginning to be pessimistic about what was achieved there'.[100] When the National Economic Development Conference (Munap), the successor to the Munas conference, convened on November 25, to address regional- ist dissatisfaction in the economic field, Husein did not attend.[101]

The Issue of Communism

Communism was increasingly becoming an issue over which the centre and the regions were in conflict. As we have seen, since December 1956 the Indonesian Communist Party had opposed the Banteng Council and other regional dissident movements. In West Sumatra itself, however, over at least the first six months of the council's existence, there seemed no absolute incompatibility between being a regionalist and being a Communist. But by September 1957 it was virtually impossi- ble to hold to both positions.

Husein had begun to adopt a more confrontational stance in July, when he appointed a military man as district head (*bupati*) in Sawahlunto Sijunjung, a district whose history of radical activity stretched back to the 1926/7 rebellion, and where even now the Communists were stronger than elsewhere in West Sumatra. Mansoer Sani, the new military *bupati*, took steps to remove all Communists, many of whom were Javanese, from civilian and military positions, arresting a few of their leaders and sending them to be imprisoned in Padang.[102]

The change can in part be attributed to the growing polarization in Jakarta, where extremist Islamic youth groups were launching grenade attacks against the headquarters of the Communist party and its labour union federation in Jakarta.[103] At the same time, through their newspapers and pamphlets, the Communist Party headquarters in Jakarta openly attacked the colonels and their supporters in the Masjumi and Socialist parties and called for arrest of Banteng Council officials.

The polarization within West Sumatra itself was exacerbated when Dahlan Djambek, the former commander of the Banteng Division, resigned his position in Jakarta and fled to Padang in late August, following a grenade attack on his home. Since the beginning of 1957, Djambek had been acting as a military liaison between army headquarters and the dissidents, and had also headed the 'liaison staff' headquartered in Medan, which Nasution had established to settle military aspects of the Sumatra problem.[104] Even earlier, he had been a voice of moderation at the first Reunion of the former Banteng Division in November 1956, where he had attempted to persuade his former military subordinates that there were legal channels through which they could assuage their discontent, arguing that

> To struggle now is not the same as in 1945. Now there is a central government, an elected parliament, and there are channels that the people must use for their complaints.[105]

But over the first half of 1957, his stance had changed. He became increasingly critical of the policies of both the central government and the army command, and when he asked to be relieved of his duties in mid-August he characterized his action as 'a protest against the way the people in power in the centre make use of that power'.[106] The Communist press had been launching accusations against him for months, and on August 17 grenades were thrown at his house in Jakarta. It is not certain that Communist elements were responsible for this attack, as it was followed immediately by a similar one against Communist Party headquarters, launched by an extremist Islamic youth organization.[107]

It appears that Djambek's flight was not merely caused by disillusionment and fear for his family's safety after the grenade attack, but was also probably a result of the charges of corruption being spread against him in the Jakarta press.[108] These accusations, as well as earlier ones charging him with involvement in an alleged Dewan Banteng conspiracy in the capital, probably originated with the Communist Party, for Djambek's religious fervor had made him the party's open adversary. When he did flee to West Sumatra, Djambek took over leadership of anti-Communist forces there and provoked ever more open enmity between the Communists and the followers of the Dewan Banteng.

During September and October, it was as leader of the anti-Communist movement in West Sumatra that Dahlan Djambek came to the fore. He was important locally not only because of his military exploits during the independence struggle, but his charisma also derived from his father, Syekh Mohd. Djamil Djambek, the outstanding Islamic scholar in Bukittinggi during the late colonial period, whose *surau* was still a centre of teaching and worship for Muslim students and townspeople there.[109] On September 4, just a couple of weeks after he arrived back in Padang,

Dahlan Djambek was instrumental in forming a Joint Movement Against Communism, known by its acronym Gebak (Gerakan Bersama Anti Komunisme), and became its secretary general.[110]

Over the succeeding months, the Gebak movement spread and became the major vehicle for launching attacks against Communists, occasionally taking on anti-Chinese overtones. In a speech in late October, Djambek blamed communism as

> one factor preventing cooperation between Sukarno and Hatta, strongly opposing the regional movements, and respecting foreign leaders such as Stalin, Mao Tse Tung etc. in the same way it respects our national leaders.

He went on to state that he believed the Communist party was receiving funding from a foreign source or from foreigners in Indonesia (presumably the Chinese).[111] Djambek also tried to use the Gebak to coordinate anti-Communist movements in other regions,[112] and in his father's Bukittinggi *surau* organized weekly sermons against the Communists.[113]

Crises in Jakarta

A rapid series of national and international incidents accelerated the burgeoning crisis between Jakarta and the regions.

The first incident took place in New York. For months, Indonesia had been mobilizing international support for its claim to West Irian, but on November 29, 1957, a United Nations General Assembly vote on whether to take up the Dutch/Indonesia dispute over this issue again fell short of the two-thirds majority needed to put it on the United Nations agenda.[114] Carrying out threats he had made over the previous weeks should the vote fail, Sukarno immediately ordered Dutch citizens to leave Indonesia and authorized Indonesian labour unions and the army to take over Dutch properties.

The following evening, November 30, when Sukarno was attending a night fair at his children's school in the Cikini neighbourhood of Jakarta, a group of youths hurled grenades at him and his party. The president narrowly escaped death, but eleven of those around him were killed, and at least thirty more severely wounded. Many of the casualties were children.

The young people carrying out the attack were members of the Jakarta-based Anti-Communist Movement (GAK, Gerakan Anti-Komunis), which had been established the previous July and was led by Saleh Ibrahim, a close associate of Zulkifli Lubis. Lubis himself was known by GAK members as Pak Haji, and members of the organization described him as its protector (*pelindung*).[115] Several of the group's young members came from the strongly Islamic areas of Bima and Dompo (on Sumbawa) and were lodged in an *asrama* close to the Cikini school. Many also belonged to the official youth group of the Masjumi party, the Indonesian Islamic Youth Movement (Gerakan Pemuda Islam Indonesia, GPII).[116] Both Lubis and Saleh

Ibrahim evaded capture after the grenade attack, and successfully escaped to Sumatra. But in the days immediately following the attack the government arrested many students from the Anti-Communist Movement (GAK). Four of them were brought to trial in April 1958, three of them eventually executed and the fourth sentenced to life-imprisonment for the murders.[117]

During the trial, the accused testified that Zulkifli Lubis was one of their principal teachers, and confessed that they had made several previous assassination attempts against Sukarno, as well as grenade attacks against Communist Party and labour federation offices. They had also tried to assassinate Colonel Nasution and one of his closest associates, Lt. Colonel Sukendro. All of the accused, and several of the witnesses, tied their Anti-Communist Movement to the regional dissidents in Sumatra, and stated that they were seeking to establish a federal state based on Islamic law.[118] Had they succeeded in assassinating Sukarno, they said, possible candidates to replace the president would have been Hatta, Wilopo, Natsir, and Sjahrir.[119] It seems likely that much of this testimony was prompted by the government.

Zulkifli Lubis always denied being responsible for the Cikini attack against Sukarno.[120] He certainly ordered some of the earlier attacks, but the November 30 Cikini affair was probably an unplanned impulsive action against the president, sparked when one of the young men happened to see Sukarno entering the school and informed his friends in the nearby *asrama*, and they resolved to take advantage of the opportunity.[121] It was an inopportune moment from Lubis' point of view, for the Fact-Finding Commission had requested that the government cancel the arrest order against him and they were in fact scheduled to interview him within the next few days.[122]

The civilian casualties, particularly the wounded and dead children, and the president's close escape enflamed the atmosphere in Jakarta. Sukarno himself left soon afterward on a six-week trip to Europe and Asia to rest and recuperate. Because several of the assassination suspects belonged to the youth wing of the Masjumi party, it was not only Lubis who was charged with being involved, but also major Masjumi leaders, particularly former prime ministers Mohd. Natsir and Burhanuddin Harahap, and Sjafruddin Prawiranegara, former head of the Emergency Government and at the time Governor of the Bank of Indonesia.

During December, newspapers accused all three men of involvement in the assassination attempt, and they received a series of abusive phone calls, while paramilitary elements jeered at them from the street. Burhanuddin Harahap, who had been closest to some of the accused young men, fled the capital in early December when he heard that he was slated for arrest in connection with the Cikini affair, as did Zulkifli Lubis. Natsir and Sjafruddin, too, finally concluded that, for the time being at least, they and their families would be safer in Sumatra, and they left Jakarta at the end of December. All four men were in Padang by the second week of January 1958.

On January 9, 1958, the dissident colonels held a meeting in Sungai Dareh, a small town on the border between West Sumatra and Jambi. The meeting had been promoted initially by South Sumatra commander Barlian, who had for weeks been trying to defuse the growing tension between the regions and the centre and find some grounds for compromise. He had hoped that Nasution might attend, but when the army chief of staff refused, Simbolon took over organization of the conference. It soon became evident to Barlian that not only Dr. Sumitro, but also Colonels Simbolon, Sumual and Lubis, and perhaps even Husein, were intent on using the meeting to embark on a path toward open confrontation with the central government. In an attempt to counter this momentum, Barlian invited the newly arrived civilian political leaders, Natsir, Burhanuddin, and Sjafruddin, to attend. He clearly hoped that they might defuse the colonels' bellicosity. But though the Islamic politicians were present they were not allowed to participate in all of the discussions. Barlian's refusal to accede to the radical actions proposed at the conference prevented any unanimous agreement being reached on the dissidents' subsequent steps.[123]

The Sungai Dareh conference, despite its inconclusiveness, sparked rumours that the colonels had decided to form a State of Sumatra, which would separate itself from the Republic,[124] a charge that the dissidents have always denied.[125] Government statements at the time, however, linked together all the antigovernment incidents of the previous eighteen months, alleging they were part of a single conspiracy. All of these statements emphasized in particular that the dissidents had drawn up plans for proclaiming a Sumatran state, which had allegedly been a focus of the discussions at Sungai Dareh. On February 4, *Waspada*, the major Medan newspaper, carried the following account of the prime minister's statement to Parliament:

> Yesterday, Monday, Prime Minister Djuanda gave the government's explanation concerning... the formation of a 'Sumatra State.' Actually rumours concerning what was called 'a Sumatra State' for the first time were heard in the middle of 1956....
> At that time voices concerning a 'Sumatra State' did not become widespread because of the series of incidents that have followed since August 1956, such as the effort to arrest Foreign Minister Roeslan Abdulgani [by Col.Kawilarang], the November 16, 1956 affair [Lubis' attempted coup], followed by the 'power seizing incident' in Central Sumatra by the 'Dewan Banteng' and the 'North Sumatra Affair' on December 22, 1956.
> Prime Minister Djuanda went on to say that reliable reports and news concerning efforts to proclaim a 'Sumatra State' or the formation of a 'new RI government that would have its headquarters in Sumatra,' are difficult to obtain...But according to Djuanda, the government knows for certain that on January 9, 1958 a meeting was held attended by a number of military and political leaders in Sungai Dareh, a small town between West Sumatra and Djambi.

Present in that meeting, among others were Col. Z. Lubis, Col. Simbolon, Col. Dahlan Djambek, Lt. Col Ahmad Husein, Moh. Natsir, Sjafruddin Prawiranegara and Sumitro Djojohadikusumo.[126]

Government spokesmen were thus tying the Sungai Dareh meeting to secret documents dating from the previous June, which the army had seized from Lubis' house in Jakarta in late January. In these documents, stated by Lubis to be authentic, Lubis *had* discussed formation of a new government, but in fact there was no mention in them of a 'Sumatra State'.[127]

Despite the reluctance of the Indonesian dissidents to contemplate splitting Sumatra from the rest of Indonesia, their American backers had actually been advocating such a strategy for several years. As early as October 1953, Secretary of State Dulles in instructions to the new U.S. ambassador to Indonesia, Hugh S. Cumming, Jr., had stated his preference for Indonesia splitting up rather than remaining united under a Communist-leaning government, stating:

> As between a territorially united Indonesia which is leaning and progressing towards Communism and a break up of that country into racial and geographical units, I would prefer the latter as furnishing a fulcrum which the United States could work later to help them eliminate Communism in one place or another, and then in the end, if they so wish arrive back again at a united Indonesia.[128]

During 1957, with the establishment of the regional councils, American policy options had focused on the possibility of a separate state being established in Sumatra.[129] By April 1958, when warfare had actually broken out, the American Joint Chiefs of Staff were discussing the 'Secession of Sumatra from the Indonesian Republic', with the U.S. recognizing Sumatra and guaranteeing its independence.[130] At about the same time, Secretary of State Dulles discussed possible 'recognition of the government of the Sumatran State', with President Eisenhower and his advisers.[131]

Ignoring Barlian's unwillingness to countenance a confrontation with Jakarta, Dr. Sumitro Djojohadikusumo returned to Singapore immediately following the Sungai Dareh conference, and on January 15 began to pin down arrangements for obtaining financial and military backing from outside powers for the regional dissidents. Husein and Sumual accompanied him. According to Sumitro, the three of them maintained 'intensive contact' with each other while they were in Singapore, after which Husein returned to West Sumatra, while Sumual went on to Tokyo, and later to Taiwan and Hong Kong, to seek aid from other Asian countries. 'Based on the discussions in Singapore with Sdr. A. Hussein and Sumual', Sumitro himself went on to Europe to represent the dissidents' interests there.[132] Sumitro in Europe, Sumual and Warouw in Asia, and Simbolon in Padang were all not only seeking outside support but, in their frequent interviews with the foreign press, were publicizing the dissidents' most extreme demands. All three stressed that Colonel Husein in Padang was about to proclaim a competing government if Sukarno did not accede to these demands.[133]

In their statements, Sumitro, Sumual, and Simbolon had clearly gone far beyond any agreements reached in Sungai Dareh and were pursuing the path to confrontation. In Singapore, together with Husein, they had worked out a course of action to force the situation to a climax which threatened to split Indonesia apart. Only by such an open confrontation could Simbolon, Sumual, and Sumitro have any hope of retrieving their earlier powerful positions; and only by focusing their opposition on the issue of communism could they hope to retain the enthusiastic backing of the United States.[134] But they had not sufficiently syncronized their statements with each other or with their more reluctant colleagues.

While Sumual's and Sumitro's statements in the foreign press became ever more bellicose, not only Barlian and some of the civilian leaders, but even Husein began to hang back. After his heady meetings with Indonesia's national leaders – and the discussions in Singapore with his former superior officers and their foreign supporters, who were pressing him to action – Husein now had to respond to the misgivings of his supporters in Padang. There the atmosphere was very different. Apprehension was widespread, and there was a general fear that events were moving too fast and going far beyond the original aims of the Banteng Council. In struggling for more autonomy and a fairer division between the centre and regions, the former Banteng soldiers and the people of West Sumatra had had no intention of splitting the country or repudiating the aims of the independence revolution and its leaders Sukarno and Hatta. Husein felt the need to respond to their anxiety and tried to take some tentative steps away from the brink of confrontation.

Sukarno was still out of the country, and in Jakarta matters remained in abeyance while political leaders sent emissaries to try to persuade the Padang leaders not to take any irrevocable steps. Members of the Masjumi party and the Indonesian Socialist Party were particularly active, with former foreign minister Mohd. Roem making several visits to Padang to meet with Natsir, Burhanuddin, and Sjafruddin in an effort to dissuade them from declaring a competing government. After the Sungai Dareh conference, Sjafruddin himself had visited Barlian and become convinced that the South Sumatra commander would never agree to any direct challenge to Jakarta. Sjafruddin then sent an open letter to Sukarno, hoping to precipitate the president's return to Indonesia to face the problems the country was confronting. Nasution, too, seemed to be trying to calm the situation. Meeting with territorial commanders in Bandung, the army chief of staff accepted a proposal from the absent Husein that a meeting with the army commanders on Sumatra be postponed. Nasution also stated he was awaiting a direct report from Husein before commenting on the Sungai Dareh meeting.[135] Believing that Lubis was now living under Husein's protection in Padang, however, he did order Husein to arrest the colonel in connection with the Cikini incident.

By early February there was a clear disjunction between the bellicose declarations from Sumitro and the colonels abroad, and Husein's hesitant stance. For it appears that in their Singapore meetings Sumual and Sumitro must have persuaded Husein that he should issue an ultimatum to the central government at the beginning of February. From Sumitro in Geneva on February 2, came a statement in English which began:

On January 30, 1958 the Djakarta regime of Sukarno and Djuanda was put on notice by Simbolon through radio Padang of a decision of crucial importance which they shall have to take very soon. Simbolon, on behalf of the National Front, demanded that the Djuanda cabinet resigned [*sic*] and the acting President, Sartono, appointed a new cabinet led by Hatta and the Sultan of Djogjakarta. This cabinet has to be free from communist influence and shall carry out a policy as outlined by the National Front and already put into operation in several Daerahs [regions] outside Java. Simbolon, furthermore, announced that the National front would set up an alternative government *for the whole of Indonesia* under the Prime Ministership of Sjafruddin Prawiranegara, if the Djuanda cabinet refused to resign....The National Front does not intend to start civil war against Djakarta, but if Djakarta would attack, the Daerahs would defend themselves against such an attempt to destroy their achievements of one year of efficient and fruitful autonomy.

Thus Djakarta's choice will decide whether there will be civil war and bloodshed or not.[136]

Meanwhile, in Tokyo Warouw stated that if Hatta were not appointed prime minister, the dissidents were 'ready to proclaim the establishment of a new central government'.[137] For his part, Sukarno, then also in Tokyo, met with Warouw, but denied receiving any ultimatum from him or any of the colonels.[138]

In Padang, Husein struggled to keep his options open. He knew that several members of the Dewan Banteng opposed any drastic action. His former commander, Ismael Lengah, had remained in Jakarta and gradually distanced himself from the dissidents. In late January, Nasution reactivated Lengah's military status, posing the possibility that the army chief of staff might appoint him to replace Husein as commander of his former division.[139] In Padang itself, several of Husein's battalion commanders – Majors Nurmathias, Johan, and Iskandar – were voicing misgivings over Husein's current course, as was his Chief of Police, Kaharuddin Dt. Rangkayo Basa.[140] But Simbolon and Djambek, his superior officers from the time of the revolution, were still strongly pushing him to act.

Husein finally compromised and on February 6 broadcast a speech over Radio Bukittinggi, denying accusations that any group was trying to establish a Sumatra state, and regretting government allegations to this effect. He stated that the meeting of the leaders in Sungai Dareh was tied to their determination to protect the Unitary State and to push the government to find a way out of the difficulties it currently faced.[141]

There was surprise and relief in Jakarta when the statement was broadcast, but there was also confusion as the politicians compared Husein's words with the bellicose statements coming from abroad.[142]

For Husein's more aggressive colleagues, it was clear that he needed to be pushed. Colonels Djambek and Simbolon addressed a meeting of the People's Action Body of Central Sumatra (Badan Aksi Rakjat Sumatera Tengah, BARST) in Padang on February 9. The meeting presented a resolution to Husein that he should send a demand

Ahmad Husein, 1976

to Jakarta for prime minister Djuanda and his cabinet to return their mandate; that Hatta and the Sultan of Yogyakarta should be appointed formateurs of a new cabinet; that the central government should cancel its ban on barter; and that the president should return to the 1950 constitution in forming a cabinet. If these demands were not met, Husein should take 'wise and strong steps'.[143]

Thus propelled, Husein finally delivered his ultimatum the following day, February 10. He demanded that the Djuanda cabinet return its mandate, that Hatta and the Sultan form a cabinet until a future general election, and that President Sukarno return to his constitutional position. If these demands were not met within the next five days, 'we hereby declare that from that moment we will consider ourselves free of any obligation to obey Dr.Ir. Sukarno as Head of State'.[144]

The Djuanda government immediately rejected the ultimatum, and Nasution froze the Central Sumatra command, ordering all units to take direct orders from the army chief of staff. A government Council of Ministers the following day suspended all land and air communications with Central Sumatra, and dishonorably discharged Husein, Lubis, Dahlan Djambek, and Simbolon for taking steps that endangered armed forces discipline and the security of the state.[145] Husein had now gone too far, and he and his followers would soon be swept away in the cataclysm that followed.

CHAPTER 9

Defeat

Onset of the Civil War

As soon as the five-day ultimatum expired on February 15, 1958, Husein proclaimed the establishment of the Revolutionary Government of the Republic of Indonesia (Pemerintah Revolusioner Republik Indonesia, PRRI) in Padang, headed by Sjafruddin Prawiranegara. In addition to holding the position of prime minister, Sjafruddin was also named minister of finance. His cabinet included several of the dissident colonels: Colonel M. Simbolon as foreign minister and Colonel Dahlan Djambek as internal affairs minister and minister of defence;[1] and from Sulawesi, Colonel Warouw as minister of development and Saleh Lahade as minister of information. Masjumi leader and former Indonesian prime minister Mr. Burhanuddin Harahap was appointed to the Security and Justice ministries, and former finance minister Dr. Sumitro Djojohadikusumo, formerly of the Indonesian Socialist Party (PSI), while remaining abroad was appointed minister of both trade and communications. Mohd. Sjafei, the long-time educator and head of the INS school in Kayutanam, West Sumatra, became education and health minister.[2] In announcing the formation of the Revolutionary Government, Husein did, however, emphasize that as soon as Hatta and the Sultan of Yogyakarta were willing and able to head a Presidential cabinet in Jakarta the PRRI would cede authority to them.

The response from Jakarta was immediate. On February 16, the day after the PRRI was proclaimed, the Djuanda government ordered the arrest of rebel cabinet members Sjafruddin, Mohammad Sjafei, Burhanuddin Harahap, Sumitro, Saladin Sarumpait, and Abdulgani Usman.[3] Nasution discharged all the rebel military leaders and further arrest orders soon followed against their civilian counterparts in both Sumatra and Sulawesi.[4] Signalling the altered situation, government planes attacked Painan, Padang, and Bukittinggi on February 21 and 22, knocking out the rebels' radio equipment and severing their principal communications.[5]

The declaration of the rebel government brought to the fore the split between Husein and South Sumatra commander Barlian, who had made clear he would never support an open break with Jakarta, and who maintained a stance of neutrality throughout the ensuing struggle.[6] Within West Sumatra itself, the military officers and members of the Banteng Council were no longer united. The most outspoken opposition came from Husein's chief of police and member of the Banteng Council, Kaharuddin Dt. Rangkayo Basa, and from Colonel Nurmathias, commander of battalion 140. Both had supported the Banteng Council, but they had warned Husein in advance they would not go along with the ultimatum and declaration of a revolutionary government.[7] Neither was willing to acknowledge the authority of the PRRI government, and as soon as it was proclaimed, they withdrew with their followers to the area of Padang Sago in the foothills of Mt. Sandikat, not far from Pariaman.[8]

The proclamation of a Revolutionary Government was a step that even the rebels' strongest sympathizers in Jakarta could not countenance. In their eyes, it betrayed the independence goals pursued by centre and regions alike since the early years of the century. Many of those West Sumatrans in both the capital and in their home region who had presented a united front throughout the revolution and in support of the Banteng Council were no longer willing to approve Husein's course. Notable among these was former Vice President Hatta, who met with Sukarno on February 19, three days after the president's return from his forty-day trip abroad. Hatta still hoped that he could use the regional unrest to return to a position of real power as the one person capable of resolving the discord, but he could not countenance the rebels' illegal action in declaring a competing government. He blamed the leaders who had fled from Jakarta for distorting the nature of the movements for regional autonomy, writing later:

> the emerging interest in developing the regions was diverted on to the path of rebellion by the political leaders from the centre, such as Sumitro, Natsir, Sjafruddin together with Colonel Lubis and others. Four times I tried to impede this in various ways, but I was unsuccessful. I emphasized that that step would achieve the opposite of what was intended and would destroy all they had created by their own efforts, as well as make West Sumatra like a field trampled by an elephant, and *last but no[t] least* strengthen the dictatorial spirit of the administration. Still I tried to save the country from destruction by putting forward four proposals to Bung Karno in our discussions of the problem, but I didn't succeed.[9]

He proposed to Sukarno that all parties should return to the constitution; that the National Council should be transformed into a sort of pre-senate with its members representing the regions; that the rebels should withdraw their ultimatum, dissolve the PRRI, and return to the situation as of January 1, 1958; and that the government should declare an amnesty and Sukarno form a presidential cabinet with Hatta as prime minister.[10] He was convinced that if Sukarno agreed to these steps no group could successfully oppose them and the rebels would have to go along. Sukarno did not reject this proposal outright, and the two met once more on March 3.

> But the government with Ir. Juanda as its prime minister didn't want to negotiate before Pekanbaru had been retaken by the Republican Armed Forces, and Army Chief of Staff Nasution had said in an earlier interview that there would be no compromise with the rebel group. So my efforts to save the country from destruction failed.[11]

The president used the fact that his discussions with Hatta had been leaked to the press as a pretext for cancelling a further meeting scheduled for a few days later. He wrote to Hatta that he was 'reluctant to continue the discussions for the time being, that is, so long as the climate of "leaking" continues'.[12] Pro-Sukarno newspapers *Pemuda* and *Bintang Timur* then published denunciations of Hatta's views.[13]

After the abortive meetings between Sukarno and Hatta there were no further attempts at compromise. By now, both army chief of staff Nasution and Prime Minister Djuanda were convinced that the situation had to be resolved militarily. The dividing lines between the two sides became even more rigid, forcing those who had tried to remain uncommitted to declare for one side or the other.

Within West Sumatra, Husein arrested not only his open opponents in the Communist camp, but also anyone who did not agree with formation of the Revolutionary Government, including several of the intermediaries sent by the Jakarta political parties to try to find a road to compromise. Among those arrested in Bukittinggi were Djoeir Moehamad of the Socialist Party (PSI) and Eni Karim, minister of agriculture, both on peace missions from Jakarta. Together with some local political leaders they were taken to Padang and interned briefly before being transferred to a jail in Muara Labuh, near West Sumatra's border with Jambi, where they were held, fifteen to a cell, along with nearly four hundred other political prisoners. Most of the prisoners were from the Murba and the Socialist (PSI) parties, but they also included members of the PNI and district heads who did not agree with establishment of the Revolutionary Government.[14] Among them were a few Communists who had been held since the formation of Dahlan Djambek's anti-Communist Gebak organization, but most of the Communists were detained in other parts of West Sumatra, principally in jails near Payakumbuh in Situjuh and Suliki.[15]

The Minangkabau people were faced with a dismal choice. Most of them, while supporting the autonomy demands of the Banteng Council, had no wish to challenge the central government militarily. But now their local and ethnic loyalties had come into conflict with their loyalty to their country, and their allegiance to their region was intensified by the fact that much rebel propaganda identified West Sumatra with Islam, and the central government with communism. Since October 1957, hundreds of Minangkabau resident in Java, particularly students and former soldiers in the Banteng Division, had been making their way back to West Sumatra, usually on their own initiative. The exodus intensified at the time of the Proclamation.[16] Meanwhile, several members of the Communist party and other groups that did not support the Banteng Council's actions, had fled to Jakarta where they formed a Sons of Minang Group (Himpunan Putera Minang), which accused the Banteng Council of being a fascist organization wishing create a Sumatra state.[17]

The two sides spent about a month preparing for the civil war that was now inevitable, and Nasution drew up his plans for defeating rebel forces before they could receive help from their friends abroad.

Once faced with a military struggle, the rebels had virtually no chance of success. Apart from the government forces' overwhelming superiority in terms of manpower and logistics, their commander, General Nasution, had training, experience, and a broad knowledge of theories of military strategy which he had studied during his years of suspension from the armed forces.[18] On the other hand, Husein's only formal military training had been by the Japanese where he had achieved the rank of second lieutenant. He received no further military schooling after independence.

General A.H. Nasution
(courtesy of Ipphos)

His army experience, other than in skirmishes against the Darul Islam in West Java, was limited to fighting a localized guerrilla war against the Dutch on the eastern front of Padang. As a battalion and regiment commander during those years, he had not been responsible for formulating or executing the overall military strategy in the region. Since he had taken over command in Central Sumatra, he had been joined by more senior and experienced officers: his former commander, Dahlan Djambek; Sjarief Usman, who had also been his superior officer during the revolution and had been responsible for integrating the militias in Sumatra into the regular armed forces; the former intelligence chief, Zulkifli Lubis; and, of course, Maludin Simbolon, who had not only been territorial commander of North Sumatra prior to the regional coups, but had also been commander in South Sumatra during the revolution.

Despite the presence of these higher-ranking and more experienced officers, it seems to have been Husein who formulated the general military strategy for the PRRI in Sumatra, and in doing so he fell back on his personal experience during the revolution.[19] He never seems to have imagined taking pre-emptive actions against government troops or even conducting an active defence of the region, but rather planned from the outset to retreat to the hills to carry on the same kind of guerrilla warfare he had pursued against the Dutch ten years previously.

Nasution and his staff, on the other hand, formulated the kind of strategy the Republic had not had either the scope or resources to pursue during the revolution. He focused his immediate attention on the most important strategic and economic targets, and only after securing them and thwarting any possibility of direct outside military support to the rebels, did he turn his attention to pushing back and defeating the armed forces of the Revolutionary Government. He appointed Col. Djatikusumo as his overall commander of operations for Sumatra and Lt. Col. Rukmito Hendraningrat for Sulawesi, coordinating his strategy between the two islands.[20] Over the first few months of his offensive he achieved spectacular success.

On March 12, two companies of government paratroops parachuted directly onto the Pekanbaru airfield and set to flight the one company of rebel soldiers defending the facility. The suddenness of the government's move prevented the rebel forces from carrying out their orders that, if threatened with an attack, they should destroy the Caltex oil fields and refinery.[21] In their flight, they left strewn on the landing strip cases of modern American-made weapons, including heavy machine guns, anti-aircraft guns, mortar bombs, and small arms and ammunition that had been dropped by unidentified planes only hours earlier.[22]

The government's rapid occupation of Pekanbaru and its oil fields dealt a devastating blow to the rebels, a blow which was, however, softened two days later, on March 16, when their ally in North Sumatra, Major W.F. (Boyke) Nainggolan, launched a coup against the pro-Jakarta command in Medan, took over the city, and forced Nasution's deputy chief of staff, Colonel Djatikusumo, to flee to the east-coast port of Belawan.[23] The rebel coup in Medan, code-named Operation Sabang Merauke, enjoyed short-lived success and was important more for its propaganda value than its military impact. Nasution immediately sent in reinforcements, and within a couple of days government forces had reoccupied the town, setting the rebels to flight toward both Aceh and Tapanuli. But despite its swift reversal, Nainggolan's action in Medan gave new heart to the rebels on the west coast, who had been demoralized by the threatened defections within their own ranks and by the government's easy victories in Pekanbaru. Writing a couple of months later, Sjafruddin gave credit to the Sabang Merauke operation for preventing the complete disintegration of Husein's military forces in West Sumatra:

> If Medan had not erupted on March 16, our defence in Central Sumatra may well have collapsed as a result of the actions of Major Noermatias and Commissioner Kaharuddin. But the eruption of Medan gave Col. Husein the opportunity to construct a tight ship [*schoon schip*] in West Sumatra. Nevertheless, up to now their influence, though not great, is still felt, above all in sections of the army and police (passive).[24]

In the face of the government's landing at Pekanbaru and its occupation of much of the eastern coastal regions of Sumatra, Husein withdrew his troops westward. As Jakarta's forces closed in on West Sumatra from the east and from the north through Tapanuli, he prepared for a guerrilla war. All government officials, including school teachers, had been ordered to leave the towns over the previous weeks, and increasing numbers of high school and college students were receiving basic military training from Banteng officers in West Sumatra's towns and villages.[25]

Conscious of the superior manpower and technical resources of the government troops and of the possibility of defections among his own men, Husein had determined that his only realistic course was to pursue a strategy of withdrawal and guerrilla warfare. This confounded the hopes of the rebels' American backers and destroyed any possibility that Washington would publicly recognize the rebel government. Up until that time, the issue had been open. Until Nasution's lightning strike on Pekanbaru, units of the U.S. Seventh Fleet stationed off Singapore had been standing ready to send in paratroops ostensibly to defend the oil fields there and evacuate American personnel. Their plans had been thwarted by the speed of Nasution's pre-emptive actions, but the ships had not yet been withdrawn. The Dulles brothers, who headed the U.S. Department of State and CIA, had not abandoned hope that Husein's forces in Padang might yet make a stand that would justify open American backing. This hope was soon disappointed.[26]

The government attack on West Sumatra, code-named 'The August 17 Operation', was headed by Colonel Ahmad Yani and employed troops from the Brawijaya and Diponegoro divisions of East and Central Java, as well as paratroop units and air and sea forces.[27] Indonesian navy warships, which had been patrolling the waters off the west coast of Sumatra, began a systematic bombardment of Padang, its port of Teluk Bayur, and the coastal areas north of the town at 4.30 a.m. on April 17. This bombardment was followed by an air attack on the town and on Padang Hill, where rebel defences were concentrated. Two hours later, government paratroopers landed near the Tabing airfield, avoiding the airstrip itself which had been mined and planted with sharpened bamboo sticks by Husein's forces (and their American advisers) in anticipation of the attack. Meanwhile, Javanese troops from the Brawijaja and Diponegoro divisions, under Yani's command, made an amphibious landing north of the town. Despite the fact that news of the impending invasion had actually been reported in the local newspaper on April 13,[28] the attacking troops met very little opposition and were able to secure Padang and its immediate surroundings before the end of the day.[29] The following day, they secured the port of Teluk Bayur and reinforcements were also being landed at Tabing airport.

It had been clear since February that Police Chief Kaharuddin and Colonel Nurmathias had withdrawn their support from the PRRI, and the Jakarta government had hopes of winning at least two other of Husein's commanders to its side. Nurmathias had commanded the northern sector of West Sumatra around Pariaman, and the government hoped that Major Iskandar, battalion commander of the southern Painan-Kerinci region, and Major Johan, battalion commander in the area from Padang Panjang to Batu Sangkar, would also defect, crippling Husein's military strength.[30]

Both Nurmathias and Kaharuddin officially defected to the government a few days after Yani's troops landed in Padang, when Brawijaya forces occupied the town of Pariaman close to where they had been hiding.[31] The following month, Jakarta appointed Kaharuddin acting governor of West Sumatra. Nurmathias, however, was reluctant to fight against his former comrades, and at his own request was transferred to Jakarta and then to the Staff and Command School in Bandung.[32] Among the others who defected to the government side at the time of Yani's landing were First Lieutenant Djohan Rivai of the National Volunteer Corps (CTN: Corps Tjandangan Nasional) in Ophir, and Captain Bainal, a captain in Major Iskandar's Battalion 142, both of whom would in 1965 be accused of involvement in the September 30 movement.[33] Despite their misgivings, neither Major Johan nor Major Iskandar

General Ahmad Yani
(courtesy of Ipphos)

went over to the government, but rather remained among Husein's most able commanders.[34]

Soon confident of their communications lines to the north and east, Yani's forces concentrated on cutting Husein's supply lines to South Sumatra, where, despite his avowed neutrality, Barlian was continuing to send in food and equipment to his former colleagues, and where Major Nawawi, who had been joined by Colonel Zulkifli Lubis, was attempting to consolidate rebel forces. By April 22, government troops had occupied Alahan Panjang and by the 27th had reached Muara Labuh, a rice surplus area and the main communications link to South Sumatra.

They also advanced as rapidly as possible to the east against fairly heavy resistance, reaching Solok on April 21 and Sijunjung the following day. Their progress toward Bukittinggi was slower. Major Johan and the units under his command were able to mount a successful defence of the narrow Anai valley until Indonesian airforce planes were brought in to strafe his troops and set them to flight.[35] Jakarta's forces did not reach Padang Panjang until May 1, and proceeded from there to the rebel capital of Bukittinggi about ten miles to the north, where they met up with other government units advancing from Medan and Tapanuli, and occupied the town on May 4-5. The rebels had already withdrawn, and with the loss of Bukittinggi they formally transferred their capital to the Permesta stronghold of Manado in northern Sulawesi, where Colonel Warouw was appointed to head the government as deputy prime minister.

The rapid and disastrous collapse of rebel resistance on the west coast was apparently a devastating shock for Sjafruddin, Natsir, and the other civilian leaders. James Mossman, a British journalist reporting on the conflict, met with both men as they emerged from the cabinet meeting at which they had learned of the rebel collapse in Padang. Sjafruddin angrily left the meeting to seek out Colonel Husein 'to find out why our soldiers did not fight', vowing that he himself would 'stay here in the jungle.

Defeat

It won't be the first time'.[36] Natsir remained alone at the untidy conference table, his face 'twisted with misery'. When asked what he would do, he replied: 'What can I do? My wife and my children are all here. Any day now they might be captured. I've given everything to these people. And now this. It's all over. I don't care. Let them capture us. Let them come. What more is there?'[37] Colonel Dahlan Djambek was more sanguine, reassuring the journalists:

> We're not done yet. We will go on, you know. We'll fight in the jungles. Attack and withdraw. Attack and withdraw. Like we did against the Dutch. We'll blow up their oil pipe-lines and wage economic war against them. They'll never be able to catch us. In the end they'll be forced to come to terms with us. You'll see.[38]

The PRRI troops divided into a northern and a southern sector, as did the Revolutionary Government's cabinet. For much of the ensuing guerrilla war, Djambek had his base in Kamang from where he headed the northern sector, while Husein from near Solok was in charge of the centre and south. At least for the first few months, Djambek was accompanied by the civilian leaders Mohd. Natsir, Mr. Assaat, and Mohd. Sjafei, while military leaders Simbolon, Lubis, and Sjarief Usman were in the southern sector, as were the civilians Burhanuddin Harahap and Banteng Council secretary Soeleiman. Shortly after Jakarta's forces landed, Sjafruddin himself tried to join Husein in the south, but the government advance toward Jambi had been much swifter than the rebels had anticipated and he was forced to retreat again north:

> Twice I tried to reach Muara Labuh. On the first attempt on April 21, my group was fired on at Lubuk Selasih (+/-22.30) for we didn't know that only that afternoon Sukarno's army had taken over the town. The second try was even closer. From a distance of about 200 meters, in front of Alahan Panjang, we were greeted with sustained gun fire. Almost all of us were finally able to escape (perhaps one was killed and three captured, up to now we don't have definite information), but we were able to save all our important supplies (money, cases filled with documents). We only had to abandon our radio transmitter.[39]

Parallels with the Revolution

This was the second time in less than ten years that soldiers and government leaders in West Sumatra had taken to the jungle with Sjafruddin Prawiranegara at their head. It was not surprising that they should feel that the same tactics that had proved successful against the Dutch then could now again eventually bring them victory against Sukarno's government. In many ways, the Revolutionary Government (PRRI) was similar in composition and tactics to the Emergency Government (PDRI) also led by Sjafruddin, which at the end of 1948 had officially stood at the head of the Indonesian state after the Dutch had occupied the Republican capital of Yogyakarta and imprisoned Sukarno and Hatta on Bangka. As at that time, the Revolutionary Government had two main centres – near West Sumatra's southern border with Jambi and in the hills north of Bukittinggi. Its military strategy was to carry out a guerrilla war, while its civilian administration functioned in the countryside down to the village level, competing with that of the occupying authorities. Again, it was the civilians who officially held most of the top positions in the local administration, though in the late 1950s the military played a much larger role than during the independence war.

Despite the many similarities, the contrast between the struggle against the Dutch and the one against the Sukarno government became evident over subsequent years. By far the most important difference was that in 1949 the goal had been clear: achieving an independent Indonesia free from foreign occupation. Now, the lack of any consensus as to the precise goal of their struggle eventually led to growing dissension among the rebel leaders, and particularly between the military and civilians. In addition, the rifts within West Sumatra society were now much deeper. During the revolutionary war, the Dutch had believed that the traditional order of Minangkabau society would stand with them in opposition to the growing power of political parties and the future threat of Javanese domination of an independent Indonesia. They had been very mistaken, for over the previous thirty years Indonesian nationalism had penetrated deeply into the society, and the vast majority of traditional, religious, and radical forces within it were united in support of their leaders in Java. At the same time, during the revolution the struggle was led by local politicians, such as Chatib Suleiman and Mr. St. Mohd. Rasjid, who, despite being members of the minority Socialist Party, had a broad enough vision to draw together the apparently contradictory elements within the society in support of the Indonesian Republic.

The situation was very different during the PRRI rebellion. The rebel leaders within West Sumatra were now overwhelmingly from the majority religious stream – the Masjumi politicians from Jakarta, and the local military commanders Husein, Djambek, Sjarief Usman, and Zulkifli Lubis – and their movement focused on isolating and opposing Communist and other radical elements both in Java and within West Sumatra itself.[40] At the same time, they derived much of their support from playing on some of the same anti-Javanese sentiments that the Dutch had unsuccessfully attempted to use during their efforts to combat Indonesian nationalism. The rebels now met with a similar failure. For, however loyal the mass of the people were to the Banteng Council, it was difficult for them to support a rebel government which, while accepting the military support of outside powers such as the United States, at the same time opposed the national government in Jakarta headed by Sukarno and other long-time nationalist leaders who had led their country to independence. The fact that so many of the Minangkabau's most respected representatives at the centre – including Mohammad Hatta and Muhammad Yamin – refused to approve the rebellion, further undermined the rebels' cohesion.

The hopelessness of their position did not become evident during the first year after Jakarta's forces attacked and occupied Padang. As had been the case during the war against the Dutch, their army's failure to resist the invaders led initially to humiliation and retreat. But again, this was followed by a period of consolidation, during which the Revolutionary Government strengthened its hold on the country-side while Jakarta's forces were mainly restricted to the large population centres.

The central government's soldiers came largely from East and Central Java, and, as the Sultan of Yogyakarta stated in early 1959, 'if the situation [had] remained short of an actual break it would have been difficult to get Javanese troops to fight in Sumatra'.[41] Reluctant to fight their compatriots, during the first few months these soldiers did not pursue a very aggressive policy against the PRRI. Jakarta's lines of communication were stretched, and the rebels were able to choose their moment to attack the government's weaker outposts, and then retreat into the jungle. For at least a year, the rebels largely held the initiative, commanding the loyalty of most of the people and easily finding a haven in the mountainous and jungle-clad country-side whenever government forces attacked. Until the end of 1959, Jakarta's troops were not even able to extend their control to Kamang, a few kilometers outside Bukittinggi, where Dahlan Djambek had his headquarters and from where he and forces of the Mobile Brigade (Mobrig) headed by Sadelbergh (a Christian from Manado), would carry out lightning attacks by jeep or on horseback against govern-ment troops even in the centre of Bukittinggi.[42]

But after the more radical soldiers of Central Java's Diponegoro division had largely replaced the Brawijaja forces in much of West Sumatra, government troops became more aggressive and began to challenge the rebels' grip on the countryside. The increasing bitterness of the struggle between the occupying forces and the PRRI stemmed mostly from the growing antagonism between the Revolutionary Govern-ment's leaders and the local Communists. This began about a month after the initial invasion, as Jakarta's forces advanced into the highlands, occupying Payakumbuh on May 20, 1958. Either because the rebel forces were scared and feared spies in their midst or because they sought retribution for the help the Communists on the coast had given to the invading forces, the PRRI carried out a brutal massacre a week later. The incident took place at Situjuh Padang Kuning, not far from Situjuh Batur, the site of the major Dutch massacre in 1949 where Chatib Suleiman and sixty-eight oth-ers had died. In 1958, many Communists had been brought to Situjuh Padang Kun-ing from all over West Sumatra and detained in a schoolhouse high in the hills over-looking Payakumbuh and the Harau valley. Before retreating from the area, on May 27, the rebels, reportedly on the orders of PRRI commanders, had burned the school-house to the ground, killing its 143 occupants.[43] This massacre further enflamed antagonisms between the Communists and anti-Communists as government forces advanced into the interior. Jakarta's soldiers were also embittered by their realization of the magnitude of foreign support of the rebels, as evidence multiplied of the Amer-ican weapons and training that had been provided to the PRRI forces.

After their landings the invading forces had released a number of bureaucrats who had been imprisoned in Padang for their opposition to the PRRI government.[44] As they advanced into the highlands, Jakarta's troops brought with them many of these officials who had been affiliated with local branches of the PKI, and appointed them to administrative positions previously occupied by PRRI supporters who had left their posts to accompany the rebels into the jungle.

Appointment of the Communist Party officials led to the kind of contest for the allegiance of the people in the countryside which the Dutch in 1949 had never been able to attempt. The rebels tried to enforce their rule by following the example of their Republican predecessors during the revolution, and again relied on mobilizing the young people to maintain communications and security in the villages (*nagari*) under their control. In 1949, the Body to Protect the Villages and Towns (BPNK) had provided the administrative sinews of the Republican administration, and in 1959 the PRRI established a similar organization, the Perlaras (Perlawanan Rakjat Semesta, Total People's Resistance) with a structure stretching from the district to the village level. Throughout West Sumatra, the Perlaras energized the village youth to confront outside attacks.[45]

But this time the occupying forces responded by creating a parallel organization tied to the local military authority in each district. It was called the Peperda (Penguasa Perang Daerah, Regional War Administration). At the district and village (*nagari*) level the Peperda was assisted by the youth organization, the OPR (Organisasi Perlawanan Rakjat, People's Defence Organization), made up largely of members of the Communist Party's youth branch (Pemuda Rakyat).[46] The army used the OPR primarily to secure and defend a town or district they had 'freed' from the PRRI, allowing the army to advance to 'liberate' new areas.[47] The approximately six-thousand young people in the OPR were divided into two groups which were charged with security and development functions as well as identifying and arresting suspected PRRI adherents.[48] The People's Defence Organization operated initially in the towns but eventually extended its activities to the countryside, intensifying and further deepening the rifts within Minangkabau society, and undermining PRRI efforts to consolidate their control. Mohd. Natsir later described the effectiveness of the members of this radical Youth Organization:

> As long as we were fighting just Javanese troops there was no problem about maintaining our guerrilla bases and controlling areas just outside towns such as Padang and Bukittinggi. While I was in the jungle we got food every day from the market in Bukittinggi... But the situation was drastically altered when the Javanese troops developed a technique for using members of the local PKI's Pemuda Rakjat [Communist Party's People's Youth] as scouts to track down the guerrillas in the jungle. Being local lads they knew every creek and path just as our people did and could guide the Javanese forces.[49]

Establishment of the Federal Government (RPI)

From late 1958, PRRI representatives overseas – notably the former military governor of West Sumatra, Mr. St. Mohd. Rasjid, who had quit his post as Indonesia's ambassador to Italy to become one of the rebels' major emissaries abroad – tried to find a path of compromise whereby a settlement could be reached between the two sides without the rebels actually surrendering. Nasution, too, once he had achieved

Mr. St. Mohd Rasjid, 1976

his major military objectives, seemed to be searching for a way to end the rebellion, which was tying down his troops and undermining their unity. Few of the government's soldiers relished fighting their former comrades in arms, and Nasution's hopes for a larger role for the military in Indonesia's government were being frustrated by the continued split within the armed forces which the ongoing rebellion represented. Nasution sent Colonel Hidayat, who had commanded the Republic's forces in Sumatra during the revolution, as an emissary to Paris, where he met with Rasjid and others and gave the impression that the army was sympathetic to the possibility of compromise although the navy and air force opposed moves in that direction, as did a 'majority of Djuanda's government'.[50]

In an effort to persuade Sjafruddin at least to consider the possibility of reaching a compromise with the central government, Rasjid wrote to him as follows:

> I can understand that you and our friends want to destroy the Sukarno regime, but I think as long as we can't destroy the Sukarno government militarily or economically it will be a long time until we can attain our wishes. We are faced with two alternatives: a) to struggle a long time with all the consequences; b) to achieve a reconciliation while saving face for both sides...
>
> Although I understand that while the Sukarno army is killing innocent people you and other friends are reluctant to reach peace with Jakarta, I am also convinced that every armed struggle has to be ended by negotiations. Even if we were to gain victory through the economic collapse of Jakarta, in view of the strength of the PKI it is not unlikely that Sukarno, an opportunist, would seek help from the Soviet Union and at least Java could come under Communist influence. To avoid this tragedy we should seek the negotiation table.[51]

But his plea fell on deaf ears, for by this time the civilian leaders of the PRRI in West Sumatra were completely opposed to any compromise with the Sukarno government. They were convinced that, through its military forces and administrative officials, it was attempting to impose a Communist order in Central Sumatra. Moreover, they remained confident of eventual victory: they felt they had stabilized the situation and that time was on their side, as they continued to anticipate the ultimate collapse of the government in Jakarta. In the meantime, they were still able to maintain their centres in the jungles and hills surrounding some of the region's more isolated small towns and villages, where their administration and educational system functioned smoothly. Most of the rebels were able to live within these small centres, only withdrawing to the surrounding hills whenever government troops came in to attack.

Rather than being willing to seek compromise, Prime Minister Sjafruddin and his colleagues became more intransigent, and, repudiating both the Sukarno government and the unitary Indonesian state, began to follow a course toward creating a competing federal order. On February 15, 1959, in a speech marking the first anniversary of the formation of the Revolutionary Government, Sjafruddin declared:

> Actually our struggle has been trying to give content to the words of the Indonesian motto: Bhineka Tunggal Ika [Unity in Diversity] – even though the people of Indonesia are made up of dozens of ethnic groups and the country of Indonesia encompasses diverse regions and islands which are often strikingly different, we still wish to remain one. Up to now, the various governments in Jakarta have given no substance to these words, and the Sukarno government even seems to wish to wipe them out.

> Moreover, the Indonesian symbol shows us the five principles that form the basis of our Provisional Constitution. But it is already clear that the Sukarno regime is acting to remove the first principle [i.e. the belief in God] from the five principles. What is clear in Central Sumatra, where the administration is critically helped by Communists, is that the government now being established is nearly completely staffed with Communist Party people or with people belonging to the same family as the Communists.

> Previously we removed the colour blue from the tricolour flag so that it became the Red and White, but now the Sukarno regime is trying to remove the white so that all that remains is the red flag.[52]

At the end of the revolution, in 1949, Sjafruddin in particular had been embittered by Sukarno's behaviour. At that time, the Republican leaders imprisoned in Bangka had ignored Sjafruddin's Emergency Government during their unilateral negotiations with the Dutch, reaching an agreement in which they were willing to settle for less than full political and economic sovereignty. Ten years later, Sjafruddin was determined that this time the struggle should not again end on Sukarno's terms. He renounced any allegiance to the unitary Republic, to which all sides had thus far paid at least lip service, and went beyond calls for decentralization and autonomy to embrace the goal of federalism.

Together with Natsir, Sjafruddin began to urge the formation of a federal Indonesia that would incorporate all of the regions under rebel control in both Sumatra and Sulawesi. In the federal system they envisaged, the centre's role was largely limited to foreign relations, defence, and communications. They also began to discuss an alliance with the major Darul Islam leaders, particularly Daud Beureu'eh in Aceh and Kahar Muzzakar in South Sulawesi. A strongly Islamic minority within the PRRI now even argued for splitting completely from Java and eventually setting up a Sumatran state; they went so far as to explore the possibility of allying such a state with the newly independent state of Malaya, but this was clearly the view of a small minority.[53]

During the second half of 1959, PRRI leaders held meetings to draw up a constitution for a federal state that would eventually embrace the whole of Indonesia, and which they called the Federal Republic of Indonesia, or the United Republic of Indonesia (RPI, Republik Persatuan Indonesia).[54] The RPI, with Sjafruddin Prawiranegara as its president, would consist of ten component states (the State of the Islamic Republic of Aceh; Tapanuli/East Sumatra [North Sumatra]; West Sumatra; Riau; Jambi; South Sumatra; North Sulawesi; Islamic Republic of South Sulawesi; North Maluku; and South Maluku). Each of these component states would choose a form of government to accord with the culture and wishes of its people.[55] After drawing up a detailed constitution, the civilian leadership proclaimed the formation of the Federal Government at a meeting held in Bonjol on February 8, 1960.[56]

The moves toward forming the RPI, and particularly the rebel leadership's approaches to the Muslim rebels in the Darul Islam, increased tensions within rebel ranks. The issue of religion had always been a sensitive one, for two of the rebel regions, North Sumatra and North Sulawesi, were predominantly Christian, and feared as much as did the Sukarno government a rapprochement with proponents of an Islamic state. Establishment of the RPI also exacerbated civilian-military tensions, as most of the top military leaders, particularly such non-Muslims as Simbolon, Kawilarang, and Warouw opposed any cooperation with the Darul Islam in its formation. The military group saw the establishment of a new federal state as 'in conflict with the Independence Proclamation of August 17, 1945'.[57] Sumitro (a Javanese without any strong religious attachment) also opposed the idea of a federal system, and continued to argue for a unitary state.[58]

Civilian-military tensions were further exacerbated by developments in Jakarta, where on July 5, 1959, President Sukarno, in a step toward implementing his Guided Democracy, proclaimed a return to the revolutionary 1945 Constitution. He nullified the 1950 Provisional Constitution, up to then in effect, and at the same time abolished the Constituent Assembly. In contrast to the 1950 Constitution where major power lay with the political parties, the 1945 Constitution posited a political order where the president was the supreme authority, and it was he who appointed a cabinet, responsible to him, which shared legislative power with an elected congress.

The return to the 1945 Constitution, which strengthened the army's role as well as the president's, had been encouraged and supported by Nasution and the army leadership, and was naturally opposed by many of the political parties.[59]

In responding to Sukarno's actions, the rebel camp split along lines paralleling those in Jakarta. The Islamic political leaders opposed the return to the 1945 Constitution, but the military leaders welcomed it, for in their eyes it seemed to open up the possibility of an advantageous accommodation with Jakarta. Rebel sources overseas had described this earlier constitution as 'compatible with our goal of forming a stable Government in Indonesia which... would not provide maneuvering room for communism because it would be controlled by a single executive body'.[60] According to Natsir, the PRRI military leaders now 'began to have second thoughts' about continuing the fight, and by late 1960 'there began something of a rift, a sort of undercurrent whereby the military began to think in terms of how to make the best of things', by reaching an accommodation with Jakarta.[61]

Defeat and Humiliation

By the end of 1959, government forces had pushed the rebels ever further back into the jungle and mountains – Kamang had been taken, and in early 1960, rebel strongholds in Lintau and near Batu Sangkar were attacked and occupied.[62] Proclamation of the new Federal Republic in February 1960 marked the beginning of the end of the rebellion. Dissensions and cleavages within the rebel ranks in both Sumatra and Sulawesi were exacerbated by the Jakarta forces moving more forcefully to crush rebel military strength. By now, in the Minangkabau heartland the more leftist Diponegoro soldiers from Central Java had largely replaced the Brawijaja troops from East Java, and these Diponegoro units pursued a much more aggressive policy, impelled by ideological as well as military considerations.

The government offensive culminated in July 1960 with their occupation of the rebel stronghold of Kototinggi. Until then, this mountain redoubt had provided the real headquarters for the rebel leadership, particularly the civilian politicians who had been able to build up an administration and maintain relatively sophisticated communications with their main pockets of support in Sumatra. After Jakarta's troops forced Sjafruddin, Natsir, Burhanuddin, and Assaat to flee from Kototinggi, they were no longer able to act effectively as leaders of the rebel government and were reduced to the status of refugees dependent on the strength and goodwill of their military commanders.

Despite these government successes, however, the rebels still controlled much of the region away from the towns and main highways. As late as June 1961, after a visit to West Sumatra, the American consul in Medan reported that 'the Government does not control or feel secure in the hill and mountain areas south and east of Padang or, indeed, in much of the remainder of West Sumatra away from the main roads'.[63]

Nasution played on the civilian-military rifts among the rebels by initiating his Operation Call Back (Operasi Pemanggilan Kembali) at the end of 1960, aimed at persuading rebel army officers to 'return to the lap of their native land' (*kembali kepada pangku ibu pertiwi*). He sent emissaries to talk with the rebels in Sumatra, Sulawesi, and also in Singapore.[64] It was the military leaders in Sulawesi, led by Kawilarang, who first responded to the policy and officially gave up the struggle in April 1961.[65]

Even before the Sumatra rebels received news of the surrenders on Sulawesi, they were contemplating abandoning the struggle. At a meeting of the cabinet of the Federal Republic of Indonesia (RPI) in early 1961, Sjafruddin and Natsir appointed Simbolon to represent the group as a whole in negotiations with the central government. Simbolon, however, evidently concluded that he and his military colleagues stood a better chance of receiving good terms from Jakarta if they split from the civilian politicians and negotiated on their own behalf with their army counterparts. So in March or April 1961, he and Husein 'dissociated themselves from the DI [Darul Islam]... dropped the RPI name' and established the Emergency Military Government (Pemerintah Darurat Militer) headed by Husein.[66]

During April and May, pockets of rebel troops began surrendering in Aceh and in North, Central, and South Sumatra.[67] Nasution apparently approached both Husein in the southern region and Djambek in the northern region of West Sumatra to persuade them to give up. In response, Husein in late May initiated lengthy negotiations with Brig. General Suryosumpeno, the commander of the August 17 Territorial Command in Padang, and on June 21 officially surrendered with about six-hundred men in Solok. He ordered all his troops in West Sumatra to follow suit, and, according to some informants, threatened that 'if they did not come down he would have them hunted down'.[68] Djambek had apparently hoped to negotiate better terms with the central government,[69] but when he heard of Husein's surrender, he ordered his followers to go down with their troops, remaining alone in the highlands of Palupuh, except for a few followers, including his adjutant, Yussari.[70]

During the balance of June and July, nearly all of the rebel units – a total of several thousand men – gave themselves up, 'although we felt our souls would die'.[71] Also, during July, Simbolon negotiated his own terms and 'returned to the Republican fold' at a ceremony in Balige on August 12, attended by Deputy Chief of Staff Gatot Subroto.[72] He was accompanied by Major Hutabarat, Nainggolan, and some four thousand followers.[73]

Without any military protection, the civilians had no alternative but to follow the example of their army colleagues. In July, Sjafruddin sent a representative to Nasution to discuss surrender terms, and after an exchange of letters made a radio broadcast on August 17, 1961, calling on all RPI forces 'to cease hostilities'.[74] Also on August 17, President Sukarno announced a general amnesty for all rebels who 'surrendered unconditionally by October 5, 1961' and swore loyalty to the constitution, the state, and the 'Great Leader of the Revolution'. The following day, Zulkifli Lubis surrendered and a week later Sjafruddin, Assaat, and Burhanuddin Harahap, along with several other civilian leaders, reported to government military authorities near Padang Sidempuan in the southeastern corner of Tapanuli, where units of the Siliwangi Division of West Java were in control.[75] Sjafruddin sent a further letter to Nasution, announcing that the forces of the RPI had ceased hostilities, and, on behalf of his government, acknowledged the 1945 constitution, offering to swear an oath to support it. He surrendered the PRRI's remaining liquid assets, twenty-nine kilograms of gold bullion, to Nasution for delivery to Prime Minister Djuanda.[76]

By the end of August, only one or two small groups in West Sumatra had not yet surrendered. Natsir, with six companions, was in hiding in the hills north of Kamang, while Dahlan Djambek was a few miles away at Laring, Palupuh.[77] As fervent Muslims and outspoken anti-Communists, both Natsir and Djambek knew they were hated by the local defence militia (OPR) and Communist military and political leaders. Djambek had already sent his wife and children back to Bukittinggi, and on September 10, he sent a letter to Suryosumpeno, stating that he refused to accept the president's offer of amnesty, but that 'I am willing to be arrested and brought before a court of law'.[78] Only after his courier had left for Padang with the message, was Djambek able to meet with Natsir, who warned him of the dangers of sending the letter and of his proposed course of action.[79] Natsir's fears were well founded. Information regarding the place where Djambek agreed to be arrested leaked from Suryosumpeno's headquarters to one of the pro-Communist officers in Bukittinggi, and from there to members of the Communist-influenced militia.[80] Early on the morning of September 13, a company of OPR militia headed by Gandi, a local Communist, came up to the house in Laring where Djambek and his aide were still sleeping. They banged on the outside wall and when the two men came out they opened fire, killing first Djambek's adjutant and then Djambek himself.[81] Fearing a reaction from Djambek's followers in the surrounding areas, the militia members threatened retaliation against the villagers if they told anyone how he had died. Over the following months and years, rumours spread that Djambek had fled to Malaysia and was living there under the name of Djamil.[82]

When Natsir received news of Djambek's death, he felt he had no alternative but to surrender to the government army. In a letter to Taher Karim Lubis a month later, he recounted the events during his last few weeks in the jungle:

> From the end of July we had no support at all. All our troops had gone down – so too had the civilian and military leaders. From the end of August in all of West Sumatra there only remained the late Col. M. Dahlan Djambek, myself, and a few friends (plus or minus 10 people). Finally only two alternatives remained: going down, which meant falling into the hands of the government army [APRI]; or holding out, which meant being encircled by the 3rd Force (Communist Party activists), who, uniformed and armed, would carry out their own operations against us. I eventually decided to pursue the first alternative. I went down on September 25. Mine was the last remaining company in Central Sumatra. Djambek had been martyred on September 13, ambushed by the 3rd force [i.e. the OPR] under an official guise (*not* in battle).[83]
> I thought I would be put directly in jail when it became clear that I was not willing to take the oath [of allegiance to the government]. But H. Damanik and Col. Sitompul from Jakarta, who had been sent by Army Headquarters, took me to Padang Sidempuan. Despite my refusal to

take the oath, I was not put in the infamous Bukittinggi jail... I arrived in Padang Sidempuan on September 28 where the 'oath' was not a problem.[84]

The way the rebels were received depended largely on the units to which they surrendered.[85] Those further north, where the Brawijaja and Siliwangi soldiers were stationed, received the most lenient treatment. One rebel who surrendered in southern Tapanuli recalled that 'the military were very polite and told us just to think we were coming back from the *rantau*. They gave us 400 rps. each', and allowed them to return to their studies.[86] Many of the students were able to return to campus, but rebels from areas in the highlands where the Communists were strong were afraid to return to their home villages, and many fled the region altogether, going to Jakarta, Malaysia, or other places where they could find anonymity.

In general, the soldiers were treated better than the civilians. Indeed, former rebels felt that during the preceding years their supporters who had stayed in the towns had suffered even more than their comrades in the jungle. In Padang, government forces and their local supporters, particularly from the OPR 'did not seem like Indonesians but like Japanese or Dutch; they were brutal; put the people in jail; slapped their faces and forced them to speak Indonesian [rather than their Minangkabau dialect]'.[87] In the years following the surrender, many of the rebels returning from the jungle experienced the same humiliations that their sympathizers in the towns had suffered over the previous years.

Aftermath of the Rebellion

The years following the rebels' surrender were the nadir for West Sumatra. The rebels had believed that under the agreement for their return no measures would be taken against them.[88] Their officers expected to be welcomed by their military colleagues, and looked forward to eventually returning to the army, even if with lowered military rank.[89] However, virtually all of the top rebel leadership – both military and civilian – were detained in jails or kept under house arrest initially in Sumatra, and at the end of 1961, all were compelled to go to Java. The followers they left behind faced discrimination and political quarantine. Those who fared the best were the younger students, many of whom were allowed to continue their studies and, in fact, received government grants to do so. Their older comrades were not so lucky. Businessmen were afraid to employ them, they were forbidden to work either for the government or army, and most of them had to live on the money their wives earned by sewing and petty trading.[90]

The August 17 Territorial Command was established on April 17, 1959, to replace the August 17 Operational Command which had carried out Jakarta's invasion of West Sumatra. The Command's territory encompassed both West Sumatra and Riau[91] and was headed and staffed principally by officers and men from the Diponegoro division of Central Java.[92] These Javanese soldiers dominated the regional government, although the former Minangkabau police chief, Kaharuddin

Dt. Rangkayo Basa, remained on in his largely powerless position of governor.[93]

Many of those who had participated in the rebellion fled the area, and wherever they found a haven were often ashamed even to acknowledge their Minangkabau identity. West Sumatra itself was like an occupied territory,[94] governed, as the American Embassy reported, by 'the horde of Javanese officials and soldiery which poured in during and immediately after the rebellion.... With the Javanese occupying most of the senior positions in the Governor's office (the Governor himself is a Minangkabau), the military and the police, the West Sumatrans see themselves as second-class citizens'.[95]

During the revolution, the Minangkabau had dreamed that in the independent Indonesia emerging from the struggle their own ideals of autonomy and egalitarianism would prevail, and that West Sumatra and the other regions would be assembled into a complex whole wherein none of the components lost its individuality. These hopes had been dashed after the transfer of sovereignty, and the subsequent years of disappointment had led the people of the region to pursue their goals by more radical means, proclaiming the Banteng Council as a way to force greater power-sharing between the centre and the regions. But they had enjoyed only a brief period in 1957 when they were able to achieve local autonomy, while at the same time harbouring the illusion that their actions were really affecting the course and character of the Republic. This short hiatus had been followed by war, defeat, and humiliation. Harun Zain – the Jakarta-born Minangkabau who would later become West Sumatra's governor and who first went to the region in 1961 as a 'flying lecturer' for the University – described the situation he encountered on his arrival: 'What had an impact on me was the sadness in the eyes of the students. In 1961 the faces were dull as if they did not have any future'.[96] In fact, the consciousness that they had suffered a humiliating defeat led to 'a kind of mental breakdown' among the Minangkabau, which would last through much of the 1960s.[97]

Integration under the New Order

Overthrow of the Old Order

The 1965 Upheaval

The night of September 30, 1965, marked the bloody end of Sukarno's 'Old Order'. That night, a group of military officers, calling themselves the 'September 30 Movement' and headed by Lt. Col. Untung, a battalion commander in President Sukarno's Palace Guard (Cakrabirawa), kidnapped and murdered six of Indonesia's top military leaders whom they accused of belonging to a 'Council of Generals' that was planning to carry out a 'counter-revolutionary coup'.[1] Those killed included the minister of defence and concurrently commander of the army Lieutenant General Ahmad Yani, who had led Jakarta's invasion of West Sumatra in 1958. Another target of Untung's group, General Nasution, escaped with a broken leg, but his young daughter and an aide were both killed.[2] Whether alive or dead, the kidnapped generals had been taken to Halim Air Base on the outskirts of Jakarta, where those still alive were murdered and all were buried.

When he broadcast to the nation early on the morning of October 1, Untung declared that his 'September 30 Movement' had acted to protect Sukarno from the threat posed by the 'Council of Generals'. He also announced the formation of a forty-five-member Revolutionary Council to govern Indonesia, and proclaimed that regional Revolutionary Councils were to be established throughout the country, down to the village level, to act as the Central Council's instruments.[3]

Strangely enough, Sukarno's name was not included among the Revolutionary Council's leaders, nor did Untung indicate that the president backed his actions. However, a statement was issued in Sukarno's name at 1.30 p.m. on October 1, probably from Halim air base, declaring that he was safe and well, that the leadership of the army was directly in his hands, and that he was temporarily appointing Major General Pranoto Reksosamudro to carry out day-to-day tasks within the army.[4] In a further announcement on October 3, and in a press conference on October 14, the president stressed that he had gone to Halim air base and later to his palace at Bogor completely voluntarily:

> He explained that when, at his own desire and not because of pressure or threats from anyone, he left Freedom Palace on the morning of October 1 to go to Halim Perdana Kusumah Air Base, those responsible for escorting and guarding him were units of the Tjakrabirawa [his palace guard], who carried out their duty most effectively.[5]

Long before Sukarno made this statement, Untung's group had been overthrown and power was firmly in the hands of General Suharto, the head of the Army's Strategic Reserve Command, Kostrad. Despite his key strategic position, Suharto had not been targeted by the September 30 Movement, and this omission later provided grounds for suspicions regarding his ties to the plotters.[6] According to his later statement, as soon as he heard of the kidnappings – at about 7 a.m. on October 1 – Suharto 'decided to assume leadership of the Army'. He then speedily and successfully mustered his forces to crush the coup group.[7] By the evening of October 1, Suharto's soldiers had seized the rebels' few footholds in or near Jakarta, including the broadcasting station and Halim air base. (Sukarno by that time had driven to his palace at Bogor.)[8] Almost immediately, Suharto and his supporters began to acccuse the Communist Party of responsibility for the attempted coup and the murder of the generals. Over the next months, they launched a campaign to exterminate the party and its adherents throughout the archipelago, while gradually easing Sukarno from power.

West Sumatra's Political Climate in the Early 1960s

Untung's proclamation of a Revolutionary Council in Jakarta on the early morning of October 1, and the murder of the six top generals, caused initial confusion throughout Indonesia. This confusion took a long time to dissipate in West Sumatra, where the centre of support for what came to be known as the Gestapu (Gerakan Tigapuluh September – September 30 Movement)[9] was among the leftist Diponegoro officers in the Third Regional Military Command. It was these officers who spearheaded any open moves to support Untung and his Revolutionary Council, while most local branch members of the Communist Party kept a low profile until they were more certain of what was actually happening in Jakarta and what would be its outcome.

In the years following the surrender of the PRRI rebels in 1961, Kodam III/17 Agustus, the regional military command for West Sumatra and Riau, headquartered in Padang, had been made up primarily of units from the Diponegoro Division of Central Java. Colonel Suryosumpeno, who headed the command at the time of the rebel surrender, was eventually succeeded by Colonel Panuju, who was commander at the time of the 1965 coup attempt.[10] Most of the Diponegoro officers who served in West Sumatra after 1958 were left-leaning, and they included two men who would later head the 1965 coup attempt in Jakarta – First Lieutenant Untung was a company commander of the Banteng Raiders in West Sumatra, and Major (later Colonel) Abdul Latief was an intelligence officer in the Third Regional Command.[11]

Among the Diponegoro officers who served in West Sumatra, however, were also such later stalwarts of the Suharto regime as Benny Moerdani – one of the first paratroopers to land in West Sumatra in April 1958,[12] Yoga Sugama (Diponegoro regimental commander in Bukittinggi in 1959-60), and his chief of staff Ali Murtopo.[13] However, during the time Ali Murtopo was operational intelligence officer in West Sumatra, he 'didn't care if he developed the influence of the Communist Party', provided that it helped him in his campaign 'to assure that the PRRI rebellion was totally neutralized'.[14]

A few of the Javanese officers within the West Sumatra military command were devout Muslims, such as Major Iman Suparto, head of the command's public relations, and Major Burhani Tjokrohandoko, head of the its Religious Affairs Section, who established an Islamic education body (PTDI, Pendidikan Tinggi Dakwah Islamiyah) where former members of the Masjumi party found a sympathetic home.[15] Muslim officers were strengthened in 1964, when Army Commander Yani, in an effort to counterbalance pro-Communist influence in the West Sumatra Command, appointed a Siliwangi officer, Colonel Poniman, as chief of staff in Padang, apparently at the suggestion of the interregional commander for Sumatra, Lt. Gen. A. J. Mokoginta.[16]

In the early 1960s, Communist Party members were prominent both in the military sphere and also in much of the local governmental apparatus. When government troops had invaded the region in 1958, many civil servants and officials accompanied PRRI forces into the jungle. As noted in the previous chapter, the invading units had frequently installed Javanese officials and local members of the Communist Party in the administrative posts left vacant by the flight of the former officials and *nagari* heads. During the ensuing years, village elders who had remained in their homes, as well as followers of the traditional religious Perti party, had felt it expedient to bend to the prevailing winds and ally themselves either with the Communist Party or one of its affiliated organizations, in order to gain positions and prestige under the new administration.[17] Because of the army's lack of manpower, many of these new local officials, together with members of the Communist youth association, were trained and armed to form the Civil Defence (Hansip) forces in the districts and villages to assist the government in maintaining security against the rebel forces.[18]

When the defeated PRRI rebels returned to their villages in 1961, they were dependent on the goodwill of these village leaders, and thus remained inactive and acquiescent in order to avoid being stamped antirevolutionary.[19] Many of them felt that, to protect their families and livelihood, they too had to join Communist-affiliated associations. For

> If there was a letter that had to be signed by the Communist Nagari
> Head, it would possibly be difficult for the person needing that letter if
> he were not a Communist Party member or sympathizer. It would be
> even more difficult if he were ex-PRRI.[20]

The same was the case with Communist-affiliated unions, such as the Transport Workers Union, SBKB (Serikat Buruh Kendaraan Bermotor):

> To get a licence to operate a vehicle on a particular route, every chauffeur had to become a member of the SBKB, which meant becoming a
> member of a PKI-supported organization. This became a dilemma for
> many chauffeurs, particularly those who were devout Muslims. If the

chauffeur didn't become a member of the SBKB his livelihood would disappear, and this was a difficult choice. Finally because of the situation, he was forced to become an official member of a Communist-affiliated organization.[21]

Nevertheless, the Communist Party in general did not succeed in capitalizing on its entrenchment within the local military and administrative order, in large part because it had become so firmly identified with the Javanese and their occupation forces.

The PRRI rebellion and its defeat had sparked the largest exodus ever of Minangkabau from their home region. West Sumatran migrants spread across Sumatra, throughout the archipelago, and even to Malaysia, but the largest numbers went to the nation's capital. The 1961 census enumerated forty-three thousand people in Jakarta who had been born in West Sumatra, but in his authoritative work on Minangkabau migration, Mochtar Naim estimated that this figure should probably be at least as high as a hundred thousand. He considered the period of the PRRI rebellion 'as the zenith of the merantau flow'.[22] Most of the migrants were petty traders and food-stall or restaurant owners. West Sumatrans had occupied prominent positions in the civil service during the 1950s, but the number of these officials diminished in the wake of the PRRI.[23] The rebellion had also destroyed the clout of many Minangkabau political leaders who had held key posts in the central government, particularly those previously identified with the now-banned Masjumi and PSI parties. It was not only participants in the rebellion, such as Natsir and Sjafruddin, who remained in jail until at least 1966, but Minang politicians who had refused to condone the rebellion, such as Socialist Party head Sjahrir, were also jailed.[24] After 1958, former Vice President Hatta, too, had lost his residual influence.

Nevertheless, several West Sumatrans not belonging to the Masjumi or PSI, some of them leaders of the Tan Malaka-oriented Murba party, retained political and economic influence at the centre. Among these were the minister of information Muhammad Yamin, the businessman Hasjim Ning (both close confidants of Sukarno), and Murba party leader Chaerul Saleh who was also close to Sukarno and was a deputy prime minister, heading several ministries during the early 1960s. It was with the backing of Hasjim Ning and Chaerul Saleh that the Berkeley-trained Minangkabau economist, Harun Zain, emerged as one of the leading players in West Sumatra's political life in the mid-1960s.

In 1961, at the age of thirty-four, Zain had been named a 'flying lecturer' at Andalas University – one of the band commuting from the University of Indonesia to help staff the newly reopened tertiary institution in Padang.[25] In 1962, Zain was appointed dean of the university's Faculty of Economics, and in 1964 was named its Rector.[26] Although of Minangkabau parentage, Zain had been born in Jakarta and had had little previous interaction with West Sumatra. Chaerul Saleh and Hasjim Ning believed that Zain's lack of ties to any of the factions in the region was an advantage, and they encouraged him to accept appointment as Rector of Andalas University.[27]

Zain had received his economic training in Berkeley, and he and his family also had important connections outside the community of Minangkabau migrants in Jakarta. His father was a noted language scholar and teacher and his eldest brother was a senior diplomat, serving successively as Indonesia's ambassador to West Germany, the United States, Switzerland, and the United Kingdom.[28] Zain himself had a high reputation as a member of the prestigious Faculty of Economics at the University of Indonesia. These ties protected him when he embarked on controversial activities within Andalas University. The Muslim Student Organization HMI (Himpunan Mahasiswa Islam), was strong at Andalas because so many of the student body and younger faculty in the university had participated in the PRRI rebellion.[29] When HMI came under attack from the Communist-affiliated student organization (CGMI – Concentrasi Gerakan Mahasiswa Indonesia), Zain attempted to protect it. Although he failed in this effort, and HMI was expelled from the University's student union in September 1964, Zain himself was not penalized. He survived not only because of his ties in Jakarta, but also because he had developed friendly relations with a few of the Muslim officers in the regional military command, notably Major Iman Suparto S.H, the head of the command's public relations division.[30]

From Jakarta, Chaerul Saleh and Hasjim Ning also encouraged the foundation of an anti-Communist newspaper in Padang, as a means both of restoring Minangkabau self-respect and also countering the Communist Party's influence in the region. Muhammad Yamin was the first to promote such a paper. In the same way that thirty years earlier he had discouraged the young businessman Anwar St. Saidi from following a career in Jakarta, and urged him instead to concentrate his energies on his home region of West Sumatra where he could have greater impact, Yamin now scolded a group of Minangkabau journalists for working in Jakarta when they could be of more use at home.[31] Four of them took his admonitions to heart and sought help from Chaerul Saleh. In his memoirs, Hasjim Ning relates how he was approached by Chaerul Saleh, who argued that an anti-Communist newspaper could be important in restoring the self-respect of the Minangkabau people who had felt powerless since the defeat of the PRRI. With Ning's financial help, the four journalists then established the anti-Communist newspaper *Aman Makmur* in Padang in 1963, which rapidly gained popularity and a wide readership.[32] Guest editor for the paper was the Minangkabau journalist Rosihan Anwar in Jakarta, Harun Zain was one of its advisors, and among those writing for it was the novelist and essayist A.A. Navis.[33] Its criticisms were not popular with the local authorities, who arrested one of its correspondents, Azinar Amin. Although the newpaper was eventually able to secure his release, it was itself banned a few months later, in March 1965, for its backing of the Body to Support Sukarnoism (Barisan Pendukung Soekarnoisme, BPS).[34]

Leaders of the Murba Party in Jakarta, in conjunction with some journalists and army officers, had sponsored the BPS in an effort to unify political opposition to the Indonesian Communist Party by putting forward 'Sukarnoism' as an alternative to Marxism.[35] This group was not welcomed by Sukarno, who believed it was using his name to advance its own agenda. Partly because of pressure from the Communist Party, he ultimately outlawed it in December 1964 and a few weeks later, on January

6, 1965, also suspended the operations of the Murba party.[36] Despite the party's suspension, Chaerul Saleh's previous loyalty to Sukarno enabled him to keep his post in the cabinet, although his influence declined.[37]

During the next few months, the army 'moved to fill the vacuum created by the outlawing of anti-Communist newspapers associated with the BPS by establishing new press organs under its own patronage'.[38] In Padang, anti-Communist officers in the August 17 Command sponsored a Padang edition of *Berita Yudha*, which later became *Angkatan Bersendjata edisi Padang*, channelling to it *Aman Makmur*'s remaining financial assets. Most correspondents from *Aman Makmur* moved to this army-sponsored newspaper, although a few of its more well-known journalists were only able to work behind the scenes.[39]

The Role of General Mokoginta

Although at the time of the attempted coup most of the military administration in Central Sumatra was still largely made up of left-leaning Diponegoro troops, elements opposing the Communist Party's ascendancy were already evident. In assessing the course of events there during and after the coup, one cannot ignore the role played by the Interregional Commander for Sumatra in Medan, Major General Ahmad Jusuf Mokoginta. Born into a minor princely family in the Bolaang Mongondow district of northern Sulawesi, Mokoginta had received his initial military training from the Dutch in Bandung at the outbreak of World War II, together with Nasution, Simatupang, and Kawilarang. He had been the original commandant of the Army Staff and Command School (SSKAD) in Bandung and retained this position for much of the 1950s.[40] A long-time opponent of Nasution,[41] he was sent to Medan in November 1964 by Commander of the Army Yani as his Deputy for Sumatra. In the following April, he was installed as Mandala-I Commander. (The Mandala Command was formed in 1964 as the front-line command in Indonesia's Confrontation with the newly established Malaysian Federation.) On May 19, 1965, Mokoginta was appointed Authority for the Execution of Dwikora (Dwi Komando Rakyat, People's Double Command) in Sumatra (Pepelrada/Sumatra).[42] As the British Consul in Medan reported in November 1965,

> It is, incidentally, a fascinating, but probably never entirely to be resolved, question, how far the MANDALA SIAGA Command in Sumatra was what it purported to be, a Confrontation Command 'for the intensification of the execution of DWIKORA' and how far a device by the Indonesian Army to contain the PKI, in what is, in terms of economic wealth, the most important area of all Indonesia. Whatever the answer, it is certain that, had the Command not existed on 30th September, there would have been a very different story to tell.[43]

In the early months of his tenure, according to the British consul, Mokoginta's position in Medan had been a weak one:

The PKI ran the press, the ANTARA bureau, the radio and the Youth and National fronts. Through SOBSI and BTI, they had a stranglehold on the port of Belawan and the estates. The Karo Batak Governor of North Sumatra, Ulung Sitepu was openly playing their game. The Chinese Consul, who was Dean of the Consular Corps throve exceeedingly. The Army, which had been robbed of its newspapers following the suppression of the BPS movement in December, 1964, appeared to be devoting itself exclusively to confrontation.[44]

During the period from November 1964 to September 30, 1965, Mokoginta succeeded in altering this situation. In February 1965, he ordered his troops to arm a company of peasants and workers in each of the military districts, a move apparently in line with Communist chief Aidit's request to Sukarno that a 'fifth force' should be formed by arming peasants and workers. As the British embassy commented, however, 'We may take it that such arming as Mokoginta is engaging in is highly selective, i.e. of peasants who, if the need arises, will side with the army rather than the PKI'.[45] In May, he faced a crisis when peasants from the Communist-affiliated BTI (Indonesian Peasants Force) on the Bandar Betsy plantation at Simalungun in North Sumatra beat to death a second lieutenant who was trying to prevent them from taking over the plantation. Despite demonstrations and protests from Communist associations, Mokoginta pressed ahead with prosecuting the thirty-six peasants allegedly responsible for the officer's death, and on June 25 they received jail sentences ranging from five to fifteen years. However, under intense pressure from the Communist Party and its peasant and labour organizations, authorities in Jakarta instructed the High Court in Medan to review the case, and in August it was moved to the capital where a new trial opened in September.[46]

During the first half of the year, Mokoginta gave backing to the Pancasila Youth (Pemuda Pancasila), a group formed to counter the Communist Party's dominant People's Youth group (Pemuda Rakyat). He broke 'the virtual PKI monopoly of the mass media' by establishing a Muslim-leaning anti-Communist newspaper in Medan and two army newspapers.[47] He supported the establishment of similar army newspapers in Padang and ensured that Siliwangi officer Poniman was sent to West Sumatra to help balance the leftist Diponegoro officers who dominated the military command there. As the British Consul in Medan wrote:

> It is indeed difficult to see how Mokoginta, given the political climate of the time...could have gone further than he actually did in his attempts to neutralise the PKI in Sumatra before 30 th September....When 30 th September came the PKI were not the rampant force they had been in May; Mokoginta's few single-minded months of erosion and harassment had put them on the defensive. In the first few days of October, it was probably this factor, as much as any, which decided the immediate fate of Sumatra.[48]

On September 30, Foreign Minister Subandrio arrived in Medan, after a two-day visit to Padang, with a large entourage, including Communist Party leader Nyoto.[49] Subandrio's group was on a visit to Langsa, accompanied by Mokoginta and Governor Ulung, when news of the coup in Jakarta reached the region on October 1.[50] Early the following day, Subandrio returned to the capital, as did Nyoto after reportedly meeting with local Communist Party members.[51]

The September 30 Movement in West Sumatra

Despite Mokoginta's efforts, at the time of the coup much of the military establishment in Central Sumatra was still in the hands of left-leaning officers.[52]

The Jakarta-sponsored trials later held in the region alleged that support for Untung's movement had been planned in West Sumatra at least two weeks in advance of the October 1 'coup' in Jakarta. In an apparent effort to counter the view that Javanese monopolized the Communist movement in West Sumatra, supporters of Indonesia's New Order made sure that one of the earliest and most publicized trials held in Padang in the aftermath of the upheaval was that of Major Djohan Rivai, the most important Minangkabau allegedly involved.[53] Reports of his 1967 trial provide the most lucid account of the actions allegedly taken in support of Untung's movement.[54] During 1957, Djohan Rivai had commanded district forces in Pasaman under Major Nurmathias, and had defected with him to the government side when Jakarta's troops landed in April 1958. He was subsequently appointed Bupati of Pasaman.[55] He was arrested on December 14, 1965, accused of plotting with Djajusman alias Mamak, Baharuddin Hanafi, and two officers from the West Sumatra Command, Lt. Col. Bainal and Lt. Col. Soekirno, 'to carry out an armed uprising to overthrow the legal Government'.[56]

At the time of the coup, Capt. Bainal glr Paduko Malano was chief of staff of the Civil Defence Forces (Hansip) in West Sumatra. He had been a company commander during the revolution and, like Djohan Rivai, had defected to the government forces when they landed in 1958 because he felt that Husein had ruined his military career.[57] Soekirno Harjodarsono, a Javanese, was Commander of the Educational Depot for the Third Regional Command.[58]

Official reports agree on the contention that the West Sumatra branch of the Communist Party's Special Bureau (*Biro Khusus*) was pivotal to the course of events in the region. Djajusman alias Mamak was its chairman. He was reportedly a retired warrant officer of the Siliwangi Division, whom the Communist Party had infiltrated into West Sumatra in 1959.[59] According to Saafroedin Bahar, once in Padang, he worked as a small-businessman in the building industry, but in fact 'led the indoctrination process of the military officers and members of the Kodam 17 Agustus'.[60] The other alleged leader, Baharuddin Hanafi, is one of the more shadowy figures involved in the movement. The official history of the August 17 Command states that he was head of the West Sumatra PKI's Special Bureau and leader of the Command Group formed to oppose the Generals Council and support the Revolutionary Council.[61] He was killed in early 1966, however, and it was Djajusman who appears in the trial testimony as the head of the Special Bureau and 'brains' of the coup group in West Sumatra. According to Saafroedin Bahar, Hanafi was in fact chairman of the PKI's Special Bureau for Central Sumatra (stationed in Riau), which subsumed West Sumatra, and he was therefore superior to Djajusman. Testimony at the trials of Bainal and Soekirno states that he died in jail in early 1966, but Saafroedin Bahar, who was at the time stationed in Riau, recalls that a military officer took him from the prison in Pekanbaru and shot him on the banks of the Siak river to prevent him revealing the Communist affiliations of other officers.[62]

Beginning on September 16, 1965, the plotters reportedly held a series of meetings in Padang where they discussed steps to oppose the 'Generals Council' and support the 'Revolutionary Council' (whose formation Untung did not announce in Jakarta until October 1). In one of the meetings on September 18 it was decided that Djohan Rivai would head the 'Revolutionary Council' of West Sumatra. The group allegedly planned to send a delegation, headed by the commander in Riau, Colonel Sumedi, to persuade West Sumatra commander Panuju to support the movement. (Sumedi, a Diponegoro officer from Solo, at the time headed the Wirabima regiment in Pekanbaru and was commander of the Military Sub-Command for Riau [Korem 31].)[63] If Panuju was unwilling to go along, he would be 'isolated' and the group would use force to take over important installations in Padang, such as the Broadcasting and Telecommunications stations.[64] Djajusman allegedly requested that military units from Bukittinggi be sent to Padang Panjang, where they would join with the Raiders company from Batusangkar, proceeding from there to Padang to 'control the situation' that was expected to result from actions of the Generals' Council.[65] Col. Madjiman S., commander of Regiment 32 of northern West Sumatra, stationed in Bukittinggi, apparently headed these troops and was to lead the takeover in Padang.[66]

The central government later elaborated this account to tie events in West Sumatra more directly to Untung's movement in Jakarta. According to the central government's 'White Book' of 1994, on September 17 the 'Head of the Special Bureau for the West Sumatra region, Rivai' met with Sjam (Kamarusman bin Ahmad Mubaidah) at his home in Jakarta (Jalan Pramuka).[67] Sjam informed Rivai of the Communist Party's plans which he agreed to carry out, they discussed problems of organization, and Sjam instructed Rivai to listen to the radio broadcasts.[68] 'Rivai, alias Baharudin Hanafi' (here the account seems to be confusing Djohan Rivai with Baharudin Hanafi) carried this information back to West Sumatra on September 18.[69] It goes on to state that on October 1, after hearing Untung's broadcasts from Jakarta announcing formation of the Revolutionary Council, the Special Bureau in West Sumatra held a further meeting where Baharudin Hanafi announced (1) that on October 2 the movement in West Sumatra would break out; (2) Colonel Sumedi was to proclaim his support for the Revolutionary Council; and (3) Battalion 132 from Bukittinggi and the Raiders unit from Batusangkar were to wait in Lubuk Alung.[70]

None of these alleged plans ever materialized. According to the government's 1994 White Paper, this was because, once it became clear that Untung's movement at the centre had failed, 'the leaders of the forces were hesitant and feared mobilizing their troops, while each of the Communist leaders tried to save himself'.[71]

For the first few days of October, people of all political affiliations in West Sumatra kept their heads down and withheld comment on the situation until it was clear what had actually happened in Jakarta. Some members of the Communist Party, believing the initial broadcasts from Jakarta that it was an internal army affair, did not express any support, 'as it was nothing to do with them'.[72] With representatives from other political parties, Communist Party leaders attended a meeting called by the Kodam chief of staff (Poniman) who explained the actions in Jakarta and urged calm.[73]

It was only after October 6, when Major Iman Suparto returned from Jakarta on the first plane to arrive after the coup, that anti-Communist activities began. Apparently surprised that the situation in Padang was so calm, compared with what was happening in the capital, Suparto encouraged anti-Communist journalists to print and distribute pamphlets criticizing the PKI. Anti-Communist graffiti were soon appearing on walls throughout the town. Shortly afterward, on October 25, a branch of the university student organization, KAMI (allied in West Sumatra with the hard-pressed Muslim students' HMI), was formed to spearhead anti-Communist activity. It was soon followed by other anti-Communist youth groups.[74]

In this situation, most members and sympathizers of the Communist Party, recalling what had happened earlier under the Banteng Council, withdrew to their villages to await further orders from the Party's Central Committee.[75] At the end of October, in Kota Laweh (Padang Panjang), the military police reportedly arrested a few of their leaders, including Rahmat, chairman of the PKI's local committee; Ainuddin, a member of the committee; and Nursalim, a Communist member of the local parliament (DPR) and assistant to the governor. The detainees were then apparently surrendered to the masses who beat them to death.[76] From then on, to avoid arrest and fearing for their lives, other Communist officials fled to areas where they could still count on some support.[77]

After the overthrow of the Old Order, it was even more difficult in West Sumatra than in other regions to distinguish those who were actually Communists or Communist supporters from those who, after the defeat of the PRRI, had just been adapting to the local power constellation. Thus the suppression of alleged Communist supporters moved relatively slowly in the region, further impeded by the fact that the top military and civilian posts in West Sumatra were still held by men from the left side of the political spectrum.[78] As we have seen, in the military command in Padang, such rightist officers as Iman Suparto and Colonel Poniman were in the minority, while Brigadier General Panuju retained the post of Kodam commander for several more months. Reportedly, after the coup attempt, Poniman's divisional superiors were so concerned about his personal safety that in early October they sent a platoon from the Siliwangi brigade in Pekanbaru to protect him.[79]

The situation among the civilian authorities in West Sumatra was also in flux. Kaharuddin Dt. Rangkayo Basa, who had served as governor since being appointed to the position after central government forces landed in April 1958,[80] had been transferred to Java on July 5, 1965. His temporary replacement was Saputro Brotodiharjo, a senior official in the Department of Internal Affairs, who was a Javanese and sympathizer of the left wing of the Nationalist Party (PNI).[81] He, too, was unlikely to move against suspected Communist elements in the region.

Suppression of the Communists in North Sumatra

In North Sumatra, however, as soon as it became clear that Suharto had crushed Untung's movement in Jakarta, most military officers rallied to General Mokoginta. At the same time, the civilian Governor Ulung was put under house arrest. (He was later accused of heading the September 30 Movement in North Sumatra and was sentenced to death at his trial in September 1966.)[82] The British Consul in Medan later reported:

> The PKI had scattered to their prepared positions, but the timing of the conspiracy had gone all wrong, and they were sitting ducks when the Army began their ruthless campaign of repression and extermination on 3rd October... Posing as saviours of the nation from a communist terror, they unleashed a ruthless terror of their own, the scars of which will take many years to heal.[83]

Central army leaders' confidence in Mokoginta was signalled by the fact that in late October the Diponegoro's compromised 'L' Battalion was sent from Yogyakarta to Pematang Siantar in North Sumatra, where it was disarmed and reorganized.[84]

The authors of the provincial commemorative history of West Sumatra contend that, in the aftermath of the destruction of the September 30 Movement, General Mokoginta decided:

> that for the regions of Sumatra he would try not to cleanse the PKI through shedding their blood. Mokoginta and his Chief of Staff Brigadier General Muskita saw that the ways of cleansing the PKI that occurred on Java that were so emotional and ferocious, should not happen on Sumatra because they would cause chaos. If there were chaos on Sumatra as on Java, Indonesia would experience a great loss because most of the state's foreign exchange came from Sumatran exports of rubber, oil, tin, bauxite and so on.[85]

If this were the aim, it does not appear to have been achieved at least in North Sumatra. From Medan in January 1966, the British consul sent a confidential report which stated:

> At the outset, the Army were arresting, converting, or otherwise disposing of, some 3,000 PKI members a week, mostly rank and file. This rate has fallen off sharply. Concentration camps and 'rehabilitation centres', of both a permanent and temporary nature have been built, mostly in the estate area, and now 'villages' are being formed to house PKI mem-

bers who have not renounced their political faith but who, it is thought, might respond to political indoctrination. The rate of killing remains high: one of the Americans at the former Goodyear estate told me he estimated the number killed on this single estate at 290.[86]

The consul did, however, note that at that time, Mokoginta was 'as adamantly opposed as ever to the banning of the PKI in Sumatra'.[87]

In November 1965, Mokoginta estimated that the PKI had about 300,000 members in all Sumatra at the time of the coup, of whom 120,000, or 40 percent, were in North Sumatra. In January 1966, he reported to the 'Fact-Finding Mission for the 30th September Affair' headed by Minister for the Interior Maj. General Soemarno Sostroatmodjo, that the number of 'repentent members of the PKI' amounted to 81,000 in North Sumatra and 45,361 in West Sumatra.[88] One member of the Fact-Finding Mission, Oei Tjoe Tat, recounted how he was taken to a Chinese school in Medan where about three- to four-hundred prisoners were being held,[89] of whom 'the majority were members of Baperki and Partindo. There were those of Chinese descent, natives of North Sumatra, people of Indian descent. And among them nearly 25% were women, and not a few scholars, pharmacists, doctors, and so on'.[90]

At the end of March 1966, the British consul in Medan reported that on some of the larger estates '300 recorded deaths occurred', and he used the recorded figures he had obtained to estimate that with 273 estates in North Sumatra, the number killed on them alone would be between 27,000 and 40,000.[91] This calculation fits well with Ann Stoler's careful estimates. She writes:

> All we do know is that on the eve of the coup, the total estate work force numbered nearly 283,000. A year later that number had been reduced by 47,000, or by 16%. What proportion of these casualties were killed – as opposed to imprisoned, fired, or missing (having fled) – is unknown. It is the case, however, that very few of the SARBUPRI union leaders, branch heads, or estate division representatives are known to be alive today.[92]

The British Consul in Medan went on to make estimates of killings for Sumatra as a whole, remarking that

> there is a respectable body of opinion here which would put the total for Sumatra at over 200,000 of which about half would be 'official' and half 'unofficial' killings. In this context, 'official' means recorded in the weekly returns rendered, e.g., by estate owners and managers, to the Army and police; the 'unofficial' killings, not so recorded were the result of the paying-off of old scores, the spontaneous reaction of villagers maddened by stories, sedulously spread by the Army, of what would have happened to them had GESTAPU succeeded, and the up-surge of anti-Javanese feeling.[93]

After securing his control over North Sumatra in October and November 1965, Mokoginta turned to other Sumatra territories. In mid-December, he visited West Sumatra, and, apparently bypassing commander Panuju, worked directly with Chief of Staff Poniman and Major Iman Suparto. They organized a meeting in Bukittinggi of religious and *adat* leaders and political parties, where Mokoginta

> urged those leaders to eliminate all leftist elements in their own fields and encouraged their organizations to form a united front which centred around political and *adat* activities....This meeting dealt a psychological blow to Panudju and the leftist officers and bolstered the prestige of Poniman among leaders of Muslim and adat groups.[94]

Anti-Communist activity in West Sumatra, however, was complicated by the region's history over the previous few years. As the official commemorative history of fifty years of independence in West Sumatra puts it:

> The problem of removing Communists from West Sumatra was intensely complex because of the PRRI background. Those involved in the PRRI affair were generally Muslim adherents, while those who opposed the PRRI were in general either members of the Communist Party or of one of their social organizations. But this matter certainly can't be viewed as black and white, because after the G.30.S/PKI there were perhaps ex-PRRI who were disappointed... who made accusations against someone who was anti-PRRI. That person could definitely not be automatically viewed as PKI. The internal conflict that occurred within West Sumatra society, beginning with the eruption of the PRRI rebellion right through the G.30.S/PKI, was indeed so very deep, that it was difficult to find a basis for accusing someone of being involved or not with the PKI. Because of this internal conflict there certainly was a group that was resentful and used the momentum of the cleansing of PKI elements to carry out their revenge.[95]

It was not until after Colonel Poniman was appointed as caretaker commander to replace Brigadier General Panuju in early-February, 1966, that really successful measures began to reorganize the political and military structure in West Sumatra to accord with the changes at the centre.[96] Poniman moved cautiously to replace leftist officers in the command, acting first against members of the Communist Youth organization, Pemuda Rakyat, and its OPR militia which the West Sumatra command had used to maintain local security. He then finally removed some of the officers most publicly affiliated with the Communist Party, including Colonel Madjiman in Bukittinggi, and began to introduce some Minangkabau into the West Sumatra command. By transferring or arresting left-leaning officers, Poniman gradually transformed the command's character.[97]

Meanwhile, Poniman appointed two Minangkabau officers, Major Achmad Sjahdin and Captain Saafroedin Bahar (who had previously been serving in Riau)[98] to build *adat* and religious associations in the area more in keeping with the New Order. These associations were to replace the traditionalist Islamic Perti and the *adat* organization, MTKAAM (High Consultative Council of the Adat of the Minangkabau World), which Poniman felt had too closely allied themselves with Sukarno's policies and those of the Communist Party.[99] The newly established religious support group, the BKPUI (Badan Kontak Perjuangan Umat Islam: Contact Body for the Struggle of the Islamic Community), was to be the coordinating body for the activities of the younger Muslims, aligned with the Muslim Student Organization, which formed the backbone of the Padang branch of the New Order's university student organization, KAMI, and high-school student organization, KAPPI.[100]

On March 18 and 19, 1966, only a couple of days after the central government had officially banned the Communist Party throughout Indonesia, together with its affiliated social and cultural organizations, Major Sjahdin and Captain Bahar organized a large conference of *adat* leaders in Padang.[101] From this emerged a new *adat* organization, the Minangkabau Adat Consultative Body or LKAAM (Lembaga Kerapatan Adat Alam Minangkabau), of which Major Sjahdin became deputy chairman and Captain Saafroedin Bahar general secretary.[102] Local followers of this *adat* organization set about removing those traditional village (*nagari*) officials who were believed to have been Communists or involved in some way with the Communist Party:

> Those village elders (*ninik-mamak*) who had been involved with the PKI were replaced by their own clan through the tradition of consultation that had strong roots in the life of the society. That is [in accordance with the saying] 'if a bird's feathers are ruffled it is its own beak that re-arranges them.'[103]

The two new organizations, LKAAM and BKPUI, strongly opposed the interior ministry's nomination of acting governor Saputro Brotodihardjo, a Javanese, for the post of governor in March 1966. Kodam commander Poniman was also outspoken in opposition to this proposed appointment, arguing that, apart from the question of ideology, 'being a "native son" was a principal requirement for the next governor of West Sumatra'.[104] Poniman's predecessor, Panuju, a week before being transferred to Jakarta, had already approached Andalas University's rector, Harun Zain, to suggest that he become a candidate for governor.[105] After Panuju's departure, Zain mentioned this suggestion to Poniman, who entered his name as a candidate. However, at their mid-March, 1966, session, the regional representative council (DPRD) selected Saputro for the post, giving him twelve votes as against Zain's nine.[106]

Throughout the early 1960s, political activity in the region had been strictly controlled. The Masjumi, along with the much weaker Socialist Party (PSI), had been banned nationally in 1960. The only political choice for Muslims in West Sumatra was, thus, the traditionalist Perti, which had repudiated its early support for the Banteng Council and adapted to the climate of Sukarno's Guided Democracy. In a speech in January 1965, the party's long-time head, Siradjuddin Abbas, branded the PRRI as 'a counter Revolutionary rebellion, working for separatism, [that] had been manipulated [*didalangi*] by the overseas imperialist group that wanted to destroy the Republic of Indonesia and wanted to rebel against the Head of State'. The following month, Communist Party leader D.P. Aidit was a keynote speaker at Perti's party congress.[107]

In this situation it was understandable that when the local representative council in West Sumatra had finally been re-established on January 1, 1961 – for the first time since it had been 'frozen' ten years previously[108] – half of its political party representatives were drawn from the Perti and the Communist Party. For the legislative period 1961-66, the representative council had a total of twenty-eight members, consisting of fourteen from the functional groups and fourteen from the political parties. Four of the political party representatives came from the Perti, three from the Communist Party, two from the Nationalist Party (PNI), and one from each of the other legal parties.[109] It was therefore not surprising that in March 1966 a majority of the remaining members of the council supported Saputro against Zain.

After the vote, Poniman went to Jakarta to discuss the situation with the authorities there, with the result that, three months later, Saputro 'was put aside', and on June 4 Zain was inaugurated as governor.[110] In welcoming his appointment, Major Iman Suparto declared that 'the people did not want a Regional Head who had personal and group ambitions, but wanted a Regional Head who was capable, simple, honest, and with a strong anti-Gestapu/PKI spirit', and that Governor Zain met these criteria.[111] Two weeks later, Perti's four representatives on the regional representative council resigned their positions, in large part because student demonstrators had expressed their dissatisfaction with them as representatives of the people.[112]

After Poniman and Zain had taken over the region's top military and civilian posts, mass actions demanding the removal of officials at lower levels of the administration, particularly if they were Javanese, soon became much more widespread and violent. On the day of Zain's inauguration, student demonstrators from KAMI and KAPPI demanded that the Mayor of Bukittinggi and his secretary be dismissed, while in Payakumbuh the students were seizing rice and other supplies from Chinese-owned businesses and demanding the re-arrest of people earlier detained in connection with the September 30 Movement, but subsequently released.[113]

Two days later, twenty-five thousand KAMI and KAPPI demonstrators attacked and occupied the office of the chief prosecutor for West Sumatra, Suwarno, and his deputy Edy Wardojo, tearing off their insignia and accusing them of being involved with the Gestapu/PKI. They took them by jeep, together with Suwarno's wife, to the Town Garrison command.[114] Both men were persuaded to leave their posts 'of their own free will'.[115] The following week, Padang's mayor, Zainul Abidin Sutan Pangeran, surrendered to the district command because of student demands for his resignation.[116] Similar actions were occurring in different parts of the region,[117] and among groups other than government officials. Particularly large numbers of teachers and school administrators were being suspended or dismissed and a few arrested.[118]

It is difficult to estimate how many of those accused of being Communist sympathizers were killed in West Sumatra, although, according to the governor, the number of people arrested and jailed as Communists or Communist supporters was 'in the tens of thousands'. Governor Zain noted that the majority of these were classified as C prisoners ('those who had merely supported PKI mass organizations without playing an active leadership role'),[119] who were soon released from jail and allowed to return to their villages. But because several of them were killed by their fellow villagers when they returned home, many of the remainder reportedly elected to go back to the detention camps.[120] This view was echoed by Saafroedin Bahar, who stated that:

> Many of the Communist sympathizers...were afraid. They ran to their own original villages and kampung, and I have information that many of their own kampung people killed them. If they surrendered to the government they were safe, but not if they went to their own villages – their fellow villagers killed them.[121]

He does not, however, believe that these killings were very extensive, estimating that 'all in all there were probably in the region of fifty killed, mostly by their fellow villagers'.[122]

Indonesian histories dealing with events in West Sumatra during 1965/66 also emphasize the lack of bloodshed in the region (in relation to Java and Bali), with Ichlasul Amal writing that 'there were almost no killings'.[123] The number of alleged Communists who died in West Sumatra was almost certainly only a small proportion of the total deaths in Sumatra, most of which apparently occurred among the Javanese plantation workers in East Sumatra and PKI members in Aceh.[124] As in East Sumatra, a considerable percentage of those killed were probably drawn from the Javanese and Chinese communities.

There were some actions, however, similar to those carried out in Java. One former youth leader of the PRRI reported that after fleeing to Riau in the early 1960s, he returned to West Sumatra following the attempted coup and participated in an *Operasi Pagar Betis* (Blocking Fence Operation) where he and his companions organized groups to patrol the roads up to about twelve kilometres outside the towns searching for Communists, and walking so close to each other 'so that not even a mouse (*tikus*) could pass between them. This was like the Ansor in Central Java where they disposed of [*mengurangi*] up to half a million'.[125]

According to a former Communist detainee, large-scale police and army actions against the Communists in West Sumatra began in January 1966. Members of the Communist Youth Group (OPR) wanted to resist, but receiving no orders, became the target of mass attacks. They fled to the jungle together with other earlier opponents of the PRRI.[126]

According to Governor Zain, as the years progressed, attitudes 'became more lenient' and by the early 1970s some of the released prisoners were returning to their villages, but 'it is very hard on these people for they bear the stigma of Communist connections', so that many of them tried to leave West Sumatra and migrate to

Java.[127] An aide to the governor estimated that in 1971 about ten- to twenty-thousand productive workers a year were leaving West Sumatra, a rate somewhat less than that occurring in the immediate aftermath of the attempted coup.[128]

Attacks against local Communists were not only being impelled by revenge, ideology, or anti-Javanese feelings, but were also being directed against the Minangkabaus' long-time economic competitors, the Chinese. This became very clear in disturbances in Bukittinggi in September 1966, where the New Order student organizations suffered their first fatal casualty. The central government's prohibition of the use of Chinese characters provided an excuse for members of the high-school students' organization, KAPPI, to attack shops in the Chinese sector of Bukittinggi and tear down their signs. On September 14, one of the demonstrators, Ahmad Karim, 'was carrying out actions to demand justice against the insults being launched by the Chinese Communist Government against the Republic of Indonesia' by tearing down characters from the front of a Chinese shop, when a man in civilian clothes emerged from the shop, and, after trying to impede the students' attacks, shot Karim dead.[129] Karim was buried in the Heroes Cemetery in Bukittinggi as an 'Ampera Hero'.[130]

In the aftermath of Karim's death, the youth organizations expanded their demonstrations, demanding the expulsion of Chinese citizens from the country and the cancellation of their trading rights.[131] It is not surprising that in this atmosphere, West Sumatra's trade declined, with overseas monthly exports in August 1966 falling by about 10 percent (from 3717 to 3369 tons) compared with those of the previous year, with a similar decrease in inter-island trade.[132]

Advent of a New Regime

General Suharto's ascent to power in 1965 did not mean the end of the Javanese military occupation of West Sumatra, for the Javanese-officered August 17 Command continued to control the region, albeit increasingly headed by anti-Communists. Nor was there any immediate rehabilitation of the soldiers and civilians who had participated in the PRRI rebellion, nor of the strongest political party in West Sumatra, the still-banned Masjumi. That regional rebellion was still viewed, at least by the military officers who soon held supreme power at the centre, as having posed one of the greatest internal threats to independent Indonesia, second only to the attempted coup of 1965. Thus, despite the change in regime, the people of West Sumatra still felt themselves to be despised inhabitants of an occupied territory.

Since the end of the Revolution and the death of Tan Malaka, the Communist strand in the Nationalist movement in West Sumatra, which had been accepted by most of the other political and religious forces striving for independence there, had become increasingly controversial. Tensions had sharpened between the followers of the Islamic and Communist parties during the long campaign leading up to the 1955 elections, and the aims and rhetoric of the PRRI rebellion had further alienated many Minangkabau from the Indonesian Communist Party (PKI) and its supporters.

More than a year of rule by the Banteng Council in 1957/58 had undercut the strength of the PKI – at that time the only major political force in West Sumatra openly opposing Husein's Council. As they spread across West Sumatra during 1958, Jakarta's occupation forces installed many Communists and members of organizations affiliated with the PKI in administrative positions at the local level, but these officials were tarnished in the eyes of most of the Minangkabau population by their dependence on the central government.

The Minangkabau Communists had always been most strongly drawn to the nationalist stream of the Communist movement headed by Tan Malaka and represented after independence by the Murba party. Even at this late date, many of these local Communists, including those allied with the Indonesian Communist Party (PKI), still viewed themselves primarily as followers of Tan Malaka, and it was the nationalist strand of communism he represented that still commanded the strongest allegiance in the region. In Payakumbuh, Pesisir Selatan and parts of Agam, Communist support derived mainly from this indigenous tradition stretching back to the 1920s, but in Sawahlunto and parts of Pasaman its major strength lay among the PKI-oriented Javanese immigrant population.[133]

After the defeat of the PRRI rebellion, the fact that the Javanese units stationed in Padang were generally pro-PKI in orientation made it easier for most Minangkabau to forget their earlier history and identify communism with the Javanese occupation and view it as an outside force. The end result of the upheavals of the mid-1960s was to complete the process and entirely remove the radical socio-economic stream in general as a legitimate element in Minangkabau society.

The traumatic events of the previous thirty years left West Sumatra at the end of the 1960s demoralized and unsure of its identity as a society and of its place within New Order Indonesia. As the Rector of Andalas University commented in 1971, the two periods of repression – the 'Javanese occupation' by left-leaning Diponegoro Division troops, beginning in 1958, and the subsequent crackdown on all those who had attempted to accommodate to them – had left the people lacking individual initiative and unwilling to pose 'any challenge to the dominant authority'.[134]

During his first term in office, Governor Harun Zain strove to restore a feeling of self-respect to the Minangkabau people, and succeeded in achieving a gradual transformation in local attitudes toward Minangkabau identity and culture. To this end, he pressed for indigenous candidates to be introduced into positions of authority in both the military and civilian sphere to replace Javanese officials. Success was slow, but by 1971 – although only two of the eight district heads (bupati) were civilians, all eight, whether military or civilian were Minangkabau.[135] Changes were even slower in the military command. Governor Zain noted that in 1971, despite his own efforts, only fifteen out of about a hundred military officers in the province of the rank of major and above were 'local boys'.[136] From his early days in office, Zain was willing to stand up to the occupying troops' arrogance and bullying of the local civilians, and he provided an example to his subordinates, reminding them that 'if the governor shows fear toward the military, the people he heads will be even more afraid'.[137]

His reputation as an economist and his connections with his former colleagues, who were now the influential technocrats in Suharto's regime,[138] enabled Zain to ensure that West Sumatra received more than its fair share of financial aid from Jakarta to develop the agricultural and communications infrastructure of the region. Within a few years, it had become clear to the local people that, under the New Order, West Sumatra was experiencing a real improvement in its economic situation. At the same time, Zain established contacts with Minangkabau migrants who had settled in Jakarta and called on them to participate in developing their home region.[139]

Equally important, he made strenuous efforts to remove some of the humiliations inflicted on the people of West Sumatra over the previous decade and begin to rebuild their pride in their Minangkabau heritage and identity. He strove to reinculcate respect for the region's history and culture[140] by emphasizing aspects of Minangkabau traditions which, while posing no threat to the centre's political and military control of West Sumatra, could bring back some of the local pride that had been destroyed with the rebellion's defeat and the region's occupation by outside forces.

He demolished the 'freedom monuments' that government troops had erected in practically every *nagari*, to commemorate its 'liberation' from the hands of the PRRI forces.[141] He also introduced traditional architecture into official buildings, attaching the symbol of the buffalo-horned roofs on all government offices in West Sumatra.

But these efforts had to be conducted within strict parameters. Minangkabau concepts of the Indonesian polity and their region's place within it had rested on two strong foundations: an adherence to Islam that permeated the whole society and its politics; and a belief in the dominant Minangkabau tradition of government that, in contrast to the Javanese hierarchical unified concept, emphasized decentralization and egalitarianism. The people of West Sumatra had seen themselves as the champion of these ideas in shaping the character of the independent Indonesia emerging from the struggle against the Dutch. In the closing years of the 1960s, these ideals had to be erased from memory. In trying to fashion a new place for West Sumatra within New Order Indonesia, Zain and his colleagues had to persuade supporters of the Masjumi party 'that they should distance themselves from distinctively Islamic positions on national issues in the interests of the region', while at the same time persuading the young people in particular not to espouse principled positions regarding egalitarianism and decentralization unpalatable to the central government, and which might undermine the willingness of Suharto and his colleagues to channel development funds to West Sumatra.[142] Governor Zain 'became the symbol of the new era because he represented a new kind of Minangkabau, one who saw West Sumatra as "just one region" rather than as an "alternative centre" or a region with a special calling to lead the Outer Islands or the forces of Islam'.[143] It had to be on these terms that West Sumatra was integrated within President Suharto's Indonesia.

CHAPTER 11

Accommodation with the Centre

New Order Rule

By the mid-1980s, West Sumatra was integrated into Indonesia to an extent that would have seemed inconceivable in the Sukarno period or even in the early years of the New Order. The centre largely dictated the terms of this integration through its pressure on the local politics of West Sumatra, which paralleled Jakarta's activities in the country as a whole. But in the process, the new regime received important cooperation from Minangkabau both within West Sumatra and in Jakarta. By the early 1990s, however, there were indications that a backlash was imminent.

In the late 1960s, as he moved to replace Sukarno's regime, Suharto made some basic alterations in the ideological and political orientation of the Indonesian government and in its economic policies. At the same time, using remnants of the colonial law still on the books and the authoritarian legislation that had earlier accompanied the introduction of Guided Democracy, the new president gradually imposed a militarily enforced 'bureaucratic authoritarian regime'¹ that gained power and coherence over the ensuing years. His regime emasculated party politics, emphasizing instead economic rehabilitation. 'Development' (*pembangunan*) became the slogan of the New Order, an operation that was firmly controlled from the centre. In the regime's early years, this 'development' was 'primarily oriented toward the interests of the elite and the white-collar middle class',² as well as of the military. The term *Pancasila*, one of Sukarno's central concepts, was not abandoned, but the 'Pancasila democracy' into which it was transformed bore little relationship to the original formulation, and was shaped and elaborated to accord with the major requirements of the new regime. Officially described as government through consensus rather than political competition, the character of 'Pancasila democracy' became increasingly authoritarian.

The new government's initial caution vis-à-vis its rival aspirants for political leadership was dictated by the weakness of Suharto's claims to power and his need to establish legitimacy. Having destroyed the Indonesian Communist Party and manoeuvred Sukarno into handing over effective power in 1966, Suharto still faced the daunting task of ensuring political stability and creating his New Order. He chose as his first priority the restoration of the Indonesian economy. Soon after his seizure of power, he brought into his government a number of American-trained economists, the so-called Berkeley Mafia, headed by Professor Widjojo Nitisastro. These technocrats established a number of priorities in 1966, most notably the ending of hyperinflation, overcoming the balance of payments problem, and, especially, restoring export production.³ At their urging, the following year the Inter-Governmental Group for Indonesia (IGGI) – consisting of Japan, the United States, the Netherlands, and twelve other Western nations – was set up to provide economic support and advice to the Indonesian government. Working in conjunction with the International Monetary Fund (IMF) and the World Bank, this aid consortium provided more than 75 percent of all Suharto's development expenditures during his early years of power.

With the economic situation stabilized, Suharto and his closest advisers embarked on a strategy aimed at consolidating their control over Indonesia and its peoples. They confronted the problems of national integration by implementing a policy of militarization and centralization that would offset any potential threat from movements for regional autonomy.

In 1969, the new military regime undertook a major structural reorganization of the armed forces, through which control was centralized within the Department of Defence and Security and a new system of regional commands was created that ensured greater subordination of the regions to the centre. To prevent any re-emergence of the warlordism that had played such an important role in the PRRI/Permesta rebellion and other regional dissidence in the 1950s, Javanese officers were appointed not only to the top echelons of the army hierarchy but also to all the regional commands. It is notable that throughout the 1970s, not a single native son held a territorial command outside Java.[4] The firmness of central military control was successful in preventing any of the previously volatile regional commands from presenting a serious challenge to Jakarta.

The new army territorial structure corresponded to the various layers of the civilian bureaucracy, and through it the regime was able to exert political pressure at each level down to that of the village. Army officers not only performed military functions within each tier of society but also monitored and largely controlled political and social developments in them.[5] To this end, the Suharto regime greatly expanded the concept of the army's dual function, or *dwi-fungsi*, originally developed by Army Chief of Staff Nasution in the 1950s. This doctrine asserted not only the army's right but its duty to participate as a 'social-political force' throughout the society, with its commanding role exercised in the civilian as well as military arena.

But by the late 1960s, although Suharto had successfully demonstrated his ability to consolidate his economic and military control over Indonesia, he still urgently needed to legitimize his regime and fulfill the expectations of the donor nations making up Indonesia's aid consortium by obtaining some form of popular mandate to govern the country. Holding parliamentary general elections was viewed as a critical step toward obtaining such credentials, particularly in the eyes of the international community. But Suharto and his colleagues were reluctant to allow any elections to take place until they were confident of ensuring a satisfactory outcome. Initially, it was unclear which route could most reliably lead to their victory. In 1966, the military leadership had considered allying with one of the existing political parties, but it rejected this course and over the next three years moved instead to weaken all the parties and finally discredit and overwhelm them. By 1969, Suharto had decided to use the Sekber Golkar (Joint Secretariat of Functional Groups, Sekretariat Bersama Golongan Karya)[6] as his principal instrument in dominating the political process.

The military's assumption of government functions that had previously been held by civilians had less impact in West Sumatra than in many other parts of the country, for that region had, of course, already been living under a Javanese military occupation since 1958, with military officers occupying nearly all administrative positions down to the district level.[7] Very conscious of West Sumatra's inherent political weakness, local leaders felt that the only way for their society to survive was to continue its accommodation with Jakarta. To this end, Governor Zain and his successors in essence struck a bargain with the centre, under which they received economic development resources in return for political acquiescence. As Ichlasul Amal has characterized the prevalent attitude:

> ... there was wide support for the idea that West Sumatra's regional in-
> terest and the ethnic interest of the Minangkabaus was best served by
> 'practical' politics, that opposition to the strong central government
> would be both futile and detrimental, that it was sensible to do whatever
> the central government wanted as long as practical benefits continued to
> flow to the region. This approach was sometimes summed up in the
> Minangkabau proverb 'if you are afraid of a rifle go to its butt.'[8]

This bargain received powerful support from migrant Minangkabau in Jakarta, several of whom occupied prominent positions among the economic technocrats of Suharto's New Order.[9] But most of those who promoted the strategy did not foresee that it would lead to the destruction of many of the societal elements that had been central to Minangkabau culture, a result which did not clearly emerge for two more decades, and formed part of the general modernization process carried out in accord with the centre's priorities.

When the bargain was first struck, it called for the most important compromises being made in the political field, as the people of West Sumatra, along with those throughout the archipelago, acquiesced in the emasculation of the political parties until they became largely irrelevant to Indonesian life. The process of depoliticiza-tion was pursued gradually and was only completed after the New Order had suc-cessfully managed its first national elections in 1971.

Destroying the Political Parties

In conjunction with efforts to strengthen Golkar forces competing in the general elections, finally held in July 1971, Suharto's military government took steps to establish its control not only over the secular parties but more particularly over the Muslim groups, many of whom had been early supporters of the new regime. Suharto was wary of both the Muslim and nationalist streams of Indonesian politics. At that time, he was convinced, as had been Sukarno before him, that the Muslim groups were still aiming to create an Islamic state, while he viewed the Marhaenism of the National Party (PNI) as 'Marxism applied to Indonesian conditions'.[10]

But even while the government stepped up its campaign against the Indonesian

National Party (PNI), the ethnic Chinese party, Baperki, and previously Communist-affiliated associations, it did permit some parties identified with the left to play a role in the first elections. The small Nationalist Communist Murba party, which had been steadfastly anti-PKI and had been dissolved by Sukarno in early 1964, was reinstated. In West Sumatra, the equally small traditional religious Perti party, which had been a prominent supporter of the earlier regime, continued in existence and its leaders were allowed to make their peace with the New Order. Before the elections were held, however, many of Perti's leaders had defected to Golkar and the party itself would eventually be incorporated into that government-sponsored organization.[11]

The elimination of the Communist Party and its sympathizers did not open the way for many prominent opponents of Sukarno's Guided Democracy to re-enter the political scene. Even former Vice President Mohammad Hatta was unsuccessful when he tried to found a party based on both religion and democracy, which he called the Muslim Democratic party. President Suharto rebuffed the proposal, writing to Hatta in June 1967 that 'the existence of either an Indonesian Islamic Democratic Movement or an Indonesian Islamic Democratic Party can not at present be agreed to'. A disappointed Hatta commented that 'democracy does not yet exist in Indonesia'.[12]

Former adherents of the banned Masjumi party were even more bitterly disappointed. In late 1966, Suharto was publicly asked if, after the restoration of the Murba party, the Masjumi and PSI could also be re-established. He responded: 'Oh, the problem of Masjumi and PSI is different from that of Murba. You yourself know the difference'.[13] When it became clear that the government would refuse to reinstate the Masjumi, its former members attempted to establish a new modernist Islamic party, the Partai Muslimin Indonesia (PMI, later Parmusi). But, while permitting the party's formation, the government refused to allow any Masjumi leaders to occupy leadership positions in it.

This was in line with the Suharto regime's policy in preparing for elections, which aimed at severing ties between the political parties and their former adherents. Lists of party candidates were strictly controlled, with many earlier representatives purged, so that the new party leaders (hand-picked by the central government) increasingly owed their positions to the regime and not to the party organization, membership, or constituents.

From the time of its establishment, the Partai Muslimin Indonesia (Parmusi) was the particular focus of government manipulation. The authorities refused to allow anyone identified with the Masjumi to be nominated to leadership positions in the new party, and only men who had no standing in the Islamic community and on whom the government could completely rely were allowed to take positions at its head. Thus, not only was former prime minister Natsir forced to distance himself from the party, but Mohamad Roem, whom party members elected as chairman, was never approved.[14] The willingness of some of the new Muslim party leadership to sacrifice Islamic principles to obtain positions of influence within the regime-dominated party led the ever-outspoken Sjafruddin Prawiranegara to comment: 'The present Islamic parties are as bad as the Communists. No, that is not right, for the Communists are willing to make sacrifices.'[15]

To ensure that the military would control the conduct and outcome of the future elections, the State Intelligence Coordinating Body (Bakin) and the Operational Command for Restoration of Security and Order (Kopkamtib) – set up on November 1, 1965, under Suharto's leadership to eradicate all alleged supporters of the September 30 Movement – monitored election preparations, and military personnel were introduced at all levels of the electoral administration. Such military control was justified as necessary to maintain public order and prevent Communist elements from taking advantage of the electoral process. Nine political parties, together with Golkar, were eventually accepted as eligible to participate in the 1971 elections. In West Sumatra, the strongest political parties, apart from Golkar, were Parmusi and Perti. The district heads (*bupati*) were charged with ensuring that Golkar emerged victorious in the competition.[16]

In controlling the political process in West Sumatra, the central government relied on elements of the Javanese military command still occupying the region. Its most important instruments were those Islamic officers who were already in Padang or had been brought from Riau to spearhead the policies of Sumatra commander Mokoginta in the immediate aftermath of the September 30 Affair. Prominent among them were Achmad Sjahdin, Saafroedin Bahar, and Iman Suparto. These officers had been largely responsible for shaping the region's *adat* and religious organizations in accord with Jakarta's policies.[17] In 1969, Saafroedin Bahar was appointed chairman of the regional branch of Golkar and succeeded in weakening the political parties by incorporating many of their most influential members into this government organization.[18] As the elections approached, local efforts were reinforced by visits from top military officers, most notably Major General Ali Murtopo and Yoga Sugama, who had earlier served in the Diponegoro forces in West Sumatra and who visited the region on the eve of the elections to muster greater support for Golkar.[19]

In the event, Golkar emerged with an even larger percentage of the vote in West Sumatra than in the country as a whole – 63.2 percent as against 62.8 percent, with the Muslim Parmusi gaining only 22.7 percent and Perti 6.9 percent.[20] As a result, Golkar representatives in the regional representative council (DPRD), including appointees, occupied 70 percent of the seats.[21] This paralleled their position in the People's Representative Council (DPR) in Jakarta, where Golkar's share was 236 seats in the 460-member body, with an additional 100 seats reserved for the armed forces.

Immediately after the elections, Suharto moved to consolidate the nine remaining political parties into only two groupings, one non-Islamic and the other Islamic. The first of these eventually became the Partai Demokrasi Indonesia (PDI), incorporating the old PNI, Parkindo, IPKI, Murba, and the Catholic party, and the second the Partai Persatuan Pembangunan (PPP), incorporating the Islamic parties – NU, Parmusi, PSII, and Perti. This fusion led to a further slight erosion of support for an Islamic political party in West Sumatra in the 1977 elections, with the new PPP obtaining only 32.4 percent[22] as against Golkar's 66.5 percent of the vote.[23]

After his similar success in the subsequent 1982 elections, Suharto took the final step in weakening the remaining political parties when he demanded that all organizations, particularly political parties, had to affirm that Pancasila was their 'sole foundation' (*azas tunggal*). This order seemed aimed at not only eroding but now destroying the religious basis of the Islamic party; when the PPP and its component associations obeyed the presidential directive, effectively repudiating their party's religious foundations, the PPP lost its Islamic character and its final raison d'etre. Signalling this, the traditional Islamic NU – whose major strength lay in rural Java and which had largely been able to resist government attempts to manipulate its leadership – withdrew from the PPP, asserting that the religious aims of the NU could be better pursued outside the political process.[24]

In the 1987 elections, the PPP's share of the popular vote in the country as a whole dropped to 16 percent (from a high of 29.3 percent in 1977), not significantly more than the 11 percent garnered by the secular PDI, a difference which narrowed even further in 1992.[25] Even in West Sumatra, the Islamic PPP's percentage continued to decline, but although the Democratic Party (PDI) increased its share of the vote, this remained miniscule (1.66 percent in 1987 and 3.51 percent in 1992).[26] It was Golkar which continued to benefit from the decline of the Islamic party.

As a result of these manoeuvres and the 'celebration of democracy' that occurred every five years in the nation-wide elections, the Suharto regime had succeeded in removing Islam as a force on the Indonesian political stage. In West Sumatra, the Islamic scholars (*alim ulama*) who had always constituted an intrinsic and important factor at all levels of government – down to that of the *nagari* – no longer had a place in the political arena, their influence now being largely restricted to the spiritual, educational, and cultural sphere.

Destruction of the Nagari

The measure that struck the most decisive blow against the indigenous structures of social control in West Sumatra was the administrative reorganization that took place at the lowest level of government. This involved replacement of the traditional extended village (the *nagari*) by a smaller administrative unit which corresponded to the Javanese *desa*.

As we have seen, although the *nagari* had for centuries been the centre of Minangkabau rural life, from the mid-nineteenth century it had undergone a series of changes as a result of interference, first, from the colonial authorities and, later, from the central Republican government. Except during the revolutionary period, the major aim of this manipulation had been to shape the *nagari* into a vehicle for implementing policies initiated from the centre, whether from the colonial authorities or the independent Republican government. But despite the fact that these changes had lessened the *nagari*'s autonomy, increasingly giving it the characteristics of the lowest administrative unit in a centralized state, it had still managed to maintain much of its traditional character as an autonomous administrative, economic, and cultural entity. Thus, in the early years of the New Order, the *nagari* had been acknowledged as possessing great potential for development,[27] and local leaders discussed how its institutions could be organized to implement the central government's plans in this sphere.[28] In 1974, Governor Zain took measures to further the democratic character of the *nagari*, making the *Nagari* Head its executive and the *nagari*'s People's Representative Council (DPRN) the legislative branch for the lowest level of the local government.

These efforts came to naught when Jakarta passed Law No. 5 of 1979, which aimed to standardize the village administrative structure throughout Indonesia. The law established a uniform function and name (*desa*) for the lowest unit of the administration, and specified its internal organization, functioning, and preroga-tives – patterning the whole structure on the Javanese village model.[29] The smaller, standardized village unit gave the central government much greater control, partic-ularly as the previously elected village head was replaced under this law by a civil ser-vant effectively appointed by the governor, and election procedures for other village officials were controlled from higher up the administrative hierarchy.[30] To achieve the uniformity envisioned in the law, it was decreed that each *desa*, irrespective of population numbers or territorial size, would receive the same amount of develop-ment funds.[31] It was left to the provincial government to decide which of the local units should become the new village-level administration.[32]

After completing two terms in office, West Sumatra's first governor under the New Order, Harun Zain, proposed in 1977 that Army Brigadier General Azwar Anas should be his successor. In Zain's opinion, Anas met the criteria needed to sat-isfy both the centre and the region.[33] Even after ten years of the New Order, Zain still believed that West Sumatra's people lacked both economic development and self-confidence. At the same time, he felt that the civilian and military authorities in Jakarta still required reassurance that the region no longer posed a centrifugal threat to the nation's stability. Azwar Anas was a Minangkabau, a pious Muslim, and a chemical engineer who had graduated from the Bandung Institute of Technology. He was also an able businessman, who had succeeded in resuscitating the near-bank-rupt cement factory at Indarung, and a former military officer with good connec-tions in Jakarta. Zain believed that these qualifications would make him acceptable to both West Sumatra and Jakarta.[34]

In implementing the 1979 Village Law, Governor Anas's administration was first inclined to designate the extended village (*nagari*) as the new *desa* administrative unit. It was recognized that such a designation would maintain harmony between the administrative, economic, and cultural functions of the traditional territorial unit, despite its change in name. But the *nagari* incorporated a territory much more extensive and populous than the village administrative unit in Java and other parts of the archipelago. This meant that if the village unit remained the *nagari*, West Suma-tra would sacrifice a large proportion of the development funds channelled by Jakarta to the *desa*.

Early in his second term, in 1983, Governor Anas introduced a law through which a section of the *nagari*, the *jorong*, rather than the *nagari* itself, became the *desa* unit. In one leap, the number of villages (*desa*) in West Sumatra increased from 543 (the number of *nagari*) to 3,138 (the number of *jorong*) – plus 408 urban districts, or *kelu-rahan*). As a result, West Sumatra now received approximately six times the amount of government development funds as previously.[35]

However, splitting the *nagari* 'also destroyed the traditional and local institutions that had existed for hundreds of years' – institutions which had regulated not only the social and cultural behaviour of the rural population, but also the economic basis of the society with respect to land, inheritance, and sawah cultivation.[36] This was because, as we have seen, the *nagari* was not simply a territorial unit, but one based on kinship groups and a wide range of functions. Legally and by well-established tradition, it could be called a *nagari* only if it had certain defining characteristics, including a mosque, council hall (*balai*), road, and public bathing place:

> The mosque is the place to perform religious duties, and the balai is the place where secular and administrative matters are discussed. Only with the existence of these two institutions can a settlement be properly called a community, in which one's responsibility to his society and to the supernatural can be integrated.[37]

Traditionally, the leadership of the *nagari* was drawn from the heads (*penghulu*) of the different kinship groups (*suku*) within it, none of which was confined to a single section (*jorong*) of the extended village (*nagari*). These kinship units spread across the *nagari* exercised rights over its agricultural land and irrigation systems. In contrast, the *jorong* was an administrative unit introduced by the Japanese during their occupation and based purely on a division of the territory, with no correspondence to the *nagari*'s traditional functions.[38] Thus, there was no way of allocating traditional rights among the *jorong* units, which were in no position to take over the *nagari*'s functions and authority. As Mochtar Naim observed in 1990,

> The potency of the concept of the *nagari* up to now clearly cannot be replaced by the *Desa*, because in the concept of the *Nagari* are assembled all the nodes of power and authority,... it is not merely a territorial unit but also a traditional kinship unit; it is not only a formal administrative unit but also an informal administration; and it does not only possess strength and authoritative power delegated from above, but also strength and authoritative power which is autonomous and independent. And more than that; it is an administration that is directly participated in and felt by the people to be their own possession.[39]

'The *Desa* Head was clearly not qualified to assume the functions and role of the *Nagari* Head' and the same was the case with the local representative council.[40] These new village institutions were seen as merely carrying out development policies determined at a higher level and not adapted to the needs and aspirations of the local people. Lacking the authority bestowed on them by traditional laws and culture, the new leaders and institutions were in no position to mobilize the villagers to participate effectively in implementing government plans for developing the local economy.

The relevant local law passed in West Sumatra in 1983 (Peraturan Daerah Tingkat I Sumatera Barat No. 13 1983) which created the new *desa* units, did attempt to retain some authority in the hands of the traditional elders of the *nagari* by establishing a Village Adat Council (Kerapatan Adat Nagari, KAN). This was an important provision, for it maintained the element in the *nagari* government that could later provide the framework for resuscitating it. Nevertheless, at the time, the council lacked any power or authority in actual governmental matters. As a result

> adat functionaries, whether or not members of the Village Adat Council (KAN), gradually lost their function within the society, because the larger part of their role was taken over by the formal institutions or bureaucracy. Their most prominent role was as figures in ceremonial functions, that at the same time indicated that their role as central figures in adat life had begun to change.[41]

This change created a disorientation in the lives of the rural people as their traditional symbolic forms of authority were robbed of all content. Viewing the new village administration as a creature of the central government, many lost their wish or ability to participate in development. Increasingly, they were content to accept the Jakarta government as the authority responsible for developing the region and leave it to the centre to perform that task. Equally important, imposition of the central government's *desa* unit symbolized for the people of West Sumatra a smothering of the vestiges of local autonomy and a reinforcement of Javanese domination.[42]

During his two terms as governor from 1977 to 1987, Governor Anas brought prosperity and development to the region, but largely on Jakarta's terms. His achievements were recognized in April 1984 when President Suharto selected West Sumatra as Indonesia's most successful province in carrying out the third Five Year Development Plan, the first province outside Java to achieve such a status.[43] According to Saafroedin Bahar, Azwar Anas's success in gaining this award for West Sumatra marked the region's complete integration into Indonesia:

> From the perspective of national integration, there was no longer the slightest risk of unrest flaring up in this region....The region of West Sumatra had become one of the standard 27 provinces of the Republic of Indonesia and – perhaps – the model of a province outside Java that had once initiated rebellion and had succeeded in rehabilitating itself.[44]

But this appearance concealed considerable discontent. Despite the region's development and prosperity, local dissatisfaction with implementation of the *nagari* law and the suffocation of the political voice of Islam in the region's affairs was growing, and combining with resentment at the heavy hand of the the central government's control.

Although much more money was now flowing to West Sumatra, tensions were increasing as boundaries became blurred and people's rights and responsibilities were obscured. These tensions on occasion erupted in bloodshed, the most serious incident occurring over a land dispute in the village of Padang Sibusuk on May 29, 1989, in which three villagers were killed and four others wounded.[45] This and less-bloody clashes demonstrated the degree to which the new law was proving incompatible with maintaining the social balance within rural communities, and led to a re-evaluation of the whole policy. Ultimately, that same year, Azwar Anas's successor, Governor Hasan Basri Durin Dt. Rangkayo Mulie Nan Kuniang, began to take decisive measures to try to overturn this government-instituted reorganization.[46]

Social and Economic Changes

Governor Hasan Basri Durin

Hasan Basri Durin was the third governor to be appointed during the New Order, and the last to carry out his full term of office. Under him, signs of popular reaction against the centralization policies – as well as the growing corruption – of the Suharto regime, gradually began to surface.

Born in 1935 in a village on the outskirts of Padang Panjang, the son of an Islamic school (*madrasah*) teacher, Durin entered the Department of Interior Affairs as soon as he graduated from high school.[47] After several years of service in Jambi he returned to West Sumatra at the end of 1969 as secretary of the regional election committee for the 1971 elections. Governor Zain then appointed him mayor of Padang, a post in which he served until 1983.[48] He was then appointed assistant to the governor, and in 1987 West Sumatra's Representative Council (DPR) elected him as successor to Governor Anas. His inauguration took place on October 30, 1987.

As head of the regional *adat* asssociation, LKAAM, Durin was very conscious of the deleterious impact of abolishing the *nagari* as the village administrative unit in West Sumatra. He saw it as leading to a lack of harmony between the social and cultural basis of rural society and its government, and a decline in the role of the traditional elders of the village vis-à-vis government bureaucrats.[49] Consequently, about a year after his inauguration he began to encourage more autonomy at the lowest level of government. He initiated a programme of regrouping some of the smallest *desa* into larger units capable of exercising some degree of economic and social autonomy. Starting with proposals to regroup *desa* of less than 250 inhabitants, the legislation expanded in several stages up to units of 1,000 inhabitants. Despite the resulting loss in rural development funds, the number of villages decreased from 3,138 in 1983 to 2,162 in 1996, with 83 of the new units being the restored *nagari*. Throughout, the emphasis was on encouraging the small units to come together voluntarily.[50]

The decrease in the number of villages was tied to an effort to reinforce the cooperation between the traditional rural leaders (the elders [*ninik mamak*], Islamic scholars [*alim ulama*], and intellectuals [*cerdik pandai*]), government officials, and local villagers in a programme of cooperative participation in development. This had been initiated under Governor Anas, under the name *Manunggal Sakato* (unified and unanimous). *Manunggal Sakato* replaced *gotong royong* as the slogan of the programme because the Minangkabau had increasingly perceived *gotong royong* as concealing an effort by the higher reaches of government to compel village cooperation in government-sponsored projects – a form of forced labour.[51] In the *Manunggal*

Sakato program 'the *nagari* was again given a strategic place in the policy of rural development'.[52] Its financial basis was also reinforced with the promotion of Nagari Credit Banks to enable small-scale improvements to be instituted within the villages.[53]

Durin also tried to reconstitute traditional forms of village government by instructing local officials to set up Village Development Discussion bodies (Musyawarah Pembangunan Nagari, MPN), made up of both *nagari* leaders and government officials.[54] These bodies discussed local problems and from their discussions proposals emerged for regrouping the local units into the earlier *nagari*.

The Changing Economy

From about 1990, in conjunction with policies to revitalize the rural areas, Governor Durin also moved to improve West Sumatra's economy by attracting investment and support from outside the region, both from Minangkabau migrants (*perantau*) and from other ASEAN countries. He was able to initiate these economic measures because a basic change in thinking was also beginning to occur at the national level.

In the early 1980s, a drastic fall in oil prices had compelled the Indonesian government to basically restructure Indonesia's economy, instituting austerity measures and devaluing the rupiah as part of an effort to promote foreign investment and increase non-oil exports.[55] In the late 1980s, the central government promulgated a series of investment deregulations which resulted in both non-oil tax revenues and non-oil exports rising dramatically.[56] Altogether, between 1981/2 and 1989/90, oil exports declined from 82 percent to 40 percent of total exports, 'while the contribution of non-oil revenues to total domestic revenues... increased substantially from 29.4% in 1981/2 to 61% in 1989/90)'.[57] The centralization policies previously pursued by the Suharto government were ill-adapted to these changes and to the increasingly globalized nature of the Indonesian economy. Over the previous two decades, all budgetary decisions and financial allocations had been made by the national planning board and central government ministries. As Adam Schwartz has written;

> For most of the New Order period...this arrangement made sense. With much of Indonesia's resource wealth located in a few provinces, a strong central body was needed if the gains of development were to be distributed equitably across the country. But the rapid growth of the manufacturing sector, the declining importance of oil taxes in the government's menu of budget revenues and the persistence of uneven regional development have combined to make this argument less compelling.[58]

By 1992, some Indonesian economists were arguing that Indonesia's 'high degree of socio-economic heterogeneity' combined with 'external shocks' and 'internal inefficiencies' were making it necessary 'for the central government to rely more on regional-owned efforts'.[59] To this end, it was argued, regional governments should

Governor Hasan Basri Durin greeting President Suharto at Padang airport, 1995

be granted a larger place in the decision-making process and greater flexibility in determining how their regions should develop and attract outside investment.

In West Sumatra, Hasan Basri Durin, in conjunction with his economic advisers, moved on a number of fronts. He instituted an 'Outward Looking Policy' in 1994 to attract outside investment and tie West Sumatra's economy with the global economy. Conscious that the west coast of Sumatra was outside the major trading nexus for ASEAN (Association of Southeast Asian Nations) which focused on the east-Sumatran ports bordering the Malacca Strait, he made a major effort to establish regional links with more prosperous ASEAN countries such as Singapore and Malaysia. As West Sumatra had land and cheaper labour, but lacked technology, he argued that it would be advantageous for the province to cooperate with Singapore which had technology but lacked land. To achieve such cooperation, West Sumatra became a member of two of the newly established 'growth triangles' which embraced regions on either side of the Strait. The most important of these was the Indonesia Malaysia Singapore Growth Triangle (IMSGT), which incorporated Singapore, Riau, West Sumatra, and the southern part of Malaysia. Within this scheme, private companies in Singapore have provided the capital for establishing labour-intensive industries on the territory of its partners, with the local governments providing facilities.[60]

Role of the Perantau

Parallel with efforts to attract foreign investment were the attempts to institutionalize financial ties between migrant Minangkabau (*perantau*) in Jakarta and their home region. The migrants from Minangkabau, spread throughout the archipelago, have always played an important role in the life of West Sumatra, not only politically and socially but also economically. Practically every family has some member who has migrated and who sends back to his home village regular amounts of money, either to support the family or to provide for other needs of the village such as financing the building of a mosque, a road, or an irrigation system.

The idea of formalizing this flow of support from the migrant population was first suggested by President Suharto when he visited the area in 1982 and was asked to provide farm machinery to the farmers of West Sumatra. In response, the president suggested that they should seek such assistance from their wealthy brethren in Jakarta, saying that 'if a million migrants only contributed Rp. 1,000 each, they would collect 12 billion Rupiah a year for West Sumatra'.[61] From this remark sprang the idea for 'The Minang Thousand Movement' (Gerakan Seribu Minang), best known by its acronym, Gebu Minang.

The proposal languished for several years but was revived in early 1989 when data collected by Professor Hendra Esmara showed that, five years after the province had been awarded the national prize for implementing development, nearly half the villages in West Sumatra were still in a state of poverty or near poverty.[62] Discussions then began as to how support from the migrant population could be regulated,[63] and Governor Hasan Basri Durin publicized a detailed plan for setting it up, drawn up by Soekisman, the head of the Padang branch of the Bank Indonesia.[64] The proposal was then taken up by a number of prominent Minangkabau residing in Jakarta, who held a meeting in December 1989 and set up a Gebu Minang Institution, headed by Professor Emil Salim.[65] Their plan was to collect enough capital to form People's Credit Banks in every *nagari* in West Sumatra to give help to all who needed it.[66] According to Emil Salim, they would provide a way for development from the grass roots, so that 'it became the responsibility of every Minangkabau that no poor *nagari* should remain in the Minangkabau'.[67]

There were frictions and dissension among promoters of the Gebu Minang, and some resentment grew within West Sumatra that the wealthy *perantau* (migrants) in Jakarta were trying to impose their own concepts of the local culture on the villages and region where they no longer lived. Such dissension ensured that the amounts remitted on an individual basis from a migrant to his family and village still greatly exceeded the funds channelled via official agencies of the Gebu Minang. But the most promising aspect of the movement was its promotion of credit banks in each *nagari* which could provide the necessary capital for small entrepreneurs to develop their businesses. The programme received a great impetus in 1995 when the Bank Nasional was reestablished in West Sumatra and cooperated with the Gebu Minang in promoting credit banks in the villages. It will be remembered that the Bank Nasional had been founded in 1930 by Anwar St. Saidi with very similar aims in mind. But a crisis in the bank's finances had forced it to shift its centre of operations to Jakarta in the 1970s. In early September, 1995, the bank's president, M. Ubaidillah Faridz, announced that it would 'return to the people' and extend credit to small industries, itinerant traders, and other similar enterprises, cooperating with the Gebu Minang in establishing thirteen People's Credit Banks in West Sumatra and three in Java.[68] The plans for establishing these credit banks were very similar to those that Anwar St. Saidi had always championed, and for which he had last attempted to gain support in 1970 when he had proposed establishing banks in each of the 500 *nagari* in West Sumatra.[69] Governor Hasan Basri Durin expressed the hope that in cooperation with the Gebu Minang the bank could now channel credit to West Sumatra's small entrepreneurs. Recognizing that 'at this time in West Sumatra there are 40,000 small industries that generally are in need of an injection of working capital', the bank's president expressed its commitment to cooperate in efforts to develop the medium and small industrial sector.[70]

Erosion of the New Order

Running parallel to the pressures in the economic field toward granting more economic autonomy to the regions, was similar discontent with the way in which centralization policies had sapped West Sumatra of its particular characteristics and strengths. In the early 1990s, Minangkabau intellectuals, particularly in Jakarta, were expressing fears that centralization had led to a lack of creativity in West Sumatra and its loss of 'comparative advantage' vis-à-vis other Indonesian provinces.[71] This criticism was directed particularly at the fact that West Sumatra no longer surpassed other regions in the quality of education its children enjoyed, and that its people no longer were relatively highly represented in Indonesia's intellectual and political life. But the most obvious place where the criticism was valid was among the Minangkabau who now staffed the governmental apparatus. Such officials, of course, profited from central government policies, and in a centralized polity their success was achieved through accommodating and deferring to the powerholders. They had also assumed other attributes of the dominant culture, which during the 1980s and early 1990s was increasingly characterized by the practice of money politics. For over the years it had become impossible to obtain a position of power and influence unless the aspirant was willing to play the game that the reform movement was later to characterize as 'Corruption, Collusion and Nepotism' (KKN – Korupsi, Kolusi, Nepotisme).

During the early 1990s, corruption and nepotism gradually permeated regional politics as they did national politics, with the payment of bribes an integral part of all investment and development projects and an acknowledged factor in the electoral process. Few officials had the integrity to resist these norms when operating in the late New Order. Thus, in West Sumatra, as in the centre, money politics became an inevitable part of the government's mode of operation, and tarnished nearly all of the officials in the administration.

But while to the outside world the practices of local government officials – in the province, district, and village – were seen as reflecting those of the society they supposedly represented, most people in Minangkabau society were well aware of the corruption and actively resented and opposed it. Not only did the ordinary people in the town and countryside realize that their own hardships and exclusion were a direct result of their unwillingness or inability to participate in the dominant culture, but the blatant corruption that characterized that culture also offended the values of both their traditions and religion.

Fifty Years of Independence

To celebrate the fiftieth anniversary of Indonesian independence, on August 17, 1995, thousands of Minangkabau, travelling by plane, ship, bus, and car, returned home together (*pulang basamo*) to participate in a series of ceremonies, ranging from formal government roll calls (*apel*) in Padang and Bukittinggi to simple commemorations in the towns and villages throughout West Sumatra. Middle-aged and elderly men and women donned shirts and blouses of printed batik bearing symbols of the '45 Generation (*angkatan '45*), specially tailored for the occasion, and came together once more to remember the time when they had all stood completely united – at least in their memories – in opposition to the outside invader. Both those veterans who had sought their fortunes abroad and those who had remained at home, journeyed around the towns and villages recalling their ideals and dreams. For a few days, the failures, dissensions, and disappointments of the years following independence were forgotten, and the dreams for a unified Indonesia imbued with the values of justice and equality for which they had fought regained credibility. In Padang on the fiftieth anniversary

> at precisely 10.10 am on Thursday, August 17 1995, the sound of a siren wailed for a full minute. The people stood transfixed by reverence. And several of them wept, overcome with emotion.

> The moments of silence provided the summit to all the memories of Indonesia's Golden Anniversary. It was as if August 17, fifty years ago had returned, and alive in the atmosphere was the feeling that the long road of three and a half centuries of suffering from colonization was completely over.[72]

Vice President Hatta's widow and daughters dedicated his former house on the outskirts of Bukittinggi as a museum and they returned to his home village of Batuhampar to commemorate the anniversary. Reporters sought out the eighty-three-year-old Leon Salim, now poor and half-blind, who seventy years earlier as a young schoolboy had embarked on his own road to revolutionary struggle, and had now returned to a simple two-room rented house on the fringes of Payakumbuh.[73] One of the journalists wrote: 'This is a reality that apparently has to be accepted by a founder of our people. A man who through his own suffering pioneered the road to independence by sacrificing all he had – his physical and mental energy – for a single aim: Independent Indonesia. Still he recognizes that the rewards of that struggle are still not enjoyed by all of his people'.[74]

Even those who had confronted each other during the rebellions of the 1950s were reconciled, as Ahmad Husein and his lieutenants were finally allowed to return from their long exile in Jakarta and were embraced by followers and opponents alike.[75] The fact that the PRRI leaders had brought fratricidal warfare into their home region was, at least for the moment, forgiven, and all were united in their pride that, in contrast to so many other regions of the archipelago, West Sumatra had not

Leon Salim, with his wife,
Payakumbuh, 1999

surrendered to the Dutch and for many months its leaders had headed the Indonesian independence struggle through the Emergency Government of Indonesia.[76]

The nostalgia of the ceremonies for the fiftieth anniversary of Indonesian independence in 1995 perhaps made people more conscious of how far the contemporary Indonesian government had strayed from the ideals of the original proclamators. This became ever clearer as the 'Corruption, Collusion and Nepotism' (KKN) within the system seemed to intensify over the next two years and become ever more rampant, with the first family personifying how far these excesses had corroded Indonesian society. After a sudden heart attack killed his wife, Siti Hartinah (Ibu Tien), in April 1996, President Suharto seemed to lose his political touch and he became even less willing to curb the greed of his children and other close associates.[77] Increasingly, these were the people he turned to for economic advice rather than to the technocrats who had successfully guided Indonesia's economy since the early days of the New Order.

After being elected in late 1993 to head the Indonesian Democratic Party (PDI), former-President Sukarno's daughter Megawati Sukarnoputri had begun to make hesitant attempts to chart a somewhat independent course for the party and had attracted widespread support, particularly among the people of Java and Bali. Indications that the Democratic Party might propose Megawati as its candidate for president in the 1997 elections sparked an unbridled government reaction. First, government authorities attempted to remove Megawati or split the party by forcing through the election of a competing government-backed leader, and then on July 27, 1996, launched a bloody attack on the Jakarta offices of her branch of the PDI.[78]

These actions can be seen as the first steps in the growing crisis that would eventually engulf the regime and force Suharto's resignation. The government seemed to have lost its sense of proportion, not only in the amount of corruption it was willing to countenance but also in the selection of its political targets and the means it was willing to employ to destroy them. It was only when the Asian economic crisis began to rock the whole of Indonesian society in mid-1997, however, that these distortions became glaring and intolerable on both a national and local level. The ensuing wave of public criticism led to the rapid collapse of the Suharto regime.

Spearheading the opposition both nationally and in West Sumatra were young people, most notably the university and college students. Despite having undergone an education from primary school to college where they had been consistently indoctrinated with the regime's view of the world and its version of history, these students still emerged in the forefront of demands for justice and equality and voiced ever more vociferous criticisms of the corruption of the powerholders.

In Padang in the fall of 1997, student demonstrations initially focused on the election for a new governor to succeed Hasan Basri Durin. In an effort to demonstrate that it was listening to the people, the Padang government polled many groups throughout West Sumatra as to who should replace Durin. But when the local legislative assembly (DPRD) published the list of candidates it intended to submit to the Department of the Interior in Jakarta, neither of the top vote-getters in the West Sumatra-wide poll was included. Widespread protests resulted, and a deputation from Andalas University came to the Parliament building in late October, 1997, to charge that the legislative assembly was not providing a channel for the aspirations of the people it was supposed to represent. The students expanded these protests to include more general economic complaints, accusing the assembly of being deaf to the hardships of the people in the southern coastal regions of the province who were suffering from widespread hunger as a result of the long period of drought.[79]

As the governor's selection process went forward, the number and scope of antigovernment demonstrations increased. Eventually, from the three candidates approved by the Ministry of the Interior, the assembly elected Durin's vice governor Muchlis Ibrahim as his successor,[80] but rumours circulated that large gifts of money had been given to the members to influence their votes.[81] These allegations were not denied, and the gifts were unsatisfactorily justified as being 'for expenses' and not for bribes.[82] The new governor's inauguration was accompanied by large protest demonstrations.

During the second half of 1997, the value of the rupiah plunged, while devastating fires burning out of control through much of Kalimantan and Sumatra made life more difficult for the people there and in the surrounding areas.[83] On January 8, 1998, the rate of the rupiah to the American dollar rose from a pre-crisis rate of Rp. 2,600 to pass the Rp.10,000 mark, while the annual per capita income in Indonesia declined from $1,200 to $300 and only 22 of Indonesia's 286 publicly listed companies remained solvent.[84] The managing director of the International Monetary Fund (IMF) urged President Suharto to adhere to the terms of the fund's $33 billion bailout plan, and newspapers around the world displayed a humiliating photograph of the president signing his agreement, with the IMF director, arms folded, standing authoritatively behind him.

In the face of the crisis, the government played for time, holding down the prices of rice and fuel in order to avoid the riots that could have been sparked by the stringent austerity measures demanded by the IMF. At the same time, it continued to protect the banks and other business interests owned by Suharto's family and cronies, which had undermined the Indonesian economy.

Making no concessions to national and international criticism, the new, largely hand-picked national People's Consultative Assembly 'elected' Suharto as president for the seventh time on March 11, 1998. He immediately signalled his defiance of national and international opinion by appointing a 'crony-studded' cabinet, naming his long-time protégé, the erratic technocrat B.J. Habibie, as vice president, his eldest daughter Tutut (Siti Hardijanti Rukmana) as minister of social affairs, and his close friend and golfing partner, the notoriously corrupt timber baron Mohamad (Bob) Hasan as minister of industry and trade. The election was openly criticized as a farce, and the largest student demonstrations in decades broke out on the college and university campuses.

Crises in the political and monetary sphere were mutually reinforcing, leading to an ever-widening swathe of protest demonstrations spreading beyond Java throughout most of the country.

Suharto's Resignation

Between March and May 1998, Indonesia's facade of political stability crumbled as student calls for reform ('*reformasi*') of the political and economic systems escalated into demands that President Suharto resign and that a special session of the People's Representative Assembly be convened to elect his replacement. The crisis point was reached on May 12, when military forces opened fire on students demonstrating outside Jakarta's Trisakti University, killing six of the students and wounding at least fifteen. A week earlier, on May 4, the government had finally implemented the price increases on fuel and electricity demanded by the international lender organizations.[85] These two incidents triggered actions by much of the urban population of Jakarta, who joined in the antigovernment protests. Riots and looting spread through Jakarta, as banks and luxury shopping malls, the most obvious symbols of wealth and corruption, were ransacked and destroyed. The crowds also increasingly targeted Chinese-owned businesses. During the rampage, stores and shopping malls were set ablaze, killing as many as five hundred of the demonstrators who were trapped in the burning buildings.

In West Sumatra, students had been holding demonstrations and free-speech forums (*mimbar bebas*) since March, and by the end of that month, the local military authorities had allowed these protests to spread outside the campuses. The students voiced demands for a complete change in the character of the government, with a major Padang newspaper reporting:

> ... they demand that the government remove the practices of corruption, collusion, nepotism and arrogance of power that restrict the political

participation of the people in the practice of Pancasila democracy, and also request a restoration and growth of the people's trust in ABRI [the armed forces] as protector of the people.[86]

The students also protested the rampant corruption in the electoral process in West Sumatra, and alleged that bribes had influenced not only the December election for governor, but also the subsequent election for mayor of Padang. Outside the building of the West Sumatra Parliament (DPR), two thousand students lowered the national flag to half mast and demanded the resignation of the governor, mayor, and regional assembly.[87]

Spurred by events in Jakarta, the demonstrations gained momentum over the following weeks, and on May 18, 1998, thousands of students occupied the Parliament building in Padang. They called for the head of the assembly to convene a special session to help bring about a change in the national leadership. The following day, two thousand students took over the Republic of Indonesia regional radio station in Padang, and persuaded its head to broadcast 'Student Announcements' reassuring the public that the student reform movement did not threaten the people's security and reiterating the student calls for Suharto to resign as president and convene a special session of the national assembly to elect his successor.[88]

When the demonstrations first broke out in Jakarta, Suharto was attending a meeting of the G-15 nations in Cairo, having made clear on the eve of his departure that major reforms would only take place after his term of office ended in 2003. As soon as he arrived back in Indonesia's capital on the morning of May 15, it was clear that he was no longer in control of the situation. He had to be driven in a convoy of a hundred military vehicles from the airport to his central-Jakarta home. Later that day, he ordered tanks onto the streets and considered the imposition of martial law. But his declaration that he himself would lead the reform movement proved hollow. Hundreds of students occupied the Parliament building in Jakarta, calling for his resignation and mocking the cabinet he had so recently appointed. It soon became clear that Suharto could no longer rely either on his hand-picked assembly, his cabinet, or on the top military command. The army made no attempt to remove the students, and Suharto's cabinet members deserted him, shifting their support to his vice president, Habibie, who appeared happy to step into his shoes. General Wiranto, the chief of the armed forces, finally met with Suharto late on the night of May 20 (National Awakening Day) to inform him that the military could no longer guarantee security in Jakarta. At 9.00 a.m. the following morning, President Suharto resigned and handed over power to his vice president, B.J. Habibie, an action welcomed in West Sumatra as throughout the nation.

Conclusion

After Suharto's fall, for the first time in forty years it seemed possible that, through a new 'Era of Reform', a democratic and decentralized Indonesian political order might ultimately be realized.

During the final decades of his thirty-two-year rule, few real cracks had appeared in the structure of Suharto's New Order state and the president had seemed impervious even to demands that he name a successor. It had been presumed that the problems of a post-Suharto leader and government would not need to be confronted until after his death; the speed and smoothness of his fall and resignation stunned the nation and the world. The popular uprising that impelled him to step down made clear that the seemingly impregnable framework he had created amounted to no more than a fragile shell covering depths of popular repugnance and dissatisfaction, which needed only the strains of an economic crisis to fracture it. In the weeks after the transfer of power to Habibie, pressure increased not only for the eradication of corruption, collusion, and nepotism (KKN) throughout the government, but also for the whole state apparatus to be dismantled. Loud and persistent calls were heard for a decentralization as well as democratization of the Indonesian polity.

Suharto's unexpected and rapid capitulation opened the way for an accession to power of Vice President B.J. Habibie that was remarkably smooth. But it also meant that, despite Suharto's resignation, almost all of the New Order structure remained in place. 'Reformasi' was the battle cry of his opponents but, until new elections could be held, steps to achieve that reform had to be implemented by the very office-holders against whom the protests were directed.

Many of the students who were still occupying the Parliament building in Jakarta on May 21, 1998, were willing to accept a Habibie-led regime as an interim measure, but a sizeable number of them instead demanded that a transitional government be formed through democratic means. Enough disagreements developed among the students for the army to move in and eject them relatively peacefully from the Parliament. From then on, the unity they had maintained throughout the crisis broke apart. The more moderate students began to work with different political parties in preparing for the elections, while the more radical rejected holding any elections under the Habibie government's auspices.[1] The misgivings of the more radical students seemed to be justified, for although some of Suharto's most notorious cronies were forced to resign and a few felt compelled to leave the country, most of the military, bureaucratic, and economic elite remained in place, headed by those who had approved and implemented the Suharto regime's policies and had benefitted from the corruption permeating the New Order apparatus. Many of them were determined to retain power, and they were still in a position to hobble the democratic process.

Born in South Sulawesi, and the first non-Javanese president of Indonesia, Habibie provided a marked contrast to Suharto. He showed himself open to criticism and listened to the advice of those around him. He made some surprising concessions: offering East Timor independence if it rejected his autonomy proposals; restoring freedoms of speech, assembly, and the press;[2] and releasing political prisoners, some of whom had been in jail for more than thirty years. However, the new president was a mercurial figure, who lacked the authority to ensure that the entrenched bureaucracy and armed forces implemented the policies he enunciated. Furthermore, his long and intimate ties with Suharto rendered him suspect in the people's eyes. Their suspicion intensified when the transcript appeared of an embarassing cell-phone conversation Habibie held with his attorney general, in which they discussed tactics to ease legal pressure on former President Suharto.[3] The deep involvement of the new president and his family in much of the economic 'collusion and corruption' endemic in the previous regime, made him so vulnerable that he was not only reluctant to prosecute Suharto and his family, but also to move against other officials who had profited extravagantly in the final years of the New Order. Although he introduced a few new faces into his 'reform' cabinet, many of the ministers Suharto had appointed two months earlier remained in office.[4]

'Reformasi' in West Sumatra

In West Sumatra, and apparently in many other parts of Indonesia,[5] it was striking how rapidly the people embraced the new freedoms and took into their own hands the responsibility for removing vestiges of the previous regime and instituting a more democratic order.[6] Not only political parties but also newspapers proliferated, as did their criticisms of all aspects of government. Dissidents and former participants in the PRRI rebellion 'who have had toothache for the past thirty-five years',[7] now felt free to express not only their criticisms of those in power but also their visions for a country more in accord with their earlier ideals. They seemed determined not to let this opportunity be lost as they believed previous ones had been.

Repugnance at the practices of the former regime immediately coalesced around the announcement that former governor Hasan Basri Durin had been appointed minister of agrarian affairs in the new 'reform' cabinet. As in Jakarta, there was widespread opposition to those who had profited from the New Order staffing the new transitional government. Durin's long tenure in office, first as mayor of Padang and later during his two terms as governor, identified him with the Suharto regime in the eyes of the Minangkabau, and allegations circulated that he and members of his family had been deeply involved in corrupt practices.[8] Hasan Basri Durin took office over the protests of at least ten groups and organizations in West Sumatra, mostly of students and intellectuals, who sent letters to Habibie asking him to cancel the appointment.[9]

A few months later, in August 1998, Durin accompanied Adi Sasono, minister of social welfare, when he came to address the students at the teachers' training college in Padang (IKIP Padang). Contending that no invitation had been issued to the former governor, dozens of students ambushed his car as he tried to leave the campus, dragged him out, and held him in the meeting hall for over three hours, yelling insults at him and demanding that he acknowledge responsibility for the corruption during his tenure. They seemed prepared to detain him all night, but finally released him when he fainted and had to be taken to the hospital. Adi Sasono was the only member of the group of dignitaries, which included Governor Muchlis Ibrahim, to remain with Durin throughout the ordeal.[10]

Resignation of the Governor

In March 1999, Muchlis Ibrahim resigned as West Sumatra's governor, accusing the Ministry of Internal Affairs in Jakarta of ignoring his nominee for vice governor and appointing an official of their own choosing.[11] His act marked the first time in independent Indonesia's history that any governor had resigned his office.[12] The background to the governor's resignation was more complicated than it appeared on the surface. It revealed the continuing strength of the political and economic forces of the Suharto regime, particularly the Golkar organization and the whole governmental apparatus tied to its practice of money politics. It also highlighted the fact that tensions between the region and the centre had not dissipated and that the central government was still intent on maintaining Golkar's power in the region.

The Interior Ministry's rejection of Governor Muchlis's choice for vice governor was only the last in a series of slights, which in his opinion demonstrated Jakarta's lack of trust in him.[13] This lack of trust can be traced back to fears on the part not only of the central government, but more particularly of the national and local Golkar organization, that Muchlis would refuse to use his power to ensure a majority for Golkar in the forthcoming elections, as he had openly declared that government officials should adopt a neutral stance.[14] Their fears had gained substance at the January 1999 ceremony to open the West Sumatra branch of the party, which was attended by prominent Golkar figures who had flown in from Jakarta. Instead of the anticipated crowd of thousands flooding the stadium, the Golkar leaders were faced with a half-empty arena, populated by only about eight-hundred party stalwarts. Rather than recognizing that this might signify a lack of local support for Golkar, its leaders instead blamed Muchlis for not using government facilities to ensure that the demonstration was a success.[15] When Muchlis' choice was overruled and the former regional secretary Zainal Bakar appointed vice governor, it was with the expectation that Bakar would guard Golkar's interests against the governor's neutrality in the forthcoming election.

Muchlis refused to accommodate this plan, nor when he resigned was he willing to go quietly. He made clear that he was offended by the actions not only of the minister of the interior, but also of Minangkabau figures in Jakarta and Golkar officials in Padang whom he believed cooperated with the centre in slighting his authority. Immediately, people throughout West Sumatra hailed him as a local hero, and his action was likened to that of Mohammad Hatta when he resigned as vice president in 1956. The general view was that both leaders showed courage and integrity in resigning their positions, and that their principled actions shone out in the midst of the corruption surrounding them.

By his resignation, Muchlis had now demonstrated his honesty. Students had previously accused him of being involved in bribery when he was elected governor at the end of 1997, with the support of Hasan Basri Durin. His inauguration had been accompanied by protest demonstrations and he was then portrayed as a puppet of the previous governor. Now, however, his denials of the earlier charges carried real force. Shortly after his resignation, he was interviewed by a *Padang Ekspres* reporter who wrote: 'With respect to the rumours that Muchlis had used bribes to smooth his way to the governorship, he burst out laughing: "I use bribes? Where did I get the money? If I did that I would have had to sell my trousers"'.[16]

On the other hand, former governor Durin, now minister of agrarian affairs in Habibie's cabinet, was bracketed with its minister of manpower, Fahmi Idris, also a Minangkabau and head of Golkar's national headquarters in Jakarta. The two were believed to have manipulated the situation to undermine Governor Muchlis Ibrahim's authority.[17] These two ministers demonstrated the degree to which the perspective of Minangkabau *perantau* in Jakarta was often closer to that of the centre than of their home region. For, now, Hasan Basri Durin supported a provision in the decentralization law whereby the central government had the final say in the appointment of a provincial governor, remarking that 'the possibility of disintegration is quite large if the governor is fully autonomous'.[18] Fahmi Idris's attitude was even clearer when he criticized Muchlis for his lack of loyalty to Golkar: '... as a soldier, Muchlis should obey the decisions of his superiors. "Since when has a soldier not followed his superior's orders. That is desertion." he stated seriously'.[19]

Amid huge student protest demonstrations in Padang, Governor Muchlis Ibrahim handed over the governorship on March 27 to Jakarta's newly appointed caretaker governor, Maj. General (rtd.) Dunidja D., up until then head of the department of social and political affairs in the Interior Ministry. Dunidja's selection was probably influenced by his proven ability to overcome difficult situations in the past in Irian Jaya and East Timor.[20]

The Era of Reform

As the hopes raised immediately after Suharto's fall paralleled those of the period following the transfer of sovereignty from the Dutch in 1950, many of the basic problems that the country now confronted also paralleled those of the past. As in the early days of independence, the rapid reversal of power revealed that the Indonesian elite, both those who headed the government and those who opposed it, underestimated the strength of the people's desire for a political order that was equitable and responsible and their willingness to act independently to remove the corruption they saw undermining the state and society. As in the earlier period, the power-holders became fearful of the forces that had been unleashed.

In 1950, the crises over rebellions in South Sulawesi and Ambon had increased the impetus for Indonesia's leaders to change its form of government from a federal to a unitary structure. Now, those in authority pointed to the sporadic outbreaks of horrifying ethnic and religious violence that had erupted in a few areas of the country – most notably Ambon, West Kalimantan, and Aceh – as evidence that decentralization could lead to disintegration. Prominent leaders of the Minangkabau community in Jakarta echoed Golkar there in warning that, if the country moved too rapidly to relax the authoritarian rule of the previous decades and introduce democratization and decentralization, security would be undermined and the result would be disruption and disintegration.[21]

But in many ways the situation in 1999 was the reverse of that in 1950. Then, suspicion of Dutch motives in creating the federal states had led to antipathy toward the whole idea of federation not only on the part of the national leaders but of all who had fought for the Republican cause. By contrast, in 1998 it was antipathy toward an Indonesian government's manipulation of the unitary system to reinforce its monopolization of power that was the motivating force behind demands for at least a decentralized if not a federal state.[22]

Other than in East Timor and Irian Jaya, the unrest that erupted in several of Indonesia's regions in the post-Suharto period did not stem from a wish to separate from the Republic, but rather was fundamentally the surfacing of internal ethnic and religious tensions which had been submerged during the repressive rule of the New Order. Bloody riots frequently reflected resentment of the indigenous people of a particular area at the economic and political injustices they had endured, and a belief that 'intruders', whether of a different ethnic group (Javanese, Chinese, Buginese, or Madurese) or religion, and whether traders or peasant transmigrants, had received preferential treatment from the central government. Jakarta's transmigration policies, which had too often been used as a means of strengthening its control over 'unreliable' regions, exacerbated the friction. As in the 1950s, during the 1990s there were also protests against Jakarta's decisions that 'give insufficient opportunity to the Regional Government to use funds in accordance with the region's needs'.[23]

The Habibie government has taken steps to assuage regional discontent by introducing a new decentralization law, which was ultimately passed by the Parliament on April 23, 1999. This law promises extensive autonomy to Indonesia's provinces in all matters except defence, foreign, judicial, fiscal, monetary, and religious affairs, and matters deemed 'strategic'.[24] It provides for the country's 306 district heads (*bupati*) and mayors to be elected by their local parliaments, and ends the practice of military officers holding posts in the bureaucracy.[25]

Most significant for such regions as Riau and Aceh, was a Law of Intergovernmental Fiscal Relations, passed the same day, under which export-producing provinces were now to receive a much larger share of the revenues from their oil, gas, and other natural resources, as well as from land and property taxes.[26] It offers these provinces '15 percent of the government's share of net oil revenue, 30 percent of gas revenue, and 80 percent of income derived from forestry, mining and fisheries'.[27] However, while providing the resource-rich provinces with a larger share of the export income they earn, the law had to be careful to preserve a sufficient flow of export revenue to the central government for it to distribute adequate funds to the resource-poor provinces, which have grown dependent upon financing from the centre. For instance, prior to implementation of the new law, the province of West Sumatra received from Jakarta four times the amount of revenues that it had collected and sent to the central government.[28] Though the fiscal law requires the central government to use at least 25 percent of its total internal revenue for block grants to the provinces, it is unlikely that the financial provisions in the law will satisfy both the resource-rich and resource-poor provinces of Indonesia.

There are certainly many difficulties in moving to dismantle the well-entrenched centralized state structure built up over the past forty years. The lack of autonomy and decision-making powers in the regions has tended to draw the most qualified people to Jakarta, while the standards for a regional official to achieve success lay in who could 'best interpret the standards of the central government'.[29]

Nevertheless, in West Sumatra, most people were confident that there would be enough qualified personnel – at least at the province level – to implement the new decentralization policies, and believed that the increased autonomy might well tempt educated migrants to return to their home area.

Those warning that a devolution of power threatened the unity of Indonesia tended to underestimate the depths of the loyalty to the ideal or 'dream' of the Indonesian nation – nourished in large part by memories of the national struggle and the independence war – that are still alive in most parts of the archipelago. As Anne Booth has perceptively written:

> The very improbability of such a huge and heterogeneous collection of islands forming itself into a single country became a source of national pride, as it remains to many Indonesians to this day.[30]

It should be recalled that when the regions rebelled in the late 1950s, their goal was not to secede from the state but rather to change its character, correct the central government's policies, and establish a just balance between central and local government power. It was only when their pleas were rebuffed that the dissidents even moved to consider a federal system, let alone secession. Now as then, what pressures there are for actual separatism spring from resentment at a government that is oppressive and too centralized, exercising its power with little concern for the needs and desires of the nation's component elements.[31]

The classic example here, of course, is Aceh. This was the one area of Indonesia not occupied by the Dutch during the revolution, and its people have always felt a justifiable pride in having fought in the very vanguard of opposition to the Dutch and providing the Republic with its most reliable base of financial support. But the brutal policies of the New Order government, which have killed at least two thousand Acehnese in the last decade, have succeeded in turning what began as a weak, locally based Free Aceh (Aceh Merdeka) movement, into a potent force, enjoying considerable popular support throughout the province. Only by granting Aceh the real autonomy it has been calling for over the past fifty years, is the central government likely to avert what has become an actual danger of secession.[32]

East Timor and, to a lesser degree, Irian Jaya, can perhaps be put in a different category. Neither experienced the history of struggle and early independence shared by most of the rest of the archipelago, and their resources have been exploited and their people repressed and savagely brutalized by what they can only view as an alien regime. Even if measures were to be taken now to respond to their grievances and redress their needs through grants of autonomy and more just policies, it remains likely that if they are offered a really free choice, East Timor at least, and possibly Irian Jaya, would elect to separate from the Indonesian Republic.

As was the case with previous decentralization laws stretching back to 1948, the draft autonomy law of 1999 envisages three autonomous levels of administration: the province, the district (kabupaten), and the town or village – with the district as the key unit. Some degree of hierarchical relationship is retained between the central and provincial government, with, for example, any governor elected by the provincial council still having to be approved by the central government.[33] But this hierarchy does not continue down the administrative ladder. The district head is autonomous of the provincial governor, who is to be responsible only for services which extend throughout the province, such as communications. In all other matters, only if the area concerned (district, town, or village) is not able to carry out specific responsibilities is it called on to surrender these to the provincial authorities. The *bupati* and mayor (or village head) are elected by the local councils, and their appointments do not need approval from the provincial governor. In fact, 'the governor no longer has authority over the *bupati* and the mayor (or village head)'.[34]

Discussion of the autonomy law intensified calls in West Sumatra for the 1979 village law to be abolished and the *nagari* restored as the lowest administrative unit in the region. Though it would be difficult to reverse the administrative system of the past decade in the rural areas, pressures for the restoration of the *nagari* seemed likely to meet with success, for they reflected nearly unanimous support from most sectors of Minangkabau society.[35] Financial drawbacks to the change also disappeared at the beginning of 1999, when the central government introduced a provision whereby funds to the province were no longer to be allocated according to its number of villages, but instead in the form of block grants. These were divided into three groups: provincial funds, kabupaten funds, and rural development funds, and though the central government was still to determine the total amount of the grant to each province, it was left to the local inhabitants to decide the allocation and use of the funds.[36]

Elections

The Indonesian people's continuing faith in democracy is surprising in view of the extent to which the term has been distorted by Sukarno's 'Guided Democracy' and Suharto's 'Pancasila Democracy'. But again, as in the 1950s, much of Indonesia's population saw the holding of free national elections as providing the only reliable way of establishing a government in which they could trust.

Nationally and locally, elections would test the strength of the New Order's residual edifice against the depth of the people's demands for change. In the run-up to the elections, it became clear that the government was still resorting to 'money politics', channelling profits from state-owned enterprises to Golkar in an effort to shore up its eroded position. When Golkar chose President Habibie as its sole candidate, over the misgivings of many of its members, it ensured its unfettered access to government funds for the campaign. In fact, Golkar reportedly planned to spend nationally as much as 350 billion rupiah on the June elections.[37] In West Sumatra, local Golkar officials used their share of this money to grant loans to villagers and small businesses.[38] And government officials were ensuring that Golkar emblems and Golkar calendars were included with food parcels distributed to the malnourished families in the famine-ridden southern coastal areas of the province.[39]

In the country at large, as in West Sumatra, if Golkar were actually to win, its victory would be widely seen as evidence that elections could still be bought and that the office-holders of the 'reform era' were as corrupt as their New Order predecessors. At the same time, the Indonesian people are not naive and know that, even if power changes hands, this would be only a first step in a democratic process, and, certainly in West Sumatra at least, few believe that those elected will be much more resistant than their predecessors to the temptations of their office if there are not strong guarantees in place against the reintroduction of money politics and corrupt administration.

Despite the concerns expressed in Jakarta and abroad that free and open campaigning would lead to violence and disruption, in most parts of the country these fears were not realized. At the outset, the proliferation of parties – 234 at first count – seemed to invite confusion and disarray. But the registration process proved efficient, and 141 survived the first hurdle, with only forty-eight eventually meeting the guidelines imposed by the team of independent figures, the so-called Team of Eleven, assigned to verify which political parties were eligible to compete in the elections.[40] (In order to meet the final test, parties had to demonstrate, among other things, that they had branches in nine provinces, with offices in at least half the districts in each of these provinces.) In West Sumatra, twenty-nine parties qualified for the ballot[41] and in mid-April ten of the Islamic parties reached an agreement to cooperate in campaigning for the election to try to ensure a victory for the Muslim forces.[42]

Although fears remained that Golkar's practice of money politics would again prove successful,[43] there appeared to be a broadly based consensus that the elections could provide the tentative first step toward creating a decentralized and democratic Indonesian polity more in line with the ideals of the Minangkabau people of West Sumatra than anything achieved in the country's previous history.

June 1999

Bibliography of Secondary Sources

Abdullah, Taufik, 'Minangkabau dalam Perspektif Perubahan Sosial', in *Perubahan Sosial di Minangkabau*, ed. Zed *et al.* (Padang: Universitas Andalas, 1992)

Abdullah, Taufik, 'Modernization in the Minangkabau World', in *Culture and Politics in Indonesia*, ed. Claire Holt *et al.* (Ithaca: Cornell University Press, 1972)

Abdullah, Taufik, *Schools and Politics: The Kaum Muda Movement in West Sumatra (1927-1933)* (Ithaca: Cornell Modern Indonesia Project, 1971)

Abdullah, Taufik, 'Adat and Islam: An Examination of Conflict in Minangkabau', *Indonesia* 2 (October 1966): 1-24

Abu, Rifai & Drs. Abdullah Suhadi, *Chatib Suleman* (Jakarta: Departemen PD & K, 1976)

Adams, Cindy, see *Sukarno*

Alfian, *Muhammadiyah* (Yogyakarta: Gadjah Mada University Press, 1989)

Alisjahbana, S. Takdir, *Perdjuangan Autonomi dan Kedudukaan Adat Didalamnja* (Jakarta: Pustaka Rakjat, n.d. [1957])

Amal, Ichlasul, *Regional and Central Government in Indonesian Politics: West Sumatra and South Sulawesi 1949-1979* (Yogyakarta: Gadjah Mada University Press, 1992)

Amalsip, 'Hadji Abdoellah Ahmad: Seorang Oelama, Journalist, Politikoes dan Organisator di Minangkabau', *Pandji Islam* 6/2, 6/3, 6/4 (January 9, 16, 23, 1939)

Ambler, John S., 'Historical Perspectives on Sawah Cultivation and the Political and Economic Context for Irrigation in West Sumatra', *Indonesia* 46 (October 1988): 39-77

Aminuddin, Dr. H., Rasyad, H.Leon Salim, Hjh. Hasniah Saleh, *H. Rahmah el Yunusiyyah dan Zainuddin Labay el Yunusy* (Jakarta: Pengurus Perguruan Diniyyah Puteri Padang Panjang Perwakilan Jakarta, 1991)

Anderson, Benedict, *Imagined Communities* 1983; revised edition (London: Verso, 1991)

Anderson, Benedict R.O'G., *Java in a Time of Revolution* (Ithaca: Cornell University Press, 1972)

Anderson, Benedict R.O'G, 'The Idea of Power in Javanese Culture', in *Culture and Politics in Indonesia*, ed. Claire Holt *et al.* (Ithaca: Cornell University Press, 1972)

Anwar, Moh. Rasjad, Iwan J. Azis, Mari Pangestu, Hadi Soesastro, 'The Indonesian Economy: Problems and Prospects', *Asian Economic Journal* 5,2 (1991): 100-136

Asnawi, Sjofian, 'Pembangunan Sumatera Barat dalam Kaitannya dengan Masalah Perubahan Sosio-kultural Setempat', in *Perubahan Sosial di Minangkabau*, eds. Zed *et al.* (Padang: Universitas Andalas, 1992)

Azis, Iwan J., 'Review of Regional Development: Equity and Foreign Exchange Accumulation,' in *Spatial Development in Indonesia: Review and Prospects*, eds Tschangho John Kim, Gerrit Knaap and Iwan J. Azis (Aldershot: Avebury, 1992), 91-128

Azwar Dt. Mangiang, 'Menyingkapkan Tabir yang Menyelimuti Peristiwa Situjuh Batur 15 Januari 1949' (typescript, n.d.)

Bachtiar, Harsja W., '*Negeri* Taram: A Minangkabau Village Community', in *Villages in Indonesia*, ed. Koentjaraningrat (Ithaca: Cornell University Press, 1967): 348-85

Bahar, Saafroedin, 'Peranan Elite Sipil dan Elite Militer dalam Dinamika Integrasi Nasional di Indonesia: Kasus Etnik Minangkabau di Daerah Sumatera Barat, 1945-1984' (PhD. dissertation, Gadjah Mada University, Yogyakarta, 1996)

Bangun, Payung, *Kolonel Maludin Simbolon: Liku-liku Perjuangannya dalam Pembangunan Bangsa* (Jakarta: Sinar Harapan, 1996)

Batuah, A.M. Datuk Maruhan and D.H. Bagindo Nanameh, *Hukum Adat dan Adat Minang-kabau Luhak nan Tiga, Laras nan Dua* (Jakarta: Pusaka Aseli, n.d.)

Benda, Harry J. & Ruth T. McVey, eds, *The Communist Uprisings of 1926-1927 in Indonesia: Key Documents* (Ithaca: Cornell Modern Indonesia Project, 1960)

Boechari, H. Sidi Ibrahim, *Pengaruh Timbal Balik antara Pendidikan Islam dan Pergerakan Nasional di Minangkabau* (Jakarta: Gunung Tiga, [1981])

Boei cho boei kenshusho [Defence Ministry Research Institute], *Nansei homen rikugun sakusen: Malai Ranin no boei, Rekishi Seinshi sosho 92 [Army Operations in Southwest Areas: Defence of Malaya and the Dutch East Indieis, History of World War II, vol. 92]* (Tokyo: Asagumo Shinbun sha, 1976)

Boekoe Peringatan 15 Tahoen Dinijjah School Poeteri Padang Pandjang (Padang Panjang: Dinijjah School Poeteri, [1938])

Bondan, Mohamad, *Genderang Proklamasi di Luar Negeri* (Jakarta: 'Kawal', 1971)

Bowen, John, *Sumatran Politics and Poetics: Gayo History, 1900-1989* (New Haven: Yale University Press, 1991)

Brugmans, I.J., *Geschiedenis van het Onderwijs in Nederlandsch Indie* (Groningen-Batavia: Wolters, 1938)

Chaniago, Hasril and Khairul Jasmi, *Brigadir Jenderal Polisi Kaharoeddin Datuk Rangkayo Basa* (Jakarta: Sinar Harapan, 1998)

Chauvel, Richard, 'Ambon: Not Revolution but a Counterrevolution', in *Regional Dynamics*, ed. Audrey Kahin

Coast, John, *Recruit to Revolution* (London: Christophers, 1952)

Cribb, Robert, ed., *The Indonesian Killings 1965-1966* (Clayton: Monash University Centre of Southeast Asia Studies, 1990)

Crouch, Harold, *The Army and Politics in Indonesia* (Ithaca: Cornell University Press, 1978)

De Graaff, S & D.G. Stibbe, *Encyclopaedie van Nederlandsch Oost-Indie*, 4 vols. (The Hague: Nijhoff, 1918-1919)

Djaja, Tamar, *Pusaka Indonesia: Orang2 Besar Tanah Air*, 4th printing (Bandung: Visser, 1951)

Djajadiningrat, Idrus Nasir, *The Beginnings of the Indonesian-Dutch Negotiations and the Hoge Veluwe Talks* (Ithaca: Cornell Modern Indonesia Project, 1958)

Djohary, Sjamsir, 'Peristiwa Situdjuh' (15 Januari 1949) (MA Skripsi, IKIP Padang, 1977)

Dobbin, Christine, *Islamic Revivalism in a Changing Peasant Economy: Central Sumatra, 1784-1847*, Scandinavian Institute of Asian Studies Monograph Series No. 47 (London & Malmo: Curzon Press, 1983)

Dobbin, Christine, 'Economic Change in Minangkabau as a Factor in the Rise of the Padri Movement, 1784-1830', *Indonesia* 23 (April 1977): 1-38

Durin, Hasan Basri, *Catatan Seorang Pamong* (Jakarta: Obor, 1997)

Enar, Fatimah, *et al.*, *Sumatera Barat, 1945-1949* (Padang: Pemerintah Daerah Sumatera Barat, 1978)

Feith, Herbert, and Daniel S. Lev, 'The End of the Indonesian Rebellion', *Pacific Affairs* 36, 1 (Spring 1963): 32-46

Feith, Herbert, *The Decline of Constitutional Democracy in Indonesia* (Ithaca: Cornell University Press, 1962)

Feith, Herbert, *The Indonesian Elections of 1955* (Ithaca: Cornell Modern Indonesia Project, 1957)

Gerakan 30 September: Pemberontakan Partai Komunis Indonesia: Latar Belakang, Aksi, dan Penumpasannya (Jakarta: Sekretariat Negara Republik Indonesia, 1994)

Gibb, H.A.R., *Modern Trends in Islam* (Chicago: University of Chicago Press, 1947)

Gibb, H.A.R., and J.H. Kramers, *Shorter Encyclopaedia of Islam* (Ithaca: Cornell University Press, 1953)

Gilsenan, *Recognizing Islam: Religion and Society in the Modern Arab World* (New York: Pantheon, 1982)

Graves, Elizabeth E., *The Minangkabau Response to Dutch Colonial Rule in the Nineteenth Century* (Ithaca: Cornell Modern Indonesia Project, 1981)

Hamid, A., *Setengah Abad Ruang Pendidik ins Kayutanam 1926-1976* (Kayutanam: Panitia Hari Ulang Tahun ke 50, 1976)

Hamka, *Kenang-Kenangan Hidup*, 2nd printing (Kuala Lumpur: Pustaka Antara, 1982)

Hamka, *Kenang-Kenangan Hidup, IV* (Jakarta: Bulan Bintang, 1975)

Hamka, *Ajahku: Riwajat Hidup Dr. H. Abd. Karim Amrullah dan Perdjuangan Kaum Agama di Sumatera*, 3rd printing (Jakarta: Djajamurni, 1967)

Hamka, *Sedjarah Islam di Sumatera* (Medan: Pustaka Nasional, 1950)

Harun, Chairul, 'A.A. Navis Salah Seorang Manusia Merdeka di Indonesia', in *Otobiografi A.A. Navis*, ed. Abra Yusra

Harvey, Barbara, 'South Sulawesi: Puppets and Patriots', in *Regional Dynamics of the Indonesian Revolution*, ed. Audrey Kahin

Harvey, Barbara, *Permesta: Half a Rebellion* (Ithaca: Cornell Modern Indonesia Project, 1977)

Harvey, Barbara, 'Tradition, Islam, and Rebellion: South Sulawesi 1950-1965' (PhD. dissertation, Cornell University, 1974)

Hasbi, Mohammad, *Masalah Pengembangan Nagari di Sumatera Barat* (Bukittinggi: Biro Publikasi APDN, 1972)

Hatta, Mohammad, 'Indonesia's Foreign Policy', *Foreign Affairs* 31, 3 (April 1953): 441-52

Hatta, Mohammad, *Indonesian Patriot: Memoirs*, ed. C.L.M. Penders (Singapore: Gunung Agung, 1981)

Hatta, Mohammad, *Memoir* (Jakarta: Tintamas, 1979)

Hatta, Mohammad, *Sekitar Proklamasi 17 Agustus 1945* (Jakarta: Tintamas, 1970)

Henley, David E.F., *Nationalism and Regionalism in a Colonial Context: Minahasa in the Dutch East Indies* (Leiden: KITLV Press, 1996)

Huitema, W.K., *De Bevolkings-Koffiecultuur op Sumatra* (Wageningen: H. Veenman, 1935)

Husein, Ahmad, *et al.*, *Sejarah Perjuangan Kemerdekaan RI di Minangkabau/Riau 1945-1950*, 2nd ed. (Jakarta: BPSIM, 1991)

Ilyas, Drs. Muslim, *Aziz Chan: Riwajat & Perjuangan* (Padang: Daerah Kotamadya Padang, 1973)

Ingleson, John, *Road to Exile: The Indonesian Nationalist Movement 1927-1934* (Singapore: Heinemann Educational Books [Asia], 1979)

Jarvis, Helen, trans., *Tan Malaka, From Jail to Jail*, 3 vols. (Athens: Ohio University Center for International Studies, 1991)

Jenkins, David, *Suharto and His Generals: Indonesian Military Politics 1975-1983* (Ithaca: Cornell University Modern Indonesia Project, 1984)

Jong, P.E. de Josselin de, *Minangkabau and Negri Sembilan: Socio-Political Structure in Indonesia* (The Hague: Nijhoff, 1980)

Joustra, M., *Minangkabau: Overzicht van Land, Geschiedenis en Volk* (The Hague: Nijhoff, 1923)

Kahin, Audrey R. and George McT. Kahin, *Subversion as Foreign Policy: The Secret Eisenhower and Dulles Debacle in Indonesia* (New York: The New Press, 1995)

Kahin, Audrey, ed., *Regional Dynamics of the Indonesian Revolution* (Honolulu: University of Hawaii Press, 1985)

Kahin, Audrey, 'The Impact of the Indonesian Independence Struggle on Minangkabau Society', in *Change and Continuity in Minangkabau: Local, Regional and Historical Perspectives on West Sumatra*, ed. Lynn L. Thomas and Franz von Benda-Beckmann (Athens, Ohio: Ohio University Center for International Studies, 1985)

Kahin, Audrey, 'Struggle for Independence: West Sumatra in the Indonesian National Revolution 1945-1950' (PhD. dissertation, Cornell University, 1979)

Kahin, George McT., 'Indonesia', in *Major Governments of Asia*, ed. G. McT. Kahin (Ithaca: Cornell University Press, 1959)

Kahin, George McTurnan, *Nationalism and Revolution in Indonesia* (Ithaca: Cornell University Press, 1952)

Kantor Wilayah Departemen Sosial DKI Jakarta, *Proyek Penulisan Riwayat Perjuangan Perintis Kemerdekaan, Tahun 1979-1980* (Disusun oleh: Leon Salim, No. Pol.21/59/PK) (Jakarta, typescript, n.d.)

Kathirithamby-Wells, J., 'The Inderapura Sultanate: The Foundations of Its Rise and Decline from the Sixteenth to the Eighteenth Centuries', *Indonesia* 21 (April 1976): 65-84.

Kato, Tsuyoshi, 'Different Fields Similar Locusts: Adat Communities and the Village Law of 1979 in Indonesia', *Indonesia* 47 (April 1989): 89-114

Kato, Tsuyoshi, *Matriliny and Migration: Evolving Minangkabau Traditions in Indonesia* (Ithaca: Cornell University Press, 1982)

Kell, Tim, *The Roots of Acehnese Rebellion* (Ithaca: Cornell Modern Indonesia Project, 1995)

Kementerian Penerangan, *Republik Indonesia: Propinsi Sumatera Tengah* (n.p., n.d.)

Kepartaian dan Parlementaria Indonesia (Jakarta: Kementerian Penerangan, 1954)

King, Dwight Y., 'Indonesia's New Order as a Bureaucratic Polity, a Neo-patrimonial Regime or a Bureaucratic-Authoritarian Regime: What Difference Does It Make?', in *Interpreting Indonesian Politics: Thirteen Contributions to the Debate*, eds. Benedict Anderson and Audrey Kahin (Ithaca: Cornell University Modern Indonesia Project, 1982), 104-16.

Kitab Peringatan terkarang waktoe telah 35 tahoen 'oemoer Sekolah-Radja oentoek Goeroe Melajoe di Boekit-tinggi (n.p., [1908])

Komando Daerah Militer III/17 Agustus, *Sedjarah Kodam III/17 Agustus* (Padang: Sri Dharma, n.d. [1970])

Kotjek, M. Junus & Leon Salim, 'Pergerakan Pemuda di Minangkabau' (typesecript dated April 28, 1962)

'Laporan Penelitian: Transformasi Pendidikan di Sumatera Barat: Kasus Adabiah School' Proyek Menteri Agama Rep. Ind./Pelaksana LPDUB Indonesia Bekerjasama dengan Pusat Penelitian Kebudayaan dan Perubahan Sosial Un. Gajah Mada, IAIAN Imam Bonjol & Yayasan Sjarikat Oesaha Adabiah, 1997/1998

Legge, J.D., *Cultural Authority and Regional Autonomy in Indonesia: A Study in Local Administration 1950-1960* (Ithaca: Cornell University Press, 1961)

Leirissa, R.Z., *prri Permesta: Strategi Membangun Indonesia tanpa Komunis*, 3rd ed. (Jakarta: Grafiti, 1997)

Lev, Daniel S., *Transition to Guided Democracy: Indonesian Politics, 1957-1959* (Ithaca: Cornell Modern Indonesia Project, 1966)

Loebis, Aboe Bakar, 'Tan Malaka's Arrest' An Eye-Witness Account', *Indonesia* 53 (April 1992): 71-78

Lubis, Mochtar, *Hati Nurani Melawan Kezaliman: Surat-Surat Bung Hatta Kepada Presiden Soekarno 1957-1965* (Jakarta: Sinar Harapan, 1986)

MacAndrews, Colin, 'The Structure of Government in Indonesia', in *Central Government and Local Development in Indonesia*, ed. Colin MacAndrews (Singapore: Oxford University Press, 1986)

Mahyuni, SY., *Peristiwa Situjuh 15.1.49* (Situjuh Batur: Lembaga Sosial Desa 'Lembah Situjuh', n.d. [1972])

Malley, Michael, 'The Centrifugal Political Effects of Economic Reform in Indonesia'. Paper presented to the Annual Meeting of the Association of Asian Studies (Washington, March 26-29, 1998)

Mansoer, M.D., Amrin Imran, Mardanas Safwa, Asmaniar Z. Idris & Sidi I. Buchari, *Sedjarah Minangkabau* (Jakarta: Bhratara, 1970)

Marsden, William, *The History of Sumatra*, Oxford in Asia Historical Reprints (Singapore: Oxford University Press, 1986)

Martimin, Mardjani, Ishaq Thaher & Amir B. Mahyuddin, *Sejarah Kebangkitan Nasional Sumatera Barat* (n.p.: Proyek Penelitian dan Pencatatan Kebudayaan Daerah, 1977-78)

Maryanov Gerald S., *Decentralization in Indonesia as a Political Problem* (Ithaca: Cornell University Modern Indonesia Project, 1958)

Marzali, Amri, 'Orang Silungkang di Jakarta' (MA thesis, Gadjah Mada University, 1973)

McDonald, Hamish, *Suharto's Indonesia* (Blackburn, Victoria: Fontana Books, 1980)

McVey, Ruth T., 'The Post-Revolutionary Transformation of the Indonesian Army', *Indonesia* 11 (April 1971): 131-76

McVey, Ruth T., *The Rise of Indonesian Communism* (Ithaca: Cornell University Press, 1965)

Memoir of the Life and Public Services of Sir Thomas Stamford Raffles, F.R.S. by his Widow (London: Murray, 1830)

Moehamad, Djoeir, *Memoar Seorang Sosialis* (Jakarta: Obor, 1997)

Moertono, Soemarsaid, *State and Statecraft in Old Java* (Ithaca: Cornell Modern Indonesia Project, 1968)

Morris, Eric Eugene, 'Islam and Politics in Aceh: A Study of Center-Periphery Relations in Indonesia' (PhD. dissertation, Cornell Univeristy, 1983)

Mortimer, Edward, *Faith and Power: The Politics of Islam* (New York: Random House, 1982)

Mortimer, Rex, *Indonesian Communism under Sukarno: Ideology and Politics, 1959-1965* (Ithaca: Cornell University Press, 1974)

Mossman, James, *Rebels in Paradise: Indonesia's Civil War* (London: Cape, 1961)

Mountbatten of Burma, Vice Admiral, the Earl, *Post-Surrender Tasks: Section E of the Report to the Combined Chiefs of Staff by the Supreme Commander, Southeast Asia, 1943-1945* (London: Her Majesty's Stationery Office, 1969)

Mrazek, Rudolf, *Sjahrir: Politics and Exile in Indonesia* (Ithaca: Cornell Southeast Asia Program, 1994)

Nagari, Desa dan Pembangunan Pedesaan di Sumatera Barat (Sumatera Barat: Yayasan Genta Budaya, 1990)

Nagazumi, *The Dawn of Indonesian Nationalism: The Early Years of the Budi Utomo 1908-1918* (Tokyo: Institute of Developing Economies, 1972)

Naim, Mochtar, 'Nagari versus Desa: Sebuah Kerancuan Struktural', in *Nagari, Desa dan Pembangunan Pedesaan di Sumatera Barat*

Naim, Mochtar, 'Merantau: Minangkabau Voluntary Migration' (PhD. dissertation, University of Singapore, 1973)

Nasroen, M., *Falsafah Adat Minangkabau* (Jakarta: Bulan Bintang, 1957)

Nasution, A.H., *Memenuhi Panggilan Tugas*, vol. 4: *Masa Pancaroba Kedua* (Jakarta: Gunung Agung, 1984)

Nasution, A.H., *Tentara Nasional Indonesia*, vol. 1, 3rd printing (Jakarta: Seruling Masa, 1970)

Nasution, A. Muluk, *Pemberontakan Sarikat Rakyat Silungkang Sumatera Barat 1926-1927* (Jakarta: Mutiara, 1981)

Navis, A.A., *Filsafat dan Strategi Pendidikan M. Sjafei: Ruang Pendidik ins Kayutanam* (Jakarta: Gramedia Widiasarana Indonesia, 1996)

Navis, A.A., *Dialektika Minangkabau dalam Kemelut Sosial dan Politik* (Padang: Genta Singgalang Press, 1983)

Navis, A.A., 'Bank Nasional dalam Sejarah Nasional' (draft manuscript, 1995)

Navis, A.A., *Alam Terkembang Jadi Guru: Adat dan Kebudayaan Minangkabau* (Jakarta: Grafiti Pers, 1984)

Navis, A.A. 'Alur Kebudayaan dalam Tingkah Laku Gerakan Politik di Minangkabau', in *Dialektika Minangkabau dalam Kemelut Sosial dan Politik*, ed. A.A. Navis

Ning, Hasjim, *Pasang Surut Pengusaha Pejuang* (Jakarta: Grafiti, 1986)

Nishijima, Shigetada, and Koichi Kishi, *Japanese Military Administration in Indonesia* (Washington: JPRS, 1963)

Noer, Deliar, *Aku Bagian Ummat Aku Bagian Bangsa* (Jakarta: Mizan, 1996)

Noer, Deliar, *Mohammad Hatta: Biografi Politik* (Jakarta: LP3ES, 1990)

Noer, Deliar, *Partai Islam di Pentas Nasional* (Jakarta: Grafiti Pers, 1987)

Noer, Deliar, *The Modernist Muslim Movement in Indonesia 1900-1942* (Singapore: Oxford University Press, 1973)

Nursuhud, *Menjingkap Tabir 'Dewan Banteng'* (Jakarta: Jajasan Pembaruan, 1958)

Oei Tjoe Tat, *Memoar Oei Tjoe Tat: Pembantu President Soekarno*, eds Pramoedya Ananta Toer & Stanley Adi Prasetyo (Jakarta: Hasta Mitra, 1995)

Oki, Akira, 'A Note on the History of the Textile Industry in West Sumatra', in *Between People and Statistics: Essays on Modern Indonesian History Presented to P. Creutzberg* (The Hague: Nijhoff, 1979)

Oki, Akira, 'Social Change in the West Sumatran Village: 1908-1945' (PhD. dissertation, Australian National University, 1977)

Oshikawa, Noriaki, '*Patjar Merah Indonesia* and Tan Malaka: A Popular Novel and a Revolutionary Legend', in *Reading Southeast Asia*, ed. Takashi Shiraishi (Ithaca: Cornell Southeast Asia Program Translation Series, 1990)

Palimo Kajo, H.M.D. Datuk, *Sedjarah Perguruan Thawalib Padang Pandjang* (Padang Panjang: Jajasan Thawalib, [1970])

Penerangan Angkatan Darat [PAD], *Kini Tabir dapat Dibuka* ([Jakarta?]: Kementerian Penerangan RI, 1958)

Poer, Julius, *Benny Moerdani: Profil Prajurit Negarawan* (Jakarta: Yayasan Kejuangan Panglima Besar Sudirman, 1993)

Poeze, Harry A., *Tan Malaka: Levensloop van 1897 tot 1945* (The Hague: Smits, 1976)

Pringgodigdo, A.K., *The Office of President in Indonesia as Defined in the Three Constitutions in Theory and Practice* (Ithaca: Cornell Modern Indonesia Project, 1957)

Proyek Penelitian dan Pencatatan Kebudayaan Daerah, *Sejarah Kebangkitan Nasional Daerah Sumatera Barat* (Jakarta: Dep. PD&K, 1982)

Radjab, Muhamad, *Perang Paderi di Sumatera Barat 1803-1838* (Jakarta: Kementerian PP&K, 1954)

Raffles, *see Memoir*

Rapport van de Commissie van Onderzoek, vol. 1 (Weltevreden: Landsdrukkerij, 1928)

Rasjid, S.M. et al., *Sejarah Perjuangan Kemerdekaan Republik Indonesia di Minangkabau 1945-1950* vol. 1, 1978; vol. 2, 1981 (Jakarta: Badan Pemurnian Sejarah Indonesia-Minangkabau [BPSIM], 1978,1981)

Rasjid-70 (Jakarta: Panitia Peringatan Ulang Tahun Mr. Rasjid Ke-70, n.d.)

Reid, Anthony, *The Blood of the People* (Oxford: Oxford University Press, 1979)

Reid, Anthony, *Indonesian National Revolution* (n.p.: Longman, 1973)

Reid, Anthony, 'The Birth of the Republic in Sumatra', *Indonesia* 12 (October 1971): 21-46

Riwayat Hidup & Perjoangan Almarhum Chatib Suleiman (typescript, Padang Panjang, Feb. 1973)

Riwayat Hidup dan Perjuangan 20 Ulama Besar Sumatera Barat ([Padang]: Islamic Centre Sumatera Barat, 1981)

Robinson, Geoffrey, '*Rawan* is as *Rawan* does: The Origins of Disorder in New Order Aceh', *Indonesia* 66 (October 1998): 127-56

Roff, William, *The Origins of Malay Nationalism* (New Haven: Yale University Press, 1967)

Rosidi, Ajip, *Sjafruddin Prawiranegara: Lebih Takut kepada Allah SWT* (Jakarta: Inti Idayu Press, 1986)

Saeed, Abdullah, *Islamic Banking and Interest: A Study of the Prohibition of Riba and its Contemporary Interpretation* (Leiden: Brill, 1996)

Safwan, 'Taher Marah Sutan: Tokoh yang Dilupakan', in *Majalah Bulanan Kebudayaan Minangkabau* [Jakarta] 1,1 (January 1974): 52-55

Said, Nawir, *Pemberontakan Silungkang 1927 Sumatra Barat* (Jakarta: Pentja, 1963)

Saidi, Anwar St., *Tugu Pemuda Sumatera* (Padang: NV Tenunan Padang Asli, 1967)

Salim, I.F.M. Chalid, *Limabelas Tahun Digul Kamp Konsentrasi di Nieuw Guinea Tempat Persemaian Kemerdekaan Indonesia* (Jakarta: Bulan Bintang, 1977)

Salim, Leon, *Khatib Sulaiman* (n.p.: 1987)

Salim, Leon, *Prisoners at Kota Cane*, trans. Audrey Kahin (Ithaca: Cornell Modern Indonesia Project, 1986)

Salim, Leon, *see also* Kantor Wilayah

Salim, Makmum, *Sedjarah Operasi2 Gabungan terhadap prri-Permesta* (Jakarta: Pusat Sedjarah ABRI, 1971)

Schiller, A. Arthur, *The Formation of Federal Indonesia (1945-1949)* (The Hague: Van Hoeve, 1955)

Schrieke, B., *Indonesian Sociological Studies*, Part One (The Hague: Van Hoeve, 1955)

Schwartz, Adam, *A Nation in Waiting: Indonesia in the 1990s* (Boulder: Westview Press, 1994)

Sediono, C.K.H.R. Surjo, *Peristiwa Tjikini* (Jakarta: Soeroengan, 1958)

Sheare, I.C., *Federal Government*, 3rd ed. (London: Oxford University Press)

Shiraishi, Takashi, *An Age in Motion: Popular Radicalism in Java, 1912-1926* (Ithaca: Cornell University Press, 1990)

Sidel, John T. 'Macet Total, Logics of Circulation and Accumulation in the Demise of Indonesia's New Order', *Indonesia* 66 (October 1998): 159-94

Sjafei, Mohammad, *Dasar-dasar Pendidikan* (Kayutanam: INS, 1976)

Sjafruddin Prawiranegara, 'Pancasila as the Sole Foundation', *Indonesia* 38 (October 1984): 74-83

Sjoeib, Let.Kol. Purn., 'Era Eksperimen Politik dari Presiden Sukarno 1956-1966'. Paper given to Seminar '50 Tahun Hubungan Indonesia-Amerika Serikat' (Depok, Jurusan Sejarah Fakultas Sastra, Universitas Indonesia, 1998): 1-25

Smail, John R., 'The Military Politics of North Sumatra: December 1956-October 1957', *Indonesia* 6 (October 1968): 128-87

Smit, C., *Het Akkord van Linggadjati* (Amsterdam: Elsevier, 1959)

Smit, C. *De Indonesische Questie* (Leiden: Brill, 1952)

Soeleiman, Soetan glr. Angkoe Tan Toeah Bg. Ratoe, *Minangkabau dengan Minangkabau-Raad* (Bukittinggi: 'Merapi,' n.d. [circa 1940])

Soemardjan, Selo, *et al.*, *Pemerintahan Desa Jilid 1: Laporan Penelitian di Daerah Propinsi ....Sumatra Barat* (Jakarta: Badan Penelitian dan Pengembangan, Departmen Dalam Negeri Kerjasama dengan Yayasan Ilmu-ilmu Sosial, 1988), 140-52

Sophiaan, Manai, *Apa yang masih teringat* (Jakarta: Yayasan 'Mencerdaskan Kehidupan Bangsa', 1991)

Staf Umum Angkatan Darat [SUAD], *prri vol 1* (Jakarta: n.d.)

Stoler, Ann Luara, *Capitalism and Confrontation in Sumatra's Plantation Belt, 1870-1979* (New Haven: Yale University Press, 1985)

Sukarno An Autobiography as told to Cindy Adams (Indianapolis: Bobbs Merril, 1965)

Sukarno, *Nationalism, Islam and Marxism*. Trans. Ruth McVey (Ithaca: Cornell University Modern Indonesia Project, 1960)

Sundhaussen, Ulf, *The Road to Power: Indonesian Military Politics 1945-1967* (Kuala Lumpur: Oxford University Press, 1982)

Swift, Ann, *The Road to Madiun: The Indonesian Communist Uprising of 1948* (Ithaca: Cornell Modern Indonesia Project, 1989)

Tamin, Djamaluddin, *Sedjarah pki, Djilid I* (typescript, n.d.)

Tamin, Djamaluddin, *Kematian Tan Malaka (19 Februari 1949-19 Februari 1965)* (typescript, n.d.)

Tamin, Djamaluddin, *Sambutan pada peringatan 19 tahun hilangnja Tan Malaka* (Jakarta: n.p., February 18, 1969)

Tan Malaka, *Dari Pendjara ke Pendjara*, vol 2 (Yogyakarta: Pustaka Murba, n.d.)

Tan Malaka, *Dari Pendjara ke Pendjara III* (Jakarta: Pustaka Murba, n.d.)

Taylor, Alistair M., *Indonesian Independence and the United Nations* (Ithaca: Cornell University Press, 1960)

Van der Plas, CH. O. 'Gegevens betreffende de godsdienstige stroomingen in het gewest Sumatra's Westkust' (Weltevreden, May 16, 1929)

Van Dijk, C., *Rebellion under the Banner of Islam: The Darul Islam in Indonesia* (The Hague: Nijhoff, 1981)

Van Hasselt, Arend Ludolf, *Volksbeschrijving van Midden-Sumatra* (Leiden: Brill, 1882)

Van Langenberg, 'East Sumatra: Accommodating an Indonesian Nation within a Sumatran Residency', in *Regional Dynamics of the Indonesia Revolution*, ed. Audrey Kahin

Van Niel, Robert, *The Emergence of the Modern Indonesian Elite* (The Hague: van Hoeve, 1960)

Van Nieuwenhuijze, C.A.O., *Aspects of Islam in Post-Colonial Indonesia* (The Hague: van Hoeve, 1958)

Vatikiotis, Michael R.J., *Indonesian Politics under Suharto: Order, Development and Pressure for Change* (London: Routledge, 1993)

Verslag van Bestuur en Staat van Nederlandsch-Indie, Suriname, en Curacao van 1929 (Landrukkerij, 1929-1930)

Ward, K.E., *The Foundation of the Partai Muslimin Indonesia* (Ithaca: Cornell Modern Indonesia Project, 1970)

Wehl, David, *The Birth of Indonesia* (London: Allen & Unwin, 1948)

Williams, Gerald, 'The Banteng Council' (typescript, n.d. [circa 1958])

Williams, Michael Charles, *Communism Religion, and Revolt in Banten* (Athens, Ohio: Ohio University Center for International Studies, 1990)

Wiwoho, B., and Banjar Chaeruddin, *Memori Jenderal Yoga* (Jakarta: Rena Pariwara, 1991)

Yamin, Muhammad, *Tan Malaka: Bapak Republik Indonesia* (n.p.: 'Moerba Berdjoeang', 1946)

Young, Ken, *Islamic Peasants and the State: The 1908 Anti-Tax Rebellion in West Sumatra* (New Haven: Yale Southeast Asia Studies, 1994)

Yusra, Abrar, ed. *Tokoh yang Berhati Rakyat: Biografi Harun Zain* (Jakarta: Yayasan Gebu Minang, 1997)

Yusra, Abrar, *Otobiografi A.A. Navis: Satiris & Suara Kritis dari Daerah* (Jakarta: Gramedia, 1994)

Zed, Mestika, *Pemerintah Darurat Republik Indonesia: Sebuah Mata Rantai Sejarah yang Terlupakan* (Jakarta: Grafiti, 1997)

Zed, Mestika, Edy Utama & Hasril Chaniago, *Sumatera Barat di Panggung Sejarah 1945-1995* (Sumatera Barat: Bidang Penerbitan Khusus Panitia Peringatan 50 Tahun RI Sumatera Barat, 1995)

Zed, Mestika, Alfan Miko and Emeraldy Chatra, eds, *Perubahan Sosial di Minangkabau: Implikasi Kelembagaan dalam Pembangunan Sumatera Barat* (Padang: Universitas Andalas, 1992)

Zed, Mestika, 'Pemberontakan Silungkang pada Tahun 1927: Suatu Studi tentang Gerakan Sosial di Sumatera Barat' (MA thesis, Gadjah Mada University, 1980)

Notes

Introduction

1 I shall not for the present deal with the contentious debate over concepts of nationalism and ethnic nationalism, though aspects of the debate will be addressed throughout the book. Two of the most significant recent books on the topic are Benedict Anderson, *Imagined Communities* 1983; revised edition (London: Verso, 1991), and David E.F. Henley, *Nationalism and Regionalism in a Colonial Context: Minahasa in the Dutch East Indies* (Leiden: KITLV Press, 1996).

2 Respectively, Mts. Singgalang, Merapi, and Sago.

3 See Benedict R. O'G. Anderson, 'The Idea of Power in Javanese Culture', in *Culture and Politics in Indonesia*, ed. Claire Holt *et al.* (Ithaca: Cornell University Press, 1972), pp. 1-70. See also Soemarsaid Moertono, *State and Statecraft in Old Java* (Ithaca: Cornell Modern Indonesia Project, 1968).

4 Anderson, 'Idea of Power,' p. 52.

5 Tsuyoshi Kato, *Matriliny and Migration: Evolving Minangkabau Traditions in Indonesia* (Ithaca: Cornell University Press, 1982), pp. 41-42. In the early 1920s, the total number of *nagari* in West Sumatra, excluding the district of Kerinci, was 567, with a total population of 1,368,991. The average population per *nagari* was about 2,375, although the smallest had 250 inhabitants and the largest 16,000. Akira Oki, 'Social Change in the West Sumatran Village: 1908-1945' (PhD. dissertation, Australian National University, 1977), p. 1.

6 *Memoir of the Life and Public Services of Sir Thomas Stamford Raffles, F.R.S.* by his Widow (London: Murray, 1830), p. 347.

7 Ibid., p. 348.

Prologue

1 The longevity of this legend can be seen from William Marsden's history of Sumatra, written in the late-eighteenth century, in which he notes that 'a warrant of recent date' from the Sultan of Minangkabau to 'a high-priest residing near Bengkulen', bears seals of: (Eldest brother) Sultan of Rum, (Second brother) Sultan of China, as well as (Youngest brother) Sultan of Minangkabau. The first lines of the warrant run: 'the sultan of Menangkabau whose residence is at Pagarruyong, who is king of kings; a descendant of raja Iskander zu'lkarnaini.' William Marsden, *The History of Sumatra*, Oxford in Asia Historical Reprints (Singapore: Oxford University Press, 1986), pp. 338-40. Thereafter Marsden recounts a variation on the legend. Ibid., pp. 341-42.

2 Versions of this origin myth can be found in A.M. Datuk Maruhan Batuah and D.H. Bagindo Nanameh, *Hukum Adat dan Adat Minangkabau Luhak nan Tiga, Laras nan Dua* (Jakarta: Pusaka Aseli, n.d.), pp. 13-26; Kato, *Matriliny and Migration*, pp. 34-36; P.E. de Josselin de Jong, *Minangkabau and Negri Sembilan: Socio-Political Structure in Indonesia* (The Hague: Nijhoff, 1980), p. 99; Taufik Abdullah, 'Modernization in the Minangkabau World', in *Culture and Politics in Indonesia*, ed. Claire Holt *et al.* (Ithaca: Cornell University Press, 1972), pp. 183-84.

3 The brothers were sons of the same mother and different fathers.

4 Abdullah, 'Modernization in the Minangkabau World', p. 186.

5 Taufik Abdullah, 'Adat and Islam: An Examination of Conflict in Minangkabau', *Indonesia*, 2(October 1966): pp. 6-7.

6 de Josselin de Jong, *Minangkabau and Negri Sembilan*, p. 76.

7 Darwis Thaib Dt. Sidi Bandaro, a nationalist political leader and influential Islamic *ulama* (*Imam*), who lived in the village of Maninjau, quoted this common saying (*patah*) to explain the situation in an interview (Maninjau), August 14, 1976.

8 de Josselin de Jong, *Minangkabau and Negri Sembilan*, pp. 74-75.

9 M.D. Mansoer, Amrin Imran, Mardanas Safwa, Asmaniar Z. Idris & Sidi I. Buchari, *Sedjarah Minangkabau* (Jakarta: Bhratara, 1970), p. 15. The *penghulu*'s position derives from his relationship to the lineage's eldest female, but needs to be approved by the lineage as a whole. See also Batuah and Tanameh, *Hukum Adat dan Adat Minangkabau*, pp. 14-26, 30-32.

10 The three form the 'Tali Tigo Sapilin'. Interview with H.A.K. Dt. Gunung Hijau, a respected Islamic leader prominent in the Muhammadiah (Padang), July 9, 1976.

11 Abdullah, 'Adat and Islam', p. 4.

12 Batuah and Tanameh, *Hukum Adat*, p. 30. On the development of an independent kingdom in one of the coastal regions of West Sumatra, see J. Kathirithamby-Wells, 'The Inderapura Sultanate: The Foundations of Its Rise and Decline, from the Sixteenth to the Eighteenth Centuries', *Indonesia* 21 (April 1976), pp. 65-84.

13 His mother was Dara Jingga, who went to Singasari on Java and married Krtanegara.

14 A.A. Navis, 'Alur Kebudayaan dalam Tingkah Laku Gerakan Politik di Minangkabau', in *Dialektika Minangkabau dalam Kemelut Sosial dan Politik* (Padang: Genta Singgalang Press, 1983), p. 80.

15 A version of this story can be found in A.A. Navis, *Alam Terkembang Jadi Guru: Adat dan Kebudayaan Minangkabau* (Jakarta: Grafiti Press, 1984), pp. 51-53.

16 Christine Dobbin, *Islamic Revivalism in a Changing Peasant Economy: Central Sumatra, 1784-1847* (London & Malmo: Curzon Press, 1983), p. 119.

17 Ibid., p. 120, Abdullah, 'Adat and Islam', pp. 12-13.

18 According to Dobbin, the Naksyabandiyah was introduced into West Sumatra possibly in the first half of the seventeenth century, and was predominant in Lima Puluh Kota and Tanah Datar. The Syattariyah was introduced from Aceh in the late-seventeenth century by Syekh Burhanuddin into the coastal areas near Pariaman, and spread from there by the trade routes to southern Agam. Dobbin, *Islamic Revivalism*, pp. 123-24.

19 Ibid., p. 121.

20 Ibid., pp. 128-31; Muhamad Radjab, *Perang Paderi di Sumatera Barat 1803-1838* (Jakarta: Kementerian PP&K, 1954); Hamka, *Ajahku: Riwajat Hidup Dr. H. Abd. Karim Amrullah dan Perdjuangan Kaum Agama di Sumatera*, 3rd printing (Jakarta: Djajamurni, 1967), p. 26. According to Hamka, the haji came respectively from the *luhak* of Agam, Lima Puluh Kota, and Tanah Datar.

21 Tuanku Imam Bonjol (1772-1864), first known as Tuanku Muda, was a follower of a student of Tuanku Nan Tuo. Through his teacher's influence Imam Bonjol became a devout follower of the reformist teachings. According to Radjab, the name *bonjol* means 'the fort built to defend the true Islamic religion'. Radjab, *Perang Paderi*, p. 27.

22 Christine Dobbin, 'Economic Change in Minangkabau as a Factor in the Rise of the Padri Movement, 1784-1830', *Indonesia* 23 (April 1977), p. 14. See also M. Joustra, *Minangkabau: Overzicht van Land, Geschiedenis en Volk* (The Hague: Nijhoff, 1923), pp. 49-61.

23 Dobbin, *Islamic Revivalism*, pp. 193-97.

24 Imam Bonjol was sent first to the Preanger Residency of Java, and then for two years to Ambon and finally to Menado, where he lived until his death in 1864. Ibid., p. 206.

25 Taufik Abdullah developed this point in a lecture to a conference in Mexico city in 1976.

26 On the coffee-cultivation system in West Sumatra, see W.K. Huitema, *De Bevolkings-Koffiecultuur op Sumatra* (Wageningen: H. Veenman, 1935), pp. 45-49, 87-90; Ken Young,

Islamic Peasants and the State: The 1908 Anti-Tax Rebellion in West Sumatra (New Haven: Yale Southeast Asia Studies, 1994), pp. 186-211; Elizabeth E. Graves, *The Minangkabau Response to Dutch Colonial Rule in the Nineteenth Century* (Ithaca: Cornell Modern Indonesia Project, 1981), pp. 60-73.

27 The use of these administrators in levying corvée labour had started during the Paderi Wars, where forced labour was used to construct the road through the Anai Pass as a communications route for transporting the coffee from the highlands to the coast. Graves, *Minangkabau Response*, p. 56.

28 Ibid., pp. 38-42.

29 Oki, 'Social Change in the West Sumatran Village', pp. 82-83. According to the 1914 Nagari Ordinance, the head of a *nagari* had to be elected by and from these 'core *penghulu*' whose *adat* position was recognized by the government. All other *penghulu* were ineligible. Taufik Abdullah, *Schools and Politics: The Kaum Muda Movement in West Sumatra (1927-1933)* (Ithaca: Cornell Modern Indonesia Project, 1971), p. 23.

30 The Budi Utomo was largely comprised of traditional Javanese aristocrats, officials, and intellectuals. The most comprehensive history of the organization is Akira Nagazumi, *The Dawn of Indonesian Nationalism: The Early Years of the Budi Utomo 1908-1918* (Tokyo: Institute of Developing Economies, 1972), pp. 1, 156.

31 Ibid., p. 156.

32 Robert Van Niel, *The Emergence of the Modern Indonesian Elite* (The Hague: van Hoeve, 1960), p. 58. The Sundanese inhabit the western region of the island of Java, and the Madurese the island of Madura off Java's north coast.

33 On the 1908 uprisings, see Young, *Islamic Peasants*, and Akira Oki, 'Social Change in the West Sumatran Village: 1908-1945', pp. 74-86, 97.

34 On the development of the SI in West Sumatra and the conflicts within it, see Abdullah, *Schools*, pp. 24-28. See also below, ch. 1.

35 George McTurnan Kahin, *Nationalism and Revolution in Indonesia* (Ithaca: Cornell University Press, 1952), pp. 67-76.

36 Takashi Shiraishi, *An Age in Motion: Popular Radicalism in Java, 1912-1926* (Ithaca: Cornell University Press, 1990), pp. 92-98.

Chapter 1

1 Hamka, *Sedjarah Islam di Sumatera* (Medan: Pustaka Nasional, 1950), p. 40. Hamka notes that schools under Minangkabau leadership were established in Tapak Tuan (Sumatra Thawalib), Kuala Simpang (Diniyyah), Bengkulu, Bintuhan, and other places.

2 Ibrahim gelar Datuk Tan Malaka was born probably in 1897 in Pandam Gadang near Suliki, West Sumatra. After attending high school in Bukittinggi he trained as a teacher in Holland. Returning to Indonesia in 1919, he taught first in a plantation in East Sumatra, then moved to Semarang in 1921, where he founded schools based on Communist principles. He succeeded Semaun as chairman of the Indonesian Communist Party (PKI) in late 1921, then was exiled by the Dutch in March 1922, going first to Holland and then to the Soviet Union, where in mid-1923 he was appointed Comintern representative for Southeast Asia. He established his headquarters in Canton in December 1923, moving to Manila in 1925, and in 1926 to Singapore. On Tan Malaka, see particularly Harry A. Poeze, *Tan Malaka: Levensloop van 1897 tot 1945* (The Hague: Smits, 1976); see also Benedict R. O'G. Anderson, *Java in a Time of Revolution* (Ithaca: Cornell University Press, 1972), pp. 269-74.

3 Ruth T. McVey, *The Rise of Indonesian Communism* (Ithaca: Cornell University Press, 1965), pp. 154-58.

4 Harry J. Benda & Ruth T. McVey, eds, *The Communist Uprisings of 1926-1927 in Indonesia: Key Documents* (Ithaca: Cornell Modern Indonesia Project, 1960), pp. 115-16. The document

relating to West Sumatra translated in this volume, 'The Course of the Communist Movement on the West Coast of Sumatra', is Chapter 1 ('De Gang der Communistische Beweging ter Sumatra's Westkust') of the *Rapport van de Commissie van Onderzoek*, vol. 1 (Weltevreden: Landsdrukkerij, 1928), pp. 1-92. The second chapter of the Commission Report, 'Oorzaken en Gevolgen van het Communisme ter Westkust', is translated (with some omissions) as 'The Development of the Communist Movement on the West Coast of Sumatra', in B. Schrieke, *Indonesian Sociological Studies*, Part One (The Hague: Van Hoeve, 1955), pp. 83-166.

5 According to Djamaluddin Tamin, Alimin, to whom Tan Malaka entrusted the instructions in Manila, did not show them to the Communist members in Singapore, saying only that Tan Malaka was sick. Interview of George Kahin with Djamaluddin Tamin (Jakarta), January 5, 1959.

6 On the dissension and Bandung's reaction, see McVey, *Rise*, pp. 328-33.

7 From May of 1925, the PKI's Padang section supervised the Party's activities in West Sumatra, with Sutan Said Ali responsible for their general direction. After Said Ali's departure in May 1926 and subsequent arrest, responsibility returned to Padang Panjang. See Schrieke, *Indonesian Sociological Studies*, pp. 87-92.

8 Benda & McVey, *Communist Uprisings*, pp. 116-17.

9 Anon., 'Militaire memorie van het patrouillegebied Padang' [1928], *Memories van Overgave*, KIT Collectie [hereafter KIT] 786, Algemene Rijksarchief [hereafter ARA].

10 Benda & McVey, *Communist Uprisings*, pp. 11, 150. See also Mestika Zed, 'Pemberontakan Silungkang pada Tahun 1927: Suatu Studi tentang Gerakan Sosial di Sumatera Barat' (MA thesis, Gadjah Mada University 1980), p. 104, who also mentions assassinations in May in Bukit Batabuh, Biaro Gadang, and Gadut.

11 Benda & McVey, *Communist Uprisings*, p. 159. On October 23, the head of the Sarikat Rakyat in Sawahlunto, Haji Bahaudddin was also arrested. A. Muluk Nasution, *Pemberontakan Sarikat Rakyat Silungkang Sumatera Barat 1926-1927* (Jakarta: Mutiara, 1981), p. 91.

12 The other two were Banten and to a lesser extent Batavia (Jakarta). On the Banten revolt, see Michael Charles Williams, *Communism, Religion, and Revolt in Banten* (Athens, Ohio: Ohio University Center for International Studies, 1990). On the brief outbreak in Batavia, see McVey, *Rise*, pp. 343-44.

13 Ch. O. van der Plas, 'Gegevens betreffende de godsdienstige stroomingen in het gewest Sumatra's Westkust' (Weltevreden, May 16, 1929), p. 3. Van der Plas was the Dutch adviser for Native Affairs.

14 See introduction, above. For good studies of these rebellions, see Dobbin, *Islamic Revivalism* and Young, *Islamic Peasants*.

15 Young, *Islamic Peasants*, p. 130.

16 A.A. Navis, 'Bank Nasional dalam Sejarah Nasional' (draft manuscript, 1995), pp. 73-74.

17 Young, *Islamic Peasants*, p. 98.

18 Dobbin, *Islamic Revivalism*, p. 122, notes that in the large *surau* even in the eighteenth century 'the students depended for their livelihood on what they could sell at the weekly market'.

19 On the links between independent Islamic groups and the commercial classes in the late-nineteenth century, see Young, *Islamic Peasants*, pp. 101-3. It was often difficult for travelling merchants to find places to stay on their travels. A.A. Navis has commented that it was in order to ensure comfortable accommodation that these merchants often had wives in each of their principal trading locations. Regarding the lack of accommodation on the upland trading routes, Sir Thomas Stamford Raffles had written in the early-nineteenth century: 'I shall not speak of the nature of the accommodation which we found at this [a place a few miles from Limau Manis] and other toll-posts, further than by observing that they generally consist of one or more large sheds, for the accommodation of the native traders and travellers, who pay a small sum for being accommodated during the night... When it rained, our whole party, consisting of not less than three hundred, was sometimes collected under one shed alone'. *Memoir of Sir Thomas Stamford Raffles*, p. 345.

20 Arend Ludolf van Hasselt, *Volksbeschrijving van Midden-Sumatra* (Leiden: Brill, 1882), pp. 360-61. He notes that there were also some southern Indian merchants in Padang, a few of whom traded directly with the highland farmers. See also Young, *Islamic Peasants*, p. 224; Elizabeth E. Graves, *Minangkabau Response to Dutch Colonial Rule* (Ithaca: Cornell Modern Indonesia Project, 1981), pp. 67-68.

21 Young, *Islamic Peasants*, pp. 228-29; and Dobbin, *Islamic Revivalism*, pp. 218-19.

22 Navis, 'Bank Nasional', pp. 72-73. A reflection of this can be seen in the frequent proximity of markets to mosques, which 'extend a symbolic canopy of religious sanctions and symbols over the market and impose, at least in theory, a qualitatively different order and code upon those who come together there'. Michael Gilsenan, *Recognizing Islam: Religion and Society in the Modern Arab World* (New York: Pantheon, 1982), p. 175.

23 Sura ii. 279-80 in H.A.R. Gibb and J.H. Kramers, *Shorter Encyclopaedia of Islam* (Ithaca: Cornell University Press, 1953), p. 471 (entry under 'Riba').

24 Abdullah Saeed, *Islamic Banking and Interest: A Study of the Prohibition of Riba and its Contemporary Interpretation* (Leiden: Brill, 1996), pp. 41-42, quoting Muhammad Asad's *The Message of the Qur'an* (Gibraltar: Dar al-Andalus, 1984), p. 633 (emphasis in the original).

25 Navis, 'Bank Nasional', pp. 73-74. Islamic law forbidding the taking of such profits (*riba*) 'did not prevent the wide spread of this arrangement in the Arabic middle ages and its influence upon European money-changing. But they [Muslims] were always conscious that a direct breach of the prohibition of riba was a deadly sin. Pious Muslims to this day therefore not infrequently refuse to take bank interest'. Gibb and Kramers, *ShorterEncyclopaedia*, p. 473.

26 Benda & McVey, *Communist Uprisings*, p. 101, quoting from *Api*, March 2, 1926. For further discussion of the effect of these issues on banking practices in West Sumatra, see, ch. 3, pp. 76-77.

27 Recent scholarship, notably that of Christine Dobbin, Jane Drakard, and Ken Young, has shown the number and strength of the contacts of the highlands of West Sumatra with the outside world long before the twentieth century.

28 Kato, *Matriliny and Migration*, p. 116. He continues: 'Yet communally-held land provided merantau-aspirants with security to fall back on and sometimes financial resources for business or the advancement of education. And the matrilineal kinship network could help the recruitment and placement of new migrants.' Ibid.

29 Syekh Ahmad Chatib was born in Bukittinggi in 1855 and became the Imam of the Sjafi'i *madzhab* at the Mecca mosque. He was reluctant to return to his home region because of his opposition to its *adat* system. See Deliar Noer, *The Modernist Muslim Movement in Indonesia 1900-1942* (Singapore: Oxford University Press, 1973), pp. 19, 31-33; see also Hamka, *Ajahku*, pp. 230-32. Hamka gives his birthdate as 1860.

30 See above, pp. 18-19 and Dobbin, *Islamic Revivalism*, pp. 128-41 and *passim*.

31 Muhammad Abduh (1848-1905) was founder of the Egyptian modernist school, and a reformer of Islamic practices and ideas. Jamal al-Din al-Afghani (1839-1897), his colleague and collaborator, was a champion of Pan-Islamic ideas and an agitator for the liberation of Muslim countries from European influence. Nevertheless, he 'attacked with the same vigor the abuses which he saw within Islam and the evils of Muslim governments'. See H.A.R. Gibb, *Modern Trends in Islam* (Chicago: University of Chicago Press, 1947), pp. 27-29, 33-35. See also Gibb and Kramers, *Shorter Encyclopaedia of Islam*, pp. 85-87, 405-407; Noer, *Modernist Muslim Movement*, pp. 32-33.

32 The attitude of Haji Rasul, Abdullah Ahmad, and Djamil Djambek also contrasted with that of another of their contemporaries, Syekh Tahir Djalaluddin, a cousin of Ahmad Chatib and also from Bukittinggi, who, though educated mostly in Mecca, spent four years in Cairo and was a close friend of Rasjid Ridha and others at the Al Azhar University. On his return from the Middle East, Syekh Tahir remained on the Malay peninsula and founded a school in Singapore as well as an influential monthly magazine, *Al Imam*. On a return visit to his home

area in 1927 he was arrested and jailed for several months by the Dutch as a subversive before eventually being allowed to return to Malaya. See also William Roff, *The Origins of Malay Nationalism* (New Haven: Yale University Press, 1967), pp. 60-62; Djamaluddin Tamim [*sic* = Tamin], *Sedjarah pki, Djilid I* (typescript, n.d.), pp. 65-66.

33 H.M.D. Datuk Palimo Kajo, *Sedjarah Perguruan Thawalib Padang Pandjang* (Padang Panjang: Jajasan Thawalib, [1970]), pp. 5-7, and Tamar Djaja, *Pusaka Indonesia: Orang2 Besar Tanah Air* (n.p.: Kementerian Pendidikan Pengadjaran dan Kebudaaan, n.d.), pp. 324-25.

34 These were at Padang Panjang, Parabek (near Bukittinggi), Padang Jepang, Maninjau, and Batu Sangkar. On the evolution of the Thawalib school system from a students' social organization at the Iron Bridge *surau* and the derivation of the name, see Noer, *Modernist Muslim Movement* and Abdullah, *Schools and Politics*, pp. 34-36.

35 *Parewa* denotes a wanderer or restless youth, who lives an adventurous life and is usually expert in martial arts (*silat*).

36 Noer, *Modernist Muslim Movement*, pp. 41-42; Hamka, *Ajahku*, p. 253.

37 However, on the shortcomings of the Sumatra Thawalib in terms of modern education, see the recollections of Hamka in his *Kenang-Kenangan Hidup*, 2nd printing (Kuala Lumpur: Pustaka Antara, 1982), pp. 28-32.

38 H.M.D. Datuk Palimo Kajo, 'Riwajat ringkas Thawalib Padangpandjang'. Paper presented at the ceremony opening a new Asrama and celebrating the 55th anniversary of the Thawalib Padangpandjang, September 11, 1966 (Typescript, in author's possession), p. 8; Djaja, *Pusaka Indonesia*, pp. 326-29. See also van der Plas, 'Gegevens', pp. 8-10 on the education in these schools, and H. Sidi Ibrahim Boechari, *Pengaruh Timbal Balik antara Pendidikan Islam dan Pergerakan Nasional di Minangkabau* (Jakarta: Gunung Tiga, [1981]), p. 101.

39 Noer, *Modernist Muslim Movement*, p. 41, and H. Abdoelmalik K.A [Hamka], 'Saja Teringat', in *Boekoe Peringatan 15 Tahoen 'Dinijjah School Poeteri Padang Pandjang* (Padang Panjang: Dinijjah School Poeteri, [1938]), p. 26.

40 Hamka, 'Saja Teringat', pp. 24-26. Hamka notes that Abdullah Ahmad's Adabiah school in Padang had accepted such a subsidy. Government subsidies were given to private schools with qualified teachers who gave at least three hours a day of instruction in such subjects as writing, reading, and arithmetic. 'Vereeniging-Vereeniging di Sumatra'. Extract from *Oetoesan Melajoe*, December 1917, No. 243 (library of the Van Vollenhoven Institute for Law and Administration in Non-Western Countries, Leiden).

41 This was the second *Al Munir* to appear in West Sumatra. A journal of the same name had initially appeared in Padang under the editorship of Haji Abdullah Ahmad. It was written in Arabic characters and was published from 1911-1915 when its printing works were destroyed by fire. Mahmud Junus, 'Peranan Surau dan Masjarakat', Paper given at the Seminar, 'Islam di Minangkabau', July 23-26, 1969 (stencil, Minang Permai), p. 10.

42 Palimo Kajo, 'Riwajat Ringkas', p. 9.

43 Tamim, *Sedjarah pki*, p. 10. Emphasis in original.

44 Hamka, *Ajahku*, p. 130. literally 'did not want to surrender under his sandal' [*tidak mau menagklukkan dirinja kebawah tjerpu beliau*]. On those alienated by Haji Rasul's authoritarianism, including his own son and son-in-law, see also Navis, 'Alur Kebudayaan', p. 85.

45 Hamka, *Ajahku*, p. 132.

46 Proyek Penelitian dan Pencatatan Kebudayaan Daerah, *Sejarah Kebangkitan Nasional Daerah Sumatera Barat* (Jakarta: Dep. PD&K, 1982), p. 95.

47 Natar Zainuddin had been born in West Sumatra but taken to Aceh as a child. He worked there as a tram conductor, until the Dutch sent him back to West Sumatra in May 1923 under the government's policy of returning all people they considered dangerous to their home areas. See Benda & McVey, *Communist Uprisings*, p. 103; and R. Kern, 'Politiek Toestand ter Sumatra's Westkust; Instelling Minangkabauraad, Adviz aan G.G. 30 Juni 1924 '.(Collection Kern:Wd Adviseur Inlandse Zaken [Adviz] 1920-1926) [hereafter Kern Collection] (Microfilm 617, Kroch Library, Cornell University), No. 144, pp. 19-21.

48 Hamka, *Ajahku*, p. 131.

49 Shiraishi, *An Age in Motion*, p. 265.

50 Ibid., p. 261-62. Haji Batuah might well have attended this Congress, and it is noteworthy that the report on Misbach's speech cited above was drawn up by Landjoemin Datuk Toemenggoeng, a Minangkabau agent of the Dutch information service, who would be instrumental in combatting Communist influence in West Sumatra over the next several years. See below.

51 Benda & McVey, *Communist Uprisings*, p. 103.

52 Kern, 'Politieke Toestand', (Kern Collection #144), pp. 21-23.They were not alone in this. *Doenia Achirat*, published in Bukittinggi [Fort de Kock], also dealt with similar questions, arguing: 'Communism does not interfere in religious affairs and every Communist can carry out his own religion... As we know, under Islam, one is told to be active among the people. Indeed, the Prophet Mohamad greatly loved the poor. This is the one thing considered most important by communism'. *Doenia Achirat*, May 24, 1924.

53 Hamka, *Ajahku*, pp. 261-62.

54 L. Dt. Toemenggoeng, 'De jongste gebeurtenissen ter Westkust van Sumatra', Nota voor den Adviseur voor Inlandsche Zaken, n.d. (Kern Collection, #148), p. 11.

55 *Doenia Achirat*, November 16, 1923, and ibid., November 26, 1923. MvO van den aftredenden Gouverneur van Sumatra's Westkust G.F.E. Gonggrijp, *Mr. 360/32* (Kol. Memories van Overgave Sumatra's Westkust), p. 2. (Algemene Rijksarkief, The Hague [henceforth ARA]).

56 *Doenia Achirat*, May 10, 1924; Proces Verbaal, Djamaloedin Tamin, December 13, 1932, in 'Hoofdparket: Opgave van te interneeren personen die daadwekelijk deelgenomen hebben aan de actie van de geheime revolutionnaire 'Partei Republiek Indonesia" (P.A.R.I.)', (*Mr.963x/33*), p. 1 (ARA); Tan Malaka, *From Jail to Jail*, translated and introduced by Helen Jarvis. 3 vols. (Athens: Ohio University Center for International Studies, 1991), 3: pp. 355-56. On his release from jail in late 1925, Tamin travelled between Java and Singapore. From the time he first met Tan Malaka in June 1926, he became one of that leader's most important lieutenants and his major liaison with Java. He was one of the three founders of Tan Malaka's Pari party in Bangkok in June 1927. (See below.)

57 'Voorstel om Natar Zainoedin en Hadji Datoeq Batoewah te Interneren, Adviz aan G.G., 23 Juli 1924' (Kern Collection, #145), p. 6.

58 Hamka, *Ajahku*, pp. 133-35.

59 According to Governor Gonggrijp, in addition to Padang Panjang, the most important sections were in Kota Lawas, Gunung Bunga Tanjung, Silungkang, Solok, and Tiakar-Dangung-dangung. MvO van Gouverneur Gonggrijp, p. 31.

60 According to Schrieke, he was expelled because of his 'communistic propensities'. See Schrieke, 'Communism on Sumatra's West Coast', p. 154. See also Leon Salim, 'Pahlawan-pahlawan Cilik', typescript, n.d., p. 5.

61 The son of a farmer and artisan, Leon Salim was born in Takur Guguk, Dangung-dangung on March 9, 1912. He attended the village elementary school from June 1919, and the secondary school from April 1922 until he was expelled in 1925.

62 Kantor Wilayah Departemen Sosial DKI Jakarta, *Proyek Penulisan Riwayat Perjuangan Perintis Kemerdekaan, Tahun 1979/1980* (Disusun oleh: Leon Salim, No. Pol. 21/59/PK) (Jakarta, typescript, n.d.), [hereafter Salim, *Riwayat Perjuangan*], pp. 1-4.

63 M. Junus Kotjek & Leon Salim, 'Pergerakan Pemuda di Minangkabau' (typescript dated April 28, 1962), pp. 1-2.

64 Ibid.

65 Salim, 'Pahlawan-pahlawan Cilik', p. 10.

66 Amri Marzali, 'Orang Silungkang di Jakarta' (MA thesis, Gadjah Mada University, 1973), p. 31.

67 Ibid.; Akira Oki, 'A Note on the History of the Textile Industry in West Sumatra', in *Between People and Statistics: Essays on Modern Indonesian History Presented to P. Creutzberg* (The

Hague: Nijhoff, 1979), pp. 147-56. Oki notes that weaving may be one of the oldest industries in the Indonesian archipelago, existing in West Sumatra well before the mid-seventeenth century. With respect to the indigenous industry, he comments: 'A speciality of West Sumatran textiles was the weaving of gold and silver threads with silk to produce luxurious cloths, since there was an abundant supply of gold in the region'. Ibid., p. 147.

68 Marzali, 'Orang Silungkang', p. 35. Nawir Said, *Pemberontakan Silungkang 1927 Sumatra Barat* (Jakarta: Pentja, 1963), p. 7. See also the entry for 'Siloengkang' in S. de Graaff & D.G. Stibbe, *Encyclopaedie van Nederlandsch Oost-Indie*, 4 vols. (The Hague: Nijhoff, 1918-1919), vol. 3, p. 774, which in describing the lack of fertile land in the area, writes, 'The women weave as a means of subsistence. Alert local women and sympathetic European women have taken the matter in hand and, for example, formed a cooperative organization that buys the material and sells the finished pieces for fixed prices either to travelling merchants or in large markets. So Silungkang has become a well known centre of textile art'.

69 Nasution, *Pemberontakan Sarikat Rakyat*, pp. 45-46.

70 de Graaff & Stibbe, *Encyclopaedie van Nederlandsch-Indie*, vol. 3, pp. 710-11; vol. 2, pp. 405-406.

71 Although it seems probable that Sulaiman Labai was part of the family of the Sulaiman Labai & Zoon clothing business, the Dutch report describes him as 'the ambitious Sulaiman Labai – whose rice business had badly suffered, especially since the creation of the Railroad Cooperative...'. It also states that he married a 'noble' [*bangsawan*] girl in 1926. Benda & McVey, *Communist Uprisings*, p. 102. The *Rapport van de Commissie van Onderzoek*, p. 125, also includes him in the category of 'socially stranded people'.

72 This story is narrated in Nasution, *Pemberontakan Sarikat Rakyat*, pp. 47-48.

73 Probably Sarikat Islam Afdeling Pandu – the youth branch of the Islamic League, though according to Gonggrijp this was not introduced to West Sumatra until the end of 1928. See *Mr* 360/32, p. 31.

74 Nasution, *Pemberontakan Sarikat Rakyat*, pp. 51-53.

75 Nawawi Arief, editor of *Suara Tambang*, was arrested in 1924 and Idrus, editor of *Panas*, in 1925. Ibid., p. 60.

76 Abdul Muluk Nasution, who was among those making grenades, writes that they made two hundred of them in three weeks. Nasution, *Pemberontakan Sarikat Rakyat*, pp. 84-86. He also reports that they were able to buy weapons from a German in Padang (ibid., p. 89). Ruth McVey writes that the Padang Panjang Communist leader, Mangkudun Sati, approached a German assistant administrator at the Sawahlunto mine who supplied revolvers and carbines. See McVey, *Rise*, p. 481.

77 They were joined by religious scholars and local professionals. Navis, 'Bank Nasional', pp. 86-88. 'Laporan Penelitian: Transformasi Pendidikan di Sumatera Barat: Kasus Adabiah School' (Proyek Menteri Agama Rep. Ind./Pelaksana LPKUB Indonesia Bekerjasama dengan Pusat Penelitian Kebudayaan dan Perubahan social,Un. Gajah Mada, IAIAN Imam Bonjol & Yayasan Sjarikat Oesaha Adabiah, 1997/1998), pp. 101-4.

78 On its aims, see also, 'Laporan Penelitian', p. 105.

79 Mohammad Hatta, *Indonesian Patriot: Memoirs*, ed. C.L.M. Penders (Singapore: Gunung Agung, 1981), p. 32. Marah Sutan had only been educated up to Grade 5 in primary school, but, in Hatta's words, 'was deeply interested in the educational advancement of the young, believing that only scientific and rational knowledge could create responsible citizens'. Ibid. See also, Mardanas Safwan, 'Taher Marah Sutan: Tokoh yang Dilupakan', *Majalah Bulanan Kebudayaan Minangkabau* (Jakarta), 1,1 (January 1974), pp. 52-55. Taher Marah Sutan headed the organization until 1940.

80 Hatta described him as 'a gentle teacher'. Mohammad Hatta, *Memoir* (Jakarta: Tintamas, 1979), p. 36, Navis, 'Bank Nasional', p. 95. See also L. Datoek Toemenggoeng, 'Geheime Nota voor den Adviseur voor Inlandsche Zaken over het communisme ter Westkust van Sumatra', July 30, 1925 (Kern Collection #146), p. 3, where he is described as 'formerly a level

headed man who later after retiring as Secretary of the Entrepreneurs' League became a Communist'.

81 Toemenggoeng, 'Geheime Nota' (Kern Collection #146), pp. 4-8, which includes a long exposition of Abdullah Ahmad's critique of H. Datuk Batuah and of the Communists' attempt to reconcile communism and Islam. See also, Amalsip, 'Hadji Abdoellah Ahmad: Seorang Oelama, Journalist, Politikoes dan Organisator di Minangkabau', *Pandji Islam* 6/2, 6/3, 6/4 (January, 9, 16, 23, 1939).

82 Hatta, *Memoir*, pp. 41-42.

83 'Laporan Penelitian', p. 117; Navis, 'Bank Nasional', p. 84.

84 See Abdullah, *Schools and Politics*, p. 25.

85 Tamin, *Sedjarah pki*, p. 15.

86 Navis, 'Bank Nasional', p. 95.

87 On Magas, see Toemenggoeng, 'Geheime Nota' (Kern Collection #146), p. 1, which states that his mother was Javanese; and 'Politieke Toestand ter Sumatra's Westkust: Instelling Minangkabauraad. Adviz aan G.G. 30 Juni, 1924' (Kern Collection #144), p. 18. According to *Pandji Islam*, however, his mother was in fact a daughter of Dt. St. Maharadjo, the outstanding modernist *adat* leader of the early-twentieth century in Minangkabau, and his father was A. Madjid Sidi Soetan, an early follower of Abdullah Ahmad and leader of the PGAI, and who had married Dt. St. Maharadjo's daughter in 1905. A. Madji glr Sidi Sutan was a trader who was administratively involved in publishing the journal *Al Achbar*. See *Pandji Islam*, February 17, March 3, 1941. Other leaders of the Padang section were A. Wahab (secretary), Hamzah, K.W.A. Wahab (a Javanese), and Kaharoedin ('Politieke Toestand').

88 'Nota voor den Adviseur voor Inlandsche Zaken: De jongste gebeurtenissen ter Westkust van Sumatra', signed L.d. Toemenggoeng (n.d.) (Kern Collection #148), p. 8.

89 He was arrested on March 7, 1924, and sentenced in November. *Doenia Achirat*, March 12, November 10, 1924.

90 Benda & McVey, *Communist Uprisings*, p. 99. According to PKI records, toward the end of 1925, the Padang section had 190 members, Padang Panjang 38, Silungkang 19, Solok 25, and Sawah Lunto, 13. Ibid., p. 106, n. 21.

91 At this time, of the original executive of the Padang Panjang section, consisting of Haji Datuk Batuah, Djamaluddin Tamin, Natar Zainuddin and Dato Mangkudum Sati, only the last remained. Other staff members of the Padang Panjang section in May 1925 were Abd. Azis, Mahmud, M.A.S. Perpatih, and Achmad Chatib. Ibid., nn. 19, 22. Mahmud, a former teacher in the Thawalib school, took over the leadership in 1925 and when he left for Singapore in July 1926, was succeeded by Arif Fadlillah. Ibid., nn.19,22, & p. 146.

92 The government expelled him in January 1924 because of his agitation over the introduction of a land tax. Ibid., p. 99.

93 George Kahin, *Nationalism and Revolution*, p. 45; McVey, *Rise*, p. 103.

94 Benda & McVey, *Communist Uprisings*, pp.105-6, 124-25.

95 On their contents and failure, see ibid., pp. 108-13.

96 Djamaluddin Tamin, *Kematian Tan Malaka (19 Februari 1949-19 Februari 1965)* (typescript, n.d.), pp. 13-14.

97 See Benda & McVey, *Communist Uprisings*, p. 139, quoting Tan Malaka, *Semangat Muda* (Tokyo, January, 1926), pp. 75-76.

98 Ibid., pp. 134, 137.

99 Among those who fled to Singapore in response to Tan Malaka's instructions were Djamaluddin Ibrahim, M. Yatim Latif, and Amir Khan, head of the IPO; Rivai Junus, who was also an IPO leader, was sent by his parents to study in Cairo; M. Yunus Kocek and Asaduddin Kimin fled to western Aceh, while Alibin, the headmaster of the People's school in Padang Panjang, hid on a Dutch plantation in Deli. According to Leon Salim, at least thirty of the principal leaders fled to Malaya or Singapore. He himself was able to remain in hiding in West Sumatra and evade Dutch detection as, at the time, he was only fourteen years old and small

for his age. Interviews with Leon Salim, Jakarta 1985, Payakumbuh, 1995, and with H. Rivai Junus, Padang, June 24, 1976. See also Salim, 'Riwayat Perjuangan'.

100 Fadlillah had been active in Padang Panjang since at least 1923, when he was frequently detained by the authorities because of articles he published in *Djago-djago*. He had spent six months in jail in 1924. *Doenia Achirat*, November 26, 1923, February 27, May 12, 1924. Djamaluddin Ibrahim soon had to leave West Sumatra to join his colleagues in Singapore. By that time, Mahmud Sitjintjin (Mohammad Jusuf) was one of the PKI representatives in Singapore. (McVey, *Rise*, p. 331.) Djamaluddin Tamin spent little time in West Sumatra after his release from jail in September 1925.

101 According to Djamaluddin Tamin, it was Sdr. Abdullah (presumably Abdullah Sutan Bandaro Panjang), a teacher at Abdullah Ahmad's Adabiah school in Padang, who selected Fadlillah to represent West Sumatra at the September meeting in Singapore. Tamim, '*Sedjarah pki*', p. 40. See also Benda & McVey, *Communist Uprisings*, p. 145.

102 Nasution, *Pemberontakan Sarikat Rakyat*, p. 93. Talaha was not a leading Communist. He was a small trader who, several years earlier, had been a well-known member of the Islamic League and a close friend of Sulaiman Labai. Benda & McVey, *Communist Uprisings*, p. 166.

103 Benda & McVey, *Communist Uprisings*, pp. 165-66.

104 Ibid.; Anon., 'Militair memorie', pp. 18-19.

105 According to the West Coast Report, his name was Sarun (Benda & McVey, *Communist Uprisings*, p. 169); according to Nasution it was Harun (Nasution, *Pemberontakan Sarikat Rakyat*, p. 94).

106 Nasution, *Pemberontakan Sarikat Rakyat*, pp. 94-95. Although the broad outlines of Abdul Muluk Nasution's first-hand account are similar to that presented in the Dutch report, it is less complex and takes less into account activities in other parts of West Sumatra.

107 Benda & McVey, *Communist Uprisings*, p. 176.

108 Nasution, *Pemberontakan Sarikat Rakyat*, p. 96. According to the Dutch report, Kamaruddin's challenge took place on the night of December 31 when the revolt broke out. See Benda & McVey, *Communist Uprisings*, p. 177.

109 The investigation committee into the uprising describes Rumuat as a corporal who had been expelled from the army because of Communist leanings on July 3, 1926, and had since then been conducting Communist propaganda among the police. Ibid., p. 161.

110 Nasution, *Pemberontakan Sarikat Rakyat*, p. 96. The garrison consisted of thirty-one men, of whom twenty-seven were Indonesians, all of whom according to Pontoh had become members of the People's League. Ibid., p. 98.

111 Benda & McVey, *Communist Uprisings*, p. 171. This Alimin (Limin) should not be confused with the major Communist Party leader Alimin Prawirodirdjo, who had earlier been Tan Malaka's messenger and who was arrested with Musso in Johore by the government of the Straits Settlements on December 18, after their return from Moscow. From May of 1926 Limin had been the major contact between Arif Fadlillah in Padang Panjang and the Silungkang section. Ibid., p. 121. Limin was only one of perhaps a hundred people who fled to Singapore at the time of the uprising in early 1927, not only from West Sumatra but also from Rengat, Banten, and Jambi. According to Djamaluddin Tamin, most of them had enough money to go directly from there on the pilgrimage to Mecca. Tamin, *Sedjarah pki*, p. 57.

112 Nasution, *Pemberontakan Sarikat Rakyat*, pp. 98-99.

113 These were, in addition to Silungkang: Siaro-aro, Air Luo, Sepajang, Sjantang, Tarung-tarung, Padang Sibusuk, Pemuatan, Kampung Baru/Batu Menjulur Sehat, Kabun, Sijunjung, Sungai Batung, Sariek Laweh/Lubuk Torok, Tanjung Balik/Sangiso, Padang Laweh, Pianggu, Tak Boncah, and Tanjung Ampolu. Said, *Pemberontakan Silungkang*, p. 25. See also, 'Overzicht der Communistische Onlusten op Java en ter Sumatra's Westkust sedert Nov. 1926', Pt. 2: 'Overzicht der onlusten welke ter Sumatra's Westkust zijn voorgevallen', pp. 9-12, dated May 1927. Indisch Archief (IA70) ARA.

114 Abdul Muluk Nasution was leading this band. See Nasution, *Pemberontakan Sarikat*

Rakyat, pp. 100-101. See also 'Overzicht der onlusten', p. 9. According to the latter report, the rebel leaders informed the guards at Muara Klaban that they were going fishing.

115 *Rasjid-70* (Jakarta: Panitia Peringatan Ulang Tahun Mr. Rasjid Ke-70, n.d.), p. 8.

116 Nasution, *Pemberontakan Sarikat Rakyat*, p. 105.

117 Interview with Leon Salim, September 4, 1995. *Rasjid-70*, p. 8. On Dahlan, see also I.F.M. Chalid Salim, *Limabelas Tahun Digul Kamp Konsentrasi di Nieuw Guinea Tempat Persemaian Kemerdekaan Indonesia* (Jakarta: Bulan Bintang, 1977), pp. 376-77; McVey, *Rise*, pp. 340-42.

118 'Overzicht der onlusten', p. 10.

119 Telegram from Padang dated January 3, 1927, signed resident Arends, *Mr.* 24x/27 and 'Relaas van het voorgevallene in den nacht van 2 op 3 Januarie 1927', signed Duboureg, January 7, 1927 *Mr.* 197/27 [ARA]. See also Said, *Pemberontakan Silungkang*, p. 27, who states that Munap went on to help the rebel forces at Silungkang, where he was killed. According to Abdul Muluk Nasution, who was a relative of his, Abdul Munap had been a teacher in the government school in Tanjung Ampalu as well as a member of the People's League. Nasution, *Pemberontakan Sarikat Rakyat*, pp. 115-16.

120 For a list of those killed, see Benda & McVey, *Communist Uprisings*, pp. 172-73.

121 See, for example, telegrams from Padang dated, January 3 [no.15], January 5 [no. 50], January 10 [no.102], 1927, *Mr.* 28x/27, *Mr.* 29x/27, *Mr.* 58x/27 (ARA).

122 Foreign Office Reports 1927, F0371/12696, signed J. Crosby, Consul General (Public Record Office, Kew, Surrey, UK, [henceforth PRO]).

123 To the Procureur-Generaal, August 30, 1927. 805 had been sentenced and 558 were awaiting trial. According to the 'Overzicht der Onlusten', pp. 12-13, by January 12, 1927, 1,300 people had been rounded up in the Silungkang-Muara Klaban-Padang Sibusuk area, and around 200 had been arrested near Sijunjung, as well as smaller numbers in other areas.

124 Said, *Pemberontakan Silungkang*, pp. 33-36. Nasution, *Pemberontakan Sarikat Rakyat*, p. 123.

125 See Nasution, *Pemberontakan Sarikat Rakyat*, pp. 125-26. He himself was sentenced to twelve years in jail, and with about seventy of his fellows was sent to Glodok jail, and later to Cipinang, Pamekasan (Madura), and Ambarawa, being released in 1938.

126 The prison camp at Boven Digul was established in 1927 to house Communist prisoners and their families. By March 1929, 2,101 people were interned there (1,124 men, 450 women and 527 children). These included Communist leaders from Batavia as well as those from Banten and West Sumatra. 'Overzicht van den Inwendigen Politieken Toestand' (April 1928-Mei 1929), *Verslag van Bestuur en Staat van Nederlandsch-Indië, Suriname, en Curacao van 1929 (Landrukkerij, 1929-1930)*. See also Chalid Salim, *Limabelas Tahun Digul*, p. 182.

127 Nasution, *Pemberontakan Sarikat Rakyat*, pp. 228-29.

128 Ibid., Said, *Pemberontakan Silungkang*, pp. 15, 37.

Chapter 2

1 See for example, page 2 of 'Huidige politieke toestand ter Sumatra's Westkust', dated April 12, 1932, from Procureur-Generaal Vonk to the Resident of Sumatra's Westkust, where the situation is described as 'in the very same phase of government defamation as in the period preceding the actual revolt at the beginning of 1927'. *Mr.* 1202 geh/32 (Fiche 1216, ARA).

2 Kolonien Memories van Overgave [henceforth MvO] van de aftredenden Resident van Sumatra's Westkust, A.I. Spits, *Mr.* 504/1937, p. 45 (ARA).

3 Hamka, *Ajahku*, p. 150.

4 Ibid., p. 151.

5 Ibid., pp. 152-53. The Muhammadiah was established in Yogyakarta in 1912 by Kyai Haji Ahmad Dahlan. Its aims were to promote Islam, and to this end, it organized schools and

sponsored meetings, establishing mosques and publishing books, journals, and newspapers. In 1920 it was expanded to the whole of Java and in 1921 to all Indonesia, but did not acquire a following in West Sumatra until 1925.

6 Ch.O. van der Plas, 'Gegevens betreffende de godsdiestige stroomingen in het gewest Sumatra's Westkust', Weltevreden, May 16, 1929 (typescript), p. 20.

7 Roff, *Origins of Malay Nationalism*, p. 75. On Syekh Tahir, see also above, p. 297 (ch. 1, n. 32).

8 Ibid., p. 62; 'Catatan - Dari Tjaya Soematra 7/7/28 mengenai penangkapan S.T.' in File for 'Sheikh Tahir Jalaluddin/sp 10/1106', in National Archives, Kuala Lumpur.

9 'Kaoem Moeda di Minangkabau, viii', *Pandji Islam* No. 12 (March 24, 1941). See also Boechari, *Pengaruh Timbal Balik*, pp. 117-18.

10 There was cooperation between West Sumatra and Java in this opposition. At a meeting in Batavia, a Partindo leader reported that a protest demonstration in Padang had been attended by ten thousand student protesters, and that Mohammad Sjafei of the ins school had been a leading speaker. 'Meeting of the Partai Indonesia held in Batavia on December 25, 1932' (*Mr.* 53x/33, January 4, 1933 [Fiche 1110, ara]). Mohammad Sjafei went to Java to persuade Ki Hadjar Dewantoro of the Taman Siswa schools to head the anti-Wild Schools Ordinance actions. Mohammad Sjafei, *Dasar-Dasar Pendidikan* (Kayu Tanam: ins, 1976), pp. 138-39. According to the Dutch records, Djalaluddin Taib, a leader of the West Sumatra Permi party, also visited Ki Hadjar Dewantoro in January 1933 to coordinate activities between the two regions. *Mr.* 357/geh/33 (January 1933), p.14 (ara).

11 John Ingleson, *Road to Exile: The Indonesian Nationalist Movement 1927-1934* (Singapore: Heinemann Educational Books [Asia], 1979), p. 204.

12 For more concerning opposition to the Wild Schools Ordinance, see Abdullah, *Schools and Politics*, pp. 216-21.

13 A.R. St. Mansur was born in 1895 and had been educated in government schools and in the Sumatra Thawalib. He was a disciple of Haji Rasul and married his eldest daughter in 1917. For his biography, see Hamka, *Ajahku*, pp. 257-60.

14 On the Muhammadiah, see Noer, *Modernist Muslim Movement*, pp. 73-83, and Alfian, *Muhammadiyah* (Yogyakarta: Gadjah Mada University Press, 1989).

15 'MvO van de aftredenden Gouverneur van Sumatra's Westkust G.F.E. Gonggrijp', *Mr.* 360/32, p. 4 (ara).

16 See ibid., pp. 5-6. It seems possible that another impetus for their leaving the Muhammadiah was Syekh Tahir's imprisonment. He had apparently come to Sumatra at the invitation of some of the older *Kaum Muda* leaders, and there were rumours in radical circles that at least Abdullah Ahmad and Djamil Djambek had colluded in his arrest. For the allegations against all three of the older generation leaders, see Tamin, *Sedjarah pki*, pp. 65-66.

17 H.M.D. Datuk Palimo Kajo, 'Riwajat ringkas Thawalib Padangpandjang', September 11, 1966 (typescript), p. 12. In 1929 there were reportedly thirty-nine Thawalib schools with an estimated 17,000 students, the two largest being in Parabek (about 800 students) and Padang Panjang (about 750 students). Van der Plas, 'Gegevens', p. 8.

18 Edward Mortimer, *Faith and Power: The Politics of Islam* (New York: Random House, 1982), p. 249.

19 See above, ch. 1, p. 37.

20 See 'Vootstel tot interneering van Hadji Moechtar Loetfi', November 23, 1933 *Parket van den Procureur-Generaal Mr.* 1451x/33, pp. 5-6 ([Fiche 1216, ara).

21 MvO Gonggrijp, *Mr.* 360/32, p. 5.

22 Van der Plas, 'Gegevens', p. 10.

23 MvO Gonggrijp, *Mr* 360/32, p. 11.

24 This traders 'association was the successor to the Saudagar Vereeniging which had been founded in 1916 by Abdullah Basa Bandaro. It had maintained close ties with the Sarikat Usaha (see above, ch. 1). On the various traders' groups, see Kementerian Penerangan, *Republik Indonesia: Propinsi Sumatera Tengah* (n.p., n.d), [henceforth *Propinsi Sumatera Tengah*], pp. 753-55. For more on the Himpunan Saudagar, see below, ch. 3.

25 Abdullah, *Schools and Politics*, pp. 64-65.

26 Boechari, *Pengaruh Timbal Balik*, p. 101.

27 Van der Plas, 'Gegevens', p. 15.

28 Noer, *Modernist Muslim Movement*, pp. 153-54; Abdullah, *Schools and Politics*, pp. 139-44. The British described *Pilihan Timoer* as the 'more violent' of the two magazines, and stated that Iljas Jacub was also foreign editor of a Surabaya paper that had formerly been Communist. 'Dutch East Indian Students in Egypt', enclosure in report, 'Native Movements', June 30, 1928, W7417/157/29, in FO371/13417 (PRO).

29 'Voorstel tot interneering van Hdji Moechtar Loethfi', pp. 3-4; Abdullah, *Schools and Politics*, pp. 148-49.

30 'Sejarah ringkas Syekh Daud Rasyidy (1880-1948)', typescript given to me by H. Rivai Junus, p. 5. Djaja's short biography of him in *Pusaka Indonesia* does not mention this trip to Mecca.

31 Djamaluddin Tamin classes him with the older Kaum Muda scholars, as being opposed to politics and opposed to the Thawalib and Diniyyah School in Padang Panjang headed by Zainuddin el-Junusiah. He also accuses him of having tricked an acquaintance of Tamin's out of money that Luthfi allegedly used to support himself while he was in Cairo. *Sedjarah pki*, pp. 78-79.

32 Djaja, *Pusaka Indonesia*, pp. 364-68. According to Djaja, Luthfi left Malaya because the parents in the family he was living with there wished him to marry their daughter.

33 Taufik Abdullah deals at length with the history of Muchtar and Iljas and other Minangkabau scholars in Egypt in his *Schools and Politics*, pp. 139-54.

34 *Mr.* 254/35 (MvO van de aftredenden Resident van Sumatra's Westkust B.H.F. van Heuven [December 31, 1934]), pp. 25, 28.

35 *Soeara Islam* [Bukittinggi], November 1, 1931.

36 Basa Bandaro and H. Djalaluddin Thaib attended the December 1931 Indonesian People's Congress in Surabaya, welcoming Sukarno's release from Suka Miskin jail. There they explained Permi's philosophy and aims to the congress as a whole and specifically to Dr. Sutomo. 'Kaoem Moeda di Minangkabau IX', *Pandji Islam*, No. 13 (March 31, 1941). In July 1932, Muchtar Luthfi visited Java and met with Sukarno, so that 'The close friendship between H. Djalaloeddin Thaib and Dr. Soetomo in the Kongres Indonesia Raya[sic]... was further strengthened by the close friendship between Moechtar Loethfi and Ir. Soekarno'. 'Kaoem Moeda di Minangkabau X', *Pandji Islam* No. 14 (April 7, 1941).

37 *Boekoe Peringatan*, pp. 14-15. See also Deliar Noer, *Aku Bagian Ummat Aku Bagian Bangsa* (Jakarta: Mizan, 1996), pp. 437-38, where he describes how the dispute between Rahmah and Rasuna was decided.

38 *Mr.*227/geh/33 (December 1932), p. 10 (ARA).

39 Ibid., pp. 6-11; *Mr* 590 geh/33 (February 1933), p. 17.

40 See *Pandji Islam* No. 14 (April 7, 1941), also for the impact this had on Sukarno and the Nationalist movement on Java.

41 On the establishment of the PSII, see Abdullah, *Schools and Politics*, pp. 122-23.

42 Van der Plas, 'Gegevens', pp. 34-35.

43 Dt. Singo Mangkuto before founding the branch of the Islamic League had headed the *adat* union in his home village of Sungai Batang, Maninjau. See Mardjani Martamin, Ishaq Thaher, Amir B. Mahyuddin, *Sejarah Kebangkitan Nasional Sumatera Barat* (n.p., Proyek Penelitian dan Pencatatan Kebudayaan Daerah, 1977-78), p. 163.

44 See Abdullah, *Schools and Politics*, pp. 123-25; Martamin *et al*, *SejarahKebangkitan*, pp. 163-65; MvO Gonggrijp (*Mr.* 360/32), pp. 13-14; interview with Dt. Kampo Rajo, Kajang, Malaysia, December 23, 1981.

45 See *Mr.* 877/34 (June 1934), p. 8 (ARA).

46 Kotjek & Salim, 'Pergerakan Pemuda', p. 7.

47 MvO Gonggrijp, pp. 34-35. See also Kotjek & Salim, 'Pergerakan Pemuda', p. 5, and

Salim, *Riwayat Perjuangan*, p. 13. On Leon Salim, see above, ch. 1; M. Junus Kotjek was from Sinabang in Western Aceh. He had been a student at the Diniyyah and Thawalib schools and treasurer/organizer of the IPO in Padang Panjang in 1925. In 1926 he fled to Aceh, but returned in 1927 to become a leader of the PMDS and El Hilaal and later of the KIM. He married Leon Salim's sister. Hasanuddin Yunus was from Sungai Puar, Damanhuri from Payakumbuh, and Mahuddin Tonek from Pariaman.

48 Apart from these two, the other Pari members with whom Kotjek and Salim report continuing contacts were: Luthan Madjid (Singapore), Djured Luthan (Kuala Lumpur, he was Leon Salim's brother-in-law [interview, Payakumbuh, September 4, 1995]), Amir Chan (Perlis), and Saleh Dja'far (India), all former members of the PMDS who had fled the region. Kotjek & Salim, 'Pergerakan Pemuda', p. 11.

49 Salim, *Riwayat Perjuangan*, pp. 21-22. Other manuals, written in Arabic, were coming from Indonesian students in Cairo and New Delhi.

50 One of seven children, Chatib Suleiman was born in Sumpur, seventeen kilometres from Padang Panjang, on the hills overlooking Lake Singkarak in 1906. He attended elementary school in Padang from 1912 to 1917, the HIS Adabiah from 1917 to 1919 and, with the help of Basa Bandaro, the MULO from 1919 to 1921. From then until he went to Padang Panjang, he earned his living as a musician. Interviews with the family of Chatib Suleiman, Jakarta, Sumpur, and Padang Panjang, 1995, and with Leon Salim, and *Riwayat Hidup & Perjoangan Almarhum Chatib Suleiman* (typescript, Padang Panjang, Feb. 1973); Rifai Abu & Drs. Abdullah Suhadi, *Chatib Suleman* (Jakarta: Department P. dan K, 1976).

51 *Boekoe Peringatan*, p. 14. M. Junus Kotjek headed the youth orchestra. Also interview with Leon Salim, Payakumbuh, September 4, 1995.

52 Kotjek, in his account, dates the split to 1929. He further notes that much documentation was destroyed during the subsequent periods of unrest in West Sumatra, and this probably accounts for the confusion over the dates.

53 At the congress, members of El Hilaal were assigned to guard the assembly. The young guards were left at their posts all day without food, and when Leon Salim protested this to Permi leader Djalaluddin Thaib, Thaib responded by pulling rank. Thus provoked, Salim withdrew his followers from alliance with the Permi. Interviews with Leon Salim, Jakarta, June 8, 1985; Payakumbuh, September 4, 1995. Kotjek & Salim, 'Pergerakan Pemuda', p. 6. See also MvO Gonggrijp, though he dates the split to May 1931.

54 Salim, *Riwayat Perjuangan*, pp. 25-26; Kotjek & Salim, 'Pergerakan Pemuda', p. 6.

55 MvO Gonggrijp, p. 28.

56 Ibid., p. 36. Zainuddin and Datuk Batuah had been arrested by the Dutch in 1923 for Communist activities in the schools (see above, ch. 1), Haji Miskin and Imam Bonjol had been leaders of the Paderi movement in the 1820s and 1830s, and Arif Fadlillah was the Padang Panjang Communist leader arrested at the time of the 1926/27 uprisings (see above, ch. 1).

57 Interview with Leon Salim, Jakarta, June 8, 1985.

58 Ingleson, *Road to Exile*, p. 169.

59 Although from then on the Partindo was led by a Javanese and the New PNI by two men from the Minangkabau, the parties can not be differentiated on an ethnic basis. It is notable, for example, that the influential Minangkabau Muhammad Yamin was a leading member of the Partindo and a close friend and follower of Sukarno, and Amir Sjarifuddin, a Sumatran from Medan, was one of the party's most promising young leaders. Similarly, several Javanese were prominent in the New PNI's leadership.

60 *Mr.* 115/geh33 (November 1932), pp. 1-3, 23-24 (ARA). Two months later the central committee granted provisional recognition to the branches, and Chatib Suleiman was appointed provisional chairman with oversight over the other sections in West Sumatra. *Mr.* 357 geh/33 (January 1933), p. 1 (ARA). Leon Salim headed the branch in Padang Panjang, Ali Umar that in Pariaman, Darwis Thaib that in Maninjau, Rahimi the Bukittinggi branch, and Nur Arif that in Padang. Salim, *Riwayat Perjuangan*, p. 31.

61 Interview with Darwis Thaib Dt. Sidi Bandaro (Maninjau), August 14, 1976.

62 *Mr.* 669/33 (March 1933), pp. 1-2 (ARA).

63 Chatib Soelaeman and M. Junus, 'Soember jang gelap?' *Kedaulatan Ra'jat*, 1/2 (November 1932). Also published in *Daulat Ra'jat* No. 46, December 20, 1932, under the title 'Sedikit Djawaban Tentang P.N.I. (Pendidikan Nasional Indonesia) di Minangkabau sambil Memperkenalkan Diri'.

64 Hatta, *Memoir*, p. 272; interview with Leon Salim. There is a reference to this incident also in Anwar St. Saidi, *Tugu Pemuda Sumatera* (Padang: NV Tenunan Padang Asli, 1967), pp. 18-19. Hatta had met with Tan Malaka ten years earlier in Berlin. See *Memoir*, pp. 146-48.

65 Interviews with Roestam Anwar (Padang, June 1985) and Leon Salim, Jakarta, June 8, 1985. See also *Mr.* 877/34 (June 1934) (ARA).

66 The fullest accounts of Pari activities appear in Tamin, *Sedjarah pki*, and Poeze, *Tan Malaka*. For a fascinating account of ties between Tan Malaka's actual activities and the stories that emerged concerning him, see Noriaki Oshikawa, 'Patjar Merah Indonesia and Tan Malaka: A Popular Novel and a Revolutionary Legend', in *Reading Southeast Asia*, ed. Takashi Shiraishi (Ithaca: Cornell Southeast Asia Program Translation Series, 1990), pp. 9-40. Concerning the legends surrounding Tan Malaka, see also below, ch. 3.

67 Tamin, *Sedjarah pki*, p. 59.

68 Tamin notes that there were about twenty-thousand Muslims in Bangkok. Ahmad Wahab was known as the *ulama* of the Wahhabi group, which consisted mostly of Siamese Muslim traders. Ibid., pp. 59-60.

69 Ibid., p. 73

70 Ibid., pp. 65-66. *Bintang Timur* was published by Parada Harahap.

71 The Dutch awarded medals to both Abdullah Ahmad and Djamil Djambek. *Pandji Islam*, February 3, 1941. Haji Rasul did not receive one. We have already seen how he antagonized the Dutch through his opposition to such policies as the Wild Schools Ordinance, and in fact, several years later in January 1941 the government arrested him and exiled him to Sukabumi. 'Dr. H.A. Karim Amroellah ditangkap?' *Pandji Islam*, January 1941; Hamka, *Ajahku*, pp. 182-88. On the award of the medals, see Hatta's contention that his own uncle, together with Syekh Djambek and Syekh Tjandung had been tricked by the Assistant Resident into accepting the medals. Hatta, *Memoir*, p. 266.

72 Tamin, *Sedjarah pki*, pp. 57, 71. Leon Salim, too, regarded Djamaluddin Ibrahim as the best (*yang paling hebat*) of all the nationalists working for independence at the time. Interview, Payakumbuh, August 22, 1995.

73 Tamin, *Sedjarah pki*, p. 64. See also Poeze, *Tan Malaka*, p. 389. Kandur was the elder brother of Baharuddin Datuk Bagindo (BDB) who was a close friend of Anwar St. Saidi and played a role in the independence struggle. Navis, *Bank Nasional*, p. 234.

74 Tamin, *Sedjarah pki*, p. 63

75 Poeze, *Tan Malaka*, p. 390.

76 Ibid., p. 402.

77 Interviews with Leon Salim, who recalled that Kandur carried the Pari publications in a bag with a false bottom.

78 At Abdullah Ahmad's death in 1933, Abdullah glr. Sutan Bandaro Panjang succeeded him as the leading Indonesian teacher at the Adabiah school in Padang. Abdullah, a brother of Assaat, taught at the school from 1915 to 1960. Interview with his daughter, Ibu Soematri Abdullah, Padang, March 30, 1999. He was, however, of a very different political persuasion from Abdullah Ahmad, being a close follower of Tan Malaka who had been his schoolmate at the Sekolah Radja in Bukittinggi.

79 Tamin, *Sedjarah*, p. 83.

80 Ibid.

81 Hatta, *Memoir*, p. 272. After independence Kandur worked in Hatta's office.

82 Abdullah, *Schools and Politics*, p. 199.

83 Ibid., p. 203. Muchtar denied many of the statements attributed to him by spies attending the meetings. See 'Proces Verbaal... van Hadji Moechtar Loetfie', August 13, 1933. *Mr.* 1451x/33 (Fiche 1216, ARA).

84 *Mr.* 849x/33 'Toestand Sumatra's Westkust', July 13, 1933 (Fiche 1167, ARA).

85 'Ten uitvoerlegging vergaderverbod', Padang, August 5, 1933. Attached to *Mr.* 1249 geh/33 (August 1933) (Dos AA122, ARA).

86 They were accompanied by a third PSII leader, Ahmad Chatib glr. Dt. Singo Maradjo, who was arrested in June 1934 for introducing political courses into PSII schools. See *Mr.* 877/34 (June 1934), pp. 9-10; *Mr.* 139/35 (December 1934), p. 6 (Dos AA133, AA141, ARA).

87 Maskun, Burhanuddin, Suska, Bondan, and Murwoto were also arrested and sent to Digul. See Ingleson, *Road to Exile*, p. 227.

88 Ibid., pp. 16-22.

89 Quoted in ibid.

90 These instructions were that (1) meetings of three or more persons should be avoided; (2) each member should join a social or economic association, and there pursue his activities to the best of his ability; (3) if in his home village there was no social or economic association he should establish one and lead and guide it in accordance with the party's programme. Salim, *Riwayat Perjuangan*, p. 37.

91 Tamin, *Sedjarah pki*, p. 71.

92 Poeze, *Tan Malaka*, pp. 401-402.

93 Tan Malaka spent most of the five years after 1932 in southern China in the Hokien/Fukien region and in Futjow, Hantjau, Shanghai, and Hongkong, before going to teach in Singapore at the end of 1937. Tamin, *Kematian Tan Malaka*, pp. 21-22.

94 Tamin, *Sedjarah pki*, pp. 80-84.

95 Ibid., pp. 83-87.

96 Poeze, *Tan Malaka*, p. 412. Dawood, the illegitimate son of a German planter and Indonesian mother, was a trader in Padang. After testing his reliability in Singapore, Tamin sent him to Tan Malaka in Shanghai for further training.

97 Ibid., pp. 451-52; interviews with Leon Salim; Hatta, *Memoir*, p. 272.

98 This was with the assistance of Parindra member Jahja Nasution. An issue appeared in October 1935 and two further issues were published in 1936. Poeze, *Tan Malaka*, p. 453.

99 Ibid., pp. 457-58.

100 Interview with Leon Salim, Payakumbuh, August 22, 1995.

101 Telephone interview with Roestam Anwar, Padang, March 30, 1999; Poeze, *Tan Malaka*, p. 458.

102 Interviews with Leon Salim and Roestam Anwar; Kotjek & Salim, 'Pergerakan Pemuda', p. 3.

103 Born in Koto Baru, Padang Luar, Bukittinggi in 1911, the son of a small trader, Tamimi Usman went to school at the Sumatra Thawalib in Parabek before going to Java where he attended courses of the New PNI party in Batavia and Bandung. He returned to Bukittinggi in 1933 at the time of the Dutch crackdown. Interview with Tamimi Usman, Koto Baru, June 22, 1976.

104 *Mr.* 510/35 (March 1935) (Dos AA141, ARA).

105 The Dutch had evidently been looking for an excuse to send Nur Arif to Digul since 1929, when he had been arrested for teaching 'extremist songs' to his class at the Thawalib school in Padang Panjang and the Dutch had found three of Tan Malaka's pamphlets in his possession. They did not at the time have sufficient evidence to send him to Digul as a Communist, but kept him under surveillance in Padang from then on. Poeze, *Tan Malaka*, pp. 410-11. According to Dutch records, Nur Arif was exiled to Digul under a Government order of February 21, 1935. They do not state the charges. *Mr.* 510/35, March 1935 (Dos AA141, ARA).

106 The account appears in Salim, *Riwayat Perjuangan*, pp. 41-43.

107 *Mr.* 212/36 (January 1936) (ARA).

Chapter 3

1 '*Duduak samo randah, tagak samo tinggi*'. On these social principles, see, M. Nasroen, *Dasar Falsafah Adat Minangkabau* (Jakarta: Bulan Bintang, 1957), pp. 134-38.

2 The influential political and adat leader from Maninjau, Darwis Thaib, explicitly tied the Minangkabau tradition of *merantau* with the strength of the concept of Indonesian national-ism, for 'when ideals of Indonesian unity arose this was easy for Minangkabau to accept and for them it was not difficult to erase regional boundaries'. Interview (Maninjau), August 14, 1976.

3 The authors of these novels appeared as Matu Mona or Yusdja. According to Noriaki Oshikawa, their real names were Hasbullah Parinduri and Yusuf Djajad, both well-known dime novel (*roman picisan*) authors. Oshikawa, 'Patjar Merah Indonesia', p. 22.

4 I have copies of three of these in my possession, namely, *Spionnage-Dienst (Patjar Merah Indonesia)* by Matu Mona (Medan: Centrale Courant en Boekhandel, 1938); *Tan Malaka di Medan* by Emnast (Medan: Doenia Pengalaman, n.d.); and *Patjar Merah Kembali ketanah Air* by Yasdja (Medan, Tjerdas, 1940). According to Oshikawa, three others were *Rol Patjar Merah Indonesia c.s.* (1938), *Panggilan Tanah Air* (1940), and *Moetiara Berloempoer, Tiga kali Patjar Merah datang membela* (1940). Oshikawa, 'Patjar Merah Indonesia', p. 22.

5 It is not surprising that several of Tan Malaka's followers expressed disappointment when they finally met with their leader in the mid-1940s.

6 'Patjar Merah dari Party Republiek Indonesia tertangkap', *Timoer Baroe*, 2, 21 (April 1, 1938), pp. 14-15, and ibid., 2, 22 (May 1, 1938), p. 10.

7 Oshikawa, 'Patjar Merah Indonesia', pp. 34-35. The story also apparently appeared in *Pewarta Deli*.

8 Djaja, *Pusaka Indonesia*, p. 213.

9 A.A. Navis, *Falsafat dan Strategi Pendidikan M. Sjafei* (Jakarta: Gramedia Widiasarana Indonesia, 1996), pp. 29-30.

10 Hjh. Zuraida Zainuddin, 'Ayahku....!' in *H. Rahmah el Yunusiyyah dan Zainuddin Labay el Yunusy* ed. Dr. H. Aminuddin, Rasyad, H. Leon Salim, Hjh. Hasniah Saleh (Jakarta: Pengurus Perguruan Diniyyah Puteri Padang Panjang Perwakilan Jakarta, 1991), p. 372.

11 The introduction of communism into the Thawalib schools has generally been credited to ideas propagated by H. Datuk Batuah after his return from a short trip to Aceh and Java in 1923, although, as we saw in chapter 1, many of these ideas had already been espoused by Thawalib pupils. The 'Red Canteen', set up by the students of the religious schools backed by Zainuddin Labai, had been in existence since 1920. And although Datuk Batuah was clearly very important to political developments in West Sumatra, the Dutch exaggerated his role and the threat he posed in order to justify their dispatch of a contingent of armed police to Kota Lawas to arrest him and his colleague, Natar Zainuddin. (Tamin, *Sedjarah pki*, p. 11.) The burgeoning of the radical movement in West Sumatra, particularly among the students and young people, was probably as much a result of their resentment at these heavy-handed actions as of the teaching propagated by Datuk Batuah himself. (This was recognized in ibid., p. 13.)

12 See Noer, *Modernist Muslim Movement*, pp. 18-19 on the most controversial problem with respect to the matrilineal system of inheritance.

13 He might have been more successful in his opposition to the establishment of a Commu-nist party in Padang had the Dutch not removed him from the local scene because of his open anticolonialism. On Abdul Muis, see Abdullah, *Schools and Politics*, pp. 32-34.

14 Noer, *Modernist Muslim Movement*, pp. 264-65.

15 Ben Anderson describes Yamin as 'Indonesia's best-known political eccentric' and says that 'it was said of him, not altogether unkindly, that he was like a horse: if you were in front of him, you were likely to get nipped; if behind him to get kicked; and if under him, to be tram-pled on. But if you were on top of him, with the reins in your hands, he would carry you fast and far'. Anderson, *Java in a Time of Revolution*, p. 288.

16 Roestam Anwar, the son of Anwar St. Saidi, stated that his father worked closely with Basa Bandaro and identified Basa Bandaro completely with Tan Malaka. Interview (Padang), June 18, 1985.

17 See above, ch. 1, pp. 44; see also 'Laporan Penelitian...Adabiah School', p. 105 and *passim*.

18 See above ch. 2, pp. 54, 300 n. 24.

19 Much of the information on Anwar is drawn from A.A. Navis, *Bank Nasional*, pp.131-81; also from interviews with Anwar's son, Roestam Anwar (Padang), June 18, 1985; with Leon Salim (Jakarta and Payakumbuh), 1985 & 1995; with Syamsulbahar (Bukittinggi), May 28, 1985, and from Salim, *Riwayat Perjuangan*. I am grateful to Roestam Anwar for checking the accuracy of the facts given here.

20 Interview with Roestam Anwar, June 18, 1985.

21 Navis, 'Bank Nasional', pp. 133-34.

22 On harmonizing religious teachings with trading practices, see also above, ch. 1, p. 35.

23 Navis, 'Bank Nasional', pp. 141-47.

24 Ibid., pp. 147-48.

25 Ibid., p. 156.

26 Ibid., pp. 155-56. The request was again refused in 1938. Ibid., p. 170.

27 Interview with Roestam Anwar, June 18, 1985.

28 *Pandji Islam*, June 16, 1941.

29 Interview with Syamsulbahar, May 28, 1985.

30 Navis, 'Bank Nasional', pp. 165-66.

31 Ibid., pp. 148-49.

32 Anwar, *Tugu*, pp. 20-21. This pamphlet contains short essays on Hatta and Yamin. See also *Mr.*1125/geh/1939 (July 1939), which notes that one of the young men was Anwar's nephew and the other the son of a postal clerk in Bukittinggi.

33 Navis, 'Bank Nasional', pp. 149-50, 166-68. The Dutch were always suspicious of Anwar. In their report on a meeting to raise funds for a new mosque in Bukittinggi, they noted the 'strange connection' between Anwar, whom they viewed as an atheist tied to the Pari party, and Syekh Djamil Djambek for whose mosque he was raising funds. (*Mr.*244/geh/39 [December 1939]).

34 Ingleson, *Road to Exile*, p. 207.

35 On the *Sekolah Raja*, see I.J. Brugmans, *Geschiedenis van het Onderwijs in Nederlandsch Indië* (Groningen-Batavia: Wolters, 1938), p. 183; Abdullah, *Schools and Politics*, p. 10. *Kitab Peringatan terkarang waktoe telah 35 tahoen 'oemoer Sekolah-Radja oentoek Goeroe Melajoe di Boekittinggi* (n.p., c. 1908.).

36 *Medan Ra'jat*, July 1, 1931, p. 110. The Mosvia in Bukittinggi closed in 1931 and the closing of the *Sekolah Raja* was announced in 1933.

37 According to a Malaysian woman, Aishah Ghani, who attended the Diniyyah school in Padang Panjang in the late 1930s, there were quite a few Malays from Islamic families on the peninsula who did not want their children to go to English schools. In the school, she also had friends from all over Indonesia – Bali, Ambon, Celebes (Sulawesi), Timur, Aceh, Halmahera. Interview (Kuala Lumpur), January 4, 1982.

38 In general, Minangkabau was the informal language spoken by most of the people, and it was frequently used as the language of instruction for children in the first three elementary grades.

39 Interview with Kamaluddin Muhamed (Krismas), (Petaling Jaya), December 21, 1981.

40 *Peringatan*, p. 16. According to Noer, the number of pupils in the girls' school was three hundred in 1933, four hundred in 1935, and five hundred in 1941; while the boys' school, which apparently separated again from the girls' in the late 1930s had only six pupils in 1938 and two hundred in 1940. Noer, *Modernist Muslim Movement*, p. 56. See also Hamka, *Ajahku*, p. 265.

41 Noer, *Modernist Muslim Movement*, pp. 54-55. Noer gives a detailed account of his inter-

views with Rahmah el Junusiah in 1957 in his autobiography, *Aku Bagian Ummat*, pp. 435-39.

42 Hamka, *Ajahku*, pp. 49-51.

43 According to informants, including Leon Salim, the replacement had been in part because Chatib Suleiman at the time was already a married man with responsibilities, while Salim had no dependents. Also, Salim as an activist was more expendable, and the political movement needed Suleiman to be free to speak and write.

44 *H. Rahmah el Yunusiyyah*, p. 90; *Mr.*808/38 (June 1938)(ARA).

45 Noer, *Aku Bagian Ummat*, pp. 436-37; *Boekoe Peringatan*, pp. 13, 16-17.

46 Interview with Datin Paduka Hajjah Aishah Ghani (at the time of the interview Minister of Welfare Services in the Malaysian government), Kuala Lumpur, January 4, 1982. She attended the Diniyyah school in Padang Panjang from 1936-40, then went on to the Islamic College in Padang from 1940-44, where she found life much freer than under the eye of Rahmah el Junusiah.

47 *Medan Ra'jat* [Padang], May 1-15, 1931. (This twice-monthly journal edited initially by Iljas Jacub, was brought out by Permi and later by students of the Islamic College.) In July 1930, Abdullah Ahmad, with the support of the Padang traders, had established a teachers' training college in Padang, the Normal Islam, with Mahmud Junus of the Islamic Teachers Union (PGAI) as director. But the Permi leaders, disenchanted with Abdullah Ahmad's ties with the Dutch, wished to have their own training school. Amalsip, 'Hadji Abdoellah Ahmad', *Pandji Islam* 6/3, January 16, 1939. This is the second part of a three-part biography of Abdullah Ahmad. The first and third parts appear in the issues of *Pandji Islam* of January 9, and January 23, 1939. See also Abdullah, *Schools & Politics*, p. 214.

48 'Kaoem Moeda di Minangkabau, 5', *Pandji Islam*, No. 9 (March 3, 1941). To be admitted to the college, students had to have completed six years of schooling and graduated from the Thawalib school, Diniyyah school, Tarbiyah Islamijah, HIS, or Schakel school, or be able to display an equivalent standard of education. *Medan Ra'jat* [Padang], April 1, 1931, pp. 58-59. According to Taufik Abdullah, 'The graduates of the government secular schools had to take a special class in order to make up for their lack of religious training.' Abdullah, *Schools and Politics*, p. 215.

49 *Medan Ra'jat*, April 1, 1931.

50 *Mr.*1061/37 (October 1937) and *Mr.* 6/38 (November 1937) (ARA).

51 *Pandji Islam*, June 16, 1941.

52 See above, p. 72. On Mohammad Sjafei and the educational philosophy he followed in establishing and heading the INS, see, for example, Sjafei, *Dasar-Dasar Pendidikan*; Navis, *Filsafat dan Strategi*; A. Hamid, *Setengah Abad Ruang Pendidik INS Kayutanam 1926-1976* (Kayutanam: Panitia Hari Ulang Tahun ke 50, 1976); Syamsulbahar, 'Mohamad Syafei (typescript, Kayutanam, May 20, 1980); anon., 'Ranting Halus dipohon Sejarah Indonesia: Sejarah INS yang ringkas,' (typescript, n.d.). Both Hamid and Syamsulbahar became teachers at the school, Hamid succeeding Sjafei as its headmaster.

53 Mara Sutan was a well-known educator and intellectual. He taught in various parts of the archipelago, moving to Batavia in 1912, where he was active in publishing and in the Indische Partij. See Syamsulbahar, 'Mohamad Sjafei', pp. 7-9. Syamsulbahar reports that there were conflicting stories as to whether Sjafei was also an illegitimate son of Mara Sutan.

54 Sjafei, *Dasar-Dasar*, p. 135. Emphasis in the original.

55 Hamid, *Setengah Abad*, p. 6.

56 From its foundation the INS taught printing, and planned to establish a publishing and printing plant that could produce books to fulfil the needs of private schools, so that they could free themselves from their dependence on Dutch school-books. 'Sedjarah INS jang ringkas', (typescript 1953), pp. 16-17.

57 Syamsulbahar, 'Mohamad Syafei', p. 2.

58 Interview with Syamsul Bahar (Kayutanam), November 26, 1976. Another of Sjafei's former pupils, the painter Nasrun, A.S., however, stated that he got his first feelings of national-

ism from Sjafei while a pupil in his school. Interview with Nasrun A.S. (Jakarta), October 4, 1976. On the Taman Siswa schools in West Sumatra, see below.

59 Mansoer, *et al.*, *Sedjarah Minangkabau*.

60 Navis, 'Bank Nasional', p. 201. This amount was F350,00 in 1934 and F402.09 in 1935.

61 He had started teaching in the Muhammadiah school after resigning his chairmanship of the New PNI. *Mr.* 255/35 (January 1935), Leon Salim, *Khatib Suleiman*, n.p., 1987, p. 17.

62 *Mr.* 220/37 (January 1937), p. 2. Also, interview with Adam B.B.'s daughter, Padang Panjang, July 27, 1995. Born in 1890, Adam B.B. was a student of Daud Rasjidi. He was a strong opponent of the Dutch and much more radical in his politics than most of the other Islamic scholars. He broke from the Thawalib schools because he maintained the traditional view of the importance of the teacher's direct relationship with his pupils, and established his own *pesantren* in Padang Panjang in 1926. He was a very close friend of both Chatib Suleiman and Leon Salim. See also Hamka, *Ajahku*, pp. 124-25, 264. Junus Kotjek had been a leader with Leon Salim of the PMDS and later of the other youth groups, El Hilaal and KIM.

63 Interview (Petaling Jaya), December 21, 1981. Aishah Ghani described the situation as: 'We had no relationships with the Muhammadiah – we did not speak in the same terms'.

64 *Kepartaian dan Parlementaria Indonesia* (Jakarta: Kementerian Penerangan, 1954), p. 431; *Riwayat Hidup dan Perjuangan 20 Ulama Besar Sumatera Barat* (Padang[?]: Islamic Centre, Sumatera Barat, 1981), pp. 67-69, 79-80; see also Noer, *Modernist Muslim Movement*, p. 221, and Abdullah, *Schools and Politics*, pp. 135-36.

65 *Mr.* 759/39 (May 1939).

66 Consul-General Crosby, 'Notes upon the native movement and upon the political situation in the Netherlands East Indies generally', May 30, 1927 (FO371/12697) PRO.

67 Schrieke, *Indonesian Sociological Studies*, pp. 132-33; the words in brackets [ ] were not included in this translation but appear in the original *Rapport van de Commissie van Onderzoek*, (p. 125), on which Schrieke based his study.

68 For a description of these officials and their functions, see, for example, Aka Malin Penghulu, 'Fungsi Orang 4 Jinih di Minangkabau', *Majalah Kebudayaan Minangkabau*, no. 13 (March 1980), pp. 10-15.

69 See above, Prologue, p. 26.

70 Oki, 'Social Change,' p. 86. Oki deals with the Nagari Ordinance and its effects in ibid., pp. 82-91.

71 Note of November 6, 1933 from Roesad glr St. Perpatih (pp. 81-82) in 'Invloed van de politieke beweging op de Volkshoofden ter SWK' *Mr.* 1376x/1933 dated November 10, 1933 (ARA).

72 Ibid., p. 85.

73 Deliar Noer expresses surprise when he was interviewing a prominent Masjumi leader in 1957 to find that he acknowledged having been a member of the PKI (Indonesian Communist Party) in the 1920s, but adds: 'But at that time the PKI formed a group of people who rejected Dutch colonialism. Besides, in Minangkabau at that time, many in Islamic circles, in fact those who were teachers at the Thawalib, were also PKI'. Noer, *Aku Bagian Ummat*, p. 434.

74 Interview with H.A. Wahab Amin (Padang) June 12, 1976. Navis differentiates them later between the M (Masjumi) and MM (Masjumi Muhammadiah). Navis, 'Alur Kebudayaan', p. 83.

75 Noer, *Modernist Muslim Movement*, p. 264.

76 *Pandji Islam*, May 12, 1941.

77 Ibid., May 19, 1941.

78 S. J. St. Mangkuto was one of the founders of the Muhammadiah branch in Padang Panjang, and was in the forefront of the struggle against the guru ordinance. *Pandji Islam*, March 10, 1941.

79 Much of the following discussion is based on talks with A.A. Navis, and ideas which he developed in his own writings, in particular his manuscript on the 'Bank Nasional'.

80 Ibid., pp. 65-66.

81 Ibid., pp. 66-67.

82 However, as Navis states, 'This does not mean that the *penghulu* [*adat* leaders] don't join in with the *ulama* [religious scholars], but in doing so they do not wear the clothing of their *penghulu* status, but of their religion'. Ibid., p. 67.

83 The Perti flag was a sun on a black background. According to one of its leaders, the sun represented the Perti and the black background symbolized the *adat*. *Mr. 505/40* (January 1940) (ARA).

84 MvO Gonggrijp (*Mr. 360/32*), p. 19. In response to the strong movements for Indonesian independence, it changed its name in 1932 to Pendidikan Islam Indonesia (PII – Indonesian Islamic Education), reverting to its old name Perti in February 1938 once the Dutch had restored calm to the region.

85 Navis, 'Alur Kebudayaan', pp. 88-89.

86 'Voorstel om Natar Zainoedin en Hadji Datoeq Batoewah' (Kern Collection #145), p. 5.

87 Letter from the Comité Permoesjawaratan Oelama-Oelama Minangkabau oentoek memperkatakan ordonnnantie Mentjatet Perkawinan Boekit Tinggi (Bukittinggi, September 19, 1937), attached to *Mr. 921/geh/37* (September 1937) (ARA).

88 Interview with Dt. Simarajo, August 22, 1976.

89 *Mr. 187/38* (January 1938), pp. 14-17 (ARA).

90 'Nota betreffende het Comité Madjelis Tinggi Kerapatan Adat Alam Minangkabau (C.M.T.K.A.A.M.)' (31 October, 1937-31 October, 1938) attached to *Mr.244* (December 1938). This note also lists the people heading the committees in Simabur and the other branches. See also *Mr. 885/39* (June 1939) (ARA).

91 See *Mr. 1230/geh/39* (August 1939), *Mr. 1406/geh/39* (September 1939).

92 They both had apparently attended the Sekolah Rajah, along with Abdullah, who taught at the Adabiah school in Padang. Djalil Jahja, 'Sedjarah 1945-50' (Typescript prepared for Badan Pemurnian Sejarah Indonesia - Minangkabau [BPSIM], c. 1976), p. 32.

93 Born in the Minangkabau, Ladjoemin Dt. Toemenggoeng had previously been a minister at the Attorney General's office in Batavia. S.M. Rasjid *et al.*, *Sejarah Perjuangan Kemerdekaan R.I. di Minangkabau 1945-1950* Vol. 1 (Jakarta, BPSIM, 1978), p. 49.

94 *Mr. 535 geh/1939* (March 1939), pp. 14-18 (ARA). Although he had apparently signed the Soetardjo petition, in his speech at the meeting in West Sumatra, 'He struck at the three basic pillars of the Minangkabau region. He struck at the "movement" [*pergerakan*] because it harmed Minangkabau, even though in these past years the movement's arena was filled by the religious group. Even if by "movement" he meant "Communist" this is also not fitting because each of these periods had its own movement, and we cannot strike too hard at that earlier spirit of '25. He criticizes the "press" because it is only good at tearing up, even though that press is one of the arenas of the intellectual group, in addition to the councils. And he also criticizes the "*penghulu* group" that should understand the economy'. *Pandji Islam*, April 3, 1939.

95 *Pandji Islam* [Medan] 51 (December 18, 1939). This article was written in response to the national leader Thamrin, who on a visit to Padang that month 'expressed his surprise that the political movement no longer existed in the Minangkabau, although the Minangkabau region was famous for its spirit of struggle'.

96 'Kesengsaraan ra'jat di Minangkabau'. *Ratoe Andalas* [Palembang], March 30, 1939.

97 This was in part the result of a marked fall in the value of exports exacerbated by a very bad rice harvest in 1938/39 which had led to famine in parts of the region. Ibid. See also Oki, 'Social Change', pp. 141,157,167.

98 See Soetan Soeleiman glr. Angkoe Tan Toeah Bg. Ratoe, *Minangkabau dengan Minang-kabau-Raad* (Fort de Kock: 'Merapi', n.d. [circa 1940]), p. 51.

99 These included Mohammad Sjafei, Fachroeddin Hoeseini, and Suleiman Paris glr. Dt. Maharadjo Diradjo from the Permi, Chatib Suleiman from the New PNI, and Hasanuddin

glr. Dt. Singo Mangkuto from the PSII. *Mr.* 470/geh/38 (April 1938) (ARA). Anwar St. Saidi also became a member of the body. Navis, 'Bank Nasional', p. 176. Other members included S.M. Latif, A. Aziz St. Kenaikan, Dr. Rasjidin, Drs. Roosma, and Mr. Haroen al Rasjid. *Pandji Islam*, April 3, 1939.

100 He later formed his own party the Parpindo (Partai Persatuan Indonesia, Indonesian Unity Party).

101 See *Pandji Islam*, February 10, 1941, which reproduces the question he raised in the Volksraad regarding the arrest of Haji Rasul.

102 In particular, with Mhd. Taher Marah Sutan (*Pandji Islam* January 8, 1940) and Anwar St. Saidi. He attempted to obtain licenses for local businesses to import cloth from abroad, but largely because of the troubled international situation was only partially successful. See *Pandji Islam*, June 16, 1941; Navis, 'Bank Nasional', pp. 180-81. In a visit to West Sumatra in December 1939, he argued against Thamrin's charges that there was no longer any political movement in Minangkabau by pointing out that Dutch restrictions had restrained the activities of all political parties (Recht van Vereeniging en Vergadering) in the region, but stating that: 'There is a great difference between the movement [*pergerakan*] and associations or meetings. Associations may live and die, but the movement is constant, like the soul with the body. The body may change and become different but the soul remains constant'. *Pandji Islam*, January 8, 1940.

103 With the help of Muhammad Yamin, Anwar received permission to establish Inkorba (Inkoops Organisatie Batik) as the first indigenous import company in West Sumatra. See 'Tindjauan Mingguan', *Sumatera Tengah*, No. 104 (March 10, 1953), pp. 3-4. (*Sumatera Tengah* was the official fortnightly journal put out by the Central Sumatra Department of Information in the early 1950s.); see also *Mr.* 378/geh/1938 (February 1938) (ARA).

104 Salim, *Riwayat Perjuangan*, p. 123. Interview with Abu Nawas, Padang, August 23, 1995. Anwar established two further enterprises, Andalas and Fort de Kock, and with the assistance of Muhammad Yamin, was able to buy a group of buildings in Bukittinggi on August 6, 1941, to house these enterprises, together with his bank. Navis, 'Bank Nasional', pp. 182-83.

105 Salim, *Khatib Suleiman*, pp. 18-19. These included a 'Fisherman's cooperative' in Sasak-Talu, a limekiln cooperative in Padang Panjang, a Tobacco Estate cooperative in Payakumbuh, and others. Abu & Suhadi, *Chatib Suleman*, p. 27.

106 Interview with Abu Nawas, Padang, August 23, 1995. Many of Chatib Suleiman's friends and colleagues stressed that while he was the fount of most of the political ideas and strategy that guided the struggle in West Sumatra, he was not practical and had to rely on others to implement his ideas.

107 After a brief earlier marriage in Padang, Chatib married Zubaidah from his home village of Sumpur in 1932. They had two children, Sjahrir, and a daughter (Nurcaya) who died while still a young girl. He took a second wife, Emma, in Padang Panjang in March 1943, and they had two children (Lasteri and Kasman) before she died in 1946. Interviews with the family of Chatib Suleiman (Padang Panjang and Sumpur, 1995) and Salim, *Khatib Suleiman*, p. 1.

108 *Mr.* 178/geh/40 (November 1939)(ARA); Abu & Suhadi, *Chatib Suleman*, pp. 25-26. Also, interview with Leon Salim, Payakumbuh, September 4, 1995.

109 During their years of cooperation in the youth movement and leadership of the New PNI, Chatib Suleiman, Leon Salim, and Junus Kotjek shared a house in Padang Panjang, which was the centre of their political, musical, and educational activities.

110 See above, p. 89. See also Chatib Soeleiman, *Sikap Moeslimin Indonesia: Artikel 177I.S. akan Ditjaboet* (Bukittinggi, 'Penjiaran Ilmoe', 1939), which reproduces his major speech on this issue. He is listed on this pamphlet as vice chairman of the Badan Permoesjawaratan Islam Minangkabau.

111 Interview with Datuk Simarajo (Simabur, Batu Sangkar), August 22, 1976.

112 Ingleson, *Road to Exile*, p. 230. As can be seen from chapter 2, I admire much of what Ingleson has written, but his study is severely handicapped by its intense Java-centrism. A

revealing indication of this is the fact that his book's cover is adapted from a cartoon from *Fikiran Ra'jat*, a weekly magazine edited by Sukarno 'which portrays Rasuna Said defiantly proclaiming Free Indonesia from inside a colonial jail'. [*Pandji Islam*, April 7, 1941]. Yet nowhere in the book is there a mention of Rasuna Said – her arrest or her role in the nationalist movement, nor of the fact that she was one of the leaders of an Islamic party in West Sumatra.

Chapter 4

1 Research Section, Far Eastern Bureau, 'Chronology of Events in Japan and Japanese Occupied Countries', April 1945 (*Procureur-Generaal bij het Hooggerechtshof in Nederlands-Indië*, No. 181, 'Nefis Counter-Intelligence Informatie'), p. 15.

2 Shigetada Nishijima and Koichi Kishi, *Japanese Military Administration in Indonesia* (Washington: JPRS, 1963), p. 148.

3 Boei cho boei kenshusho [Defence Ministry Research Institute], *Nansei homen rikugun sakusen: Malai Ranin no boei, Rekishi Seinshi sosho 92 [Army Operations in Southwest Areas: Defence of Malaya and the Dutch East Indies, History of World War II, vol. 92]* (henceforth *Army Operations*) (Tokyo: Asagumo shinbun sha, 1976), p. 90.

4 The full story of this incident appears in Leon Salim, *Prisoners at Kota Cane* (Ithaca: Cornell Modern Indonesia Project, 1986).

5 The earlier version of this history, which was compiled by some of the principal Minangkabau actors during the Revolution, recounts how all Dutch armed forces, including the police, had been withdrawn and concentrated in their barracks, and at midnight on the 16th all of their weapons had been registered and stored in warehouses. 'There was no longer a single Dutchman who was brave enough to show himself on the streets'. Rasjid *et al.*, *Sejarah Perjuangan Kemerdekaan*, vol 1, p. 68.

6 Ahmad Husein *et al*, *Sejarah Perjuangan Kemerdekaan RI di Minangkabau/Riau 1945-1950*, 2nd ed. (Jakarta: BPSIM, 1991), vol. 1, p. 43.

7 Navis, 'Bank Nasional', pp. 207-209; also interview with Roestam Anwar, March 30, 1999. Navis also says that Chatib Suleiman requested Sukarno to intervene on Anwar's behalf.

8 See Anwar St. Saidi, *Tugu Pemuda Sumatera* , pp. 22-24. Japanese suspicions were probably increased by the fact that before his departure van der Plas had given money to at least some Indonesians, including Gerindo leader Amir Sjarifuddin, to develop underground operations against the Japanese.

9 *Sukarno. An Autobiography as told to Cindy Adams* (Indianapolis, Bobbs Merril, 1965), pp. 165-66.

10 Ibid., p. 158.

11 'Between hope and reality there was a sharp contradiction. The hope was freedom, independence and prosperity. But the reality was colonialism, oppression and suffering'. Abu & Suhadi, *Chatib Suleman*, p. 34.

12 Navis, 'Bank Nasional', p. 213. Interviews with Leon Salim, Roestam Anwar, Ismael Lengah.

13 Tamimi Usman kept in touch with Sjahrir, visiting Jakarta in 1944. On his instructions, Sjahrir's followers in West Sumatra formed cadre in several districts, which do not seem to have been very active until the very end of the occupation, when they organized weapons seizures. Interview with Tamimi Usman, Koto Baru, June 22, 1976. Others claimed that while ostensibly working for the Japanese they formed cells of activists under the leadership of Abdullah, and carried out anti-Japanese activities, including killing Japanese whenever an Indonesian was killed. Interviews with Djalil Jaya and Z. Arifin Aliep (Jakarta), May 13, 1976 (Padang) August 5, 1976. I have seen no other reports of such activities.

14 Abu & Suhadi, *Chatib Suleiman*, p. 34. See also Navis, *Bank Nasional*, pp. 210-12.

15 Navis, 'Bank Nasional', pp. 214-15.

16 Kementerian Penerangan, *Propinsi Sumatera Tengah*, p. 79; Abu & Suhadi, *Chatib Suleiman*, pp. 36-37; and *Riwayat Hidup ...Chatib Suleiman*, p. 8.

17 After the 1927 uprising Achmad Arif Dt. Madjo Orang had been appointed assistant chief (*demang*) of *adat* affairs, becoming chief of *adat* affairs in 1940. Husein *et al.*, *Sejarah Perjuangan*, p. 23.

18 Interviews in Tokyo with I. Wakamatsu (December 17, 1976) and Mrs. Aminah Madjid Usman (December 13, 1976). Madjid Usman, younger brother of the medical doctor A. Rahim Usman, had studied at Meiji University in Japan in the early 1930s and married a Japanese there. He was editor of the Padang newspaper *Radio* and a leading member of the town council in the late 1930s. He and his family were arrested by the Dutch shortly before the Japanese landed and were under detention in Bandung when Japanese forces arrived. (Interview with Mrs. Aminah Madjid Usman.) Madjid Usman was also an old friend of Muhammad Yamin, and Yamin sent the Partindo leader Chatib Salim back with him to Padang. Navis, 'Bank Nasional', pp. 210-11.

19 He first established a nine-member *adat* council, the Research Office on Minangkabau Society (Balai Penjelidikan Masjarakat Minangkabau) to which Roesad Dt. Perpatih Baringek belonged, and then an Islamic one, the High Council of Islam (Madjelis Islam Tinggi) which had leaders from both the Muhammadiah and Perti, including Mansur Daud Dt. Palimo Kayo and Syekh Mohammad Djamil Djambek. Interviews with Dt. Simarajo (Simabur), August 22, 1976, I. Wakamatsu (Tokyo) December 1976, and Fachrudin H.S. Dt. Majoindo (Situjuh Batur), August 1, 1976. See also Dai nijugogun gunsei kanbu, *Dai Nijugogun gunsei nenpo* [25th Army Hq., *The 25th Army Annual Report of the Military Administration*] (n.p., July 1943), p. 125.

20 Interview with I. Wakamatsu (Tokyo), December 17, 1976.

21 Interview with Mr. St. Mohd. Rasjid (Jakarta), April 9, 1976. According to Rasjid, Ahmad Husein's father, Idrus, was his deputy and when Rasjid later became Resident, he appointed Idrus public prosecutor.

22 Mahmud Junus, a Cairo-educated scholar, represented the High Islamic Council (MIT, Majelis Islam Tinggi) of West Sumatra in the Japanese-sponsored advisory bodies. He was a founder of Islamic high schools including the Normal Islam Padang, as well as a religious writer. See above, chapter 3, and Rasjid *et al*, *Sejarah Perjuangan*, pp. 122-23.

23 *Army Operations*, p. 447. No such voluntary armies were to be established in east Indonesia.

24 The Army of the South Seas was predicting such an attack throughout the latter part of 1943. At their meeting of November 17-21, 1943, the command decided to emphasize two prongs of defence against such an attack, with Burma to the north and North Sumatra to the south. Ibid., pp. 135-37.

25 Interview with Mrs. Aminah Madjid Usman, who acted as Yano's interpreter in these meetings, (Tokyo) December 13, 1976. Yano himself wrote: 'Actually before my trip to Java [in January 1943], I had suggested to my superior (Commander Tanabe of the Japanese Occupation Army in Sumatra) that, when we recruited another volunteer army, we should give more encouragement to the Indonesian people concerning their independence. I believed that if we did this the Indonesian people would certainly cooperate whole-heartedly. Commander Tanabe gave me full authorization to proceed'. Yano Kenzo, 'Sukarno no shokenzan: Dokuritsu eno prelude' [The First Meeting with S.A. Soekarno: Prelude to Independence] *Sekido hyo* (Tokyo), 17 (January 10, 1966). His proposal stemmed from the failure of efforts to recruit West Sumatrans into the Hei ho – the support troops integrated into Japanese army units.

26 Kenzo Yano, 'Sodateta minzoku noyume' [Fostering the Indonesian Dream] *Sekido hyo* 79 (January 10, 1967). I am grateful to Dr. Yoshiko Yamamoto for translating this and other materials from the Japanese.

27 Ibid. He noted that the number of applicants in West Sumatra exceeded twenty thousand.

28 Interviews with Ismael Lengah, (Jakarta) April 17, 1976, Dt. Simarajo, (Simabur) August 22, 1976.

29 In both West Sumatra and when he began recruitment campaigns for the adjacent areas of Riau, Jambi, and Pekanbaru, it was always the age and occupation of potential officer candidates that he noted. Diary of Chatib Suleiman, January 31, 1944. (I am grateful to Chatib Suleiman's widow, Yunidar Suleiman, for letting me copy this and other of her husband's papers.)

30 Interview with two of the instructors, Yuichi Sakamoto, (Tokyo) December 16, 1976, (Ithaca) May 14, 1977, and K. Kurita, (Tokyo) December 11, 1976.

31 Ibid., also interviews with Ismael Lengah, Dahlan Ibrahim (Jakarta, 1976), and with Mansoer Sani, Abu Nawas and other former members of the Giyu gun (Padang, August 1995).

32 Interviews with Ismael Lengah, Dahlan Ibrahim, and Sjarief Usman. See also Navis, 'Bank Nasional', pp. 217-18.

33 This is a free translation of part of the Indonesian text. I am grateful to Leon Salim for giving me a copy of the original typescript of the words and music.

34 Interviews with former members of the Giyu gun, Padang, August 1995.

35 Ibid., *Haluan Minggu*, August 29, 1976. In his diary, Chatib Suleiman notes that the wife of Dt. Toemenggoeng was also prominent in the organization. Chatib Suleiman's diary, January 21-22, 1944.

36 Salim, *Riwayat Perjuangan*, pp. 127-28. Chatib Suleiman's diary shows him attending meetings to organize support groups for the Giyu gun in Padang on January 8, 1944, Pariaman and Bukittinggi on the 10th, Bukittinggi on the 12th and 13th, Batu Sangkar on the 15th, Solok on the 18th, Padang on the 19th, Talu on the 20th, and Air Bangis on the 23rd.

37 Interview with Leon Salim, August 1995.

38 These included the Wild Tiger Unit (Barisan Harimau Liar) and the Flying Dragon Unit (Barisan Naga Terbang), and were to be thorns in the side of the Indonesian Republic after it was established in 1945.

39 Fukuin kyoku shiryo, *Nanpo sakusen ni tomonau senryochi gyosei no gaiyo*: Besusatsu 3 [The Outline of Military Administration in Sumatra Appendix 3] (Tokyo: Fukuinkyoku, 1946), p. 14.

40 Kenzo Yano, 'Saigo no kaigi' [The Last Conference], *Sekido hyo*, 82 (April 10, 1967).

41 According to Yano's recollections Tanabe would frequently ask his advice because Tanabe himself was 'neither satisfied with reports by the Military Administration Headquarters nor with their military policy. Further, he was very much interested in policies toward the native people'. Ibid.

42 According to Yano he resigned immediately after the conference. Ibid. Other accounts state that he was dismissed.

43 Interview with Yuichi Sakamoto, (Ithaca) May 14, 1977, and Kyoshi Kono 'Sumatora Kyoiku memo' [Memorandum of Education in Sumatra] *Sekido hyo*, ed. T. Sato (Tokyo, 1975), pp. 422-23. (*Sekido hyo* refers to both the book edited by T. Sato, and published in 1975 and the periodical issued by the Tokyo-based organization. The periodical is signified by a date and the book by a page number.)

44 The most notorious of these was at Logas, near Pekanbaru on construction of a rail line.

45 Interview with Ambassador S. Saito, (Tokyo) December 10, 1976. The Japanese military headquarters in Bukittinggi appointed a research team, made up of Anwar St. Saidi, Iskandar Tedjasukmana, and Djoeir Moehamad, which travelled throughout Sumatra to find whether the people would accept Sumatran independence, but they discovered that all wanted to be part of Indonesian independence. Interview with Djoeir Moehamad, (Jakarta) July 24, 1995.

46 On this body, see Anderson, *Java in a Time of Revolution*, pp. 61-62.

47 The three were Teuku Mohammad Hassan, a lawyer from Aceh, Dr. Mohammad Amir, a doctor of Minangkabau origin but long resident in Medan, and Abdul Abbas, a Mandailing Batak lawyer long resident in Lampung. See Anthony Reid, 'The Birth of the Republic in Sumatra', *Indonesia* 12 (October 1971), pp. 27, 30.

48 See Mohammad Hatta, *Sekitar Proklamasi 17 Agustus 1945* (Jakarta: Tintamas, 1970), pp. 20-27.

Chapter 5

1 Kementerian Penerangan, *Propinsi Sumatera Tengah*, pp. 85-86.

2 See Anthony Reid, *The Blood of the People* (Oxford: Oxford University Press, 1979), pp. 152-53; 155-56.

3 On the decision to make Sumatra a single province, see below.

4 Principal among these were Tamimi Usman and Arifin Aliep. See above, chapter 4.

5 Originally, their area of responsibility embraced only Sumatra, but it was extended to include all of the Dutch East Indies. Admiral Mountbatten was informed in Potsdam in late July, 1945 both of this extension and of the projected use of the atom bomb against Japan; but because of the secrecy surrounding the latter he could do no open planning until he officially assumed command of the larger territory on August 15, 1945. See Idrus Nasir Djajadiningrat, *The Beginnings of the Indonesian-Dutch Negotiations and the Hoge Veluwe Talks* (Ithaca: Cornell Modern Indonesia Project, 1958), pp. 15-16; David Wehl, *The Birth of Indonesia* (London: Allen & Unwin, 1948), pp. 31-32; Vice Admiral, the Earl Mountbatten of Burma, *Post-Surrender Tasks: Section E of the Report to the Combined Chiefs of Staff by the Supreme Commander, Southeast Asia, 1943-1945* (London: Her Majesty's Stationery Office, 1969), p. 282.

6 Mountbatten, *Post-Surrender Tasks*, p. 283.

7 E.L.F. Couvreur, 'Chronologisch Overzicht: Hoofdstuk SVI, August-December 1945', p. 29 (Sectie Krijgsgeschiedenis, Staff van de Bevelhebber der Landstrijdkrachten, The Hague).

8 '1946 Feb. Operations Dulcie and Parakeet re-occupation of Padang and Medan Sept-Dec 1945, Naval Report', War Office File WO 203/5388 (PRO).

9 There was a battalion of gurkhas in Bukittinggi for the first few weeks, but it was withdrawn at the time of the clashes in December 1945.

10 The brutality of this murder was also condemned by Indonesians, and according to both Indonesian and Dutch accounts the culprits were apparently six Buginese who were possibly former members of the KNIL. 'Nefis Buitenkantor Padang', Dagrapport nr. 6, July 23, 1946 (Proc.Gen. Nr. 861. ARA); see also account by Johnny Anwar, the former police chief of Padang, who interviewed one of the accused in jail (*Haluan* [Padang], October 8, 9, 11, 1976.) According to Barbara Harvey, however, this is unlikely, for Buginese were not accepted into the KNIL in this century because of their tendency to run amuck. (Personal communication.)

11 The British reported a total of 199 houses burned down, in addition to the barracks and the BPPI office. 'Politiek Verslagen betreffende Sumatra Jan. 1946-Oct. 1948' for the period ending January 1, 1946, p. 20 (Algemene Secretarie Batavia II [ARA]).

12 On these militias, see below.

13 See above, chapter 4. The son of an Islamic scholar, Sjarief Usman had been arrested several times by the Dutch during the 1930s for his anticolonial writings. He was one of the first group of officers in the People's army during the Japanese occupation.

14 Interview with Sjarief Usman, November 1, 1976.

15 See above, chapter 2.

16 During the Japanese occupation the INS had become the Indonesia-Nippon School, and it was now called the Indonesia National School.

17 According to Mr. Rasjid, Jahya Jalil asked Sjafei to assume the Residentship around August 22 or 23, stating that his request was supported by Mr. Rasjid and other intellectuals. Before accepting, Sjafei went to Bukittinggi to consult with Chatib Suleiman and Anwar St. Saidi. (Interview with Mr. Rasjid, [Jakarta] April 9, 1976).

18 See above, chapter 1.

19 See Salim, *Limabelas Tahun*, pp. 376-77, for an account of Dahlan's attempted escape from Digul and presumed death. Roesad reportedly had officiated at the marriage of his brother Dahlan's widow with another Communist and former Digulist, Usman St. Keadilan (Uska)[see ibid., pp. 145, 378-80], a leading member of the Communist party in West Sumatra during the Revolution. Interview with Leon Salim, July 1995.

20 Some later accounts state that he was merely appointed on a temporary basis until the administration was in place.

21 Interview with Mr. St. Mohd. Rasjid, (Jakarta) April 9, 1976.

22 Chatib Suleiman's diary, March 17, 1946.

23 In addition, as was repeatedly stressed by local informants, his strength lay in conceptualizing plans and energizing the people and he lacked the practical skills a Resident was likely to need. His reluctance may also have been personal, as his wife Emma had died less than a week previously (on March 11) leaving him with two infants. He married Emma's younger sister, Yunidar, four months later. They would have three children – Sudarman and twins Surakhman and Erman.

24 Tan Malaka, *Dari Pendjara ke Pendjara Bahagian kedua* [vol.2] (Yogyakarta: Pustaka Murba, n.d.), pp. 117-27.

25 Muhammad Yamin, *Tan Malaka: Bapak Republik Indonesia* (n.p.: 'Moerba Berdjoeang', 1946), p. 2.

26 The other two men were Wongsonegoro and Iwa Kusuma Sumantri. For conflicting accounts of this 'political testament' and Tan Malaka's role in it, see Tan Malaka, *Dari Pendjara ke Pendjara III* (Jakarta: Pustaka Murba, n.d.), pp. 51-52; George Kahin, *Nationalism and Revolution*, pp. 148-51; Anderson, *Java in a Time of Revolution*, pp. 278-80.

27 Yamin, *Tan Malaka*, pp. 12-13.

28 Anderson, *Java in a Time of Revolution*, p. 292.

29 Also arrested were Abikusno Tjokrosujoso and Soekarni and later Djamaluddin Tamin and Subardjo. On the arrests, see ibid., pp. 322-37, and Aboe Bakar Loebis, 'Tan Malaka's Arrest: An Eye-Witness Account', *Indonesia* 53 (April 1992), pp. 71-78; Tan Malaka, *Dari Pendjara ke Pendjara III*, p. 143. Helen Jarvis translates Tan Malaka's account as follows: 'it has become clear that the...arrests were carried out by a triumvirate from a certain party – Sjahrir-Amir-Sudarsono – certainly with the approval of President Sukarno and Vice-President Hatta and reportedly on the urging of the British/Dutch delegation, so as to expedite the Dutch-Indonesian negotiations with the aim of achieving cooperation between the Dutch (who are still colonialists) and the Indonesian people, who proclaimed their 100 percent independence on 17 August 1945'. *From Jail to Jail*, vol. 3, p. 210.

30 The Masjumi in West Sumatra was formed by a fusion of two Islamic organizations that had existed under the Japanese, the High Council of Islam (MIT – Majelis Islam Tinggi), which incorporated many former adherents of the Permi, and the Muhammadiah, still under Haji Rasul's son-in-law A.R. Sutan Mansur.

31 On the Perti, see above. It was still under leadership of its founder, Syekh Sulaiman Arrasuli of Candung, and of H. Siradjuddin Abbas.

32 Among its most prominent leaders were Chatib Suleiman, Leon Salim, Tamimi Usman, Iskandar Tedjasukmana, Anwar St. Saidi, Dr. Rahim Usman, Djoeir Muhammad, and Darwis Taram. *Oetoesan Soematera*, February 26, 1946.

33 The son of Haji Said, a merchant and supporter of the Permi, Bachtaruddin was Rasuna Said's half brother, and was born and raised in Maninjau. He went to school at the HIS and MULO in Jakarta, and worked as a colonial official in Medan. He was briefly a boxer in Singapore, and during the Japanese occupation was a member of the police force in Padang. Other Communist Party leaders were Usman St. Keadilan and Haji Dt. Batuah, who returned from exile in early 1946 and was the official head of the PKI in West Sumatra until his death in August 1948.

34 It is interesting that Muhammad Yamin refers to the Struggle Union as a Volksfront in his pamphlet, *Bapak Republic Indonesia*. Informants in West Sumatra all stressed the independence of the Volksfront from the Struggle Union on Java.

35 Kementerian Penerangan, *Propinsi Sumatera Tengah*, pp. 112-13.

36 Bariun A.S., a member of the Indonesian Workers' Party and editor of the Padang newspaper, *Oetoesan Soematera*, was the husband of Rasuna Said.

37 Iskandar Tedjasukmana had studied law in Jakarta, and taught at the Islamic teachers' training college in Padang from 1937 or 38. He carried out legal studies for the Japanese in Bukittinggi during the occupation. Interview (Jakarta), April 1, 1976. On Dahlan Ibrahim, see chapter 4, and Audrey Kahin, 'Struggle for Independence: West Sumatra in the Indonesian National Revolution, 1945-1950' (PhD. dissertation, Cornell University, 1979), pp. 136-37.

38 It was reportedly at Anwar St. Saidi's suggestion that the 100-rupiah note was removed as legal currency. For a full treatment of this issue, see Kahin, 'Struggle for Independence', pp. 139-42 and Kementerian Penerangan, *Propinsi Sumatera Tengah*, pp. 112-21 and 478-82.

39 On the social revolution in East Sumatra, see Reid, *Blood of the People*, pp. 225-51 and Michael Van Langenberg, 'East Sumatra: Accommodating an Indonesian Nation within a Sumatran Residency', in *Regional Dynamics of the Indonesian Revolution*, ed. Audrey R. Kahin (Honolulu: University of Hawaii Press, 1985), pp. 123-25.

40 Interview with Tuanku nan Putih's son, Kalmar Rahman (Bukittinggi), February 18, 1991. When a boy of 11 Kalmar Rahman had been a team leader in the Pemuda Nippon Raya. (On the Pemuda Nippon Raya in West Sumatra, see above, ch. 4.)

41 Ibid., and interview with Dt. Sandi (Kupung Bibik, Baso), February 19, 1994.

42 Interviews with Kalmar Rahman and Karelmaniar (his son and daughter), 1991 and 1994. At Baso they also built a metal folding machine to make sugar cane meal. Interview with Dt. Serai (Sungei Sarik, Baso), February 18, 1991.

43 Estimates of their number varied between 25 and 50.

44 Interview with Kalmar Rahman, February 18, 1991; Interview with Dt. Sandi, February 19, 1994. Resident Djamil was also apparently in the group, as was the local district head. According to Dt. Serai (interview February 18, 1991), Bachtaruddin, Dr. Rivai, and Mr. Rasjid also accompanied him.

45 Boerhan was born in 1915 of the same mother but a different father. According to informants, his nickname, 'the black one' (nan Hitam), was because of his skin colour. Tuanku Nan Putih means the white or pure one.

46 The Japanese were given Minangkabau names – St. Marajo was skilled in machines, St. Diatih in medicine, and Malin Kuning (Sukaguchi) in social science. Interview with Kalmar Rahman. One other Japanese joined them in February 1946 after having been in hiding in the caves near Payakumbuh since the capitulation. Interview with Dt. Sandi (Baso), February 19, 1994.

47 Interview with Dt. Serai.

48 According to Tuanku Nan Hitam's brother-in-law, it was the Communist leader Rustam Effendi who made a speech telling the people they could steal and rob, and both brothers tried to stop them. Interview with Rabali Sutan Rumah Panjang and Malin Mauri (Baso), February 19, 1994.

49 According to Agussalim Dt. Rangkayo Mulie (interview with Azmi, July 17, 1976), those killed included Demang Azinar from Koto Gadang Bukittinggi, and his assistant demang, Anwar.

50 Interview with Nasrun, A.S.(Jakarta), October 4, 1976. Informants in Baso stated that the Javanese *romusha* were responsible for these deaths.

51 Interview with Abdul Halim (Jakarta), May 14, 1976.

52 Interview with Sjarief Usman (Jakarta), October 23, 1976.

53 Interview with Abdul Halim, May 14, 1976. Among the local people who lost their lives were Angku Pawang, Tuanku Bagindo, Dt. Kayo Kayo, Fakih Kayo. Another brother of Tuanku Nan Putih, Dt. Serai, was also arrested but later freed, and subsequently founded Tan Malaka's Murba party in Baso. Interview with Jamarin Pakih Satih (Sungei Sarik), February 18, 1991.

54 According to Tuanku Nan Putih's son, 'The difference between the Volksfront and my father's movement was that my father didn't have a public or Dutch school education but he

had many followers among the villagers and rural people; however, Chatib Suleiman and his friends had received a Dutch education and had influence among intellectuals in Padang Panjang and among the townspeople'.

55 Van Langenberg, 'East Sumatra', pp. 123-24; Reid, *Blood of the People*, pp. 225-38.

56 Interview with Halim. It is interesting to note the contradictory hindsight views from the opposing factions concerning the relevance of the Baso affair to the later history of the Republic in West Sumatra. Halim claims that had the Baso leaders not been suppressed, a Communist rebellion similar to that at Madiun might also have broken out in West Sumatra in 1948; while the followers of Tuanku Nan Putih contend that had their movement not removed several of the former colonial officials, the Dutch might well have succeeded in their efforts in 1949 to create a Dutch-sponsored Minangkabau state in the region.

57 Interview with Volksfront leader Iskandar Tedjasukmana (Jakarta), April 1, 1976

58 'Regionale Berichten betreffende de politieke ontwikkeling op Sumatra' (Alg. Sec. van de Ned-Ind Regering 1942-1950: Nefis Pub. No. 6), p. 36 (ARA).

59 Interview, Feb. 15, 1991. According to a religious official in the West Sumatra administration, Nasaruddin Thaha, members of the Baso movement had unsuccessfully attempted to kill Syekh Arrasuli. Interview (Padang), October 1976.

60 Interview with Azwar Dt. Mangiang (Padang), August 22, 1995. After the action against the Baso movement, Azwar felt obliged to resign from the police and join the army instead, 'because I was a Baso person and people from around Baso had respected very much the calling of Tuanku Nan Putih, and I was young at the time. And they were old and respected'.

61 He describes Dahlan Djambek as general representative of the Islamic group, and Bachtaruddin as general representative of the Communist Socialist group of Mr. Amir Sjarifuddin and Sutan Sjahrir. Djamaluddin Tamin, *Sambutan pada peringatan 19 tahun hilangnja Tan Malaka* (Jakarta, February 18, 1968), p. 12.

62 Interview with Mr. Rasjid, May 18, 1976. There were also two executive members, initially Mr. Rasjid and Dr. A.Rahim Usman. (Kementerian Penerangan, *Propinsi Sumatera Tengah*, pp. 131-32). Chatib Suleiman later became one of these members.

63 The full text of the Proclamation (20/46 of May 21, 1946) outlining arrangements for establishing the *nagari* councils and what their functions would be can be found in Kementerian Penerangan, *Propinsi Sumatera Tengah*, pp. 331-36.

64 On these elections, see Audrey Kahin, 'The Impact of the Indonesian Independence Struggle on Minangkabau Society', in *Change and Continuity in Minangkabau: Local, Regional and Historical Perspectives on West Sumatra*, ed. Lynn L. Thomas and Franz von Benda-Beckmann (Athens, Ohio: Ohio University Center for International Studies, Monograph No. 71, 1985), pp. 303-20.

65 To avoid unnecessary alienation of these traditional heads, it was emphasized that the new Wali Nagari and *nagari* Councils would not interfere in *adat* affairs.

66 Estimate of Mr. Sutan Mohd. Rasjid (Jakarta), May 18, 1976.

67 The federal state would consist of the Republic of Indonesia (Java and Sumatra), Borneo, and the Great East (Sulawesi, the Lesser Sundas, the Moluccas and West New Guinea). On the Linggadjati agreements see C. Smit, *Het Akkoord van Linggadjati* (Amsterdam: Elsevier, 1959), and Djajadiningrat, *Beginnings of the Indonesian – Dutch Negotiations*.

68 On the discussions in Padang, see Kahin, 'Struggle for Independence', pp. 172-76.

69 Interviews with Sjuib Ibrahim and Maksum, leaders of the Hizbullah, (Padang) July 1, 1976. Kahin, 'Struggle for Independence', pp. 197-99; and Rasjid *et al.*, *Sejarah Perjuangan*, vol. 1, pp. 422-23.

70 The son of a traditional scholar, S.J. St. Mangkuto was born in 1901 at Pitilah near Padang Panjang. He completed secondary education in 1917 and had a range of jobs, from most of which he was fired because of his quarrelsome nature. He learned about the Muhammadiah on a trip to Yogyakarta from Haji Bachruddin, and in 1926 established a branch of the organization in Pitilah. He became chairman of the regional executive board of the Muhammadiah

in 1929, but was always outspoken and frequently disagreed with the moderate stance of the rest of the organization's leadership. In 1945 he became a member of the National Committee in West Sumatra and was appointed District Head (*bupati*) of Solok in January 1946. On S. J. St. Mangkuto, see above, chs. 2 and 3. See also Abdullah, *Schools and Politics*, pp. 84-85, 90-95; and Hamka, *Kenang-Kenangan Hidup*, IV (Jakarta: Bulan Bintang, 1975), p. 59.

71 Born near Padang Panjang, Adam B.B. (Balai-Balai) studied under Syekh Daud Rasjidi who treated him as a son. He disagreed with establishment of the Sumatra Thawalib and founded his own school in Padang Panjang in about 1926, at which in the 1930s Chatib Suleiman and Leon Salim were among the teachers. Like S.J. St. Mangkuto he was aggressive and nonconformist. See Hamka, *Ajahku* , p. 264; interviews with Leon Salim, October 17, 1976, Ismael Lengah, April 17, 1976, and Rosinah Adam, September 1995.

72 Fatimah Enar et al., *Sumatera Barat, 1945-1949* (Padang: Pemerintah Daerah Sumatera Barat, 1978), pp. 143-52.

73 Interview with Dt. Simarajo, (Simabur) August 22, 1976.

74 Rasjid et al., *Sejarah Perjuangan*, vol. 1, p. 423.

75 Posters at the meetings apparently portrayed an army major with a woman in his arms, with captions accusing the military leaders of enjoying themselves while their soldiers had to fight at the front without adequate clothing or supplies. 'Politiek Verslag Sumatera', March and April 1947, signed by J.J. van de Velde, Medan, May 1, 1947 (Proc. Gen. 824) (ARA).

76 Rasjid et al., *Sejarah Perjuangan*, vol. 1, pp. 423-24. According to this account, there were rumours that the Republican central government's intelligence body, headed by Zulkifli Lubis, was at least peripherally involved in the coup attempt, being aware that it was to take place, but not informing any of the local government leaders. Two officers of Lubis's P 002 organization, Anwar Inderakesuma Doos and A. Malik, were part of Zubir Adam's delegation, and, according to the Dutch report, issued the orders for the arrests of residency leaders. 'Politiek Verslag', May 1, 1947. loc. cit.

77 Among those kidnapped in Bukittinggi were: Eni Karim; Dr. & Mrs. Rusma; Gafar Djambek; Abdul Murad (Bupati of Payakumbuh); Anwar St. Saidi; and Makinuddin. In Padang Panjang: Taher Samad and Richard, the deputy head of the town's police; in Payakumbuh: Dr. Anas and Bupati Murad; in Pariaman: Muchtar Taub. Others included: Daranin in Maninjau, Roesad Dt. Perpatih Baringek and Dr. Adnan. Interview with Eni Karim, April 15, 1976; Daranin St. Kayo, August 14, 1976. 'Politiek Verslag Sumatera', Medan, May 1, 1947 (Proc.Gen.824) (ARA). Kementerian Penerangan, *Propinsi Sumatera Tengah*, p. 148; Enar, *Sumatera Barat*, p. 148; Husein et al., *Sejarah Perjuangan*, p. 455.

78 Among those who escaped capture were Dahlan Ibrahim, Leon Salim, Jahja Djalil, and Nasrun A.S. (Rasjid et al., *Sejarah Perjuangan*, vol. 1, p. 429).

79 'Nefis Buitenkantoor Padang Dag. Mil. Nr. 41 Bijlage II' (attached to Min. of Col. *Mail-rapport* nr. 728/gen/1947) (ARA).

80 Among those arrested were Saalah J. St. Mangkuto (Muhammadiah), Nazaruddin Dt. Rajo Mangkuto (MTKAAM), Bachtiar Junus (Hizbullah), Yusuf Ali, nicknamed Black Cat, from the regular army, and the religious leader Adam B.B., as well as the two members of the Sumatra command. See Enar, *Sumatera Barat*, p. 144.

81 Politiek Verslag, May 1, 1947 (ARA). According to this report they all received six yards of cotton material and F. 60.

82 Chatib Suleiman was one of the delegates from West Sumatra, and his diary notes for March 6 give reasonably accurate information on the major actors in the affair.

83 Included in the team were A.R. St. Mansjur, Marzuki Yatim, and Udin. Enar, *Sumatera Barat*, p. 144.

84 Interview with Ismael Lengah (Jakarta), October 22, 1976. When Hatta ordered him to return the weapons and he refused, he did not at the time inform his fellow officers. But he did speak with Anwar St. Saidi, who had been among those arrested and who agreed with him. In the interview, Lengah commented, 'Perhaps this was the reason Hatta was not pleased with me'.

85 Ahmad Husein, who earned the name 'Tiger of Kuranji' (*Harimau Kuranji*) because of the exploits of his battalion, was the son of Mancu Kahar, the head of the Hizbullah's treasury. Interview with Maksum (Padang), July 1, 1976.

86 The other two subcommands were headed by A.K. Gani (South Sumatra) and Teuku Daud Sjah (North Sumatra). A.H. Nasution, *Tentara Nasional Indonesia* vol. 1, 3rd printing (Jakarta: Seruling Masa, 1970), p. 344.

87 Interview with Sjoeib, April 19, 1976, Ismael Lengah, October 22, 1976, Dahlan Ibrahim, April 20, 1976, Sjarief Usman, November 1, 1976. Komando Daerah Militer III/17 Agustus, *Sedjarah Kodam III/17 Agustus* (Padang: Sri Darma, n.d. [1970]), p. 114. (At the time, Sjoeib, a former lieutenant in the Giyu gun, had been appointed commander of some of the irregular forces on the Padang front.)

88 *Kedaulatan Rakjat*, September 6, 1946.

89 Interviews with Sjuib Ibrahim and Maksum, July 1, 1976.

90 See below. On the confusion and anarchy in many parts Sumatra in the face of the Dutch advance, see Anthony Reid, *Indonesian National Revolution* (n.p.: Longman, 1973), p. 115.

91 'Outline of Vice President's Statement on the Situation in Sumatra' [English translation made available to the Committee of Good Offices, at a meeting in Yogyakarta, January 17, 1948] (in my possession). Originally established in Medan, the Sumatra government under Governor Hassan had moved to Pematang Siantar in 1946, in the aftermath of the social revolution. Reid, *Blood of the People*, p. 244.

92 Aziz Chan had been Mayor of Padang since August 14, 1946. Members of his family who went to the hospital allege that when his body was brought in his only wound was from a blow to the back of his head, and that the bullet wounds were administered after his death. His body was not released to the Republicans until the following day. Drs. Muslim Ilyas, *Aziz Chan: Riwajat & Perjuangan* (Padang: Daerah Kotamadya Padang, 1973), pp. 76-78. For the Dutch report of the event, see Kahin, 'Struggle for Independence', p. 210. The date given there for the incident of July 20 is apparently erroneous, and the death occurred the previous day, Saturday, July 19.

93 Mohd. Nasrun replaced Djamil as Subgovernor of Central Sumatra in April 1947 when Djamil was appointed to head the preparatory committee for a University of Sumatra in Bukittinggi. On Nasrun, see Kahin, 'Struggle for Independence', p. 248, n.11.

94 Husein *et al.*, *Sejarah Perjuangan*, vol. 1, p. 542. Mr. Rasjid gave more dramatic figures of 18,000 to 150,000 in interviews, May 11, October 12, 1976.

95 This committee was made up of three representatives: Belgium, chosen by the Netherlands; Australia, by Indonesia; and the United States as the third member acceptable to both sides.

96 Alistair M. Taylor, *Indonesian Independence and the United Nations* (Ithaca: Cornell University Press, 1960), pp. 93-97, 311-21; Kahin, *Nationalism and Revolution*, pp. 215-29; Reid, *Indonesian National Revolution*, pp. 113-14.

97 'Politiek Verslag Sumatra', Batavia, June 1, 1948 (ASBII Old Nr. 374) (ARA).

98 Interview with Mr. Rasjid, October 12, 1976.

99 Nasution was a Mandailing Batak, born in Tapanuli in 1918. He had received his military training under the Dutch, attaining the rank of second lieutenant in the KNIL. In May 1946, he became the first commander of the Siliwangi Division.

100 George Kahin, *Nationalism and Revolution*, p. 263.

101 Interview with A.H. Nasution (Jakarta), October 23, 1976.

102 Interviews with Banteng officers, including Ismael Lengah, Sjarief Usman, Ahmad Husein, Dahlan Ibrahim, Abdul Halim, 1976.

103 The quotation is from a Dutch report, 'Overzicht en Ontwikkeling'. Nr. 105, December 11, 1948 (ARA). See also Husein et al., *Sejarah Perjuangan*, p. 705.

104 In an interview General Hidayat noted that he should initially have taken up the post in September, but because of the Madiun rebellion had to delay his departure until November.

He was angered by the attempts of the local troops in Sumatra to make him think they had more weapons than they actually possessed by passing them round from one unit to another as each was inspected. Hidayat later recognized, however, that he had been too brusque in the way he had tried to reduce the number of officers and men. Interview (Jakarta), October 7, 1976. The Banteng officers complained of his peremptoriness and resented his use of Dutch, the language in which he clearly felt most at ease. Husein *et al.*, *Sejarah Perjuangan*, pp. 708-709.

105 The best biography of Sjahrir is Rudolf Mrázek's *Sjahrir: Politics and Exile in Indonesia* (Ithaca: Southeast Asia Program, 1994). There has not yet been a good political biography of Amir.

106 George Kahin, *Nationalism and Revolution*, pp. 268-69.

107 Musso was born in Kediri in 1897. He was actually abroad when the 1926 uprisings broke out. He was arrested by the government of the Straits Settlements in Johore in December 1926 (see above, ch. 1, p. 298n.111), and after his release returned to the Soviet Union.

108 The best study to date of the conflict is Ann Swift's *The Road to Madiun: The Indonesian Communist Uprising of 1948* (Ithaca: Cornell Modern Indonesia Project, 1989).

109 Interview with Mr. Rasjid (Jakarta), May 18, 1976. He was given the titular rank of lieutenant general. This was a change of heart for Hatta, who had prevented Rasjid from being promoted to the position of Governor of Central Sumatra in June 1948. In the face of this humiliation Rasjid had gone to Java for medical treatment, but was appointed to the new position only about a month later.

110 Siliwangi officers Kawilarang, Ibrahim Adjie, and Akil, as well as Sumatra commander Suhardjo were on the same plane. Interview with Mr. Rasjid, October 12, 1976.

111 Interview, Ahmad Husein (Jakarta), April 12, 1976; Idris Madjidi (Solok), July 17, 1976; Nurhakim Taruman (Solok), July 17, 1976. Nazir St. Pamuncak was a friend of Hatta and had studied with him in the Netherlands. He had worked in the Dutch underground during the war and shortly after liberation was a member of the First Chamber of the Dutch Parliament.

112 Mr. St. Mohd. Rasjid, May 18, 1976, Leon Salim (Jakarta), October 24, 1976, Ismael Lengah (Jakarta), April 17, 1976. 'Politiek Verslag Sumatra', Batavia, October 2, 1948.

113 Most of these were detained by Col. Husein who was angered by reports from Java that Musso was declaring that Husein and his Kuranji battalion were among his followers.

114 Swift, *Road to Madiun*, p. 23.

115 According to Helen Jarvis, the newspaper mentioned the GRR as early as February 1948 and she believes it was probably formed the previous month. See Tan Malaka, *From Jail to Jail*, vol. 1, p. cxlii.

116 See George Kahin, *Nationalism and Revolution*, pp. 280-81.

117 And when fighting was already taking place in Surakarta among forces loyal to Amir and those of the pro-Tan Malaka GRR (People's Revolutionary Movement), as well as Siliwangi and air-force units. On the Solo affair, see Swift, *Road to Madiun*, pp. 67-73.

118 Tan Malaka, *From Jail to Jail*, vol. 3, p. 9.

119 See Kahin, *Nationalism and Revolution*, pp. 314-15.

120 Tan Malaka, *Dari Pendjara ke Pendjara III*, p. iv. See also Helen Jarvis's version in her translation of the volume, *From Jail to Jail*, vol. 3, pp. 6-7. Adam Malik informed Helen Jarvis in an interview in 1980, that Abdullah was in fact this representative. Ibid., pp. 213-14.

121 Husein, *Sejarah Perjuangan*, p. 689; interviews Lengah, Halim, and Salim.

122 Tan Malaka, *From Jail to Jail*, vol. 1, pp. cxviii-cxix.

123 Helen Jarvis, in ibid., p. cxx, citing *Anetz* of January 15, 1949. Probably this should read: 'the Indonesian Trotskyist Tan Malaka'.

124 Hamka, *Kenang2-an Hidup* vol. 4 (Jakarta: Bulan Bintang, 1975), p. 179.

1 'Overzicht, Rondschrijven, 19/12/48-22/12/48' [Sectie Krijgsgeschiedenis, 158-X 206-3].
2 'Overzicht Situatie', Padang, December 28, 1948 (Min. of Col., *Mailrapport*, nr. 25/geh/49) (ARA); Sjamsir Djohary, 'Peristiwa Situdjuh (15 Januari 1949). Skripsi presented to the History Faculty of the IKIP Padang (Padang, 1971).
3 'Overzicht en Ontwikkeling van de Toestand Nr 1 van 19/12/48 - 22/12/48', Padang, December 23, 1948 (Sectie Krijgsgeschiedensis, Doos 0117-56; 157-xa). The Dutch estimated a total of 1,600 tree trunks across the road between Kayutanam and Padang Panjang.
4 'Overzicht Rondschrijven', 19/12/48-22/12/48.
5 The only town not evacuated was Padang Panjang, where the Dutch attack apparently came before it was expected. The Dutch reported the people of the town standing by the roadside waiting to be evacuated (ibid.). The Dutch Resident wrote that virtually all of Bukittinggi had been evacuated, though here and in Solok most Chinese had remained. He reported Solok pretty much evacuated and Padang Panjang not at all. Almost all the kampungs along the road were deserted, except for a few old people and children. 'Overzicht Situatie', Padang, December 28, 1948.
6 These included the army command complex, the electricity generating station, the railway station and post office, as well as all radio-communications facilities. 'Overzicht en Ontwikkeling Nr. 1', Padang, December 23, 1948.
7 George Kahin, *Nationalism and Revolution*, p. 337.
8 For a full account of the attack and occupation of Yogyakarta, see ibid., pp. 337-39.
9 Interview with Sjafruddin Prawiranegara, (Jakarta) September 30, 1976.
10 After their attack on Yogyakarta, the Dutch had arrested Sukarno, Hatta, Sjahrir, and most of the Republican cabinet, including foreign minister Haji Agus Salim. On December 22, they flew most of the detainees to the island of Bangka off the east coast of Sumatra. For the first month Sukarno, Sjahrir, and Salim were separated from the other prisoners and detained in Brastagi and Prapat in North Sumatra. When Sukarno and Salim were allowed to rejoin their comrades on Bangka, Sjahrir was permitted to go to Jakarta as he was not at the time an official member of the Republican cabinet. See George Kahin, *Nationalism and Revolution*, pp. 337-38.
11 For the other members of the cabinet and their positions, see Audrey Kahin, 'Struggle for Independence', p. 291.
12 Interview with Sjafruddin Prawiranegara, September 30, 1976; Kementerian Penerangan, *Propinsi Sumatera Tengah*, pp. 170-71.
13 Mestika Zed, 'PDRI Penyelamat Republik', *D&R [Detik dan Romantika]*, August 16, 1997. Zed has recently published the first history of the Emergency Government: *Pemerintah Darurat Republik Indonesia: Sebuah Mata Rantai Sejarah yang Terlupakan* (Jakarta: Grafiti Press, 1997).
14 Interview with Mr. Rasjid, (Jakarta) November 2, 1976. It was also an area which Rasjid had been familiar with since he was a boy when he accompanied his father, a district officer, around the region.
15 John Coast, *Recruit to Revolution* (London: Christophers, 1952), p. 221. The air force had handed over a number of powerful transmitters to the PDRI and many of the regimental commanders in West Sumatra and Tapanuli already had their own transmitters. Interviews with Abdul Halim, October 15, 1976; Dahlan Ibrahim, April 20, 1976.
16 Interviews with Commodore Soejono (who was commander of the air force in Sumatra) and Wiweko Soepeno, who brought radio equipment to Aceh at the beginning of 1949. Wiweko was flying charter flights mostly between Bangkok and Rangoon to raise money to buy arms and equipment for the Republic. Interviews, (Jakarta) August 23 and 29, 1995; see also *Angkasa* [Jakarta] 5,11 (August 1995), pp. 27-28; 43 ff. Both Sjafruddin and Rasjid were able to make radio contact with India. Interviews, (Jakarta) September 30, 1976; November 2, 1976.

17 This appears in the attitude expresssed by villagers in Kamang and accounts of soldiers fleeing from the front, such as that of Anas Malik from Regiment 3 in 'Pengalaman Seorang Prajurit' (typescript, n.p., n.d.), given me by Ahmad Husein with his 'Aggressie ke II 19 Desember Tahun 1948'.

18 A few weeks later they did realize the importance of this area to the Republican struggle, and when a new KNIL infantry battalion arrived it was sent to conduct clearing operations through the region. A report of February 7 noted: 'There are three known resistance centres, namely north and south of Payakumbuh (towards Suliki and Fort v.d. Capellen [Batu Sangkar); Matur (by Minanjau) and north of Bonjol in the direction of Lubuk Sikaping. In the last place, Mr. Rasjid and his staff must be staying'. 'Overzicht Situatie', Padang, February 7, 1949 (Min. of Col., *Mailrapport* nr. 249/geh). Although this report wrongly located Mr. Rasjid's headquarters, its general assessement of the main areas of Republican strength was accurate.

19 'Perhubungan Tentara, Pemerintah dan Rakjat' [Relations between the Army, the Government and the People], Instruksi No. 8/GM, January 11, 1949 in Bahagian Penerangan, Staf Gubernur Militer Daerah Sumatera Tengah, *Himpunan Instruksi Gubernur Militer Daerah Sumatera Barat* (typescript, n.d.) [hereafter *Himpunan Instruksi*], p. 9.

20 Djohary, 'Peristiwa Situdjuh', pp. 53,59.

21 Other leaders killed included Lt. Col. Munir Latif from Painan, Capt. Tantawi and Lt Azinar from the Merapi Battalion and three members of the military governor's staff, Sjamsul Bahry, Rusli, and Sjamsuddin. SY Mahyuni, *Peristiwa Situjuh 15.1.49* (Situjuh Batur: Lembaga Sosial Desa 'Lembah Situjuh', n.d. [1972]), p. 18.

22 There is no mention in contemporary Dutch accounts of the role played by Kamaluddin. The military report of the operation does not mention any Indonesian spy, and in fact does not appear to have known the identity of most of the people killed or the nature of the meeting they were attending. According to the report, the attack was launched against a 'Company post of the CII Regiment'. The report identified only one army officer, Munir Latif, by name, although it notes that other army officers were killed and that when the defenders returned the Dutch fire 'the post was completely eliminated with the enemy suffering many dead'. 'Terr./Tpn. Co. Mid. Sum, 1e kwartier 1949 14-20/1/49' (Sectie Krijgsgeschiedenis, File Nr. 0117-4, 160-X).

23 Interviews with Azwar Dt. Mangiang (Padang), August 22, 1995 and with Djamaris Yoenoes, Padang, March 19, 1999. Yoenoes had been one of the people Kamaluddin met with after his flight from Situjuh and was present when the local commander Nurmathias advised the fugitive to go to Payakumbuh to have his wounds treated.

24 Interview with Djamaris Yoenoes. For a plausible account arguing that Kamaluddin was merely a scapegoat, see Azwar Dt. Mangiang, 'Menyingkapkan Tabir yang Menyelimuti Peristiwa Situjuh Batur 15 Januari 1949' (typescript, n.d.).

25 One of the elements of the rationalization plans that was implemented was the separation of Riau from the territory under command of the Banteng Division.

26 Rasjid *et al.*, *Sejarah Perjuangan Kemerdekaan R.I. di Minangkabau 1945-1950*, vol 2 (Jakarta, BPSIM, 1981), pp. 106-7.

27 In blocking the Dutch advance north, Dahlan Djambek's forces (PDD – Pasukan Dahlan Djambek) cooperated with those of the Police Mobile Brigade (Mobrig).

28 Husein *et al.*, *Sejarah Perjuangan Kemerdekaan*, vol. 2, p. 579.

29 They were T. Daud Beureu'eh (Aceh, Langkat and Tanah Karo); Dr. F.L. Tobing (East Sumatra and Tapanuli); Mr. St. Mohd. Rasjid (West Sumatra); R.M. Utojo (Riau); and Dr. A.K. Gani (South Sumatra and Jambi). Hidayat issued the order from Rao, on his treck north to Aceh.

30 'Maklumat Bersama dari Partai2 Politik se-Sumatera Barat', 'Pedoman Pendjelasan Keterangan Bersama Partai2 se-Sumatera Barat', 'Pembentukan Pasukan Mobiel Teras BPNK', Instruksi No.24/GM, April 5, 1949, in *Himpunan Instruksi*, pp. 50-56.

31 'Pendjelasan Instruksi B.M. No. 24', in ibid., pp. 57-58.

32 'Badan Pengawal Negeri dan Kota (BPNK)', Instruksi No 13/GM, February 2, 1949, in Badan Penerangan Staf Gubernur Militer Daerah Sumatera Tengah, in *Himpunan Instruksi*, pp. 19-22.

33 The quotation is from 'Overzicht Situatie', Padang, March 1, 1949 (Min. of Col., *Mailrapport* Nr. 263/geh/49) (ARA).

34 These ranged from Major Titular for the District Head to Lt. 1 Titular for the head of the *nagari* or extended village. See Kementerian Penerangan, *Propinsi Sumatera Tengah*, p. 181.

35 The DPD was headed by Mr. Rasjid with Lt. Col. Dahlan Ibrahim as his deputy. Its members from the executive were Dr. Ali Akbar and Orang Kayo Ganto Suaro, while Abdullah (Murba), Bachtaruddin (PKI), and H. Siradjuddin Abbas (Perti) represented the people's organizations. Kementerian Penerangan, *Propinsi Sumatera Tengah*, p. 172; Husein *et al*, *Sejarah Perjuangan*, vol. 2, p. 97.

36 The PMT was established at the end of March 1949. See Audrey Kahin, 'Struggle for Independence', p. 317.

37 On the tax-raising and other economic policies of the local Republican government, see below and Kahin, 'Struggle for Independence', pp. 319-34.

38 Most important were the Body to Help the Front Lines (Badan Pembantu Barisan Muka, BPBM), which became the Body to Help the Families of War Victims (Badan Pembantu Keluarga Korban Perang, BPKKP), which was an outgrowth of the Hahanokai women's association of the Japanese period; and the Daughters of the Indonesian Republic (Keputrian Republik Indonesia) which was formed in September 1945, with branches throughout West Sumatra and which was particularly active on the front lines.

39 For more details on collection of the taxes and other local government economic policies, see Audrey Kahin, 'Struggle for Independence', pp. 328-34.

40 'Overzicht Situatie', Padang, March 1, 1949 (Min. of Col., *Mailrapport* No. 263/geh.) (ARA).

41 When the new Dutch currency was introduced into Java and Sumatra in March 1946, it became the sole legal tender in the Dutch-occupied territories, and was exchanged at the rate of 3 NICA guilders for 100 Japanese rupiah. 'AFNEI Intelligence Review, October 45-November 46 Part VI (ARA).

42 Kementerian Penerangan, *Propinsi Sumatera Tengah*, pp. 116-17. At that time, they had received very little of the promised new Republican currency from Java (ORI).

43 Ibid., p. 151.

44 In West Sumatra the Division 9 command was responsible for producing the banknotes, as it possessed printing machinery, but it operated under supervision of the banks and of the residency civilian authorities. In 1947 and 1948 the residency government printed a total of 1,500 million ORIPS, which were used to pay the army's debts and the salaries of civilian officials, as well as provide loans to farmers.

45 The Linggajati agreement of early 1947 officially recognized *de facto* Republican control of Sumatra, and local residency officials tried to legitimize this trade. In West Sumatra they attempted to establish their own customs post in Teluk Bayur, the port of Padang, through which they planned to export such goods as cassia, coffee, rubber, copra, and resin in exchange particularly for clothing, but they were unable to reach any agreement with the Dutch before the first Dutch 'Police Action' of July 1947 destroyed the possibility for any such trade. *Mailrapport* 1219/geh/AGSU, April 23, 1947; *Mailrapport* 1944/geh/AGSU, Padang, June 21, 1947 (ARA).

46 He spent three months in Singapore, probably early in 1944. One of the Chinese merchants had been a friend of Anwar's brother, the Pari leader Djamaluddin Ibrahim, and one of the Minangkabau entrepreneurs, the owner of an antique shop in Singapore, had been born in Anwar's home village of Sungai Puar. The weapons included several colts, grenades, and disassembled rifles, with ammunition. (Navis, 'Bank Nasional', pp. 221-22, 225. Also interview with Roestam Anwar [Padang], June 18, 1985.) At this time Anwar St. Saidi also succeeded in

obtaining a letter of cooperation from a branch of the Yokahama Bank in Singapore for his National Bank. As a result his bank in Bukittinggi was able to operate freely during the Japanese occupation. (Ibid., pp. 186-87.) He was helped in his relations with the Yokahama bank by Dr. Gaus Mahyuddin, a Minangkabau doctor, who had beeen educated at the University of Tokyo, had married a Japanese, and later opened a practice in Singapore. (Ibid., pp. 186, 219.)

47 Tamimi Usman was principally in charge there. Ibid., p. 225.

48 Ibid., pp. 229-32; interviews with Roestam Anwar (Padang), June 18, 1985, Ismael Lengah (Jakarta), April 17, 1976.

49 During the interregnum, British forces seized large numbers of Japanese weapons, which the Allied command ordered them to dump or destroy so that they did not fall into the hands of either the Dutch or the Republic. Instead, the British stored a considerable portion of these arms on Kudap island, and until 1948 Republican forces conducted a brisk trade with the Singapore British military police, bartering gold and quinine for the Kudap weapons. Interview with the head of the supply section of Division 9, Dahlan Ibrahim (Jakarta), April 20, 1976.

50 Interviews with Roestam Anwar (Padang), June 18, 1985, Leon Salim (Jakarta), June 8, 1985, Syamsulbahar (Bukittinggi), May 27, 1985.

51 Pekanbaru was also within the territorial command of Division 9. The office was run by Li Ban Seng, a Chinese trader with family and business connections in Singapore. (Interview with Dahlan Ibrahim, April 20, 1976.)

52 Interviews with Mohd Hatta (Jakarta), October 6, 1976, St. Mohd. Rasjid (Jakarta), October 12,1976. See also Rasjid *et al.*, *Sejarah Perjuangan*, vol. 1, p. 586.

53 The Dutch reported this company was earning about $100,000 a month in 1948, but this is certainly an exaggeration. See 'Politiek Verslag Sumatra', June 1948 (*Mailrapport* 367/geh./ 48). *Mailrapport* 726/geh/48 (ARA). reported that the State Bank (Bank Negara), Resident Rasjid, and Chatib Suleiman had important interests in the Sumatra Banking and Trading Corporation. See also Rasjid *et al.*, *Sejarah Perjuangan*, vol, 1, p. 586, which states that Abdul Aziz Latif was its president-director.

54 During the revolution Anwar St. Saidi's National Bank played virtually no role, because he had handed over its assets in April 1946 to Army commander Dahlan Djambek to be used in the national interest. The bank had been little affected by inflation because early in the Japanese occupation it was decided that the bank's reserve capital should be in the form of gold, and in 1946 this capital reportedly amounted to Rp.2,072,600.00. This amount was handed over to the Republic. Navis, 'National Bank', pp. 184,188.

55 Rasjid *et al.*, *Sejarah Perjuangan*, vol. 2, pp. 215-16, and Enar, *Sumatera Barat*, p. 293. According to the latter source, the Republic had received about 4 tons of opium from India, and it was a part of this supply that was transferred to Bukittinggi. A total of about thirty cadets were sent to India to be trained as pilots. Interview with Wiweko (Jakarta), August 29, 1995.

56 Rasjid *et al.*, *Sejarah Perjuangan*, vol 2, p. 216.

57 The maximum value of the opium was about Straits $1,000 per kilogram, but the most usual price was between $600 and $800 per kilogram.

58 This was called the Emergency Government's Struggle Supply Center (Pusat Perbekalan Perjuangan - PPP PDRI), Rasjid *et al.*, *Sejarah Perjuangan*, vol. 2, pp. 218-19.

59 Shortly after the supply section re-established contact with the Chinese community in Dutch-occupied Bagan Siapiapi in mid-February 1949, their Chinese messenger was able to bring out to their headquarters in Tanah Putih about twenty tons of goods from Bagan Siapi-api, including salt, cloth, and medicines. Radiogram, April 6, 1949, signed by Capt. Dipandjaitan, and Zainal Zinur, P3PDRI. (Typed copy in my possession. This and later cited documents are from a collection of typed or handwritten reports, etc. of the PDRI and Military Governor of West Sumatra [henceforth Arsip PDRI], which were in the custody of Sjamsul Bahar, who kindly gave me access to them.)

60 In his orders of January 1, 1949, Hidayat suggested that Chinese or Indonesian merchants could use the opium as exchange for articles such as clothing, printed cotton, and salt-dried fish, and eventually perhaps weapons and ammunition from outside Indonesia (Hidayat memorandum 'Provisions and Financing Sub-Territory of West Sumatra', January 1, 1949), Arsip PDRI. Later, orders from both Hidayat and from the Emergency Government stipulated that the opium must principally be used to obtain food and clothing, with only 10-20 percent of it to be used to obtain arms. (Hidayat, 'Pembagian Supply Hasil2 Pangaraian', and P3 [Pusat Perbekalan Perdjuangan], 'Usaha P3 PDRI', April 1, 1949.) Ibid.

61 On the BFO see George Kahin, *Nationalism and Revolution*, pp. 386-90, and C. Smit, *De Indonesische Questie* (Leiden: Brill, 1952), pp. 174-75.

62 The DISBA had first been established in Padang in August 1947 after the first Dutch 'Police Action'.

63 Contending that no village head was able to exercise authority unless he was also a *penghulu*, the Dutch Resident commented: 'Among broad sections of the population the disregarding of the adat authorities has never been accepted and orders from a negeri head who is not at the same time a penghulu are never or rarely obeyed'. 'Overzicht Situatie', Padang March 1, 1949 (*Mr.* 263/geh)(ARA).

64 See Kementerian Penerangan, *Propinsi Sumatera Tengah*, p. 327, where the *adat* leaders are characterized as 'feudal remnants' who were 'tools' of the Dutch government. They are there held responsible for the disappearance of real democracy in the Minangkabau: 'and what was left behind was "a mockery of democracy" [*demokrasi pura-pura*], which actually signified complete power for the *adat* group as long as they stood on the side of the colonial government'.

65 'Overzicht Situatie', Padang, June 1, 1949 (Min. of Col. *Mr.* 563/geh) (ARA).

66 'Overzicht Situatie', Padang, March 29, 1949, and July 4, 1949 (*Mr.* 351/geh and 639/geh) (ARA).

67 On the Republican intelligence apparatus, see Audrey Kahin, 'Struggle for Independence', p. 342, n. 142.

68 'Overzicht Situatie', Padang, June 1, 1949 (ARA).

69 'Biographi pegawai2 jang bekerdja pada Belanda Sedjak Desember 1948' [Biography of officials who worked for the Dutch after December 1948], signed Lt. Muda Jahja 'Commandan PMT/Barisan Guerila Rakjat, Brigade Kota BKt' (ARSIP PDRI).

70 As noted above, many of these were the same routes earlier used by the political activists of the Pari. Essential in the effort were the Chinese traders in Singapore and Kuala Lumpur, as well as in the east-coast ports of Sumatra. Interviews with Tamimi Usman (Koto Baru, Padang Luar Bukittinggi), June 22, 1976; Dahlan Ibrahim, April 20, 1976, Roestam Anwar. See also Navis, *Bank Nasional*, pp. 186-225.

71 The *bupati* was usually coordinator for all affairs in his District while the main duties of the District head (*camat*) were to implement the taxing system and distribution of resources.

72 Interview with Sjafruddin Prawiranegara (Jakarta), September 30, 1976. In a statement of April 9, 1949, Sjafruddin declared that a ceasefire order could only be issued by the Emergency Government and not by the president and vice-president who were under Dutch arrest. 'Vijandelijke Radioberichten [Intercepts] & MINOGS: 19 april-3 mei, 1949' (Sectie Krijgsgeschiedenis, File 228-4: 'Mil. & Pol. Overzichten').

73 Interview with Dahlan Ibrahim (Jakarta), October 19, 1976.

74 Also in the delegation were Dr. Johannes Leimena, Dr. Halim, and Mohd. Yamin. Enar, *Sumatera Barat*, p. 310.

75 *Waspada*, July 16, 1949.

76 Interviews with Sjafruddin Prawiranegara (Jakarta), September 30, 1976 and Mohd. Natsir, October 16, 1976.

77 *Mr.* Nr. 991/geh /1949 (ARA).

78 *Mr.* Nr. 1084/geh. 20-12-49 (ARA).

79 Although he left Australia with his wife and seven children in October 1945, the Dutch pressed the British to arrest him in Kupang (Timor). He was detained for several months there and on Labuan and St John before being allowed to return to West Sumatra. See Mohamad Bondan, *Genderang Proklamasi di Luar Negeri* (Jakarta: 'Kawal', 1971), pp. 10, 44-45; see also Rasjid *et al.*, *Sejarah Perjuangan*, vol 1, pp. 245-46.

80 Tamar Djaja, *Pusaka Indonesia*, p. 372; Barbara Harvey, 'Tradition, Islam and Rebellion: South Sulawesi 1950-1965' (PhD. dissertation, Cornell University, 1974), p. 223.

81 Bondan, *Genderang Proklamasi*, pp. 44-45; Rasjid *et al.*, *Sejarah Perjuangan*, vol. 1, pp. 244-45.

82 Abdullah Ahmad and Haji Rasul died before the proclamation of independence (Abdullah Ahmad in 1933 and Haji Rasul in June 1945, having been as stubborn in confronting the Japanese as he had earlier been in defending his principles against both the Communists and the Dutch – refusing, for example, Japanese orders to bow toward Japan).

83 According to Djoeir Moehammad, Chatib Suleiman instructed Suska, the journalist, to protect Hamka when he fled from Medan. Interview (Jakarta), July 24, 1995.

84 The fourth volume of his memoirs, *Kenang2-an Hidup*, recounts his experiences during the period.

85 Ibid., pp. 57-68, 101-4.

86 Interviews with Ibu Naimah Djambek and former associates of Dahlan Djambek (Bukittinggi), March 29, 1999. Zainal Abidin Djambek succeeded his father in his *surau* in Bukittinggi, and another son, Saaduddin, had moved to Java. Noer, *Saya Bagian Ummat*, p. 439.

87 On Natar Zainuddin, see Reid, *Blood of the People*, pp. 61, 79-80, 244-45 and *passim*.

88 Real leadership of the Communist party, however, was in the hands of Bachtaruddin, who initially headed the Communist militia [Temi, Tentera Merah, Red Army] and succeeded Dt. Batuah as head of the PKI in 1948.

89 Bondan, *Genderang Proklamasi*, p. 14; Navis, 'Bank Nasional', p. 234.

90 He served as head of the Banteng Division's Investigation Body and Communications with the People from 1946 to 1948, after which he became head of Social Investigations (Penyelidik Masyarakat [Pema]) on the Governor's staff, with the rank of captain. 'Riwayat hidup Perintis Kemerdekaan' (typescript, n.d.).

91 Interview with Leon Salim (Jakarta), October 24, 1976.

92 He was appointed to the Central Joint Board, the national body overseeing implementation of the ceasefire, and then went on to the Indonesian foreign office.

93 Hamka, *Kenang2-an Hidup*, 4, p. 216.

94 They also included some of the most respected and senior military officers. Ismael Lengah, as we have seen, had been forced to leave in December 1948. At the end of 1949 he was followed by Abdul Halim and Dahlan Ibrahim. On the reasons behind their departures, see below, chapter 7.

95 See Jarvis, 'Introduction', *From Jail to Jail*, pp. cxxi-cxxvi, where she brings together the most reliable accounts she can find of events surrounding Tan Malaka after he fled Kediri.

96 These indications will be dealt with in the following chapter.

97 'Overzicht Situatie', Padang, September 12, 1949, Min. of Col. *Mailrapport* nr. 781/geh/1949 (ARA).

Chapter 7

1 There were a total of 'seven states, nine other constitutional units of lesser status, and several minor areas of lower rank'. A. Arthur Schiller, *The Formation of Federal Indonesia (1945-1949)* (The Hague: Van Hoeve, 1955), p. 337. See also George Kahin, *Nationalism and Revolution*, pp. 435 ff.

2 Westerling was reportedly born in 1919 of mixed Turkish, Dutch, and Greek descent. He

lived in Java before the war, and then in the UK from 1942-45 where he received commando training and a commission as a reserve officer in the Dutch East Indies Army. He was parachuted into Sumatra in late 1945 and went to Sulawesi in early 1946, where he led an extermination campaign against Indonesian guerrillas in the countryside. According to a British report, his wife had been murdered by Indonesians. He finally resigned in July 1949 because of a rank dispute. By November of that year he had mobilized three- to five-thousand troops mostly from his former command, a number that had expanded to approximately eight thousand at the time of his rebellion in Bandung. See Report from Mr. H.C. Druce, dated January 25, 1950, incorporated in cable January 26, 1950 to Foreign Office (FO371/83689) PRO. See also, Barbara S. Harvey, 'South Sulawesi: Puppets and Patriots', in *Regional Dynamics of the Indonesia Revolution*, ed. Audrey Kahin (Honolulu: University of Hawaii Press, 1985), pp. 218-19.

3 On these events, see Schiller, *Formation of Federal Indonesia*, pp. 337-41; Kahin, *Nationalism and Revolution*, pp. 446-66. The Indonesian army launched an attack on Ambon in September 1950 and was finally able to crush the RMS by the end of the year when its remaining leaders fled to the neighbouring island of Ceram. From that time on the movement posed no further threat to the Republic, though its prime minister, Soumokil, was not captured until twelve years later in 1962. See Richard Chauvel, 'Ambon: Not Revolution but a Counterrevolution', in *Regional Dynamics*, pp. 258-59.

4 Mohammad Hatta, 'Indonesia's Foreign Policy', *Foreign Affairs* 31,3 (April 1953), pp. 441-52, p. 449.

5 Herbert Feith, *The Decline of Constitutional Democracy in Indonesia* (Ithaca: Cornell University Press, 1962), pp. 94-96; Kahin, *Nationalism and Revolution*, pp. 464-65.

6 Gerald S. Maryanov, *Decentralization in Indonesia as a Political Problem* (Ithaca, N.Y: Cornell University Modern Indonesia Project, 1958), p. 25 and in general, pp. 20-27.

7 K.C. Wheare, *Federal Government*, 3rd ed. (London: Oxford University Press), p.15. Citing Sir Robert Garran in the Report of the Royal Commission on the Australian Constitution (1929), p. 230.

8 Schiller, *Federal Indonesia*, p. 342.

9 They were empowered to deal with the 'household affairs' of the region, which were eventually listed as 'irrigation, maintenance of roads and public buildings, supervision and development of agricultural programs, control of fisheries, maintenance of health services, maintenance of veterinary services, matters of social welfare, supervision of marketing and distribution'. J.D. Legge, *Cultural Authority and Regional Autonomy in Indonesia: A Study in Local Administration 1950-1960* (Ithaca: Cornell University Press, 1961), p. 29.

10 Maryanov, *Decentralization as a Political Problem*, p. 70.

11 Regional heads (*kepala daerah*)also existed at the district and the village levels, but there seemed little disagreement that the role of these heads should be largely as people's representatives. Government spokesmen seemed to agree that 'these regional heads have to be men close to and known by the people of the region'. However, 'the government was of the opinion that direct election with free choice for the regional head at the present time can only be for the regional head of level III [i.e. the village].... With regard to the regional head of levels I and II [the province and the district] the government believes it is enough in this time of transition for the regional head to be chosen by the local council of the region concerned'. *Haluan*, April 23, 1955.

12 As Legge has pointed out, this marked a reversal of the situation under colonial rule where 'the head of the local government system at each level was the central government's chief executive officer in the region'. Legge, *Central Authority and Regional Autonomy*, p. 36. Legge treats the position of the *kepala daerah* at length in ibid., pp. 35-40.

13 Ibid., p. 39. The central government's interior ministry was usually able to reject the local candidates on the grounds that they lacked the necessary administrative experience.

14 Cited in Maryanov, *Decentralization as a Political Problem*, p. 39.

15 Interview with Djoeir Moehamad (Jakarta), July 24, 1995. The most wide-ranging Parliamentary debate on this issue occurred in 1954 when Djoeir Mohammad led proponents of a law to make Aceh an autonomous region. See the debates in *Ichtisar Parlemen*, for June 25, July 15, 16, and October 15, 1954.

16 See the reports of the discussions in Parliament appearing in *Haluan*, April 23, 25, 26, 27, 1955.

17 The other provinces were West, Central, and East Java, Kalimantan, Sulawesi, Maluku, and Nusatenggara.

18 See Maryanov, *Decentralization as a Political Problem*, pp. 100-101; John R. Smail, 'The Military Politics of North Sumatra: December 1956-October 1957', *Indonesia* 6 (October 1968), pp. 134-38.

19 Maryanov, *Decentralization as a Political Problem*, p. 100.

20 After Sjafruddin ceded his powers as president of the Emergency Government (PDRI), President Sukarno appointed him deputy prime minister and authorized him to act on behalf of the central government in 'decreeing government statutes for Sumatra which would later be subject to central government review'. Eric Eugene Morris, 'Islam and Politics in Aceh: A Study of Center-Periphery Relations in Indonesia' (PhD. dissertation, Cornell University, 1983), pp. 169-70.

21 'Salah saham dan ragu2 tentang pembentukan Prop. Sumatera Utara tidak ada lagi' [Misunderstandings and hesitation concerning formation of the Province of North Sumatra no longer exist], radio speech by Mohd. Natsir, January 23, 1951, *Suara Penerangan*, 2,5 (January 30, 1951), pp. 3-5, 8.

22 For a full account of the developments in 1950-51 in Aceh, see Morris, 'Islam and Politics in Aceh', pp. 172-86; see also Feith, *Decline of Constitutional Democracy*, pp. 345-46.

23 Kementerian Penerangan, *Propinsi Sumatera Tengah*, pp. 305-308.

24 On the events surrounding the dispute, see ibid., pp. 395-407.

25 Ichlasul Amal, *Regional and Central Government in Indonesian Politics: West Sumatra and South Sulawesi 1949-1979* (Yogyakarta: Gadjah Mada University Press, 1992), p. 42.

26 Kementerian Penerangan, *Propinsi Sumatera Tengah*, p. 412.

27 Interview with Mohd. Natsir (Jakarta), October 16, 1976.

28 Roeslan was confirmed as governor seven months later, on June 27, 1951. Djawatan Penerangan Sumatera Tengah, *Dunia Seminggu* (20), July 16, 1951, pp. 3-4.

29 Local frustration with the 'freezing' of their representative council can be seen throughout these years. See the official publication of the Information Agency for Central Sumatra, *Dunia Seminggu* for June 18, 1951 (25), pp. 3-4, which describes the 'Catch-22' situation into which the freezing of the council had placed the region. See also Kementerian Penerangan, *Propinsi Sumatera Tengah*, pp. 425-26, describing attempts by the political parties of Central Sumatra to persuade the central government in 1952 and 1953 to 'fill the vacuum of democracy in Central Sumatra' by re-establishing the local representative councils.

30 This account is based on, and all the quotations taken from, the long extracts from the proceedings of the conference, appearing in 'Otonomi Daerah: kesan2 dari konperensi DPDS2 kab/kota se Sumatera Tengah', appearing in the monthly publication of the province's Department of Information, *Sumatera Tengah* No. 123/124, January 25, 1954, pp. 8-14, 19.

31 One estimate, by a respected journalist/publisher, was that in 1956 71 percent of Indonesia's exports came from Sumatra (21 percent from North Sumatra, 15 percent from Central Sumatra, and 35 percent from South Sumatra). S. Takdir Alisjahbana, *Perdjuangan Autonomi dan Kedudukan Adat Didalamnja* (speech before the All-Sumatra Adat Congress, Bukittinggi, 12-20 March, 1957 (Jakarta: Pustaka Rakjat, n.d.), p. 16.

32 The *Panca Sila*, first outlined by Sukarno in a speech before the Investigating Committee for the Preparation of Independence on June 1, 1945, was the major philosophical basis for independent Indonesia. The Five Principles were Nationalism, Internationalism or Humanitarianism, Representative Government, Social Justice, and Belief in one God. For long

excerpts from Sukarno's initial formulation, see George Kahin, *Nationalism and Revolution*, pp. 122-26.

33 For the background of Kartosuwirjo in the Islamic League (psii) and later Masjumi, see C.A.O. van Nieuwenhuijze, *Aspects of Islam in Post-Colonial Indonesia* (The Hague: van Hoeve, 1958), pp. 167-70.

34 See C. van Dijk, *Rebellion under the Banner of Islam: The Darul Islam in Indonesia* (The Hague: Nijhoff, 1981), p. 10; Deliar Noer, *Partai Islam di Pentas Nasional* (Jakarta: Grafiti Pers, 1987), pp. 179-83.

35 Feith, *Decline of Constitutional Democracy*, pp. 212-14. See Harvey, 'Tradition, Islam and Rebellion', pp. 240-53, for an account of Kahar's disaffection with Republican army leaders and his ultimate decision to join with the Darul Islam.

36 Harvey, 'Tradition, Islam and Rebellion', p. 253.

37 Morris, 'Islam and Politics', p. 200.

38 Roem was, however, still a member of the cabinet.

39 See Morris, 'Islam and Politics', pp. 339-48 for the effect of the Masjumi's exclusion on the Aceh revolt.

40 In mid-1955, for example, the governor openly criticized the centre for not providing any money at all to fund capital expenditures in the region 'for construction of roads and bridges, school buildings, hospitals, irrigation, buying ships, and so forth'. *Haluan*, June 13, 1955.

41 Ibid., June 4, 1955.

42 *Haluan*, April 18, 21, 1955.

43 In East Java, the nu received more votes than any other party: 3,370,554, as against its nearest rival, the pni's 2,251,069; the Masjumi came fourth with 1,109,742. In Central Java, the nu ran behind both the pni and pki, receiving 1,772,306, (as against their 3,019,568 and 2,326,108 respectively) but it still gained nearly twice as many votes as the Masjumi (902,387). See Herbert Feith, *The Indonesian Elections of 1955* (Ithaca: Cornell Modern Indonesia Project, 1957), p. 66.

44 Ibid., p. 68. See also *Haluan*, October 14, 1955.

45 The Masjumi obtained only 25.4 percent of its vote in East and Central Java (51.3 percent in Java as a whole) and 48.7 percent of its vote outside Java. See Feith, *Decline of Constitutional Democracy*, p. 437; see also Audrey R. Kahin & George McT. Kahin, *Subversion as Foreign Policy: The Secret Eisenhower and Dulles Debacle in Indonesia* (New York: The New Press, 1995), p. 50.

46 *Haluan*, October 14, 19, 21, 1955.

47 Gerald Williams, 'The Banteng Council', typescript circa 1958, based primarily on his visit to the area and a comprehensive analysis of the Padang newspaper, *Haluan*, for 1956.

48 Interview with a group of former officers of the Banteng Division (Padang), August 9, 1995.

49 Letter from Deputy Chief of Staff of the Armed Forces Col. T.B. Simatupang to Colonels Hidajat, Simbolon, Lt. Cols. Kawilarang and Dahlan Djambek and Major Akil on Sumatra, dated August 10, 1949. I am grateful to former Col. Alwi St. Marajo for giving me a copy of this letter.

50 In his initial discussions with the pdri, Leimena expressed Yogyakarta's confidence that the regular army would obey the ceasefire but its uncertainty regarding the attitude of the *lasjkars* (militias). 'Minutes of meeting between the central government delegation with pdri, tni officers, etc.', July 7, 1949 (Arsip pdri).

51 'Surat Perintah' No. 25/Org. July 11, 1949, signed Kom. Sub. Terr. IX 'Brig' Bant. Lt. Kol. Dahlan Djambek (Arsip pdri). They appointed a Rationalization Commission to prepare and smooth the road to rationalization. It was headed by Major Thalib, and Captain Leon Salim was one of its four members. Husein *et al.*, *Sejarah Perjuangan*, vol. 2, pp. 792-93.

52 Interview with Dahlan Ibrahim (Jakarta), October 19, 1976. Husein *et al.*, *Sejarah Perjuangan Kemerdekaan*, vol. 2, p. 579.

53 Husein *et al.*, *Sejarah Perjuangan*, vol. 2, p. 579.

54 Interview with Abdul Halim (Jakarta), October 15, 1976.

55 Husein *et al.*, *Sejarah Perjuangan*, vol. 2, p. 580. Also interviews with former Banteng officers. After having failed to stop the central government from destroying the autonomy of West Sumatra's Banteng forces, a number of senior officers, including Chief of Staff Abdul Halim and former West Sumatra commander Dahlan Ibrahim, also resigned from the army and returned to civilian life.

56 Rasjid *et al.*, *Sejarah Perjuangan*, vol. 2, p. 492. These battalions were the Kuranji, Pagar Ruyung, Kinantan, Gumarang, Buaya Putih, and Sibinuang.

57 Estimates vary widely: According to a group of former officers, it was reduced from thirty thousand to seven thousand; individual officers state from twenty-three to seven thousand and from twenty to five thousand. Interviews Padang, 1995.

58 For details of the changes in composition of the battalions, see Kementerian Penerangan, *Propinsi Sumatera Tengah*, pp. 593-98; *Sumatera Tengah* No. 113/114 (August 17, 1953), p. 48.

59 Husein *et al.*, *Sejarah Perjuangan*, vol. 2, pp. 581-91; interview with Sjoeib (Jakarta), April 19, 1976. Sjoeib had been active in the early revolution in the Padang area and was put in charge of the battalion in which the irregular forces were regrouped. He was one of the instructors in the first West Sumatra military academy in 1946, and later headed one of the battalions in Husein's eastern sector. Sofyan Ibrahim had been security officer for the West Sumatra command after the second attack. Azwar, *Menyingkapkan tabir*, p. 17.

60 The government had expected trouble in West Kalimantan, because of Sultan Hamid and the continuing presence there of KNIL forces, but in fact there were apparently no problems. The situation was different in West Java. There the soldiers from West Sumatra had no idea who were Darul Islam (DI), and 'there was no way of knowing who were friends and enemies and the DI were protected by the people'. Interview with Abu Nawas, who was chief of staff of the Pagar Ruyung battalion (Padang), August 23, 1995.

61 *Sumatera Tengah*, No. 105, March 25, 1953, p. 3.

62 *Merdeka*, May 16, 20, 1953. The mutiny of the battalion was reported in *Trompet Masjarakat* (May 18, 1953). See Ruth McVey, 'The Post-Revolutionary Transformation of the Indonesian Army', *Indonesia* 11 (April 1971), p. 174.

63 *Merdeka*, July 11, 22, 1953.

64 The Kuranji battalion was in West Java from December 1950 to December 1951, Kementerian Penerangan, *Propinsi Sumatera Tengah*, p. 594.

65 Interview with Ahmad Husein (Jakarta), June 1985.

66 Ahmad Husein's father had been an assistant in the pharmacy of the Dutch military hospital, and in the Muhammadiah had been a close friend of S.J. St. Mangkuto. He became treasurer of the West Sumatra branch of the Masjumi party. Husein was born on April 1, 1925 in Padang, and studied at the Taman Siswa school until the Japanese invasion. He had been a member of the Muslim Boy Scouts' organization, the Hizbul Wathan, during the colonial period, and was in the second group of Giyu gun candidates during the Japanese occupation, serving under Ismael Lengah and reaching the rank of 2nd lieutenant. Interview (Jakarta), April 12, October 18, 1976.

67 These were the conditions described by a delegation headed by Governor Roeslan Moeljohardjo, which Husein took on a tour of the army barracks in Padang, Teluk Bayur, Solok, and Padang Panjang in August 1956.

68 Interview with Ahmad Husein (Jakarta), June 1985. Nasution says there was a meeting on September 21, 1956, attended by 123 people, most of them from Jakarta. The representatives from Central Sumatra were Husein, Capt. Nurmathias (Comm. Batt. 140), 1st Lt. Bustanudin (Staff Reg. 4), Kamarudin Datuk Makhudum (ex-Capt), Sulaeman, (ex-Major ALRI), and 1st Lt. St. Badarudin from Bandung. (A.H. Nasution, *Memenuhi Panggilan Tugas*, vol.4: *Masa Pancaroba Kedua* [Jakarta: Gunung Agung, 1984], p. 57). Djambek had recently returned from London where he had been serving as military attaché in the Indonesian embassy.

69 A Reunion committee was formed at a meeting in Padang on October 11, where it was also decided that Colonel Ismael Lengah, Colonel Dahlan Djambek, and Colonel Simbolon should be advisers to the committee. Nasution, *Memenuhi Panggilan Tugas*, vol. 4, p. 57.

70 Regarding the preparations for the Reunion, see Saafroedin Bahar, 'Peranan Elite Sipil dan Elite Militer dalam Dinamika Integrasi Nasional di Indonesia: Kasus Etnik Minangkabau di Daerah Sumatera Barat, 1945-1984' (PhD. dissertation, Gadjah Mada University, Yogyakarta, 1996), p. 196.

71 *Sumatera Tengah*, 159 (Special Issue, 'Peristiwa 20 Des'.) February 15, 1957, p. 9; Feith, *Decline of Constitutional Democracy*, p. 523.

72 *Sumatera Tengah*, February 15, 1957, p. 9.

73 These included: Husein himself; Major Sjoeib (see above, n. 59) who was now attached to the Army General Staff in Jakarta; Major Anwar Umar, Chief of Staff of Regiment I; Hasan Basri, former commander of Regiment IV (Riau) of the Banteng Division; Capt. Nurmathias, commander of Battalion 140 of Regiment IV; Lt. Sebastian, an officer from Inderagiri, and Col. (retd.) Ismael Lengah, one of the founders of the Banteng division and its commander from 1946 to 1948, before being removed by Hatta just before the Second Dutch attack. (See above, ch. 5.)

74 Kaharuddin Dt. Rangkajo Basa, who had headed the provincial police in the region since the Japanese occupation and was currently chief of police for Central Sumatra (*Harian Penerangan*, January 4, 1957, Nasution, *Memenuhi Panggilan Tugas*, vol. 4, p. 59), and Sutan Suis, chief of police for the city of Padang.

75 A delegation made its way from the province to Jakarta. Officially consisting of Banteng Council members Ali Loeis and Hasan Basri, together with a government official Sidi Bakaruddin (these first two were from Jambi and Riau; Sidi Bakaruddin had been a member of West Sumatra's government throughout the revolution and was Bupati of Tanah Datar in 1949), the delegation had the backing of some of the most illustrious of the division's veterans who had attended the Reunion, including Dahlan Djambek, and two of his former regimental commanders, Dahlan Ibrahim and Abdul Halim. (Halim was now a businessman and Dahlan Ibrahim the IPKI minister of veterans' affairs in the Ali Sastroamidjojo cabinet.) The delegation had intended to meet with the president, vice president, members of the cabinet, and other leaders, but their only official meeting was with Mr. A.G. Pringgodigdo, head of the President's Secretariat, although Prime Minister Ali did receive them at his home. On December 15, council member Sutan Suis expressed regret that the central government had thus far disregarded the delegation's attempts to present the Reunion's demands. See *Sumatera Tengah*, February 15, 1957, p. 10.

76 Ibid., p.6. See also Hasril Chaniago and Khairul Jasmi, *Brigadir Jenderal Polisi Kaharoeddin Datuk Rangkayo Basa* (Jakarta: Sinar Harapan, 1998), pp. 227-28.

Chapter 8

1 At the death of General Sudirman on January 19, 1950, his position of armed forces commander was abolished. In its place, Prime Minister Hatta and Minister of Defence Sultan Hamengkubuwono appointed Simatupang as Chief of Staff of the Armed Forces, Nasution as Army Chief of Staff, Suryadarma as Chief of Staff of the Air Force, and Subijakto as Navy Chief of Staff, with Colonel Hidayat appointed the top-ranking officer within the Ministry of Defence. All of these men were former KNIL officers. See Ulf Sundhaussen, *The Road to Power: Indonesian Military Politics 1945-1967* (Kuala Lumpur: Oxford University Press, 1982), p. 52.

2 Ibid., pp. 63, 65, 68; McVey, 'Post-Revolutionary Transformation', p. 145. The group charged Nasution and his colleagues with being supporters of Western imperialism and too strongly influenced by the Dutch advisory military mission (MMB) still operating in Indonesia. See also Manai Sophiaan, *Apa yang masih teringat* (Jakarta: Yayasan 'Mencerdaskan Kehidupan Bangsa', 1991), p. 317.

3 Feith, *Decline of Constitutional Democracy*, p. 249.

4 The best and most extensive treatment of the October 17 Affair appears in Feith, *Decline of Constitutional Democracy*, pp. 246-73; see also Kahin & Kahin, *Subversion as Foreign Policy*, pp. 48-49; Sundhaussen, *Road to Power*, pp. 65-73; McVey, 'Post-Revolutionary Transformation', pp. 143-50.

5 Sundhaussen, *Road to Power*, pp. 89-92.

6 Nasution, *Tjatatan-tjatatan sekitar Politik Militer*, cited in Feith, *Decline of Constitutional Democracy*, p. 403.

7 Feith, *Decline of Constitutional Democracy*, pp. 487-500.

8 McVey, 'Post-Revolutionary Transformation', p. 153.

9 Simbolon's future position had not been announced; Warouw was to become military attaché in Beijing; Kawilarang was to go to Washington as military attaché, and Lubis was to replace Simbolon in North Sumatra. Lubis' replacement as deputy chief of staff was Nasution stalwart Gatot Subroto.

10 Interview with Nasution (Jakarta), May 7, 1991.

11 McVey, 'Post-Revolutionary Transformation', pp. 171-72; Sundhaussen, *The Road to Power*, p. 64.

12 Interview with Zulkifli Lubis (Jakarta), May 10, 1991. Rasjid, it will be recalled, was the former military governor of West Sumatra, had gone to the foreign office and was now about to be appointed Indonesian ambassador to Italy.

13 For a detailed treatment of these events, see McVey, 'Post Revolutionary Transformation', pp. 165-71.

14 Staf Umum Angkatan Darat (SUAD), *prri*, vol. 1 (Jakarta, n.d.), pp. 70-71. On the discussions among the officers in Bandung, see McVey, 'Post-Revolutionary Transformation', pp. 171-73.

15 Payung Bangun, *Kolonel Maludin Simbolon: Liku-liku Perjuangannya dalam Pembangunan Bangsa* (Jakarta: Sinar Harapan, 1996), pp. 211-15. This volume carries the full text of the December 4 Idea and the joint oath of the North Sumatra officers.

16 Ibid., pp. 216-21, carries the text of Simbolon's declaration of December 22.

17 Ibid., pp. 224-30. The fullest account of this affair can be found in Smail, 'Military Politics of North Sumatra', pp. 140-55; see also Kahin & Kahin, *Subversion as Foreign Policy*, pp. 59-61. The central government made certain that Gintings would dare to act against his commander, by appointing his deputy as his replacement should he not make such a move.

18 Kahin & Kahin, *Subversion as Foreign Policy*, pp. 61-62, 65-66.

19 As noted above, Warouw had then been appointed military attaché in the Indonesian embassy in Beijing.

20 By far the best account of the rebellion in Sulawesi is Barbara Harvey's monograph *Permesta; Half a Rebellion*.

21 According to Husein, Nasution ordered the ship carrying these weapons to go via the Padang port of Teluk Bayur, where Husein was able to take over the arms. 'We had been using Enfield rifles before that, but these were all new Italian weapons, five thousand of them'. Interview with Ahmad Husein (Jakarta), June 1985.

22 *Haluan*, February 2, 1957. There were also reports that the cabinet and ministry of defence had wanted Nasution to postpone the conference. Ibid., February 4, 1957.

23 Ibid., March 27, April 1, 1957.

24 Legge, *Central Authority and Regional Autonomy*, p. 237. Exports from Padang in 1956 were valued at Rp.187,300.000 compared with Rp.2,090,000,000 for North Sumatra and Rp.3,324,000,000 for South Sumatra.

25 Viewed in this context, it was estimated that in the nine months from January to September 1956, Central Sumatra earned Rp.1,137,000,000 in foreign exchange. The taxes collected in the region every month amounted to Rp.170,000,000 of which only Rp.20,000,000 were retained locally, while the rest went to the central government, which returned only

Rp.40,000,000 to the region to maintain local government agencies. SUAD, *prri*, p. 59. In other words, the centre received Rp.110,000,000 of the taxes and Central Sumatra Rp.60,000,000.

26 Interview with Yunidar Chatib Suleiman (West Jakarta), August 30, 1995.

27 *Haluan*, July 11, 1957. Sukarno actually came to West Sumatra in June 1948, travelling on a plane of the UN Committee of Good Offices (GOC).

28 The money came from a subsidy given by the central government to the region.

29 *Haluan*, February 25, March 3, May 29, July 11, 1957. Interviews in Padang with Azmi, February 12, 1991; Syofyan Asnawi, February 14, 1991; Anwar Z.A., February 16, 1991; Mansoer Sani, August 20, 1995.

30 These members were, respectively, Syekh Ibrahim Musa Parabek, one of West Sumatra's outstanding traditionalist *ulama* (for a biography, see *Haluan Minggu*, June 16, 1957); H. Darwis Taram Dt. Tumenggung, a member of the Masjumi party who had served the Republic as a *bupati* in West Sumatra from the early days of the revolution; Dt. Simarajo, one of the traditional elders of Minangkabau, who was founder of the *adat* party in West Sumatra (MTKAAM) and had headed it since its establishment in 1938; Ali Luis, *bupati* and deputy governor of Central Sumatra; H. Abd. Manaf, *bupati* of Kabupaten Merangin, Jambi, and Saidina Ali, head of the office of Social Welfare in Kabupaten Kampar, Riau.

31 Soeleiman, head of the Bureau for National Reconstruction (BRN), was born in Central Java and educated in Yogyakarta. He had been one of the participants in the Zeven Provincien mutiny, and then later became a teacher in the Taman Siswa schools. He was transferred to the Taman Siswa school in Padang in 1936, and had lived in West Sumatra ever since, teaching in the INS in Kayutanam, serving in the Republic's Navy, and being a founder of the IPKI party in West Sumatra. For a biography, see *Haluan Minggu*, January 27, 1957.

32 Among them, Mr. Nazaruddin, a lawyer and teacher at Pancasila University in Padang who was active in economic development, and Egor Hakim, also a lawyer, who was in charge of coordinating financial affairs. Interview with Ahmad Husein (Jakarta), May 9, 1991; SUAD, *prri*, p. 42.

33 *Haluan*, January 3, March 13, December 19, 1957.

34 Interview with Syofyan Asnawi (Padang), February 14, 1991.

35 *Haluan*, January 2, 1957; *Sumatera Tengah* 159, p. 13. For Ismael Lengah's statement regarding his other meetings with the president, and prime minister, see SUAD, *prri*, p. 42.

36 Nursuhud, *Menjingkap Tabir 'Dewan Banteng'* (Jakarta: Jajasan Pembaruan, 1958), p. 22. The pamphlet was dated Bukittinggi, December 20, 1957. It is interesting that in this pamphlet it is the Socialist Party (PSI) that is singled out as being the *eminence grise* of the Dewan Banteng; the writer cites various instances of the Communist party holding out a hand of friendship to members of the Masjumi.

37 *Haluan*, January 16, 1957. Those arrested were Sobsi members Djanizar, Djaman, and Nur Rauf, and Zarkawi Latif and Sjahruddin Djalal from Perbum Pekanbaru. Ibid., January 12, 1957.

38 Ibid., January 16, 22, 26, 1957.

39 See ibid., February 5, 15, 1957.

40 Nursuhud, *Menjingkap Tabir*, pp. 29-30. Nursuhud deplores the passivity of the party members and their unwillingness to recognize the fascist nature of the Council. The PKI head from Sawahlunto Sijunjung, for example, issued a statement of support for the Banteng Council (*Haluan*, March 11, 1957), and a PKI branch leader in Suliki left the party to join supporters of the Council (ibid., November 19, 1957).

41 Interviews with Azmi, and Imran Manan (Padang), February 12, 1991.

42 *Haluan*, January 9, 10, 19, 1957.

43 Disagreement with the formation of three provinces was voiced by the head of the Partai Islam Indonesia, H.A. Darwis Djambek, who stated that it would split the Minangkabau people and also questioned why it should be applied only in the civilian and not in the military field. *Haluan*, July 18, 1957.

44 Feith, *Decline of Constitutional Democracy*, p. 528.

45 *Haluan*, August 9, 1957; Legge, *Cultural Authority and Regional Autonomy*, p. 67.

46 *Haluan*, October 15, 1957.

47 Legge, *Cultural Authority and Regional Autonomy*, p. 77.

48 *Haluan*, January 11, 16, 1957.

49 Kahin & Kahin, *Subversion as Foreign Policy*, pp. 66-67.

50 *Haluan*, March 15, 1957.

51 Ibid., February 21, 1957.

52 This 'Provisional Constitution of the Republic of Indonesia' was ratified when the Federal Indonesian State (RIS or RUSI) was dissolved and the unitary Republic of Indonesia established on August 17, 1950. A Constitutional Assembly was still discussing a permanent constitution. See Feith, *Decline of Constitutional Democracy*, pp. 92-99. For a definitive treatment of the subject, see A.K. Pringgodigdo, *The Office of President in Indonesia as Defined in the Three Constitutions in Theory and Practice* (Ithaca: Cornell Modern Indonesia Project, 1957).

53 *Haluan*, March 20, 1957.

54 Ibid., April 9, 1957; Kahin & Kahin, *Subversion as Foreign Policy*, p. 67.

55 *Haluan*, April 6, April 20, 1957. These rumours had centred on Hatta's role in depositing government gold reserves in a bank in Bukittinggi during the revolution. There were also rumours during March 1957 that there would be an attempt to kidnap Hatta (ibid., March 21, 1957).

56 Ibid., April 23, 1957.

57 See Legge, *Central Authority and Regional Autonomy*, pp. 68, 236; Feith, *Decline of Constitutional Democracy*, pp. 534, 552. Under the decentralization legislation, the number of Indonesia's provinces was increased from nine to fifteen; district heads were to be elected by local councils rather than appointed from Jakarta, and municipalities were re-established in Central Sumatra.

58 *Haluan*, April 25, 1957.

59 Ibid., April 27, May 3, 1957.

60 Ibid., April 25, 1957.

61 The long drawn-out negotiations on the issue appears in ibid., June 18, 20, 24, 26, 27, July 9, 10, 13, 20, 1957.

62 Ibid., June 25, 1957.

63 *Waspada*, May 29, 1957.

64 *Haluan*, July 11, 1957.

65 *Haluan* May 11, 13, June 6, 1957. Several officers from West Java were arrested in Bandung and Jakarta in connection with a grenade attack on Communist headquarters.

66 Ibid., August 6, 21, 1957.

67 Ibid., May 23, 1957; *Waspada*, May 20, 1957; 'Dr. Sumitro Flees to Central Sumatra rather than face interrogation of Alleged Corruption', Foreign Service Despatch, Ambassy, Jakarta, June 14, 1957 (756D.00-1457) (National Archives).

68 For full examination of contacts, particularly of Simbolon and Sumitro with American agencies, see Kahin & Kahin, *Subversion as Foreign Policy*, pp. 102-6. At the time John Foster Dulles was Secretary of State, and his brother Allen Dulles headed the CIA.

69 *Haluan*, August 23, 1957. The conference was promoted by various factions including Roeslan Abdulgani and Army Staff and Command School officers. Ibid., August 23, 27, 1957.

70 Ibid., September 3, 1957. One other proposal being aired at the time was that any real National Conference should embrace all four major contending parties in Indonesia, namely: (1) Sukarno, Nasution, and the current national civilian and military leadership; (2) Lubis, Simbolon, Husein, and the other dissident military officers; (3) Hatta and other moderate civilian groups in Jakarta; and (4) Kartosuwirjo, Daud Beureu' eh, and Kahar Muzakkar, representing the rebel forces of the Darul Islam. Ibid., September 4, 1957.

71 Cable, Jakarta to Secretary of State 649, September 7, 1957 (756D.00(W)/9-757) (National Archives).

72 Attending this conference, in addition to Nasution, were Col. Gintings from Military Territory (TT)1, Kosasih from TTIII, Suhartomo from TTIV, Sarbini from TTV (West, Central, and East Java), and Kusno Utomo from TTVI (Kalimantan). Cable, Djakarta to Secretary of State, No. 575, August 31, 1957, 756D.oo(W)/8-3157.

73 *Haluan*, September 5, 1957. On Djambek's flight from Jakarta to West Sumatra and its causes, see below.

74 *Haluan*, August 30, 1957.

75 This conference held from September 8-11 was instrumental in drawing the lines more starkly between Islamic and Communist forces. See below.

76 See Penerangan Angkatan Darat [PAD], *Kini Tabir dapat Dibuka* (Jakarta: Kementerian Penerangan R.I., 1958), p. 30 and Daniel S. Lev, *Transition to Guided Democracy: Indonesian Politics 1957-1959* (Ithaca: Cornell Modern Indonesia Project, 1966), pp. 36-37. For the full text of the Palembang Charter see also Nasution, *Memenuhi Panggilan Tugas*, vol. 4, Appendix 2, pp. 446-49, and Sumitro 'Searchlight on Indonesia' (typescript, c. February 1959), p. 6.

77 *Mutiara* 832 (30th year), October 1-7, 1996.

78 I am grateful to Rudolf Mrazek for noting this point.

79 Cable: Djakarta to Secretary of State, #761, September 19, 1957, 7567D.oo/9-1957 (National Archives).

80 Cable from Whitney, Office of the Special Assistant Intelligence London to Secretary of State, Roger Channel, No. 2222, October 2, 1957. This accords with Sumitro's account, where he states that their general strategy 'should be based on the regions' functioning as a spearhead in a national front, adopting the objectives as formulated in the Palembang Charter as its political platform'. Sumitro, 'Searchlight on Indonesia', pp. 8-9.

81 For details on these contacts, see Kahin & Kahin, *Subversion as Foreign Policy*, pp.102, 105, 120-21.

82 *Haluan*, September 13, 14, 1957.

83 Ibid., September 17, 1957.

84 PAD, *Kini Tabir Dapat Dibuka*, p. 47. The publication incorporates documents seized from Lubis' house in Jakarta in January 1958. Lubis confirmed in an interview that the documents are authentic. Interview with Zulkifli Lubis (Jakarta), May 10, 1991.

85 Ambassador Allison commented that the 'meeting of dissident leaders [in] Palembang probably contributed [to the] unanimity [of] their position at national conference Djakarta which is said to have impressed Sukarno'. Djakarta to Sec. of State #761, September 19, 1957.

86 *Haluan*, September 10, 11, 1957. Representing West Sumatra, in addition to Husein, were West Sumatra Resident, Mr. Abu Bakar Djaar, and Moh. Sjafei. They were joined in Jakarta by General Simatupang, whom they had chosen to represent their area, and the Banteng Council's Commissioner in Jakarta, Ramawi Izhar. (*Haluan*, September 10, 1957.)

87 Ibid., September 18, 1957. The full text of Husein's speech can be found in R.Z. Leirissa, *prri Permesta: Strategi Membangun Indonesia tanpa Komunis*, 3rd ed. (Jakarta: Grafiti, 1997), pp. 269-81. The translated sentences appear on pp. 276 and 278.

88 *Haluan*, September 19, 1957. This extended trip to China had long been planned and Hatta had postponed his departure in order to participate in the MUNAS. The trip and the speeches Hatta made in China must have reinforced the colonels' alienation from him.

89 The committee was headed by President Sukarno and the other members were former Vice-President Hatta, Prime Minister Djuanda, Third Deputy Prime Minister Dr. Leimena, former minister of defence, Sultan Hamengku Buwono IX, Minister of Health, Dr. Azis Saleh, and Chief of Staff Nasution.

90 Interview with Ahmad Husein (Jakarta), May 9, 1991.

91 *Haluan*, September 19, 1957.

92 Sumitro, 'Searchlight on Indonesia', section 2, 'History of the Daerah Movement', pp. 7-8.

93 PAD, *Kini Tabir Dapat Dibuka*, pp. 45-47.

94 Sumitro, 'Searchlight on Indonesia,' section 2, p. 8.

95 George Kahin's interview with Hamengku Buwono IX (Jakarta), February 25, 1959. The Sultan explained that the face-saving compromise called for dropping all political charges against the dissident colonels and then going through the motions of an investigation of criminal charges which would be found to be without basis and dismissed.

96 *Haluan*, September 22, 1957.

97 Ibid., September 25, 1957.

98 The quotations come from a letter from Hatta to Col. Dahlan Djambek of November 2, 1957. Hatta's younger sister was married to Djambek's elder brother, M. Zein Djambek. See Deliar Noer, *Mohammad Hatta: Biografi Politik* (Jakarta: LP3ES, 1990), pp. 521-23.

99 *Haluan*, October 14, 1957.

100 Ibid., October 25, 1957.

101 Ibid., November 25, 1957.

102 Mansoer Sani succeeded a civilian *bupati*, Bagindo Darwis, and was the only military *bupati* in all of West Sumatra. Interviews with Mansoer Sani (Padang), August 20, 1995, March 21, 1999. See also *Haluan*, September 5, 1957, which reproduces an article that had appeared in a Medan newspaper criticizing the Communist role in the 1927 rebellion.

103 C.K.H.R. Surjo Sediono, *Peristiwa Tjikini* (Jakarta: Soeroengan, 1958), pp. 178-79.

104 *Haluan*, February 2, 3, 1957. He had also accompanied Nasution on some of his trips to Sulawesi to meet with the Permesta leaders.

105 At the Reunion meetings, Dahlan Djambek had clearly been trying to act as conciliator, urging his former colleagues against taking too drastic steps, and recommending that the discussion should take into account pressing national problems and not be localistic. He stressed that unity among the leaders of the Banteng Division had been one of its strengths and that the Division's collapse had come from outside, because of a change of organization of the army, not from arguments among the local commanders. He had suggested that the Reunion send a delegation to Jakarta to meet with the central government and West Sumatran members of Parliament to present their views, a course which, as we have seen, they followed without success.

106 *Haluan*, August 25, 1957.

107 Ibid., August 18, 1957. See below. This organization had launched a similar attack against Communist Party headquarters a few weeks earlier.

108 Ibid., September 2, 5, 1957.

109 Interviews with Azmi (Padang), February 12, 1991; Sjamsul Bahar (Bukittinggi), May 3, 1991; Ahmad Husein (Jakarta), May 9, 1991.

110 *Haluan*, October 8, 1957. Interviews with Ibu Naimah Jambek and former associates of Dahlan Djambek (Bukittinggi), March 27, 29, 1999.

111 *Haluan*, October 25, 1957.

112 Ibid., November 1, 1957.

113 Interview with Azmi (Padang), February 12, 1991.

114 The vote was 40 in favour, 25 against, with 11 abstentions, including the United States. Kahin & Kahin, *Subversion as Foreign Policy*, pp. 110-11.

115 According to testimony at the trial of the accused, the organization was also known as the Religious Fighters against Communism (Pejuang Agama anti-Komunis) or the Lubis Movement (Gerakan Lubis). Sediono, *Peristiwa Tjikini*, p. 40, and *passim*.

116 Ibid., p. 113.

117 The accused were Jusuf Ismail from Bima, Sa'adon bin Mohamad from South Sulawesi, Tasrif bin Hoesain from Bima, and Mohamad Tasim bin Abubakar from Dompo, Sumbawa. The first three were sentenced to death on August 13, 1958, but were not executed until May 28, 1960, when they died before a firing squad. These were reportedly the first executions to be carried out in Indonesia after the transfer of sovereignty. Department of State telegram 3408: Jakarta to Sec. of State, May 31, 1960.

118 Sediono, *Peristiwa Tjikini*, p. 89. One of them, Tasrif bin Hoesain, went so far as to repeat

the regions' demand for establishment of a pre-senate to represent the regions. Ibid., pp. 101, 108.

119 Ibid., p. 114.

120 In an interview, Lubis stated that when Saleh Ibrahim came to him shortly before the action, Lubis told him he was opposed to an assassination attempt and counselled him to urge the boys to 'go to the mosque to pray'. Interview with Zulkifli Lubis (Jakarta), February 24, 1971.

121 Wahab bin Arsjad bin Wahab Pena, a major witness at the trial, stated that he was the first to see Sukarno enter the school and informed his friends that the president was there. According to him, Saleh Ibrahim 'answered that it was not necessary to carry out the grenade attack against the President because "there was a new development" and Z. Loebis had not yet ordered another attack after the two previous failures to ambush the president'. Jusuf Ismail had disagreed, and later the witness heard the grenade explosions and was informed that the attack had been carried out. Sediono, *Peristiwa Tjikini*, p. 131.

122 Interview with Zulkifli Lubis, February 24, 1971; Zulkifli Lubis, 'Komandan Intelijen Pertama Indonesia', *Tempo*, July 29, 1989, pp. 51-65.

123 SUAD, *prri*, p. 186.

124 *Haluan*, January 16, 18. 1958.

125 In a letter to me, dated August 16, 1988, Simbolon denied that the issue was ever discussed at Sungai Dareh. He stated: 'the idea of a separatist state had never entered the mind of those present. The struggle had been designed since the very beginning to be nation wide, embracing the whole territory of Indonesia'. Statements by Barlian in an earlier interview confirmed this. He stated that at Sungai Dareh 'the others' not including himself, 'wanted a counter government but not a separate state'. Interview (Jakarta), February 23, 1971.

126 *Waspada*, February 4, 1958.

127 PAD, *Kini Tabir Dapat Dibuka*, *passim*. Despite this, the newspaper reports on the documents allege that Lubis was advocating a Sumatra State, or a New RI government. *Haluan*, January 21, 23, 29, 1958; *Waspada*, February 4, 1958.

128 Papers of John Foster Dulles, Harvey Mudd Library, Princeton University, Princeton, N.J. For further details and a full discussion of Dulles' attitude toward the split up of Indonesia, see Kahin, & Kahin, *Subversion as Foreign Policy*, pp. 75-79.

129 Ibid., pp. 83-89.

130 Record of Howard P. Jones, 'Secretary State/British Ambassador Discussion of What Actions to Take re. Indo and PRRI'. Political Scene File, Box 17, Hoover Library.

131 'Memorandum of Conversation with the President', April 15, 1958.

132 Sumitro's full description of these, and his subsequent activities up to April 1958, in organizing foreign aid for the rebels, appear in 'Memorandum: Usaha/pekerdjaan diluar negeri' dari S.D. [Sumitro Djodjohadikusumo], undated, but apparently written in about April/May 1958. (PRRI Document #116. This is a collection of internal correspondence and memoranda among rebels in Sumatra and their representatives abroad. These documents are lodged in the ISEAS library in Singapore and will be referred to by the number they are assigned in this collection.) See also Leirissa, *prri Permesta*, p. 205. According to Leirissa, Sumual was accompanied by Arie Supit and J.M.J. Pantouw, and Pantouw continued on to the United States.

133 In Tokyo Warouw reported Sumual's statement that if their demands are not met, 'those attending the secret meeting are ready to proclaim the establishment of a new Central Government', *Haluan*, February 5, 1958. Meanwhile, in Padang, Simbolon told *Time* correspondent James Bell that the meeting at Sungai Dareh had decided to form a competing government headed by Sjafruddin and proclaim an ultimatum demanding dissolution of the Djuanda government and formation of a national anti-Communist government under Moh. Hatta. If this demand was not met, the emergency government would become a competing government. Ibid., February 5, 1958.

134 A full discussion of American policy toward the regional dissidents, the encouragement

and support the United States provided them after October 1957, and the pressures it exerted to persuade the dissidents to break with Jakarta appear in Kahin & Kahin, *Subversion as Foreign Policy*. See especially pp. 120-27, 132-34.

135 *Haluan*, February 8, 1958.

136 Sumitro, 'Indonesia's National Front', typescript, with notation: 'this summary was made from the documentation of Dr. Sumitro and approved by him for information purposes. Geneva, February 2, 1958'. Emphasis in original. There is no report in *Haluan* of Simbolon's alleged broadcast on January 30.

137 *Haluan*, February 5, 1958.

138 Ibid., February 6, 1958.

139 Ibid., January 29, February 2, 1958; *Waspada*, February 3, 1958.

140 On Kaharuddin's ambiguous relationship with the Dewan Banteng from the time of its formation, see Chaniago & Jasmi, *Brigadir Jenderal Polisi Kaharoeddin*, pp. 231-36.

141 *Waspada*, February 7, 1958. He has always maintained this position, stating in an interview in 1985: 'From the beginning to the end not a single step did we take to separate with the other islands. We had Javanese (Sumitro, Suleiman and others) and people from all the other islands to put it all together'. Interview (Jakarta), June 1985.

142 *Haluan*, February 8, 9, 1958.

143 *Waspada*, February 11, 1958. Natsir and Sjafruddin were also present at the conference but neither spoke.

144 'Piagam Perdjuangan' 'Menjelamatkan Negara', signed by Lt. Col. Ahmad Hussein, Padang, February 10, 1958 (typescript). See also *Waspada*, February 12, 1958.

145 Ibid., February 13, 1958.

Chapter 9

1 Dahlan Djambek only held the post of internal minister for a few weeks, after which it was taken over by Mr. Assaat, who by then had also left Jakarta to join with the PRRI. Ajip Rosidi, *Sjafruddin Prawiranegara: Lebih Takut kepada Allah SWT* (Jakarta: Inti Idayu Press, 1986), p. 212.

2 Other cabinet members announced at this time were Saladin Sarumpait as minister of agriculture and of labour; Lt. Col. Muchtar Lintang as minister of religion; and Abdul Gani Usman as social minister. It is noteworthy that neither Masjumi head Mohd. Natsir nor Zulkifli Lubis held posts in the government.

3 Dua Tahun Kabinet Karya; *Waspada*, February 17, 1958.

4 Kahin & Kahin, *Subversion as Foreign Policy*, p. 145; Makmum Salim, *Sedjarah Operasi2 Gabungan terhadap prri-Permesta* (Jakarta: Pusat Sedjarah ABRI, 1971), pp. 17-18.

5 Air force planes also launched bombing raids against Manado.

6 Interview with Barlian, February 23, 1971. Barlian, however, refused Nasution's order that he should arrest his deputy Nawawi, and withdrew to Lahat where he remained inactive until he was dismissed and replaced by his chief of staff, Sohar.

7 Interview (Jakarta), Saafroedin Bahar, May 3, 1991. Husein, however, contended that 'at the time of the ultimatum all the members of the Dewan Banteng were one. The reasons Kaharuddin and Nurmathias turned against us were that they had expected Hatta and Sjahrir to back the movement'. Interview (Jakarta), Ahmad Husein, May 9, 1991. Kaharuddin himself wrote that his refusal to join the PRRI was influenced by information from Rasuna Said in Jakarta that Hatta disagreed with its formation. Chaniago and Jasmi, *Brigadir Jenderal Polisi Kaharoeddin*, p. 241.

8 Ibid., pp. 244-46. The new prime minister of the Revolutionary Government, Mr. Sjafruddin Prawiranegara, believed that personal feelings had also influenced Nurmathias. He wrote shortly afterwards that Nurmathias 'had objections to several members of the

Dewan Banteng, in particular Major Sofjan Ibrahim, head of the Civil Staff, who practically replaced Gov. Roeslan Moeljohardjo earlier. According to Noermathias this man was incapable and corrupt. How far he is corrupt I am not able to say, but as an officer, he has certainly issued several orders that have only increased feelings of weakness and panic. But he is loyal to the PRRI'. Letter from Mr. Sjafroeddin Prawiranegara to E. Pohan in Singapore, May 18, 1958. (PRRI documents #16). Hostility between the two, however, may well have stemmed from the Situjuh Batur incident during the revolution. Interviews with Buchari Tamam (Jakarta), May 6, 1991; Azwar (Padang), August 22, 1995.

9 Nasution, *Memenuhi Panggilan Tugas, 4,* pp. 214-15, quoting an interview Hatta gave on February 1, 1963. 'last but no least' is given in English.

10 George Kahin, interviews with Hatta (Jakarta), December 12, 1958, January 8, 1959.

11 Hatta's interview of February 1, 1963, in Nasution, *Memenuhi Panggilan Tugas, 4,* p. 215.

12 Mochtar Lubis, *Hati Nurani Melawan Kezaliman: Surat-Surat Bung Hatta Kepada Presiden Soekarno 1957-1965* (Jakarta: Sinar Harapan, 1986), pp. 50-52.

13 Noer, *Mohammad Hatta,* p. 535.

14 Interviews with Djoeir Moehamad (Jakarta), January 14, 1991, July 24, 1995.

15 Interviews with Anwar ZA (Guguk, Payakumbuh), February 16, 1991; Zulkifli Lubis (Jakarta), May 10, 1991. Djoeir Moehamad, *Memoar Seorang Sosialis* (Jakarta: Obor, 1997).

16 For example, Abu Nawas, who was serving with Army Information in Jakarta, had fled in October 1957 because he had heard he was going to be arrested. According to him, many others, including Dahlan, Col. Sjoeib, deputy commander of the Banteng Division, and Nusirwan did so for the same reason. Interview (Padang), August 23, 1995. Among those returning from Bandung in the early months of the PRRI were Major Sofinar Biran, who became a regimental commander, Major Harlan Darwin, and Major Badar Gafar. Interview (Padang), February 20, 1991. Also, interview with a returnee from Yogyakarta (Padang), February 14, 1991.

17 *Haluan,* January 23, 1958.

18 And he was supported by a much more highly educated staff, many of whom had recently received specialized military training in the United States.

19 Simbolon, for example, asserted to a British journalist who was with the rebels in March and April, 1958, that he would have followed a very different strategy after the government landing at Pekanbaru. James Mossman, *Rebels in Paradise: Indonesia's Civil War* (London: Cape, 1961), p. 112.

20 Initially, Rukmito led operations in East Sumatra, and once those were completed Nasution appointed him as commander of operations against Permesta. George Kahin interview with Rukmito (Jakarta), May 27, 1971.

21 It was hoped that if they set the oil fields alight and took the American personnel there prisoner, the American 7th Fleet, waiting in the waters off Riau, would have an excuse to intervene. See Sjoeib, 'Era Exsperimen Politik dari Presiden Sukarno 1956-1966' in '50 Tahun Hubungan Indonesia-Amerika Serikat' (Jurusan Sejarah Fakultas Sastra, Universitas Indonesia, 1998), pp. 24-25. See also Kahin & Kahin, *Subversion as Foreign Policy,* n. 46, p. 282.

22 Nasution, *Memenuhi Panggilan Tugas* 4: 223-28; Salim, *Sedjarah Operasi2,* p. 21-25. See also Mossman, *Rebels in Paradise,* pp. 109-10.

23 'Pidato dari Komandan Operasi Sabang Merauke, Henry Siregar, berkenaan dengan peringatan ulang tahun pertama Operasi Sabang Merauke, tgl 15 Maret 1959' (PRRI doc. #14).

24 Sjafruddin's letter of May 18, 1958 (PRRI doc. #16). Presumably by 'passive' (*pasif*) he means that the army and police had not been acting aggressively in response to the government's invasion.

25 Interviews, Sophiaan Mochtar (Padang), February 13, 1991; Jalal Ibrahim (Lintau), February 3, 1991; Imran Manan (Padang), August 10, 1995.

26 On American moves toward recognition of the rebels and the discussions over giving fur-

ther support to the Padang forces, see Kahin & Kahin, *Subversion as Foreign Policy*, pp. 160-63, 166.

27 For the full listing of government forces, see Kodam III/17 Agustus, *Sedjarah Kodam III/17 Agustus*, p. 161.

28 Ibid., p. 162.

29 For an account by one of the paratroopers leading the attack, see Julius Poer, *Benny Moerdani: Profil Prajurit Negarawan* (Jakarta: Yayasan Kejuangan Panglima Besar Sudirman, 1993), pp. 158-62. See also Nasution, *Memenuhi Panggilan Tugas* 4: 241-43; Salim, *Sedjarah Operasi2*, pp. 33-40. For the account of an English journalist who witnessed the government's advance on Padang and met with Yani, see Mossman, *Rebels in Paradise*, pp. 149-59.

30 See USARMA to Secretary of State No. cx 108, 120545 z, April 13, 1958, which quotes a Jakarta intelligence officer, Lt. Col. Sukardjo's erroneous report that both Johan and Iskandar had revolted against Husein.

31 Kodam III/17/Agustus, *Sedjarah Kodam III/17 Agustus*, p. 164. Yani reportedly sent a delegation to meet with the defecting officers, who had been hiding out for past two months in Padang Sago, and accompany them back to Padang. Chaniago & Jasmi, *Brigadir Jenderal Polisi Kaharoeddin*, pp. 256-57.

32 Interview with Djamaris Yoenoes (Padang), March 19, 1999. At the time Sjafruddin wrote that Nurmathias 'is under house arrest because he is unwilling to be sent to Pematang Siantar to lead Sukarno's forces there'. Sjafruddin's letter of May 18, 1958.

33 Bainal's refusal to join the PRRI was apparently based on a personal grievance against Husein, stemming back to the end of the revolution when Husein refused to assign him to the kind of position he felt his service deserved. Interview with Djamaris Yoenoes (Padang), March 19, 1999. See also Kodam III/17 Agustus, *Sedjarah Kodam III/17 Agustus*, p. 165. This military history lists a number of other defectors.

34 Johan described his decisions as follows: 'We were then faced with a difficult problem; and rather than being concerned with the national issues it became for us an issue of loyalty to one's comrades merely, to the people we had fought with since 1945'. Interview with Colonel Johan (Bandung), February 26, 1994.

35 Interview with Colonel Johan (Bandung), February 26, 1994; Ahmad Husein (Jakarta), May 9, 1991; Sjafruddin letter, May 18, 1958.

36 In his letter to Mr Pohan in Singapore a month later, Sjafruddin was much less critical of the rebels' defence, speaking of 'the tremendous resistance our forces gave against the aggressors. We were only compelled to withdraw, because we could not effectively protect ourselves against the air attacks, which were very accurate in bombing their targets'. He accused the government of using Czech pilots, and gave particular praise to the rebel volunteers: 'The volunteers, such as the student army, the highschool corps and the new and young units in general were not so influenced by feelings of panic and despair. The enthusiasm for resisting and fighting is still good. And they are actually the ones who every time they had the opportunity inflicted many losses and casualties on Sukarno's army'. Letter of May 18, 1958 (PRRI doc. #16). It was, of course, in the rebels' interest to present as good a face as possible to their supporters abroad.

37 Mossman, *Rebels in Paradise*, pp. 165-66.

38 Ibid., p. 172.

39 Sjafruddin letter of May 18, 1958. Benny Moerdani was heading the RPKAD forces which ambushed the Sjafruddin group at Alahan Panjang, and according to his recollections they killed about twenty of the rebels. Poer, *Benny Moerdani*, p. 164.

40 During 1958 the lines between the 'international oriented Communists' of the PKI and the 'nationalist Communists' of the Murba became blurred in the eyes of the PRRI leaders, and all were targeted for arrest or detention.

41 George Kahin interview with Sultan of Yogyakarta, Hamengku Buwono IX, January 13, 1959; see also Nasution, *Memenuhi Panggilan Tugas 4*, p. 182.

42 Interviews with Abu Nawas (Padang), August 23, 1995; Dt. Ahman (Kamang), February 6, 1991.

43 Visit to Situjuh, June 17, 1985 and discussions with residents there; interviews with Zulki-fli Lubis (Jakarta), May 10, 1991; Anwar za (Guguk, Payakumbuh), February 16, 1991. There was at least one other jail where Communists were held, at Suliki, but it is unclear what happened to the prisoners there. Saafroedin Bahar cites reports of other massacres, notably at Bancah, Payakumbuh on May 23 where forty-seven Communist youths were killed. Bahar, 'Peranan Elite Sipil dan Elite Militer,' p. 212. The non-Communist prisoners held in Muara Labuh were all released by the rebels before the government forces arrived. Djoeir Moe-hamad recalls that their release was ordered by Zulkifli Lubis, Burhanuddin, and Sjafruddin Prawiranegara. Moehamad, *Memoar Seorang Sosialis*, pp. 281-82; interview with Djoeir Moe-hamad (Jakarta), January 14, 1991.

44 At the same time, however, they arrested a number of Socialist Party (psi) leaders, appar-ently on the advice of local Communists who targeted them as supporters of the prri. These psi leaders were never heard from again, and their colleagues presumed that they had been killed. Among those arrested and presumably killed were A. Murad Saad, who had been one of the prisoners at Kota Cane in 1942, Bahar Dt. Bandaro Kuning, Bustami, and Ali Amran, a middle-school teacher. Interviews with Nukme Zein St. Mangkuto and Leon Salim (Paya-kumbuh), September 2, 1995. This was confirmed on March 4, 1999 by A. Murad Saad's niece, Eli Sudarman Khatib.

45 Interview with Mansoer Sani (Padang), August 20, 1995; Salim, *Sedjarah Operasi2*, pp. 52-54.

46 Ibid., p. 52. The opr officially replaced the People's Security Organization (Organisasi Keamanan Rakyat, okr) on September 19, 1959. Sejarah Kodam iii /17 Agustus, *Sedjarah Kodam III/17 Agustus*, p. 167.

47 Ibid., p. 310.

48 Their total number was actually 6,341. Group A (numbering 1,665) was assigned specifi-cally to security and Group B (4,676), in addition to security tasks, were also supposed to help with development. Ibid., pp. 161-62. According to Saafroedin Bahar, Pranoto, who had suc-ceeded Yani as territorial commander diverged from the central command's orders of July 1958 when he set up the okr. These orders had stated that the okr in any region should not exceed one company, i.e. 150 men and should not be influenced by any single social group. Interview, Jakarta, February 21, 1999; Bahar, 'Peranan Elite Sipil dan Elite Militer', p. 226.

49 Interview with Mohammad Natsir (Jakarta), January 23, 1971.

50 Letter from Agus Ramedhan to prri representatives, December 2, 1958 Paris (prri doc. #38) and Ramedhan to prri European Representatives, December 7, 1958 (prri doc. #2).

51 Letter from Rasjid to Sjafruddin, Geneva, November 20, 1958 (prri doc. #40).

52 Speech by Sjafruddin over the Radio prri, February 15, 1959 (prri doc. #13).

53 Letter from Geneva to Sdr. tkl [Tahir Karim Lubis] in Singapore, December 12, 1958 (prri doc. #86). The writer of this letter (code-named 183) raises the possibility of the new state 'later joining with Malaya if it could be agreed'. Mentioning the danger to newly inde-pendent Malaya of the large Chinese population of Singapore, the writer states: 'We see the only way to defend the later position of Malaya would be for it to join with Sumatra or the Fed-eral Indonesian State. If your discussion succeeds with Tengku Abdulrahman, then higher level discussions will need to be held, so it will be necessary to try as fast as possible to have Sdr. M. Natsir and/or Mr. Assaat come to Malaya'. As this could be difficult to arrange, he proposes as an interim measure a meeting between Tengku Abdul Rahman and Mr. Rasjid. Ibid.

54 'United Republic of Indonesia' was the translation favoured by Sjafruddin. Interview (Jakarta), February 21, 1971. Rasjid, as the rpi's deputy minister of foreign affairs, said that the new government would be known as the 'Federal Republic of Indonesia', and this was how it was usually rendered in English. Copy of draft note from Mr. Rasjid enclosed in Foreign

Service Despatch #208 from the U.S. Resident Delegation and Consulate General, Geneva, March 15, 1960.

55 'Undang-Undang Dasar Republik Persatuan Indonesia'(typescript, n.d.), Paragraph 179, p. 62. The RPI constitution consists of 113 typewritten pages, with a further forty-one pages of appendices made up of proclamation documents. The date of the document is February 8, 1960.

56 Letter from M. Natsir to Chief of Staff of the Army, from Padangsidempuan, December 22, 1961, p. 7. (typescript in my possession.) Sjafruddin stated that 'It was difficult to get concurrence of all groups with regard to this constitution, but negotiations took place with Aceh and Minahassa by cable and radio'. Interview (Jakarta), February 21, 1971. Also interviews with Dt. Ahmad (Kamang), February 6, 1991; Anwar AZ (Guguk, Payakumbuh), February 14, 1991.

57 Bangun, *Kolonel Maludin Simbolon*, p. 310. Apparently Husein initially went along with establishment of the RPI, but was bitterly opposed by Major Johan. See Salim, *Sedjarah Operasi2*, p. 54. In Sulawesi, Sumual reluctantly went along. For his and other Permesta reactions to formation of the RPI, see Harvey, *Permesta*, pp. 128-29.

58 Interview with Sjafruddin (Jakarta), February 21, 1971.

59 For further details, see Lev, *Transition to Guided Democracy*, pp. 235-57; and George McT. Kahin, 'Indonesia', in *Major Governments of Asia*, ed. Kahin, esp. pp. 662-65.

60 This story appeared in the Jakarta daily *Merdeka*, cited in Foreign Service Despatch [841[, Amembassy Jakarta to Department of State, April 5, 1959 (756 D.00/4-559).

61 Interview with Mohammad Natsir (Jakarta), May 31, 1971.

62 Kodam III/17 Agustus, *Sedjarah Kodam III/17 Agustus*, pp. 166-67.

63 Foreign Service Despatch #126 from Amconsul Medan, June 19, 1961, 'Military and Security Conditions in West Sumatra and Riau'. In a trip the consul took from Padang to Sawahlunto, via Padang Panjang, the military convoy accompanying him sometimes consisted of as many as '40 soldiers in seven vehicles with a heavily armored car bringing up the rear'. Ibid.

64 Bangun, *Kolonel Maludin Simbolon*, p. 307.

65 Somba, as military commander of North Sulawesi, led the negotiations, supported by Kawilarang. On the events in Sulawesi at this time, see Harvey, *Permesta*, pp. 146-47.

66 See British Consulate Medan to British Embassy, Jakarta, 20 September 1961. According to Simbolon, he outlined to Husein the hopelessness of their position and told him 'that our only solution was to surrender on the best terms available. With this he agreed'. Bangun, *Kolonel Maludin Simbolon*, p. 307.

67 These were mostly in response to appeals by Jakarta's commanders in these regions for the rebel leaders 'to return voluntarily to the fold of the Republic', with promises 'that those who did so 'openly and with sincere hearts' would be treated well and given 'suitable positions''. Amconsul Medan Despatch #119, May 11, 1961, "Operation Persuasion': An Intensified Effort to Persuade Rebels to Surrender'.

68 Interview with Dt. Ahman (Kamang), February 6, 1991. See also, Hasjim Ning, *Pasang Surut Pengusaha Pejuang* [seperti dituturkan kepada A.A. Navis], (Jakarta: Grafiti Press, 1986), p. 159.

69 He delayed responding to Nasution's initiative until he heard from Sjafruddin, still officially president of the RPI. According to one of his close followers at the time, Djambek intended to ask Nasution to evacuate one region, preferably in Riau, where the rebel forces could consolidate during negotiations. They would then have one region under their control should the discussions break down. Interview with Nizar and others (Bukittinggi), March 27, 1999.

70 Nizar stated that Djambek ordered them to go down, but would not surrender himself because if he did so he would be unable to face the women in the villages whose sons and husbands had no such alternative because they had been killed in the struggle.

71 Interview with Mansoer Sani (Padang), August 20, 1995. He surrendered with about thirty men in Balai Selasa. Also interviews with Imran Manan (Padang), August 10, 1995; Abu Nawas (Padang), August 23, 1995; and other rebel soldiers. See also Herbert Feith and Daniel S. Lev, 'The End of the Indonesian Rebellion', *Pacific Affairs* 36,1 (Spring 1963), p. 43. According to them, Husein surrendered with 13,500 men and Simbolon with 11,000 men.

72 Bangun, *Kolonel Maludin Simbolon*, pp. 320-23.

73 British Military Attaché (Colonel Boyle) memo, August 14, 1961 (FO 371/159961) PRO.

74 He refused to use the term 'surrender'. Interview with Sjafruddin (Jakarta), February 21, 1971.

75 Interview with Sjafruddin (Jakarta), May 21, 1971.

76 Interviews with Sjafruddin (Jakarta), February 21 and May 21, 1971. Rosidi, *Sjafruddin Prawiranegara*, pp. 216-18. See also British Embassy Jakarta to Foreign Office, September 4, 1961 (FO371/159960) PRO.

77 Interviews with Buchari Tamam (Jakarta), May 6, 1991 and with HMS Dt. Tan Kabasaran (Bukittinggi), March 29, 1999, both of whom were with Natsir; and with Sjamsul Bahar (Bukittinggi), May 1985. According to Tamam, the head of the RPI's police, Sabiruddin Dt. Rajo Indah headed another group that had not yet surrendered.

78 Copy of Letter dated 10 September, 1961 to the Panglima Kodam III/17 Agustus Kolonel R. Soerjosoempeno di Padang (typescript in my possession. I am grateful to Col. Djambek's sister, Ibu Naimah Jambek, for giving me a copy of this letter). In it Djambek refused to accept the offer of amnesty because it involved swearing an oath that was forbidden by the Qu'ran. According to other informants, he was asking to be brought to trial to clear his name of the corruption charges made against him when he fled Jakarta in August 1957 to join Husein in Padang. Interviews with Saafroedin Bahar (Jakarta), May 3, 1991; Buchari Tamam (Jakarta), May 6, 1991.

79 H.M.S.Dt. Tan Kabasaran, 'Mengenang Kepergian Kolonel M. Dahlan Jambek Tokoh anti Komunis yang Konsekwen, 13 September 1961-13 September 1996' (typescript, in my possession). Interview with Dt. Tan Kabasaran (Bukittinggi), March 29, 1999.

80 According to Saafroedin Bahar, the officer was Colonel Sumedi, chief of operations of the central government forces in Bukittinggi, interview, May 3, 1991; according to Buchari Tamam, it was Retno Moyo, the Korem Intelligence head, interview, May 6, 1991. Djambek's family and followers confirmed that Retno Moyo was the officer concerned. (Interviews, March 27, 29, 1999.)

81 Interview with two of the villagers who witnessed the killing, Usman and Khatib Suleiman (Laring), March 29, 1999. Natsir's letter of December 22, 1961; and interviews with Syofyan Asnawi (Padang), February 14, 1991; and with Syamsul Bahar, who was related to Djambek (Bukittinggi), May 1985.

82 I visited the graves of Djambek and Yussari, about a kilometer from Laring, on March 29, 1999.

83 Emphasis in the original. Reports put out by the government stated that Djambek had been killed in a clash with government forces. See, for example, Letter from A.P. Makatita to Head of Protocol, The Foreign Office, dated September 28, 1961, stating that 'Colonel Mohamad Dahlan Djambek... fell yesterday in a fight against Djakarta troops in Central Sumatra'. (FO371/159961) PRO.

84 Letter from Natsir to Taher Karim Lubis, Padang Sidempuan, October 15, 1961. (PRRI doc. #6).

85 The rebels in Sulawesi also received generally better treatment than those in Sumatra. See Feith & Lev, 'End of the Indonesian Rebellion', p. 44.

86 Interview with Syofyan Asnawi (Padang), February 14, 1991.

87 Interview (Padang), February 12, 1991.

88 The president's order of August 17, 1961 granted them amnesty and abolition, with the explanation: '1) With the granting of amnesty, all criminal measures against the people con-

cerned in sections 1 & 2 [which spell out the rebels] are erased; and 2) with the granting of abolition all procedures are cancelled against these people'. Keputusan Presiden Republik Indonesia No. 449 Tahun 1961, August 17. 1961.

89 Immediately after his surrender, Simbolon 'maintained that all [rebels] had been given a free pardon...that promises had been made that after a period of suspense (two to three years) ex-regulars would be given the chance of being re-absorbed into the Army; that in any case adequate help would be forthcoming to rehabilitate all who had returned'. J.A. McKay's report of his interview with Colonel Simbolon in 'Despatch #15 from British Consulate Medan, to Sir Leslie Fry, British Ambassador, Jakarta', dated September 20, 1961. (F0371/159961) PRO. Major Johan was the highest ranking officer among the few who were allowed to continue in the army. One captain, Yamur Yamin, and about seven first lieutenants and about fifteen second lieutenants were also retained at lower ranks, but the regular soldiers were all deactivated. Interview with Mansoer Sani (Padang), August 20, 1995.

90 Interview with Abu Nawas (Padang), August 23, 1995. He spent the next seven years (until 1968) on a boat borrowed from a friend sailing among the coastal islands, while his wife supported his family by her sewing. Darmansjah, too, was unable to work for the next seven years, relying on his wife's sewing earnings. Interview (Padang), August 23, 1995.

91 Kodam III/17 Agustus, *Sedjarah Kodam III/17 Agustus*, p. 181.

92 The Third Military District had its headquarters in Padang, and its three sub-area commanders had their headquarters at Solok, Bukittinggi, and Pekanbaru. Foreign Service Despatch #126, from Amconsul Medan, June 19, 1961, p. 2.

93 Amal, *Regional and Central Government*, pp. 94-95; Chaniago & Jasmi, *Brigadir Jenderal Polisi Kaharoeddin*, pp. 286-95.

94 Interview with Harun Zain (Jakarta), July 25, 1995.

95 'The West Sumatran Political Scene', Airgram to Department of State from Floyd L. Whittington, Counselor of Embassy for Political Affairs #A-69, July 19, 1963.

96 Interview with Harun Zain (Jakarta), July 25, 1995.

97 It was so described by Syofyan Asnawi, a student leader who joined the PRRI. Interview (Padang), February 14, 1991.

Chapter 10

1 'Statements of the September 30th Movement: Initial Statement of Lieutenant Colonel Untung', broadcast at approximately 7.15 a.m. on the morning of October 1, 1965. *Indonesia* 1 (April 1966), p. 134. These were translations of texts appearing in *Antara (Warta Berita)*, October 1, and *Harian Rakjat*, October 2, 1965.

2 The other generals killed were Major General Suprapto, Major General S. Parman, Major General Harjono M.T., Brigadier General D.I. Pandjaitan, and Brigadier General Sutojo Siswomihardjo. 'Statements by the Indonesian Army Leadership', Ibid., p. 158.

3 Ibid., pp. 136-37. Most council members had been appointed without their knowledge; the only Minangkabau among them was K.H. Siradjuddin Abbas, head of the Perti party. Ibid., p. 138.

4 At the time Pranoto was Third Assistant to the Minister/Commander of the army. In the late 1950s he had been chief of staff of the Diponegoro Division at a time when Suharto was its commander. According to Harold Crouch, 'Suharto was dismissed in 1959 because of his involvement in smuggling after complaints were made by Pranoto... Pranoto was widely respected because of his simple style of living and apparent incorruptibility'. Harold Crouch, *The Army and Politics in Indonesia* (Ithaca: Cornell University Press, 1978), p. 129. Pranoto had been commander of Kodam III in Padang from July 1958 to March 1959 and had been responsible initially for establishing the OKR (Organisasi Keamanan Rakjat) militia in November 1958. Bahar, 'Peranan Elite Sipil dan Elite Militer', pp. 225-26.

5 *Indonesia* 1 (April 1966), pp. 151-55.

6 A leading member of the September 30 Movement, Col. Abdul Latief, has always maintained that he had informed Suharto of the impending actions of the movement several days before they took place, and that Suharto did nothing to prevent them.

7 The main forces which Untung used, in addition to the first Cakrabirawa battalion of the palace guard, were Battalions 454 and 530 from Central and East Java (which were in Jakarta to march in a long-scheduled armed forces day parade), as well as air force elements. 'Speech by Major-General Suharto on October 15, 1965, to Central and Regional Leaders of the National Front', ibid., pp. 166-68.

8 Ibid., pp. 160-73.

9 The acronym was coined by the director of the army newspaper *Angkatan Bersenjata*, with the German 'Gestapo' in mind. Crouch, *Army and Politics*, p. 140.

10 Both men actually served twice as panglima of the Third Regional Military Command, Suryosumpeno from March to September of 1959 and from January 1960 to October 1963, and Panuju from September 1959 to January 1960 and from April 1964 to February 1966. The other two commanders were Colonel Pranoto Reksosamudro (July 1958-March 1959) and Colonel Suwito Harjoko (October 1963 to April 1964). Kodam III/17 Agustus,*Sedjarah Kodam III/17 Agustus*, pp. 181-82.

11 Interviews with Governor Harun Zain (Padang), April 20, 1971, Saafroedin Bahar (Jakarta), May 3, 1991, February 21, 1999; B. Wiwoho & Banjar Chaeruddin, *Memori Jenderal Yoga* (Jakarta: Rena Pariwara, 1991), p. 149; *Tempo*, October 8, 1977. According to Zain, both Untung and Latief came to Padang in August 1958 and at least Untung stayed until the middle of 1959. He commented that 'because of the experience in 1958-59 with Untung, people in West Sumatra were incredulous when it was announced that Untung was in charge of the attempted coup. Neither they nor I can understand why the PKI should have chosen someone of so little consequence to lead it'.

12 See above, ch. 9; see also Pour, *Benny Moerdani*, pp. 158-62.

13 Wiwoho & Chaeruddin, *Memori Jenderal Yoga*, pp. 102-108. Ali Murtopo became one of Suharto's closest associates and headed Opsus, the organization formed to carry out 'special operations' for the president. In the late 1960s, while Ali Murtopo was in charge of foreign intelligence, Yoga Sugama was responsible for domestic intelligence. Crouch, *Army and Politics*, pp. 307-8.

14 Interview with Saafroedin Bahar, Jakarta, February 21, 1999.

15 Amal, *Regional and Central Government in Indonesian Politics*, pp. 97, 98.

16 Mestika Zed, Edy Utama, Hasril Chaniago, *Sumatera Barat di Panggung Sejarah 1945-1995* (Sumatera Barat: Bidang Penerbitan Khusus Panitia Peringatan 50 Tahun RI Sumatera Barat, 1995), pp. 183-84.

17 One example of the balance of power in an extended village not far from Payakumbuh in the mid-1960s was given by Harsja Bachtiar. He reported that in the village of Taram at that time, the village head (*wali nagari*) was a 30-year old villager, a tailor, and a member of the Communist Party (PKI), who had been a leader of the OPR in the area and had a reputation during the PRRI of being 'very harsh, if not cruel, in his actions'. One of the most respected *adat* authorities in Taram at the time was Pituhan Datuk Paduko Basa, a member of the Communist Party, whom his fellow elders had appointed *wali nagari* in 1950. In the mid-1960s, with the Masjumi banned, the largest political party in Taram was the Perti, with the PNI second, 'and the smallest but seemingly best organized party' was the PKI, 'which achieved its present political ascendancy in *negeri* Taram because it was the only political party without any member involved in the recent uprising against the central government'. Harsja W. Bachtiar, '*Negeri* Taram: A Minangkabau Village Community'*Villages in Indonesia*, ed. Koentjaraningrat (Ithaca: Cornell University Press, 1967), pp. 348-85 .

18 *Sedjarah Kodam III/17 Agustus*, p. 310.

19 Ibid., p. 308.

20 Zed, Utama, & Chaniago, *Sumatera Barat*, p. 188.

21 Ibid., p. 189.

22 Mochtar Naim, 'Merantau: Minangkabau Voluntary Migration' (PhD. dissertation, University of Singapore, 1973), p. 140. He considered Lance Castles' figure of sixty thousand in 1961 as too low, particularly in view of Jakarta Governor Ali Sadikin's claim in 1971 that there were then half a million Minangkabau in the city. Ibid., pp. 169-71.

23 Ibid., pp. 171-81. Naim notes that Minangkabau were also prominent in journalism, constituting perhaps 30 percent of the journalists in Jakarta.

24 Non-Minangkabau leaders of both the Masjumi and PSI parties were also jailed, such as Mohd. Roem, Prawoto Mangusasmita, Anak Agung, and Subadio Sastrosatomo,.

25 Abrar Yusra, ed., *Tokoh yang Berhati Rakyat: Biografi Harun Zain* (Jakarta: Yayasan Gebu Minang, 1997); Interviews with Imran Manan (Padang), August 10, 1995, and Adrin Kahar (Padang), August 9, 1995. Andalas University had been moved from Bukittinggi to Padang following the rebellion 'for security reasons'. Interview with Kamal, Mayor of Bukittinggi, April 16, 1971.

26 Interview with Harun Zain (Padang), April 20, 1971, (Jakarta), July 25, 1995.

27 Ibid.

28 Yusra, ed., *Tokoh yang Berhati Rakyat*, pp. 2-13, 119-21.

29 Interviews with Azmi and Imran Manan (Padang), February 12, 1991.

30 This is based on Amal, *Regional and Central Government*, p. 97. See also Yusra, *Tokoh yang Berhati Rakyat*, pp. 131-42 for a fuller account of Zain's tenure as rector.

31 Zed, Utama & Chaniago, *Sumatera Barat*, p. 179. For Yamin's earlier advice to Anwar St. Saidi, see above, ch. 3.

32 Ning, *Pasang Surut Pengusaha Pejuang*, p. 197. These four were Marthias Doeski Pandoe, Syaifullah Alimin Dt. Ibadat, M. Hamidy, and Darmalis. *Singgalang*, October 9, 1997.

33 Ibid., Abrar Yusra, *Otobiografi A.A. Navis: Satiris & Suara Kritis dari Daerah* (Jakarta: Gramedia, 1994), pp. 105-6, 129; Yusra, *Tokoh yang berhati rakyat*, pp. 143-45.

34 Yusra, *A.A. Navis*, pp. 130-31; *Aman Makmur* [Padang], November 10, 1966.

35 Crouch, *Army and Politics*, p. 65.

36 Rex Mortimer, *Indonesian Communism under Sukarno: Ideology and Politics, 1959-1965* (Ithaca; Cornell University Press, 1974), pp. 112-13; 376.

37 Ibid., p. 377. See also Crouch, *Army and Politics*, p. 66, where he details Saleh's loss of influence.

38 Mortimer, *Indonesian Communism*, p. 386.

39 Bahar, 'Peranan Elite Sipil,' p. 245; Yusra, *Otobiografi A.A. Navis*, p. 131.

40 Sundhaussen, *Road to Power*, pp. 14, 64, 101. He was appointed to the team of seven after the National Conference of September 1957 to investigate the military complaints of the dissident regional councils. See Bahar, 'Peranan Elite Sipil', p. 73 for more details.

41 He was commandant of SSKAD at the time of Nasution's arrest of Lubis' supporters there. See above, ch. 8.

42 Confidential Despatch to James Murray, British Embassy, Jakarta, from J.B. Wright, British Consul in Medan, dated January 3, 1966 (FO371/186027) PRO.

43 Confidential letter to James Murray, in the British Embassy in Jakarta from J.B. Wright, British Consul in Medan, dated November 22, 1965 (FO371/180309)PRO. This was reiterated in a report of January 3, 1966, where the consul noted: 'The Mandala-1 (Confrontation) Command, was formed in April [1965], but brought none of the heightening of confrontation it was ostensibly designed to achieve. Its preoccupations were internal rather than external, and since the 30th of September it has devoted most of its time to PKI-hunting and guarding of the estates'. (FO371/186027)

44 Confidential Despatch on 'the course of events in North Sumatra during 1965', from Consul J.B. Wright, in Medan to J. Murray in Jakarta, dated January 3, 1966, attached to letter to the Rt. Hon. Michael Stewart from James Murray, Chargé d'affairs in Jakarta, dated January

20, 1966 (FO371/186027). Sobsi was the labour union and BTI the peasants' union, both affiliated with the Communist Party.

45 Letter to D. Tonking, SEA Department Foreign Office from S.J.G. Cambridge, British Embassy Jakarta, dated March 3, 1965 (FO371/181455). Harold Crouch is in accord, writing: 'By implementing the PKI's proposal in his own way, Mokoginta had ensured that the number of trained peasants and workers would be very small and under the army's control'. Crouch, *Army and Politics*, p. 90.

46 Crouch, *Army and Politics* pp. 87-88. 'The Bandar Betsy Affair', attached to Confidential report from the British Embassy, Jakarta, to The Rt Hon Michael Stewart M.P. dated August 4, 1965 (FO371/180315); Wright to Murray, November 22, 1965, op. cit.

47 Wright to Murray, November 22, 1965, op. cit.

48 Ibid.

49 Subandrio and Nyoto, with their party, had arrived in Padang on September 29. Interview with Harun Zain (Padang), April 20, 1971.

50 Confidential Despatch from Consul Wright in Medan to J. Murray in Jakarta, January 3, 1966, p. 3. The consul writes that the visit to Langsa was 'ostensibly to seal off the area as an invasion zone, but possibly to secure it as an area where Chinese arms and supplies to nourish the PKI rising planned for 7th October could be landed. He is believed to have set up a similar zone at Padang before coming on to Medan'. I've seen no evidence for this interpretation.

51 *Antara Warta Berita*, June 20, 1966 (Trial of Peris Pardede).

52 According to Saafroedin Bahar three military district (*korem*) commanders in Central Sumatra were all Communists, Col. Madjiman and Col. Imam Sugandi in West Sumatra, and Col. Sumedi in Riau. Interview (Jakarta), February 21, 1999.

53 This interpretation was put forward by Ichlasul Amal, who notes that there was no doubt Rivai 'was a leftist officer, but the extensive publicity given to his role, which was much greater than that given to the role of higher ranking Javanese officers who played key roles in the leftist movement, suggests that the authorities were concerned to make an ethnic point, that is that leftist ideology was not a Javanese monopoly but was also shared by Minangkabau officers'. See his *Regional and Central Government*, p. 113.

54 'Ketua "Dewan Revolusi" Sumbar Dihadapkan ke Mahmillub Padang,' *Antara Warta Berita*, July 28, 31, August 3, 1967.

55 Kodam III /17 Agustus,*Sedjarah Kodam III/17 Agustus*, pp. 165, 217; Bahar, 'Peranan Elite Sipil', p. 235.

56 'Ketua "Dewan Revolusi" Sumbar Dihadapkan ke Mahmillub Padang', *Antara Warta Berita*, July 28, 1967, p. 17.

57 See above, ch. 9. Interview with Djamaris Yoenoes (Padang), March 19, 1999.

58 Dan Dodik Dam III, *Antara Warta Berita*, July 28, 1967.

59 *Antara Warta Berita* (Dalam Negeri), July 31, 1967, p. 4, August 3, 1967, p. 4. Interview with Saafroedin Bahar, February 21, 1999.

60 Interview with Saafroedin Bahar. See also Bahar, 'Peranan Elite Sipil', p. 235.

61 Kodam III /17 Agustus, *Sedjarah Kodam III/17 Agustus*, p. 313.

62 Interview with Saafroedin Bahar, February 21, 1999. According to Bahar, this was First Lt. Hanrito, the brother of a member of the Communist Central Committee. See also *Haluan*, August 21, 1974. Despite the circumstances of his death eight years earlier, Hanafi's written testimony was still accepted in the trials of Bainal and Soekirno in 1974. *Haluan*, August 1, 1974.

63 *Antara Warta Berita*, July 28, 1967; *Haluan*, July 31, 1974, August 1, 1974 (trial of Bainal and Sukirno). Saafroedin Bahar alleges that while in Bukittinggi in 1961 Sumedi was one of those responsible for ordering Dahlan Djambek's murder when he was attempting to surrender. Interview with Saafroedin Bahar (Jakarta), May 3, 1991. Others accused of being less centrally involved in the 1965 plot were Capt. Bachtiar Latief, deputy commander of battalion 132; Capt. Budjang Kasi (possibly the same person who appears as Captain Zanawi Bud-

jang or Budjang Bazoka in the *Antara* reports); Major Hadiprajitno, chief of staff of military district 0304 Agam/Bukittinggi; Warrant Officer (Peltu) Bahar Kirai, 2nd Lt. Sudjono, and AKBP Asmaun, a former officer in the Police Area Command Staff (SKOMDAK), who was later transferred to Surabaya. *Antara Warta Berita*, August 3, 1967. This report states that all these suspects, with the exception of Asmaun, were then under arrest. A further participant appears in the report of August 8: Mansur alias Ahmad, a member of the West Sumatra Communist Party Special Bureau. *Antara Warta Berita*, August 8, 1967. Another alleged member of the Special Bureau, Syamsoel Bahri, appeared as a witness in the 1974 trials. *Haluan*, July 30, 1974.

64 *Antara Warta Berita*, July 28, 1967, and *Haluan*, July 30, 31, 1974.

65 *Haluan*, August 1, 1974.

66 *Antara Warta Berita*, July 31, August 3, 1967, p. 8.; Interview with Harun Zain (Padang), April 20, 1971; Kodam III/17 Agustus, *Sedjarah Kodam III/17 Agustus*, pp. 313-14, which lists the units that were ready to be deployed in the action as Battalion 132, one and a half companies of Battalion 131, one company of Battalion 130, and the Raiders company.

67 *Gerakan 30September: Pemberontakan Partai Komunis Indonesia: Latar Belakang, Aksi, dan Penumpasannya* (Jakarta: Sekretariat Negara Republik Indonesia, 1994), p. 89. As head of the Special Bureau, Sjam was allegedly the key contact between Communist Party head Aidit and the plotters.

68 Ibid., p. 80.

69 Ibid., p. 89.

70 According to testimony at Bainal's 1974 trial, on the night of October 1, he ordered live ammunition to be issued to a two-hundred-man volunteer combat support unit, 'Tiger of Champa' (Harimau Champa), made up mostly of members of the Communist youth group (OPR). This unit was ordered to go to Bukittinggi (possibly rendezvousing first with the other units in Lubuk Alung). *Haluan*, August 3, 1974.

71 *Gerakan Tigapuluh September*, p. 113.

72 Tape of an interview with Nourmatias, a former member of the West Sumatra PKI's secretariat, August 8, 1988. I am grateful to Jim Siegel for giving me access to this taped interview.

73 Ibid.

74 Zed, Utama and Chaniago, *Sumatera Barat*, pp. 203-6.

75 Kodam III/17 Agustus, *Sedjarah Kodam III/17 Agustus*, pp. 317-19. Also taped interview with Nourmatias: according to him, they also considered sending a messenger to Jakarta to find out exactly what had happened.

76 Taped interview with Nourmatias. Other reports, such as interview with Saafroedin Bahar, February 21, 1999, confirmed that they had been killed in late 1965.

77 These areas included the foothills of Mt. Singgalang and the northern and southern coastal areas near Pariaman and in Pesisir Selatan. Kodam III/17 Agustus, *Sedjarah Kodam III/17 Agustus*, p. 119; taped interview with Nourmatias. Most journeys between their various refuges were made by sea. Even if these fugitives wished to go from Padang Panjang to Painan they would go overland to Pariaman and then travel south by ship.

78 Kodam III/17 Agustus, *Sedjarah Kodam III/17 Agustus*, p. 319.

79 Zed, Utama & Chaniago, *Sumatera Barat*, p. 202.

80 And after Kaharuddin had defected from his support of the Banteng Council. See above, ch. 8.

81 Zed, Utama & Chaniago, *Sumatera Barat*, p. 193; interview with Adrin Kahar (son of Kaharuddin), Padang, August 9, 1995; interview with Harun Zain (Jakarta), July 25, 1995.

82 *Antara Warta Berita*, September 19, 23, 1966.

83 Despatch from Wright to Murray, January 3, 1966, loc. cit. [above, n. 44].

84 Letter from J.B. Wright (Medan) to S.J.G. Cambridge at the British Embassy, Jakarta, November 9, 1965 (FO371/180309)PRO.

85 Zed, Utama & Chaniago, *Sumatera Barat*, p. 221.

86 'Confidential Report' from Consul Knight, January 3, 1966 (FO 371/186026).

87 Ibid.

88 J.B. Wright to M.J.T. McCann, British Embassy, January 10, 1966 (FO371/186027).

89 He speculated: 'Perhaps all the prisons were already too full so that school buildings had to be used as police and army detention camps'. Oei Tjoe Tat, *Memoar Oei Tjoe Tat: Pembantu President Soekarno*, ed. Pramoedya Ananta Toer & Stanley Adi Prasetyo (Jakarta: Hasta Mitra, 1995), p. 190.

90 Ibid. Baperki was the peranakan Chinese party and Partindo was the small left-Nationalist Party, composed of all ethnic groups, to which Oei Tjoe Tat himself belonged.

91 'The Liquidation of the Indonesian Communist Party in Sumatra', report by Consul Wright, Medan, March 30, 1966 (FO371/186030). Appendix 'B': 'Assessment of Numbers of PKI and Affiliated Organisations Killed in North Sumatra since September 30, 1965'.

92 Ann Luara Stoler, *Capitalism and Confrontation in Sumatra's Plantation Belt, 1870-1979* (New Haven: Yale University Press,1985), pp. 163-64. SARBUPRI = Sarekat Buruh Perkebunan Republik Indonesia, Union of Indonesian Plantation Workers.

93 Consul Wright, 'The Liquidation of the Indonesian Communist Party'.

94 Amal, *Regional and Central Government*, p. 112.

95 Zed, Utama & Chaniago, *Sumatera Barat*, p. 208.

96 Amal, *Regional and Central Government*, p. 113. Poniman was confirmed as commander on April 22. Ibid., p. 114.

97 Zed, Utama & Chaniago, *Sumatera Barat*, p. 224. Governor Zain noted in 1971 that all three Diponegoro regimental commanders who were in the province when he took office in 1966 had been arrested and were at that time still in jail in West Sumatra. He stated that 'many other officers were arrested and some are still being investigated, with some arrests continuing'. Interviews with Governor Harun Zain (Padang) April 11, 20, 1971.

98 Saafroedin Bahar, 'Ali Akbar Navis Cadiak Pandai Minangkabau', in *Otobiografi A.A. Navis*, ed. Yusra, p. 349. Bahar had served six years in Riau and returned to West Sumatra in 1966 where he would remain for the next ten years. Interview, February 21, 1999.

99 Quoting an interview with Poniman, Zed, Utama, and Chaniago, stating that the MTKAAM had been infliltrated by the Communist Party, which had also influenced the Perti and its leader Siradjuddin Abbas. Zed, Utama & Chaniago, *Sumatera Barat*, p. 223. Siradjuddin Abbas was accused of direct involvement in the September 30 Movement, but nevertheless had returned to an influential position within the Perti by the end of 1966. See *Aman Makmur*, December 2, 1966.

100 As an organization, however, the BKPUI apparently lacked the prestige of the Sumatra Islamic Scholars' Council (MUI Sumatera) headed by Mansur Daud Dt. Palimo Kayo, the old Permi and later Masjumi leader. Zed, Utama & Chaniago, *Sumatera Barat*, p. 222.

101 *Antara Warta Berita*, March 17, 18, 1966.

102 It was headed by Baharuddin Datuk Rangkayo Basa, who also headed the provincial government's information department. See Bahar, 'Ali Akbar Navis', in *A.A. Navis*, pp. 352-53. See also Amal, *Regional and Central Government*, pp. 114-15. In anticipation of the conference various *nagari* appointed new *penghulu* to replace those who had allegedly been involved in the September 30 Movement. *Antara Warta Berita*, March 18, 1966.

103 '*kusuk bulu, paruah nan manyalasaikan*'. Zed, Utama & Chaniago, *Sumatera Barat*, p. 223. The results of this policy were seen in November 1966, when in Nagari Sintuk in Pariaman forty-three new village elders (*ninik-mamak*) were appointed to replace those allegedly involved in the 'Gestapu/PKI' while a short time previously in a *nagari* in Batu Sangkar twenty new elders had been appointed for the same reason. *Aman Makmur*, November 25, 1966.

104 Amal, *Regional and Central Government*, p. 117.

105 Interviews with Harun Zain (Jakarta), July 25, 1995, February 22, 1999. Panuju apparently said they would also appoint a deputy governor, and Zain speculated that 'they might have hoped I would be a weak governor and they could control me through the deputy'.

106 Perti and the PNI voted for Saputro, while IPKI, the NU, the Catholic party, Parkindo, the PSII and the Functional Group voted for Zain. Amal, *Regional and Central Government*, p. 117.

107 Siradjuddin Abbas, 'Perti dan Revolusi', *Suara Perti* 30, 1 (January 1965), p. 10. In the same speech, Syekh Siradjuddin Abbas also defied history when he stated that Perti had been established to oppose Dutch colonialism and defend Islam, and that it never received any subsidies from the colonial government. Ibid., pp. 8, 9. See also *Suara Perti*, 30, 2 (June 1965).

108 See above, ch. 7. For the remainder of the Guided Democracy period it was called the Dewan Perwakilan Rakyat Daerah-Gotong Royong (DPR-GR; i.e. People's Regional Representative Council - Mutual Help)

109 These were the NU, PSII, Partai Murba, Partindo, and the Catholic Party. The Functional group representatives were drawn from the following groups and associations: State Police; Veterans/People's Youth Organization (OPR); farmers and workers; officials; Islamic religious scholars; Christian religious scholars; *adat* representatives; artists; youth; women; intellectuals; cooperatives and national enterprises; education and culture; and journalists. See Zed, Utama & Chaniago, *Sumatera Barat*, p. 190.

110 *Antara Warta Berita*, June 5, 6, 1966; *Singgalang*, October 9, 1997.

111 *Antara Warta Berita*, June 5, 1966.

112 Ibid., June 17, 1966. They were soon followed by a representative of the *adat* group, M. Sarah Dt. Sati.

113 *Antara Warta Berita*, June 6, 1966. Bukittinggi mayor Anwar Maksum and his secretary Indra Sjamsu were soon targets of an investigative team set up by the new governor. *Antara Warta Berita*, June 18, 1966.

114 Ibid., June 10, 1966. Mrs. Suwarno was accused of having connections with the Communist Women's Movement, Gerwani.

115 Amal, *Regional and Central Government*, p. 116. A couple of days later the prosecutor was replaced by Lt. Col. Sudjadi S.H. *Antara Warta Berita*, June 11, 1966. It was not until the end of 1966 that Brig. Gen. Poniman announced that trials of those allegedly involved in the September 30 Movement would probably begin in early February 1967. *Aman Makmur*, December 14, 1966.

116 *Antara Warta Berita*, June 20, 1966.

117 For incidents against goverment officials in Pasaman and Sawahlunto, see ibid., June 24, July 2, 1966.

118 For example, out of 630 teachers and officials in West Sumatra's Educational and Cultural Organization (Perwakilan PDK), 115 had been suspended and 34 fired; 448 others were awaiting a decision. All those suspended, fired, pensioned, and made non-active had been members of the Communist Party or its social organizations. *Antara Warta Berita*, June 25, 1966.

119 Crouch, *Army and Politics*, p. 224.

120 Interview with Harun Zain (Padang), April 20, 1971.

121 Interview with Saafroedin Bahar (Jakarta), February 21, 1999. From 1966 to 1968 Major Bahar served as head of the social communications bureau of Kodam III in West Sumatra, and he was on the military tribunal which tried Djajusman alias Mamak in 1967.

122 Ibid.

123 Amal, *Regional and Central Government*, p. 113. See also Zed, Utama & Chaniago, *Sumatera Barat*, pp. 221-22.

124 Stoler, *Capitalism*, pp. 163-64; Robert Cribb, ed., *The Indonesian Killings 1965-1966* (Clayton: Monash University Centre of Southeast Asian Studies, 1990), pp. 23-26; Eric Morris estimates the number of alleged Communists killed in Aceh at only between two thousand and six thousand people. See Morris, 'Islam and Politics in Aceh', p. 246. In the Takengen district of Central Aceh's Gayo region alone, however, John Bowen states that 'estimates of the number killed range from eight hundred to three thousand', including Gayo and Javanese, mostly from former contract-labour camps, but few if any Chinese. John Bowen, *Sumatran*

Politics and Poetics: Gayo History, 1900-1989 (New Haven: Yale University Press, 1991), pp. 120-21.

125 Interview with Bagindo Fahmi (Padang), September 4, 1995. The Ansor was the NU's youth organization, which was held responsible for much of the anti-Communist activity in Java.

126 Taped interview with Nourmatias. He recounted approaching the village of Malalak where he came upon a large government army operation, involving perhaps a thousand civilian supporters, against a village suspected of being sympathetic to the Communists. As he approached the village, 'I heard someone sobbing, it was an ulama who said: 'I've been beaten by the masses and they left me as they thought I was dead. The others were thrown into the river'. A hundred metres further on he saw an armed group crossing the river carrying lamps. When he and his companions went down from the hills they found the village deserted.

127 Interview with Harun Zain (Padang), April 20, 1971.

128 Interview with Hendra Esmael (Padang), April 13, 1971.

129 *Antara Warta Berita*, September 16, 1966. According to Zed, Utama & Chaniago, who cite as their sources an interview with a KAPPI activist in Bukittinggi, Makmur Hendrik, and an account by Hasril Chaniago which appeared in *Singgalang* on November 10, 1985, this man was in fact a soldier, Corporal Asbar, who belonged to Battalion 0132 of the Bukittinggi regimental command that had been headed by Colonel Madjiman. Zed, Utama & Chaniago, *Sumatera Barat*, p. 207.

130 *Antara Warta Berita*, September 16, 17, 1966.

131 Ibid., September 23, 1966.

132 Ibid.

133 In Pasaman, however, there were still many relatively strong indigenous Communist groups.

134 Interview with Dr. Busra Zahir, Rector of Andalas University (Padang), April 12, 1971. He noted that even then 'investigations are still going on with respect to leftist affiliations stemming from this accommodation of expediency in the post-rebellion period'.

135 Interviews with Harun Zain (Padang), April 11, 1971, and Dr. Busra Zahir (Padang), April 12, 1971.

136 Interview with Harun Zain (Padang), April 11, 1971.

137 Zed, Utama & Chaniago, *Sumatera Barat*, p. 219, citing an interview with Hasan Basri Durin, then an official in the governor's office.

138 Zain had been the classmate of several of them when he attended the University of California at Berkeley in 1958-60. Interview with Harun Zain (Padang), April 20, 1971.

139 Zed, Utama & Chaniago, *Sumatera Barat*, p. 221.

140 Interview with Harun Zain (Jakarta), July 25, 1995.

141 Soewardi Idris, 'A.A. Navis dan Cerpen Dunia Akhirat', in *Otobiotgrafi A.A. Navis*, pp. 385-92.

142 Amal, *Regional and Central Government*, pp. 139, 193.

143 Ibid., p. 193.

Chapter 11

1 See Dwight Y. King, 'Indonesia's New Order as a Bureaucratic Polity, a Neo-patrimonial Regime or a Bureaucratic-Authoritarian Regime: What Difference Does It Make?' in *Interpreting Indonesian Politics: Thirteen Contributions to the Debate*, ed. Benedict Anderson and Audrey Kahin (Ithaca,: Cornell University Modern Indonesia Project, 1982), pp. 104-16.

2 Crouch, *Army and Politics*, p. 273.

3 Hamish McDonald, *Suharto's Indonesia* (Blackburn: Fontana Books, 1980), p. 78.

4 Javanese consistently occupied between 74 and 80 percent of the positions listed in the

'Current Data on the Indonesian Military Elite' prepared by the editors of the journal, *Indonesia*. See, for example, *Indonesia* 26 (October 1978), p. 161 and *Indonesia* 29 (April 1980), p. 157.

5 For a table of the parallel military and civilian bureaucacies and their interaction, see David Jenkins, *Suharto and His Generals: Indonesian Military Politics 1975-1983* (Ithaca: Cornell University Modern Indonesia Project, 1984), p. 46.

6 The functional groups had their origins under Sukarno's Guided Democracy, but the Joint Secretariat was developed in the early years of Suharto's rule by Ali Murtopo into an electoral machine through which the army could ensure its success. A brief reliable account of the process can be found in Crouch, *Army and Politics*, pp. 264-72.

7 According to Governor Zain, during the early years of his tenure 70-80 percent of district heads (*bupati*) were military officers. Interview, February 22, 1999.

8 Amal, *Regional and Central Government*, p. 193. This Minangkabau proverb (Min.: *takuik di ujuang badia, lari ka pangkanyo* [Ind.: *takut diujung bedil lari ke pangkalnya*]) is also quoted by Zed *et al.* in describing the attitude of the West Sumatra people in the immediate aftermath of the PRRI defeat. At that time, of course, it had meant accommodation with the leftist forces of the late Sukarno era, rather than with Suharto's military regime. Zed, Utama & Chaniago, *Sumatera Barat di Panggung Sejarah*, p. 171.

9 Notable among these was Emil Salim, a graduate of Berkeley and head of the technical team for stabilizing the economy from 1967-69.

10 Jenkins, *Suharto and His Generals*, p. 34. Marhaenism was a political philosophy elaborated by Sukarno, which emphasized the importance not only of the proletariat but of all the 'destitute people of Indonesia'. See Sukarno, *Nationalism, Islam and Marxism* (Ithaca: Cornell University Modern Indonesia Project Translation Series, 1960).

11 The Perti was extensively purged in 1966 and once more before the 1971 elections.

12 *Antara Warta Berita*, June 17, 1967. He later noted that in refusing his request, Suharto had given the excuse that the Parliament (MPRS) had passed a regulation forbidding establishment of any new parties, though it soon permitted a new modernist Muslim party to be formed. Interview with Mohammad Hatta (Jakarta), January 19, 1971.

13 *Aman Makmur*, November 17, 1966. Although the Socialist Party (PSI) was never revived, many of its foremost leaders were very influential in the New Order government, either as advisers to the army leadership or in the economic field.

14 Interview with Mohamad Roem (Jakarta), January 25, 1971.

15 Interview with Sjafruddin Prawiranegara (Jakarta), May 21, 1971. A detailed history of the Parmusi's establishment and early history can be found in K.E. Ward's *The Foundation of the Partai Muslimin Indonesia* (Ithaca: Cornell Modern Indonesia Project, 1970). On government manipulation of the Muslim party, see also Crouch, *Army and Politics*, pp. 259-63.

16 Interviews with several *bupati* in West Sumatra in April 1971. The most outspoken was Kamarudin, *bupati* of Agam, who acknowledged that the major problem he faced in his region was political: 'to ensure that Golkar wins'. He expressed worry that 'the old followers of Masjumi are so strong and Parmusi may defeat Golkar in Agam and Bukittinggi'. Interview (Bukittinggi), April 16, 1971.

17 See above, ch. 10.

18 He later explained how he made a consistent effort to attract the traditionalist *ulama* from the areas of West Sumatra outside the heartland, from their former allegiance to Perti: 'at the periphery the mystic organizations were influential among the population, particularly the Tarbiyah. Taking advantage of my military experience, I courted the *ulama*, giving them holy books, sarongs, kerosene lamps. As long as the *ulama* were happy all of them would support Golkar'. Interview with Saafroedin Bahar (Jakarta), February 21, 1999.

19 *Haluan*, June 4, 8, 1971.

20 On Golkar's tactics in the campaign, see Bahar, 'Peranan Elite Sipil', pp. 302-12. In Agam, Golkar gained 47 percent of the vote in the district as against 33 percent for Parmusi and just

under 10 percent for Perti. Thus Bupati Kamarudin succeeded in obtaining a Golkar victory, though it fell short of the 50 percent considered adequate by Golkar headquarters.

21 See Amal, *Regional and Central Government*, pp. 143-47.

22 In the 1971 elections the combined vote of the four Muslim parties in West Sumatra was 34.6 percent.

23 Zed, Utama & Chaniago, *Sumatera Barat*, p. 300 . The authors note, however, that in the 1977 election Golkar was defeated by the PPP in the towns of Bukittinggi and Padang Panjang, and barely beat the PPP in Padang (49,825 to 49,245 votes). This contrasted with the situation on a national level, where Golkar retained its 62 percent, as against 29 percent for the PPP and 9 percent for the PDI. Golkar's subsequent slighting of one of the leaders of the Syattariyah sect led to its share of the vote in West Sumatra dropping slightly to 64 percent in 1982, though the PPP's percentage increased only marginally.

24 Sjafruddin Prawiranegara was also an outspoken opponent of the measure, sending an open letter to Suharto on July 17, 1983, which provided detailed arguments against its enforcement. See Sjafruddin Prawiranegara, 'Pancasila as the Sole Foundation', *Indonesia* 38 (October 1984), pp. 74-83.

25 When PPP obtained 17 percent and PDI 15 percent.

26 Zed, Utama & Chaniage, *Sumatera Barat*, p. 307.

27 Zed, Utama & Chaniago, *Sumatera Barat*, p. 294. In his book discussing the history and outlook for regional autonomy in Indonesia, John Legge also recognized the potential of the *nagari*, as opposed to the Javanese *desa*, as a suitable foundation for the third level of government: 'The *negeri* of Minangkabau, though it is approximately equal in size of population to a Javanese *desa*, covers a more extensive area, and it has already had some experience in the operation of a council system modified by Dutch regulation. Moreover, it controls more adequate sources of revenue – e.g., unlike the Javanese *desa* it secures income from market administration which is a *kabupaten* [district] or municipal preserve in Java. It may well prove a suitable subject for experiment as an autonomous unit of the third level'. Legge, *Cultural Authority and Regional Autonomy*, pp. 93-94.

28 Mohammad Hasbi, *Masalah Pengembangan Nagari di Sumatera Barat* (Bukittinggi: Biro Publikasi APDN, 1972).

29 For the law's implementation in the province of Riau, see Tsuyoshi Kato, 'Different Fields Similar Locusts: Adat communities and the Village Law of 1979 in Indonesia', *Indonesia* 47 (April 1989), pp. 89-114.

30 Colin MacAndrews, 'The Structure of Government in Indonesia', in *Central Government and Local Development in Indonesia*, ed. Colin MacAndrews (Singapore: Oxford University Press, 1986), p. 39.

31 The government subsidy for each *desa* had begun at 100,000 rupiah a year in 1969 (the initial year of the first Five Year Development Plan), and rose to Rp.4.5 million a year per *desa* by 1990. Sjofian Asnawi, 'Pembangunan Sumatera Barat dalam kaitannya dengan masalah perubahan sosio-kultural setempat', in *Perubahan Sosial*, pp. 89-93.

32 Interview with Hasan Basri Durin (Jakarta), February 18, 1999.

33 Interviews with Harun Zain, July 25, 1995, February 22, 1999.

34 Ibid. In the DPRD session on October 8, 1977, Anas defeated his two rivals, receiving twenty-five votes to eight votes for Yanuar Muin and five for Anas S.H. *Singgalang*, October 10, 1997.

35 Asnawi, 'Pembangunan Sumatera Barat'; Zed, Utama & Chaniago, *Sumatera Barat*, pp. 290-91.

36 For an enlightening discussion of the impact of the new law on irrigation systems in West Sumatra, see John S. Ambler, 'Historical Perspectives on Sawah Cultivation and the Political and Economic Context for Irrigation in West Sumatra', *Indonesia* 46 (October 1988), pp. 39-77, particularly pp. 69-77.

37 Taufik Abdullah, 'Adat and Islam: An Examination of Conflict in Minangkabau', *Indonesia*

2 (October 1966), p. 12. Other characteristics defining a *nagari* can vary. According to a 1988 study of village administration throughout Indonesia, a *nagari* should also have wet and dry rice fields, cattle, households, and four kinship groups (*suku*). 'Laporan Penelitian di Daerah Propinsi Sumatra Barat', in *Pemerintahan Desa*, vol. 1, ed. Selo Soemardjan et al. (Jakarta: Badan Penelitian dan Pengembangan Departemen Dalam Negeri kerjasama dengan Yayasan Ilmu-Ilmu Sosial, 1988), p. 142.

38 Traditionally the *nagari* developed from the grouping of a number of *koto*, which were settlements possessing some characteristics (e.g. a meeting place [*balai*]) but not all, of the *nagari*. See Kato, *Matriliny and Migration*, pp. 75-77; Bachtiar, '*Negeri* Taram', pp. 360-62.

39 Mochtar Naim, 'Nagari versus Desa: Sebuah Kerancuan Struktural', in *Nagari, Desa dan Pembangunan Pedesaan di Sumatera Barat* (Sumatera Barat: Yayasan Genta Budaya, 1990), p. 54. In this section I have relied heavily on this volume, which contains the proceedings of a seminar held in 1989 in Payakumbuh on the problems of village government.

40 Zed, Utama & Chaniago, *Sumatera Barat*, p. 296.

41 *Nagari, Desa dan Pembangunan*, p. 95. As Hasan Basri Durin described the situation, 'The KAN's functions only concerned *adat*, and they had no right to interfere in government functions. That caused a disintegration of the *adat* community which became weaker, and also the *desa* as a government unit became weaker because there was no support from the *adat* community'. Interview (Jakarta), February 18, 1999.

42 On the impact of the dissolution of the *nagari*, see Hasan Basri Durin, *Catatan Seorang Pamong* (Jakarta: Obor, 1997), pp. 101-104.

43 The name of the award was the 'Prasamya Purnakarya Nugraha Pelita III'. The awards for the First and Second development plans had gone to East and West Java. Ibid. See also Bahar, 'Peranan Elite Sipil', pp. 326-27, concerning the award, and Zed et al., *Sumatera Barat*, pp. 171-76 for a description of the award ceremony.

44 Bahar, 'Peranan Elite Sipil', p. 331.

45 A full account of the incident and its background appears in Zed, Utama & Chaniago, *Sumatera Barat*, pp. 284-86.

46 Hasan Basri Durin defeated two other candidates for the post of governor, getting thirty-two votes in the regional assembly while the Rector of Andalas University, Professor Jurnalis Kamil, got seven votes and Haji Fauzan, Assistant Rector of IAIN Imam Bonjol, Padang, got five votes. *Tempo*, September 26, November 7, 1987.

47 The Department of Interior Affairs supported his education at Gadjah Mada University in Yogyakarta, from which he graduated in 1960. He served in the civil service in Jambi, spent a year of study at Wayne State University in Detroit, and was appointed acting mayor of Jambi in 1966.

48 He was elected to the post in 1973 and 1977. *Amanah* 97 (March 23-April 5, 1990), p. 94. See also Zed et al, *Sumatera Barat*, p. 361, and Durin, *Catatan Seorang Pamong*, pp. 5-7, for a fuller biography.

49 Durin, *Catatan Seorang Pamong*, pp. 101-102. There were other reasons for the decline in the role of the village elders. These stemmed in large part from many of the rural youngsters leaving to pursue their education in distant cities, which led to a growing number of unqualified *penghulu* (clan heads) in the *nagari* and a lack of respect toward *mamak* (uncles, head of Kin group) on the part of their *kemanakan* (nephews or followers) who had become more worldly. (On these issues, see Zed et al., *Sumatera Barat*, p. 324.)

50 Durin, *Catatan Seorang Pamong*, p. 105-106.

51 *Gotong royong* or mutual cooperation, is a traditional way throughout the Indonesian archipelago by which people of a community come together to carry out a project that is usually of mutual benefit to all. It has been misused on occasion by governmental authorities, such as during the period of the Japanese occupation, to force all the people to participate in a government-sponsored project.

52 Zed et al., *Sumatera Barat*, p. 340.

53 *Singgalang*, October 11, 1997. Also see below.

54 Zed *et al.*, *Sumatera Barat*, pp. 340-41.

55 Moh. Arsjad Anwar, Iwan J. Azis, Mari Pangestu, Hadi Soesastro, 'The Indonesian Economy: Problems and Prospects', *Asian Economic Journal* 5,2(1991): 100-136.

56 Iwan J. Azis, 'Review of Regional Development: Equity and Foreign Exchange Accumulation', in *Spatial Development in Indonesia: Review and Prospects*, ed. Tschangho John Kim, Gerrit Knaap and Iwan J. Azis (Aldershot: Avebury, 1992), pp. 91-128.

57 Anwar *et al*, 'The Indonesian Economy', p. 108. See also Michael Malley, 'The Centrifugal Political Effects of Economic Reform in Indonesia'. Paper presented to the Annual Meeting of the Association of Asian Studies (Washington, March 26-29, 1998), p. 15.

58 Adam Schwarz, *A Nation in Waiting: Indonesia in the 1990s* (Boulder: Westview Press, 1994), p. 62.

59 Azis, 'Review of Regional Development,' p. 110.

60 The other, and less important of the schemes was the IMTGT (Indonesia Malaysia Thailand Growth Triangle) which excludes Singapore. The components of this triangle are Aceh, North Sumatra, Riau, and West Sumatra, the northern part of Malaysia (Kedah and Langkawi), and the southern part of Thailand. This triangle is aimed mostly at the coordination of tourism in the region. Interviews with Professor Dr. Sjafrizal (Padang), February 16, 1999; Hasan Basri Durin, Jakarta, February 18, 1999.

61 *Otobiografi A.A.Navis*, p. 194. Pak Navis notes that every year about Rp. 41 billion in money orders were sent home from outside West Sumatra. These, however, were not coordinated, but sent individually to the migrants' families and villages.

62 Saafroedin Bahar, 'Ali Akbar Navis', in ibid., p. 356. According to this data 179 of the 600 *nagari* were in a state of poverty, and 120 were in a state of near poverty. Ibid., p. 199.

63 Ibid.

64 Soekisman, 'Gebu Minang: Suatu Pemikiran ke arah Operasionalisasi (Untuk Bahan Diskusi Lebih Lanjut)', typescript, dated January 17, 1989.

65 Durin, *Catatan Seorang Pamong*, pp. 145-47. Others prominent in the organization were former governors Zain and Anas and Saafroedin Bahar.

66 *Tempo*, January 6, 1990.

67 *Panji Masyarakat*, 644 (April 11-20, 1990). The character of a migrant's ties with his home region and his willingness to support its development was to a large extent based on his own clan (or *suku*) and his own *nagari*. In his native loyalties, the *jorong* meant nothing, nor did the other administrative divisions above the extended village level. The growth in the economic importance of the Gebu Minang to the development of West Sumatra must then have been a further impetus for Governor Hasan Basri Durin to encourage the return to the *nagari* as the administrative unit in the countryside of West Sumatra.

68 *Singgalang*, September 5, 1995. By 1996 the number had grown to 19.

69 S.M. Rosman, 'Tentang Bank Desa: Apa maksud Anwar St. Saidi? Mungkinkah ditiap2 Negari didirikan Bank Desa?' [Concerning Village Banks: What does Anwar St. Saidi mean? Is it possible to establish a Village Bank in each Nagari?], *Haluan*, January 22, 23, 1970.

70 *Singgalang*, September 5, 1995.

71 See, for example, Taufik Abdullah, 'Minangkabau dalam Perspektif Perubahan Sosial', in *Perubahan Sosial di Minangkabau*, ed. Zed *et al.*, especially pp. 28, 30.

72 *Singgalang*, August 18, 1995. I witnessed the ceremony in Bukittinggi, where the atmosphere was the same.

73 'Perintis Kemerdekaan Leon Salim: Adil dan Makmur Baru Milik Segelintir Rakyat' [Independence Pioneer Leon Salim: Justice and Prosperity are possessed by only a sliver of the people], *Singgalang*, August 16, 1995.

74 Ibid.

75 Interview with Ahmad Husein (Padang), August 20, 1995. Interviews with veterans (Padang), August 1995.

76 Interviews with a group of former officers of the Banteng Division (Padang), August 9, 1995.

77 As early as 1989 the Central Intelligence Agency (CIA) estimated the Suharto family's assets as US$30billion. *New York Times*, May 22, 1998.

78 A detailed account of the attack appears in *Tempo* Interaktif, July 27, 1996.

79 They also cited the Assembly's refusal to help merchants whose stalls had been burned down in markets in Sungai Limau and in Bukittinggi. (Rumours circulated that at least the destruction of the Upper Market [Pasar Atas] in Bukittinggi had been initiated by developers wishing to replace the market stalls by a large Western-style supermarket.) *Haluan*, October 25, 1997; *Singgalang*, October 25, 1997.

80 *Haluan*, November 25, 30, 1997.

81 It was reported that on December 27, 1997, two days before the election, nine-hundred million rupiah from the Supplementary Expenses Budget was divided equally among forty-five members of the legislative assembly. *Republika*, March 27, 1999.

82 *Kompas* Online, March 26, 27, 1998.

83 Not only Indonesia, but also Malaysia and Singapore suffered from the smoke and smog.

84 *Far Eastern Economic Review*, January 22, 1998.

85 On the interplay of economic and political forces in the crisis, see John T. Sidel, 'Macet Total, Logics of Circulation and Accumulation in the Demise of Indonesia's New Order', *Indonesia* 66 (October 1998): pp. 159-94.

86 *Haluan*, March 28, 1998. This was a demonstration by the Islamic students' organization, HMI. See also *Haluan*, March 27, for the on-campus protests at the teachers' training college.

87 *Kompas*, April 17, May 2, 1998.

88 *Kompas*, May 19, 20, 1998. Students participated from all the major tertiary institutions in Padang, including Andalas University, the teachers' training college (IKIP), and Bung Hatta University.

Conclusion

1 *Kompas*, May 20, 1999.

2 The new minister of information, Yunus Yosfiah, seems to have taken the initiative in the moves to liberalize the entire news media, though the 'open air' policy of the last years of the Suharto regime had permitted sections of the population, particularly the students and the middle class, access to satellite communications from around the world. Their ability to hear views from outside the country regarding globalization, corruption, and human rights had undoubtedly had an influence on their demands for a more responsive government in Indonesia. After being appointed to the cabinet, Minister Yunus permitted these opinions to have broad circulation throughout the population. Born in 1944 in South Sulawesi, Yunus was a lieutenant general in the armed forces, a member of Kopassus, who served in East Timor before 1978 and was commander in Dili from 1985 to 1987. He reportedly killed Fretilin chief Lobato in 1978. He is married to an East Timorese.

3 I have a copy of the tape cassette in my possession. For the transcript of the conversation, see *Panji Masyarakat*, February 24, 1999.

4 Half of the ministers in Habibie's thirty-six-member 'Reform Development Cabinet' had served in Suharto's last cabinet.

5 See, for example, Gerry van Klinken's analysis 'Is Indonesia Breaking Down?' in *Far Eastern Economic Review*, March 18, 1999, with respect to West and Central Java and northern Sumatra.

6 By May 1999 it was reported that as many as fifty of the country's 306 district chiefs had been replaced since Suharto's downfall, 'often under pressure from the local populace'. Ibid., May 13, 1999.

7 This remark was made to me by a veteran of the PRRI at a meeting the group held in Padang, February 14, 1999.

8 For several of the accusations against Durin and his family, see *Singgalang*, March 25, 1999. Durin dismissed these allegations as slander (*fitnah*), possibly made by frustrated people who had not received the appointments they desired during his tenure. Interview with Hasan Basri Durin (Jakarta), February 18, 1999.

9 *Kompas*, May 25, 29, 1998. Some of the people with whom I spoke, while not contesting the involvement of Durin and his family in corruption, believed that particularly during his second term he had only gone along with practices that were by then endemic throughout the administration, from the central to the village government level.

10 Account of a faculty member of IKIP who witnessed the incident. Interview (Padang), March 27, 1999. See also *Gatra* March 27, 1999.

11 The governor's nominee was Ir. H. Nurmawan, a former Bupati of Solok and head of the Regional Development Board, and Jakarta's choice was a former regional secretary, Zainal Bakar.

12 He submitted his letter of resignation on March 13, and the ceremony for transferring power to his successor took place on March 27.

13 The government had earlier rejected his nominees for mayor of Payakumbuh and mayor of Padang Panjang. *Gamma*, March 28, 1999.

14 This stance accorded with professed government policy that all civil servants should remain neutral during the campaign and no party should be able to use state finances or facilities.

15 Interviews with Professor Mestika Zed of the Department of History and Professor Imran Manan of the Department of Anthropology (Padang), March 23 and 24, 1999.

16 *Padang Ekspres*, March 20, April 1, 1999.

17 'Tekanan dari Rantau', in *Gatra*, March 27, 1999. Durin was said to resent Muchlis' not using his authority to secure Durin's release when he was kidnapped by IKIP students the previous August. Interviews in Padang, March 24, 27, 1999.

18 Interview with Hasan Basri Durin, Jakarta, February 18,1999.

19 *Gatra*, March 27, 1999.

20 Reportedly he was involved in gaining the release of Western hostages taken by local dissidents in Irian in 1996 and had been sent to East Timor after the Santa Cruz massacres. *Bijak* 3,1 (29 March - 4 April 1999), p. 5.

21 Interviews with various Golkar members and Minangkabau migrants in Jakarta, February 1999.

22 There was still a general reluctance to discuss the possibility of federalism for Indonesia, and in early 1999 the only people I found willing to entertain and even advocate a federal system for Indonesia were a few intellectuals in West Sumatra and some former adherents of the PRRI.

23 *Singgalang*, September 23, 1997.

24 See *International Herald Tribune*, April 24-25, 1999. In the draft law, the exceptions were 'foreign affairs, defence and security, justice and fiscal/monetary policy, together with other fields decided by government regulation'. Ch. IV, paragraph 7 of *Rancangan Undang-undang Nomor – Tahun 1999 tentang Pemerintahan Daerah*', p. 3. (So, in the final law Parliament added 'religious affairs' to those initially within the purview of the central government.) This is, of course, a far cry from the limited fields over which the government would retain control in a federal order – usually only defence, foreign affairs, postal services, and other communications. And some of the fields are amorphous enough for there to be considerable latitude of interpretation.

25 *Far Eastern Economic Review*, May 13, 1999.

26 It was projected that in the year 2000/2001, Aceh, for example, would receive 15 percent of the government's share of oil revenue from the region, and 90 percent of the province's land

and property taxes (with 10 percent going to the central government.) Altogether it was estimated that Aceh would receive as its share of the profits and taxes on all its resources Rp. 2.5 trillion, compared with a previous figure of Rp. 350-500 billion. *Kompas*, May 27, 1999.

27 *Far Eastern Economic Review*, May 13, 1999.

28 Interview with Prof. Dr. Sjafrizal, Dean, Faculty of Economy, Andalas University (Padang), February 16, 1999.

29 *Jakarta Post*, July 14, 1995, reporting a statement by Taufik Abdullah. This was in response to a trial decentralization project inaugurated in April 1995 whereby the central government gave greater authority and responsibility to twenty-six selected district (kabupaten) administrations throughout the archipelago. In West Sumatra, Tanah Datar was the designated kabupaten.

30 Anne Booth, 'Can Indonesia Survive as a Unitary State?', *Indonesia Circle*, No. 58 (June 1992), p. 33.

31 *Mimbar Minang*, April 19, 1999.

32 For good accounts of the growth of rebellion in Aceh see Tim Kell, *The Roots of Acehnese Rebellion* (Ithaca: Cornell Modern Indonesia Project, 1995) and Geoffrey Robinson, '*Rawan* is as *Rawan* does: The Origins of Disorder in New Order Aceh', *Indonesia* 66 (October 1998), pp. 127-56.

33 There were loud protests from the regions when this provision was included in the draft law, but it appears to have been retained in the final version.

34 *Gatra*, February 20, 1999.

35 See for instance *Gatra*, February 20, 1999; *Singgalang*, March 20, 1999; *Padang Ekspres*, March 4, 24, 1999.

36 Interview with Professor Sjafrizal, February 16, 1999.

37 *Far Eastern Economic Review*, May 20, 1999.

38 Ibid.

39 *Kompas*, May 22, 1999.

40 The Team included leading scholars, lawyers, and student activists. For a full list of the parties that qualified, see *Jakarta Post*, March 5, 1999.
In the event, in the national elections held on June 7, 1999, the top five parties obtained 86.7 percent of the vote, with the remaining forty-three parties sharing only 13.3 percent. Megawati Sukarnoputri's PDIP (Partai Demokrasi Indonesia-Perjuangan, Indonesian Democratic Party of Struggle) gained the largest number of votes: 35,689,073 (33.8 percent), with Golkar a poor second with 23,741,749 (22.5 percent). The PKB, headed by NU leader Abdurrachman Wahid and the Islamic PPP were runners up with 13,336,982 (12.7 percent) and 11,329,905 (10.7 percent) respectively, while Amien Rais' PAN was fifth with only 7,578,956 (7.1 percent). *Kompas Online*, July 27, 1999.

41 *Haluan*, March 23, 1999.

42 *Mimbar Minang*, April 19, 1999.

43 In West Sumatra the vast majority of votes went to Islamic parties, but Golkar finally did edge out the Modernist Muslim party (PAN-Partai Amanat Nasional), headed by former Muhammadiah chief Amien Rais for first place. In the general elections, Golkar received 459,577 (23.6 percent) out of 1,912,230 valid votes, with PAN receiving 430,848 (22.1 percent). The Islamic PPP received 400,702 votes (20.6 percent) and Megawati Sukarnoputri's PDIP received 202,520. Thus Golkar was entitled to four seats in the national parliament, both PAN and PPP three seats and the PDIP 2 seats. *Mimbar Minang*, June 21, 1999.

Index

Abbas, Syekh (of Padang Jepang), 37
Abduh, Muhammad, 36, 293n. 31
Abdul Muis, 36, 45, 74
Abdul Rahman Tuanku nan Putih, 118-19, 121,
 122, 317n. 45
Abdullah glr. Sutan Bandaro Panjang, 102, 158,
 190, 309n. 92
 as member of dpd, 122
 and Sukarno, 195-96
 and Tan Malaka, 64, 134, 136-37, 158, 297n.
 101, 303n. 78, 321n. 120
Abdullah, Taufik, 44
Abubakar, 180
Aceh, 55, 189, 226
 kingdom of, 23
 in Revolution, 127, 141, 144, 154-55
 in early 1950s, 169, 170-71, 174, 180
 and Darul Islam, 175-76, 188, 224
 in 1965, 248, 353n. 124
 under Habibie, 275, 276-77, 361n. 26
Adabiah School, 44, 51, 102, 293n. 40
Adam B.B., 83, 91, 124, 308n. 62, 319n. 71
Adam, Zubir, 124, 125
adat, 16-17
 and Islam, 74, 84-88, 309n. 82
 leaders (traditional authorities), 25, 36, 40, 57,
 85, 86-87, 111, 190, 235, 245, 290n. 29, 352nn.
 102, 103
 under Japanese, 102, 312n. 19
 during Revolution, 108, 123, 152, 156, 326nn.
 63, 64
 during prri, 235
 under New Order, 258-59, 261-62, 352nn. 102,
 103
 KAN (Village adat Council), 260
 See also lkaam; mtkaam; nagari, penghulu
Adityavarman, 21, 23, 289n. 13
Ahmad, Haji Abdullah, 36, 44, 51, 54, 63, 294n.
 41, 303n. 71, 327n. 82
Aidit, D.N., 191, 239, 247
Ainuddin, 242
al-Afghani, Jamal al-Din, 36, 293n. 31
Al Azhar, 36, 55
Al Munir, 37, 63, 294n. 41
 See also newspapers
Alamsjah, St. Nur, 68-69
Alimin (Limin), see Limin

Alimin Prawirodirdjo, 72, 291n. 5, 298n. 111
Alwi Sutan Marajo, 145
Amal, Ichlasul, 248, 254
Ambarawa, 49
Ambon and Ambonese, 143, 166, 180, 328n. 3
America, American, See United States
Amrullah, Syekh Abdul Karim. See Rasul, Haji
Anai valley, pass, 31, 33, 68, 138, 217, 290n. 27
Anas, Azwar, 258, 260-61, 357n. 34
Andalas University, 23, 236-37, 246, 250, 268,
 348-49n. 25
Anderson, Benedict R. O'G., 16
Anderson, Major, 109, 315n. 10
anticommunism, 197, 202-5, 208, 213, 219, 227,
 242, 245, 248-49, 343nn. 40, 43, 349n. 43
 See also gak; Gebak
Anwar, Rosihan, 237
Anwar St. Saidi, 75-78, 149, 237, 265, 306nn. 16,
 33, 310nn. 102, 103,
 arrests of, 77, 97-98
 and Hatta, 62, 78
 and Chatib Suleiman, 83, 90, 91
 and National Bank, 76-77, 83
 in revolution, 111, 141, 158, 316n. 38, 325-
 26nn. 46, 54
 See also National Bank
Arif, M. Nur, 69-70, 304n. 105
Arisun, Bupati, 143
armed forces:
 British, 108-9, 314n. 5, 315nn. 9, 11 10
 Dutch, 95, 103 (See also KNIL)
 Japanese, 95
 Indonesian (during revolution), 114, 116, 126,
 160, 323n. 16
 BKR, 108, 109
 TKR, 109
 TRI, 126
 TNI, 127, 148, 151
 in the 1950s, 179, 184-86, 198, 222, 333n. 1,
 337n. 72
 under Guided Democracy, 225, 238
 under Suharto, 253, 254, 270, 272, 355nn. 4, 7
 See also Banteng Division; Javanese troops; mili-
 tias; rationalization; sskad
Arrasuli of Candung, Syekh Suleiman, 84, 91,
 122, 316n. 31, 318n. 59
ASEAN (Association of Southeast Asian Nations),
 262

Assaat, 64, 170, 172, 218, 225, 226, 340n. 1
assassination attempts. *See* Cikini
Australia, 96, 130, 157
autonomy, 17, 19, 167, 168, 169, 171, 173-74,
   179, 182, 188-90, 193-97, 208, 209, 212, 213,
   224, 253, 260, 265, 329nn. 9, 10
   regional movements for, 184, 188-89, 213, 229
   See also decentralization; centre-regional relations

Bachtaruddin, 116, 117, 122, 134, 135, 160, 176,
   316n. 33, 327n. 88
Bahar, Saafroedin, 240, 241, 246, 248, 256, 260,
   353n. 121
Bainal glr Paduko Malano, 216, 240, 241, 342n.
   33, 351n. 70
Bakar, Zainal, 273
Bakin (Intelligence Coordinating Body). *See*
   Intelligence services
Banda Neira, 78, 97
Bangkok, 63, 303n. 68
banks and banking, 76-78, 150, 264
   village credit, 262, 264
   See also National Bank
Banteng Charter, 182-83, 184
Banteng Council:
   aims of, 184, 195-96, 208, 213
   formation of, 182-83, 333nn. 73, 74, 75
   membership of, 183, 335nn. 30, 31
   opposition to, 202-3,
   policies of, 188-92, 193, 219, 229
   splits in, 209, 211-12
Banteng Division, 18-19, 99
   in revolution, 110, 120, 126-27, 131-32, 144,
   321n. 104
   and trade, 149, 150
   disbanding of, 178-82, 331nn. 51, 55, 56, 57
   reestablishment of, 182-84, 189, 191
   reunion of, 182-83, 332nn. 68, 70, 338n. 105
Bariun A.S., 117
Barlian, 182, 187, 192, 198-201
   at Sungai Dareh, 206-7
   neutrality of, 208, 211, 217, 341n. 6
Basa Bandaro, Abdullah, 44, 54, 56, 58, 75, 78, 82,
   300n. 24, 300n. 36, 306n. 16
Baso, 118-22, 317nn. 42, 45, 46, 48, 49, 53, 54, 56,
   317n. 56, 318nn. 59, 60
Batuah, H. Datuk, 39, 40, 53, 59, 78, 88, 157-58,
   305n. 11, 316n. 33, 327n. 88
Beureu'eh, Teungku Daud, 170-71, 175, 224
Bodi Caniago, 21-22, 86
Boerhan Malin Kunieng (Tuanku Nan Hitam),
   118-19, 122, 317n. 45
Bonjol, Tuanku Imam, 25, 59, 289n. 21, 290n. 24
Booth, Anne, 276
Bosselaar, Resident, 97
Boven Digul, 40, 49, 50, 52, 63, 65, 67, 69-70,

112, 156-58, 299n. 126, 304n. 105
BPNK. *See* militias, village
BPPI. *See* Youth Information Office
Brawijaya Division, 216, 220, 225, 228
British, 199, 243, 244, 314n. 5
   See also armed forces, British
Budi Utomo, 26-27, 290n. 30
bureaucracy. *See* officials

Cairo, 36, 54, 55, 87
Central Trading Corporation, 150
centre-regional relations:
   in revolution, 125-26, 127-33, 144, 160-61, 168,
   173-74, 176, 178, 179
   in 1950s, 183, 185, 192, 195, 197, 200, 202, 206,
   208, 212, 229, 258, 330nn. 29, 31, 331n. 40,
   334n. 25
   under Suharto, 251, 253, 273
   See also decentralization
Chambers, Major General H.M., 109
Chan, Aziz, 129, 320n. 92
Chatib, Syekh Ahmad, 36, 292n. 29
China, Chinese:
   community, 42, 75 150, 151, 159, 244, 247, 248,
   249, 255, 269, 351-52n. 90
   Republic of, 200-1, 204
   See also traders, Chinese
Chuo sangi in (Central Advisory Council), 104
Christians and Christianity, 168, 188, 220, 224
   missionaries, 34, 89, 92
Cikini, 204-5, 208, 338nn. 115, 117, 339nn. 120,
   121
Cipinang, 40, 49, 67
civil service.*See* officials
coffee, 26, 27, 35, 150, 325n. 45
   cultivation system, 26, 35, 290n. 27
Collins, Foster, 199
Communist & communism, 31-32, 35, 49, 249-
   50
   and Islam, 27-28, 39-41, 44, 45, 53, 74, 86, 88,
   294n. 52, 308-9n. 73
   and the PRRI, 199, 202-4, 220, 222-23, 228
   in 1965/6, 240, 242, 248-9, 353-54n. 124, 354n.
   126
   See also anticommunism
Communist party. *See* pki
Constituent Assembly, 169, 177, 224
Constitution:
   of 1945, 224-25, 227
   of 1950, 194, 210, 224, 336n. 52
coups and attempted coups, 165-66, 186, 215
   of October 17, 1952, 184-85
   of November 1956, 186
   of September 30, 1965, 233-34, 238, 242, 245,
   247-49, 256, 347nn. 2, 6, 7, 9, 350nn. 50, 62, 63,
   351n. 66, 70
   See also March 3 affair

Cumming, Hugh S., Jr., 207
currency, 117, 148-49, 150, 268, 316n. 38, 324-25nn. 41, 42, 44

Daan Jahya, 132
Dahlan, 48, 315n. 19
Darul Islam, 175, 176, 180, 188, 214, 224, 332n. 60
Darwis Thaib Dt. Sidi Bandaro, 22
Datuk Batuah, H. *See* Batuah, H. Datuk
Dawood, 67, 304n. 96
decentralization, 16, 19, 251, 335n. 43, 361n. 29
  under Japanese, 104-5,
  economic, 189-90, 262-63
  calls for, 167-69, 173-74, 183, 198, 224, 329n. 15
  law of 1948, 168, 173
  legislation of 1957, 195, 336n. 57
  law of 1999, 275, 277, 361nn. 24, 26, 33
  See also centre-regional relations
de Josselin de Jong, P.E., 22
Digul. *See* Boven Digul
Diniyyah schools, 17, 34, 54, 55, 79, 307n. 40
  establishment of, 37-38, 53
  for girls, 32, 56, 80-81, 306n. 37, 307nn. 40, 46
  student organization of (pmds), 57-58, 80-81
Diponegoro Division, 243
  in West Sumatra, 216, 220, 225, 228, 238, 250, 352n. 97
Disba. *See* Special Region
Djago-djago, 39, 41, 44
  See also newspapers
Djajusman alias Mamak, 240, 353n. 121
Djalaluddin, Syekh Tahir, 52, 63, 293n. 32, 300n. 16
Djambek, Dahlan
  in Giyu gun, 102, 106
  as Banteng commander, 110, 119, 120, 122, 126, 157, 179, 180
  after Dutch attack, 144, 145-46, 160, 323n. 27
  and Banteng Council, 182, 189, 198, 338nn. 98, 105
  anticommunism of, 203-4, 213, 219
  and prri, 209, 210, 211, 214, 218, 220, 340n. 1, 345nn. 69, 70
  death of, 227-27, 345n. 78, 346nn. 82, 83
Djambek, Syekh Mohd. Djamil, 36, 44, 51, 63, 99, 111, 122, 126, 157, 203, 303n. 71
Djamil, Dr. Mohammad, 111, 112, 114, 117, 119-21, 171, 320n. 93
Djamil Djaho, Syekh Muhammad, 84
Djamin, Mr. Dt., 77
Djatikusumo, 214
Djaya, Tamar, 72
Djoeir Moehamad, 213, 329n. 15
Djuanda Kartawidjaja, 194-95, 196, 198, 206, 209, 210, 211, 213, 222

Doos, Anwar, 125
dpd. *See* Regional Defence Council
dpr. *See* People's Representative Council, Parliament
dprst. *See* People's Representative Council
Dulles, Allen, 197, 216
Dulles, J. Foster, 197, 207, 216
Dunidja D., 274, 360n. 20
Durin, Hasan Basri, 261, 263-65, 268, 272-73, 357nn. 41, 46, 47, 48, 360nn. 8, 9, 17
Duski Samad, 122
Dutch:
  East India Company (voc), 25
  officials, 109
  First "Police action" (1947), 128-30
  Second "Police action" (1948), 131, 133, 137, 138-42, 145-46, 159, 160, 322nn. 5, 10
  See also economy; repression, Dutch
dwitunggal (duumvirate), 184, 188, 193-94, 195, 198-200, 202

East Indonesia, 185, 187
  under Japanese, 95
East Indonesia State (NIT), 157, 166
economy:
  under Dutch, 90, 310nn. 97, 102
  under Japanese, 103-4
  in revolution, 117, 120, 147-48
  postrevolutionary, 174, 176, 184, 189-90, 200, 202, 334nn. 24, 25
  under the New Order: 251-53, 258, 262-65, 268-69, 272, 357n. 43, 358nn. 60, 62
education:
  Islamic, 74, 78
  Western, 34, 36, 72, 78, 111
educational institutions. *See* schools
egalitarianism, 17, 71, 74
El Hilaal (Crescent Moon). *See* youth organizations
Eisenhower, Dwight D., 207
elections, 166-67, 168, 168, 265, 270, 271
  during revolution, 122-23, 177
  in 1955, 176-78, 184-85, 249, 331nn. 43, 45
  under Suharto, 253, 255-57, 261, 267, 268, 269, 355n. 16, 356nn. 20, 23, 359n. 81
  in 1999, 273, 361-62n. 40, 362n. 43
Elephant Council (Dewan Gajah), 186-87
Emergency Government (PDRI), 138-41, 151, 153, 154, 179, 218-19, 223, 267, 326nn. 59, 60, 327n. 72
Entrepreneurs' League (Sarikat Usaha), 44, 75
Esmara, Hendra, 264
European & Eurasian community, 42, 75

Fadlillah, Arif, 46, 47, 59, 85, 297n. 100
FDR. *See* People's Democratic Front
Federal Consultative Assembly (BFO), 152, 154

Federal Republic of Indonesia (RPI), 221, 224-25, 226, 344nn. 54, 55, 56, 57
federalism and federal system, 152, 165-67, 205, 224, 318n. 67, 361n. 22
  in Minangkabau, 22
  See also RIS
Fujiyama, Colonel, 97, 98, 99

Gaharu, Sjahmaun, 189
GAK (Anti-Communist Movement), 204-5, 338n. 107
Gandi, 227
Gani, A.K., 109-10
Garuda Council, 187
Garuda Division, 187, 192
Gebak (Joint Movement against Communism), 204, 213
Gebu Minang(Minang 1000 Rupiah movement), 264, 358n. 67
Gerindo (Gerakan Rakyat Indonesia), 90
Gintings, Djamin, 187, 334n. 17
Giyu-gun (People's Volunteer Army) 18, 99-103, 107-8, 111, 118, 126, 313nn. 25, 27, 29
Giyugun koenkai (support organization), 102, 108, 147, 313n. 36
Glodok, 49, 66
Gobée, E., 66
gold, 24, 25, 150, 227, 295n. 67, 325n. 49
Golkar (Functional Groups) 253-54, 355n. 6
  Party, 253, 255, 256, 257, 355n. 15, 356nn. 18, 20, 23
Gonggrijp, G.F.E., 54
Good Offices Committee, UN, 130, 320n. 95
government: concepts of, 16, 153, 156, 161
governor, role of, 168, 171-73, 229, 242, 246, 247, 258, 260-61, 268, 270, 272, 329nn. 11, 12, 13, 357nn. 34, 46, 361n. 33
  See also Roeslan Moeljohardjo; Zain, Harun; Azas, Anwar; Durin, Hasan Basri; Ibrahim, Muchlis
GRR (Gerakan Revolusi Rakyat) *see* People's Revolutionary Movement
Guided Democracy, 246-47, 252, 255
guru ordinansi. See teachers' ordinance

Habibie, B.J., 269, 270, 271, 272, 360n. 4
Hahanokai, 102, 324n. 38
  See also women's organizations
Halim, Abdul, 119, 137, 144, 145, 146, 328n. 94, 331n. 55, 333n. 75
Hamengku Buwono IX, Sultan of Yogyakarta, 196, 201, 209, 210, 211, 220
Hamid II, Sultan, 166, 320n. 60
Hamka, 38, 39, 137, 157, 160, 327n. 83
Hamzah, Djamhur, 191
Hanafi, Baharuddin, 240, 241, 350n. 62
Harahap, Burhanuddin, 177, 205, 206, 208, 211, 218, 225, 226

Hassan, Tengku Mohd., 107, 118, 128, 129, 135, 140
Hatta, Mohammad:
  as prewar leader, 36, 44, 50, 56, 59-61, 64, 73-74
  exiled, 65-66, 97
  under Japanese, 98, 104
  as prime minister, 130, 132, 133, 134, 135, 138-39, 144, 159, 166
  as vice president, 107, 114-16, 120, 125, 129-31, 160-61
  under Dutch arrest, 153-55, 322n. 10
  resignation of, 178, 183, 273
  and regional dissidents, 199, 201, 210, 212-13, 337n. 88, 338n. 98
  after prri, 236, 255
  economic ideas of, 78, 150
  followers of, 59-60, 77, 86, 91, 192-94
  and Sukarno, 59-60, 196, 200, 212
  and Tan Malaka, 62, 115-16, 121
  views on decentralization, 128, 166, 171
Hazairin, Professor, 173
Hidayat, Col., 132-33, 139, 141, 144, 145, 146, 151, 154, 159, 179, 222, 321n. 104, 326n. 60, 333n. 1
Hirose, Vice Admiral Sueto, 109
Hitam, Tuanku nan. *See* Boerhan Malin Kunieng
Hizbul Wathan. *See* youth organizations
Hizbullah, 103, 110, 116, 124, 125, 126
  See also militias
Hokokai. *See* Patriotic Service League
Husein, Ahmad:
  biog. of 181-82, 332n. 66
  in revolution, 126, 134, 145, 320n. 85, 321n. 113
  and Banteng Council, 182-83, 186, 190, 192, 195, 196, 209-10, 250
  and Nasution, 193, 334n. 21
  and other dissidents, 197, 198, 209-10, 217, 240, 266, 341n. 7, 342n. 33
  and Munas, 200-201
  and outside support, 199, 207, 208
  and prri, 211, 214-15, 218, 219, 340n. 141
  surrender of, 226, 345n. 66
Hutabarat, 226

Ibrahim, Dahlan, 102, 117, 125, 126, 142, 144-45, 179, 182, 328n. 94, 331n. 55, 333n. 75
Ibrahim, Djamaluddin, 41, 46, 57, 58, 62, 63-64, 65, 66-67, 75, 77, 78, 158, 297n. 99
Ibrahim Melawas, 49
Ibrahim, Muchlis, 268, 273, 360nn. 11, 12, 13, 17
Ibrahim Musa Parabek, Syekh, 40
Ibrahim, Saleh, 204, 339n. 120
Ibrahim, Sofyan, 180, 182, 332n. 59, 341n. 8
IGGI (Inter-Governmental Group for Indonesia), 252-53
IMF (International Monetary Fund), 253, 268-69

India, Indian, 130, 150, 159, 244
  nationalist movement, 55
  traders, 24, 292n. 20
Ingleson, John, 52, 59-60. 92
Inkorba, 90, 310n. 103
INS school, 52, 72, 82-83, 111, 190, 307n. 52,
  308n. 56, 315n. 16
Insulinde party, 72
Intelligence services:
  American (cia), 199, 216
  British (cid), 66
  Dutch (pid), 68, 72, 111
  Indonesian, 124, 319n. 76, 348n. 13
    Pema, 137, 328n. 90
    Kopkamtib, 256
  Japanese, 158, 185
ipo (International Scouting Organization), 41,
  43, 57
Irian Jaya (West Irian) 204, 277
Iron Bridge surau. See Surau Djembatan Besi
isdv (Indies Social Democratic Association), 27
Iskandar, 209, 216, 342n. 30
Islam, 17, 84, 251, 312n. 19
  and adat, 84-87, 88
  and banking, 35, 76-77, 292n. 25
  and communism, 27, 39, 40, 41, 45, 53, 74, 88,
    294n. 52, 308-9n. 73
    (see also pki Lokal Islamy)
  and nationalism, 53, 55-56, 60-61, 64, 74
  and politics, 64, 219
  and trade, 24, 34, 35, 71, 292nn. 18, 19, 22, 25
  Islamic colleges, 79, 82, 307nn. 47, 48
  See also schools, Islamic
Islamic law, 177, 205
Islamic League (Sarikat Islam, SI), 27, 31, 32, 36,
  39, 42-43, 45, 51, 92, 118
  See also PSII
Islamic political parties, 17, 50, 175, 219, 246,
  249, 255-56, 257, 356nn. 20, 23
  (see also Masjumi; Perti; Parmusi; PPP)
  youth branch of, 203-5, 237, 246, 359n. 86
  See also youth organizations
Islamic scholars, leaders (ulama), 22, 34, 50-53,
  74, 87, 102, 175, 190, 198-99, 245-47, 257,
  309n. 82
Islamic State, 175, 224
Ismail, Rasimah, 56

Jacub, Iljas, 53-55, 65, 78, 87, 156-57, 171-72,
  300n. 28, 327n. 79
Jalaluddin, Haji, 46
Jambi, 43, 141, 150. 169, 173, 183, 190, 191-91,
  198, 218, 219, 261
Jamil, Damanhuri, 40, 41, 57
Japanese:
  invasion, 49, 67, 92, 95, 113, 311n. 5
  occupation, 18, 70, 74, 95-106, 107, 118, 259,
    313n. 24

capitulation, 104, 107
officers, in independence struggle, 101, 118,
  119, 317n. 46
Javanese:
  contract workers, 42, 169, 248, 354n. 124
  immigrant population,169, 202, 248, 250
  labor (romusha), 118-19
  relationship with Minangkabau, 16, 17, 23-24,
    152, 156, 190, 219, 260
  troops in West Sumatra, 220-21, 228, 235, 250,
    254, 346-47n. 92
  See also officials, Javanese; centre-regional rela-
    tions
Jazir, 62
Johan, 209, 216, 217, 342nn. 30, 34
Junus, Bachtiar, 124
Junus, Mahmud, 87, 99, 101, 111, 313n. 22
Junus, Mohamad. See Kotjek
Jusuf Sampono Kajo, M., 49

Kaharuddin Dt. Rangkayo Basa, 190, 209, 211,
  215, 216, 228-29, 242, 333n. 74, 340n. 140,
  341n. 7
Kamal, Mustafa (Kamal Attaturk), 37, 41, 55
Kamaluddin (alias Tambiluak), 144, 323nn. 22,
  23, 24
Kamaluddin Muhamed (Krismas), 79
Kamang, 33, 145, 218, 220, 225, 227
Kamaruddin gelar [alias] Manggulung, 47, 49
Kandur St. Rangkayo Basa, 62, 63-64, 67, 158,
  303nn. 73, 77
Karim, Ahmad, 249
Karim, Mr. A. 150
Karim, Eni, 213
Karim M.S., Abdul, 107, 135
Kartosuwirjo, S.M., 175, 330n. 33
Kasimo, 170
Kaum Muda (Young Group), 31, 44, 51, 86
Kaum Tua , 31, 54
Kawilarang, Alex E., 103, 185, 224, 226, 238,
  334n. 9
Kern, R., 40
Ketemanggungan, Datuk, 19, 21, 23
KNI, KNIP (Komité Nasional Indonesia [Pusat]).
  See also National Committee
KNIL (Koninklijke Nederlandsche Indische
  Leger), 157. 165, 166, 179, 323n. 18
Koiso Declaration, 104
konsepsi of Sukarno, 193, 196, 200
Kopkamtib (Operational Command for Restora-
  tion of Security and Order). See Intelligence
  services
Kostrad (Army's Strategic Reserve Command),
  234
Kotjek, Mohamad Junus, 57, 58, 59, 83, 91, 102,
  301n. 47, 308n. 62, 311n. 109
Koto Piliang, 21-22, 86

Kototinggi, 141, 151, 225, 322n. 14
Kraink, Dt., 68
Krtanagara, 23

Labai, Sulaiman. *See* Sulaiman Labai
Labai, Zainuddin. *See* Zainuddin Labai el Junu-
siah
Lahade, Saleh, 187, 211
Landjoemin Dt. Toemenggoeng, 89, 119, 294n.
50, 309-10n. 94
language, 73, 82, 83-84, 228, 306n. 38
Lasjmi, 110, 124
See also militias, Islamic political parties, Perti
Lathif, H. Abdul, 55
Latief, Abdul, 234, 347n. 6, 348n. 11
Legge, John, 189, 192
Lengah, Ismael:
in Giyu gun, 102
in revolution, 108, 126, 137, 149
and March 3 affair, 123-24, 127, 319-20n. 84
dismissal of, 132, 144, 328n. 94
and Banteng Council, 182, 191, 209
Leurs, Mr., 48
Liem, Roland, 199
Limin (Alimin), 46, 47, 298n. 111
Linggajati Agreement, 123, 125, 130, 154, 325n.
45
LKAAM (Minangkabau Adat Consultative Body),
246, 261
See also adat
Logas, 118, 314n.44
Long Declaration. *See* Plakaat Panjang
Lubis, Taher Karim, 227
Lubis, Zulkifli, 334n. 9
background, 185
attempted coup of, 186-87, 202
and dissidents, 193, 196-99, 206, 210, 212
and Cikini, 204-5, 208, 339n. 120
in PRRI, 214, 217, 218, 219, 226
Luthfi, Muchtar, 53, 54, 55, 65, 78, 80, 87, 157,
301n. 31

Madiun. *See* rebellion
Madjiman S., 241, 245, 350n. 52, 354n. 129
Madjo Orang, Dt., 98, 99, 111
Magas Abdul Madjid, 44-45, 296n. 87
Mahmud, 46
Malacca Strait, 33, 35, 59, 63, 149, 150, 151, 185,
263
Malaya, Malaysia, 71, 75, 79, 149, 224, 263, 344n.
53
Mangkuto, Dt. Singo, 56-57, 301n. 43
Mangunkusumo, Dr. Tjipto, 66
Mansoer Sani, 202, 338n. 102, 345n. 71
Mansur, A.R. Sutan, 53, 87, 300n. 13
Mansur Daud Dt. Palimo Kajo, 37, 177, 352n. 100
Marah Sutan, Muhamad Taher, 44, 75, 77, 78, 82,
296n. 79

Maramis, Mr., 140
March 3 affair, 123-26, 127, 157, 177, 319nn.
75, 76, 77, 80, 84
Maryanov, Gerald S., 169
Masjumi party,
in West Sumatra, 123, 125, 157, 160, 171, 176,
177, 235, 251, 316n. 30
national party, 125, 172, 175, 176, 177, 191,
193, 203, 208, 219, 255
in 1955 elections, 17, 177, 331nn. 43, 45
banning of, 246, 249
youth group of 204-5
matrilineal system, 17, 24, 36, 57, 84, 98, 292n. 28
Mecca, 36, 54, 55
Megawati Sukarnoputri, 267
merantau. *See* migration
Merapi, Mt., 31
1926 eruption of, 32, 49
Merapi Institute, 83
merchants. *See* traders
Merchants' Group (Himpunan Saudagar), 54, 75,
76
migrants (perantau), migration, 19, 36, 71, 74, 88,
196, 236, 248-49, 251, 254, 262, 263, 273, 305n.
2, 348nn. 22, 23, 358nn. 62, 67
military-civilian relations, 151, 219, 224, 225,
355n. 7
militias, 110, 116, 119, 145, 146, 313-14n. 38,
331n. 50
district, 146
village: (BPNK), 146-47, 221
(Perlaras), 221
of the political parties, 110, 116, 123, 124, 126-
27, 145, 175
See also Hizbullah; Sabilillah; Lasjmi; Temi
Minangkabau Harmony (Kerukunan Minangkabau), 99, 100
Minangkabau Raad (Minangkabau Council), 90,
108, 174, 310n. 99
Minangkabau State. *See* Special Region
Minangkabau Trading Company, 150
Misbach, H. Mohammad, 39, 42, 53
Moerdani, Benny, 234, 343n. 39
Mokoginta, Ahmad Jusuf, 235, 238-40. 243-44,
245, 256, 349nn. 40, 41, 45
Mossman, James, 217
Mountbatten, Admiral Lord Louis, 108, 314n. 5
MTKAAM (Majelis Tinggi Kerapatan Adat Alam
Minangkabau), 89, 92, 124, 246, 352n. 99
See also adat, LKAAM
Muhammadiah, 51, 53, 73, 82, 83, 87, 89, 182,
299n. 5
schools of, 83-84
Muis, Abdul. *See* Abdul Muis
Munap, 'General' Abdul, 48
Munas (National Conference 1957), 198, 199,
200-201, 336n. 70, 337nn. 86, 88

Murba party, 137, 158, 199, 213, 236, 237, 238, 250, 255
Murtopo, Ali, 234, 256, 348n. 13, 355n. 6
Muskita, 243
Musso, 134, 135, 298n. 111, 321n. 107
Muzakkar, Kahar, 175, 224, 330n. 35
myths:
    origin, 21-24, 288nn. 1, 2, 289n.3
    re Tan Malaka, 62, 71-72

nagari (extended village), 16, 21-22, 75-76, 102, 146-47, 153, 257-58, 259, 262, 265, 288n. 5, 348n. 17, 357nn. 37, 38, 358n. 62
    councils of, 22, 26, 122-23, 174, 258, 318n. 65 (See also adat)
    elections (1946) in, 122-23, 147. (See also elections)
    government of, 86, 246, 260, 261, 348n. 17, 352nn. 102, 103, 356n. 27
    heads of, 26, 123, 152, 235, 258, 318n. 65, 326n. 63, 357n. 49
    ordinance (1914), 26, 85-86, 290n. 29
    1979 law. See village law, 1979
    1983 law, 259, 260, 261, 357nn. 36, 41, 42
    security organizations (MPRN, BPNK), 147, 148, 153
    See also militias, village, penghulu
Nahdlatul Ulama (NU), 176, 177, 193, 257
    in 1955 elections, 177, 331n. 43
Naim, Mochtar, 236, 259
Nainggolan, W.F. (Boyke), 215, 226
Naksyabandiyah, 24, 88, 289n. 18
Naoaki, Hattori, 104
Nasrun, Mohd., 91, 129, 131, 171, 320n. 93
Nasution, A.H., 103, 320n. 99
    in revolution, 131-32, 134, 135, 144, 160,
    as army chief of staff, 180, 184, 188, 198, 203, 206, 209, 253
    dismissal and reinstatement of, 185
    opposition to, 186, 205, 333n. 2
    relations with Husein, 189, 193, 195, 208, 334n. 21
    on Committee of Seven, 201
    actions against PRRI, 210, 211, 212, 213, 214-16
    negotiations with rebels, 221-22, 225-26
    in 1965, 233
Nasution, Abdul Muluk, 47, 48, 49, 296n. 76
Nasution, Jahja, 64
National Bank, 76-77, 83, 98, 264-65, 325-26nn. 46, 54
National Committees
    central (KNIP), 125
    local (KNI), 107, 108, 111, 112, 114, 117, 120, 122
National Conference (1957) see Munas
National Council, proposal for, 193, 195-96, 200, 212

nationalism, 14, 156, 305n. 2, 314n. 45
    and Islam, 53, 55-56, 60-61
    and democracy, 60-61
Natsir, Mohammad:
    and Persis, 74
    and Aceh, 154-55, 175
    as Masjumi head, 125, 205, 255
    as prime minister, 170-71, 172, 176
    with the rebels, 206-7, 208, 212, 217-18, 221, 224, 225
    surrender of, 226-28, 345n. 77
Navis, A.A., 23, 34, 87, 237
Nawawi, 217, 341n. 6
Nazaruddin Dt. Rajo Mangkuto, 124, 125, 157, 319n. 80
Nazir St. Pamuncak, 134, 321n. 111
Nehru, Jawaharlal, 139
New PNI. See PNI Baru
newspapers and journals, 37, 39, 40, 41, 44, 58, 63, 79, 213, 237, 238, 239, 242, 272, 294n. 52, 300n. 28, 307n. 47
Ning, Hasjim, 236, 237
NIT. See East Indonesia State
Noer, Deliar, 87
Noer, Jusuf, 182
Nur Ibrahim, Mohammad, 46
Nurmathias, 209, 211, 215, 216, 240, 341nn. 7, 8, 342n. 32
Nursalim, 242
Nusjirwan, 182
Nyoto, 240, 350n. 49

Obor, 58, 62, 64, 67
    See also newspapers, Pari
Oei Tjoe Tat, 244
officials, bureaucracy, 167, 220, 221, 235, 246, 250, 254, 261, 262, 265, 355n. 7, 360n. 6
    under Dutch, 22, 95, 106, 119, 125, 152
    under Japanese, 95, 99, 104, 106, 112-13, 125
    in revolution, 108, 112, 119, 123, 124, 125, 129, 156, 324n. 34, 327n. 71
    Javanese, role of, 169, 235, 242-43, 246, 247, 250, 253
oil and oilfields, 95, 99, 215, 216, 243, 262, 341-42n. 21
Oki, Akira, 86
Ombilin: mine, 32, 42, 43, 47, 54
    river, 15
opium, 150-51, 325n. 55, 326nn. 57, 60
OPR (People's Defence Organization), 221, 227, 228, 245, 248, 343-44nn. 46, 48, 348n. 17, 351n. 70
    See also nagari security organizations; youth organizations

Padang
    as trade centre, 25, 27, 34, 35, 42,

in 1927 rebellion, 32, 36, 43-45, 46, 49,
   as nationalist centre, 54, 56, 60, 64, 68
   Sukarno in, 96-98
   in revolution, 108-9, 120, 124, 129, 156, 181
   in PRRI, 211, 216, 219
Padang Panjang
   as educational centre, 31, 34, 37-41, 57
   as political centre, 32, 36, 38-42, 45, 57, 60, 67,
    68-69, 291n. 7, 297n. 91
   in 1927 rebellion, 46-47, 49
   in revolution, 137, 138, 141, 322n. 5
Paderi movement, wars, 24-25, 27, 33, 34, 35, 36
Pagarruyung, 22
Pagar Ruyung battalion, 180
Palembang Charter, 198-99, 337n. 85
Pancasila (Five Principles), 19, 223, 252, 257,
   330n. 32
'Pancasila Democracy', 252, 270
Pancasila Youth (Pemuda Pancasila), 239
Panuju, 234, 241, 242, 245, 347n. 10, 352n. 105
Pari (Partai Republik Indonesia), 58, 59, 62-64,
   73, 75, 77, 158, 325n. 46, 327n. 70
Parliament, 184, 185, 195, 196, 268, 270
   See also People's Representative Council
Parmusi (Partai Muslimin Indonesia), 255, 256,
   356n. 20
Partindo (Partai Indonesia), 50, 56, 59, 60, 61, 65,
   244. 302n. 59
Patriotic Service League (Hokokai), 99, 107, 108,
   113
Payakumbuh, 54, 139, 141, 142, 155, 159, 250,
   266
PDI (Partai Demokrasi Indonesia), 256, 257, 267
PDRI. *See* Emergency Government
Pekanbaru, 64, 77, 149, 150, 191, 212, 215, 216,
   241, 242
Pema. *See* Intelligence services, Indonesian
Pemandangan Islam, 39, 40, 41, 44
   See also newspapers
penghulu (lineage heads), 16, 21, 22, 26, 152, 259,
   289n. 9, 309n. 82, 326nn. 63, 64, 352nn. 102,
   103, 358n. 49
   See also officials; adat; nagari
People's Army. *See* Giyu gun
People's Consultative Assembly (MPR), 269,
   355n. 12
People's Democratic Front (FDR), 133, 135
People's Front (Volksfront), 114, 117, 119-22,
   317n. 54
   See also Struggle Union
People's League (Sarikat Rakyat), 32, 40, 43, 45,
   46, 47, 53, 73, 118, 291n. 11
People's Representative Council:
   in Jakarta (DPR), 256, 269-70, 271
   in West Sumatra (DPRD), 171-73, 178, 242, 246,
   247, 256, 261, 268, 270, 330n. 29, 353n. 108
   See also Parliament

People's Revolutionary Movement (PRM), 135,
   321n. 117
People's School (Sekolah Rakyat), 31, 40, 41
perantau. *See* migrants
Perhimpunan Indonesia, 36, 82
Permesta (Piagam Perjuangan Semesta Alam),
   187-88, 217, 342n. 20
   See also rebellions; PRRI/Permesta
Permi (Persatuan Muslimin Indonesia)
   formation of, 53-54
   membership, 55, 60, 75, 89
   platform, 54, 55-56, 61, 74, 86-87
   and schools, 58-59, 67, 79, 80-81, 302n. 53,
    307n. 47
   repression of, 50, 65, 67, 102, 156-57
   and Minangkabau Council, 90
Perpatih nan Sebatang, Datuk, 21, 23
Persatuan Islam (Persis), 74
Persatuan Perjuangan. *See* Struggle Union
Perti (Persatuan Tarbiah Islamiyah), 84, 88, 111,
   176, 177, 193, 235, 246, 247, 255, 256, 309n. 84,
   316n. 31, 348n. 17, 352nn. 99, 106, 352-53n.
   107, 355n. 11, 356n. 18
Peta (Pembela Tanah Air, Japanese volunteer
   army on Java), 103, 184
PGAI (Persatuan Guru-guru Agama Islam), 54
PKI (Partai Komunis Indonesia)
   formation of, 27, 31, 38
   and 1926/27 rebellion, 31-33, 39, 43-47, 134,
    297n. 91
   splits in, 62, 73
   militia (Temi), 116
   in revolution, 134-35, 158
   in 1955 elections, 177, 249, 331n. 43
   and Banteng Council, 190-91,196, 199, 202-4,
    250, 335nn. 36, 40
   and PRRI, 220-21, 235-36, 343n. 43, 348n. 17
   under Guided Democracy, 193, 197, 237-38,
    247
   in 1965, 234, 239, 242-45, 250, 252, 255
   Special Bureau (biro khusus), 240-41
   See also communism, anticommunism
PKI Lokal Islamy, 88
Plakaat Panjang (Long Declaration), 25, 27, 33
PMDS (Students' League of Diniyyah Schools).
   See Diniyyah
PNI (Indonesian National Party), 59, 133, 173,
   176, 177, 193, 243, 247, 254-55, 331n. 43
PNI Baru (Pendidikan Nasional Indonesia), 50,
   59-62, 65, 66, 67, 70, 73, 86, 89, 90, 302n. 59
"Police" actions. *See* Dutch
political parties, 19, 50, 71, 126, 249, 254-57, 271,
   353n. 109, 355n. 12
   See also Islamic political parties, and under
   party names
Poniman, 235, 239, 242, 245, 246, 247, 353n. 115
Pontoh, Sergeant Major, 47

Poorten, Gen. Hein Ter, 95
Potsdam Agreements, 108
PPP (Partai Persatuan Pembangunan), 256, 356n. 23
Pranoto Reksosamudro, 233, 343n. 48, 347n. 10
PRRI government 211-13, 218-19, 340nn. 1, 2
PRRI/Permesta rebellion. *See* rebellion
PS (Socialist Party), 111, 116, 133
PSI (Indonesian Socialist Party), 133, 191, 203, 208, 211, 213, 246, 255, 335n. 36, 343n. 44, 355n. 13
PSII (Partai Sarikat Islam Indonesia), 51, 56, 57, 60-61, 65, 67, 73, 74, 86-87, 89, 90, 304n. 86
PST. *See* Sumatra, East
PUSA (All Aceh Ulama Union), 170-71
Putih, Abdul Rahman Tuanku nan. *See* Abdul Rahman

Raffles, Sir Thomas Stamford, 16-17, 292n. 19
Rahmah el Junusiah, 56, 80-81, 83
Rahmany, H. Uddin, 56m 64, 65
Rahmat, 242
Rasjad, Sabilal, 65
Rasjid, Mr. St. Mohd., 99, 111, 112-13, 114, 134, 141, 159, 160, 171, 219, 221-22, 328n. 92, 334n. 12
  as Resident, 120, 121, 123, 123, 125, 129, 131, 135, 139, 172, 321n. 109
  as military governor, 146, 147, 148, 149, 151, 155
Rasul, Haji (Syekh Abdul Karim Amrullah), 36, 37, 38, 39, 40, 44, 51, 52, 53, 54, 63, 87, 157, 303n. 71, 327n. 82
Rasyad, Suhaimi, 40
Rasyidi, Syekh Daud, 55, 118
rationalization (of the armed forces), 131, 132, 134, 144, 179, 184, 185, 324n. 25, 331n. 51
rebellion, 174
  1908 tax, 27, 33, 34
  1926/27 Communist, 17, 18, 28, 31, 43, 46-49, 50, 51, 85, 111, 112, 134, 296n. 76, 298nn. 111, 113, 119, 299n. 123
  Madiun, 134-35, 321n. 117
  Islamic, 176, 180, 188
  5/Permesta, 17, 18-19, 99, 179, 192, 197, 211-29, 234, 235, 236, 245, 247, 253, 266, 272, 343nn. 36, 43, 44
  surrender of, 226-29, 345nn. 66, 67, 70, 71, 346n. 88
  See also Darul Islam
reform movement (reformasi), 265, 269, 270, 271, 272, 360n. 4
Regional Defence Council (DPD), 122, 136, 147, 318n. 62, 324n. 35
Renville agreements, 130, 132, 133, 134, 135, 154, 175
repression

Dutch, 45, 49, 50, 51, 65, 82, 89-90, 92, 96, 156
Japanese, 97-98, 104, 106, 112, 118
by Republican government, 116, 119, 121-22, 144
by Suharto regime, 243-44, 248, 255, 276-77
revolutionary government. *See* PRRI government
Riau, 110, 169, 171, 173, 174, 183, 190, 191-92, 198, 248, 263, 275, 324n. 25
  archipelago, 149, 150, 169, 171, 192
riba (usury), 35, 292n. 25
Ridha, Said Rasjid, 37, 41, 53, 293n. 32
RIS (Republik Indonesia Serikat), 15, 165-67, 328n. 1, 336n. 52
Rivai, Djohan, 216, 240, 241, 350n. 53
RMS (Republik Maluku Selatan), 166, 328n. 3
Roem, Mohamad, 153, 176, 208, 255, 330n. 38, 348n. 24
Roem-van Royen agreements, 153-54, 155
Roesad Dt. Perpatih Baringek, 48, 54, 86, 89, 90, 99, 111-12, 122, 315n. 19
Roeslan Moeljohardjo, 172, 176, 180, 182, 183, 330n. 28, 331n. 40
Round Table Conference, 154, 165
RPI. *See* Federal Republic of Indonesia
Rukmito Hendraningrat, 214, 342n. 20
Rumuat, 47, 298n. 109
Rustam, 40

Saalah J. St. Mangkuto, 87, 124, 125, 157, 172, 318-19n. 70, 319n. 80
Sabilillah, 110, 116, 124
  See also militias; Islamic political parties; Masjumi
Sadelbergh, 220
Sadikin, Ali, 182
Sago, Mt., 142
Said Ali, Sutan, 33, 44, 45, 78, 85, 291n. 7, 296n. 80
Said, Rasuna, 56, 65, 78, 80, 102, 196, 311n. 112, 316n. 33
Saleh, Chaerul, 116, 119, 236, 237, 238
Salim, Haji Agus, 36, 45, 57, 74, 161, 322n. 10
Salim, Emil, 264, 355n. 9
Salim, Leon:
  as youth leader, 40-41, 57-59, 78, 295n. 61, 297n. 99, 302n. 53
  and New PNI, 60, 62, 67, 68-69, 90, 302n. 60, 307n. 43
  and Chatib Suleiman, 58, 91, 98, 102-3, 158-59, 311n. 109
  arrests of, 70, 81, 96, 98
  and Pema, 137, 158-59, 327n. 90
  in old age, 266-67
Saputro Brotodiharjo, 242-43, 246, 247, 352n. 106
Sari, Ratna, 102, 196

Sarikat Islam. *See* Islamic League
Sarikat Rakyat. *See* People's League
Sartono, 59, 209
Sarumpait, Saladin, 211
Sasono, Adi, 272-73
Sastroamidjojo, Ali, 173, 176, 177, 186, 192
Sawahlunto, 32, 33, 42, 45, 47, 48, 54, 202, 250, 291n. 11
sbkb (Transport Workers' Union), 235-36
Schiller, A. Arthur, 167
schools and education, 41, 43, 78-84, 247, 265, 353n. 118
  government (Western), 40, 58, 72, 79, 82
  private, 18, 40, 44, 52, 79, 82, 83
  Islamic, 31, 34, 36, 37, 38, 40, 41, 45, 51, 62-63, 67, 71, 79-82, 83, 313n. 22
  See also Islamic colleges, People's School; Diniyyah, Sumatra Thawalib
Schwartz, Adam, 262
Semaun, 28
September 30 Movement. *See* coups
Shiraishi, Takashi, 39
Shu sangi kai (provincial assembly under Japanese), 99, 108
Siliwangi Division, 131, 132, 144, 180, 185, 226, 228, 235, 239, 240, 242, 321n. 110
Silungkang, 32, 33, 36, 42-43, 45, 46, 47, 48, 49, 295n. 68
Simarajo, Dt., 92. 99, 101, 124
Simatupang, 103, 238, 333n. 1
Simbolon, Maludin, 188, 339n. 125
  as North Sumatra commander, 182, 185, 186-87, 214, 333n. 9
  with Banteng Council, 190, 193, 197, 198, 201, 206, 209
  overseas ties, 199, 207, 208
  and prri, 211, 214, 218, 224, 340n. 133, 341n. 19
  surrender of, 226, 345n. 66
Simons, Lt. W.F.H.L., 48
Singapore, 35, 46, 59, 62-64, 66, 67, 71, 77, 91, 95, 104, 141, 149-50, 207, 208, 263
Singkarak Charter, 124
Siradjuddin Abbas, Syekh, 84, 111, 247, 316n. 31, 347n. 3, 352-53n. 99, 353n. 107
Situjuh Batur, 42-44, 159, 323nn. 21, 22
Situjuh Padang Kuning, 213, 220, 343n. 43
Sjahdin, Achmad, 246, 256
Sjafei, Mohammad, 52, 72, 82-83, 91, 99, 101, 104, 105-6, 125, 140, 169, 190, 193, 211, 218, 307-8n. 53
  as Resident, 107, 111, 315n. 17
Sjafruddin Prawiranegara, 139, 170, 205, 255, 329n. 20, 356n. 24
  as head of Emergency Government, 139-41, 144, 151, 153-56, 159, 179, 327n. 72
  with Banteng Council, 206-208

as head of prri government, 209, 211, 215, 217-18, 222-24, 225, 226-27, 341n. 8, 343n. 36
Sjahrir, Sutan, 50, 60, 65, 74, 91, 98, 111, 114, 116, 120, 133, 137, 161, 205, 236, 312n. 13, 322n. 10
Sjam (Kamarusman bin Ahmad Mubaidah), 241
Sjarif, Gani, 64
Sjarifuddin, Amir, 64, 113, 116, 119, 120, 128, 130, 133, 135, 137, 312n. 8
Sjoeib, 180, 182, 331n. 59, 341n. 15
smuggling. *See* trade
sobsi (Communist Labour Federation), 191, 239
social revolution, 117, 119, 127
Socialist Party. *See* PS, PSI
Soedarsjono, Dr., 116
Soedjatmoko, 137
Soekirno Harjodarsono, 240, 241
Soeleiman, 190, 218, 335n. 31
South Moluccas.*See* rms
Soviet Union, 134
Special Region of West Sumatra (disba), 152-53, 326n. 62
Spits, Governor A.I., 50, 95, 109
sskad (Army Staff and Command School), 186, 187, 216, 238
Starkenborgh Stachouwer, Gov. Gen. A.W.L. Tjarda, 95
Stoler, Ann, 244
Struggle Union (Persatuan Perjuangan), 114-16, 117, 135
students' organizations. *See* youth organizations
Subakat, 58, 62, 63, 66
Subandrio, 239-40, 349n. 49
Subroto, Gatot, 226, 334n. 9
Sudirman, General, 140, 153, 154, 184, 333n. 1
Sugeng, Bambang, 185
Suhardjo Hardjowardojo, 110, 132
Suharto: 234, 243, 251, 252, 253, 256, 257, 264, 267, 268, 269, 347n. 6, 359n. 77
  regime, 19, 251, 252, 254, 273
  resignation of, 270
Sukarno
  and Partindo, 50, 56, 59,
  under Dutch arrest, 65-66, 144, 153, 219, 322n. 10
  under Japanese, 96-98, 104
  as president, 107, 109, 127, 129, 130, 155, 185, 189, 195, 208, 226, 254
  and Guided Democracy, 193, 194, 196, 209, 222, 223, 225, 237-38, 239
  assassination attempt against, 204-205
  overthrow of, 233-34, 252
  and Hatta, 60, 200-202, 204, 212-13
  and Tan Malaka, 114-16. 120
Sukendro, 205
Sukiman, Dr., 140, 172, 176
Sulaiman Labai, 32, 33, 42, 46, 49, 78, 85, 295n. 71

Sulawesi, 184, 185, 187, 214, 217, 224, 225, 226, 328n. 2
Sulawesi, South, 157, 175, 188, 224
Suleiman (of Youth Party), 117
Suleiman Arrasuli, Syekh. *See* Arrasuli, Syekh Suleiman
Suleiman, Chatib, 302n. 50, 311nn. 107, 109, 315n. 23
    and prewar politics, 58, 60-61, 67, 78, 81, 83, 90-91, 302n. 60, 307n. 43, 310-11, n. 106
    arrests of, 96-97, 98, 120
    under Japanese 98, 99, 104, 106, 113
    and Giyu gun, 100-101, 102, 113-14, 313nn. 29, 36
    and residency government, 111, 112-13, 114, 141, 158-60, 219
    and Volksfront, 117, 120, 121
    strategies of, 136, 141-42, 146-47, 158, 219
    death of, 142-44, 220
Sultan of Yogyakarta. *See* Hamengku Buwono IX
Sumatra, East, 55, 117, 119, 127, 149, 158, 169, 248, 314n. 38
    State of (PST), 166
    See also Sumatra, North
Sumatra, North, 184, 185, 215, 226, 239, 243-44
    See also Sumatra, East
Sumatra, South, 55, 78, 169, 184, 187, 192, 211, 214, 217, 226
Sumatra Banking and Trading Corporation, 150
Sumatra state, issue of, 206, 207, 213, 224, 339nn. 125, 127, 344n. 53
Sumatra Thawalib, 17, 34, 37-40, 52, 53, 54, 55, 56, 57, 79, 80, 293n. 34, 300n. 17, 305n. 11
Sumedi, 241, 350nn. 52, 63
Sumitro Djojohadikusumo, 197, 198, 199, 201, 206, 207, 208, 211, 224
Sumual, H.N. Ventje, 186, 187, 188, 198, 199, 200, 207, 208
Sungai Dareh conference, 206, 208, 209, 339n. 125, 340n. 133
Suparto, Iman, 235, 242, 245, 247, 256
Surau Djembatan Besi, 37, 54, 55
    See also Sumatra Thawalib
Suripno, 134
Suryosumpeno, 226, 227, 234, 347n. 10
Susanto, Mr. 140
Sutomo, Dr., 76, 77
Suwarno, 247
Syattariyah, 24, 27, 33, 88, 289n. 18

Tabing, 109, 216
Tahir Djalaluddin, Syekh. *See* Djalaluddin, Syekh Tahir
Talaha gelar Rajo Sampono, 46
Taman Siswa, 52, 83
Tamin, Djamaluddin, 38, 39, 40, 46, 53, 57, 58, 62, 66-67, 78, 122, 158, 294n. 56, 316n. 29

Tan Malaka, Ibrahim gelar Datuk
    biography of, 290-91n. 2, 304n. 93
    and PKI, 31, 32, 33, 36, 46, 53, 134, 135, 250, 291n. 5
    and 1926/27 rebellion, 43, 46, 49
    followers of, 38, 41, 45, 54, 59, 63, 74, 75, 88, 111, 118-19, 121-22, 127, 134, 136, 148, 158, 250
    and Pari, 58, 60, 62, 66, 158
    myths about, 71-72
    return to Indonesia, 114-16
    and struggle union, 115-16
    imprisonment of, 120, 136-37, 322n. 123
    death of, 160, 328n. 95
Tanabe, Lt. General Moritake, 100, 104, 109, 314n. 41
Tapanuli, 55, 169, 187, 215, 226, 228
Taram, Darwis, 125
taxes, 25, 27, 262
    war tax, 147-48, 153
teachers' ordinance (guru ordinansi), 51, 52, 53, 79
Tedjasukmana, Iskandar, 117, 316n. 37
Teluk Bayur (Emmahaven), 42, 109, 216
Temi (Tentara Merah Indonesia). *See* PKI
Terauchi, Marshal, 104
Thaib, Darwis, Dt. Sidi Bandaro, 18, 60, 62, 78
Thaib, H. Djalaluddin, 54, 55, 64, 65, 78, 157, 301n. 36, 302n. 53
Thalib, Ahmad, 142, 180, 181
Tjokrohandoko, Burhani, 235
Tobri, Rachmat, 124
Tonek, Mahyuddin, 57, 59
trade, 249, 330, 334nn. 24, 25
    barter, 149, 185, 325n. 49
    Islamic law re, 76-77
    items of, 75-76, 150, 151, 185, 243, 262, 325nn. 45, 49, 326nn. 59, 60
    (*See also* coffee, gold, opium),
    networks, 75-76, 77, 150-51, 326n. 70
    organizations, 44, 75, 90-91, 98, 150, 263, 300n. 24, 325n. 53
    during revolution, 148-51, 325nn. 45, 46, 49, 51, 53
    routes, 31, 35, 42, 149, 150, 263
    for weapons, 98, 131, 149, 150, 151, 325nn. 46, 49, 326n. 60
    under Suharto regime, 259, 358n. 60
traders, 18, 31
    Chinese, 35, 44, 75, 77, 149, 151, 247, 249, 269, 325n. 51, 326nn. 59, 60, 327n. 70
    European, 34, 35, 44, 75, 77
    indigenous, 18, 35, 36, 42, 44, 77, 310nn. 102, 103, 104
    support for schools, 34, 44, 292n. 19
    See also Islam and trade

ulama. *See* Islamic scholars
Ulung Sitepu 239, 240, 243
United Nations130, 139, 140, 153, 155, 204,
   338n. 114
United States, 197, 199, 225
   aid to PRRI, 207, 208, 215-16, 219, 220, 339n.
   132, 340n. 134, 342n. 21
Untung, 233, 234, 240, 241, 243, 347n. 7, 348n.
   11
Usman, A. Rahim, 172, 312n. 18, 318n. 62
Usman, Abdulgani, 211
Usman, Madjid, 98, 172, 312n. 18
Usman, Sjarief, 102, 110, 119, 122, 125, 126, 127,
   214, 218, 219, 315n. 13
Usman, Tamimi, 67, 98, 304n. 103, 312n. 13

van der Plas, Ch. O., 33, 52, 97, 312n. 8
Van Mook, H.J., 130
van Royen, Dr. J.H., 153
van Straten, L.B., 148
village law (1979), 19, 258-59, 356n. 31
   See also nagari
villages, extended. *See* nagari
voc. *See* Dutch East India Company
Volksfront. *See* People's Front
Volksraad (People's Council), 27, 90

Wahab, Syekh Ahmad, 63, 303n. 68
Wahhabis, 24-25, 36
Wakamatsu, I. , 98, 99
Wardojo, Edy247
Warouw, J.F., 185, 187, 207, 209, 211, 217, 224,
   333-34n. 9, 340n. 133
West Irian. *See* Irian Jaya
Westerling, Captain R.P.P. 'Turk', 165-66, 328n.
   2
Whitlau, Assistant Resident, 40
Widjojo Nitisastro, 252
Wild Schools Ordinance, 52, 56, 79, 83, 299-
   300n. 10
Wiranto, 270
women
   education of, 32, 56, 80-81, 306n. 37, 307n. 40
   organizations of, 102, 147-48, 324n. 38

political role of, 56, 65, 80-81, 98
   See also matrilineal system, Hahanokai
World Bank, 253
World War I, 31, 35
World War II, 90

Yamin, Muhammad, 23, 64, 74, 77, 90, 114, 116,
   120, 219, 236, 305-6n. 15, 310nn. 102, 103, 104
Yani, Ahmad, 216, 217, 233, 235, 344n. 48
Yano Kenzo, 98-99, 100, 105, 313n. 25, 314n. 42
Yatim, Marzuki, 91
Yoga Sugama, 234, 256, 348n. 13
Young Group. *See* kaum muda
Young Troop (Barisan Muda), 40. 41, 57
Youth Information Office (BPPI), 108, 109
Youth organizations, 43, 57, 80, 221, 237, 242,
   268, 271, 359nn. 86, 88
   El Hilaal (Crescent Moon), 58, 59, 302n. 53
   Hizbul Wathan, 59
   HMI (Muslim Student Organization), 237, 242
   KAMI, 242, 246, 247
   KAPPI, 246, 247, 249, 354n. 129
   KIM (Kepanduan Indonesia Muslim), 58, 59
   Pemuda Rakyat (Communist Youth), 221, 235,
   239, 245, 248
   Pemuda Nippon Raja, 98, 118, 317n. 40
   SIAP, 43, 59, 295n. 73
   See also Diniyyah; IPO; Islamic youth; OPR; Pan-
   casila Youth; Young Troop
Yunus, Hasanuddin, 57, 59
Yunus Yosfiah, 359-60n. 2
Yussari, 226, 346n. 82

Zain, Harun
   as Rector, 236-37, 246
   as Governor, 23, 229, 247, 248, 250-51, 254,
   258, 261, 352n. 105, 354n. 138
Zainuddin Labai el Junusiah, 37, 38, 39, 53, 56,
   63, 72-73, 78, 80, 305n. 11
Zainuddin, Natar, 40, 59, 157-58, 294n. 47, 305n.
   11
Zainul Abidin Sutan Pangeran, 247
Zed, Mestika, 140